MAGILL'S
LITERARY ANNUAL

1994

MAGILL'S LITERARY ANNUAL

1994

*Essay-Reviews of 200 Outstanding Books
Published in the United States during 1993*

With an Annotated Categories List

Volume One
A-Len

Edited by
FRANK N. MAGILL

SALEM PRESS
Pasadena, California   Englewood Cliffs, New Jersey

LIBRARY OF CONGRESS CATALOG CARD NO. 77-99209
ISBN 0-89356-294-7

FIRST PRINTING

PUBLISHER'S NOTE

Magill's Literary Annual, 1994, is the thirty-ninth publication in a series that began in 1954. The philosophy behind the annual has been to evaluate critically each year a given number of major examples of serious literature published during the previous year. Our continuous effort is to provide coverage for works that are likely to be of more than passing general interest and that will stand up to the test of time. Individual critical articles for the first twenty-two years were collected and published in *Survey of Contemporary Literature* in 1977.

For the reader new to the Magill reference format, the following brief explanation should serve to facilitate the research process. The two hundred works represented in this year's annual are drawn from the following categories: fiction; poetry; literary criticism, literary history, and literary theory; essays; literary biography; autobiography, memoirs, diaries, and letters; biography; history; current affairs; science, history of science, and technology; ethics and law; fine arts and film; philosophy and religion; psychology; sociology; and women's issues. The articles are arranged alphabetically by book title in the two-volume set; a complete list of the titles included can be found at the beginning of volume 1. Following a list of titles are the titles arranged by category in an annotated listing. This list provides the reader with the title, author, page number, and a brief description of the particular work. The names of all contributing reviewers for the literary annual are listed alphabetically in the front of the book as well as at the end of their reviews. At the end of volume 2, there are two indexes: an index of Biographical Works by Subject and the Cumulative Author Index. The index of biographical works covers the years 1977 to 1994, and it is arranged by subject rather than by author or title. Thus, readers will be able to locate easily a review of any biographical work published in the Magill annuals since 1977 (including memoirs, diaries, and letters—as well as biographies and autobiographies) by looking up the name of the person. Following the index of Biographical Works by Subject is the Cumulative Author Index. Beneath each author's name appear the titles of all of his or her works reviewed in the Magill annuals since 1977. Next to each title, in parentheses, is the year of the annual in which the review appeared, followed by the page number.

Each article begins with a block of top matter that indicates the title, author, publisher, and price of the work. When possible, the year of the author's birth is also provided. The top matter also includes the number of pages of the book, the type of work, and, when appropriate, the time period and locale represented in the text. Next, there is the same capsulized description of the work that appears in the annotated list of titles. When pertinent, a list of principal characters or of personages introduces the review.

The articles themselves are approximately two thousand words in length. They are original essay-reviews that analyze and present the focus, intent, and relative success of the author, as well as the makeup and point of view of the work under discussion. To assist the reader further, the articles are supplemented by a list of additional reviews for further study in a bibliographic format.

LIST OF TITLES

vii

LIST OF TITLES

LIST OF TITLES

LIST OF TITLES

TITLES BY CATEGORY

ANNOTATED

TITLES BY CATEGORY

TITLES BY CATEGORY

page

page

BIOGRAPHY

TITLES BY CATEGORY

page

CURRENT AFFAIRS

TITLES BY CATEGORY

CONTRIBUTING REVIEWERS FOR 1994 ANNUAL

Edward Abood
California State University,
Los Angeles

McCrea Adams
Independent Scholar

Michael Adams
Fairleigh Dickinson University

Terry L. Andrews
Independent Scholar

Jennifer Ward Angyal
Alamance County School
System

Stanley Archer
Texas A&M University

Edwin T. Arnold
Appalachian State University

Jean Ashton
Columbia University

Bryan Aubrey
Maharishi International
University

Dean Baldwin
Pennsylvania State University,
Erie
Behrend College

Dan Barnett
California State University,
Chico and Butte College

Robert A. Bascom
United Bible Societies

Richard P. Benton
Trinity College, Hartford

Charles Merrell Berg
Kansas State University

Mary G. Berg
Radcliffe College

Harold Branam
Savannah State College

Gerhard Brand
California State University,
Los Angeles

Cynthia K. Breckenridge
Independent Scholar

Peter Brier
California State University,
Los Angeles

Jean R. Brink
Arizona State University

Charles Cameron
Independent Scholar

Thomas J. Campbell
Pacific Lutheran University

Ethan Casey
The Bangkok Post

Thomas J. Cassidy
South Carolina State College

Richard Hauer Costa
Texas A&M University

Peter Crawford
Independent Scholar

Jeff Cupp
University of Charleston

Frank Day
Clemson University

Bill Delaney
Independent Scholar

Robert P. Ellis
Worcester State College

Robert Faggen
Claremont McKenna College

Bruce E. Fleming
United States Naval Academy

Robert J. Forman
St. John's University, New York

Raymond Frey
Centenary College, New Jersey

Leslie E. Gerber
Appalachian State University

Sidney Gottlieb
Sacred Heart University

Daniel L. Guillory
Millikin University

Donald E. Hall
California State University,
Northridge

John W. M. Hallock
Temple University

Terry Heller
Coe College

Peter P. Hinks
Yale University

William L. Howard
Chicago State University

Philip K. Jason
United States Naval Academy

Shakuntala Jayaswal
University of New Haven

Jane Anderson Jones
Manatee Community College

Steven G. Kellman
University of Texas at
San Antonio

W. P. Kenney
Manhattan College

Karen A. Kildahl
South Dakota State University

James B. Lane
Indiana University Northwest

Eugene Larson
Los Angeles Pierce College

Leon Lewis
Appalachian State University

Elizabeth Johnston
Lipscomb
Randolph-Macon Woman's
College

Liesel Litzenburger
Independent Scholar

Janet Lorenz
Independent Scholar

R. C. Lutz
University of the Pacific

Janet McCann
Texas A&M University

Mark McCloskey
Independent Scholar

Philip McDermott
Independent Scholar

Margaret McFadden
Appalachian State University

Ric S. Machuga
Butte College

Paul Madden
Hardin-Simmons University

Paul D. Mageli
Independent Scholar

Maria Theresa Maggi
University of Idaho

Lois A. Marchino
University of Texas at El Paso

Peter Markus
Western Michigan University

Liz Marshall
Independent Scholar

Charles E. May
*California State University,
Long Beach*

Laurence W. Mazzeno
Ursuline College

Kenneth W. Meadwell
*University of Winnipeg,
Manitoba, Canada*

Leslie B. Mittleman
*California State University,
Long Beach*

Robert A. Morace
Daemen College

Gregory L. Morris
*Pennsylvania State University,
Erie
Behrend College*

Robert E. Morsberger
*California State Polytechnic
University, Pomona*

Edwin Moses
Bloomsburg University

Daniel P. Murphy
Hanover College

John M. Muste
Ohio State University

Stella Nesanovich
McNeese State University

George O'Brien
Georgetown University

William T. Obsorne
*Florida International
University and
Florida Memorial College*

Lawrence J. Oliver
Texas A&M University

Lisa Paddock
Independent Scholar

Robert J. Paradowski
*Rochester Institute of
Technology*

David Peck
*California State University,
Long Beach*

John Powell
*Pennsylvania State University,
Erie
Behrend College*

Cliff Prewencki
The College of Saint Rose

Rosemary M. Canfield
Reisman
Troy State University

Carl Rollyson
*Baruch College of the City
University of New York*

Joseph Rosenblum
*University of North Carolina at
Greensboro*

Robert L. Ross
University of Texas at Austin

John K. Roth
Claremont McKenna College

Barbara Elman Schiffman
Independent Scholar

Glenn J. Schiffman
Independent Scholar

Francis Michael Sharp
University of the Pacific

T. A. Shippey
Saint Louis University

R. Baird Shuman
*University of Illinois at
Urbana-Champaign*

Anne W. Sienkewicz
Independent Scholar

Thomas J. Sienkewicz
Monmouth College, Illinois

Harold L. Smith
University of Houston, Victoria

Kay H. Smith
Appalachian State University

Ira Smolensky
Monmouth College, Illinois

Gerald H. Strauss
Bloomsburg University

James Sullivan
*California State University,
Los Angeles*

William L. Urban
Monmouth College, Illinois

Ronald G. Walker
Western Illinois University

Qun Wang
*University of Wisconsin, River
Falls*

Harry M. Ward
University of Richmond

Bruce Wiebe
Independent Scholar

John Wilson
Independent Scholar

Michael Witkoski
Independent Scholar

Susan Wladaver-Morgan
*Western Association of Women
Historians*

Elizabeth Zanichkowsky
*University of Wisconsin
Centers, Waukesha*

Laura Weiss Zlogar
*University of Wisconsin, River
Falls*

MAGILL'S
LITERARY ANNUAL

1994

ACROSS THE BRIDGE

Author: Mavis Gallant (1922-   )
Publisher: Random House (New York). 198 pp. $19.00
Type of work: Short stories
Time: The 1930's to the 1980's
Locale: Primarily Montreal, Canada, and Paris, France

Eleven new stories, most of them from The New Yorker *magazine, by one of Canada's most acclaimed masters of the short story form*

Mavis Gallant's *Across the Bridge* was among the fourteen titles (including six works of fiction) chosen by the editors of *The New York Times Book Review* for the list of Best Books of 1993. Gallant has been publishing short stories, almost exclusively in *The New Yorker*, since the late 1940's. It is difficult, however, to place her in any of the better-known generic traditions of the short story, even those usually described as *New Yorker* stories. Although Gallant has been compared to Henry James and Anton Chekhov, she is probably more related to Jane Austen. As a result, she poses a problem for readers expecting stories that seem to have a patterned point, a metaphoric texture, or a sense of closure. Rather, Gallant's stories seem to be so forthrightly focused on the everyday lives of her characters that there is little to say about them. They certainly do not appear to need interpretation, the only mystery about them being the mystery of what they are about. Indeed, with everything so clearly laid out in realistic detail, there does not seem to be much "aboutness" about them.

Of course, both James and Chekhov were also accused of presenting little ado about not very much, but Gallant's stories do not have James's convoluted syntax, reflecting the complexity of his characters; nor do they have Chekhov's calculated conciseness, suggesting that more is left out than put in. In fact, Gallant's characters do not seem very complex at all, at least self-consciously, and Gallant appears to say everything that needs to be said about them. Instead of moving toward some explicit or implicit patterned intention, as readers have come to expect in the short story form, Gallant's stories seem as if they could go on and on, creating a novelistic "feel" that violates the reader's usual expectation that short stories will meaningfully lead somewhere. Trying to find out where the meaning lies or how meaning is communicated in a Gallant story is not so much challenging as apparently beside the point. Readers either get so caught up in the creation of character and milieu that they do not care what the story means, or else they tire of the seemingly inconsequential nature of the story and just stop reading.

Like Jane Austen, Gallant presents characters within a circumscribed social world going about their usual manners and morals business without obvious conflict, analytical self-doubt, or troublesome introspection. The comedy of manners that results is a form that is usually too leisurely and too detailed for the relatively short space of the short story, being better served by the novel form. The first four stories in this new collection, because they focus on significant points in the life of one

Montreal family, are typical of the novelistic tendency of Gallant's technique. Upon reading the stories, however, one realizes very quickly that if Gallant had put together eleven or twelve stories about this same family—enough to fill the book—the result would still have been a collection of short stories rather than a novel. The reason for this distinction between novel and short story derives from Gallant's selectivity of focus and detail as well as her ironic style. On closer analysis, the reader begins to realize that her stories are not quite as realistically inconsequential as they first appear.

The first story, "1933," introduces Mme Carette and her two daughters, Berthe and Marie, shortly after the death of her husband has forced the little family to move to a smaller place. The strict social conventions of the middle-class Carette family are revealed by the fact that the daughters never see their mother wearing a bathrobe, and that the only English she thinks they need to know are the phrases: "I don't understand," "I don't know," and "No, thank you." The central, most telling, statement in the story is the mother's insistence that the children never refer to their mother as a seamstress, but must say instead, "My mother was clever with her hands." The thematic point of the story, if indeed "point" is the appropriate word here, is the fear and loneliness of the Carette family because of the loss of the husband/father; its artistry lies in the subtle way Gallant conveys that fear and loneliness.

"The Chosen Husband" focuses on the family in 1949 after Mme Carette receives a legacy of eighteen thousand dollars from a brother-in-law whom she has suspected of various social offenses, not the least of which is being a Freemason. The daughters, now in their early twenties, are in a position to fill the emptiness left by the death of their father by marrying. And indeed, the plot of this relatively long story is Marie's courtship with Louis Driscoll—a courtship that seems straight out of Jane Austen, especially in the language Gallant uses to describe it. For example, when Driscoll makes his first call and chokes on one of his own chocolates, Gallant says "He was in trouble with a caramel," and the Carettes look away so that he can "strangle unobserved." The story ends with the marriage; Berthe reflects that, being Montreal girls, she and Marie have not been trained to accompany heroes, or to hold out for dreams, but rather just to be patient.

The last two stories in the mini-saga of the Carette family, "From Cloud to Cloud" and "Florida," focus on Marie's son Raymond: first, after the death of his father, when he enlists in the American army during the Vietnam era, and then afterward when he settles in Florida and marries a rather common (by traditional Montreal social standards) young divorcée. The story ends with Raymond storming out after a minor quarrel, leaving Marie and Raymond's pregnant wife without a man in the house, just as Marie and her sister and mother were in the first story in the series, "1933." In addition to the basic theme of the ultimate breakup of the rigid social structure of Montreal in the relatively classless society of Florida of the 1970's, what holds the story together is a nicely ironic metaphor of Marie's being plagued with static electricity. For example, when she gives a plant a kiss, the flower "absorbed a charge and hurled it back." She exchanges sparks with everything; when she eats a peppermint, she feels it detonating in her mouth. The story ends with Marie warning

Raymond's wife that everything around is electric and that they will have to be careful because of the baby and make sure that they are all grounded. In her excitement she lapses into French, Gallant writes, but it did not matter, because the baby, although still in the mother's womb, could hear her and knew what she meant. Although in such stories it may not be obvious what Gallant means, the detail of the static electricity is typical of her technique of using seemingly insignificant particulars in ironic ways.

The title story, the longest piece in the collection, is similarly lacking in plot but is rich in ironic suggestiveness. "Across the Bridge" differs from other stories in the book, however, in being told in the first person; thus, it seems somewhat flat by comparison because of the relatively unsophisticated nature of the protagonist/ narrator. The bridge in the story is at first merely a physical presence, for the story begins with the narrator Sylvie walking across a bridge in Paris with her mother, who has the invitations to her wedding in a leather shopping bag. Sylvie, however, is not so acquiescent as Berthe and Marie, the restrained young ladies from Montreal, in marrying a man she does not love. When she demurs, her mother says that loving a man takes "patience," like practicing scales.

Sylvie has her mind on another young man, saying she has thoughts of throwing herself off the bridge if she is forced to marry the family choice, Arnaud, and not allowed to marry her own choice, Bernard. In response, her mother dumps the invitations off the bridge, and, in an imagistic metaphor that reverberates throughout the story, Sylvie watches as the envelopes fall in a slow shower and float apart on the dark water. The rest of the story is an ironic/comic treatment of the family's efforts to match Sylvie up with Bernard, who, it turns out, in spite of Sylvie's romantic idealizations, has no interest in her at all.

The story ends in a typical drawing-room comedy way with Sylvie falling in love with her family's original choice for her after all. The key scene in the story is a dinner engagement Sylvie has with Arnaud in which their future life together is presaged. The first personal thing he says to her is that she is not eating her dessert. Although the food has been paid for, Sylvie cannot eat the flan because the restaurant has mistaken it for a piece of quiche and put parsley on it. As Arnaud scrapes off the parsley and begins to eat the flan for her, Sylvie says to herself that he must love her or otherwise the dessert would be disgusting. The story ends in romantic poignancy as Sylvie takes the long way home after seeing Arnaud board his train, for she thinks it unfair to arrive home before he does. She says she will never tell anyone about this, that it will remain a small and insignificant secret that belongs to the "true life" she is almost ready to enter. This is the bridge-crossing reflected by the title of the story and the book, for these small and seemingly insignificant secrets are what give Gallant's stories life. In one of her essays, Gallant has said that the only question worth asking about a story is "Is it dead or alive?"

Young women struggling with the roles expected of them by the old social order are not the only central characters in Gallant's stories; there are also Old World men as well, such as Dr. Dominic Missierna in the story "Kingdom Come," a scholar who has created a grammar of a little-known language spoken on a small island and who returns to Europe after twenty-four years to find out that no one really cares. Similar characters are Blaise Forain in the story "Forain," literary executor of a writer, Adam Tremski, who has just died, and keeper of an entire flock of little-known writers with only a modest estimation of their own gifts; and M. Wroblewski in the story "A State of Affairs," who misconstrues an offer from a bank for a line of credit for an account from which his wife can draw money when he dies. Missierna, Forain, and Wroblewski are the last remnants of the old Europe, just as the Carette family are the last remnants of the old Montreal. They live in a new world of changed conditions in Eastern Europe, where everything costs too much, young people are ignorant and rude, and there are no books worth reading.

Gallant's stories are notoriously irresolute, lacking the kind of patterned tidiness that often characterizes the short story form. It is a bias that she has held since the beginning of her professional life. When she was writing a weekly column about radio for the *Montreal Standard* newspaper in the late 1940's, she described one writer's plays as being unlike the usual radio play because they did not come to a traditional fictional climax. She defended this practice by noting that the people portrayed in the plays were "case histories," arguing that real problems do not always resolve themselves in tidy ways and that if stories seem incomplete, that is because they are true.

In spite of this apparent dismissal of the rhetorically patterned in favor of the realistically detailed, in one of her better-known essays, "What is Style?", collected in the anthology *Paris Notebooks* (1986), Gallant claims that style is intentional and inseparable from structure; it is part of whatever the writer has to say, she claims, concluding—as Henry James might well have—that content, meaning, intention, and form make up a unified whole that must have a reason to be.

The stories of Mavis Gallant are an acquired taste, delicate constructions that seem to be artless vignettes rather than carefully patterned stories. Gallant's stories are like the static electricity that plays around the person of Marie Carette: They create sparks and mild shocks in ways that many may miss unless they are paying careful attention. Gallant's characters do not seem significant in the large scheme of things, but then who determines what is large and what is small? As Gallant said in one of her essays, no life is more interesting than any other; what really matters is what is revealed and how.

Charles E. May

Sources for Further Study

Library Journal. CXVIII, September 1, 1993, p. 225.
Maclean's. CVI, October 18, 1993, p. 66.
The New York Times Book Review. XCVIII, September 12, 1993, p. 7.
Publishers Weekly. CCXL, July 12, 1993, p. 68.
The Washington Post Book World. XXIII, December 19, 1993, p. 6.

THE AGE OF FEDERALISM

Authors: Stanley Elkins (1925-   ) and Eric McKitrick (1919-   )
Publisher: Oxford University Press (New York). 925 pp. $39.95
Type of work: History
Time: 1789-1801
Locale: The United States

   A history of government and political ideas during the administrations of George Washington and John Adams

               Principal personages:
               GEORGE WASHINGTON, first president of the United States, 1789-1797
               JOHN ADAMS, second president of the United States, 1797-1801
               ALEXANDER HAMILTON, U.S. secretary of the treasury, 1789-1795
               THOMAS JEFFERSON, U.S. secretary of state, 1790-1793, and vice president,
                  1797-1801
               JAMES MADISON, member of the U.S. House of Representatives, 1789-1797

   This book presents a reasonably definitive treatment of the George Washington and John Adams presidential administrations, 1789-1801. Although a number of worthy biographies of the founding fathers, monographs, and excellent general studies, such as John C. Miller's *The Federalist Era, 1789-1801* (1960), have been previously published, there has been need for an in-depth analysis of American national government and politics between the inaugurations of Washington and Jefferson. Stanley Elkins and Eric McKitrick pull together all the threads and themes to present a judicious and freshly interpretive account of the shaping of the new government of the Republic. Although often excessively wordy, the book achieves considerable vitality in depicting the personalities of the important participants and even of lesser ones. Somewhat obtrusive, however, are the flashback biographical sketches of persons. For the major figures, the authors demonstrate a consistency in intellectual development.
   The book has something of a split personality, partly due to dual authorship, but mostly because the chronological coverage allows for a shifting of emphasis in the political process. First, ideas had to be tested in the practical arena of establishing government and formulating the direction of its policies. Then, as settled government emerged, events, domestic and worldwide, had sway in affecting the course of decision making and in causing the rise of oppositional politics.
   The great men who influenced decisions, some at odds with each other as Federalists versus Democratic-Republicans, had in common a desire to fashion government and its policies so that successive generations of Americans would be best served. The authors recognize a "Court-Country" division in American politics of the Revolutionary era, bearing some resemblances to alignments in Georgian England; in America, besides the competition between the "ins" and the "outs," there were the contending forces of nationalism, promoting commercial and industrial development, versus advocacy of agrarianism and a weak central government. The authors state that "a

central question for this book" is "exactly how the 'Court option'—the Federalist version of a republican future—was smothered in the 1790s, and the degree to which it smothered itself." With the rise of a party system, "the response of Federalism was that of righteousness under siege, and amounted to little more in the end than a sterile defense of constituted order against the forces of insubordination and sedition."

The authors discuss personal attributes of the great men of the age—notably George Washington, John Adams, Thomas Jefferson, James Madison, and Alexander Hamilton—but are not very successful in penetrating beyond the public to the inner man. Washington certainly honed virtues of restraint during his Virginia legislative and Congressional experiences and as commander in chief under the superintendence of Congress, as the authors contend. Yet this side of the man was as much affected during the French and Indian War years, when he learned how to handle interpersonal relationships in the context of driving ambition. The authors are also too selective in composing profiles of Jefferson, Adams, Madison, and Hamilton. Interpretations of lesser figures, such as Timothy Pickering, are more revealing.

Washington, whom the authors depict as a true republican, set his sights on establishing legitimacy, even reputation, for the new government. Having already long acquired a sense of "an additional self," Washington tried his best to follow the highest, most disinterested standards in administration. His quest not for the best men but for the "First Characters" was compromised somewhat, however, by insistence that appointees come from different segments of the broad geographical constituency.

Readers will find many insights in the discussions of the establishment of the executive and judicial branches, the enactment of the Bill of Rights, and foreign and Indian relations and diplomacy. Throughout the book, legislative debates and maneuvering are covered alongside executive actions.

The authors allege a "massive personal and political enmity" between Hamilton and Jefferson, but do not substantiate this assertion beyond discussing the clash of their policy ideas and principles. The "Federalist-Republican polarity" that developed was expressive of commerce and money versus agriculture, nation versus states, and elitism versus democracy. Philosophically, the cleavage between Hamilton and Madison, dating back to the duality of the *Federalist* papers, was an emphasis on power versus balance in government.

A strong case is made that Hamilton's hopes for a strong nationalist and mercantilist state were predicated upon ideas expounded in the writings of Scotsman David Hume. Though differing with Hume regarding the funding of national debt, Hamilton believed, as did Hume, that the public good was best promoted by the use of governmental power to stimulate commerce and industry. An urban, orderly, and commercial society suited the advancement of the economy and of human dignity.

The compelling criterium of the Hamiltonian program, according to the authors, was one of projection—"an ordering of facts and circumstances into patterns which present conditions have not as yet made actual but which future ones will." It is a vision of future growth. "The problem was one of execution, of how the potential was to be made real." The administration of Washington is evaluated in this context, with attention to the success of the Hamiltonian program in establishing public credit and its attempts to create an expansive government in the economic life of the nation.

The "bank war" is fully explained as it unfolded in the cabinet and Congress. Interestingly, the authors show that Hamilton's views in this instance derived not from Hume but from the Bank of England's charter, the ideas of Adam Smith, Malachi Postlethwayt, and Adam Anderson, and, by example, the career of William Pitt the Younger as chancellor of the exchequer and prime minister. The Madison-Jefferson and Hamilton debate over the constitutionality of a national bank—strict construction versus implication—has a deeper meaning of vested interests in government versus protection from government usurpation.

Jefferson's ideas of an agrarian democracy and his toughness concerning commercial rivalry with England reflected the influence of French Physiocrats and his own long-standing distrust of Britain, dating back to the pre-Revolutionary War years. The authors' contention that the 1769 nonimportation movement in Virginia (which never really caught on) was determinant upon Jefferson's views is overdrawn.

Little effort is made to gauge nationwide the growing party alignments—who, where, and why—as they began to appear after late 1791. The authors consider that the primary reason for the mounting opposition against Hamilton lay in perceptions that the Treasury was attempting to dominate the American national government. Jefferson and Madison were determined to prevent the triumph of Hamiltonian ideology and to thwart completion of the remainder of the Hamiltonian program— particularly protective tariffs, bounties, premiums for manufactured goods, and the government's creation of a model manufacturing corporation.

A shortcoming of the book is its failure to analyze substantially the intense, growing sectionalism in politics. Treatment of the question of establishing a new national capital concerns only cultural aspects. No issue was more volatile and divisive than the heated controversy, in Congress and out, over the capital's location, exacerbating bitter feelings between Yankees and Southerners. For further development of party rivalry, the authors give attention to the Philadelphia newspaper wars and the dissensions over Western policies, including the Spanish-Mississippi question. Although the authors fail to give adequate treatment of Democratic-Republicans and Federalists at the grassroots, they do afford a fresh interpretation of the Democratic societies that proliferated in 1793-1794 and then quickly disappeared. These societies are viewed mainly as simply another category among many associational groups. Though inspired by the Jacobin Clubs in France and republican ideas, they never obtained much popular support and therefore exerted little pressure on government. Nevertheless, even with minimal influence, they contributed to organizational tactics of the Jeffersonian Republicans. The authors declare that "the real drama of the French Revolution in America . . . was one not of foreign policy but of domestic partisanship." Public opinion was not so much affected by personalities or issues as by sentiment.

The rising indignation over British discrimination against American commerce, the retention of the Western posts, and encouragement of Indian resistance, according to the authors, brought the country to the verge of war with Great Britain. Anthony

Wayne's victory at Fallen Timbers in August, 1794 and the Jay Treaty, even though it sparked bitter popular opposition initially, defused an impending crisis. Though Republicans were the immediate losers with the treaty, in the long run the accompanying popular agitation aided their cause. The Pinckney Treaty of 1795, reaffirming Florida's boundary with Spain by the Treaty of Paris (1783) and permitting Americans an outlet for goods down the Mississippi, gained further approval for Federalist foreign policy.

The authors downplay economic disparity as a cause for the Whiskey Rebellion of 1794. Western farmers could pass the whiskey excise tax on to the consumer, they had access to the Mississippi and thus did not have to rely on Eastern markets, and the government, for military purposes, heavily purchased provisions and whiskey in western Pennsylvania. The main problem was that all stills, large and small, were taxed the same. While these factors are noted and participants are aptly profiled, the authors do not give a satisfying explanation for the crisis. Hamilton is viewed as having little to do with actual interference in law or government to bring a military solution.

Elkins and McKitrick emphasize that all the founding leaders embraced principles of republicanism but had different projections for the future. Washington, Hamilton, and Adams, unlike Jefferson and Madison, feared factions and the propensity for anarchy in an unbridled democracy. Jefferson and Madison were apprehensive of a too centralizing and encroaching government. Like other Federalists, Adams, whom the authors depict as aristocratic in outlook, saw the necessity of one-party government, allowing little leeway for dissent. To Adams, republican government had to have energy in order to control factions. Adams' political philosophy meant balanced powers among governmental branches, presided over mostly by an elite of merit. To Adams, the Federalist Congress was totally responsible for its legislation, good or bad, not in any measure owing to the direction of the Federalist president.

"XYZ fever" was at the heart of the political disingenuity of the late 1790's. With France allowing for the seizure of British goods on American ships, the country again came perilously close to war in 1798-1799. Adams refused to press for a declaration of war, not so much because of his own independent initiative as because his cabinet was divided for and against war.

While absolving Adams of any responsibility for enactment of the Alien and Sedition acts, the authors consider his lack of opposition to them and uncritical enforcement to be an expression of his basic fears of overzealous republicans of the Jacobin mold. The authors do not probe very far into the Alien-Sedition crisis—the government prosecutions and reactions.

The Quasi War with France, 1798-1799, in which the American government ordered armed retaliation against French search and seizure on the high seas, led to provision for a standing army to be used in a larger war. Some rapprochement occurred between Federalists and Democratic-Republicans, because Southerners feared a French invasion from the Caribbean, one that might incite slave insurrection. The war scare quickly subsided, and the intended army was never fully enlisted. The authors miss some of the nuances in the rancorous discontent over Adams' ranking of top officers, as suggested by Washington in retirement, and even Washington's own overzealous support for war preparations. The authors might have noted Adams' payback to Henry Knox for his refusal to serve under Hamilton and Charles Cotesworth Pinckney by refusing Knox's son a naval officer's appointment. Interestingly, the authors point out that Hamilton, always the "grand projector," declined a seat in the Senate in the expectation of leading the "New Army."

Adams' feud with Hamilton and the cabinet reorganization underscored the frailty of Federalist rule. Adams was vindicated in his foreign policy with the adoption of the Convention of 1800, which abated the American-French rift.

The final chapter, "The Mentality of Federalism," generally evaluates the Alien-Sedition crisis, suggesting that the repressive measures were not too severe, at least in comparison with the kind of actions taken in Great Britain during the same period. The Fries Rebellion of 1799, against the federal property tax to pay for war mobilization, accentuated public disfavor with the Federalists. The Virginia and Kentucky resolutions, written by Madison and Jefferson respectively, stating opposition to the Alien and Sedition acts while advocating states' rights and strict construction of the Constitution, really were intended for partisan propaganda. The election, or "revolution," of 1800 was a victory for popular sovereignty and a legitimation of change in government by those from the outside. With the lesson accomplished, the Jeffersonians, following a good Madisonian doctrine, projected a country reconciled and united.

Elkins and McKitrick's tome is a masterful narrative of the testing of ideas and public policy under the aegis of government by anointed guardians of American republican destiny. Federalism as a political entity was doomed to failure because of its own conceit and affinity for English Whig government. Americans needed to come to terms with a broad-based democracy.

The Age of Federalism does a great service in tracing opposing ideologies in America and showing how their proponents sought to develop them into a vision of stability and progress. The authors have researched significantly, but not exhaustively, published primary and secondary sources. Annotation is thorough and often expository. A bibliography is not included. Though the authors are often too selective in presenting evidential support of their interpretations, they have broadened the contours of understanding of the formative years of the Republic.

Harry M. Ward

Sources for Further Study

The Atlantic. CCLXXII, December, 1993, p. 134.
Booklist. LXXXIX, July, 1993, p. 1940.
Chicago Tribune. October 3, 1993, XIV, p. 1.
Choice. XXXI, February, 1994, p. 987.
The Christian Science Monitor. September 13, 1993, p. 13.

Colonial Homes. XX, February, 1994, p. 34.
Library Journal. CXVIII, October 1, 1993, p. 109.
Los Angeles Times Book Review. September 26, 1993, p. 2.
The New York Times Book Review. XCVIII, November 7, 1993, p. 15.
The New Yorker. LXIX, December 6, 1993, p. 144.
Publishers Weekly. CCXL, June 14, 1993, p. 54.

ALWAYS STRAIGHT AHEAD
A Memoir

Author: Alma Neuman (1912-1988)
Publisher: Louisiana State University Press (Baton Rouge). 165 pp. $24.95
Type of work: Memoir
Time: The 1930's to the 1980's
Locale: Upstate New York, New York City, Alabama, Mexico, and East Berlin

The wife of James Agee and the German writer Bodo Uhse tells all in a remarkably frank manner

Principal personages:
ALMA NEUMAN, a member of bohemian leftist circles in the United States and Europe
JAMES AGEE, her first husband, an American writer
BODO UHSE, her second husband, a German writer
JOEL AGEE, her son with Agee
STEFAN UHSE, her son with Uhse
ALFRED MILLER, her lover

In the late 1970's, long after his death (1955), Alma Neuman received a letter from her first husband, the famous American journalist, novelist, and film critic James Agee. Written in 1953, the letter had taken more than twenty years to reach her. A "stranger" had found the letter among Agee's manuscripts shortly after his death, misplaced it, and then found it again years later and sent it on. Agee had remarried, was the father of two children by his second wife (Alma was the mother of Agee's first child, Joel), had taken an "Irish girl" as lover, and yet, despite all the intervening years, confessed in this long-lost letter that he still loved Alma more than his second wife and his mistress.

Receiving this letter was a great shock for Alma Neuman, who had built an entirely different life for herself after Agee had fallen in love with another woman while she was pregnant with Joel. In 1941, when the couple separated, Alma took Joel to Mexico on what was supposed to be a long vacation. Agee eventually journeyed to Mexico to bring her and his son back to the United States, but she chose to return to Mexico and stay with a German émigré writer, Bodo Uhse, who offered her the emotional stability that Agee was unable to provide.

Uhse was also a marvelous father to Joel, and Alma was as grateful for his attention to the child as she was touched by his adoration of her. There was, however, a problem. Sex with Uhse was not what it had been with Agee; indeed, the absence of true passion with this man eventually drove Alma to take as her lover Uhse's best friend in Mexico, Alfred Miller, a fellow émigré and Communist who lacked Uhse's intellect but radiated compassion and was able to satiate Alma's sensual needs. Eventually, however, Miller died of a sudden heart attack. After a series of other misunderstandings, this time involving Uhse's attraction to another woman, Alma and Uhse realized that their bond was a true one, and Alma agreed to accompany him after the war to East Germany, where he was welcomed back as a respected anti-Fascist and Communist writer.

The woman who opened Agee's letter in the late 1970's had long since resettled in New York after Uhse's attempted suicide in Berlin. Her burning desire to answer Agee's poignant love letter was translated into the decision to write the present memoir. Her complete truthfulness would be her way of meeting Agee's desperate love call across the years that had separated them in life and now, as well, in death. Alma Neuman died in 1988, and her son Joel published the memoir in 1993.

So much for the bare outlines of her story. There is much more that could be told: the tragic fate of Uhse and Alma's son, Stefan, who accompanied his mother back to New York and eventually threw himself out of a window in despair over his incurable schizophrenia; in a lighter vein, Alma's working as a receptionist in a Mexico City art gallery and befriending Pablo Neruda, the great Chilean poet, and the greatest Mexican artists of the day, Diego Rivera and David Siqueiros; the important witnessing of Agee's visit in Alabama with the Tingle family, the impoverished sharecroppers Agee would immortalize in his famous book-length essay *Let Us Now Praise Famous Men* (1941); or the high drama of being physically threatened by a mob in June of 1953 when East German workers rose in revolt against the Communist regime.

Despite the honesty and unpretentious manner in which Alma Neuman shares with the reader the unusual and often searing incidents of her life, one has the impression, finally, that it was a life that happened to her rather than a life that she, in any purposeful way, made happen. She herself announces at regular intervals throughout the narrative that she always felt herself swept up in circumstances over which she had no control. This is true of all lives, to a certain extent, but Neuman suggests that she actually came to depend on these twists of fate to redirect her life without taking full responsibility for it, to experience the uplift of new beginnings without personally initiating the will to earn it. "Always straight ahead"—with someone or something else at the reins—was Neuman's guiding principle. She led a bohemian life, and in all fairness it must be acknowledged that bohemian women are more or less at the mercy of their self-indulgent bohemian male partners. In this case, however, Neuman's passivity cannot be easily dismissed; she was no mere artist's model or casualty of the gender politics of the literary world.

The child of an unimaginative but devoted businessman and a brilliant and artistic mother, Alma was drawn in her teens to the Saunders family, patrician Protestants who welcomed the Jewish girl to their enclave of high culture. She fell in love with the Saunders son and was a welcome addition to Professor Saunders' string quartet. (She became an accomplished violinist and played recitals in middle age when she was in Berlin.) It was at the Saunders home that Alma met James Agee, a Harvard senior at the time. The unexplored tensions resulting from Alma's suppressing of her Jewishness rose to the surface in Mexico, when she befriended refugees from Nazi Germany and connected with Bodo Uhse, her future husband, who, although a fervid anti-Nazi Communist when they met, confessed that he had been a member of the National

Socialist Party in the early 1930's. When Alma followed Uhse back to Germany after the war, she was mindful of the fact that she was now living among the people who only a very short while ago were subjecting Jews to their greatest persecution in two thousand years; nevertheless, her essential detachment prevailed. She felt isolated in Germany because she did not speak the language, but she blended with the East German intelligentsia without too much difficulty.

All through the memoir, the reader is never sure just how much or how little a Communist Alma Neuman was—in the United States, in Mexico, or in East Germany. Her circumspection on this point may have much to do with her perception of American attitudes toward American Communists, attitudes that she probably sensed were still considerably hostile in the 1970's and 1980's. The way she dealt with politics is similar to the way she dealt with the Holocaust. So close to moments of great significance in world history, Neuman never quite impresses us as really having been there.

This holds as well for her relationships to the two writers she married. Both were prominent. Uhse was as much admired in Berlin as Agee was in New York. Alma may have been a muse to both men, but she gives no sign of having been seriously touched by what they wrote. This is very different, for example, from the witnessing of Eileen Simpson, the wife of the brilliant but disturbed American poet John Berryman. In her memoir *Poets in Their Youth* (1982), Simpson captures the vitality of Berryman and his fellow poets—Randall Jarrell, Delmore Schwartz, Robert Lowell—and their dedication to their craft as well as the underlying troubles that contributed to their tragic early deaths. Neuman renders Agee's eccentricities, but the man himself eludes her. Uhse's literary art remains distant from her because her German is not up to it, while the man seems an anomalous combination of compassion, repression, courage, and self-indulgence. As the memoir unfolds, Uhse's essential incredibility seems to have more to do with Alma Neuman's limitations of perception than with her husband's actual character.

The most haunting moment in the entire memoir is not the sudden and mysterious arrival of Agee's long-lost letter. What stands out is the powerful scene in the memoir's epilogue between Alma, now more than sixty years old (remarried, for the last time, to a New Yorker named Bill Neuman) and her second son, Stefan, only an hour before his suicide leap from the high window of his room. Stefan gestures with his hands, a blessing of "healing" according to Alma, and without ever touching his mother encases her in an imaginary shelter of love and apology: "And always his hands were moving and halting, up and down, some three inches from my body." Alma interprets Stefan's parting gift to her as an occult gesture reaching for "the etheric field or aura around me." Maybe so, but the reader cannot help but see in this strange oedipal farewell one last example of Alma Neuman's curious isolation, even quarantine, from the tumultuous tragedy of her own life.

Peter Brier

Sources for Further Study

Belles Lettres. IX, Fall, 1993, p. 39.
Kirkus Reviews. LXI, January 1, 1993, p. 47.
Library Journal. CXVIII, February 15, 1993, p. 174.
Publishers Weekly. CCXL, February 1, 1993, p. 83.

AMENDING AMERICA
If We Love the Constitution So Much, Why Do We Keep Trying to Change It?

Authors: Richard B. Bernstein (1956-   ) with Jerome Agel
Publisher: Times Books (New York). 392 pp. $25.00
Type of work: History
Time: 1787 to the present
Locale: The United States

A historical look at the many attempts, since its adoption in 1788, to amend the U.S. Constitution

The United States Constitution remains as the oldest written constitution in continuous operation anywhere in the world. Originally designed to address the needs of a small and young nation of about four million people, it now governs the most powerful nation on earth.

One of the central questions raised by the authors of *Amending America: If We Love the Constitution So Much, Why Do We Keep Trying to Change It?* is whether the Framers were intent on producing a document to endure "for all time" or simply to address the shortcomings of the Articles of Confederation, the document that preceded the Constitution. Shortly after the delegates met in Philadelphia in 1787, it was clear that revising the Articles of Confederation, which had gone into effect in 1781 and had proved inadequate for the effective government of the United States, would not suffice. It was agreed that an entirely new document was necessary in order to ensure the political and financial stability of the young republic.

One of the major problems with the Articles was the impossibility of amending the document. Proposed amendments needed the consent of all the state legislatures—a requirement that proved unworkable. If even one state voted against an amendment, it was defeated. The solution, which became Article V of the new constitution, was that a proposed amendment could be considered whenever two-thirds of both houses of the legislature deemed it necessary. If three-fourths of the state legislatures subsequently approved, the amendment would become part of the Constitution.

Thus, the authors point out, the designers of Article V had two goals in mind. Since the impossibility of amending the Articles of Confederation made them an ineffective form of government, the Framers of the Constitution produced a document that could be adapted to changing circumstances and needs. At the same time, they wanted to ensure that changes would be made only when the majority of the citizens desired it and that changes would be considered only in serious cases, in order to maintain the stability of the document. When one looks over the span of almost two hundred years, it is evident that their hopes have been realized. During this time, the Constitution has been amended only twenty-seven times, and if the first ten amendments, which make up the Bill of Rights, are taken as one "mega-amendment" ratified in 1789, the number drops to seventeen. Yet more than ten thousand prospective amendments have been introduced or formally recommended to Congress during that time.

The first major change to the new Constitution was the demand by several states for a bill of rights. Many delegates, while agreeing that a strong federal government was necessary to the survival of the United States, also believed that the power of such a government must be limited if the rights of the people were to be protected. Thus Article V placated the strong opposition to the new Constitution and established some of the most basic individual rights cherished by American citizens: freedom of religion, freedom of speech, freedom of the press, freedom of assembly, the right to keep and bear arms, protection against unreasonable searches and seizures, and due process of law, among others.

Perhaps the greatest test of the amending process was the controversy over slavery. Taken together, the Thirteenth, Fourteenth, and Fifteenth Amendments, sometimes known as the "slavery amendments," reestablished the principles of individual rights and equal justice in America. Although they were originally ratified in order to put an end to the institution of slavery, in later years their guarantees of social and economic independence, equal protection of the laws, and the right to vote for emancipated blacks would sow the seeds of the Civil Rights movement in the twentieth century. The principles of individual rights and equal justice embodied in these amendments would help to shape the future of the American republic almost as profoundly as the Bill of Rights itself.

Between 1870 and 1913, no new amendments were added to the Constitution. Then suddenly, between 1913 and 1920, in response to the Progressive movement, which dominated American politics and society from the late 1890's through World War I, four new amendments were ratified. The Sixteenth Amendment, ratified in 1913, authorized Congress to levy and collect taxes on income, thus giving the American people more of a voice in how the federal government spent money. The Seventeenth Amendment, also ratified in 1913, gave the American people more control over the government by subjecting a key institution of the federal government, the U.S. Senate, to their authority; it required senators to be elected directly by the people rather than being chosen by state legislatures. The Eighteenth Amendment, ratified in 1919, outlawed the sale and use of alcoholic beverages, thus promoting such Progressive principles as sobriety, hard work, and morality among all classes of society. Finally, the Nineteenth Amendment, following the principle established by the Fifteenth Amendment (which allowed blacks to vote), extended the right of suffrage to women. Even the Twenty-first Amendment (1933), which repealed the Eighteenth and put an end to Prohibition, was considered a Progressive victory because it illustrated the ability of the American people to correct constitutional mistakes.

Not all amendments that have aroused widespread interest and public support were successful. A case in point was the proposed Equal Rights Amendment (1972): "Equality of rights under the law shall not be denied or abridged by the United States or by any State on account of sex." Although it seemed the amendment would be quickly ratified (by 1973, thirty of the necessary thirty-eight states had done so), it fell short by three states, even after the seven-year time limit for ratification had been extended three more years to 1982. Well-organized conservative opponents of the ERA successfully blocked ratification—a development that dramatically illustrates the difficulty of the amending process.

Other proposed amendments have met a similar fate, among them an amendment proposed in 1861 to prevent the federal government from interfering with the labor laws and practices of any state (which was actually an attempt to preserve the institution of slavery), a 1924 amendment to prohibit child labor, and a proposed amendment in 1978 to grant full self-government and representation for the citizens of the District of Columbia. Proposed amendments of this type usually fail to win ratification because they endeavor to use the Constitution as a legislative tool. Others, such as the Eighteenth Amendment and the attempt in 1989 to add an amendment prohibiting flag burning, deal with issues that are of concern only to a particular time. Most Americans have viewed their Constitution as a document that should primarily address universal concerns, and the consensus has usually prevailed that amendments that confine themselves to the problems of a particular era do not belong in the Constitution.

Some of the most troublesome features of the Constitution deal with the office of the presidency; indeed, four of the seventeen amendments after the Bill of Rights are concerned with adjustments to the executive branch. The Twelfth and the Twenty-second Amendments were designed to rectify defects in the process of choosing the president, the Twentieth Amendment changed the date at which the presidential term would begin, and the Twenty-fifth Amendment clarified the process for dealing with presidential illness and disability. The changes brought about by these amendments have been relatively minor, and although politicians have attempted to utilize the amendment process to expand, restrict, or restructure presidential powers even further, they have not succeeded. The durability of the office of the chief executive illustrates the brilliant balance of power established between the federal government and the people by the Constitution. Recognizing the need for a strong executive, the Framers marked out the boundaries of attempts to revise the office, but through the amending process, the people's ability to exercise responsible change in their system of government has been preserved.

As the authors assert in the subtitle of the book, Americans continue to love and revere their Constitution. But if this is the case, why has it been changed twenty-seven times, and why have there been more than ten thousand attempts to amend the document, including dozens of suggestions to replace the Constitution altogether? "If we love the Constitution so much, why do we keep trying to change it?"

Part of the answer is that the nation has changed dramatically in the more than two centuries since the United States declared its independence from Great Britain. In spite of the Framers' intentions to produce a document that would not only serve their immediate concerns but also address the problems and crises of generations to follow, they could not possibly have conceived what the United States of America would become. They also could not envision the moral and legal dilemmas created by modern technology and the complexities of American social and political life. Thomas

Jefferson argued in 1788 that no generation should be bound by any obligations contracted by its predecessors. He thus foresaw a day, not too far in the future, when the Constitution would be replaced by a document that more accurately reflected the problems and concerns of some future generations of Americans. Yet others, such as James Madison, were more cautious. Madison feared that too-frequent constitutional revision and replacement would undermine the political and social stability of free government.

Despite Jefferson's call for frequent constitutional reform, the United States still governs itself according to a constitution adopted in 1788, with relatively few revisions thereafter. Although there have been a few calls for a second constitutional convention, the ability to amend the Constitution through the process outlined in Article V has subdued most attempts to return to the constitutional drawing board.

Yet the question remains whether the Constitution can continue to be an effective document in the light of the dramatic and continuing improvements in transportation, communications, medicine, weaponry, and other forms of technology. For example, could the Framers have anticipated that a future president would have at his or her disposal the awesome power of nuclear weapons capable of destroying the entire world? Advances in medical technology have also made questions of life and death difficult to resolve constitutionally, and areas such as genetic engineering and biotechnology bring up hundreds of unforeseen constitutional questions.

Richard Bernstein and Jerome Agel believe that as the pace of American life continues to accelerate and legal and political issues continue to arise for which the document provides no clear solution, there will be increasing political pressure to amend the Constitution. Unfortunately, the defenders of the new Constitution in 1787-1788 left few clues regarding their thoughts on how Article V should be used to amend the document. Their primary concern at the time was to secure the adoption of the Constitution, and consequently they were reluctant to point out any inherent defects. All that is known is that they intended Article V to be used to correct future defects of the Constitution as they became apparent, or to adapt it to changing circumstances.

The question for future generations, as additional amendments are added to the Constitution, is at what point the amendment process should cease and, because of the large number of changes, an entirely new document be drafted. The authors conclude *Amending America* by suggesting that a time may come when the American people consider the Constitution no longer adaptable to the changing conditions of American social and political life and in need of a full-scale revision. Even though the majority of American people continue to regard their Constitution as an almost timeless and sacred document, it remains to be seen just how far they will trust its political adaptability.

Raymond Frey

Sources for Further Study

Booklist. LXXXIX, March 15, 1993, p. 1278.
Choice. XXXI, September, 1993, p. 218.
Detroit News. August 11, 1993, p. A11.
Human Rights. XX, Summer, 1993, p. 9.
Kirkus Reviews. LXI, February 1, 1993, p. 107.
Library Journal. CXVIII, April 1, 1993, p. 114.
National Journal. XXV, May 1, 1993, p. 1075.
Publishers Weekly. CCXL, January 25, 1993, p. 70.
The Washington Post Book World. XXIII, September 5, 1993, p. 6.

ANAÏS
The Erotic Life of Anaïs Nin

Author: Noël Riley Fitch (1937-   )
Publisher: Little, Brown (Boston). 525 pp. $24.95
Type of work: Literary biography

The demystification process that this book launches is healthy and long overdue, but the author leaves the reader only more in awe of Anaïs Nin's struggle and achievement

> *Principal personages:*
> ANAÏS NIN, a diarist and fiction writer
> ROSA CULMELL-NIN, her Cuban-born mother
> JOAQUIN NIN, her musician-composer father
> HUGH P. GUILER (IAN HUGO), her banker husband, who became an engraver and filmmaker
> RENATE DRUKS, her artist friend and confidante
> EDUARDO SANCHEZ, her cousin and sometime suitor, whom she considered her psychic twin
> OTTO RANK, an Austrian psychoanalyst who became her mentor and lover
> HENRY MILLER, an American novelist and essayist who was her lover in the 1930's and friend thereafter
> JUNE MILLER, Henry's wife, Nin's alter ego during the early 1930's
> LAWRENCE DURRELL, a British novelist and friend to Miller and Nin
> LUISE RAINER, an actress she befriended
> GORE VIDAL, an American novelist, who helped her gain commercial publication
> RENÉ ALLENDY, her French psychoanalyst
> GONZALO MORE, a Peruvian expatriate revolutionary, manager of Nin's Gemor Press, and another of her lovers
> JEAN VARDA, an American painter-collagist
> RUPERT POLE, an actor, outdoorsman, and teacher with whom Nin lived the last third of her life in California

After the seven volumes of *The Diary of Anaïs Nin* (1966-1980), the four volumes of *The Early Diary of Anaïs Nin* (1978-1985), *Henry and June* (1986), and *Incest* (1992), with more volumes of unexpurgated material to come, why would anyone want to attempt the biography of a woman who spent most of her own life creating an intimate self-portrait? There are many answers to this question. One answer is that such an attractive subject needs to be cut down to a manageable size. Noël Riley Fitch's 410 pages of biographical text do just that; fortunately, this concentration of interpreted information heightens rather than merely reduces its subject. Another answer is that Nin's diaries are factually unreliable, and a careful researcher such as Fitch (who provides almost eighty pages of acknowledgments and notes) can fill in and emend the record. Finally, Nin's sense of herself, as recorded in her own words, is illusory. Fitch is able to attend to these image distortions as well as to their causes and effects.

Fitch's Nin (there will be others) emerges as a woman of dramatic paradoxes. At once (or in turn) vain and insecure, prudish and nymphomaniacal, willful and yielding,

Nin managed the pieces of her fragmented nature like an artist working in mosaic. A control freak often ready to fly into pieces, she found her life's work and worth in a career of self-making centered in the diary enterprise. The discipline of the diary held her together—or at least kept her from further destruction and dispersion. She took William Wordsworth's dictum that we half create what we perceive and applied it to her very self as much as to the world around her. Fitch's careful and compassionate study reveals the psychic and textual machinery of this process.

Nin's life, as Fitch relates it, can be compared to a psychological game of hide-and-seek, with Nin playing both parts. Playing, that is, as in acting. Addicted to disguises and deceits, Nin is a creature of costume, set design, and cosmetic transformation. For her, the domestic skills of sewing and home decorating become the magic of a theater of illusion in which she was eternally the awakened sleeping princess. A single leading man could not bring out the range of possibilities imagined by this woman, who was always experimenting in search of the core self. She was her perfectionist father's little girl hiding out as junior socialite wife to bank officer Hugh Guiler; lover, supporter, and literary helpmate to vagabond genius Henry Miller; rival and enamorata of Henry's wife June; patient, assistant, and seductress to psychoanalyst Otto Rank; and (briefly) mistress to that father by whom she felt abandoned—and this is merely to rehearse her better-known roles. What is most remarkable about this particular group of parts is that during the 1930's Nin could play many of them in a single day, sometimes before different sets in the same theater.

Although she could momentarily realize herself in each of these parts (and a succession of others), Nin could not find rest in any of them. Some other need led her to make quick escapes and costume changes. Indeed, she made her life so complicated that it seems as if she wanted to trip herself up and be found out. Maybe if she was discovered (or uncovered), she would find the source of her dissatisfactions. In less obvious ways, she sought discovery as a prelude to punishment. She was a woman of many pleasures, but they may have all been rooted in pain and guilt.

Fitch's major contribution to the understanding of Nin's often erratic behavior—indeed, one might call this insight the thesis of her book—is the assertion that as a young girl Nin was sexually abused by her father. Nin's repression and sublimation of this trauma is a key factor in Fitch's reading of Nin's oddly patterned existence. It lies behind *The Diary of Anaïs Nin* as firmly as the diary lies behind the fiction.

The strength of Fitch's argument lies more in how well it explains the patterns of Nin's life and work than in its evidentiary rigor. Only fragments of evidence for the traumatic scene emerge. Yet Fitch's extrapolation is skilled and compelling. Wisely, she does not make too much of it, and thus she avoids the risk of an absurdly reductive approach. She knows that this buried trauma, while it adjusts the reader's vision, does not explain everything. It does not account for Nin's enormous reservoirs of energy and perseverance. It does not make her an admired writer. It does not make her manufactured self a role model for countless women.

Fitch helps readers understand the shaping forces in Nin's life with a detailed look at Nin's parents and their families, especially the maternal branch. Nin's intimate lifelong relationship with her cousin Eduardo Sanchez, whom she considered a kind of double, helps to explain her literary concern with the proximity of self-love and incest. Nin always needed a closed world that she could manage even while striving to achieve a stature dependent upon the attention of many. Her husband's partial estrangement from his own family consequent upon his marriage to this ungenteel Catholic young woman also helps to explain the very private world that the young Guilers made for themselves in Paris. Fitch's analysis of sexual dysfunction and denial during the early years of the Guiler marriage prepares the reader to understand Nin's volcanic sexuality some years later, while it is itself understood in terms of her traumatic past.

Of particular interest is Fitch's portrait of Nin's later years, which were spent largely in California; her long, restorative relationship there with Rupert Pole (during which time she maintained her East Coast front with her only legal husband, who had taken the name Ian Hugo); and the blessings and costs of fame following the publication of her diary volumes. Yet the chapters of the book that cover Nin's post-New York career cover many more years in far fewer pages than do the chapters on earlier periods of her life. In this regard Fitch has followed the proportional attention of Nin's own record. She has trusted, perhaps inevitably, Nin's sense of where the drama lies.

One of Fitch's primary interests, an interest that justifies her biographical project, is to examine the ways in which the diaries are themselves duplicitous. She attends to Nin's practice of revising while recopying and typing the original manuscript diaries, and she suggests that even in their original state the diaries were heightened and shaped versions of Nin's life. She also sharpens one's awareness of the editorial process that brought Nin's reconstituted and reconfigured life to the attention of a largely admiring public. Furthermore, Fitch underscores Nin's habit of revealing more about herself in works prepared and presented as fiction than in (published) diary material on the same life events and relationships. In these matters Fitch is not breaking new ground. Benjamin Franklin V and Duane Schneider in their *Anaïs Nin: An Introduction* (1979) and Nancy Scholar in her *Anaïs Nin* (1984) are among theseveral earlier scholars who have noted many of these same characteristics of the diary and the fiction. Fitch orchestrates such insights effectively, enlarges upon them, and makes them an important part of her overall portrait. Moreover, she includes considerations of Nin's unpublished work as well as early drafts to help fill in the picture.

Most of the time, literary biographers have to stay clear of finding the life in the works. While a knowledge of the life might help to elucidate the works, the opposite tactic is fraught with dangers both obvious and not so obvious. Biographers must credit the imaginative powers of their artist-subjects. In Nin's case, however, the biographer can legitimately make cautious deductions from the fiction. As Nin herself admitted, she was not able to make credible anyone's experience but her own. Furthermore, as publication of the "unexpurgated" diaries makes clear, Nin often drew slavishly upon this material for her stories and novels. Many of the revelations in *Henry and June* (1986), for example, had been made much earlier in thinly veiled fictional disguise in a story called "Djuna," published as part of the limited edition *The Winter of Artifice*

(1939) and later suppressed. Though Nin long denied the dependence of her fiction on the diary, the denial was one of many deceptions. Nevertheless, the fiction must be handled with care, and Fitch so handles it. Indeed, she handles all of her sources with imagination and, given the incendiary nature of the material, with tact.

Fitch achieves a new dimensionality for her subject by having fruitfully absorbed the scant public record; the published and unpublished correspondence, diaries, and fiction; the published comments of Nin's friends and associates; and the relevant work of other scholars. (One should note here that many diary volumes have not yet been made available to Fitch or to other scholars.) She has added to this material insights gathered from scores of interviews and from privately held correspondence between Nin and others. The weave is smooth, dexterous, and thematically focused. In this way (if not in others), Fitch's book on Nin is more successful than her earlier *Sylvia Beach and the Lost Generation* (1983), a monument in modern literary history. One possible artistic blemish in *Anaïs: The Erotic Life of Anaïs Nin* is Fitch's decision to employ the historical present tense, a decision that creates a breathless, forward-pushing prose that in turn fosters an artificial sense of immediacy and urgency. Given the story and character being revealed, such a stylistic strategy is hardly needed and may be, for some readers, counterproductive.

Though impressively careful in her presentation of facts, Fitch slips up on a few occasions. She perpetuates Nin's own error by naming a book by Otto Rank *Don Juan and His Double*. There is no such book. What Nin had read was a French translation of two Rank essays bound in one volume as *Don Juan: Une étude sur le double* (1932). This volume was published by Bernard Steele, the man who gave it to Nin. Fitch's treatment of the Rank affair is strangely attenuated, given its importance, and her claim that it was essentially over before February 1935 can certainly be challenged. On one occasion, Fitch misdates Nin's second book of fiction (as 1936 rather than 1939), though the correct date is given in numerous other references. Nevertheless, these problems are few and their import minuscule in the light of the vast amount of information Fitch has unearthed, mastered, and presented with vividness and clarity.

Just as Nin's own writings have led many women to a greater sense of security, possibility, and understanding, so Fitch's biography will further—though with modifications—the Nin legend and its consequences. Although a jacket blurb by Erica Jong announces that Fitch "solves riddles and answers the questions," such is not ultimately the case—nor can it be. The questions Fitch answers only raise new ones. The demystification process that begins with this book is healthy and long overdue, but in putting a more human, more accessible face on the many faces of Anaïs Nin, Fitch leaves her readers only more impressed with Nin's struggle and achievement. The newly displayed warts do not take anything away. Nin's need for illusion does not have to infect her readers, those to whom her writings bring a unique mixture of excitement, comfort, and insight. She can be admired for who she was just as much as for the woman (or women) she thought she was and wanted to be.

Philip K. Jason

Sources for Further Study

Booklist. LXXXIX, August, 1993, p. 2030.
Boston Globe. October 3, 1993, p. 39.
Chicago Tribune. October 24, 1993, XIV, 3.
Detroit News. November 24, 1993, p. C3.
Library Journal. CXVIII, September 1, 1993, p. 183.
Los Angeles Times Book Review. December 26, 1993, p. 6.
The New York Times Book Review. XCVIII, October 17, 1993, p. 18.
Publishers Weekly. CCXL, June 28, 1993, p. 61.

ANGELS AND INSECTS
Two Novellas

Author: A. S. Byatt (1936-   )
First published: 1992, in Great Britain
Publisher: Random House (New York). Illustrated. 339 pp. $21.00
Type of work: Novellas
Time: 1859-1875
Locale: England

In the guise of Victorian romance, these two loosely linked novellas explore timeless questions of life and love

Principal characters:
> WILLIAM ADAMSON, a naturalist
> HARALD ALABASTER, a former clergyman, now a baron
> GERTRUDE ALABASTER, his wife
> EDGAR ALABASTER, their son
> EUGENIA ALABASTER, their oldest daughter
> MATTY CROMPTON, a distant, dependent relative of the Alabasters
> ARTURO PAPAGAY, the captain of the *Calypso*
> LILIAS PAPAGAY, his wife
> SOPHY SHEEKBY, Lilias Papagay's housemate and a spiritual medium
> RICHARD JESSE, a retired sea captain
> EMILY TENNYSON JESSE, his wife, a sister of Alfred, Lord Tennyson
> ALFRED, LORD TENNYSON, the Victorian poet laureate
> ARTHUR HENRY HALLAM, his friend and Emily Tennyson's fiancé

In *Possession* (1990), A. S. Byatt's previous work of fiction, the late twentieth century academics Roland Mitchell and Maud Bailey pursued the lives of fictional Victorian poets Randolph Ash and Christabel LaMotte. The novel's structure allowed Byatt to re-create a nineteenth century world and to contrast that period with that of the late twentieth century. She indicated that in the Victorian era sex was more difficult but love was simpler, and that what modernity has gained in knowledge it has lost in feeling.

Angels and Insects returns to the Victorian era, but it now appears as vexed as the reader's own. The title suggests one of the novellas' central concerns: Which term better describes humanity? Byatt offers no definitive answer, but her posing of the question combines historical romance and philosophical disquisition.

The first novella, *Morpho Eugenia*, takes its title from a Brazilian butterfly and the lovely Eugenia Alabaster (*morpho* in Greek means lovely, well-formed). This dual significance introduces a theme that pervades the narrative, the similarity between human behavior and that of the social insects. Even the architecture of Bredely Hall suggests this parallel. For example, Harald Alabaster's study is "hexagonal in shape, with wood-panelled walls and two deep windows, carved in stone in the Perpendicular style: the ceiling too was carved stone, pale grey-gold in colour, a honey-comb of smaller hexagons." The description demonstrates Byatt's skill in re-creating Victorian settings in loving detail, but her word paintings move beyond mere decoration. Alabaster's study, with its hexagonal construction, suggests a beehive and so links him and his household to the insect world.

Alabaster, a former clergyman who became a baron on the unexpected death of his older brother, retains his clerical garb and religious preoccupations. Byatt pointedly begins the novella in 1859, the year Charles Darwin published his *On the Origin of Species by Means of Natural Selection*, which challenged the biblical account of creation and shook the foundations of religious belief for many. Born in an age of faith, when the Bible could be taken literally, Alabaster has lived to find "a world in which we are what we are because of the mutations of soft jelly and calceous bone matter through unimaginable millennia." Byatt thus demonstrates that culture shock is not an exclusively late twentieth century phenomenon.

To combat his doubts, Alabaster is writing a book arguing that belief in a Creator remains possible after Darwin. He enjoys discussing his ideas with William Adamson, a naturalist who had formerly supplied him with specimens and who was shipwrecked on his return from a decade in the Brazilian jungles. Though reared by a strict Methodist father, Adamson cannot share Alabaster's religious views. He rejects arguments of design and analogy, but as he studies the workings of anthills and beehives he ponders the same mysteries that prey on Alabaster.

Even on his first night at Bredely Hall, Adamson observes the butterflylike qualities of Alabaster's three oldest daughters. Lady Gertrude Alabaster resembles a queen bee or ant. Secluded in her bower, she is fed sweet foods and drink, and her only function appears to be the production of offspring. She has given birth to eight; Bredely Hall is aptly named. Despite her lassitude, Adamson senses that she provides the vital force of the household, that without her the family would cease to function, just as a hive or anthill cannot survive without its queen.

In another analogy with the insect world, after marrying Eugenia, Adamson discovers that his conjugal life assumes a cyclical pattern, for sex is banned during Eugenia's frequent pregnancies. Pointedly, Adamson's second honeymoon, in 1861, coincides with the mating flight of the local ants.

The servants also remind Adamson of insects. In his jungle hut he had a nest of wasps on his roof. They did not bother him, and they controlled the flies and cockroaches. The servants at Bredely Hall also live just below the roof. They dress in drab outfits, and among their duties is ridding the house of unwanted beetles. During an attack of slave-seeking sanguinea on a wood-ant colony, Adamson observes that captured wood-ant larvae will serve their masters despite their different birth and appearance. He also comments that *Polyergus refescens* depend on slave ants for all their bodily needs; the master ants can only kill and carry off more slaves. Set against the English class system with its unproductive aristocracy and the backdrop of the American Civil War, Byatt's story indicates yet another Darwinian parallel between human and insect society.

Morpho Eugenia challenges the notion of human uniqueness. It also questions the distinction between civilization and barbarism. Again, Adamson's first encounter with the Alabasters introduces this theme. The family is hosting a dance, and Lady Alabaster encourages Adamson to participate. Her son Edgar adds, "Not much dancing in the jungle." Adamson replies that Christian festivals in Brazil involve weeks of dancing, and the Indians have their own versions that last for hours. The English ball provokes memories of a *festa* in South America, and Adamson recognizes beneath the fancy dress and decorous posing the same mating impulse that underlies the Brazilian palm-wine dance.

Adamson's early encounter with Edgar foreshadows other unpleasantries between them. Shortly before Adamson's marriage, Edgar, drunk, challenges his soon-to-be brother-in-law. Edgar's behavior reminds Adamson of the antics of intoxicated Brazilian natives. After Edgar leaves the room, Robin Swinnerton (who is engaged to Rowena Alabaster) calls the quarrelsome young man an anachronism, whereas he himself and Adamson represent civilization. Yet even the parlor games and the wedding at Bredely Hall suggest jungle festivals. The cultural distance between the English countryside and the Amazon is less than the geographical.

A keen observer of insects and analogies, Adamson is not aware of the incestuous relationship between Eugenia and Edgar. To enlighten him, Matty Crompton, who has unobtrusively been guiding Adamson's life at Bredely Hall, writes an insect fable that combines Homer, Aesop, and Jean de La Fontaine. In *Possession* Byatt demonstrated her facility with ventriloquism, creating with equal agility Victorian poetry and postmodern academic prose. The same talent manifests itself here. Crompton's story tells of Seth's capture and enchantment by a Circe-like figure who is the counterpart of Eugenia. He is rescued by Mistress Mouffet, Matty Crompton's alter ego. The fable again emphasizes the similarity between people and insects. Even Eugenia's incest, an anagram for "insect," suggests the insect world, in which the queen mates with her own offspring.

Adamson cannot decode the fable (or the anagram). Only when Adamson finds brother and sister together in the latter's bedroom does he learn what the other members of the household have known for years. This confrontation is engineered mysteriously, as if in the motions of an anthill. Together with Matty, Adamson sails for Brazil aboard the *Calypso* in 1863. Commanding the ship is Captain Arturo Papagay.

Twelve years later, in the second novella, Lilias Papagay is still waiting to hear from her husband. To support herself she has taken a lodger, Sophy Sheekby, and the two women earn a living as spiritual mediums. Each week they visit the Jesses for a séance. Mrs. Papagay hopes to hear from her husband, Mrs. Hearnshaw seeks to communicate with her five dead daughters, all named Amy, and Mrs. Jesse wants to learn about her dead fiancé, Arthur Henry Hallam.

In this novella Byatt retells the love story of Emily Tennyson's engagement to Hallam and of his tragic, premature death in 1833. Emily mourned for nine years, but her brother grieved for seventeen before publishing *In Memoriam* (1850), large chunks of which are quoted in the course of the narrative. Emily recognizes the poem's greatness but believes that with it her brother has stolen her own lost love.

At the end of this novella she is offered a chance to reclaim him. Arthur appears to her as half of a Swedenborgian conjugal angel—the source of the novella's title—and says that in Heaven Emily will become his other half. Even her husband, Richard Jesse, is surprised when she rejects this arrangement, preferring to remain with her spouse in the afterlife.

The account of Emily Tennyson's—and her brother Alfred's—love of Arthur Hallam is well told, but Byatt's treatment of spiritualism strains the reader's credulity. One expects a debunking of automatic writing, table rapping, and spectral visions. Instead, Mrs. Hearnshaw's dead children reveal what none of the others at the Jesse séance can know, that their mother is pregnant again. Separated by many miles, Sophy Sheekby and Alfred, Lord Tennyson have coinciding visions. When Mrs. Papagay transcribes from spiritual dictation, her handwriting resembles that of the dead speaker.

These novellas offer two visions of humanity. *Morpho Eugenia* regards people as another evolutionary form differing little from the social insects. *The Conjugal Angel* accepts the soul's immortality and religious mysticism. The former revolves around doubt and infidelity; the latter, apart from a minor episode involving an ill-mannered clergyman, tells of love and reunion. Both are entertaining. If the darker vision appears the truer, perhaps Byatt is challenging the reader to ponder why.

Joseph Rosenblum

Sources for Further Study

Belles Lettres. IX, Fall, 1993, p. 28.
London Review of Books. XIV, November 19, 1992, p. 18.
Los Angeles Times Book Review. June 13, 1993, p. 8
The New Republic. CCIX, August 2, 1993, p. 41.
New Scientist. CXXXVII, March 20, 1993, p. 41.
New Statesman and Society. V, November 6, 1992, p. 49.
The New York Times Book Review. XCVIII, June 27, 1993, p. 14.
The New Yorker. LXIX, June 21, 1993, p. 98.
The Observer. October 18, 1992, p. 60.
Publishers Weekly. CCXL, March 1, 1993, p. 40.
The Spectator. CCLXIX, October 24, 1992, p. 32.
The Times Literary Supplement. October 16, 1992, p. 22.

ANTHONY TROLLOPE

Author: Victoria Glendinning
First published: Trollope, 1992, in Great Britain
Publisher: Alfred A. Knopf (New York). 551 pp. $30.00
Type of work: Biography
Time: 1815-1882
Locale: England and Ireland

A well-written, detailed biography of one of the most prolific English novelists of the Victorian era—or any other

> *Principal personages:*
> ANTHONY TROLLOPE (1815-1882), a Victorian novelist
> FRANCES (FANNY) TROLLOPE (1780-1863), his indomitable mother, a prolific and celebrated writer in her own right
> ROSE TROLLOPE (1821-1917), his devoted wife of thirty-nine years
> TOM TROLLOPE (1810-1892), his older brother, who became their mother's caretaker and a serious collector of Italian art
> KATE FIELD (1838-1896), an accomplished young American activist

Even a superficial perusal of Anthony Trollope's life presents a conundrum: how to reconcile this most conventional, "clubbish, roast-beef" Englishman, this lifelong public servant, with his fantastic literary output, consisting of forty-seven novels plus travel writing, short fiction, and an autobiography. In part, it was the pedestrian nature of Trollope's existence that allowed for this extraordinary creative effort. Clearly, the same habit of regularity that contributed to Trollope's successful forty-three-year career with the Post Office permitted him to rise every day at 5:00 A.M. (later 6:00) and turn out between 20 and 120 pages per week, each page containing precisely 250 words (he counted every one of them).

However admirable Trollope's discipline, it does not explain the high quality of most of his work; neither does it explain the extraordinary sensitivity and insight manifested in the novels toward his characters, particularly the females. In life Trollope exhibited unremarkable passions for politics and fox hunting, and he married a dutiful and seemingly unremarkable woman to whom he apparently remained faithful. Where then did he acquire—indeed, find the time to acquire—the wide-ranging psychological acumen displayed so abundantly in his literary work?

For answers Victoria Glendinning turns to Trollope's childhood, which while not as conspicuously harrowing as that of his contemporary Charles Dickens, nevertheless contained more than enough trauma to mark any moderately sensitive child for life. To begin with, there were his parents.

His father, Thomas Anthony, a barrister educated at Winchester and an Oxford college, had all the appropriate credentials, but as his son Anthony put it later in life, he was a "mixture of poverty and gentle standing." While continuing to declare himself a gentleman, the elder Trollope steadily—and seemingly inexorably—reduced his family's circumstances to a state of bankruptcy. One of the most poignant and amusing scenes from the novelist's early life occurred just as his father fled the country to escape his creditors. When the eighteen-year-old Anthony returned home after taking his father to catch a boat bound for Belgium, as he later noted in his *Autobiography*, "a scene of devastation was in progress, which was not without its amusement." As the bailiff's men carried furniture out the front door, Anthony's sisters and three neighbor girls were snatching up anything they could carry and absconding with the goods to the neighbors' house.

Fortunately, Fanny Trollope possessed enough energy and good humor to make up for her husband's instability, poor health, and even poorer disposition. In order to rescue her family from destitution, she turned to writing, exhibiting a level of industry and discipline that surely influenced Anthony's later workmanlike approach to the craft. But she, too, deserted the family because of financial exigency, going off to America to seek her fortune when she was forty-seven and Anthony only thirteen. Unlike her husband, she returned from exile and made something positive of her adventures by writing a celebrated book, *The Domestic Manners of the Americans*— the first of many literary efforts—but her nearly four-year absence must have cost young Anthony dearly.

From very early in their childhood, it was made clear to all the Trollope children that Anthony's eldest brother, Tom, five years his senior, was Fanny's favorite. Thus alienated from the affections of the only real source of stability during his early years, Anthony developed a sense of inferiority that was soundly reinforced by the beatings he received from Tom when both were schoolboys at Winchester College. Sullen, clumsy, antisocial, and an academic ne'er-do-well, the young Anthony seems nevertheless, at the nadir of adolescence, to have found the resolve eventually to succeed, to rescue for himself the gentle standing his father had squandered. Once redeemed, it was a status Trollope worked tenaciously to preserve.

If Trollope realized his father's status, he got there by emulating his mother's industry, and he did not get there alone. It was only after meeting and becoming engaged to Rose Heseltine at age twenty-eight that Trollope began his literary career. It may have been the prospect of increased financial responsibilities that initiated his first novel, *The Macdermots of Ballycloran* (1847), but clearly his marital alliance with Rose, who served as his amanuensis and read every word he wrote before anyone else did, smoothed the way for his prolific output (he averaged two novels a year).

Rose also served as a different sort of inspiration in her husband's writing. Glendinning connects Rose with what she calls the "Ur-story" of Trollope's romantic plots, in which the author comments on the difficulties of committing oneself to another and the pain of loving two people simultaneously. In Trollope's Ur-story the hero falls in love with a poor, unsophisticated, but respectable country girl to whom he spontaneously proposes, perhaps only because of her proximity and availability. The hero then returns home to the city, only to become involved there with another more worldly and sexually sophisticated woman. An even-handed exploration of the agonies of both the hero and his trusting fiancée ensues.

Comparisons between the naïve Ur-heroine and Rose seem inevitable. Trollope's family clearly thought that in marrying Rose, a bank manager's daughter who had neither fortune nor any notable beauty, he was "marrying down." Trollope himself never directly indicated any disaffection with his "Dearest Love" (as he addressed Rose in letters throughout his life with her). Nevertheless, Trollope's equilibrium was considerably unsettled when, in the sixteenth year of his marriage, he met Kate Field, then twenty-two years old, a dynamic, liberated, and highly attractive American woman. Field cultivated literary figures, and Trollope was not the first to succumb to her charms, but her effect on him replicated the prolonged and painful anxieties experienced by many a Trollope Ur-hero in the throes of an involvement with the "other woman."

In his posthumously published *Autobiography* (1883), Trollope made scant mention of Rose; neither did he have much to say about Kate Field. Such was his integrity, however, that he was compelled to bear witness to her impact on his life:

> There is an American woman, of whom not to speak in a work purporting to be a memoir of my life would be to omit all allusion to one of the chief pleasures which has graced my later years. In the last fifteen years she has been, out of my family, my most chosen friend. She is a ray of light to me, from which I can always strike a spark by thinking of her. I do not know that I should please her or do any good by naming her. But not to allude to her in these pages would amount almost to a falsehood.

Glendinning evidently uncovered no evidence of a sexual relationship with Field. Plainly, however, she played an important role in Trollope's life—if only by embodying one aspect of the romantic myth that occupied his imagination and informed his fiction.

Glendinning thus goes a long way toward reconciling the personage once called "the dullest of Britons" with his phenomenal literary creativity. The wealth of detail she provides in her lengthy book itself helps to personalize Trollope and breathe life into the times in which he lived. In her introduction, for example, she makes use of an ancillary but interesting tidbit she uncovered in researching his life: his near obsession with women with healthy teeth (a rarity in Victorian England). In a footnote she observes that because the last report of the happening occurred in 1850, as a young postal clerk in London Trollope could have heard nightingales singing in Berkeley Square.

Anthony Trollope is more life than literary analysis. Nevertheless, although Glendinning does not devote lengthy passages to exegesis of the novels, she does a good job of interweaving Trollope's biography with his works in order to explain his legacy. Trollope acquired an enormous readership in his own time, and his popularity has continued more or less unabated. Today virtually all of his works are in print, and although this fact doubtless owes something to a serialization on television of the Palliser and Barchester novels, it is worth noting that unlike the works of some other critically favored writers, Trollope's have never gone out of favor with readers.

Trollope's reputation has been repeatedly assailed by critics on grounds that his novels are too firmly rooted in the status quo, diminished by smugness. His contemporary Thomas Carlyle wrote that Trollope was "irredeemably imbedded in common-place, and grown fat upon it." To be sure, any writer exhibiting such fecundity as Trollope did is bound also to exhibit flaws—Glendinning duly notes his defective spelling (often, she asserts, the fault of Rose's transcriptions) and his frequent confusion of such detail as characters' names and occupations—but his loyal and constant readership attests his skill at addressing the interests of their lives. It is a tribute to him that these interests persevere—and not only among general readers. As no less a commentator than Henry James, who was not always a friendly witness, observed, "Trollope did not write for posterity; he wrote for the day, the moment; but these are just the writers whom posterity is apt to put into its pocket."

This is not to say that Trollope novels are slice-of-life. Throughout his own life Trollope harbored political ambitions—perhaps not unrelated to his driving hunger for gentlemanly acceptance—and after retiring from the Post Office, he mounted an unsuccessful parliamentary candidacy. In his political novels, better known as the Palliser series, Trollope exhibits an understanding of politics and politicians that equals or surpasses his portrayal of the lives of English landed gentry in the Barchester novels. And in what is arguably his greatest work, *The Way We Live Now* (1875), he perused the whole of British society and its institutions, from the Church of England to financial dealings in London, to record what he saw as the deceptions of the modern world.

Glendinning's work is, as befits a biography of Anthony Trollope, an external rather than psychological portrait. Yet by examining an abundance of external detail, Glendinning admirably conveys a sense of the inner complexity that compelled Trollope to pursue writing with an intensity that he himself compared to addictions like drinking and gambling. Glendinning's biography serves as a welcome corrective to the critical notion that Trollope is solely a purveyor of nostalgia and a chronicler of convention.

Lisa Paddock

Sources for Further Study

The Christian Science Monitor. February 1, 1993, p. 11.
London Review of Books. XIV, November 5, 1992, p. 8.
Los Angeles Times Book Review. June 27, 1993, p. 5.
New Statesman and Society. V, September 4, 1992, p. 41.
The New York Review of Books. XL, April 8, 1993, p. 9.
The New York Times Book Review. XCVIII, January 31, 1993, p. 1.
The New Yorker. LXIX, March 15, 1993, p. 123.
Publishers Weekly. CCXL, January 4, 1993, p. 63.
Smithsonian. XXIV, April, 1993, p. 156.
The Times Literary Supplement. August 28, 1992, p. 3.
The Wall Street Journal. February 10, 1993, p. A12.
The Washington Post Book World. XXIII, February 7, 1993, p. 9.

APPROPRIATING SHAKESPEARE
Contemporary Critical Quarrels

Author: Brian Vickers (1938-   )
Publisher: Yale University Press (New Haven, Connecticut). 508 pp. $40.00
Type of work: Literary criticism and theory

Wide-ranging argument that recent schools of criticism, deriving largely but not exclusively from French structuralism, have distorted William Shakespeare's texts to support their own ideologies and now threaten the survival of independent critical analysis

As editor of a six-volume work entitled *Shakespeare: The Critical Heritage* (1974-1981), surveying all Shakespearean criticism from 1623 through 1801, Brian Vickers is in an excellent position to assess the state of Shakespearean criticism. *Appropriating Shakespeare: Contemporary Critical Quarrels*, however, is not a considered work of literary history; Vickers intended this highly polemical work to provoke controversy in academic circles. He sets out to demonstrate the fallacies of recent schools of literary theory and criticism, which he charges have willfully appropriated the texts of Shakespeare to fit their critical theories or ideologies. The book is organized into two parts, part 1 analyzing critical theory and part 2 describing critical practice. In part 1, Vickers' methods involve critically commenting on the theories of his opposition and then countering them with the views of scholars with whom he concurs. Each of his two long theoretical chapters concludes with a reading of Othello.

In the first chapter of part 1, "The Diminution of Language: Saussure to Derrida," Vickers traces damaging developments in modern literary theory to French theorists whose works were regarded as avant-garde in the 1960's. He claims that Ferdinand de Saussure, widely recognized as the father of modern linguistics, was also the founder of structuralism, a methodology that was later applied to anthropology by Claude Lévi-Strauss and to semiology by Roland Barthes. Labeling Jacques Derrida, Michel Foucault, and Jacques Lacan neostructuralists, Vickers accuses these thinkers of ignoring language as it is used in everyday life for communication. He concludes his survey of structuralism with an interpretation of Shakespeare's *Othello*, entitled "A Test Case for Language Theory." Vickers contends that any theory of language serviceable for interpreting literature must illuminate meaning and respect the "context of utterance," defined as who is speaking, to whom, under what circumstances, and for what purpose. Denying that a "play" can have agency independent of its author, Vickers insists that intentionality should be attributed to the characters in a drama rather than to the "play," which is an aesthetic whole that organizes meaning. In fact, what Vickers offers is a close reading of *Othello* that pays particular attention to words and imagery relating to language.

By the title *Appropriating Shakespeare*, Vickers means "the interested, self aggrandizing, social possession of systems of discourse," a definition taken from Frank Lentricchia's *After the New Criticism* (1980). Vickers' second chapter, entitled "Creator and Interpreters," maintains that the theoretical schools deriving from Barthes and Foucault are destructive, attacking the concept of the author as a creative intelligence shaping a literary work. Vickers is particularly concerned with their attempts to suggest that we misread works of literature if we look for a coherent meaning.

In response to these theories, Vickers offers a brief essay on convention and the way it dominates representation, citing as examples the tendency to believe a slanderer in Renaissance drama and the existence of character types such as "the melancholic lover, the quarrelsome braggart, the dignified king." He concludes with an overview of Shakespeare's adaptation of major English sources, Raphael Holinshed's *The Chronicles of England, Scotlande, and Irelande* (1577) and Sir Thomas North's translation of Plutarch's *Parallel Lives of the Greeks and Romans*. To show that Shakespeare had a sense of organic unity he offers a detailed study of how he adapted Othello from Giambattista Giraldi Cinthio's *Hecatommithi* (1565; one hundred tales).

Part 2 contains five chapters, each of which concerns the critical practices of a theoretical school that Vickers finds either biased or harmful to Shakespearean criticism. He takes to task "deconstruction," "New Historicism," "psychocriticism," and "feminist stereotypes," and then devotes his final chapter to Christians and Marxists, concluding with an epilogue entitled "Masters and Demons."

Tracing the theoretical underpinning of deconstruction to Jacques Derrida, he characterizes it as a largely American phenomenon, suggesting that American theorists have been far too willing to espouse a theory already regarded by Europeans as suspect. Quite interestingly, Vickers obliquely acknowledges the debt of deconstruction to the New Criticism of the 1940's and 1950's by mentioning that it sets out to locate ambivalence or indeterminacy in a text, a procedure followed by William Empson, but neglects to develop this fruitful insight into its history. After lengthy exegesis of the works of Paul de Man and J. Hillis Miller, Vickers examines and finds wanting the deconstructionist criticism of Miller, Gary Waller, John M. Kopper, Howard Felperin, Malcolm Evans, and others. Vickers concludes that the inevitable result of deconstruction is to reduce drama to the level of mere language and to manipulate the language until it validates a Derridean theory.

New Historicism, according to Stephen Greenblatt, moves away from the formalist isolation of New Criticism by attempting to contextualize literary works as products of the culture producing them. In fact, Greenblatt has affirmed that "Cultural Poetics" is a better descriptive label for his theory than New Historicism. Vickers justly warns that "the alternative to 'isolation' can be irrelevant contextualisation." To demonstrate that Greenblatt is culpable on precisely these grounds, he exhaustively examines Greenblatt's studies of the love test in act 1 of *King Lear*, transvestism in *Twelfth Night*, devil lore in *King Lear*, and interpretations of *The Tempest* and *Henry V* as parables of colonialism. Many of Vickers' objections are valid, but his highly contentious tone is likely to alienate even a sympathetic reader. Reprimanding Greenblatt for misreading *Henry V*, Vickers denounces him for assuming that any character who assumes an ethical position must be hypocritical:

This exemplary story of the emergence of a supremely successful and legitimate ruler can be of little interest to the avowedly politicised New Historicist, disillusioned after Vietnam, Watergate, the Gulf War, or any of a dozen episodes in contemporary history that reveal our governors in the worst possible light. The jaundiced idealist Greenblatt, preferring to side with "rotten opinion" and "base newsmongers," writes a sustained indictment of Hal.

Vickers' sustained indictment of Stephen Greenblatt (and only incidentally his work) may have the reverse effect of what Vickers intends.

Vickers finds the psychocriticism inspired by Sigmund Freud monotonous, but he is particularly concerned that this movement ignores questions of genre, style, and historical context. He illustrates psychoanalytic critics' distortion and omission by analysis of work by Ruth Nevo, Kay Stockholder, Marjorie Barber, and Stanley Cavell. Here Vickers seems less antagonistic to the theory than to the practice; he seems willing to concede a potential value to Freudian models as long as they are applied with scrupulous care.

In "Feminist Stereotypes: Misogyny, Patriarchy, Bombast" (which is likely to provoke more controversy in academic circles than it deserves), Vickers begins by differentiating feminism as a political movement designed to correct discrimination from feminist criticism, which he thinks too frequently politicizes literary works in ways that violate their integrity and individuality. Vickers endorses the goals of the political movement, but instead of squarely addressing the problems of conflating a long-overdue political movement with the promotion of women's studies, he says that he is not hostile to women's studies and merely wishes to correct the "injustice done to Shakespeare."

Vickers' history of feminist criticism begins with the publication of *The Woman's Part* (1980) and traces admittedly uncritical notions of patriarchy to Lawrence Stone's influential *The Family, Sex, and Marriage in England, 1500-1800* (1977). Vickers acknowledges that Stone has been corrected by historians, but concludes that "for the great majority of feminist Shakespeare critics, however, blissfully unaware of the weakness of Stone's thesis, patriarchy continues to serve as a monolithic, reified bogey-man." Since Vickers' book appeared in 1993 and he had an opportunity to add notes citing articles appearing as late as 1992, this kind of charge ought to be supported by reference to works appearing after Stone's work was reviewed. The lack of chronological rigor is troubling. Articles appearing in 1980, probably written a year or two earlier, are treated as representative of "current" feminist criticism. Vickers works against his own argument by citing studies written before corrections of Stone's theories had been fully absorbed. Returning to *Othello*, Vickers finds feminist criticism guilty of ignoring Iago. Again, the articles cited were published in 1980, 1981, 1986, 1981, and 1980, respectively; more recent feminist scholarship on *Othello* is ignored.

In conclusion, Vickers compliments the achievements of feminist history because the new social history draws upon a body of material not previously subjected to critical analysis. He is less sanguine about the addition of women writers to the canon, explaining that these women were amateurs and thus subject to the same difficulties experienced by amateur men writers, "cut off from the public arena which discourages so many of the untalented, and exposes those who do find a footing to the necessity of satisfying a reading or theatre-going public." Vickers concludes that "the writings of most amateur writers, male or female, hardly repay prolonged study." Helen Vendler, whom Vickers cites as agreeing with his conclusion, may be willing to overlook Emily Dickinson, but few Renaissance scholars will be willing to accept "professionalism" as an index of literary quality. Given a choice between including Mary Sidney Herbert and Thomas Tusser in an anthology of Renaissance literature, Vickers himself would be unlikely to choose the professional over the amateur.

Vickers concludes his discussion of feminist criticism with a tribute to the contributions of women scholars to current understanding of the Renaissance, but adds that their contributions "have been neglected of late as not fitting the current political paradigms." His inference is clear—women scholars are not the problem, but feminist scholarship is. Vickers' call for fresh interpretive models for feminist criticism is legitimate, but his polemical tone may obscure the valid issues he raises.

Linking Christian and Marxist approaches to Shakespeare, Vickers sees these ideologically based kinds of criticism as not only ignoring dramatic structure and experience but also turning the characters themselves into allegorical figures. He has a veritable field day with Christian allegorists, especially those who use psychoanalytic models. Marxism he finds much more restrained, though inclined to be as dull as naïve Freudianism. The British equivalent to the American New Historicism is classified by Vickers as neo-Marxist.

On the charge frequently voiced by Alan Sinfield and others that requiring Shakespeare on examinations has accustomed schoolchildren to an unjust social order, Vickers is scathing. He points out that the alternative to rewarding a new petty bourgeoisie based on education would be to base social advancement on family connections. His opposition to these attacks on Shakespeare is fueled by his own experience: Stating that he grew up in a miner's cottage in South Wales and owed his education to the 1944 Butler Education Act, he modestly declines to add that he later won the Harness Shakespeare Essay Prize at Cambridge.

Vickers' epilogue, not unfairly, describes the academy as a battleground in which pugnacious theoretical cliques battle for ascendancy. Repeating his charges that Marxists, feminists, and other theoretical cliques have distorted Shakespeare's works in order to promote their ideologies, he laments that literary criticism has been politicized by these theorists. Nevertheless, he concludes on a positive note by advocating objectivism, rationality, and pluralism—principles that he insists ought to inform discourse inside and outside the academy.

Jean R. Brink

Sources for Further Study

Choice. XXXI, November, 1993, p. 458.
The Chronicle of Higher Education. XXXIX, June 23, 1993, p. A10.

The Observer. April 18, 1993, p. 63.
The Sewanee Review. CI, Fall, 1993, p. cxvii.
The Times Literary Supplement. April 23, 1993, p. 20.
The Washington Post Book World. XXIII, June 6, 1993, p. 13.

ARABIAN JAZZ

Author: Diana Abu-Jaber
Publisher: Harcourt Brace (New York). 374 pp. $21.95
Type of work: Novel
Time: The 1960's to the 1990's
Locale: Euclid, New York

A novel that traces an Arab American family's struggle to balance and reconcile two cultures in a small poor-white community in upstate New York

> *Principal characters:*
> JEMORAH RAMOUD, a young Arab American woman
> MELVINA RAMOUD, her sister, a head nurse
> MATUSSEM RAMOUD, their father, who plays drums in a jazz band in his leisure time
> FATIMA MAWADI, Matussem's sister
> ZAEED MAWADI, Fatima's husband

Even though Edward W. Said and Anwar Abdel Malek are recognized as two of the most distinguished scholars in the United States today, Arab American literature remains largely neglected in the study of American ethnic literatures and cultures. The American reading public is probably more familiar with names of Arab writers such as Naguib Mahfouz and Ghassan Kanafani than with works produced by Arab Americans. The problem is partly occasioned by the fact that English is not first-generation Arab American immigrants' native language and partly by the fact that Arab Americans do not belong to any of the four established ethnic minority groups. Nevertheless, as is demonstrated by Diana Abu-Jaber's *Arabian Jazz*, the second- and third-generation Arab American writers are ready to take on the challenge of diversifying the ethnic voice in America.

Abu-Jaber's is a fresh voice in Arab American literature. *Arabian Jazz* is her first novel; it describes an Arab American family's struggle in Euclid, New York, a small poor-white community. The thematic power of *Arabian Jazz* is generated by the collision between the past and the present, dream and reality, and the ways of "the Old Country" and the lifestyle in the New. Structurally, the novel's humor relies heavily on the anachronistic appearance of characters whose faith in "the Old Country" brings into question their cantankerous relationship with the present. Yet Abu-Jaber's thematic treatment of the conflict between traditional Arab culture and modern American culture goes beyond the conventional exploration of irony. It reveals a painful paradox built on what African American scholar W. E. B. Du Bois in *The Souls of Black Folk* (1903) calls the experience of "double consciousness," or "a peculiar sensation, . . . the sense of always looking at one's self through the eyes of others, of measuring one's soul by the tape of a world that looks on in amused contempt and pity."

It is true that in *The Souls of Black Folk* Du Bois' argument mainly focuses on displaying how the influence of the mainstream culture can sometimes obscure, or even obliterate, a person's ontological relationship with his or her ethnic cultural heritage. As is shown in *Arabian Jazz*, however, as well as in Ralph Ellison's *Invisible Man* (1952) and Alice Walker's *Possessing the Secret of Joy* (1992), too much pressure to identify oneself with an ethnic group can produce an equally detrimental effect on the individual's sense of identity. This is especially true for people who are born into a family with two cultures, which is the case of the protagonist, Jemorah Ramoud, in *Arabian Jazz*.

Jemorah's father, Matussem, is a first-generation Arab immigrant in the United States; her mother Nora, who died of typhus on a trip to Jordan when Jemorah was three years old, was white. Because of her mother's untimely death and her father's close ties to his relatives who live in Syracuse's Arab community, Jemorah feels constantly under pressure to conform to traditional Arab customs she does not quite understand. She complains to her sister, Melvina,

> I'm tired of fighting it out here. I don't have much idea of what it is to be Arab, but that's what the family is always saying we are. I want to know what part of me is Arab. I haven't figured out what part is our mother, either. It's like she abandoned us, left us alone to work it all out.

Fast approaching thirty, Jemorah becomes the main topic in her Arab relatives' gossip. Aunt Fatima Mawadi, for example, simply cannot stand the fact that Jemorah is still single. Fatima has strong faith in the traditions of "the Old Country" and is obsessed with the idea of wanting to join the social committee of the local Syrian Orthodox Church, whose roles include, among others, "marriage makers and shakers, preservers of Arabic culture and party throwers, immigrant sponsors, and children-police." Because she does not have children, Fatima believes that it is her responsibility to help find a fitting bridegroom for Jemorah within the family, so that the family's name and honor can be preserved.

Family pressure is one reason that Jemorah is struggling with her identity and her relationships with other people. Even though she has met and dated several men, Jemorah cannot decide which relationship is worth pursuing. There is Gilbert Sesame, a dreamer and free spirit who eschews commitment and responsibility but is very good at pinball; there is Ricky Ellis, who was Jemorah's high-school sweetheart and appears just as purposeless in life as Jemorah's wandering soul; there is also Auntie Rein's son Nassir, an Arab scholar who completed his baccalaureate and graduate degrees in science and anthropology at the Universities of Cambridge and Oxford and is on his way to Harvard University to work in a postdoctoral program.

If Jemorah's friendships with Gilbert and Ricky suggest, empirically, the possibilities and choices she has in life, it is Nassir who, despite his inclination to philosophize about life (which explains why he has only one good eye), helps Jemorah to recognize those possibilities:

> To be the first generation in this country, with another culture always looming over you, you are the ones who are born homeless, bedouins, not your immigrant parents. As you and your sister just said, everything and nothing. You're torn in two. You get two looks at a world. You may never have a perfect fit, but you see far more than most ever do.

Indeed, getting two looks at the world can be a confusing experience to some people, but to others it can be a blessing. Sometimes all it takes to cross the line that separates freedom and bondage is knowing that one is free to choose. In Melvina's words, as she explains to Jemorah what she believes their mother would like to see happen to both of them, "What it boils down to is the sense that she didn't want us to be tied down to anything. She would say 'I want my girls to be free.' "

Before she meets Nassir, Jemorah seriously considers moving back to Jordan to be with family, people with whom she shares name and appearance. Now, however, she sees that the relationship between physical displacement and cultural disorientation is not only dialectical but also relative to individuals' choice. That belief is further confirmed by the pictures of Jordan that Matussem brings back from his recent visit to that country, pictures that look just as foreign to Jemorah as mainstream American culture is difficult for her.

Matussem also brings home a new theory about drumming that he developed "while lying awake on the Castro convertible in his sister Rima's rumpus room, surrounded in a valley of her grandchildren's toys." His theory posits that drumming

tapped into the heart and broke the spirit free, all the colors and the flavors of the life a person had lived. There were things hidden in the core of a person, feelings and memories so deep, that with the right music the spirits of people could be liberated, new life conceived, and the dead given rest.

After his wife's death, Matussem had decided to move the family to Euclid to leave behind unpleasant memories and his suspicious, hostile American in-laws. It is in music, however, that he finds peace. Matussem's hobby is to play drums in a jazz band after work. In music Matussem has learned how to deal with the loss of his wife and how to conquer his sense of emptiness and chaos. In music Matussem has found ways to connect the past and the present, memory and reality, and the world of life and that of death, for "only at his drums did he seem to focus, concentrate with the purpose of remembering, steering rhythms into line, coaxing a steady—in his word, *peripatetic*—pulse out of air." The drumbeat reverberates Matussem's heartbeat and the tapping in music, the rhythm of life.

Matussem's new theory on music helps Jemorah realize that Arabian jazz, as cacophonous as the term sounds, creates a new form of music by bridging two seemingly incompatible worlds. Now Jemorah can "hear the sound of the drums . . . jazz and trills of Arabic music, bright as comet tails, and through this, the pulse of the world." She knows that she is ready to find her way "along a path of music"; she is ready to compose her own song.

The cadence of *Arabian Jazz* is as rhythmic and musical as its tone is humorous. Melvina, for example, personifies commitment, dedication, and professionalism. Both Jemorah and Melvina work at Johnson-Crowes Hospital, but one out of necessity and the other out of "destiny." Her mother's untimely death might be what led Melvina to the decision to "pursue the greatest of professions, the most physically, emotionally, and intellectually demanding of any field, the most misunderstood and martyred, the closest to divinity: nurse." Jem, however "knew that one reason Melvie made such an excellent nurse was not because of any kindly nature, but because she was annoyed by illness and held patients personally responsible for their own diseases. *A weakness of will*, she'd heard Melvie say more than once."

Melvina's exposure to illness and death has provided her with a perspective on life that is radically different from Jemorah's, and she therefore takes it as her responsibility to make Jemorah aware of reality. When Jemorah complains, "I've started to see better, like the way I don't fit in. I haven't put together a life. I'm still living at home, I've been working at a job I hate. I'm so tired of being a child, being good, wanting people to like me," Melvina tries to reassure her by saying, "Americans don't like anybody! Americans don't like Americans!"

Melvina's counterpart in the book is Aunt Fatima, a bona fide representative of values and traditions of "the Old Country" whose anachronistic appearance in the book creates comic irony by itself. Fatima immigrated to the United States, according to Matussem, so that she could keep an eye on her brother; to abide by the "Law of Mohammed," Fatima forces her husband, Zaeed, to take a mistress. Fatima is also the self-appointed guardian of her American nieces, even though she is certain that Jemorah and Melvina will send her "to the mental hospital with so much worries about who are they ever going to marry." At the age of forty-nine, Fatima claims she is too old to move back to Jordan.

Despite some of the book's minor flaws such as the sometimes burlesque and farcical portrayal of Arab characters, *Arabian Jazz* presents a witty, lyrical, and balanced depiction of lives in the Arab American community.

Qun Wang

Sources for Further Study

Booklist. LXXXIX, June 1, 1993, p. 1780.
Boston Globe. August 17, 1993, p. 49.
Chicago Tribune. June 27, 1993, XIV, p. 1.
The Christian Science Monitor. June 18, 1993, p. 14.
Library Journal. CXVIII, June 1, 1993, p. 186.
Los Angeles Times. June 24, 1993, p. E5.
The New York Times Book Review. XCVIII, July 18, 1993, p. 9.
The New Yorker. LXIX, August 2, 1993, p. 83.
Publishers Weekly. CCXL, April 12, 1993, p. 45.
The Washington Post Book World. XXIII, June 13, 1993, p. 6.

THE ARABISTS
The Romance of an American Elite

Author: Robert D. Kaplan
Publisher: Free Press (New York). Illustrated. 333 pp. $24.95
Type of work: History
Time: The 1820's to 1991
Locale: Washington, D.C., and the Near East

A well-written and exciting account of the Americans who, for over a century, interpreted the Arab world for their fellow citizens

> *Principal personages:*
> DANIEL BLISS, a nineteenth century American missionary and educator in Lebanon
> LOY HENDERSON, a distinguished American diplomat
> JOSEPH SISCO, the head of the State Department's Bureau of Near Eastern Affairs, 1969-1974
> APRIL GLASPIE, the U.S. Ambassador to Iraq, 1989-1990

Robert Kaplan's *The Arabists: The Romance of an American Elite* is an engaging book that recounts the rise and fall of a little-known band of Americans who dominated their countrymen's perceptions of the Arab world for over a century. Ironically, the Arabists' hold on American policy toward the Arabs persisted only as long as the Middle East and North Africa remained exotic and marginal realms, outside the interests of most Americans. This situation changed dramatically with the birth of the state of Israel in 1948. Suddenly, millions of Americans were passionately concerned with the politics of the Middle East, and the Arabists, sharing the chagrin of their Arab coadjutors, found themselves facing their greatest challenge. Over the next four decades, the influence of the Arabists withered away before the reality of America's commitment to Israel, leaving them a vilified remnant in the foreign policy establishment. Only the burgeoning prospects for peace between Israel and its Arab neighbors promises to revive the Arabists' importance. As Kaplan points out, however, it will be a new and different breed of Arabists who will play a role in the unfolding of a new order in the Middle East.

Kaplan is well suited for the task of bringing this tale to the American public. A contributing editor of *The Atlantic* and the author of books about the famine in Ethiopia, the war in Afghanistan, and the breakup of Yugoslavia, he gracefully blends history and journalism in his work. Kaplan expertly abridges a mountain of scholarship in the first quarter of his book, in which he explains the origins of American involvement in the Middle East and the emergence of the Arabists as a class. Kaplan devotes the balance of his pages to a brilliant study of the travails of Arabists in the State Department, drawing heavily on numbers of interviews with survivors of the "Foggy Bottom's" bureaucratic wars. *The Arabists* is thus useful both as an introduction to the tangled relations between the United States and the Arab world and as a primer on twentieth century American foreign policy in the Middle East.

"Arabist" is an elusive term; it has meant many things over the years. Perhaps the most famous Arabists of all were the British explorers and soldiers who, in a series of brilliantly evocative books published in the late nineteenth and early twentieth centuries, created an enduring image of the Arab world as a scene of romantic adventure. The man who best embodied the exotic qualities of the British Arabists was T. E. Lawrence, known to legend as Lawrence of Arabia. A British political officer charged with fomenting an Arab rebellion against the Ottoman Turks during World War I, Lawrence embraced aspects of Arab culture even as he exploited the Arabs as a people. In the process, he self-consciously wove a myth around himself as a man caught between two ways of life and increasingly alienated from both, a moral drama all the more powerful for being enacted against the stark backdrop of the Arabian desert. Lawrence's literary genius and his poetic re-creation of the moral and physical bleakness of his Arabian landscape captured the imagination of succeeding genera-tions of Arabists, infusing their labors with an unmistakable, if sometimes ethically murky, glamour. The iconic figure of a morally deracinated Arabist striding through deserts and streets in Arab garb never died away, at least not in the minds of the Arabists themselves.

Yet the British Arabists, for all their lyric orientalism and swashbuckling enterprise, were in the end unabashed agents of Great Britain's imperial interests. American Arabists, while entranced by the silver pens of their British colleagues, proved to be a decidedly different lot. Lacking the Britons' literary panache, they also lacked their political ambitions. The first American Arabists came not as imperial janissaries but as missionaries, imbued not with the spirit of conquest but of uplift.

The American engagement with the Arab world was an enthusiastic emanation of the Second Great Awakening, a powerful religious revival of the early nineteenth century, which inspired American Protestantism with an evangelical zeal that spilled beyond the borders of the United States. Congregationalist ministers, fired by their fervor for Protestant Christianity and American republicanism, believed that mission-aries from the United States were destined to convert the Near East, precisely because of the absence of any compromising American interests in the region. Beginning in the 1820's, American missionaries spread throughout the Ottoman Turkish Empire, most significantly taking up station at Beirut, the leading city of a territory then known simply as "the Lebanon."

The Americans in Beirut made few converts. Islamic Arabs demonstrated little inclination to abandon the faith of their fathers. Indeed, the American missionaries even failed to get along with the local Marionite Christians, whom they held to be a degenerate flock. The American mission in Beirut was saved through the labors of a remarkable man named Daniel Bliss, who possessed the courage and vision to transform the nature of the American role in Lebanon.

Bliss began his long career as an Arabist in 1855, as a typical Congregationalist missionary. Soon realizing the futility of operating along traditional missionary lines in the Arab world, he decided that the most effective way to minister to the Arabs and help them improve their lives was through education. American missionaries had already established a number of schools for their charges. Wishing to extend and complete this work, Bliss called for a nondenominational college, open to all the peoples of the region and operated along the best American lines. In 1866, Bliss helped found the Syrian Protestant College in Beirut, forerunner of the American University of Beirut, which in time would become the moral center of American Arabism and the most influential American institution in the Middle East.

Bliss and his successors dedicated themselves to instilling in the Arabs the Protestant values of democracy, free and rational intellectual inquiry, and hard work. Yet while they hoped to bring "civilization" to the Arabs, they did not intend to produce mirror images of themselves. The founders of the college originally intended that all instruction would be in Arabic. This ultimately proved impractical because of the impossibility of obtaining modern textbooks in that language; thus classes were taught in English. Nevertheless, the college's strong commitment to the study of the Arabic language and its literature became its distinctive purpose, distinguishing it from the educational institutions established by Europeans. In Beirut, a rival school run by French Jesuits prided itself on producing students steeped in French culture, Frenchmen in form if not fact; the Americans strove to create something different, a new man, the modern Arab. Hence the Syrian Protestant College, and later the American University of Beirut, became a nursery of Arab nationalism. Even before the founding of the college, American missionaries had brought the first Arabic printing press to Syria and established the first Arab cultural society. It was a group of young men educated at the college, however, who began the modern Arab nationalist movement by forming a secret political organization in 1875. The American educators in Beirut allowed their institution to become an important intellectual center for the opposition to Ottoman Turkish rule and the European mandates that succeeded it. Graduates of the American University of Beirut would play important roles in twentieth century Middle Eastern politics.

Never disinterested spectators of the Arab struggle for national self-determination, American missionaries and educators fell easily into an emotional attachment to the cause. Their bond with the Arabs often blinded them to faults in the people they served. They developed a psychological reflex that excused Arab misdeeds, attributing them to differences in culture. They exhibited the missionary trait of emphasizing the positive in their interlocutors, eager above all to maintain a relationship. The Beirut Arabists' solicitude for the nationalist aspirations of the Arab people became an important factor in American foreign policy, as an impressive number of the sons of Lebanese missionaries and educators entered the foreign service. Many more State Department Arabists imbibed these attitudes after being sent to Beirut to learn Arabic. This intense engagement with Arab opinion would prove the Achilles heel of both the Beirut and the State Department Arabists. Instinctively hostile toward Israel after 1948, they would prove incapable of adjusting to a new American role in the Middle East and oblivious to the dangers of espousing increasingly radical Arab programs and leaders. The American educators in Beirut would pay the price of their idealism in the 1970's and 1980's, when several of their number were assassinated or kidnapped by

Lebanese extremists. The State Department Arabists would suffer a succession of rebuffs before their final humiliation at the hands of Saddam Hussein in 1990.

One of the ironies of the State Department Arabists' story is that it was a non-Arabist who canonized their anti-Zionism. Loy Henderson made his name as an expert in Soviet affairs. His extensive experience in the Soviet Union made him an early and acute critic of the Stalin regime, and an embarrassing liability when the Soviets became American allies during World War II. Henderson was exiled to the State Department's Near Eastern Affairs Bureau, known as NEA. As head of NEA, Henderson was strategically placed to comment on the postwar Palestinian crisis and the birth of Israel. For Henderson, ever conscious of the emergent Cold War with the Soviet Union, it seemed obvious that American policy should favor the Arabs over the Israelis. The Arabs overwhelmingly outnumbered the Israelis, controlled enormous oil reserves vital for the West's economy, and sat athwart important geographic crossroads. Henderson believed that support for a Jewish homeland in Palestine was a sentimental folly that risked driving the Arab world into the Soviet camp.

President Harry Truman granted American recognition to Israel against the unanimous opposition of State Department officials. Though Henderson lost his battle in 1948, his line became orthodoxy for State Department Arabists. For twenty years, officials at NEA would fight a holding action against Israeli interests. These Arabists became notorious in Zionist circles and were routinely charged with being anti-Semitic. Kaplan is careful to acknowledge that most Arabists were not motivated by hostility. They simply loved Arabs and were able to rationalize their feelings by arguing that good relations with the Arab states were necessary for the containment of the Soviet Union.

The Arabists could not indefinitely resist the weight of history. The Six Day War of 1967, in which Israel routed the armies of its Arab opponents, merely accentuated the handwriting on the wall. With the new administration of President Richard Nixon came an inevitable reformation. Joseph Sisco, the new head of NEA, ruthlessly winnowed the ranks of the Arabists, bringing to the fore men and women willing to take a more evenhanded approach to the Arab-Israeli conflict. For the first time, experience in Israel and a knowledge of Hebrew advanced a U.S. diplomat's career. Kaplan regards Sisco as the greatest head of NEA since Henderson and credits him with bringing a new balance and realism to the State Department's understanding of the Middle East. For his pains Sisco earned the undying enmity of the Arabists. It could be argued, however, that Sisco's rough medicine saved the Arabists from a worse and more conclusive fate.

Old habits die hard. One such habit for the surviving Arabists was the conviction that Iraq, with its large middle class and sophisticated economy, was poised to become the first fully modern, perhaps even democratic, state. Despite abundant evidence to the contrary, the hard-core Arabists persisted in this delusion. It lay too close to the missionary impulse at the heart of their vision. Thus, when the United States threw its weight behind Iraq during the Iran-Iraq War of 1980-1989, the Arabists rallied to this policy with enthusiasm. Even when the Iranian danger had receded and the brutal ambitions and methods of Iraq's leader Saddam Hussein were becoming increasingly apparent, the Arabists abetted the administration of President George Bush in assisting and appeasing this menacing new Arab military power. The unfortunate paladin of this doomed policy was April Glaspie, appointed ambassador to Iraq in 1989. A pioneering feminist in the State Department and the first woman to become an ambassador to an Arab country, Glaspie was a thoroughly conventional Arabist, too concerned with the importance of maintaining a dialogue with Saddam Hussein to perceive the necessity of challenging him. In a notorious interview with the dictator in July, 1990, Glaspie failed to warn him that aggression against Kuwait would be strenuously opposed by the United States. Her efforts to placate Saddam may have even encouraged him to invade his neighbor. Glaspie flew home for a vacation less than a week before Saddam launched his war. Within six months, the United States would be waging its first major war against an Arab state.

Glaspie's blunder was a microcosm of a larger failure of the American Arabists. They loved too well, and often none too wisely. Nevertheless, Kaplan is charitable in his assessment of the Arabists. Even in their errors, they reflected much of what is best in the American character, an idealism and openness rooted deep in the nation's history. Kaplan's book is a sobering record of American mistakes in assessing the world; yet it is also an inspiring chronicle of a remarkable experiment in cross-cultural communication. No one can finish Kaplan's book without the conviction that the future of Arab-American relations can be bright.

Daniel P. Murphy

Sources for Further Study

Booklist. XC, October 15, 1993, p. 399.
Foreign Affairs. LXXII, November, 1993, p. 175.
Library Journal. CXVIII, September 15, 1993, p. 90.
Los Angeles Times. October 27, 1993, p. E2.
The New Republic. CCIX, November 22, 1993, p. 39.
The New York Times Book Review. XCVIII, October 17, 1993, p. 3.
Publishers Weekly. CCXL, August 16, 1993, p. 92.
San Francisco Chronicle. October 24, 1993, p. REV8.
The Wall Street Journal. September 16, 1993, p. A18.
The Washington Post Book World. XXIII, October 24, 1993, p. 6.

ARC D'X

Author: Steve Erickson (1950-   )
Publisher: Poseidon Press (New York). 298 pp. $20.00
Type of work: Novel
Time: The mid-eighteenth to early twenty-first centuries
Locale: Virginia and Paris in the 1700's, Berlin in the 1990's, and a postapocalyptic California

A fictional meditation on the nature of history, centered on the figure of Sally Hemings, Thomas Jefferson's slave who chooses love over freedom and thus changes the future of a country and ultimately the world

> *Principal characters:*
> THOMAS JEFFERSON, author of the Declaration of Independence
> SALLY HEMINGS, his slave and mistress
> GANN HURLEY, her husband in a later manifestation
> POLLY HURLEY, her daughter
> WADE, a homicide detective in a future dystopia
> MONA, a dancer in the Arboretum
> ETCHER, a clerk who works for Church Central
> ERICKSON, a novelist in Berlin
> GEORGIE VALIS, a member of the Pale Fire gang in Berlin

"What if," the scientist Professor Seuroq asks in the last part of the twentieth century, "time is relative not simply to the perspective of motion, not simply to what the eye sees from a passing train or a rocket hurtling at the speed of light, but to the heart as well, and the speed at which it travels?" What is history, he further asks, but the "heart's arc across the course of lifetime," and many lifetimes beyond? The arc of the heart is the central metaphor of Steve Erickson's constantly inventive and challenging *Arc d'X*, a novel that begins in the middle of the eighteenth century and ends, or pauses, in the first years of the third millennium. A philosophical mixture of history, alternate histories, science fiction, and fantasy, the book perceives the cause of far-reaching events in the actions of the human heart. Like *Absalom, Absalom!* (1936), William Faulkner's fictional contemplation on history and love and freedom, to which this book is kin, *Arc d'X* requires its readers to reconsider the nature of knowing, the truth of story, and the extensive ramifications of the individual choice.

Erickson's novel contains four major story lines, each ultimately focused on the character of Sally Hemings. The first narrative is historical, reconstructing Thomas Jefferson's supposed affair with his fourteen-year-old slave Sally. Erickson's Thomas (only once is he given the last name Jefferson, although Jefferson's life and character are clearly the antecedent for Erickson's creation) is a passionate, conflicted man. "I'm only as bright as the whitest light in any man can be, tempered as it is in every man by whatever black impulse he can't ignore," he confesses. "At my best I have only been the slave of a great idea." Thomas, the author of the Declaration of Independence, in essence *creates* the United States of America, but in Erickson's portrayal he is able to do so because he expends his "black impulses" in his loving and abusive relationship with Sally, the child he rapes and keeps enslaved in a sexual bondage. Sally, for her part, both loves and hates Thomas, yearns to worship him and to kill him. In Paris (where she has come with Thomas' daughter Polly to join him and his other daughter Patsy), Sally realizes that she is free, that the legal rights of the slaveholder do not apply. At the same time she finds herself growing more enslaved by the sexual and emotional relationship that develops with Thomas, so that when he must return to America, her decision to return with him, to forfeit her legal rights in France, takes on immense importance. This decision reverberates throughout the rest of the novel.

The first hint that this novel will challenge the conventional occurs when Sally tries to kill Thomas, stabbing him in bed. Fleeing into the city, she witnesses the fall of the Bastille, then wanders into a bizarre countryside, a land of ash and rock, and discovers a house in the crater of a volcano. In the house she confronts her own image and then an older man whose thick glasses make his eyes "loom like blue crystal balls." She has, for the moment, traveled through time, confronted her own grown daughter and the man she will come to love two centuries hence. Fleeing from this scene and returning to Paris, she finds Thomas unharmed and resubmits herself to him, goes with him to America, and becomes his acknowledged mistress in Virginia.

Sally next appears in a futuristic world, the very one seen in her earlier vision. This world is apparently a postcataclysmic, theocratic Los Angeles, now called Aeonopolis, ruled by Church Central. The city is bounded by Church Central tower to the west, overlooking the sea; by the Arboretum, a sprawling construction of buildings and underground passages in which inhabitants live beyond the rule of the Church, to the northeast; and, rising above both, by the volcano in the east which blocks out the sun until near noon each day. "If Church Central was anxious about the disorder of human desire that lurked in the Arboretum, it genuinely feared . . . the volcano because it represented the most alarming of possibilities: that there was indeed a God, who manifested himself daily in the mix of volcano smoke and ocean fog that the residents called the Vog." Here Sally is discovered in a hotel, in bed beside a murdered man. Sally is now revealed to be married in this world to an actor, Gann Hurley, who is the father of her daughter Polly (the name also of Thomas' daughter). Her attempted murder of Thomas in Paris two centuries before seems to have replayed itself, except that this man has been bludgeoned rather than stabbed. The murder investigation is led by Wade, a huge black man who realizes that Sally is innocent and is haunted by her beauty and sadness. Wade's search leads him into the Arboretum, where he finds another strange death, that of a young white man covered with tattoos. In the Arboretum Wade meets Mona, a stripper from the North, from the land of Ice, with whom he becomes involved in an inverse version of Sally and Thomas' relationship.

The third story intersects with that of Wade and Mona. Etcher, who also comes from the Ice, works as a clerk in the archives of Church Central. There he sees Sally and Polly, who have come to learn more about Madison Hemings, one of Thomas and Sally's children. Etcher follows Sally home, and they soon begin an affair. By accident, Etcher makes a profound discovery at Church Central when one of the priests leaves a key in the door to a little-used room. There Etcher finds volumes of books labeled "Unexpurgated Volumes of Unconscious History": "In them were listed events Etcher had never heard of. The volumes told of people no one had ever known and countries no one had ever seen. He read of lives no one had ever lived and pored over maps of places no one had ever been." Inspired by his love for Sally and her inherent need for freedom, Etcher quietly begins to steal the books and their concealed history, until he has them all in his possession and thus becomes a great threat to the Church and its power. Unlike Thomas (one of the "people no one had ever known"), Etcher attempts to free Sally, to help her escape from Aeonopolis and the threat of imprisonment for murder.

The fourth narrative concerns Erickson, a middle-aged novelist whose last books have failed. In 1998 he reads of Professor Seuroq's discovery of time's alternate passage, the conclusion that between the last day of December, 1999, and the first day of January, 2000, a missing day would occur, "twenty hours and seven minutes and thirty-four seconds to be precise, the accumulation, according to Seuroq's calculations, of all the moments over the millennium that grief and passion had consumed from memory and then dribbled back into the X of the arcs of history and the heart, past and present and future rushing toward a dense hole of time into which all of history would collapse." In the third millennium "history would measure itself not by years but by memory, where the heart is a country." To be present for this day, the writer Erickson goes to Berlin, the city of the Wall, the central image of freedom and captivity in the twentieth century. In Berlin he meets Mona, who will end up in Aeonopolis after the collapse of history, and Georgie Valis, a teenage leader of a postpunk gang called the Pale Fire which does battle with another, secret group called Neuwall Brigade. Georgie is the tattooed boy who will eventually be found dead in the Arboretum by Wade, but in Berlin he represents the divided city at the moment of its collapse.

> Now in Berlin, in the last spring of the second millennium, on X-257 . . . every nineteen-year-old with a computer was a reich unto himself. He created his own German state and programmed it to last not a thousand years but ten thousand. He invaded weak peoples, wiped out impure races, torched effete cultures, claimed natural living space, and added seventeen new definitions to the term Final Solution. All he needed was the right softwear and a sector of the city where the juice hadn't been shut off.

Erickson, who shares his name with the author of the book, ends up dead, killed by Georgie and his gang; Georgie, who takes on Erickson's identity, inspired and tortured by the idea of "America," of "the pursuit of happiness," of "freedom," goes to the United States, to the West Coast, reversing Erickson's journey, to await X-Tag, the missing day of the heart's history. There he has his own rendezvous with Thomas and Sally.

Even this brief summary of the novel suggests the complexities of its story. Beginning as history, it forsakes linear development and comes to question the whole nature of history. Thomas, the rational, intellectual father of American independence, is reinvented as a man haunted by his passions. Originally opposed to slavery, he comes to embrace it out of his need for the slave Sally, whom he cannot let go. His love for her, and her love for him, which causes her to return to America, results in Jefferson's betrayal of his earlier ideals and thus, Erickson implies, charts the course of the nation away from emancipation and toward self-destruction.

Each of the narratives in this novel centers on the often-conflicting demands of love and freedom. As Seuroq's study reveals,

> Beyond three hearts in tandem was history, and when he reduced the meaning of history he was left not with the common denominator of love but rather that of freedom. . . . One calculation based itself on history's denial of the human heart and the other on history's secret pursuit of the heart's expression: if one heart's story was the pursuit and denial of love and if history was the pursuit and denial of freedom, what lay at the arcs' intersection except the missing moments consumed by memory . . . ?

These are the kinds of questions asked by Faulkner in *Absalom, Absalom!* and by Thomas Pynchon in *Gravity's Rainbow* (1973), two books often reflected in *Arc d'X*. At the intersection of the arcs is always the memory of the heart.

Etcher, who steals the Church's "Unexpurgated Volumes of Unconscious History," begins to rewrite the pages before he returns them to Church Central, revising the past world in accordance with his new knowledge engendered by love and sacrifice. Near the end of the book, Erickson himself offers an alternate history, another convergence of lives and hearts. What if, he asks, Sally had not returned with Thomas? How then would the world have been changed? He offers an insurgent Jefferson, a mad prophet leading black armies of militant slaves he has set free and made master over himself. "It's the final resolution of the dilemma of power," he tells John Adams, "to be at once both king and slave. To at once lead an army and be its waterboy." Erickson also shows Sally in France, inspiring yet another revolution in Europe and altering again the development of events.

Arc d'X is a fascinating book, daring and questioning and revisionist. Stories and characters and images echo each other throughout, from the Rue d'X in Paris where Thomas lives to the Fleurs d'X club in the Arboretum, where Mona dances to Day X when time collapses at the end of the millennium. The book sometimes overreaches. Characters sometimes intrude with first-person monologues that add little to the reader's understanding. Not all the minor episodes are integrated effectively into the larger narrative. The Berlin section is not as successful as the earlier ones, and the character of Erickson seems somehow unnecessary, as if he is brought into the story only for the shock of being killed off. Nevertheless, this is an important work, a novel that provokes and demands and, above all, rewards.

Edwin T. Arnold

Sources for Further Study

Booklist. LXXXIX, March 15, 1993, p. 1297.
Boston Globe. May 9, 1993, p. 13.

Chicago Tribune. May 19, 1993, V, p. 3.
Library Journal. CXVIII, March 15, 1993, p. 104.
Los Angeles Times. April 1, 1993, p. E4.
The New York Times Book Review. XCVIII, May 2, 1993, p. 9.
Publishers Weekly. CCXL, March 22, 1993, p. 59.
Time. CXLI, May 10, 1993, p. 70.
The Washington Post Book World. XXIII, May 9, 1993, p. 4.

AROUND THE CRAGGED HILL
A Personal and Political Philosophy

Author: George F. Kennan (1904-   )
Publisher: W. W. Norton (New York). 272 pp. $22.95
Type of work: Political theory and social commentary

Reflections on human nature, religious faith, ideology, and U.S. public policy (both foreign and domestic) by the leading American diplomat in the Cold War period

The literary critic I. A. Richards was famous for asking students to evaluate a poem without first knowing the identity of its creator. This technique produced strikingly bold and heterodox judgments. A similar strategy might be usefully employed on readers of public affairs and political thought. Deprived of the knowledge that such-and-such writing is the work of John Kenneth Galbraith, Robert Heilbroner, William F. Buckley, Amitai Etzioni, Jeremy Rifkin, Daniel Patrick Moynihan, or James Fallows, the reader would simply confront an array of titles and texts. The result might be a refreshing new sense of where convergencies and differences lie, a revisioning of the spectrum of positions and persuasions.

But how might such a reader react to *Around the Cragged Hill: A Personal and Political Philosophy*? Here is a book with the following discomforting elements: (1) an argument for a theology that deprives God of any responsibility for creating and sustaining the natural order in which we are "compelled" to live; (2) a description of the sex act as "brief, bestial, and potentially humiliating, so much so as to require elaborate rituals for concealment, disguise, cant, and prevarication just in order to be made even approximately compatible with the decencies of normal social inter-course"; (3) the suggestion that the United States would be better off if reorganized as a system of nine "constituent republics, absorbing not only the powers of existing states but a considerable part of those of the present federal establishment"; (4) an appeal for a revitalization of the institution of domestic service on the grounds that there are people "for whom service in or around the home pretty well exhausts their capabilities for contributing to the successful functioning of a society"; (5) an indict-ment not only of television but also of "radio, the rock-and-roll cassette player, the movie, [and] even the passive watching of sport in the open."

Assuming that our naïve reader had not in fact abstained from cinematic pleasures, she might at this point paraphrase a famous Western: "Who *is* this guy?" Indeed, who would dare to include in the same relatively short volume chapters on "Man, the Cracked Vessel," "Faith," "Dimensions" (on the disadvantages of bigness), "Egalitari-anism and Diversity," and "Foreign Policy, Military"? Who would—in the book's epilogue—describe *himself* in words as oblique and fey as these?

Eccentric as might be the figure he presented on the present national scene—esoteric in its social and cultural origin, slightly *dépaysé* by the many years spent abroad, and colored by membership in a generation now close to total disappearance—he still thought of himself as an American (what else could he be?) and felt some sense of responsibility in that capacity.

The answer to these questions is, of course, George Kennan. And because that is the answer, making light of *Around the Cragged Hill* is simply impossible. For as Peter de Leon has rightly said, George Kennan is "a national asset."

Kennan's contribution is a threefold one. First, as a career diplomat, he exercised decisive influence on the entire course of postwar foreign policy. An expert on Germany, the Baltic States, and the Soviet Union, he produced the famous 1946 "Long Telegram" from the embassy in Moscow and the 1947 "X-article" in *Foreign Affairs* that laid the intellectual basis for the Cold War strategy of containment. Kennan here depicted the Soviets as inherently expansionist, needing to be "firmly contained at all times by counter-pressure which makes it constantly evident that attempts to break through this containment would be detrimental to Soviet interests."

Kennan's early analysis seems particularly prescient in light of the 1991 breakup of the Soviet Union. He believed that expansionism was necessary to mask the profound weaknesses and pathologies of Soviet society. These had pre-Marxist origins, but that ideology—especially in its glorification of the Communist Party— could serve the interests of post-Czarist despots like Joseph Stalin. By countering both the international machinations of the Communist Party and the specific thrusts of the Red Army, the West would force the Soviet Union to rely upon its own resources. Since these were inherently faulty, Kennan claimed, "Soviet Russia might be changed overnight from one of the strongest to one of the weakest and most pitiable of national societies."

Kennan's second contribution has been as a diplomatic historian. After serving as U.S. ambassador to the Soviet Union in 1951-1952, he retired from the Foreign Service. His hopes for an appointment as secretary of state were thwarted both by his enmity toward John Foster Dulles and by the failure of Adlai Stevenson's presidential campaigns. Although he was ambassador to Yugoslavia during the Kennedy years, he mainly served as a Princeton University scholar and mainstay of its Institute for Advanced Study. In this capacity he turned out a remarkable series of books: *Soviet-American Relations, 1917-1920* (volume 1 in 1956, volume 2 in 1958), *Soviet Foreign Policy, 1917-1941* (1960), *The Decline of Bismarck's European Order* (1979), and *The Fateful Alliance: France, Russia, and the Coming of the First World War* (1984). Kennan's memoirs of his years as an active diplomat constitute a standard for this genre.

Third, Kennan has functioned as a brilliant gadfly and controversialist. Often characterized as a "mystic," "romantic," or "alienated intellectual," Kennan has been a biting critic of domestic mass culture in North America. At the same time, he developed highly unorthodox views on McCarthyism, Vietnam, atomic warfare, the student Left, environmentalism, and governmental reform. It is into this last category that *Around the Cragged Hill* fits.

The first five chapters of the book constitute part 1 and are, in Kennan's words, "an effort to call attention to certain congenital imperfections in human nature and to show how these affected, everywhere, the indispensable institutions of government and politics." Although Kennan cites his great philosophical and theological mentor

Reinhold Niebuhr only occasionally, the latter's influence is everywhere apparent. Thus, in conceptualizing human nature Kennan does not start with humans' capacity for rational self-development or the fulfillment of higher potentials. Rather, he focuses on prerational impulses, psychic insecurity, sexual passion, susceptibility to collective egoisms, and the allure of the demonic. Like Niebuhr, Kennan construes political reality as primarily a place where individuals seek to cure their insecurities through the exercise of power. "It is here," he writes, "in and around government, in the competition for . . . position and the enjoyment of it, once attained, that the human ego becomes most deeply and helplessly engaged."

Present in the Soviet Union in its earliest decades, Kennan did not—as did Niebuhr—pass through a Marxist phase; yet he has never been an enthusiast for unregulated capitalism. While reluctantly accepting free enterprise as a superior economic system, he has consistently expressed abhorrence at the commercialism, giantism, and urban chaos that American capitalism seems to engender. The chapter titled "Ideology" voices these views once again. Niebuhr shared many of Kennan's feelings, but he was far more inclined to evaluate economic systems from the standpoint of justice and the achievement of power balances between labor and capital. Kennan's views seem curiously patrician—that is, lacking sufficient concern for the recent sharpening of class divisions in American society. "What we are confronted with today in practically all Western countries are societies composed very largely of one, vast middle-class, uniform in outlook even where it is not uniform in income," he writes. A very un-Niebuhrian complacency about relative economic justice is betrayed here.

Part 2 of *Around the Cragged Hill* focuses on domestic problems in the United States. In many ways, this section appears to be the work of a pure reactionary. Put more charitably, Kennan follows here not Niebuhr but Edmund Burke and Alexis de Tocqueville. He laments the unavailability of household servants. He decries forced desegregation and pleads for neighborhood schools. He argues for a rehabilitation of the concept of a social elite—a class deserving deference and respect because of the offices it holds. The democratic techniques of initiative and referendum receive his censure. For Kennan, everything in the United States is too big: population, cities, bureaucracy, the rate of immigration, and the federal deficit.

Worse than this, Americans have become "a people of bad social habits." They are "addicted" to the private automobile, so much so that they have come to accept both its community-destroying effects and its massive waste of resources. Television is a second addiction, which Kennan sees in the broader context of "the extensive domination of almost every kind of public communication by the advertisers." Thus, his discussion links (1) the trend toward "info-tainment," (2) attention-span curtailment, (3) the ways advertisers legitimate their activities by associating products with doctors, priests, and other trusted social servants, and (4) the near ruination of the U.S. Postal Service by junk mail. The nostalgia that underlies Kennan's critique is nicely captured in this remark:

It has sometimes seemed to me that the child who has never had the experience of finding itself left to itself on a rainy day in a room with nothing greatly interesting but a filled bookcase, with the rain streaking down the window, with no television set, and nothing to do but to pick up a book and read, is truly deprived.

It would thus be tempting simply to dismiss Kennan's book. Well aware of the dated and "old-fashioned" character of his views, Kennan often invites the reader to do exactly that. But the invitation is ironically put, for Kennan is aware that he has often been uncannily far-sighted. Mary McGrory observed in 1989 that Kennan's tendency is to be "prematurely and unfashionably right." For example, his angry *Democracy and the Student Left* (1968) presaged not only the decline of that movement but also the rise of environmental activism. So while many readers will be put off by Kennan's high Presbyterian snobbishness and his dedication to values such as decorum, dignity, elegance of expression, and aesthetic cultivation, they write him off at some risk.

Around the Cragged Hill deserves a careful reading for another reason. Alienated though he is from American society, Kennan's patriotism constantly urges him to propose schemes for reform. These dot the book and interrupt its pessimism in interesting ways. For example, he has a detailed plan for rehabilitating the office of secretary of state, one that entails dispensing with the National Security Council. The chapter titled "What Is to Be Done?" contains a six-point agenda for developing "a permanent, non-political advisory body—one that permits the tapping of the greatest sources of wisdom and experience that the private citizenry of the country can provide." This body, which would occupy itself "only with long-term questions of public policy, . . . restricting itself to the identifications of the preferable principles and directions of action," would be appointed by the president but would be fiscally independent of annual appropriations. Known as the Council of State, it would allow the country to take advantage of an untapped well of creative insight available in the personages of "ex-presidents, ex-cabinet members, ex-governors, former distinguished legislators or jurists, retired diplomats, and many others." Elder leaders from business, the academy, journalism, and science would also be appointed.

Like many in the book, this is a splendid (and quite practical) suggestion. It is put forward with the engagement of one who still cares greatly for the fate of the nation. From the safe haven of his large Pennsylvania farm, George Kennan may celebrate his remoteness from the swirl of American public life. The truth of the matter, however, is that he remains very much at the center of it, and we are all the richer because of that fact.

Leslie E. Gerber

Sources for Further Study

Booklist. LXXXIX, November 15, 1992, p. 562.
Chicago Tribune. January 3, 1993, V, p. 1.

Kirkus Reviews. LX, November 1, 1992, p. 1355.
Library Journal. CXVIII, January, 1993, p. 146.
The New York Review of Books. XL, February 11, 1993, p. 3.
The New York Times Book Review. XCVIII, January 3, 1993, p. 7.
The New Yorker. LXVIII, February 8, 1993, p. 113.
Publishers Weekly. CCXXXIX, December 7, 1992, p. 52.
The Times Literary Supplement. May 21, 1993, p. 17.
The Washington Post Book World. XXIII, February 11, 1993, p. 11.

ASSEMBLING CALIFORNIA

Author: John McPhee (1931-   )
Publisher: Farrar Straus Giroux (New York). 304 pp. $21.00
Type of work: Science

In his fourth book on geology, John McPhee explores the geological origins of California and the revolutionary vision of plate tectonics

Assembling California is the final book in John McPhee's geological tetralogy, *Annals of the Former World.* "Assembling" refers coyly to the two-decade-old theory of plate tectonics, which the three preceding books (*Basin and Range*, 1980; *In Suspect Terrain*, 1982; and *Rising from the Plains*, 1986) explained for those readers who survived the exposure to thick geological nomenclature. Tectonic geologists have embraced McPhee as one of their own, given his immersion in the topic and skill at discussing it. He dedicates *Assembling California* to Kenneth Deffeyes, the geologist who accompanied him to the Western states to look at road cuts, the freeway builder's gift to students of rocks. But when McPhee entered California near Tahoe with the ever-prescient Deffeyes, the geologist was stumped by rock he did not recognize, and referred the author to his California alter ego, Eldridge Moores. *Assembling California* is the fruit of trips with Moores over several years during the 1980's.

Geology is not humanities or anthropology, as the time charts on the book's endpapers make clear. The most recent geological era is the Cenozoic, which traces time back a mere 65 million years. The three preceding eras begin with Precambrian time, which originates in the Hadean Eon, dated at 4,600 million years before the present. In that four-era-long wealth of time, plate tectonicists assert, the earth has been in a constant state of topographical rearrangement, such that supercontinents have more than once formed, broken apart, and re-formed. McPhee imparts this perspective with as much expertise as a lover of the subject can develop, professionals included. The earth, he writes, is "a planetary shell so mobile that nothing on it resembles itself as it was some years before, when nothing on it resembled itself as it was some years before that." Geology addresses infinity, the persistent replacement of land with oceans and vice versa, and the continuance of all this in the present at the same, to human senses, immeasurably slow pace. McPhee's explication of this phenomenon, parts of it admittedly hypothetical, is as close to an act of worship as a three-hundred-page book can come without ever invoking the name of God.

The art of John McPhee has always been to wrest marvels from the mundane. He can write about whiskey, oranges, canoe building, tires, Alaska, roadkill, Atlantic City, or Bill Bradley, and the reader is hard-pressed to decide if it is the subject that fascinates or McPhee's energized consciousness of it. He brings a poet's sensibility to the most tangible things. Writing about geology, this feaster on the detail beneath the detail asks readers to follow him into a subject as complex as a medical subspecialty with the accompanying technical lingo. Because McPhee is writing, the reader most likely will comply.

In *Assembling California*, McPhee's strategy remains what it has been in many of his books: He stage-manages the presence of a man or woman who knows the subject. The world is not facts, he tacitly proposes, but personalities generating ideas, attitudes, products, and lives. To know California's geology, one gets to know Eldridge Moores, a geologist who works out of the University of California, Davis. McPhee is interested in presenting geology as a subject while showing how the subject comes into being. Plate tectonics is a new vision. It exists as the community of geologists senses it, defines it, modifies it, fights it, and believes it. The work of human thought and perception, making discoveries and diving deep into time through stone, is as major a drama for McPhee as the earthquakes—past, present, and future—which are the most dramatic effects of tectonic action. If the world is assembling and disassembling itself as tectonics proposes, so is the scientist's evolving vision. Geologists relish the uncertainty. McPhee quotes a volcanologist in this regard: "In the next ten years, our confusion will reach new heights of sophistication."

Much of *Assembling California* recounts trips McPhee took with Moores into California's Sierra Nevada Mountains, where the evidence of tectonics can be most easily read. In this high range, sloped gradually to the west, dropped abruptly from its summits to the basin floor to the east, Moores demonstrates through the visible rock the subduction which caused the range to form. In "subduction," a central concept for plate geology, one plate pushes under another as the two plates meet. A shape like the Sierra Nevada is formed, much like the effects on a car fender in a collision, a collision which consume centuries and blends rock and leaves debris at a messy joint and at new elevations. As McPhee noted in *Basin and Range*, and repeats here, "The summit of Mount Everest is marine limestone." Whether the geologist looks at the Sierras, the Alps, or the Himalayas, he is reading the junction of plate contact.

A vintage McPhee analogy gives the reader some sense of what the geologist is seeing at such a "suture." Imagine an attic that houses pieces of furniture differing widely in date and style:

> You also see, lined up in close ranks, a Queen Anne maple side chair, a Federal mahogany shield-back side chair, a Chippendale shell-carved walnut side chair, and a William and Mary carved and caned American armchair. Stratigraphically, they are out of order. How did that happen? Why are they here? Only one thing is indisputable: this is some loft.

Earlier geology presumed that the earth—its rock layers, stratigraphy, readable zones of difference—arose and wore away on a vertical plane. But that attic of random chairs was puzzling, and only the effects of plate collisions and subductions could account for the disorder. Moores tells McPhee: "To see through the topography and see how the rocks lie in three dimensions beneath the topography is the hardest thing to get across to a student. . . . Left handed people do it better." Readers who struggle to follow McPhee's unabashed geological vocabulary—sheeted diabase, spreading center, terrane, batholith, abyssolith, and so on—are sensing their relative proclivity as left-handers, if not simply their curiosity about the globe they live on every day.

McPhee provides other geological perspectives which do not necessitate line-by-line recourse to a dictionary. First, he explores the Gold Rush history of California, an apt digression since gold shows up where plates come together. California was populated more or less instantly, as a result of gold fever; thus its inhabitants' "assembly" in the place curiously resulted from the docking of one plate with another. McPhee will not explicitly point out that odd causation, but vividly juxtaposes the earth's behavior and man's such that the reader holds the image throughout the book. The incongruity of geological phenomena and human behavior is a variously spun theme. The geologist's purity of intent—to know the life of stone ("It was fine-grained diabase, in magnification asparkle with crystals—free-form, asymmetrical, improvisational plagioclase crystals bestrewn against a field of dark pyroxene")—contrasts with the greed-driven, furious, but brief tearing and blasting of California in the 1850's.

The dance of a riffraff of gold miners on the juncture of two vast plates made history for students in grade school, but the earth keeps its plates in motion, and the towns of the miners are gone. What of more sustained mining, for which geological surveys exist, in part, to establish? McPhee visits Cyprus with Moores, Cyprus being a piece of visible ocean crust attracting Moores's study, and dilates on the smelting of copper which began there in 2760 B.C. "At Skouriotissa, southwest of Peristerona, the concurrence of geologic time and human time had been long enough to approach a record. A very large working strip mine there had been in operation for four thousand three hundred years." Cyprus copper made the battles in Homer's *Illiad* possible, and other copper turned bronze from Cyprus armed Darius the Persian's forty thousand soldiers. Most of humankind uses the earth's metals to kill and buy things with, but Moores tells McPhee about "the joy of being alone with the geology."

Moores himself, in a chapter McPhee devotes to the geologist's Arizona boyhood and college years, seems a pure product of the earth, naturally studying and "producing" his nurturing mineral source. He grew up in a tiny mining village, accessible only by dangerous mountain roads. His father mined with mediocre success, and the teenage Moores admitted to his parents that it was not the life he wanted to lead. At the California Institute of Technology, however, the only major he considered was geology: "He wondered still about those colors in granite. He may not have cared how the gold got out of the mountains, but he did want to know how the mountains came there to receive the gold."

So the world grows, like other natural forms. There once was no California, there is now, there will not be one in the future. Though the historical scale of these motions is difficult for most minds to care about, the fact of it becomes all-important when an earthquake occurs. The world's inhospitality is geological. That simultaneous incongruity of life—the globe's and humanity's—is suddenly manifested when an astoundingly beautiful city, San Francisco, is shaken. McPhee quotes Bay Area columnist Stephanie Salter responding to the 1989 Loma Prieta quake:

> A traumatic experience . . . started in the depths of the earth and wreaked damage all the way to the depths of the psyche. . . . Or maybe the truth is, earthquake time is the most real time of all, a time when all the bull ceases and the preciousness of life is understood most acutely.

The final fifty pages of *Assembling California* McPhee reserves for the San Andreas fault and the cities it threatens, particularly San Francisco and Los Angeles. "Of the two most direct routes from southern to northern California, always choose the San Andreas Fault. If you have adequate time, it beats the hell out of Interstate 5." The fault region is wired by seismologists, for the sake of knowledge but equally in the hopes of offering warning of impending quakes to the populated cities. To give a feeling of the wave motion of a quake, the quake being the shock created by those plates moving against each other, McPhee provides a moment-by-moment narrative of the 1989 quake which delayed the World Series. It was not a San Francisco earthquake, in fact, but a Watsonville-Santa Cruz earthquake which ultimately arrived in San Francisco with a much-spent share of its epicentered power. McPhee uses the present tense to drive home the details of what people near the epicenter experienced:

> On Summit Road, near the Loma Prieta School, a man goes up in the air like a diver off a board. He lands on his head. Another man is thrown sideways through a picture window. A built-in oven leaves its niche and shoots across the kitchen. A refrigerator walks, bounces off a wall, and returns to its accustomed place. As Pearl Lake's seven-room house goes off its foundation, she stumbles in her kitchen and falls to the wooden floor. In 1906, the same house went off the same foundation. Her parents had moved in the day before. . . . Ryan Moore, in bed under the covers, is still under the covers after his house travels a hundred feet and ends up in ruins around him.

Those who experienced the earthquake that struck Los Angeles in 1994 will find that McPhee's account could have been written about them.

Some McPhee readers will question his geological preoccupations, and wonder why their favorite writer has led them so relentlessly into science with *Assembling California* and its predecessors. He might shrug and say this topic is that much larger than any he has presented before. Or he may be as indifferent to his readers as the earth is to those living on it. It is more likely that these books are the fulfillment of his concentration on what is around us, as in any of his books, to give himself and his readers a sense of where we are. To quote his quote of Moores:

> People look upon the natural world as if all motions of the past had set the stage for us and were now frozen. . . . They look out on a scene like this and think, It was all made for us—even if the San Andreas Fault is at their feet. To imagine that turmoil is in the past and somehow we are now in a more stable time seems to be a psychological need.

Bruce Wiebe

Sources for Further Study

Booklist. LXXXIX, December 1, 1992, p. 633.
The Christian Science Monitor. March 3, 1993, p. 13.
Kirkus Reviews. LX, December 1, 1992, p. 1485.
Library Journal. CXVIII, January, 1993, p. 162.
Los Angeles Times Book Review. January 13, 1993, p. 1.

New Scientist. CXXXIX, July 24, 1993, p. 37.
The New York Times Book Review. XCVIII, March 7, 1993, p. 9.
Publishers Weekly. CCXL, January 4, 1993, p. 67.
Time. CXLI, April 5, 1993, p. 62.
The Washington Post Book World. XXIII, March 7, 1993, p. 5.

AT THE HIGHEST LEVELS
The Inside Story of the End of the Cold War

Authors: Michael R. Beschloss (1955-   ) and Strobe Talbott (1946-   )
Publisher: Little, Brown (Boston). 498 pp. $ 24.95
Type of work: History
Time: 1982-1993
Locale: The United States of America and the Soviet Union

Drawing on once-secret material, Michael Beschloss and Strobe Talbott intimately chronicle the decisions by American and Russian statesmen which ended the Cold War

Principal personages:
MIKHAIL GORBACHEV, leader of the Soviet Union from 1985 to 1991
GEORGE BUSH, the forty-first president of the United States, 1989-1993
JAMES BAKER, U.S. secretary of state under Bush
EDUARD SHEVARDNADZE, the Soviet foreign secretary under Gorbachev
BORIS YELTSIN, the first president of the post-Soviet Russian Republic
BRENT SCOWCROFT, national security adviser under Bush
SADDAM HUSSEIN, president of Iraq

One of the most fascinating aspects of *At the Highest Levels: The Inside Story of the End of the Cold War* is the book's total fulfillment of its promise to provide readers with an insider's view of what happened at key policy meetings, superpower summits, and supposedly secret conversations at the end of the Cold War. In their direct quotes and uncannily close descriptions of the talks, actions, and plans of leaders such as George Bush, Mikhail Gorbachev, James Baker, and Eduard Shevardnadze, historian Michael Beschloss and former journalist Strobe Talbott reveal their amazing access to the world players who have made recent history.

Written in part during the crucial years 1989 to 1991, *At the Highest Levels* tells its remarkable story in roughly chronological fashion and headlines each chapter with a personal quote by one of the statesmen involved. This method establishes a strong sense of immediacy, if not suspense, and allows the reader to live again through those influential times when a world order was suddenly overturned. An outline of the events under discussion, which is printed in front and back of the book, greatly helps the reader to keep track.

At the Highest Levels opens with a quick succession of state funerals in Moscow, as Ronald Reagan's vice president George Bush attends these ceremonies occasioned by the demise of one superannuated Soviet leader after another. When fifty-four-year-old Mikhail Gorbachev assumes command in the spring of 1985, the course of Soviet foreign policy changes dramatically: This relatively young, fresh leader seems determined to end the old enmities between the Soviets and the West which had given the Cold War its name.

Once George Bush is inaugurated as president in January, 1989, Beschloss and Talbott chronicle in great depth how the leaders of the two superpowers try to establish a political and, soon enough, personal relationship through which to set the tone and pace of their wide-ranging negotiations. The authors are careful not to let hindsight cloud their description of Bush's initial reluctance to maintain the breakneck speed at which Gorbachev and Reagan had come to operate in their mutual efforts to change superpower relations. Right from the beginning, and indicative of things to come, the reader is given a front-row seat at the newly elected American president's first private policy seminar on relations with the Soviets, which Stanford professor Condoleezza Rice organized at Bush's vacation home in Kennebunkport.

On the Soviet side, *At the Highest Levels* provides a similar level of intimate knowledge, as its pages reveal in vivid detail Gorbachev's anger at Bush's overly cautious proceedings. Almost a year passes before the two meet face-to-face at the "seasick summit" in Malta in December, 1989. By this time, as Beschloss and Talbott show, the world has changed dramatically. Gorbachev's decision to release the Soviet satellites in Eastern Europe results in the fall of the Berlin Wall and the astonishingly quick and relatively bloodless collapse of virtually every Communist regime in the region during the *annus mirabilis*, or "wonderful year "of 1989. Suddenly, the authors demonstrate, statesmen and diplomats in the East and the West see their hands forced by unforeseen, rapidly unfolding external events.

Yet pressure on foreign policy also arises from domestic difficulties. On the American side, there is George Bush's lingering vulnerability to charges of betrayal from the Republican right; in the Soviet Union, a deteriorating economy together with an increasing desire for independence in the Baltics and a nascent civil war in the Transcaucasus hamper Gorbachev's freedom of action and severely erode his popularity at home.

Given the domestic troubles of the two leaders, it is easy to see why, as Beschloss and Talbott reveal, Bush privately assures Gorbachev that he will overlook some Soviet actions against opponents within the Union, as long as violence is avoided. As a result, a close relationship develops between the two men, and the world sees a reunified Germany which is a member of the North Atlantic Treaty Organization (NATO), and the forging of the remarkable anti-Saddam Hussein alliance, which succeeds in throwing the Iraqi invader out of Kuwait.

Its focus on people who shape history is a major strength of *At the Highest Levels*. The authors take the reader into Gorbachev's darkest moments, when hardliners attempt to depose him during the critical days of August 18 to 21, 1991, less than three weeks after another meeting with Bush. Returning to Moscow, the man who had worked hard to end the Cold War and released Eastern Europe into freedom finds himself presiding over the breakup and end of the Soviet Union.

While the momentous events of the years between 1989 and 1991 are told primarily from the perspective—and often in the very words—of the key players at the centers of political power, Beschloss and Talbott augment their narrative by providing a concise review of the larger, and even the more technical political and diplomatic decisions. Thus, *At the Highest Levels* often moves beyond the offices and homes of the two world leaders and their aides and adversaries to include an overview of the political issues debated, deliberated, and negotiated as the Cold War waned.

Nevertheless, the authors never lose sight of their primary interest in the people behind the shifting positions and the articulation of new treaties. Their book is about men and women in charge of change who grapple with the problem of fundamentally redefining American-Soviet relations, and Beschloss and Talbott make this a very interesting story.

One telling example is representative of their success in capturing the human dimension of their story. The authors provide a detailed account of the influential meeting between James Baker and Eduard Shevardnadze on Baker's ranch in Wyoming in September, 1989. With wit and a keen sense for the telling detail, Beschloss and Talbott not only highlight the revolutionary Soviet concessions but also present the hunt to determine Shevardnadze's hat size, so that Baker's present of a Stetson hat would fit perfectly.

Not surprisingly, the questions of arms control, disarmament, and conventional force reduction debated in Wyoming make up the bulk of the pro-active political work of the period aimed at reversing old trends. In this field, the representatives of both superpowers do not have to react to sudden challenges, but rather seek a diplomatic breakthrough for log-jammed issues that had defined the stalemate of the Cold War, complete with its ever-increasing stockpiles of costly weaponry. Throughout these often very technical negotiations, the narrative nicely brings together personal actions, specific policy issues, and the larger diplomatic picture.

Beschloss and Talbott point out cogently how the meeting in Wyoming becomes instrumental in firmly establishing the remarkable friendship between Baker and Shevardnadze. The two move on to revolutionize not only the atmosphere but also the substance of superpower relations. One year after their ministers' groundbreaking Wyoming meeting, Bush and Gorbachev sign a treaty reducing conventional forces in Europe (the CFE treaty); another year later, in 1992, the long awaited Strategic Arms Reduction Treaty (START) is signed in Moscow.

Lest the reader forget the momentousness of these treaties, *At the Highest Levels* gives ample space to the objections voiced by conservatives in both countries. On the American side, there is the almost indecent pressing of the American advantage by Brent Scowcroft, Bush's hardline national security adviser, who is often seen trying to squeeze the last ounce of blood out of a former opponent. On the Soviet side, the authors show the persistent resistance of hardliners, who try to derail Gorbachev's bold initiatives.

Ultimately, however, it is not the hardline opposition that undoes Gorbachev, but the rising star of his rival, Boris Yeltsin. Unable to raise domestic living standards and presiding instead over a slow economic decline, Gorbachev becomes increasingly unpopular at home while his reputation soars abroad. At the time of the failed Soviet coup in August, 1991, Beschloss and Talbott show how Boris Yeltsin's resignation from the Communist party in July of 1990 and his election to Russian president in June of 1991 turn him into a powerful popular figure. He has become a real alternative to the reform-minded, but still committed Communist Gorbachev.

Their chronicle of Yeltsin's rise and his subsequent dismantling of the Soviet Union in favor of the new Commonwealth of Independent States (CIS) reveals that Beschloss and Talbott had far less direct access to Yeltsin and his aides. There are few personal quotes, and the reader feels that the doors to Yeltsin's inner chambers have remained closed to the two authors. Perhaps tellingly, none of Yeltsin's words are used as a chapter headline.

Its focus on the actions of people at the center of power works rewardingly for most of *At the Highest Levels* and could not be more appropriate for the era of George Bush, who placed such great emphasis on personal contacts. He achieved his biggest triumph, the forging of the anti-Saddam coalition, by following this strategy, and, together with Mikhail Gorbachev, effectively ended the Cold War.

In their epilogue, however, Beschloss and Talbott warn of the pitfalls of such an approach. They observe that Bush and Gorbachev fell from power because of large-scale domestic problems which their personal efforts could not mitigate. At the end of their book, the reader cannot help but see the stark irony that Bush and Gorbachev, whose foreign policies changed the world, were both ultimately overcome by domestic opposition based on economic difficulties at home.

The greatest strength of *At the Highest Levels* lies in the astonishingly detailed and far-ranging amount of information which the authors' extraordinary access to people in power has yielded. Beschloss and Talbott have wisely refrained from any attempt at a large-scale analysis of their fresh material. Instead, they leave it to their reader to establish an informed opinion of his or her own.

Finally, in view of President Bill Clinton's appointment of Talbott, his former Oxford roommate, as ambassador-at-large to the former Soviet Union in 1993 and his subsequent nomination of Talbott for the post of deputy secretary of state, the reader may look forward to seeing how well the former journalist is able to put into practice the lessons that are suggested by this extraordinary chronicle.

R. C. Lutz

Sources for Further Study

Arms Control Today. XXIII, March, 1993, p. 30.
Chicago Tribune. January 31, 1993, XIV, p. 3.
The Christian Science Monitor. July 29, 1993, p. 14.
Foreign Affairs. LXXII, Summer, 1993, p. 200.
Los Angeles Times Book Review. March 21, 1993, p. 7.
The New York Times Book Review. XCVIII, February 14, 1993, p. 9.
The New Yorker. LXVIII, February 1, 1993, p. 105.
Newsweek. CXXI, February 1, 1993, p. 62.
Publishers Weekly. CCXL, January 4, 1993, p. 64.
Time. CXLI, February 15, 1993, p. 62.
The Wall Street Journal. March 8, 1993, p. A10.

BALKAN GHOSTS
A Journey Through History

Author: Robert D. Kaplan
Publisher: St. Martin's Press (New York). 307 pp. $22.95
Type of work: Current affairs
Time: The 1980's and early 1990's
Locale: Albania, Bulgaria, Romania, Greece, and the states of the former Yugoslavia

In this literate, well-written travel book by a journalist who spent a decade visiting and living in the Balkans, the author strives to demonstrate how the region's problems in the 1990's stem from its history

Principal personages:
> ROBERT D. KAPLAN, the author, who travels through the Balkan countries
> GUILLERMO ANGELOV, Kaplan's Bulgarian journalist friend
> WILFRED BURCHETT, a famed Australian Communist writer who settled in Bulgaria
> ALOJZIJE STEPINAC, Archbishop of Belgrade during World War II
> ANDREAS PAPANDREOU, Prime Minister of Greece

The region of southeastern Europe known as the Balkans returned with a vengeance to newspaper readers' awareness during the early 1990's. At the beginning of the twentieth century, with bitter ethnic wars in 1912 and 1913, the region had spawned a term, "balkanization," that entered regular English usage. One *Webster's* dictionary defines the verb "to Balkanize" as "to break up into small, mutually hostile political units, as the Balkan States after World War I." Sarajevo, the capital of Bosnia-Herzegovina, was the site of the 1914 assassination of Archduke Franz Ferdinand of Austria—the catalyst of that war. Some of World War II's bitterest and bloodiest fighting took place in Yugoslavia, between the Ustasha secret police of the Fascist state of Croatia and the Partizan resistance led by Marshal Josip Tito.

Tito's highly personalized Communist dictatorship and his talent for keeping a political balance among Croats, Serbs, Muslims, and other groups kept Yugoslavia unified and relatively stable until, in the wake of revolutions elsewhere in Europe, it collapsed. In December of 1991, Croatia and Slovenia, two of Yugoslavia's constituent republics, declared themselves independent. Their recognition by the European Community—insisted on by Germany, the EC's most powerful member—was the signal for a bloody war between Croatia and Serbia and the eventual near-destruction of Bosnia-Herzegovina, haplessly caught in the middle with a population that was a volatile ethnic mix.

Robert D. Kaplan began visiting the Balkans in the early 1980's, when few others were going there. Though his book's publication was well timed to coincide with heightened interest in the area, he is more interested in the region as a whole—which he defines as including Albania, Bulgaria, Romania, and Greece, as well as the states of the former Yugoslavia—and the historical roots of the several countries' current plights than in the headline-grabbing tragedy of Bosnia-Herzegovina. Though *Balkan*

Ghosts: A Journey Through History is billed as a travel book, it really is more a series of essays linked thematically by Kaplan's musings on history and chronologically by his visits. "On the road, when I met people, I asked them always about the past," he writes. "Only in this way could the present become comprehensible."

> Belgrade, Bucharest, Sofia, Athens, Adrianople. These were once the datelines of choice for ambitious journalists—the Saigon, Beirut, and Managua of a younger world," he notes. "Ernest Hemingway filed his most famous dispatch from Adrianople (now Edirne, in Turkish Thrace) in 1922, describing Greek refugees 'walking blindly along in the rain,' with all their possessions piled on oxcarts beside them. The Balkans were the original Third World, long before the Western media coined the term. . . . Whatever has happened in Beirut or elsewhere happened first, long ago, in the Balkans.

Kaplan divides his book into four parts. Part 1, "Yugoslavia: Historical Overtures," includes chapters on Croatia, Serbia and Albania, Macedonia, and Belgrade, the capital of Serbia. The second and—perhaps surprisingly—longest section (110 pages long, out of 287 pages of text) is on Romania, which geographically need not be defined as part of the Balkans. The short but memorable third part is on Bulgaria. Part 4 is on Greece, a country many in the West think of more as an eastern outpost of Western Europe than as a Balkan country. Kaplan is at pains to show—and does show, persuasively—that Greece (where he has lived) indeed is "Balkan" and is hardly much better off economically or politically than its sad neighbors.

He uses British novelist Rebecca West's classic travel book *Black Lamb and Grey Falcon: Record of a Journey Through Yugoslavia in 1937* (1941) as a touchstone for his chapters on Yugoslavia. West became obsessed with Yugoslavia the day in 1934 when she heard on the radio, while lying in a hospital bed, that the king of Yugoslavia had been assassinated. Her ambitious, massive book (still in print as a Penguin paperback) is more or less *the* book to read in English on Yugoslavia, so Kaplan's somewhat proprietorial reading of it is a bit tiresome, as is his questionably accurate insistence on calling its author "Dame Rebecca." (West was not made a Dame of the British Empire until 1959, two decades after her time in the Balkans.)

He is right to assert that "Yugoslavia [is] a story of ethnic subtlety atop subtlety that resisted condensation on the news pages"; therein lies the value of his book as well as of West's. "Politics in Yugoslavia perfectly mirrors the process of history and is thus more predictable than most people think," he claims. He also discusses the legacy of Alojzije Stepinac, the complex, tortured Roman Catholic archbishop of Belgrade, who collaborated with but also resisted the Fascist regime in Croatia during World War II. "Croatia's tragedy was that its modern nationalism coalesced at a time when fascism was dominant in Europe, forcing its proponents to become entangled with Nazism," he writes. He prescribes a "brave and unambiguous appraisal of the past . . . to untangle these threads." He summarizes the Bosnian mess competently:

> Bosnia represents an intensification and a complication of the Serb-Croat dispute. Just as Croats felt their western Catholicism more intensely than did the Austrians or the Italians, precisely because of their uneasy proximity to the Eastern Orthodox and Muslim worlds, so the Croats of Bosnia—

because they shared the same mountains with both Orthodox Serbs and Muslims—felt their Croatianism much more intensely than did the Croats in Croatia proper, who enjoyed the psychological luxury of having only their ethnic compatriots as immediate neighbors. The same, of course, was true of the Serbs in Bosnia. Complicating matters in Bosnia was the existence of a large community of Muslims. These were Slavs, whether originally Croat or Serb, who had been converted to Islam in the late Middle Ages by the Turkish occupiers and whose religion gradually became synonymous with their ethnic identity.

Balkan Ghosts is not the best primer on the bloodletting in the former Yugoslavia; that is *The Fall of Yugoslavia: The Third Balkan War* by BBC Central Europe correspondent Misha Glenny, a Penguin paperback published in 1992 in Great Britain and the next year in the United States. Glenny's book is necessarily rather breathlessly narrated but well written, informed and lucid. The value of Kaplan's book is its wider scope, both geographic and historical.

Kaplan's chapter on the city of Salonika in Greece well illustrates his concerns. Almost within living memory, Salonika (the Thessalonica to whose early Christians the apostle Paul wrote epistles) had been overwhelmingly Jewish, populated by Sephardic ("Spanish") Jews forced to leave Spain and Portugal during the Inquisition of the late fifteenth century. At the turn of the twentieth century, writes Kaplan,

> the reactionary tyranny of the Turkish sultans was finally collapsing. But fear and uncertainty loomed: in a region of great ethnic diversity, the Jews had carved out a niche. The intolerant— perhaps because it was so long repressed—nationalism of Bulgarians, who occupied the hinterland around Salonika, and of the Greeks, who occupied all the territory to the south, represented a much more threatening tyranny than that of the imperial Turks.

A huge fire in 1917 followed a 1916 Greek occupation. Then World War II came. "Of all the cities in Nazi-occupied Europe," writes Kaplan, "Salonika ranked first in the number of Jewish victims: out of a Jewish population of 56,000, 54,050—96.5 percent—were exterminated at Auschwitz, Birkenau, and Bergen-Belsen." Kaplan uses the genocide of Jewish Salonika, and contemporary Greeks' refusal to ponder its legacy, to introduce his important and cogent argument that Greece is a Balkan country. The Cold War, he writes, separated Greece artificially from its northern neighbors. "Only Westerners like me, living in Greece, realized how Balkan Greece was. Those on the outside were determined to see Greece as a Mediterranean and Western country only: the facts be damned." Kaplan punctures Western ideals of the "Greek tourist myth" that developed during the 1960's, as well as what he sees as a simplistic Western belief in "Greece" as the founder of Western civilization. "In the learning centers of the West," he writes, ". . . the most recent 2,000 years of Greek history were virtually ignored in favor of an idealized version of ancient Greece."

He illustrates his point by narrating the sordid career of Greek Prime Minister Andreas Papandreou, as well as the wounds inflicted on the Greeks' national pride by the International Olympic Committee's decision to award the Olympic Games in 1996—the hundredth anniversary of the modern Olympics—to Atlanta instead of to Athens. In the same context he discusses Greeks' refusal to remember Salonika, as well as what he sees as their paranoid refusal to recognize the independence of former Yugoslav Macedonia because of a proprietary feeling about the country's name. Greece's "naive trust" in promises made by the "romantic philhellene" British prime minister David Lloyd George during World War I led to the rise of what became known as the "Great Idea": "the return of every inch of historic Greece to the motherland." This, notes Kaplan, was "the same old Balkan revanchist syndrome: each nation claiming as its natural territory all the lands that it held at the time of its great historical expansion." A glance at a map of the Balkans suggests vividly how this syndrome can and does wreak havoc and bloodshed throughout the region.

The book ends perfunctorily, with Kaplan asserting that "the Enlightenment was, at last, breaching the gates of these downtrodden nations. A better age would have to follow." The conclusion rings false and suggests an editor's or publisher's—or author's—need for an upbeat ending. Kaplan insists sometimes tiresomely on a hackneyed dichotomy between the enlightened, rational "West" and the instinctive, romantic "East" (ill-defined terms in this book, as elsewhere).

Nevertheless, *Balkan Ghosts* is admirable and refreshing in its pointed ignoring of exciting, marketable headlines and in its readable discussion of the region's history. An interview with Kaplan in *Publishers Weekly* of March 29, 1993, offers a fine depiction of a dogged writer determined to follow his own vision of what is worth writing about. "The hard-news media does not cover the world; it covers the foreign extensions of America's domestic obsessions," Kaplan tells interviewer Paul Elie.

Kaplan's friendship with an intrepid, voluble Bulgarian journalist, Guillermo Angelov, is the book's most memorable episode. Angelov pressed his friendship on Kaplan in a seedy hotel staircase in 1981. He introduced Kaplan to Wilfred Burchett, a legendary Australian Communist writer whose books include *My War with the CIA* (1973), which he ghost-wrote for Prince Norodom Sihanouk of Cambodia. Burchett, writes Kaplan, "spoke several Asian languages and had been on intimate terms with Mao, Ho Chi Minh, Kim il Sung, and others whom few (if any) Western journalists had access to. . . . He showed up at the 1953 Korean War peace talks as a kind of semi-official spokesman for the North Korean delegation. . . . In the 1950s, the Australian government revoked his passport, so Burchett globetrotted with a *laissez passer* provided him by North Vietnam's Communist regime." By the time Kaplan met him, Burchett had married a Bulgarian and settled down. He died two years later, in 1983.

Angelov was enamored of Burchett and urged the young Kaplan to emulate him. Though Kaplan quotes Angelov's earnest exhortations with tongue in cheek, they serve as a worthy epigraph to what he has attempted—largely with success—to do in *Balkan Ghosts.* "Grabbing me by the arm, he said, 'A man, Robby, a man is not a man until he is on the open road! . . . Write books, Robby! Go deep. Be like Wilfred Burchett. Don't be a hack!'"

Ethan Casey

Sources for Further Study

Booklist. LXXXIX, February 15, 1993, p. 1028.
Business Week. April 12, 1993, p. 15.
Kirkus Reviews. LXI, February 1, 1993, p. 119.
Library Journal. CXVIII, February 15, 1993, p. 179.
The New Leader. LXXVI, June 14, 1993, p. 17.
The New York Times Book Review. XCVIII, March 28, 1993, p. 3.
The New Yorker. LXIX, April 26, 1993, p. 119.
Publishers Weekly. CCXL, March 29, 1993, p. 30.
The Wall Street Journal. May 13, 1993, p. A12.
The Washington Post Book World. XXIII, March 28, 1993, p. 1.

BECKETT'S DYING WORDS
The Clarendon Lectures, 1990

Author: Christopher B. Ricks (1933-   )
Publisher: Clarendon Press/Oxford University Press (New York). 218 pp. $25.00
Type of work: Literary criticism

Ricks's lectures illuminate not only the theme of death in Beckett's writings, but also that theme in philosophy and literature

By "dying words," Christopher Ricks does not mean to discuss, literally, Samuel Beckett's deathbed utterances. If Beckett had indeed articulated some final words, Ricks has nothing to report to his readers—nor to his audience during the 1990 Clarendon Lectures, from which this volume derives. To be sure, Ricks had been acquainted—but only casually—with Beckett. He met the playwright twice, briefly; and the two exchanged a terse correspondence, mostly on technical linguistic topics. After Beckett's death in December of 1989, a London newspaper requested Ricks to write an obituary, but he declined. Several years earlier, he had written a tribute to Beckett for the *Sunday Times* (London). Yet in a sense, *Beckett's Dying Words* is a definitive obituary for the man, just as it is a supreme tribute. Ricks focuses upon the essential theme of Beckett's lifetime work as an artist: the quest for dying.

From Beckett's earliest publication, an essay treating James Joyce, *Our Exagmination Round His Factification for Incamination of Work in Progress* . . . (1929), to his last posthumously published work, *Dream of Fair to Middling Women* (1992), the dour Irishman penned his "dying words"; all his inquiries into death, from *Whoroscope* (1930) to *Nohow On* (1989), center around words that come to terms with dying—with puns, tricks of language, play of ideas, private and public ironies. Fully to appreciate Beckett as a person and as an artist, the reader must observe, without flinching and without distaste, the writer obsessed with death. Ricks's special contribution to our understanding of Beckett is his steady, empathetic observation of the writer's death-words. In a true sense of the word, Beckett is consumed with *morbidity*, that is the matter of dying, and with language that expresses a condition of dying.

Ricks divides his study, as presumably he had organized his lectures, into four main parts, which are chapters of the book. The chapter subtitles describe the content of each part: "Death," "Words That Went Dead," "Languages, Both Dead and Living," and "The Irish Bull." A brief "Postscript" dated December, 1989, concludes the volume with commemorative pages.

Once the reader manages a passage through the turbulence of chapter 1, the rest of the book is smooth sailing. In that first part Ricks argues that the death instinct in literature is quite as powerful as that of vitality. Moreover, he insists that the "wish to die" is every bit as keen as the urge to endure. Although Beckett is at the center of this investigation, he is by no means the only advocate. Ricks cites, among others, Philip Larkin, Robert Lowell, John Berryman, A. E. Housman, Sébastien Chamfort, and Thomas Hardy. A unifying argument of these sometime advocates of death-over-life is expressed without equivocation by the chorus in Sophocles' *Oedipus at Colonus*: that it is better to be dead than alive; that the greatest good is never to have been born. Whereas the notables mentioned above—and other writers as well—have been quoted on occasion to approve Sophocles' sentiments, Beckett of all writers is most persistent in his philosophical assent. Just as *The Oxford Book of Death* (1983) provides an anthology of brief readings on the topics of dying and death, so Beckett's work, taken in totality, offers his readers a similar "anthology," but one that is philosophically unified.

Ricks treats this matter, one which may trouble some admirers of Beckett's writings, forthrightly and with sympathy. His approach is never condescending, as from a healthy to an unhealthy mental consciousness. For Ricks, Beckett's point of view is not curious, odd, or unwholesome. To him Beckett is *morbid* not in a pejorative but a descriptive sense of the word. Moreover, Ricks places Beckett's morbidity into the context of philosophical discourse, rather than psychological aberration. Although aware of Freud's concept of the death impulse beyond the "pleasure principle," Ricks chooses not to examine Beckett from a Freudian stance. To put the issue bluntly, Ricks appears to believe that the Irishman's viewpoint is correct, or at least defensible. With wit and sanity he examines the larger implications of the death-urge. More than a study of Beckett's dying words, Ricks's slender volume is one of the great twentieth century essays on the subject of dying.

In Ricks's judgment, Beckett was aware of different kinds of death. One form of literary death is the demise of language, of words that no longer are "alive" with meaning. Ricks shows how Beckett parodies words that have become "abstracted to death"; phrases that are merely clichés; words that have achieved a "resurrection" into different usage; and words (as well as ideas) that deserve an obituary. To probe Beckett's language, Ricks uses both English and French versions of the writer's work. Because Beckett customarily translated his writing from one language to the other, he was acutely sensitive to the slightest variation in the tone of different speech forms. Ricks is similarly sensitive to language. A master of French, Ricks perceives the finest nuances of meaning that Beckett had intended to suggest in words from both tongues. Indeed, *Beckett's Dying Words* ought to be useful for translators, no matter what languages they use; for Ricks understands perfectly the art—and dangers—of translation.

As a matter of fact, as a stylist Ricks at times appears to be a continuation of Beckett. Such praise is great, but not excessive. Close, attentive reflection upon Beckett's language has had the admirable effect upon Ricks of imitating many of the master's virtues. Like Beckett's prose, Ricks's is spare, direct, musical, incantatory. His principle is one of condensation—of making the most of the fewest words; and of clarity—of making the obscure appear obvious. These stylistic talents are also gifts of the poet. At his best, Ricks's prose resembles poetry.

At no point in the book is the virtue more apparent than in the final section, "The Irish Bull." Defined by the *Oxford English Dictionary* (*OED*) as "a self-contradictory proposition . . . in modern use an expression containing a manifest contradiction in terms or involving a ludicrous inconsistency unperceived by the speaker," the Bull is further defined as "often with [the] epithet *Irish*," although the word "had been long in use before it came to be associated with Irishmen." Ricks cites the *OED* definition, as well as the one from Brewer's *Dictionary of Phrase and Fable*: "A blunder, or inadvertent contradiction of terms, for which the Irish are proverbial."

Although the definitions quoted are from impeccable sources, Ricks begs to differ—or rather to quibble—with these standard interpretations. First, he examines the Irish Bull in terms of literary and linguistic history of usage, including such modern variations as malapropisms by former vice president of the United States Dan Quayle. Older examples of the Bull include those by Thomas Carlyle, John Milton, Jonathan Swift, Dr. Johnson, and others. With scholarly delight Ricks examines the classic "Essay on Irish Bulls" (1802) by Maria Edgeworth and Richard Lovell Edgeworth. After this extensive survey, Ricks argues his own point of view. To him a definition of the Irish Bull must allow for some perception that the speaker (or the reader) is aware of the presumed blunder—indeed, that the blunder may not at all events be so.

For Ricks, the matter is more than a scholarly quibble over definitions, because he believes that Beckett's use of the Bull is a necessary part of the artist's vision. Embedded within the logical inconsistencies of the Bull may be a different kind of logic, a different reality. Ricks shows how Beckett's presumed inconsistencies and presumed blunders parody logic, yet—often with comic effect—revitalize "dead" forms of logic. To make his point clear, he cites a "bouquet" of fifteen Bulls from Beckett, both in English and French. So carefully has Ricks prepared his readers for this lesson, that he does not have to analyze the content of the Bulls. The reader understands.

Perhaps the major contribution of Ricks's study to the already vast accumulation of Beckett criticism is the writer's ability to get into the Irishman's mind. Ricks plays with the same tricks of language. As a consummate teacher, he shows his readers (or his audience at the Clarendon Lectures) not simply how to understand particular passages in Beckett, but how to learn Beckett's habits of thought. An example of Ricks's pedagogy is his brief but cogent exposition of the playwright's Gaelic borrowings. In order fully to appreciate the wit of an Irishman, Ricks holds that one should think like an Irishman. Because Beckett's Irish is at once modern and retrospective to the older traditions, Ricks explains how Beckett uses "dead languages, . . . mother tongues, and . . . stepmother tongues." Once Ricks completes his lesson, his readers are able to puzzle out Beckett without help, even from the critic's sensitive guidance. Consider, for example, the title Ricks has chosen: "Beckett's Dying Words." With the addition of a single word, the phrase becomes an Irish Bull—a seeming contradiction which is nevertheless true. That word turns a supposed blunder into a paradoxical reality: Beckett's dying words *live*.

Leslie B. Mittleman

Sources for Further Study

Bostonia. Winter, 1993-1994, p. 78.
The New Criterion. XXII, January, 1994, p. 65.
New Statesman and Society. VI, July 16, 1993, p. 39.
The New York Review of Books. XL, December 16, 1993, p. 42.
The Spectator. CCLXXI, August 28, 1993, p. 31.
The Times Literary Supplement. October 1, 1993, p. 7.

BENJAMIN BRITTEN
A Biography

Author: Humphrey Carpenter (1946-   )
First published: 1992, in Great Britain
Publisher: Charles Scribner's Sons (New York). 677 pp. $30.00
Type of work: Biography
Time: 1913-1976
Locale: England

A thorough compilation of details about the personal life of Benjamin Britten, this book relies heavily on speculation to connect the life of the composer to his music

> *Principal personages:*
> BENJAMIN BRITTEN, a musical composer, performer, and conductor
> ROBERT BRITTEN, his father
> EDITH BRITTEN, his mother
> PETER PEARS, his companion of thirty-seven years
> W. H. AUDEN, his friend, mentor, and collaborator

His mother was determined to make him the fourth *B*, the twentieth century representative in the pantheon of Bach, Beethoven, and Brahms. Indeed, his very birthday fell on the feast day of the patron saint of music and seemed to confirm Edward Benjamin Britten's destiny. Born in Lowestoft in East Anglia on November 22, 1913, Beni, as his family called him, was shaped for musical greatness.

Humphrey Carpenter's biography of Benjamin Britten carefully documents the composer's journey from a pampered childhood, through a rather miserable public school career, struggles for musical acceptance, and self-doubts about his personal life, to the recognition that honored his last years. Referencing diaries, letters, and extensive interviews with those who knew him, Carpenter scrupulously tries to gain a consensus from his sources about Britten's personal life.

Two of the pervasive issues in this book are the composer's preoccupation with his sexual orientation and his keen interest in the theme of innocence endangered. After the nurturing environment of his family home, Britten found the English public school environment inhospitable. His diary and letters reflect his revulsion at disciplinary beatings and bullying. Eric Crozier, librettist and producer of several early Britten operas, maintains that the composer told him that he had been raped by a schoolmaster. This event perhaps was the source of his later protectiveness toward young boys and his proclivity for operatic texts on the theme of the vulnerability of innocence.

Britten began to compose at the piano as early as age five or six, producing pieces that, as he put it with some irony, were "inspired by terrific events in my home life." "Do You No That My Daddy Has Gone to London Today," dated 1919, for piano and vocal duet, is one of those surviving pieces. At ten, he was encouraged by his piano teacher to attend concerts in Norwich. Particularly impressed by Frank Bridge's *The Sea*, he was studying with Bridge by age fourteen.

At sixteen, he won a scholarship to London's Royal College of Music based on some of his compositions. Carpenter describes the British music scene at this time as divided between Edward Elgar and the Brahms imitators and the English pastoralists, including Ralph Vaughan Williams, Gustav Holst, and John Ireland. Impatient with these composers, Britten seems to have charted another course. His diary records favorable impressions of Arnold Schönberg, Alban Berg, Igor Stravinsky, and Dmitry Shostakovich. On the strength of his *Sinfonietta* and two works entitled *Phantasy*, Britten, by age nineteen, was being classified with William Walton as one of the rising stars in England's music firmament.

Britten's was an uphill struggle, however, for contemporary music was not well received. Epitomizing this state of affairs was the 1936 performance of his satiric, experimental *Our Hunting Fathers*. In a rehearsal he conducted, which he referred to as "the most catastrophic evening of my life," members of the London Philharmonic Orchestra mocked the work and its twenty-three-year-old composer.

To earn a living in this early period of his career, Britten turned to writing soundtracks for General Post Office documentary films. His first assignment was "to concoct *some* rubbish about a Jubilee Stamp." Yet the job had the fortunate effect of introducing him to W. H. Auden, who wrote text for the films. Seven years his senior, bohemian, leftist, and openly homosexual, Auden had an important influence on the young composer. Britten said that Auden was "in" all of his operas, although they actually collaborated on only one, *Paul Bunyan* (1941). In turn, Auden regarded Britten as possessing an extraordinary sensitivity to the English language and ability to ally music with it.

Aside from their professional relationship, Auden influenced Britten's personal life. In 1936, he wrote, with characteristic boldness, poems offering his impression of the composer as cold and numb and urged him to give himself up to passion. Christopher Isherwood confirms that he and Auden probably took it upon themselves "to bring [Britten] out."

The deaths of his father in 1934 and mother in 1937 seem to have freed Britten to make a decision about his sexuality. Only a month after his mother's death, a diary entry describes a luncheon with a homosexual schoolmate who urged him "to decide something about my sexual life. O, for a little courage." Carpenter notes that in June of 1938, after eleven years of faithful recordings, Britten's diary abruptly comes to an end. He speculates that this date may have marked the beginning of a relationship that Britten wished to keep discreet.

It was around this period that he met Peter Pears, the man with whom he would eventually spend the last thirty-seven years of his life. Pears, a preparatory school master, was a frequent guest at the Old Mill, Britten's home in the marshlands near Aldeburgh. He and Britten formed a musical partnership—Britten as composer and pianist, Pears as tenor—that lasted for the rest of Britten's life.

In 1939, the pair toured America, perhaps to get away from the inevitable war with Germany. After the war broke out, embassy and friends advised them to remain there. Besides the danger posed by warfare, as pacifists they risked going to prison. The longer they remained away from home, however, the more their reputations were hurt back in England. Complicating matters was Britten's commission from the Japanese government to write *Sinfonia da Requiem* for that country's twenty-six-hundredth anniversary. Some in England construed this as traitorous (although England was not at war with Japan, nor was the United States at that time).

Auden, also in America at the outbreak of the war, wrote the libretto for *Paul Bunyan*. Characteristically, he was also more than willing to offer advice. Art, he asserted, was a mixture of order and chaos, bohemianism and bourgeois conventions. In his view, Britten leaned too far toward conventional and technical skill and evaded "the demands of disorder." In his personal life, this explained "your attraction to thin-as-a-board juveniles, i.e. to the sexless and innocent."

Britten's eventual return to his homeland seems to have been the result of nationalistic longing. Having read an article by E. M. Forster on George Crabbe, the late eighteenth and early nineteenth century poet who was born at Aldeburgh, Britten procured a copy of *The Borough* (1810), which featured a story about Peter Grimes, a fisherman whose apprentices died under mysterious circumstances. Reading the poem and Forster's article led Britten to the conviction that he wanted to write an opera about Grimes and to go home.

Back in England, Pears and Britten had the sense of being social outsiders because of their conscientious objector status and their homosexuality. In 1940's and 1950's England, it was illegal for consenting adults to engage in homosexual acts even in privacy. Although no charges were brought against him, Britten was interviewed by Scotland Yard. That his sex life was considered abnormal created enormous tension in him, which Carpenter suggests accounts at least partially for the power of his art.

Such tension is reflected in the opera *Peter Grimes* (1945). As Britten puts it, the alienation he and Pears felt "led us to make Grimes a character of vision and conflict, the tortured idealist he is, rather than the villain he was in Crabbe." This vision informed subsequent operas such as *The Rape of Lucretia* (1946) and *Albert Herring* (1947) as well. The Sadler's Wells singers, who performed *Peter Grimes* in 1945, complained about the difficulty and cacophony of the music and about Britten and Pears's pacifism and homosexuality. Although the performance led to fourteen curtain calls, many of the singers refused to perform for a recording of the work.

In 1947, Britten and Pears moved from the Old Mill to Crag House in Aldeburgh, from which they planned the first of what would be twenty-eight arts festivals in Britten's lifetime. Invited to speak was Forster, who lectured on differences between Peter Grimes in the poem and in the libretto. Forster helped write the libretto for Britten's next opera, *Billy Budd* (1951), in which Pears played Captain Vere, the man who must decide the fate of the consummately innocent Budd, convicted killer of the evil Claggart. Although Forster wanted the story to be about the redeeming power of homosexual love and the vanquishing of twisted perversion, Britten preferred to focus on Captain Vere and the ethical dilemma he faced. Carpenter believes that in doing so, Britten avoided "bringing his own dark side out of the cupboard again."

From being on the margins of English society, Britten moved in his middle and later years to a position in which he received much respect; he was named a peer of the throne in the last year of his life. Britten's growing popularity might be attributed to his sense that music should be written for a particular audience, place, soloist or ensemble: "almost every piece I have ever written has been composed with a certain occasion in mind." Perhaps the most notable example of this was his commission to compose an opera, which he named *Gloriana* (1953), for the coronation of Elizabeth II.

Carpenter's exhaustive concentration on the psychosexual is occasionally varied with more musically based analyses that give a broader sense of Britten's accomplishments. For example, John Ireland, Britten's former teacher, thought *The Turn of the Screw* (1954), a chamber opera with only thirteen instruments plus voices, remarkably original in spite of its operating on a diatonic or tonal basis. The influences of Balinese gamelan music and the Japanese Noh play, which Britten encountered on a world tour, are also traced. The former was incorporated into *The Prince of the Pagodas* (1957) and the latter in *Curlew River* (1964).

Britten's musical output was prolific and continued almost nonstop until poor health slowed it in 1972. Fearful that he would never complete his opera *Death in Venice* if he underwent surgery for aortic valve disease, he delayed the operation until 1973. Not successful, the surgery was complicated by a slight stroke that left his right arm partially paralyzed and essentially ended his career as a pianist.

Letters between him and Pears in late 1974, when Pears was performing *Death in Venice* (1973) in America, Britten too sick to accompany him, provide a fitting tribute to the two men's shared love and artistry. Britten writes, "What *have* I done to deserve such an artist and *man* to write for?" Pears replies, "I am here as your mouthpiece and I live in your music—And I can never be thankful enough to you and to Fate for all the heavenly joy we have had together for 35 years." Carpenter argues that *Death in Venice* is Britten's anguished autobiography. Rather than a celebration of pedophilia, it promotes restraint rather than abandon, respect rather than degradation. Britten stated, "*Death in Venice* is everything that Peter and I have stood for." Upon Britten's death in 1976, Queen Elizabeth sent condolences to Pears, which to the composer's longtime companion signified "a recognition of the way we lived."

William L. Howard

Sources for Further Study

The Economist. CCCXXV, October 10, 1992, p. 112.
Library Journal. CXVIII, June 15, 1993, p. 70.
London Review of Books. XV, February 11, 1993, p. 3.
The Manchester Guardian Weekly. CXLVII, October 11, 1992, p. 29.
The New York Times Book Review. XCVIII, July 11, 1993, p. 9.
The New Yorker. LXIX, July 5, 1993, p. 86.
The Observer. September 27, 1992, p. 51.

Opera News. LVIII, October, 1993, p. 56.
Publishers Weekly. CCXL, May 10, 1993, p. 64.
The Spectator. CCLXIX, October 3, 1992, p. 28.
The Times Literary Supplement. November 13, 1992, p. 5.
The Washington Post Book World. XXIII, June 20, 1993, p. 8.

BERNARD SHAW
Volume IV: 1950-1991, The Last Laugh

Author: Michael Holroyd (1935-   )
First published: 1992, in Great Britain
Publisher: Random House (New York). 490 pp. $35.00
Type of work: Literary biography
Time: 1950-1991
Locale: Mostly England, occasionally the United States

This is a coda to a triple-decker biography that ranks among the twentieth century's most distinguished studies of literary lives

> *Principal personages:*
> GEORGE BERNARD SHAW, the British playwright, who left much of his
>   money to efforts to popularize a phonetic English "alfabet"
> CHARLOTTE SHAW, his wealthy wife, who also left an idiosyncratic will
> BARBARA SMOKER, an arch-campaigner for Shavian causes
> FRITZ LOEWENSTEIN, Shaw's bibliographer, candidate for custodianship of
>   "Shaw's Corner"

In three previous volumes, Michael Holroyd chronicled and analyzed in fluent, lucid, and often witty language the career of one of the most productive, elusive, and long-lived writers in the history of literature. The first book, subtitled *The Search for Love* (1988), took George Bernard Shaw from his 1856 birth to 1898; the second, *The Pursuit of Power* (1989), to 1918; the third, *The Lure of Fantasy* (1991), to his death in 1950. This fourth tome is a pendant tracing the posthumous career of the considerable Shavian fortune and offering an often humorous sketch of the characters, places, and institutions associated with Shaw's name. It also includes four appendices: the full text of Bernard Shaw's will (fourteen pages) and of Charlotte's (nine pages), a record of principal purchases from the Shaw Fund by Ireland's National Gallery, and a list of the films made from Shaw's works (eighteen, from 1921 through 1968). Then follow the source notes for all four of Holroyd's texts, since he had decided to delay publication of all his references to his final volume, so as to avail himself and readers of the latest scholarship. Finally, a fifty-two-page cumulative index concludes the monumental enterprise.

When Bernard Shaw's will was published in March, 1951, the gross value of his estate amounted to £367,233, equivalent to between $12.5 million and $13 million in 1993 purchasing power. Holroyd emphasizes that the will's promulgation coincided with a time, for the British, of severe austerity. Hence, when a Shaw Memorial Fund was launched that same spring to subsidize young authors, dramatists, and musicians as well as to promote the presentation of Shaw's plays at festivals, it fell embarrassingly short of its goal of £250,000. By 1990 it had reached but £416—a total disaster. Instead, persuaded by such influential luminaries as lady Nancy Astor, Rebecca West, and T. S. Eliot, the government decided to break Shaw's trust, particularly since most of his money had been marked for the creation of two private trusts, the first of which would support a statistical inquiry to determine how much time and money English speakers and writers could save by using Shaw's proposed simplified alphabet, while the second would transliterate his play *Androcles and the Lion* (1912) into such a phonetic alphabet, publishing a bialphabetic edition with the traditional alphabet on one side and Shaw's "alfabet" on the other. Shaw hoped that the resulting dissemination and publicity would eventually persuade the English-using world to adopt his orthography, whose written signs would be as simple as its spoken sounds.

Also contested by the government was Charlotte Shaw's will, which bequeathed £94,000 (more than $3 million) to bring masterpieces of fine art within the reach of all classes in Ireland, to teach the Irish people the secrets of self-control, elocution, oratory, and deportment, and to endow a chair at an Irish university for instruction in all these arts. The Chancery Division of the High Court in London declared Charlotte's testamentary wishes valid, but the money has been distributed in esoteric ways, such as planting village halls in rural Irish communities. No university chair has as yet been established to teach social skills and ethical conduct.

Bernard Shaw's will was hotly contested in Chancery Court. Holroyd provides a dexterous and dramatic description of such eccentric court watchers as Barbara Smoker, who had no paying job but always kept herself busy, this time as secretary of the Phonetic Alphabet Association and assistant secretary of the Shaw Society. She was aghast to discover that the attorney general with the Dickensian name of Baulkwill, acting as public trustee of Shaw's will, "knew nothing of Jesperson and Zamenhof, or even the difference between inflected and agglutinated language!" She therefore slipped into the bulging briefcase of the attorney general's counsel a daily avalanche of linguistic lore. The leading opponent of the government's authorization of the will's bequests for alphabet reform was Sir Charles Russell, representing two residuary legatees: the British Museum and the Royal Academy of Dramatic Art. He concluded his argument by asking the presiding judge whether a line from *Androcles and the Lion*, "Did um get an awful thorn into um's tootsum wootsum?" could be efficiently phonetically transliterated. Justice Harman apparently decided it could not, for he ruled that Shaw's will had created no valid charitable trust and was therefore void. The three residuary legatees were therefore entitled to come into their inheritance. Hence the British Museum, the Royal Academy, and Ireland's National Gallery each received one third of the estate—after legal expenses and annuities for servants had been paid.

Smoker and an ally, spelling reformer James Pitman, teamed up to publicize their protests against this decision in the media, and to threaten a legal appeal. The public trustee approved a consolation price for their interests by funding a competition for a new phonetic alphabet. It attracted 467 valid entries by the end of 1958. Four of these were declared "semi-winners," and their devisers were each awarded £125. The public trustee also authorized the 1962 publication of fifty thousand copies of *Androcles and the Lion* in parallel texts; it sold poorly. Unfortunately or otherwise, the public at large could not have cared less about alphabet reform.

The British Museum has benefited hugely from Shaw's estate, particularly through the posthumous windfall from the musical adaptation of Shaw's phonetic romance *Pygmalion* (1912). *My Fair Lady* opened on Broadway in March, 1956, and did not close its run there for six and a half years, "by which time $55,000,000 had already been made from performances round the world, plus another $10,000,000 from recordings and film rights." Holroyd worries about how the British Museum has spent Shaw's millions, with the institution's trustees free to disburse them as they wished. They have determined not to make public disclosure of the annual amount and disposal of money from the Shaw estate, fearing that such revelations would cause Treasury officials to scant the museum's governmental grants.

The British Museum's secrecy may well be practical, considering what happened to the Royal Academy of Dramatic Art (RADA). The RADA forced the resignation of its principal, John Fernald, who was highly regarded artistically but lacked financial acumen. The academy then acquired a larger building, but the Treasury canceled its grant to RADA in 1967, so that only the income from Shaw's will is enabling it to operate. As for the National Gallery of Ireland, it chose to publicize its acquisitions funded from the Shaw estate, including an excellent piece by Nicolas Poussin, some fine Italian Baroque paintings, and some creditable Irish pictures. Holroyd concludes that Shaw would have been pleased by the gallery's use of his money.

He takes care to point out Shaw's considerable private benefactions, during his lifetime, to such organizations as the Actors' Orphanage, the Royal Literary Fund, the National Flood Distress Fund, Zionist appeals, Stratford's Shakespeare Memorial Theatre, and many, many more. Publicly, however, Shaw played the scrooge. "It is useless to ask him for money: he has none to spare," read a card he composed in 1949. Dan H. Laurence, a leading Shaw scholar, calls him "probably the most charitable professional man of his generation." The public, however, ascribed Shaw's reason for not providing his trust with his money to sheer meanness, and did not realize that he simply wanted to stretch his funds as far as possible so as to benefit an enormous number of individuals and institutions.

On March 17, 1951, the distinguished actress Dame Edith Evans declared "Shaw's Corner" at Ayot St. Lawrence open to the public. So little did the residents of the village where Shaw had lived for a generation welcome their worldwide fame that they organized raiding parties to uproot thirty Automobile Association direction signs. The National Trust was placed in charge of Shaw's home, and many Shavians expected its trust curator to be Fritz Loewenstein. He had been Shaw's bibliographer and ardent admirer, and he campaigned openly for the position. He never got it. Lady Astor disliked his unctuousness; Shaw's former secretary, Blanche Patch, could not stand his undue servility; and his Jewishness probably did not endear him to the locals. In the end, Loewenstein was poorly treated by the Shaw estate's public trustee, who refused to honor Shaw's wish in his will that Loewenstein be "consulted and employed" in all matters involving Shaw's posthumous literary interests. Bitterly, in 1955 Loewenstein took himself and his family back to Germany, where, as a refugee from the Hitler regime, he was entitled to a modest compensation by the state.

Holroyd adroitly steers a tactful path through the reefs and shoals of Shaw scholarship and criticism. He salutes Dan H. Laurence for his towering contribution of scrupulously editing four volumes of Shaw's *Collected Letters* (1965, 1972, 1985, and 1988) and producing a comprehensive two-volume bibliography in 1983. In the 1980's the number of books about Shaw rose to more than three hundred, including Stanley Weintraub's two-volume, annotated edition of *The Diaries* (launched in 1986), Bernard F. Dukore's *The Collected Screenplays of Bernard Shaw* (1980), A. M. Gibbs's *Shaw: Interviews and Recollections* (1990), and Dan H. Laurence and James Rambeau's *Agitations: [Shaw's] Letters to the Press, 1875-1950* (1985).

Among critical studies Holroyd singles out two: Eric Bentley's incisive *Bernard Shaw* (1947; second edition, 1967), and Raymond Williams' *Drama from Ibsen to Eliot* (1952; revised as *Drama from Ibsen to Brecht*, 1968). He notes Williams' doubt that Shaw's work would survive the twentieth century. Holroyd discusses an extraordinary discovery by the American researcher B. C. Rosset: Contrary to Shaw's recollection that his mother had waited one or two years before following her music master and possible lover, Vandeleur Lee, from Dublin to London, Rosset found that Mrs. Shaw had followed Lee to London only a few days after his departure, on her twenty-first wedding anniversary. Since Rosset had quoted GBS without having received permission from the Shaw estate, however, his book was withdrawn from publication by England's Society of Authors; Rosset died soon after this disappointment.

Holroyd ends his essay on Shaw's posthumous fortunes and misfortunes by rehearsing the history of his own biographical relationship to the master. In 1970 the Shaw estate decided to commission an authorized biography and turned to the thirty-four-year-old Holroyd, who "had no experience of politics or theatre, no academic qualifications, and no record of having worked on Shaw." Busy with research for his biography of the painter August John (1974), Holroyd did not begin his Shavian explorations until 1975. He found himself "encumbered with help," since "there is a Shaw distribution throughout the world." He has attempted to uncover Shaw's "concealed humanity" behind his panache of heterodox opinions, and he insists that "under the play of his paradoxes . . . moves a current of passion. . . . It is this that I have sought to navigate." On the strength of his performance in this four-volume voyage, Michael Holroyd has proved one of the most discerning pilots among contemporary biographers.

Gerhard Brand

Sources for Further Study

Boston Globe. April 18, 1993, p. 42.
Choice. XXXI, September, 1993, p. 117.
London Review of Books. XIV, November 5, 1992, p. 8.
The New York Times Book Review. XCVIII, April 18, 1993, p. 22.

San Francisco Chronicle. June 6, 1993, p. REV7.
The Spectator. CCLXVIII, May 9, 1992, p. 27.
The Times Literary Supplement. May 8, 1992, p. 32.
Washington Times. June 20, 1993, p. B7.
World Literature Today. LXVII, Spring, 1993, p. 391.

BERTRAND RUSSELL
A Life

Author: Caroline Moorehead (1944-   )
First published: 1992, in Great Britain
Publisher: Viking (New York). 596 pp. $30.00
Type of work: Biography
Time: 1872-1970
Locale: England, the United States, and China

A lucid and discriminating narrative of Bertrand Russell's long life as philosopher, popular writer, and political activist

> *Principal personages:*
> BERTRAND RUSSELL, a British philosopher
> LADY RUSSELL, his formidable grandmother
> JOHN RUSSELL, his older brother
> ALYS PEARSALL SMITH, his first wife
> DORA BLACK, his second wife
> MARJORIE SPENCE, his third wife
> EDITH FINCH, his fourth wife
> LADY OTTOLINE MORRELL, his mistress
> LUDWIG VON WITTGENSTEIN, his student and fellow philosopher

Caroline Moorehead provides an acute and entertaining biography of one of the most controversial figures in twentieth century culture. Given Bertrand Russell's long life and many interests, she does an admirable job of surveying and assessing the highlights, judiciously noting his triumphs and failures and demonstrating how they evolved out of his character. Inevitably, a biographical narrative cannot do justice to the intricacy of his philosophical arguments, but the main points of his important books are introduced.

Russell was the descendant of an aristocratic family. The Russells were Whigs—members of the political party that fought for a constitutional monarchy and did much to establish England's tradition of civil liberties and individual conscience. Bertrand Russell was expected to make his contribution to that tradition by taking a prominent role in politics. Although he eventually decided in favor of philosophy, he remained active in politics—running for Parliament twice—and he exhibited a fierce dedication to human rights throughout his life.

Russell discovered Euclid at the age of eleven during a school holiday, when his older brother Frank offered to teach him some mathematics. Russell was entranced with the elegance of algebra. In his autobiography he called it "one of the great events of my life, as dazzling as first love. I had not imagined that there was anything so delicious in the world."

That Russell was virtually a born philosopher is suggested by the fact that he immediately wanted to know why Euclid's axioms had to be accepted as true. How did Frank know they were true? Perhaps many inquisitive children would ask the same question, but Russell was persistent in his determination not to stop asking such questions. They are what brought him to his major contribution to philosophy, his *Principia Mathematica* (1910-1913), written in collaboration with Alfred North Whitehead. This two-volume work, along with much of Russell's other philosophical writing, attempts to show the connection between mathematics and logic—indeed to prove that logic and mathematics are virtually identical. This premise has not been accepted by either mathematicians or philosophers, but it is a measure of his brilliance that he made both rethink the basis of their disciplines.

Russell was born in the last third of Queen Victoria's reign, and he attended the University of Cambridge while she was still on the throne of England. His early attitudes toward women and sex were Victorian: He regarded women as delightful companions but certainly of a lower intellectual order than men. He would later modify these attitudes and show himself remarkably adaptable to changing values and manners, but his early Victorian and aristocratic upbringing continued to inform his rather cavalier and sometimes cruel treatment of women.

Russell's first wife, Alys Pearsall Smith, was from a Quaker family. She seems to have appealed to Russell because of her combination of bold thinking (she was an advocate of free love) and submissive devotion to him. She did not succumb immediately to his courtship; in fact, he would woo her for several years before she consented to a marriage opposed by both of their families. His grandmother, Lady Russell, did not want him to marry an American. Her family, while charmed by English culture, rejected the class-ridden conventions to which their daughter would have to subject herself. Eventually, however, both families were placated after Russell and Smith agreed to a trial three-month separation to test the strength of their love.

Initially enraptured with Smith, Russell's interest in her paled as he concentrated on developing a career and intellectual pursuits that he found difficult to share with her. She was not philosophically minded, although her accomplishments in campaigning for women's rights were not negligible. The young Russell was gradually throwing off the mental and sexual restraints of his Victorian upbringing, putting into practice ideas of free love that his faithful wife preached but did not practice.

There is a passage in Moorehead's biography that wonderfully captures the moment when Russell discovered his life's work. The biographer's words convey not merely the content of Russell's vision but a peculiar and almost comic picture of the philosopher wrapped up in his vision. Russell and his wife are on their honeymoon in Germany:

> Russell had one of his momentous flashes of understanding, when his entire life appeared to open out before him. Walking one day in the Tiergarten, thinking about Hegel and about the future, he suddenly became convinced that he should devote his life to producing two strands of work, the first a series of books on the philosophy of the sciences, the second a parallel series on social questions. His idea, which he held to for most of his life, was that the two might eventually meet in a "synthesis at once scientific and practical."

Thus was born the writer who produced both *The Principles of Mathematics* (1903; the study which preceded *Principia Mathematica*) and such popular works as *Mar-*

riage and Morals (1929). For Russell, his great work would be to show how the world was made coherent by reason in science, politics, and society at large.

Such an ambitious enterprise reflected a dynamic personality that could not be bound by the conventions of academic or married life. He alienated many of his contemporaries, including his academic colleagues, by taking a strictly rationalist attitude toward learning, social conventions, and politics. He was ruthless in opposing what he considered to be outdated theories and inimical social policies. He became a militant pacifist during World War I, seeing absolutely no justification for the loss of thousands of men in war. His stand was very unpopular and eventually led to his dismissal from Cambridge, but Russell was never one to back away from his principles.

A compassionate man, he could nevertheless behave brutally once he had decided he no longer rationally believed in an idea or relationship. Thus he rejected his first wife as soon as he discovered that he no longer loved her. In this respect, he did not seem quite human. "He has not much body of character," Virginia Woolf observed. "Nevertheless, I should like the run of his headpiece," she concluded.

Russell did not immediately divorce Alys, for he was still thinking through his position on institutions such as marriage. Yet he engaged in a number of affairs, most notably with the literary hostess Lady Ottoline Morrell, who spoke to his need for a more passionate and cosmopolitan relationship. Married to the politician Philip Morrell, however, she was never able to offer him the complete devotion he still expected in the women he loved. Indeed, no woman seemed to offer that kind of all-encompassing interest in his life until the advent of his fourth wife, Edith Finch, the companion of his last twenty years.

Russell was fearless as a political activist and philosopher. He spent six months in prison for his pacifist beliefs, yet he had the courage to reverse his position and support England's entry into World War II, recognizing that pacifism was not sufficient to quell Hitler's evil. Similarly, he did not merely write about education but started his own school with his second wife, Dora Black, spending much of his own money to support it. When he lost faith in the school, he abandoned it in a way that seemed cruel to Black but that again was in accord with his rationalist principles.

It is a tribute to Moorehead's sense of balance and of human character that Russell's wives, with the exception of Marjorie Spence, are vividly presented. That Spence seems shadowy is probably not the biographer's fault, since Spence said little about her marriage to Russell and became a recluse after their divorce. Indeed, Moorehead is not certain whether Spence is still alive. Spence's main purpose seems to have been to cater to Russell during his difficult six-year period in America, when he taught at several universities and tried to earn enough to support his wives and his two children by Black and one by Spence.

Russell as a father receives a very mixed review. On the one hand, he seems to have loved children—his own and others'. He enjoyed their company, inventing whimsical stories for them—telling them, for example, that Hungary used to be named "Yum Yum" but decided to change its name to something more dignified. On the other hand, he was often oblivious to the things children most needed. Because childhood fears seemed irrational to him, he would treat them as such, neglecting to comfort his son John during a violent storm in the belief that it would lead to indulging and spoiling him. When John expressed his terror of the sea, his father told him that he was ashamed of him. Naturally, his children grew chary of telling him about their anxieties. As his daughter Kate put it, their fears "grew and grew and grew, secretly, in John as in me, festering quietly and sapping our vitality." Of such childrearing, Moorehead concludes: "It was all a little bleak."

After World War II, Russell became an extraordinary performer on BBC radio. He gave serious talks on nuclear disarmament, but he also appeared on game shows. Moorehead shows how this was part of Russell's plan to write and speak on all levels, from the most abstract to the most concrete. He wanted the serious attention of his fellow philosophers and of the public at large.

Russell was rarely daunted by anything. When he was, it seems worth noting. He was taken aback, for example, by his brilliant pupil Ludwig von Wittgenstein, who challenged and perhaps surpassed him as a philosopher. Wittgenstein was not merely tactless in argument—capable of calling Russell's work rubbish; he was vicious and so austere in devotion to his discipline that Russell once said Wittgenstein made him feel like a "bleating lambkin."

In his last years, Russell's fame was enhanced by his antinuclear campaigns and his organization of a war crimes trial indicting the United States for its atrocities in Vietnam. Moorehead is careful to show how serious Russell was in his dedication to world peace, yet she admits that many of his statements were irrational products of a lifelong ambivalence about the United States, which at various times he compared to Nazi Germany and Stalinist Russia. Moorehead clearly dissents from Russell's extreme views, but she is unable to make clear why Russell was so vehement in his denunciations of the United States.

Moorehead also portrays some of Russell's important friends and adversaries in vivid vignettes, including D. H. Lawrence, Joseph Conrad, and T. S. Eliot and Eliot's first wife, Vivienne. Russell's brief but intense friendship with Conrad seems to have been a mystery to him and to his biographer. How a novelist who placed little faith in human rationality and a philosopher who touted reason reached rapport is not clear. It may be that Conrad had a way of helping Russell to see the dark, irrational side of himself that the philosopher did not otherwise know how to acknowledge or comprehend.

Carl Rollyson

Sources for Further Study

The Atlantic. CCLXXII, October, 1993, p. 123.
Library Journal. CXVIII, September 15, 1993, p. 85.

London Review of Books. XIV, November 19, 1992, p. 8.
New Statesman and Society. V, October 2, 1992, p. 44.
The New York Times Book Review. XCVIII, October 31, 1993, p. 7.
Newsweek. CXXII, November 1, 1993, p. 70.
The Observer. October 25, 1992, p. 64.
Publishers Weekly. CCXL, August 30, 1993, p. 81.
The Spectator. CCLXIX, October 3, 1992, p. 29.
The Times Literary Supplement. October 2, 1992, p. 13.

THE BIRTH-MARK
unsettling the wilderness in American literary history

Author: Susan Howe (1937-   )
Publisher: Wesleyan University Press/University Press of New England (Hanover, New Hampshire). 189 pp. $40.00; paperback $16.95
Type of work: Literary history

An eclectic, original, brilliant rereading of American literary history from the Colonial era through the nineteenth century

A member of a group known since the 1970's as the Language Poets (which also includes Charles Bernstein, Ron Silliman, and others), Susan Howe has mapped a career protesting the ways in which editorial policies and traditional rules of syntax and form have stifled spiritual development and freedom of expression in poets. Detaching language from convention meant producing, at times, an unreadable text, but one that did not impose on either the writer's or the reader's freedom. In such collections of poetry as *Articulation of Sound Forms in Time* (1987) and *Singularities* (1990), as well as her critical work *My Emily Dickinson* (1985), Howe demonstrated this freedom in her own poems while arguing against the imposition of convention on the poetry of Emily Dickinson. Her *The Birth-mark: unsettling the wilderness in American literary history* marks a continuation of this argument. (Indeed, the argument begins with the very form of the title: In keeping with her challenge to intrusive editorial control, Howe herself deliberately does not use standard form for the subtitle, omitting capitalization.) Consisting of an extensive introduction, five essays, and a reprint of an interview with Howe from *Talisman* magazine (Spring 1990), *The Birth-mark* argues that "the issue of editorial control is directly connected to the attempted erasure of antinomianism in our culture." This thesis carries the reader through an eclectic, brilliant—at times unreadable—restructuring of American literary history.

Antinomy suggests conflict of authority as well as paradox. For Howe, the distinctive mark of the American literary voice is antinomianism, not primarily as a matter of religious belief (its usual understanding) but as a way of expression and a resistance to stricture in all of its forms: ecclesiastical, political, socioeconomic, and literary. Taking her title and one of her epigraphs from Nathaniel Hawthorne's 1843 story "The Birth-mark," Howe parallels the efforts of Aylmer, the husband in the tale, to remove his wife's distinguishing mark with those of Colonial church officials to silence the spirited rebel Anne Hutchinson and those of later editors to create standardized texts at the expense of the authors' creativity. In Hawthorne's story, Aylmer's attempts to remove what he sees as his wife Georgiana's flaw leads to her death; so, in Howe's view, the brilliance of prophets and the inventiveness of women writers in particular have been slain or, at least, disfigured by preemptive authority.

Supporting her arguments with extensive research into original manuscripts and facsimile editions, Howe unearths the distortions of several early American texts at the hands of editors. Included in her discussion are, most notably, the autobiographical writings of Thomas Shepard, the minister of the First Church of Cambridge from 1637 to 1645 and one of the accusers of Anne Hutchinson during the 1636 antinomian controversy; the journals of John Winthrop, minister and later governor of the Massachusetts Bay Colony; the captivity narrative of Mary Rowlandson; and the poems and letters of the nineteenth century poet Emily Dickinson. Figures receiving less extensive discussion include Elizabeth Hawthorne, the sister of Nathaniel; Herman Melville; Sara Coleridge, daughter of Samuel Taylor Coleridge and a writer and editor; Mary Dyer, an associate of Anne Hutchinson and a midwife, who was later hanged; and Anne Bradstreet and her sister Sarah Dudley Keayne. The predominance of female figures here arises from Howe's contention that, from its beginnings, antinomianism has been "feminized and then restricted or banished." The wilderness alluded to in Howe's subtitle is, then, both actual and metaphorical. Hutchinson suffered actual banishment because she chose to express her views; that which is free, spirited, and unsettling in literary expression, particularly in the work of women writers, is also banished to a wilderness of unpublished manuscripts or seen as undisciplined and wild, in need of taming.

Clearly a feminist text in its implications, Howe's work also offers a broader context for discussion of American literature than is found in many standard scholarly works. As the author points out, F. O. Matthiessen's *American Renaissance: Art and Expression in the Age of Emerson and Whitman* (1941), considered by many a classic study of nineteenth century American literature, omits Margaret Fuller and Emily Dickinson. As Howe demonstrates, Matthiessen's letters and journals indicate that he originally thought to include both women, but later he bowed to scholarly rules which did not, in the 1930's and 1940's, include women as part of the literary canon. Matthiessen also neglected, Howe contends, to include the American Civil War and its impact in his discussion. His personal enthusiasm for the poems of Percy Bysshe Shelley and the homosexual poems of Walt Whitman, revealed again in Matthiessen's letters to his lover, was also squelched in order to follow "T. S. Eliot's insistence on 'form' and 'impersonality' in poetry." Howe records, "In 1941 the author of *American Renaissance*, under the influence of Eliot's critical dismissal of Shelley, downplayed his influence on Melville and deplored it in Hawthorne." A similar fate afflicted Elizabeth Hawthorne, who borrowed thousands of volumes for her brother from the Salem Athenaeum, knew what influenced his writing, what he actually read, and the marginalia he recorded as he read. Hawthorne's biographer, James T. Fields, explored Elizabeth and Nathaniel's relationship through a series of letters he elicited from Elizabeth but chose to ignore them in his composition. Other scholars, notably Perry Miller and Kenneth Murdock, discounted the importance of the antinomian controversy and the witchcraft trials, though Cotton Mather, Howe argues, "would not have agreed in 1700, the year he finished writing 'the Church History of this countrey,' " his *Magnalia Christi Americana*.

Through her wide reading of letters, journals, original texts, and later scholarship, Howe shows that many scholars rule out not only the feminine and female writers but also important spiritual and moral issues that were ineluctable influences on the development of a distinctive American literary voice. Home, politics, family, history, ideology, and art are inseparable in Howe's view. What was the flaw in Billy Budd's speech, Howe asks, the mark on Georgiana, that so possessed Captain Vere and Aylmer that they sought to destroy the persons as well as the flaw? Citing Charles Olson's study of Melville, *Call Me Ishmael* (1947), Howe says in the *Talisman* interview that "the stutter is the plot."

> It's the stutter in American literature that interests me. I hear the stutter as a sounding of uncertainty. What is silenced or not quite silenced. All the broken dreams. Thomas Shepard writes them down as soon as 1637. And the rupture from Europe. . . . All that eccentricity.

"Eccentricity," "lawlessness," "antinomianism," "the wilderness," and "spiritual enthusiasm," at times, become nearly synonymous in Howe's text—key phrases reverberating around a central conflict of freedom and restraint, the core issue for emigrants to America during the Great Migration of the 1630's. America was the great educator for these people, who were fleeing political, religious, and economic constraints in Europe yet faced a wilderness that demanded attention to issues of control if they were to survive. The Colonial captivity narratives and journals are, for Howe, bridges to the nineteenth century. In works such as the autobiographical writings and notebooks of Thomas Shepard, Howe finds evidence of antinomianism. His "T {My Birth & Life:} S" contains two halves, though editors have consistently ignored the eighty-six-page blank center and the reversed story contained in the "S" section. In his small reversible notebooks, Shepard, an accuser of Hutchinson, recorded the conversion experiences and religious testimonies of fifty-one men and women, mostly midwives, servants, and widows, whose names are indicated by masculine appropriation—for example, "Goodman Luxford His Wife." Since the usual practice was for a male to speak for a woman before a congregation, these notebooks reveal that "although Shepard thought women should defer to their husbands in worldly matters, in his theology of conversion they were relatively independent."

In Rowlandson's captivity narrative, the paradox is found in the contrasts between her descriptions of horrendous violence, the killings of her children and relatives, and the scriptural passages interposed to serve as reminders that Providence is evident in these events—passages, Howe suggests, that were inserted by the Reverend Joseph Rowlandson, Mary's husband, after the first edition, of which no copy is known to exist. Again, where Mary Rowlandson found the Indian chief King Philip (Metacomet), her captor, at times kind, taking her hand to help her from the mud at one point, she conflicted with the authoritative view of the Indian leader as the devil incarnate, a savage killer. Like Rowlandson, Anne Bradstreet violated Puritan strictures, not so much by her views but by the very fact that she wrote in her own voice. Like Rowlandson, moreover, she was saved by her tone and the fact that her poems were first published by her brother-in-law, without her knowledge, in 1647.

Hawthorne and Melville too, according to Howe, reflect the stylistic idiosyncrasy found in the work of Cotton Mather through their combining "history, fiction, Scripture, and Elizabethan and baroque drama." More directly, Hawthorne alludes to antinomianism in a number of his works, most notably in the opening passage of *The Scarlet Letter* (1850), which contains a reference to Anne Hutchinson. Books in the library of Herman Melville reveal underlined passages in Hawthorne's *Twice-Told Tales* (1837, 1842) referring to antinomianism or antinomian characters. Dickinson's poetry and letters also reveal a combining of ideas, a deliberate rejection of publication—which would require standardization of her poems—idiosyncratic line breaks, and variant word lists that indicate her experimentation with poetry as a visual form. All these writers found relevance for antinomian ideas in their literary texts and in their modes of expression.

Howe as well is highly idiosyncratic in sections of *The Birth-mark*. Her method is to amass numerous instances of antinomianism in subject, voice, and expression and to cite fragments of texts, often in random sequence, without interlinking passages except thematically or linguistically—that is, through word associations. A reference, for example, to one writer's description of himself as a library cormorant might open to a passage from Noah Webster's original *An American Dictionary of the English Language* (1828) defining "strand," since the cormorant is a strand bird. Lest the author be guilty of the same editorial sins she denounces in such editors as Thomas H. Johnson, whose *The Complete Poems of Emily Dickinson* (1951) Howe believes violated the integrity of Dickinson's texts, she avoids telling the reader what to think through interpretation. Rather, she writes in response to the texts she duplicates through facsimile reproductions and citations. What ties her work together is her extensive introduction and the *Talisman* interview, which serves as a conclusion and reiterates her aims. Though a carefully reasoned and exceedingly well-supported argument, at times Howe's work is frustrating, but it is well worth the effort for the insights and original thought it offers regarding American literary history. Though the style of *The Birth-mark* is turbulent, the book is a brilliant piece of scholarly investigation. Though it occasionally lapses into fragments, run-on sentences, and unreadable syntax, these deliberate breaks with convention illustrate precisely the thesis the author is arguing.

Stella Nesanovich

Source for Further Study

The Times Literary Supplement. December 3, 1993, p. 12.

BLACK HOLES AND BABY UNIVERSES
AND OTHER ESSAYS

Author: Stephen Hawking (1942-   )
Publisher: Bantam Books (New York). 182 pp. $21.95
Type of work: Essays; autobiography and science
Time: The twentieth century
Locales: England, Europe, and the United States

This collection of thirteen autobiographical and scientific essays and a concluding interview ranges over a wide variety of topics, both personal and cosmological, which reveal Hawking as a visionary scientist and a fascinating human being

Principal personages:
> STEPHEN HAWKING, a British theoretical physicist whose work on black holes and the space-time structure of the universe revolutionized cosmology
> JANE (WILDE) HAWKING, Stephen Hawking's wife who helped him live after he developed motor neurone disease and who gave him something to live for
> ALBERT EINSTEIN, German-American theoretical physicist whose theory of relativity profoundly influenced Hawking's work

One of the great surprises of recent publishing history was the extraordinary success of Stephen Hawking's *A Brief History of Time: From the Big Bang to Black Holes*, which, since its publication in 1988, has sold more than five and a half million copies, been translated into thirty-three languages, and entered the *Guiness Book of Records* for appearing more weeks on the London *Times'* best-seller list than any previous book. In many ways *Black Holes and Baby Universes and Other Essays* is a sequel to *A Brief History of Time*, since it seeks to satisfy readers' curiosity about Hawking's personal history generated by the popularity of his account of the universe's history. He wrote *A Brief History of Time* to raise money to pay for his daughter's school fees and to inform the general public that cosmologists were discovering wondrous things about the nature and structure of the universe. He wrote *Black Holes and Baby Universes* to pay for his nurses and to show that ordinary people can understand the really big questions about the universe—How did it begin? Where is it going? If, when, and how will it end? Hawking's new book contains items from talks and articles he composed between 1976 and 1992. They range from two autobiographical sketches through his analysis of *A Brief History of Time*'s success to a series of essays detailing his past and present views on cosmogony and cosmology. The book concludes with an interview, "Desert Island Discs," in which Hawking gives, interspersed with autobiographical reminiscences, an account of some of his favorite classical (Mozart's *Requiem*) and popular (the Beatles' "Please Please Me") recordings.

Since it is unlikely that Hawking will ever write a full-fledged autobiography, the memoirs contained in this book are probably the closest we are likely to get to Hawking's view of his own life. In this they are similar to Albert Einstein's *Autobio-*

graphical Notes in both authors' reluctance to deal with personal matters and in their enthusiasm for detailing the evolution of their scientific ideas. Though these limitations seriously curtail the usefulness of Hawking's reminiscences for scholars and those interested in probing deeply into his character, they are nevertheless full of insights into his own life and times and those of twentieth century cosmology. He sprinkles his essays with humor, references to popular culture, and well-directed barbs meant to deflate pomposities in and out of science. Indeed, one of the reasons for the great popularity of his talks and writings is his talent for luring the reader into sharing his passion for exploring the most profound truths about this universe. As a companion with Hawking on these voyages of his intellect and imagination, the reader comes to share the author's sense of wonder about the strange phenomena in our cosmos, including black holes that are not really black, imaginary time that has nothing to do with the imagination (but that founds a universe that has not been created and will not be destroyed), and baby universes, small, self-contained worlds that fickly branch off from our region of the cosmos (and may just as fickly join on again).

In his role as cosmic messenger, Hawking sees himself as an heir to Galileo Galilei, who himself explored the universe with his telescope and wrote about it in his *Sidereus Nuncius* (1610), which has been translated as *The Messenger from the Stars*. Hawking likes to note that he was born on January 8, 1942, exactly three hundred years after the death of Galileo. He was born into a time as turbulent as Galileo's. England was in the midst of World War II, and because a German bomb almost hit his parents' London house, his mother gave birth to Stephen in Oxford, where his father had studied medicine and where his mother had studied philosophy, politics, and economics. (The Germans had agreed not to bomb Oxford and Cambridge if the British did not bomb Heidelberg and Göttingen.) His mother remembers Stephen as a normal boy in most respects, though he learned to read much later than his sisters. He recalls that he loved trains and enjoyed building model airplanes and boats. In his analysis of these early interests he sees the same motivation to know how things work and to control them that exists in his adult work in cosmology. Knowledge, for him, became a form of control.

After the war's end, he went to school in St. Albans and then to University College at Oxford, where his father had become an expert in tropical medicine but where Stephen studied mathematics and physics, much to his father's displeasure. Lonely and infected by the lackadaisical attitude of many of his fellow students, Hawking worked, according to his own calculation, on average only an hour a day for the three years he was at Oxford. Toward the end of his time there, a number of things happened that radically altered his life. A fall downstairs that left him temporarily without memory caused him to see a doctor to have his reflexes tested. The doctor diagnosed Hawking as having amyotrophic lateral sclerosis (ALS), a disease caused by the degeneration of the nerve cells in the spinal cord and brain that control voluntary muscular movement, while leaving the mind unaffected (it is called motor neurone disease in England and Lou Gehrig's disease in the United States). His mother was told that her son would probably be dead in about two to three years. Hawking was told that the disease was unpredictable but incurable. Unknown to Stephen, his father was trying all kinds of things to save his son, including getting in touch with the virologist D. Carleton Gajdusek (later to win a Nobel Prize), who had researched a related disease called kuru, a neurological disorder caused by a slow-acting virus and transmitted by cannibalism. All these efforts, however, proved fruitless.

After getting a first-class degree from Oxford, Hawking went to the University of Cambridge to pursue doctoral studies in cosmology, but his disease initially progressed so rapidly that he saw little reason to work diligently since he expected to be dead before he could receive his doctorate. As time went on, however, the disease slowed down, and he met Jane Wilde, who helped him to see that his life was worth living and that he could actually do the many things he wanted to do. After their marriage in 1965, he also had to plan for a job and the family that they both desired. With Jane's encouragement, he was able to master Einstein's general theory of relativity, which explains gravitational effects in terms of the curvature of space, and to make progress in his own research on singularities, which result from powerful gravitational forces that cause matter to have infinite density in an infinitesimal volume. Hawking believed that the history of a massive star ended in a catastrophic collapse that continued until a singularity of infinite density was reached. Since such a collapse could result in a black hole, Hawking's work on singularities and black holes was closely connected.

Black holes are extremely small regions of space-time with a gravitational field so intense that nothing can escape, not even light. (John Wheeler coined the name when he got tired of calling them "gravitationally completely collapsed objects.") To do creative work on black holes, Hawking found that he needed to develop new mathematical techniques. With Roger Penrose, who had already done important work on the gravitational collapse of giant stars, Hawking derived a series of singularity theorems that showed how space-time becomes highly curved at extremely small distances. Hawking then got the idea of adapting Penrose's analysis of star collapse to the collapse of the entire universe. By this time the big bang theory of the universe's origin had been well established, and he visualized the present universe, which was a consequence of this cosmic explosion some fifteen billion years ago, run backward to what he thought might be a singularity, which was also a beginning of time. Hawking's analysis revealed, however, that relativity theory breaks down under the special circumstances of the universe's beginning, and this deeply concerned him, for he wanted the laws of science to work in every place, at every time, and under every condition.

In 1970, shortly after the birth of his daughter Lucy, Hawking conceived the idea that led to his famous discovery that black holes are not completely black. The idea was to use the uncertainty principle to investigate the behavior of very small particles in the curved space-time near a black hole. The uncertainty principle states that the position and speed of atomic particles cannot be precisely determined at the same time, and Hawking showed that this principle allowed particles to leak out of a black hole at a steady rate. Space is filled with particles and antiparticles, but near a black hole, one particle may fall inside while its unpaired mate appears as radiation emitted by the black hole (now called "Hawking radiation" in his honor). This work combined quantum mechanics (the science of the very small, of which the uncertainty principle is an essential part) and general relativity, which actually forbade any particle's escape from inside a black hole. Einstein, who made important contributions to both theories, never accepted the uncertainty principle as a final explanation of reality, and his statement illustrating this attitude is famous: "God does not play dice with the universe." Nevertheless, Stephen Hawking's rejoinder to this quip is also becoming famous: "Not only does God play dice, he sometimes throws them where they cannot be seen."

Hawking deepened his analysis of the "evaporation" of black holes by discovering that particles escape very slowly from a big black hole but extremely rapidly from a small one. So fruitful was his combination of relativity and quantum mechanics that he tried to develop his insights as they applied to the entire universe. In the big bang theory, the state of the universe at one time can be calculated on the basis of a previous time, that is, the universe is as it is now because of how it was in the past. Einstein's equations, however, could not explain why it was as it was just after the big bang, and this bothered Hawking, so he formulated a different universe in which space-time was finite but had no boundary. Just as the earth's surface is finite in area but has no boundaries or edges, the universe's space and time are also finite but closed up on themselves without boundaries or edges. If this no-boundary universe is correct, then the laws of physics hold everywhere, even during the earliest stages of the big bang. Some scientists and theologians have interpreted Hawking's no-boundary universe as meaning that reality has no absolute beginning and so no need exists for a Creator. Others have interpreted the absence of a beginning in time to indicate the need for a Creator different from the "watchmaker God" who created the universe and then let it run by itself. For them, Hawking's cosmology lends itself to a timeless and sustaining God to whom all moments have a similar relationship and by whom the universe is maintained in existence. Hawking himself sidesteps the question of God's existence, although his theory removes God as the answer to *how* the universe began but leaves him as a possible answer to *why* it began or exists at all.

Two events occurred in the mid-1980's that dramatically altered Hawking's life: he completed the manuscript of *A Brief History of Time* and he caught pneumonia while on a visit to Geneva, Switzerland. Although he received a lifesaving tracheostomy operation, this operation eradicated his ability to speak. For a time, the only way he could communicate was by signaling with his eyebrows as someone pointed to letters on a spelling card. Fortunately, an American computer expert learned of Hawking's plight and sent him a program that enabled him to choose words from a series of menus on a computer screen. A synthesizer could then translate his words into speech.

Despite his need for twenty-four-hour nursing care and his nearly total loss of motor-muscle control, Hawking continued to develop new ideas about the universe. He began to wonder what would happen to such objects as spaceships and human beings if they fell into a black hole. His answer was that their matter might end up in baby universes of their own. The identify of the spaceship and its inhabitants would not be preserved, however, since the massive gravitational forces would rip everything into "spaghetti," to use Hawking's word. During the 1980's, he also investigated the future of our universe. Will it go on expanding forever, or will it reach a point of maximum expansion and then collapse to what he calls the big crunch? The key variable in answering these questions is the average density of matter in our universe. If the density is not large enough, the universe will continue to expand forever. Hawking himself believes that the density is sufficient to bring about the big crunch.

Against this backdrop of the birth and death of universes, Hawking analyzes some of the most basic mysteries of human existence, including the value of life, the meaning of free will, and the significance of death. He admits that death has always been in the background of his own life, but he realizes that, even though his life will end in death, he can in some way control this inevitability by reflecting on the end of the universe. To him, a real universe exists outside of himself that is waiting to be investigated, but nothing in this universe makes any sense until a theory exists to understand it. Scientists work to develop theories and laws that will completely determine the evolution of the universe, but Hawking finds some room for free will in this picture. The human brain contains a hundred septillion (10^{26}) particles, much too many for any scientist to derive and solve the immeasurable number of equations necessary to predict how a certain brain would behave under particular conditions. Hawking believes that all events in the universe are determined, but they might as well not be since humans can never know what is determined. Humans must therefore act as if they had moral responsibility.

Throughout the essays in this book Hawking has, for the most part, followed the qualitative approach of *A Brief History of Time*, but unlike that book, whose approach was unified, *Black Holes and Baby Universes* derives from a series of self-contained talks and writings, each of which was intended for a different audience. For example, one talk before the International Motor Neurone Disease Society was for a general audience, whereas the *Scientific American* article on "The Quantum Mechanics of Black Holes" was obviously intended for people with some background in science. This variety of approaches leads to repetitions and may occasionally present difficulties for readers who have never studied science. Another of the book's deficiencies is its lack of illustrations. In his essay "A Brief History of *A Brief History*," Hawking remarks that he thinks in pictorial terms and his aim in his popularizations has been to describe these mental images. Even the *Scientific American* article appears in this book without its original diagrams and illustrations. Since Hawking emphasizes his own views about the nature and history of the universe throughout *Black Holes and Baby Universes*, the reader may easily be misled into thinking that all the author's views are widely accepted, whereas the truth is that several of them are very controversial. For example, substantial observational evidence for his interesting theories about black holes is still lacking. If controversies about his cosmological views are downplayed, so, too, are controversies about his personal life. A few years before this book was written, Hawking, after a marriage of more than two decades, left his wife and moved in with one of his nurses. He refuses to explain his action either in the autobiographical essays or in the interview of this book. Some of Hawking's biographers have discovered that his agnosticism about God's existence may have played a role in his rift with his wife, a religious woman.

For many people, one of the most fascinating things about Stephen Hawking is his seemingly indomitable spirit. His ALS has influenced but not seriously impeded his personal and scientific life. Despite a disease that has progressively taken the control of his own body away from him, his restless mind continues to explore the universe. He himself does not see his disease as much of a handicap: In his words, it is "rather as if I were color blind." He tries to lead as normal a life as he can and believes he is actually happier now than before he became ill, mainly because of the great satisfaction and success he has found in his scientific work. Yet he also admits that he finds physics "completely cold" and that he could not carry on with his life if he only had physics, for like everyone else, he needs "warmth, love, and affection." Thus science gives him the most gratification when he can give it away, in other words, when he can find congenial listeners to stimulate and who stimulate him. Though he can now barely move, his agile mind continues to generate mind-expanding ideas, and his scholarly and popular writings can spread these ideas throughout the world. This is the glory and the grace of communication, scientific and otherwise—to stretch minds so that they never return to their previous states.

Robert J. Paradowski

Sources for Further Study

Byte. XVIII, October, 1993, p. 49.
The Economist. CCCXXIX, November 6, 1993, p. 120.
Library Journal. CXVIII, September 1, 1993, p. 217.
New Scientist. CXL, November 20, 1993, p. 40.
The New York Times Book Review. XCVIII, October 24, 1993, p. 22.
Publishers Weekly. CCXL, July 12, 1993, p. 61.
Science News. CXLIV, October 2, 1993, p. 210.
Time. CXLII, September 27, 1993, p. 80.
The Wall Street Journal. September 13, 1993, p. A14.
The Washington Post Book World. XXIII, September 12, 1993, p. 6.

BODY AND SOUL

Author: Frank Conroy (1936-   )
Publisher: Houghton Mifflin/Seymour Lawrence (Boston). 450 pp. $24.95
Type of work: Novel
Time: From 1945 to the 1970's
Locale: Mainly New York City

The romantic history of a musical prodigy's development from humble beginnings to concert fame as a piano virtuoso

> *Principal characters:*
> CLAUDE RAWLINGS, the pianist-hero through whose eyes all the novel's action is revealed
> EMMA, his mother, a taxi driver and left-wing activist
> AL, a black maintenance man who becomes Emma's lover
> WEISFELD, a music-store owner, Claude's first teacher and mentor
> FREDERICKS, Claude's later teacher, whose tutelage helps him refine his art
> ALDO FRESCOBALDI, a famous violinist, Claude's sponsor
> IVAN ANDERSON, Claude's sophisticated friend and lifelong confidant
> PRISCILLA (LADY) POWERS, a brilliant young woman whom Claude meets at college, marries, and divorces
> CATHERINE MARSH, Claude's first love object, Priscilla's cousin
> LORD LIGHTNING, a jazz pianist of mixed ethnic origin who is revealed to be Claude's father

Frank Conroy's first novel, published in his fifty-seventh year, harks back to a distinguished tradition in fiction: the "life" novel, the story of passage, the experience of a spiritual education. *Body and Soul* is an expansive novel that reconnects serious fiction to the Victorian chronicler of the painful but ultimately rewarding growing-up of David Copperfield, to the later breaking out of soul's prison of Philip Carey in W. Somerset Maugham's *Of Human Bondage* (1915) and Paul Morel in D. H. Lawrence's *Sons and Lovers* (1913), down to the struggles to find a self that allows growth in the autobiographical American heroes of Sherwood Anderson, Thomas Wolfe, and Ernest Hemingway. Perhaps even more than his English-language forebears, Conroy's Claude Rawlings is fictional offspring of Jean Christophe, the composer genius of French novelist Romain Rolland's early twentieth century novel cycle of that name.

Unlike *Jean Christophe* (1904-1912), which was published just before France and Germany went to war in 1914 and reflects the author's high-minded notions about "heroes," there is nothing lofty about Claude Rawlings' rise to become a famous pianist. Except for his obsession to develop into virtuosity a talent whose origins are graphically traced, Claude is portrayed as persistently naïve, almost ordinary. The workings of ego and narcissism, usually standard traits of the artist-hero, are nowhere apparent. Except for his devotion to music, Claude goes through life like a Pip without many great expectations.

At the age of six, Claude discovers in the back room of the Manhattan tenement where he lives in poverty with Emma, his six-foot, three-hundred-pound taxi-driver mother, "up against the back wall, half buried under piles of books and sheet music, a small, white console piano with sixty-six keys and a mirror over the keyboard." From that moment, Claude is absorbed by music. Not even the shocks of various personal crises—his first girlfriend, at fifteen, who jilts him, the discovery that he and his wife cannot have children, a painful divorce—produce any extended introspection. In so unabashedly romantic a novel as *Body and Soul*, the hero may age, but from the moment he renews the constancy of the piano keys, he remains fixated on the same ecstatic mood of his first recital (at fifteen): "launched . . . into a trance, like an infant at his mother's breast or a true believer before the moment of communion."

This is, as Will Blythe puts it in his capsule *Esquire* review, "a genuinely happy novel, in which virtue and fidelity are rewarded and joy made as plausible as divorce or nuclear meltdown . . . a book that in its form and aspiration owns a kind of Dickensian grandeur."

Part 1—thirteen chapters, 246 pages—carries Claude into his sixteenth year and establishes the two most vital relationships of his life. The earliest, with his mother, is always mysterious, with Emma functioning as his minimal caretaker who lives a shadowy underground life from which he is excluded. While their two-room basement apartment, with its dual sound conductors—a tiny radio and, above all, the piano—fills the imaginative center of Claude's life, it is for Emma only a place to cat-nap between taxi runs. Conroy, who in a brief afterword calls *Body and Soul* "to some extent a historical novel," uses Emma less as Claude's only blood family than as a reference for the era: 1945-1954, a time of suppressions of left-wing politics by government vigilante groups and of blacks just before civil rights were legislated. Emma Rawlings' taxi is barely a cover for clandestine political activities (she is eventually arrested by the Federal Bureau of Investigation and forced to inform on her Communist friends). She will become the lover of her son's friend Al, a black maintenance man. The reader will not learn the identity of Claude's father until near the end of the novel.

The out-of-wedlock mother's desperate life cannot include more than an unknowing glimpse of the prodigy-in-the-making. That pleasure is deservedly reserved for Aaron Weisfeld, owner of a music store on Third Avenue. Claude finds in the piano bench a piece of sheet music for "Honeysuckle Rose." Never shy about things that fuel him, he takes it to Weisfeld, who gives him a minirecital. "I have to learn how to do that, with the music," Claude exclaims. Recognizing the youngster's gift, Weisfeld agrees to teach him the basics. From then on, with Weisfeld's help, Claude rises, though with none of the agonizing setbacks that are the usual lot of fictional artist-heroes, to the heady world of Aldo Frescobaldi (violin virtuoso) and other patrons on two continents.

Part 2, three chapters, seventy-five pages, moves Claude nearly five years ahead. He is a senior scholarship student in English at Cadbury, a small Quaker college between Philadelphia and Princeton with 430 male undergraduates (in the mid-1950's Frank Conroy attended Haverford, a small private liberal arts college of the highest academic standing). Triumphant in his first recitals and concert appearances, which bring him into the orbit of the aristocratic Fisks, Senator Barnes, and others, he is nevertheless rejected by his first love, Catherine Marsh, a scion of wealth. Weisfeld, to whom Claude returns frequently even during college, warns him not to trust apparent sponsors like the Fisks: "To them, the artist is a high-class entertainer. They don't even know they don't know anything. . . . So don't expect anything. Be careful with those kind of people."

Conroy devotes little description to Claude's senior year at Cadbury except to make it the occasion for meeting Priscilla (Lady) Powers, a senior at nearby Hollifield College whom he marries at the end of the section. That she happens to be a first cousin of the young woman who jilted him is the first of several important instances in which Conroy exploits the long arm of coincidence. In the tradition of rites-of-passage fiction, the hero is usually humiliated by his social betters, but Conroy plays a variation on this theme. During a wild party hosted at a mansion by Lady's Bryn Mawr friend Caroline, Claude emerges as the hit. Seeking consolation for his discomfort, he sits down at the piano and blends Art Tatum into Fats Waller into Jelly Roll Morton in a cascade of improvisational jazz. Pleased by her date's uncharacteristic letting-go, Lady brings him briefly into the presence of her parents. It is early morning after the party, and the lights in the luxurious house are still on. "It's not in the pattern," she said. "The pattern is one Scotch and soda for her, two for him, and then upstairs with ginger ale to their respective bedrooms. It never varies."

What does vary from the usual angst-ridden "passage" novel is Claude's confidence in his exclusivity as an artist. His life with his mentor Weisfeld—their devotion to his career-to-be—enables Claude to soar above any darkness. In a remarkable sentence of concision, Claude sums up his separateness from the ordinary entrapments of life: "How strange people were, he thought, subject to all kinds of invisible forces, dealing with hidden devils and all the while keeping up appearances."

Novelist David Plante, reviewing *Body and Soul* in *The New York Times Book Review*, finds it easy to believe in Claude's obsession but difficult to believe that he has so few tantrums. The hero's placidity, which carries until Weisfeld's death eighty pages from the end, produces a bloodlessness that confirms a truism from theater: A character in motion will always upstage the stationary figure at center stage, no matter how much talking the latter does. Claude's two most compassionate sponsors—Aaron Weisfeld, for the prodigy-in-progress, and violin virtuoso Aldo Frescobaldi, for the evolved artist—take on scene-stealing capability. Conroy, who supported himself for years by playing jazz piano in clubs, knows the patter that passes among musicians, impresarios, conductors, and agents. The richest spinoff from Conroy's insights into the world of music is contained in the larger-than-life portrait of Frescobaldi: "A veritable mountain of fat, his huge liquid neck as wide as his head. Even his eyes bulged, under black eyebrows so thick and wild they looked like exotic caterpillars. His hand covered Claude's like a pillow." Claude is similarly overwhelmed by the man's generosity.

In part 3—the final eight chapters and 120 pages—Conroy brings his life novel to culmination by deploying some of the conventions of classic models. Like Maugham's Philip Carey, who finally sheds the bondage represented by the pathetically despicable

Mildred, Claude divests himself of Lady. Theirs, however, is a divestiture on the late twentieth century's terms—a sort of no-fault estrangement and divorce. Unable to conceive a child, they try for adoption, only to learn that the prospective baby belongs to one of Lady's students. Lady is traumatized when she realizes that the biological mother's anonymity has been violated. The death of Weisfeld and the dissolution of his marriage follow in catastrophic tandem.

Just as the orphaned Pip learns who he is at the end of *Great Expectations* (1860-1861), Claude must be given clues to his birth. The plot often creaks as Conroy is obliged to contrive a series of unlikely developments to reveal the booklong secret of Claude's bastardy: (1) Lady's father's private investigation, which leads to the disclosure that Claude's mother, long under surveillance by the House Committee on Un-American Activities for Communist ties, is living with a black male—a taboo, (2) Claude's awakened interest in who he is and his fear that discovery will threaten his precious pursuits, and (3) his mother's disclosure, under pressure from Claude, that she married a Canadian soldier, a show-business acquaintance, two days before he shipped out. She doubts, however, that he was Paul's father.

For 421 pages, until the penultimate chapter, Conroy has angled his artist-hero novel entirely from Claude's viewpoint. To resolve his hero's—and the novel's—identity crisis, Conroy uses jazz pianist Lord Lightning, "whose *café-au-lait* complexion was the only obvious indicator of his Negro blood," as the lens through whom the reader will learn *Body and Soul*'s final secret. To bring Claude's past and present into alignment, the famous pianist, now also a composer of promise, goes to London for the London Symphony Orchestra's performance of his first major composition. He visits a jazz club featuring Lord Lightning, who invites him to sit in. The number Claude chooses is the piece he first took to Weisfeld at ten. Claude is astounded by his perfect musical rapport with Lord Lightning; they play "Honeysuckle Rose" with improvisations each recognizes. As for recognition in the literary sense—that is, in the drama's denouement, its point of no return—Conroy leaves Claude characteristically unsure. The reader is left convinced: The black jazz pianist and Claude are father and son.

With Claude professionally fulfilled and reunited in London with his first love, with Weisfeld dead and his suffering in the Holocaust revealed, and with Emma finding solace with Al, *Body and Soul* concludes, just as it has proceeded all along, on a note of déjà-vu. Conroy's novel breathes air from an earlier America—that of the late 1940's and 1950's—not yet overwhelmed by nonconformity (1960's), blandness (1970's), greed (1980's), and violence (1990's). This book returns fiction to a momentary nostalgia for a time when heroes—artist-heroes in particular—stood above the forces that later became all too committed to diminishing them.

Richard Hauer Costa

Sources for Further Study

Chicago Tribune. September 26, 1993, XIV, p. 1.
The Christian Science Monitor. October 14, 1993, p. 13.
Los Angeles Times Book Review. September 19, 1993, p. 3.
The Nation. CCLVII, October 25, 1993, p. 471.
The New York Times Book Review. XCVIII, October 3, 1993, p. 7.
Newsweek. CXXII, September 27, 1993, p. 74.
Publishers Weekly. CCXL, June 21, 1993, p. 82.
Time. CXLII, September 27, 1993, p. 91.
The Wall Street Journal. October 6, 1993, p. A14.
The Washington Post. October 5, 1993, p. D1.

BONE

Author: Fae Myenne Ng (1956-   )
Publisher: Hyperion (New York). 194 pp. $19.95
Type of work: Novel
Time: The 1960's through the 1980's
Locale: San Francisco's Chinatown

Lei's story of growing up in Chinatown as the daughter of first-generation Chinese immigrants is haunted by the recent suicide of her sister Ona

Principal characters:
> LEILA "LEI" FU LOUIE, the narrator of the novel, a schoolteacher in San
> Francisco
> DULCIE "MAH" LEONG, her mother, who has worked most of her life as a
> seamstress and now owns a children's clothing store
> LEON LEONG, her stepfather, a retired seaman
> NINA LEONG, her half-sister, who lives in New York and leads tours to China
> ONA LEONG, another half-sister who has recently committed suicide
> MASON LOUIE, Lei's husband, a car mechanic

The children of immigrants have often been called upon to translate for their parents. Their ability to switch from the language of their parents to the English of their birthplace makes them the bridge between the customs of the old world and the expectations and demands of the new. Not only are these children faced with a generation gap, but they must also cope with a cultural gap. This enormous responsibility can become an overwhelming burden. In Fae Myenne Ng's first novel, *Bone*, the narrator Lei, the "First Girl," and her younger sister Nina, the "End Girl," confront this burden over a dinner conversation.

> Nina's voice went soft. "Look, you've always been on standby for them. Waiting and doing things their way. Think about it, they have no idea what our lives are about. They don't want to come into our worlds. We keep on having to live in their world. They won't move one bit."
>
> She looked straight at me. "I know about it too. I helped fill out those forms at the Chinatown employment agencies; I went to the Seaman's Union too; I listened and hoped for those calls: 'Busboy! Presser! Prep man!' And I know about *should*. I know about *have to*. We should. We want to do more, we want to do everything. But I've learned this: I *can't*."

Nina's inability to shoulder this burden of translation has caused her to move to New York, far away from San Francisco's Chinatown where her parents live. Lei, the eldest sister in the family of three daughters, remains in San Francisco, uncomfortably but inextricably connected to the family and the community. Yet it is the self-imposed silence of the "Middle Girl," Ona, that is at the center of this novel.

Ona has committed suicide by jumping off the M floor of one of Chinatown's housing projects. She left no note, and although the police reported that she was on downers, there was no apparent cause for the suicide. Lei's attempts to come to terms with her sister's death, and thereby her own life, lead her to muse about incidents from their childhood and the everyday circumstances of the present. The author, Fae

Myenne Ng, does not seek to solve the mystery of Ona's death in this novel—it is a mystery that is unsolvable; rather, through the narrative voice of Lei, she explores the languages and silences of love, grief, assimilation, avoidance, anger, guilt, and finally acceptance.

The novel begins with the language of gossip: "We heard things. 'A failed family. That Dulcie Fu. And you know which one: bald Leon. Nothing but daughters.'" Whispers are heard behind children's backs—a failed family because there were no sons, because Dulcie had left her first husband, because Dulcie and Leon fought and Leon had moved out, because Nina had moved to New York, because Ona had committed suicide, because Lei had moved in with Mason Louie and then married him in New York without the benefit of the traditional banquet. At the beginning of the book, Lei has just returned from New York and must tell her parents that she married Mason while there.

There is no hesitation in speaking to Leon, her stepfather—he is the first person Lei wants to tell. Leon is the one who had dismissed the gossipmongers: "People talking. People jealous. . . . Five sons don't make one good daughter." Leon always had assured his stepdaughter, "It's time that makes a family, not just blood." Telling her mother is much more difficult for Lei, because the announcement inevitably will wound Mah's Chinese pride.

The conversation jumps between languages, as Lei's attempt at accommodation by approaching her mother in Chinese falls away in the American reality of her deed; she must speak in English. Her mother counters in her ancient language, one that goes back to primitive grunts, to express her displeasure and provoke guilt in her daughter. Not only does Mah have a Chinese vocabulary to draw on, but she can invoke the universal language of motherhood. Lei survives the encounter because she chooses not to retaliate against her mother by reminding her of her own failed marriages; instead, she reaches across the divide of affection by shifting the focus to Mason.

> "You don't like Mason, is that it?"
> "Mason," Mah spoke his name soft, "I love."
> For love she used a Chinese word: to embrace, to hug.
> I stepped around the boxes, opened my arms and hugged Mah.

Although two gossipy women have witnessed the altercation between mother and daughter, Lei no longer cares about their tales. When she sees them leave, knowing that they are off to pass on their news, she dismisses them from her concern: "Let them make it up, I thought. Let them talk."

Gossip gives way to lies when Lei begins to work through her relationship with Leon. Leon needs a steady source of income to pay his rent at the resident hotel he moved into after Ona's suicide. When Lei finally convinces him that he can still earn some money while collecting social security, he agrees to apply for his benefits. Lei accompanies him to the social security office, where she and the interviewer try to sort through the morass of aliases and multiple birthdates Leon has claimed over the years. He had entered the United States illegally, taking on someone else's name and life history. Once in the country, he followed "old-timer logic: If you don't tell the truth, you'll never get caught in a lie. What Leon didn't know, he made up. Forty years of making it up had to backfire sometime." These are the lies that Leon had used to survive and support his family in a society that patronized him and devalued his masculinity. At one point during the interview, a frustrated Leon resorts to cursing in broken English. His stepdaughter realizes in a bitter moment that what English he knows, he had learned from shipmates cursing him.

The social security interviewer sends them home to find proper documentation. What Lei finds is a suitcase full of papers, neatly sorted by year and rubber-banded by decade—a history of rejections, letters from Mah when he had shipped out, photographs, newspaper clippings, receipts of money sent to China, official documents that contradicted each other, and finally the needed certificate of identification and entry into the country. The contents of the suitcase attest a life created by papers—writing that is at once sacred and duplicitous, a testimony to the difficulties of sustaining an existence in an alien society. Lei realizes that Leon Leong had to imagine himself into being: "I'm the stepdaughter of a paper son and I've inherited this whole suitcase of lies. All of it is mine. All I have is those memories, and I want to remember them all."

These threads of affection and memories, spun of gossip and lies, draw Lei and the reader into the fabric of the family's life that was rent by Ona's suicide. The fabric was never tightly knit. Mah had married Leon for his green card, and their life together was defined by hard work; they worked so their children could marry for love. Family life was punctuated by Leon's long absences, when he was shipped out on voyages to Hong Kong and Gibraltar and Australia. During one of the voyages, Mah had had an affair with her boss; Leon found out and moved out of the apartment, but moved back in after another voyage. A failed venture into the laundry business with a dishonest partner tore apart friendships, trust, and Ona's romance.

Everyone in the family longs for escape: Leon from the humiliations of failure, Mah from loneliness, and the daughters from the expectations and needs of their parents. They long to escape from the boundaries of Chinatown, from their own lives. The children are drawn away by fast cars, drugs, casual sex, the world of American youth—but each is bound more or less tightly by complexities of loving and living in the ambiguous reality of two languages. Nina, the youngest daughter, is the least bound and escapes across the continent; she declares her independence by refusing to lie in order to appease her parents. Ona, the middle child, was caught in the middle; she learned too well how to keep secrets. Her escape, chosen or accidental, was to fly out the window. Lei, the translator from one language to another, finally succeeds in moving across town, but even as she leaves, she realizes the truth of what Leon once told her: "The heart never travels."

Fae Myenne Ng's *Bone* is eloquently understated. She explores how the force of words—whether in English or Chinese, whether spoken or left unsaid—determines the course of lives. Perhaps it is the words not said that haunt the book most tellingly. Was there a conversation, a secret revealed, a word said that might have saved Ona?

What does one do with those secrets, those unspoken promises that are the bones of every family?

Jane Anderson Jones

Sources for Further Study

Belles Lettres. VIII, Spring, 1993, p. 21.
Chicago Tribune. February 25, 1993, V, p. 3.
Library Journal. CXVIII, January, 1993, p. 166.
Los Angeles Times. January 14, 1993, p. E5.
Ms. III, May, 1993, p. 75.
The New York Times Book Review. XCVIII, February 7, 1993, p. 7.
The New Yorker. LXVIII, February 8, 1993, p. 113.
Publishers Weekly. CCXXXIX, November 9, 1992, p. 71.
The Washington Post Book World. XXIII, January 10, 1993, p. 8.
Women's Review of Books. X, May, 1993, p. 27.

BOOK OF THE FOURTH WORLD
Reading the Native Americas Through Their Literature

Author: Gordon Brotherston (1939-   )
Publisher: Cambridge University Press (New York). Illustrated. 478 pp. $39.95
Type of work: Literary history

Literary history and philosophy, with particular interest given to the pre-Columbian iconic or hieroglyphic languages and literature of Mayan, Aztec, Incan, and North American Indian cultures

The problem of patterning order out of chaos is solved by many cultures by the introduction of heroes who translate or decode images from the source, which are then recorded as creation stories. In many creation stories, the creative cultural hero has a younger or a twin brother, the trickster/destroyer. The Creator/Destroyer twin motif brings order to the chaotic clash between benevolent and malevolent forces.

Book of the Fourth World: Reading the Native Americas Through Their Literature is about making order out of chaos. Gordon Brotherston is our trickster/author; his book is about strange lands, incomprehensible cultural symbols and archetypes, and an indecipherable language. Indeed, Brotherston does not simply write "about" making order; rather, he plunges the reader into unfamiliar territory, confusing at first. From this initial confusion, a strange but compelling order gradually emerges.

On the opening page, Brotherston asks "How many worlds define this planet?" "Where is the heart of each, and its frontier?" Among the issues he addresses in answering these questions are "script and how to define it," "modes of embodying and mapping space," "calendars as the reckoning of tribute in kind or labor," "the pastoralism peculiar to the Andes," and the "links of food production and the shape of the cosmogony," which he describes in terms of "native coherence." Let's focus on the word "coherence," beginning with a brief review of Western (Cartesian) reasoning.

Factual truths and logical truths are not the same. Statements within a system differ from statements about a system. Factual truths describe *actual* events. Factual truths are contingent upon something having happened or something happening—"it is raining." Logical truth stems from formalized relationships between symbols. Logical truth necessitates. "Water is wet. Rain is water. Rain is wet."

The factual/logical split has generated the "coherence" theory and the "correspondence" theory of truth. A story is coherent because it is internally consistent to collectively accepted paradigms. A story may have to be interpreted if the receiver of the story is not acquainted with the coherent structure.

The key issues Brotherston addresses are explained by simply making statements in the native coherence of the subject matter. His manner of proceeding is neither "factual" (the historical and mythological literature of the Americas cannot be judged by standards of factual verification) nor "logical" (since this literature was handed across time in iconic-based languages, which are far from being logical and mathematical.) Brotherston unsettles those of us who habitually employ the Cartesian dichotomies of splintered truth, and are not literate in pre-Columbian MesoAmerican content. The native coherence which Brotherston uses as explanation is best described as "truth as accurate description." Thus, truth is a matter of degree, because some stories in MesoAmerican Indian traditions are mystifying to Western audiences, and would not be called stories in our linear terminology.

In MesoAmerica, home of woven screenfold books, play is characteristically made not just with the act of writing, as, for example, the image of a tongue pen used for a singing lesson; but with the very surface written upon—paper or skin. The Aztec poet identifies the threads of his song with the fibers of the screenfold paper page, and a Maya inscription at Copan contrives to weave its hieroglyphic thread into the grain in the stone. Text is a framed composition, an "authorized" example of discourse which has its own inner structure and capacity to reflect upon itself while forming part of the larger literary system. MesoAmerican iconic texts translated into phonetic Spanish or English lose their authorial motive and are profaned by our translations of them; profaned because in iconic languages space is modulated, rather than sound, and in iconic reckoning time operates in a circle and exists in many different dimensions. Translating the cyclic, rhythmic reasoning of iconic languages (which are often read as chants and incorporate sounds for meanings) into linear phonetic codes victimizes truth. There is a mismatch.

Brotherston's intellect, knowledge of the subject matter, and control of the English language thus truthfully describe the rich iconography of the ancient inscriptions and screenfold books which set the schemes of the Fourth World cultures. The genius of Brotherston is that he employs phonic English words *as icons* and weaves these into his descriptions of the intricate stories of cataclysms, metamorphoses, and epic quests of the cosmogonies of the Fourth World. Also, he does not temporalize, thus trivialize, in the Western sense. He describes the time schemes of MesoAmerica as they are and not as "quaint" in comparison to Christian-era time schemes. In general, Western civilization imposes diachronic time on all of its interpretations of all texts from all cultures. To impose such a linear structure on, for example, the texts of the Nahuatl, Mixtec, or other MesoAmerican languages destroys the ingenious visually integrated structure of the literature. There is bivalence to the European system, multivalence to the MesoAmerican structures. Bivalence is profane. We do not know the facts and we do not understand the logic. To his credit, Brotherston is not profane with his accurate descriptions, sonorous though they may be.

Nonphonetic languages register sound concepts, but they also (in Brotherston's words) "conform by turns to a chronicled narrative, an icon or map, or a mathematical table. Indeed, integrating into one holistic statement what for us are separate concepts of letter, picture, and arithmetic, these languages flout received Western notions of writing. Round fruits on a tree count out units of time; the sign for a place also denotes a date in the Era; a bird serves to characterize and date the space through which it flies." Phonetic languages do not translate this kind of coherency. Phonetic language codes and grammatical ciphers are logical truths. Credit must be given to Brotherston for retaining accuracy. He declares the native text to be an entity unto itself. He describes, but does not question, the structure of the embedded sequence of episodes common to languages coded by an iconic cipher.

Coherency in MesoAmerica is also based on the life-nexus logic of body paradigms. Whole vocabularies use gesture or sign language, time is measured in cycles and multiples of cycles, ritual logic provides grammatical ciphers, people's names are represented by pictures depicting the metamorphosis from soul to mask, and landscapes are linked to architecture. The creators of this literature used it to structure history, settle accounts, theorize, and picture geography all in one holistic reflexive design with the force of natural law behind it.

Brotherston's recurring theme is that westerners must not impose their cultural assumptions on the literature of the indigenous peoples of the Americas. He underlines this theme by comparing a Zuni story with a European fairy tale. "Turkey Girl" is to "Cinderella" as the Popol Vuh is to its Spanish translation.

Cinderella is banished to cleaning the hearth because it is a dirty job which her stepsisters will not do. In Native America, women who, with cedar boughs, sweep the ashes of the hearth are rekindling and renewing new life. Among the Aztecs, rekindling fires at the ends of eras was a profound ceremony undertaken with much circumstance at stake.

As in Cinderella, the action of Turkey Girl centers around a major ceremonial dance. Unlike Cinderella, Turkey Girl is drawn to a place, not a person.

Turkey Girl inhabits "Wind Place," one of the first towns inhabited by Zuni after emerging into *this* world. Turkey Girl lives in a spiritually charged landscape, dealing with birds which function sacrificially, ornamentally, and as domesticated animals. Wild turkeys are known for their ferociousness, stealth, and extraordinary patience, which makes them difficult to hunt. Turkey Girl, who communicates with and domesticates this very difficult creature, is considered sacred and is held apart. She yearns to rejoin her people.

The whole action centers on the dance. The dance becomes the funnel through which the solitary Turkey Girl, living on the other side, comes to belong to the Zuni People. The dance being performed is the Yaaya (Sacred Bird Dance). Turkey Girl, in going to the dance, returns to her People and brings with her an ancient spiritual contract with the "other side" in the songs she sings. She finds her own center at the "Place in the Middle." When Turkey Girl does not return to the other side, the turkeys leave their domesticated life and continue their own epic emergence journey up the Zuni River to the top of the sacred mountain. They sing their own song and chant the place names of the landscape and make their prints on the rocks. Told orally and cued from icons, the story of Turkey Girl ends here. No glass slipper, "no happily ever after." Through this story, which is chanted and danced, the Zuni are reminded of their own emergence myth and of their sacred contract with those that provide food, clothing, amusement, and tests for the People. And the children learn that there is no greater interactivity than to sing and dance a story in a ritual space.

Gordon Brotherston is faithful to the texts of the Fourth World. He imposes no alien system or structure, he seeks no right and wrong, he is not self-righteously romantic about the sophistication of the noble savage, he does not react pompously to the savagery of the pagans on the frontier, nor is he looking for a new "publish or perish" spin to an old top.

He is trickster, doing his job, bringing order out of chaos, naming, administering, and designating terrestrial space signs or icons which symbolize the cosmogonical occurrences of such spaces; which consecrate and thus make each territory the center of the world, in order to advise our culture during periods of change.

Glenn J. Schiffman

Sources for Further Study

Antiquity LXVII, December, 1993, p. 900.
The Guardian. July 27, 1993, p. 11.
New Statesman and Society. VI, August 13, 1993, p. 40.
The Times Literary Supplement. July 16, 1993, p. 12.

BURNS
A Biography of Robert Burns

Author: James Mackay (1936-   )
First published: 1992, in Great Britain
Publisher: Mainstream Publishing (Edinburgh). Distributed by Trafalgar Square (North Pomfret, Vermont). 749 pp. $34.95
Type of work: Biography
Time: 1759-1796
Locale: Scotland

A definitive biography of Robert Burns, using all the tools of rigorous scholarship to arrive at an accurate account of his life

Principal personages:
ROBERT BURNS, the eighteenth century Scottish poet
WILLIAM BURNES, his father
AGNES BROWN BURNES, his mother
JEAN ARMOUR BURNS, his wife
MARGARET CAMPBELL (HIGHLAND MARY), a young woman Burns loved
AGNES CRAIG MCLEHOSE (CLARINDA), an unhappily married woman with
     whom Burns was involved

As a highly respected scholar who has devoted his life to the study of Robert Burns, James Mackay was eminently qualified to produce his biography. For fourteen years, Mackay served the Burns Federation as editor of its *Burns Chronicle*; in addition, he compiled both *The Complete Works of Robert Burns*, which was published by the Federation in 1986, and a Burns concordance, *Burns A-Z: The Complete Word Finder* (1990). To his latest project Mackay has brought not only encyclopedic knowledge but also the objectivity that many of the previous biographers of Burns have lacked. While no one would accuse Mackay of having less than warm feelings toward his subject, his motive in researching and writing this volume is clearly the loftiest aim of scholarship: not to advance a particular point of view but to ascertain the truth.

Where the life of Burns is concerned, this task is particularly difficult. Long before he became a famous poet, Burns had become the subject of gossip. Along with a group of high-spirited friends, he drew the criticism of conservative Calvinists, who suspected that he was a freethinker as well as a drunkard. In addition, he seemed to be almost irresistible to women, and soon he was being credited with even more living proofs of his virility than he actually fathered. Once Burns became famous, it seemed that almost everyone had a story to tell about him. Unfortunately, after his death many of these anecdotes were reiterated in biography after biography, until they attained the status of undisputed truth. What Mackay has done in this monumental volume is to move systematically through the brief life of his subject, pointing out obvious errors of fact in previous accounts and, where there is conflicting evidence, showing how he has arrived at some conclusion, which in many cases must be labeled merely a probability or a possibility. *Burns: A Biography of Robert Burns* is thus of interest in two very different ways. On one hand, of course, its readers will gain a much clearer idea as to what Burns was really like, but in addition, since the biographer conducts them step by step through each analysis, they will have an opportunity to see a fine scholarly mind at work.

In method Mackay is not unlike Arthur Conan Doyle's fictional detective, Sherlock Holmes. Even in relatively minor matters, such as the circumstances of Robert Burns's birth, Mackay takes nothing for granted. Since it is known that the end of January, 1759, was exceptionally stormy, the dramatic account of William Burnes's fording a river at night, desperately seeking a midwife to attend at the birth of his child, has long been accepted without question. After relating the story, however, Mackay pauses to take a long look at it. In Holmesian fashion, he initially wonders how, once having crossed the swollen river, Burnes would have got the midwife back to his home in Alloway. Then he turns to contemporary documents, where he finds, first, that there is no record that Robert Burns was born late at night, as the narrative supposed, and, second, that the village midwife could have arrived as soon as Agnes Brown Burnes went into labor, since she lived next door to the Burneses. Clearly, the river anecdote, though colorful and certainly harmless, is untrue.

Mackay takes pains to find an explanation for some of the confusing details that students must face. For example, while the poet's father spelled his surname "Burnes," the parish register records the birth of Robert "Burns" on January 25, 1759, as well as his christening the following day. The biographer notes that the spelling "Burns" reflects the Ayrshire pronunciation. Furthermore, by looking at the early letters of Robert Burns himself, he has found that the poet seems quite early to have adopted that spelling, except on a few occasions when he used still another variant, "Burness."

The fact that Mackay is so meticulous sometimes results in what might be perceived as a defect in his work. Whenever a name is mentioned, for example, that of the Reverend William Dalrymple, who christened Robert Burns, or even those of the witnesses, James Young and John Tennant, the biographer pauses in his narrative to relate all that is known about the person identified, not only such significant matters as his later associations with Robert Burns and the references to him found in Burns's letters and poetry, but also details about his later life which can hardly be considered relevant to the subject at hand. In defense of Mackay, however, one must recognize the fact that as a definitive biography, this work will probably be used as an encyclopedia as often as it will be read from cover to cover. Therefore in many cases the demands of the narrative must be sacrificed to the needs of later scholars.

Where a number of issues are concerned, no one would wish Mackay's research to be any less thorough or less extensive. For example, some nineteenth century biographers reported that William Burnes was a poor businessman, and perhaps also a dishonest one, who very nearly went to prison because of his dealings with his landlord David McClure. Mackay marshals facts to prove that William Burnes was in the right in this case and, indeed, that he was generally careful in his dealings and scrupulously honest.

Since the twentieth century has brought its own obsessions to the study of Burns, Mackay is also forced to spend considerable time pointing out how patently ridiculous it is for critics such as Alan Dent, author of *Burns in His Time* (1966), to insist that the poet had homosexual leanings. After quoting Dent as he imagines Burns on a Sunday walk with a male friend, Mackay makes it clear what he thinks of "this ludicrous picture of two Wildean aesthetes in the woods" and of the "cheap jibe" at admirers of Burns with which Dent follows his own fiction. Although in examining evidence Mackay is admirably objective, such clear-sighted comments remind one that every biographer is to some degree a character in his own book. With his wit and his perspicacity, Mackay is a pleasant companion on this leisurely journey through Burns's life.

Because Burns has often been accused of habitual drunkenness, and indeed, since his early death was frequently attributed to alcoholism or to general debauchery, Mackay considers it essential to look at the supposed proofs of such charges. He points out, for example, that most of the references to drinking found in Burns's letters are clearly exaggerated for the sake of humor. Moreover, readers of eighteenth century literature should recognize the fact that Burns's bacchanalian songs are much like the love poems of the staid bachelor poet Robert Herrick, conventional exercises in a common form rather than heartfelt expressions of personal experience.

Having agreed with the physician-writers of the 1920's who dismissed the idea that the use of alcohol had anything to do either with Burns's periodic ill-health or with his death, Mackay also questions whether Burns suffered as a result of rheumatic fever, as had been previously thought. Instead, the biographer offers proof that early in his life Burns was subject to attacks of clinical depression, while later he sustained physical injuries in riding accidents, which indeed made it impossible for him to continue farming. His final illness may well have been brucellosis, or undulant fever, which could easily have been contracted from the milk of infected cattle. Unfortunately, Burns's physician did not have the benefit of modern medical knowledge, and he probably killed his patient by prescribing mercury for him, thus causing his kidneys to fail. Mackay hastens to point out that although mercury was also commonly used for the treatment of venereal diseases, there is absolutely no reason to believe that Burns's death had anything to do with his susceptibility to feminine charm.

Not surprisingly, some of Mackay's most interesting discussions concern the women who inspired some of Burns's best poems and then later kindled the passions of scholars. There is a hilarious account of the running conflict between the "Episodists" and the "Mariolaters," who disagreed as to whether "Highland Mary"—whose name in fact was not Mary, but Margaret Campbell—was the mother of a baby later found buried with her, perhaps a child of the poet, or instead the unspotted virgin of the earlier tradition, in whose honor Burns wrote some of his loveliest works. Mackay also clears up a number of questions about Agnes Craig McLehose, the abandoned wife with whom, as "Clarinda," Burns maintained a voluminous and rather sentimental correspondence.

Nevertheless, the biographer stresses his belief that the only woman Burns truly loved was Jean Armour, his devoted wife. Although in many of the other lives she was treated as a barely literate symbol of fecundity who would have bored any man as brilliant as Burns, Mackay shows that Jean had a much better education than most country girls would have received. From the polished style and thoughtful content of her surviving letters, as well as from Burns's own casual comments, one must conclude that Jean was a more interesting person than the shadowy figure of earlier biographies. In this volume, Mackay presents details that give Jean a real identity and, in addition, make it clear how much Burns really cared about her. For example, a servant girl at Mill Hole Brae recalled Burns's being concerned because his busy wife was often a little "out of order," or less than genteel in appearance. In order to remedy the situation, she said, Burns would buy Jean the finest clothing he could afford, and thus she became "one of the first ladies in Dumfries to wear a gingham gown," a real distinction since that new fabric was "rather costly, and almost exclusively used by persons of superior conditions." If one is to see both of the Burnses clearly, this glimpse of their home life must be given as much importance as Burns's own accounts of his womanizing.

Mackay believes that, as with his drinking, in the area of sexual conduct the poet was largely responsible for blackening his own reputation. In his letters and poems, Burns frequently adopts the role of a heartless rake. The biographer cites instances of his use of military metaphors to describe the process of courtship; despite the evidence that many women, such as Agnes McLehose, went to great trouble to get acquainted with the good-looking celebrity, Burns liked to pretend that it was he who took the initiative and who thus should be credited with the conquests. Most readers also find distasteful the boastful manner in which Burns announces the births of his children, seemingly denying any participation, even any humanity, to the mothers. Yet anyone who has observed human nature must recognize the fact that Burns is hardly the first man to crow about such matters for the benefit of his male friends, nor will he be the last. In Mackay's opinion, Burns should be judged not by the poses that he struck on such occasions but by his characteristic behavior. In reality, Burns was no libertine. Though admittedly he was unfaithful to his wife, he did indeed love and cherish her, and he certainly intended no harm to the other women with whom he became involved. Moreover, it must be said in his defense that, whenever possible, he did take responsibility for his illegitimate offspring.

The Robert Burns who emerges from this new biography is in fact a decent, hardworking, disciplined man. Those reviewers who judge that Mackay was too sympathetic toward his subject to present a true picture of him must argue not only with the biographer's conclusions but also with the supporting evidence that he so painstakingly has accumulated and so candidly presented to his readers. This impressive volume is not simply another work about Robert Burns; it should take its proper place as the definitive biography of one of the world's greatest poets.

Rosemary M. Canfield Reisman

Sources for Further Study

Kirkus Reviews. LXI, June 15, 1993, p. 771.
The Observer. November 22, 1992, p. 63.
Publishers Weekly. CCXL, June 14, 1993, p. 54.
The Times Educational Supplement. October 23, 1992, p. 7.
The Times Literary Supplement. January 1, 1993, p. 3.

THE BUTCHER BOY

Author: Patrick McCabe (1955-   )
First published: 1992, in the United Kingdom
Publisher: Fromm International (New York). 215 pp. $19.95
Type of work: Novel
Time: The early 1960's
Locale: A small town in Ireland

A novel that traces an Irish boy's inexorable descent into madness

    Principal characters:
        FRANCIE BRADY, a troubled young boy
        BENNY BRADY, his alcoholic father
        ANNIE BRADY, his emotionally unstable, suicidal mother
        JOE PURCELL, his friend and trusted comrade
        PHILIP NUGENT, a priggish new boy in town
        MRS. NUGENT, Philip's mother, the target of Francie's rage and resentment

Patrick McCabe has published two novels, *Music on Clinton Street* (1986) and *Carn* (1989), and one book for children, *The Adventures of Shay Mouse* (1985), in England and Ireland. *The Butcher Boy* marks his impressive introduction to the American reading public. Inspired by a grisly news story that McCabe first encountered in the form of a radio play when he was eight years old, the novel draws on other sources as well. Although McCabe composed the novel while living in England, where he was teaching learning-disabled children, the small town which is its principal setting resembles, in its size and its remoteness from any cosmopolitan center, the town of Clones in Ireland's County Monaghan, where McCabe was born and reared. McCabe has noted that his early loss of his father contributed significantly to the intensity of feeling he generates in the book. Although Francie Brady, McCabe's protagonist, is certainly very different from his creator, McCabe's memories of his own loss and the longing that followed it have helped carry him to his character's emotional center.

The emotional truth thus achieved has no doubt contributed to the laudatory responses of critics, who have made comparisons not only to J. D. Salinger and Anthony Burgess but also to such masters as Mark Twain, James Joyce, Samuel Beckett, and Feodor Dostoevski. In England the book was shortlisted for the prestigious Booker Prize, and it was awarded Ireland's Aer Lingus Prize for 1992.

The story McCabe tells is a chilling one. Even in the relatively benign opening pages, which focus on what might easily be regarded as the pranks that pervade the typical boys' book, the first thing one learns about Francie Brady is that he will be hunted for something he has done to Mrs. Nugent. While progressing for the most part in straightforward chronological order, the narrative also moves in the direction of a gradual illumination of Francie's fatal act.

Francie is an impressive creation, both as protagonist and as narrator. To capture the quality of Francie's voice, a voice the reader is made to hear, McCabe frequently deviates from the conventions of sentence structure and punctuation. While this may constitute an initial obstacle to some readers, especially those not familiar with the patterns and rhythms of Irish speech, it more than justifies itself by the achievement of authenticity and immediacy. McCabe makes of the narrator's vernacular an instrument that is eloquent, flexible, and often plain funny. It is not surprising that critics have been reminded of Salinger's Holden Caulfield and even of Mark Twain's Huckleberry Finn.

Like Holden and Huck, Francie belongs to the tradition of the boy narrator who has so far avoided becoming completely civilized. These narrators have a freshness and innocence of perception; they have not internalized the conventions by which the more respectable members of society, especially the grown-ups, organize their lives. As a result, the narrator effortlessly and more or less unconsciously assumes an ironic perspective on the social environment.

All this is true of Francie, and a result is a sometimes scathing, often hilarious portrait of provincial Irish life. Yet the direction in which Francie is moving, a direction one senses early in the novel, makes him frightening in ways that Huck and Holden are not. A major accomplishment of this novel is that although it is Francie who speaks, McCabe lets the reader see truths beyond what Francie is able to articulate: truths about the community, about the other characters, about Francie himself. The power of the novel rests not only in what Francie sees but also in how he is seen.

The act that sets the novel in motion arises from a prank played by Francie and his friend Joe Purcell. That Philip Nugent, the new boy in school, has been to a private school in England impresses Francie and Joe not at all. His comic-book collection is another matter. They must have it, and by a ruse they play on Philip, they soon get it. Mrs. Nugent, Philip's mother, will naturally not tolerate this. She shows up on the Bradys' doorstep to denounce Francie. There she goes too far. After all, she demands, what could one expect of a boy like Francie, since all civilized people know that the Bradys are pigs?

In fact, the Bradys are far from an ideal family. Benny Brady, Francie's father, is an abusive alcoholic. Francie's emotionally unstable mother is obsessed with suicide, and soon after Mrs. Nugent's visit she makes a feeble attempt at it. She is sent to the garage, as Francie calls it; Francie knows that "the garage" is really a mental institution, but his jokes about the repair job being done on his mother provide some distraction from the ugly truth of the situation.

There is an even uglier truth that Francie cannot let himself recognize or utter. Part of him believes that Mrs. Nugent is right. Worse, part of him wishes he were in Philip's place, the son of the genteel Mrs. Nugent and her teetotaling, pipe-smoking husband, rather than of the pathetically dysfunctional pair who are his actual parents. It is more than idle curiosity that sets him to peering into the Nugents' window, and it is not pubescent sexuality but his longing for a nurturing mother that generates the fantasies in which Mrs. Nugent offers him her breast.

The impossibility of acknowledging such emotional betrayal motivates the fervor of Francie's pledge to his mother, extracted by her just after she has given him a beating, that he will never let her down. Of course, he cannot keep that promise.

Following a disastrous visit from his uncle Alo, whose supposed success in England turns out to be a fraud, simply a family myth, and whose presence brings to the surface all the intensity of family bitterness, Francie runs away.

He runs all the way to Dublin, but he cannot live with his disloyalty. He is soon on his way home, bearing a gift for his mother: a plaque bearing the legend "A mother's love's a blessing."

His discovery that his mother has drowned herself is shattering, especially since it is too easy for the boy, whose burden of guilt is sufficiently heavy, to accept his father's drunken accusation that his mother's death is all Francie's fault. At the deepest level, Francie knows that he had rejected his mother even before he ran away.

Since this knowledge is intolerable, Francie allows himself to recognize only a distorted version of it: His mother's death is all the fault of Mrs. Nugent. He now embarks on a series of direct and indirect attacks on her; it is some measure of McCabe's art that even as one sees Mrs. Nugent through Francie's rages, one is made aware that she is nothing worse than a limited, understandably confused woman of ordinary decency. Finally Francie breaks into the Nugents' house and defecates on the floor. This time he is caught and sent to an industrial school, run by priests. Like his father before him, he finds himself in a "home."

Before he is released, Francie has become the object of the advances of a pederastic priest. What is more disturbing is that on his release, he finds that his relationship with Joe is no longer what it was. In one of the novel's most painful moments, its narrative turning point, Francie hears Joe tell a cousin of Mrs. Nugent that he and Francie are not friends any longer.

Francie is never able to accept Joe's rejection. "They" made him say it, Francie convinces himself. Yet Francie has other things on his mind. Having failed his mother, as he supposes, he vows that he will never let his father down. He even goes to work in the slaughterhouse. He thus assumes the role of the butcher boy. This involves the literal killing of a piglet, which, given his internalization of the epithet "pig," must to some degree involve a symbolic self-destruction. Further, Mrs. Brady's favorite ballad told of a young woman who kills herself because she has been betrayed by the butcher boy. Francie can neither recognize nor articulate the emotional pressures that are being brought to the boiling point here, but the explosion begins to seem inevitable.

Then the youth learns that his father has died. Francie has been making his promises to a rotting corpse. When this is discovered, it is Francie's turn to go to "the garage." His life increasingly seems an uncanny repetition of his parents'.

Francie is pulled in two directions. Part of him looks for a new beginning; he will bid goodbye to the old Francie, to Francie the Bad Bastard. On the other hand, he seeks a return to the good times with Joe. A kind of nostalgia leads him to the town where his parents spent their honeymoon and where, he had always understood, they had known a few days of love and happiness. Yet the happiness of the Bradys is just another family myth. The owner of the boardinghouse remembers with disgust the Benny Brady who behaved unforgivably toward a priest and whose poor bride never saw him sober.

Frustrated in his search for a blessed past, Francie is all the more urgently determined to effect a reconciliation with Joe. When he tracks Joe down at the college he and Philip Nugent now attend, Francie suffers a rejection that is painful, humiliating, and final.

It is, of course, all Mrs. Nugent's fault. Francie now takes his horrible revenge. He is ready to hang for what he has done, but as a sergeant of the local police, who is unable to withhold his sympathy entirely, tells him, they no longer hang people in Ireland. Francie tells this story, he does not know how many years later, from the institution in which he will spend the rest of his life.

The power of McCabe's novel undeniably arises in part from the sheer force of its grisly subject matter. Yet if this were all, the novel would possess only the power to shock and, ultimately, to repel. *The Butcher Boy* works at much deeper and more satisfying levels.

In part, this may be attributed to McCabe's unobtrusive mastery of structure. The motif of butchery, including its complex relationship to the theme of betrayal, and the variations on pig imagery provide strong organizing principles, in addition to their functions at the level of content. The partial revelation of the novel's denouement at the beginning is a highly effective compositional device, contributing to an air of inevitability that approaches the tragic.

That air of inevitability is supported by the novel's sheer narrative drive, as Francie is carried relentlessly to his fate. Yet this drive is always under the firm control of an artist. The turn that determines Francie's irreversible isolation, Joe's assertion that he and Francie are no longer friends, is placed at almost the exact center of the novel. The novel is also full of formal echoes. Francie's time in the home repeats his father's childhood experience; his time in the mental institution mirrors his mother's stay at "the garage." Francie's claim, while in the home, that he has had religious visions finds an echo in the Traynor girl's claim, on the weekend of the Cuban missile crisis, that the Blessed Virgin Mary is about to make an appearance in Francie's hometown.

It is in the treatment of Francie, however, that McCabe achieves his greatest triumph. The complexity of the character contributes to the tonal richness of the novel, as humorous as it is horrific, and—a most impressive accomplishment—never more harrowing than humane. At his most brutal, Francie never moves beyond the boundaries of the reader's sympathy. The tears that stream down Francie's face at the end of the novel certainly suggest a kind of purification; they may also find a counterpart in the response of the reader.

W. P. Kenney

Sources for Further Study

Chicago Tribune. July 11, 1993, XIV, p. 4.
Library Journal. CXVIII, May 1, 1993, p. 116.

Los Angeles Times Book Review. June 13, 1993, p. 6.
The New York Review of Books. XL, October 7, 1993, p. 28.
The New York Times Book Review. XCVIII, May 30, 1993, p. 9.
The New Yorker. LXIX, August 23, 1993, p. 160.
The Observer. March 21, 1993, p. 62.
Publishers Weekly. CCXL, April 5, 1993, p. 62.
The Times Literary Supplement. April 24, 1993, p. 21.
The Washington Post Book World. XXIII, May 16, 1993, p. 4.

THE CHILDREN OF MEN

Author: P. D. James (1920-   )
First published: 1992, in Great Britain
Publisher: Alfred A. Knopf (New York). 241 pp. $22.00
Type of work: Novel
Time: The year 2021
Locale: England

A futuristic novel about a world in which children have not been born for a quarter of a century, set in a Britain ruled by a dictator who suddenly is challenged by five unlikely rebels

> *Principal characters:*
> THEODORE (THEO) FARON, an Oxford historian who unintentionally becomes mentor and leader of the rebels
> XAN LYPPIATT, Warden of England, the country's dictator and Faron's cousin
> JULIAN, one of the rebels, who draws Theo into the group and becomes the first woman to conceive since 1995
> ROLF, her husband
> LUKE, a former Anglican priest, her lover and the father of her child
> MIRIAM, a Jamaican, one of the rebels and a midwife

The Children of Men is P. D. James's twelfth novel since the 1962 *Cover Her Face*, a book that critics and readers compared to works by Marjory Allingham, Agatha Christie, Dorothy Sayers, and other writers of classic detective fiction. Since this auspicious debut, James has ignored the familiar constraints of the mystery genre to produce denser, more complex narratives in which the puzzle to be solved is only one of many narrative and thematic elements. Further, in character development she always moves beyond the stereotypical whodunit probing of motive to psychological analysis, and her settings are not only suitable venues for crimes but also breeding places for social and moral conflicts that disturb people's psyches, such as guilt and remorse, the inability to relate to others, and the unexpected emergence of love.

After seven such full-length fictions that added luster both to the genre and to her reputation, James in 1980 produced *Innocent Blood*, an atypical novel in which neither of her detectives, Adam Dalgliesh and Cordelia Gray, is present. Not a whodunit but a search for identity by an eighteen-year-old girl who was adopted at birth and wants to learn the identity of her biological parents, it received mixed reviews. Importantly, though, reviewers treated it as a mainstream novel rather than merely as a genre work, thereby according James a degree of attention she long deserved. Two years later, in *The Skull Beneath the Skin* (1982), James reverted, as she put it, "to the traditional detective story with a closed circle of suspects," but at the same time "bringing these well-worn conventions up to date . . . confronting them with the courage, the dispassionate intelligence, and the cool common sense of my young contemporary, female detective." Not as prolific as most detective-fiction writers, she produced only two more novels in the 1980's, mysteries featuring Scotland Yard's Dalgliesh, an introspective and detached man, a sometimes poet whose life has been permanently scarred by a central tragedy, the death of his wife and only child (a son) in childbirth.

In 1992, James embarked on her fourth decade in the craft with *The Children of Men*, a totally different mainstream novel with no detective-fiction conventions but with themes and characters that recall her previous books. A futuristic work set in England during 2021, it portrays a world in which women no longer can conceive. Babies have not been born since 1995, called Year Omega. For some time after the apparent onset of this universal infertility, hope persisted, but when the Omegas (children of 1995) reached sexual maturity, they proved to be infertile. Nevertheless, they are the elite of this dying society, fawned over and studied to the point that many have become arrogant and cruel, even joining marauding gangs (called Painted Faces) that waylay travelers and engage in banal rituals as preludes to murder and destruction. There is a pervasive negativism and malaise among their elders, with the most desperate of them committing suicide and others finding solace in the continuing reproductive abilities of cats, treating kittens like their own newborn and having them—and even dolls—baptized. The established churches moved in the mid-1990's "from the theology of sin and redemption to a less uncompromising doctrine: corporate social responsibility coupled with a sentimental humanism." By 2021, all but the largest have been abandoned, and only a few evangelists prosper, one of whom has the Beatles' "All You Need Is Love" as her theme song.

Middle-aged Oxford historian Theodore (Theo) Faron, whose diary entries make up much of the book, is the story's protagonist and moral center, observing with despair the social and economic decay that pervades Britain's infertile, increasingly phleg-matic population. He recalls how the sciences and particularly medicine, which were the people's gods, promised relief but failed to determine why the deadly phenomenon occurred and come up with a cure. "For all our knowledge, our intelligence, our power, we can no longer do what the animals do without thought," Theo notes in his diary, and then suggests that the decadence of the early 1990's may be the cause. For fifteen years, his cousin and childhood companion, the oddly named Xan Lyppiatt, has been Warden of England, originally elected but now a despotic ruler supported by a massive security network and private army. Having served briefly as an observer-adviser at the Warden's council meetings, Theo has become an apolitical loner, turning to his Victorian studies as a retreat from personal sorrows (remorse over accidentally killing his baby daughter and the subsequent breakup of his marriage). His passive stability comes to an end, however, when an erstwhile student asks him to intercede with Xan on behalf of a small resistance group, the Five Fishes.

Julian is one of them. The other renegades are Rolf, her husband; Miriam, a former midwife; Luke, an Anglican priest without a parish; and Gascoigne, a long-distance truck driver and explosives expert. They want Theo to ask Xan to hold elections, call a halt to mandatory semen testing and gynecological examinations (from which Julian and Luke are exempt because they are physical rejects due to her withered arm and his epilepsy), end the Quietus (a supposedly voluntary mass-suicide program for the elderly), improve conditions at an island penal colony and stop sending convicted offenders there, and give civil rights to Sojourners (immigrant laborers) and cease deporting them when they reach the age of sixty. Though he believes that the outcome is predictable, Theo meets with the Warden and his Council. Xan warns him: "Tell your friends, whoever they are, to be sensible. If they can't be sensible, tell them to be prudent. I'm not a tyrant, but I can't afford to be merciful. Whatever is necessary to do, I shall do."

Lacking prudence, the quintet circulates a manifesto setting forth their demands, a foolhardy act to which Theo reacts unsympathetically. Thinking that most people "carried their burden of sorrow and regret with such fortitude as they could muster," he wonders, "by what right did the Five Fishes seek to impose upon these stoical dispossessed the futile burden of heroic virtue?" In other words, he is questioning the purpose of resistance and rebellion in a world without a future.

Notwithstanding such skepticism toward the Five Fishes, Theo has become increasingly disturbed about his cousin's regime, though without being able to offer credible alternatives. Philosophical musings become moot, however, when Miriam tells him that Julian is pregnant. She assures him that this is not a false alarm, one of the imagined pregnancies to which women have been increasingly prone since Year Omega. At about the same time, Gascoigne is captured while setting explosives to destroy a Quietus bridge. The rebel group is imperiled, certain that torture will lead Gascoigne (who is unaware of the pregnancy) to reveal their identities and whereabouts. Still, they are determined to remain free at least until the child is born. The second half of the novel, therefore, is a compelling narrative of fugitives on the run, risking capture to obtain provisions and transportation. James is at her best in this second part, for she is creating situations, like those in her other books, that dramatize (as she said in an interview) "this sense of the extraordinary fragility of life." Also, focusing now on a smaller number of people, she develops them as credible, three-dimensional human beings.

Rather than strengthening the rebels' ties to one another and to their common cause, the pending birth exposes the tenuousness of their commitment and their individual weaknesses. Rolf, the putative father, revels in his singularity, not wanting the Warden to "take over," proclaiming the birth to the world on television and "showing my child to the nation"; that, he announces, is "for me to do, not him." To Theo's comment that the "birth is the concern of the whole world" and the baby "belongs to mankind," Luke replies, "The child belongs to God." Theo at first thinks that Miriam supports Rolf's position because she wants to be "midwife to the first of a new race," but he soon realizes that she is completely selfless, confident in her skill and determined to respect Julian's wishes. As their desperate odyssey continues, Rolf becomes increasingly authoritarian and even looks forward to replacing Xan: "If they want my sperm they'll have to take me. They can't have one without the other. I could do the job as well as he does." Theo charges him with inconsistency and betrayal, for the course of action he proposes after his takeover ironically exposes him as being little different from Xan.

After an attack by a gang of Painted Faces in which Luke is the sacrificial victim, Rolf learns that Julian is not carrying his child but Luke's. Devastated, he deserts, shifting his allegiance to "the source of power," which, says Julian, always has fascinated him. His caring more for the group than for her, she explains, had made her want to punish him and had turned her to Luke in what she calls an act of self-indulgence. Theo is dismayed and labels the whole situation tawdry.

His disappointment with her revelation is profound because of his growing respect and love for her; he already has come to understand her insistence on having the child in private rather than under the aegis of Xan, a personification of evil. Although her obstinacy so far has cost the lives of two of the five—including the baby's father—she trusts that eventually goodwill will prevail. Indeed, her faith is rewarded then a healthy boy is born, but then Miriam goes in search of food and water, and the Grenadiers, Xan's militia, kill her.

Soon after, there is the inevitable confrontation between Xan and Theo. The Warden comes forward alone, his gun in a holster and the glittering emblem of authority, the "wedding ring of England," on a finger of his left hand. Unaware that the birth has occurred, he has come to take Julian, preside over her care and that of the child, and then be married to her. He asks Theo to return to the Council as his lieutenant. When Theo refuses, Xan aims to shoot. Theo also has a gun, however, and he is the better marksman; he kills his cousin with a shot through the heart. He removes Xan's ring, and when the Council members and Grenadiers emerge from the forest, he raises it, deliberately places it on a finger, and then shows the back of his hand to them—a defiant yet instinctive gesture "to assert authority and ensure protection."

Later, reflecting on the power now within his grasp, he tentatively removes the ring but then replaces it. When Julian says, "That wasn't made for your finger," he replies, "It's useful for the present. I shall take it off in time." As the first exercise of his new authority, he christens the baby, making the sign of the cross on the boy's forehead "with a thumb wet with his own tears and stained with [Julian's] blood." If not at hand, political as well as spiritual redemption is a likely prospect. That James wants to conclude her grim look into the future optimistically is apparent from the titles of the two books into which she divides her novel; whereas she calls the first "Omega," the second is "Alpha."

Julian's stubborn denial of reality during the fugitives' hapless flight and Theo's reluctant but total embrace of both a cause and its people exemplify a central credo of P. D. James. Though "personal tragedy and in particular physical pain can break anybody," she said in 1986, "we all need to believe that love is stronger than death, that the human spirit is indestructible, can surmount almost anything that fate can throw against it." Indeed, the statement could serve as an epigraph for *The Children of Men*.

Gerald H. Strauss

Sources for Further Study

The Christian Science Monitor. March 16, 1993, p. 14.
Commonweal. CXX, April 23, 1993, p. 26.
Locus. XXX, April, 1993, p. 17.

Los Angeles Times Book Review. April 4, 1993, p. 12.
New Scientist. CXXXVII, March 20, 1993, p. 41.
The New York Times Book Review. XCVIII, March 28, 1993, p. 23.
The New Yorker. LXIX, March 22, 1993, p. 111.
Time. CXLI, March 1, 1993, p. 69.
The Times Literary Supplement. September 25, 1992, p. 26.
The Wall Street Journal. February 19, 1993, p. A12.

CITY POET
The Life and Times of Frank O'Hara

Author: Brad Gooch (1953-   )
Publisher: Alfred A. Knopf (New York). Illustrated. 532 pp. $30.00
Type of work: Literary biography
Time: 1926-1966
Locale: Massachusetts, Michigan, New York City, and Europe

An exhaustive, fact-filled biography of Frank O'Hara, one of the most innovative of modern American writers

Principal personages:
> FRANCIS (FRANK) O'HARA, "New York School" poet and curator at the Museum of Modern Art
> LARRY RIVERS, a painter, his friend and lover
> JOHN ASHBERY,
> JAMES SCHUYLER, and
> KENNETH KOCH, his friends and fellow "New York School" poets
> JANE FREILICHER and
> GRACE HARTIGAN, painters, his friends and muses
> VINCENT WARREN, a ballet dancer, his lover

Since his accidental death in 1966 at the age of forty, Frank O'Hara has been surrounded by a gauze of myth that has effectively silenced serious evaluation of his poetry and sustained documentation of his life. Only Marjorie Perloff's careful and important study of his work in relation to contemporary New York artists and modernist writers, *Frank O'Hara: Poet Among Painters* (1977), succeeds in clearing a path through the tangle of anecdotes in which O'Hara has mostly lived. In various memoirs he has been portrayed as an intensely vital urban sprite who nevertheless brooded darkly about mortality and actively courted death himself. Alternatively, he has been reduced to a propulsive, campy Pan, gulping a breakfast vodka and grapefruit juice, dashing off his occasional "I do this I do that" poems on lunch breaks from his job at the Museum of Modern Art before heading downtown for yet another bout of boozing and erotic sparring with Greenwich Village artists at the Cedar Tavern or the San Remo Bar. Academic critics have largely been responsible for perpetuating this latter view of O'Hara as a negligible if witty writer of impromptu verse for a small, incestuous circle of friends, a dilettante in both artistic and literary worlds.

Both views inadequately capture the richness and interest of O'Hara's poetry and personality, and to some extent Brad Gooch's biography does offer a more comprehensive picture of the artist. It lays to rest certain popular myths while supplying foundational support for others. Moreover, in its sheer amplitude the book captures something of its subject's unbridled generosity, the seemingly limitless flow of O'Hara's talk, its capacious range and suggestive juxtapositions. Gooch has assembled the results of many interviews, and readers can now know exactly what films O'Hara saw and with whom, what music he listened to as a boy with his family, what bars he frequented as a Navy Shore Patrol officer in San Francisco, what friends he proposi-tioned and with what results. The book is astonishingly easy and enjoyable to read, full of incidents and personalities both comic and pathetic, a kind of high-level gossip. What is sadly missing in the recital of facts, however, is any real sense of O'Hara's enthusiasm, his high-spirited irreverence and poisonous wit. Again and again O'Hara's friends testify to the poet's richly affectionate nature, his charm, his passionate attentiveness to people, art, cities. Little of this comes across. Gooch is a plodder, choosing to place pertinent material from the life in a clear chronological connection with the actual work, but without registering much of a reaction to the frequently melodramatic nature of the events he narrates. His neutrality is very likely a deliberate rhetorical choice to counter earlier partisan accounts, yet the biography could do with a more argumentative edge. Gooch fails to offer much of a case for O'Hara's significance as a poet or his originality as an artist. He does not argue for the innovative way (intoxicating to younger poets such as David Shapiro and Daniel Berrigan) that O'Hara transformed his life into his poems, for his nonchalant craft in blending the two and creating, as critic Helen Vendler has said, "a new species." O'Hara's readers will not find here any particular analysis of *why* some of these poems are among the most loved of any written in the last century.

The only point on which Gooch does mount something like an argument is O'Hara's homosexuality. Practically every interviewee is asked to weigh in on the question of O'Hara's sexuality. If Gooch does have a thesis, it is to show that O'Hara was suppressed as a young Catholic boy, but once away from the provincial Massachusetts town of his youth and embarked on the journey to Harvard University, New York City, and Europe, he could freely express his gay identity and become the great gay "city poet" of midcentury, the logical successor to Walt Whitman. The introverted, earnest, well-read mama's boy could evolve into the witty, gregarious avant-gardist of art and sex. Gooch catalogs O'Hara's male love affairs assiduously, from the passionate and artistically productive relationships with painter Larry Rivers and dancer Vincent Warren to the turbulent, often violent couplings with men met in streets, bars, and subway lavatories. One learns that O'Hara glorified straight males, pursued an episodic and compulsive promiscuity, and eroticized the teaching of younger men who throughout his life gathered enthusiastically around him.

All of this fills in important gaps in the biography, though the detailed accounts of O'Hara's drunken evenings in bed with this or that reluctant or eager partner can become, after a time, deadening. More illuminating would have been to tease out the warmth, humanity, and romantic sentiment of O'Hara's sexual life, since these overwhelmingly color his poetry. O'Hara knew that he worked best as a love poet, that he was most prolific when he was in love: His two years with Vincent Warren (1959-1960) resulted in more than one hundred lyrics, his first openly gay love poems. During the next two years, after their breakup, he wrote fifty poems, in 1964 fourteen, in 1965 two, in 1966 one. When romance deserted him, the muse soon followed.

Still, the mercurial figure of O'Hara does transcend the stodgy handling of his biography. Readers see the young Francis in his youth, surrounded by loving parents and doting aunts (teachers, librarians, nuns), reading widely (especially James Joyce), playing the piano and pronouncing grandly on music (his favorites Sergei Rachman-inoff and Paul Hindemith), and avidly going to the cinema. Fastidious and bookish, ferocious in his passions and discoveries, O'Hara also educated himself about art.

He left this hothouse existence to join the Navy in 1944, and his two-year tour did much to pry him away from his family and his religion and give him a new self-reliance. Yet it was really his years at Harvard, from 1946 to 1950, that shaped the man he was to become. When his father died suddenly during the winter of 1947, O'Hara turned his back on his increasingly alcoholic and dependent mother and charged into the heady atmosphere of those postwar years in Cambridge. Within a year O'Hara had turned from music to poetry, staking out his identity as a writer. Francis had become Frank.

Cambridge in the late 1940's boasted a literary scene of compelling brilliance: John Ashbery, Robert Bly, John Updike, Alison Lurie, Harold Brodkey, Donald Hall, Robert Creeley, Kenneth Koch, and Adrienne Rich were all O'Hara's contemporaries there, and a young John Ciardi presided over a creative writing class where literary battles erupted between Audenites (O'Hara) and Yeatsians (Hall). O'Hara's meeting with Ashbery was the crucial event for redirecting his poetry from dandyism to a more robust eclecticism, in which films, popular culture, music, and literature came together in a surrealistic wash of witty, polished verse. He developed at this time too the writing habits that would remain throughout his career and that continually amazed his friends. He wrote quickly and revised sparingly; he loved to write in public or in collaboration; he was notoriously careless about keeping copies of his poems (many survive simply because they were written out in letters to friends who kept them); he was, despite a competitive streak and a healthy ego, largely unconcerned about publication and indifferent to reviews. He wrote, so it seemed, as naturally as he talked or breathed—he called it "playing the typewriter."

After graduation, Ciardi arranged a position for him in the University of Michigan's Creative Writing Program, and in his first ten months in Ann Arbor he produced ninety poems and two plays. In the Midwest he came under the spell of William Carlos Williams and wrote poems of greater simplicity and directness, with more colloquial, less mannered speech and rhythms.

Gooch is at his best in conjuring up the New York Village scene in those early and mid 1950's, the jazz clubs, the artists' bars, the long nights of epic drinking and smoking and fighting. O'Hara was drawn to the world of the Cedar Tavern, where the New York School expressionists, now giving rise to a second generation of artists like Larry Rivers and Jane Freilicher, proved a generous audience for his poems. He proved just as stimulating to their painting. He had a completely assured eye and a ready tongue; his focus was always on the things he loved, and what he loved he loved ardently. He had the power to tell artists where they had been and to suggest where that might lead. No wonder they loved him, painted him, and collaborated with him.

New York was the inspiration for O'Hara's poetry—its art and artists, but also the city itself. He wrote, in "Meditations in an Emergency," that "I can't even enjoy a blade of grass unless I know/ there's a subway handy, or a record store or some/ other sign that people do not totally *regret* life." He fed on the urban noise and crush and energy, the ballet, the theaters, the galleries, the gay bars, the friends. Beginning with a job selling postcards at the Museum of Modern Art (MOMA) and writing short reviews for *Art News*, he worked his way up to be an associate curator at MOMA, handling the first exhibitions of contemporary American art to travel internationally. Although unorthodox in practice and without proper academic credentials, he did know the artists and their work intimately, and he put together a string of successful European touring shows that effectively placed Abstract Expressionism on the map as a peculiarly American contribution to international culture.

Yet as eventful and demanding as this full-time job was, O'Hara managed to make it merge with his hectic social life outside the museum. He was magnetic, the bridge between people otherwise separated. He mixed Downtown with Uptown, even East Coast and West Coast. His readings with Allen Ginsberg and championing of Gregory Corso made him more popular among the San Francisco Beats than were other New York School poets.

At about this time (1959) O'Hara wrote his mock-manifesto "Personism," originally intended for Donald Allen's anthology but published in LeRoi Jones's little magazine *Yugen*. Prompted by a beery lunch with Jones where the two poets decided to "think of a movement," O'Hara, fortified by a bourbon and water and Rachmaninoff's Third Piano Concerto, sat down and wrote:

> After lunch with LeRoi Jones on August 27, 1959, a day in which I was in love with someone . . . I went back to work and wrote a poem for this person. While I was writing it I was realizing that if I wanted to I could use the telephone instead of writing the poem, and so Personism was born.

As glib as this sounds, it had substantial implications for O'Hara's language. He valued the informal diction of telephone conversations over the verbal structure of the printed page. Poetic language should come spontaneously to mind under the impact of immediate experience and not sound as if, by virtue of authoritative, carefully constructed verses, it has the power to register some metaphysical truth free from the contingencies of the poet's life. Language does not assert its own authority or impose some order on experience, but moves with it, reacts to it, captures the vibrancy of the moment, the concrete details, the authentic sounds. This all has its own music, and O'Hara was nothing if not a musical writer.

The City Lights edition of *Lunch Poems* (1964) was probably the first volume of O'Hara's to get him a wider public, but it was Donald Allen's landmark collection *The New American Poetry: 1945-1960* (1960) that dared to present O'Hara's poems as anything other than amusing coterie trifles. A volume that Ginsberg hailed as a "great blow for poetic liberty," the anthology made available the work of post-World War II poets who had charted a new and bold direction: away from T. S. Eliot and the pantheon of modernist masters, away from institutionalized high culture and toward jazz, abstract painting, popular culture. Grouped into New York School, Black Mountain,

Beat Generation, and San Francisco Renaissance, the forty-four poets in Allen's anthology raised fresh voices to counter the elegance and formalism of the prevailing academic tradition.

Yet in O'Hara's last years his world and his friends were changing. Old pals were marrying and withdrawing from the bohemian life; Pop Art and Neo-Realism were the new passwords. Andy Warhol (whom Willem de Kooning blamed for the death of painting) had arrived and rejected the expressive brushstroke in favor of mechanical means of representation. O'Hara was uncomfortable with these changes but neatly sidestepped into sculpture and continued his frenetic round of openings, retrospectives, readings, and Fire Island weekends. It was during one of these weekends in July, 1966, that O'Hara, after a night of eating, drinking, and dancing, walked into the path of a beach buggy and died a day later of internal injuries. Shocking as it was, the accidental nature of his death seems oddly in keeping with O'Hara's insistence on the contingent, the moment-by-moment experience of living. Yet it is paradoxical, too, that this poet who was so vitally attentive to each moment was extinguished in a moment of inattention. In 1956, rocked by Jackson Pollock's death in a car accident at age forty-four, he had written a poem about his own funeral in which he urged people not to come, a poem that ends with lines that capture as well as any the poet's credo for living:

> When I die, don't come, I wouldn't want a leaf
> to turn away from the sun—it loves it there.
> There's nothing so spiritual about being happy
> but you can't miss a day of it, because it doesn't last.

Thomas J. Campbell

Sources for Further Study

Booklist. LXXXIX, May 15, 1993, p. 1670.
Boston Globe. July 13, 1993, p. 30.
Library Journal. CXVIII, May 15, 1993, p. 68.
Los Angeles Times Book Review. June 27, 1993, p. 3.
The New Republic. CCIX, August 2, 1993, p. 33.
The New York Times Book Review. XCVIII, June 20, 1993, p. 18.
The New Yorker. LXIX, July 19, 1993, p. 71.
Publishers Weekly. CCXL, May 17, 1993, p. 57.
San Francisco Chronicle. July 11, 1993, p. REV1.
The Washington Post Book World. XXIII, August 29, 1993, p. 5.

COLLECTED EARLY POEMS, 1950-1970

Author: Adrienne Rich (1929-   )
Publisher: W. W. Norton (New York). 435 pp. $27.50
Type of work: Poetry

Adrienne Rich's early poems are assembled in one volume that traces the accomplishment and development of this important American poet

Adrienne Rich's *Collected Early Poems, 1950-1970* is an impressive collection. The mode is primarily lyric, although a few of the poems have narrative elements and some are strong thematic statements. One critic, Helen Vendler, has divided Rich's poetry into the psychological and the didactic. The first two sections in this collection are decidedly psychological, but the third, "Snapshots of a Daughter-in-Law," shifts the balance to the didactic poems; in these poems Rich often takes a strong feminist stance. Rich's poetry tends to be direct and forceful, with little of the mystification of such poets as James Merrill and none of the abstruse learning of a poet like Robert Lowell. Her poems are also not structurally complex; she tends to use the simile more than any other figure and to use a loose iambic meter, although many of the poems after "Snapshots of a Daughter-in-Law" are in free verse. In addition, Rich does not use difficult language or private symbolism but creates a speaker who confronts or examines the problems of living a genuine and full life; that speaker does, however, consistently reject the call of an inhuman ideal. Rich has a reputation as a feminist poet, but this collection demonstrates her power and shows her to be not only one of the finest contemporary poets but also one who is continually expanding her range and changing her style.

The first poem in the collection is in the section "Change of World," and it identifies the speaker and her world memorably. "Storm Warnings" portrays both outer and inner weather. The outside weather cannot be resisted; "clocks and weatherglasses cannot alter" it. It will penetrate "the unsealed aperture." The poem ends with a recognition that one must endure the onslaught of weather; nothing can prevent the intrusion of this outside force. Those who "live in troubled regions" take the necessary steps, but the force of cold will penetrate and make its presence apparent. One of Rich's greatest achievements is to create a speaker who acknowledges the imperfections and dangers of the world in which she must exist but refuses to be overwhelmed by the situation.

"Aunt Jennifer's Tigers" is a more programmatic poem that contrasts the roles of women and men. The first stanza presents the tigers Aunt Jennifer is working in wool as active and unafraid. In contrast, Aunt Jennifer is not free; she finds it hard to pull even an "ivory needle." "The massive weight of Uncle's wedding band" oppresses her. The weight of the ring and the "ivory needle" are wonderful images of the oppression of ordinary things. The first stanza resolves the conflict by showing Aunt Jennifer's creation, the tigers, continuing to be active, proud, and "unafraid," while Aunt Jennifer remains incomplete; she is "mastered" by her husband. The poem makes a statement that is echoed by many feminist critics: Women's creations survive even if the creators are defeated by a patriarchal society.

"At a Bach Concert" is the most interesting poem in the first section. The poem presents two nameless speakers contrasting the art of the day, which is "out of love with life," with the art of Johann Sebastian Bach, which represents a love that is "not pity." The experience of the Bach concert alters their perception of love as it "renews belief in love yet masters feeling." The last stanza clarifies the contrasting elements. "A too-compassionate art is half an art./ Only such proud restraining purity/ Restores the else-betrayed, too human heart." It is an impressive poem that connects love to the control of form rather than the exigencies of passion. Furthermore, the poem itself displays just that control and measured form in its regular meter and alternating rhyme.

"Afterward" seems to be a personal poem in which the speaker contrasts the uncompromising early life with the necessary acceptance of an imperfect world and self which age brings. "We who know limits now give room/ To one who grows to fit her doom." Many of the early poems deal with the subject of time and the necessary but begrudging accommodations one must make to it.

The next section, "The Diamond Cutters," contains a number of fine poems. "Living in Sin" is one of Rich's most amusing poems; it contrasts the expectations of an ideal love affair with the sordid realities—another attempt to explore the gaps between the ideal and the real. The speaker "thought the studio would keep itself;/ no dust upon the furniture of love." There would be "a plate of pears,/ a piano with a Persian shawl, a cat/ stalking the picturesque amusing mouse/ had risen at his urging." The reality, however, is very different. There is "the milkman's tramp" at five each morning, and the picturesque mouse becomes a pair of threatening "beetle eyes." Above all, her lover would yawn and find the piano out of tune while she turned to necessary dusting. The last few lines point to a resolution. That evening she is back in love, "though not so wholly," since "she woke sometimes to feel the daylight coming/ like a relentless milkman up the stairs." The simile is a perfect modern figure that ironically portrays the coming of dawn as forbidding rather than promising. It also contains not the expected visual image of the coming of dawn but an aural image—the pounding steps of a milkman.

The last poem in the section, "The Diamond Cutters," metaphorically compares the cutting of a diamond to creating a poem. The cutter must "be serious, because/ The stone may have contempt/ For too familiar hands." So too must the poet respect his or her material if the poem is to live. The poet and the cutter must be "hard of heart" to "liberate" what is there and not impose "desire" upon the object and ruin it. The last stanza speaks of the necessary judgment of the work of the creator as "false" or "true," and ironically points not to the joy of creation but to the work that remains, since "Africa/ Will yield you more to do."

The title poem of "Snapshots of a Daughter-in-Law" is a very direct and effective feminist poem. The ten sections of the poem portray the state of women. In the first section, the protagonist's mind is "mouldering like a wedding-cake,/ heavy with useless experience." Her accomplishments are of no use, and she has no true role in the world. Other sections bring in women from history such as Emily Dickinson and

Mary Wollstonecraft. The enemy is clear: "Time is male." Time in the earlier poems was an enemy of the ideal, but now it speaks of patriarchal oppression. The last section, however, suggests the triumph rather than the subjection of women.

> Her mind full to the wind, I see her plunge
> breasted and glancing through the currents,
> taking the light upon her
> at least as beautiful as any boy
> or helicopter,
>   poised, still coming,
> her fine blades making the air wince
> but her cargo
> no promise then:
> delivered
> palpable
> ours.

The metaphor of women as a helicopter is startling, especially since Rich's earlier use of the simile is conventional, and the announcement of their arrival into their own universe is powerful and convincing.

The next section, "Necessities of Life," shows feminism to be a central concern of Rich. There is, for example, a poem on Emily Dickinson, "I Am in Danger—Sir—." The speaker in the poem is searching for the true Emily Dickinson; is she "half-cracked," as some would have it? Or is she to be found "afterward famous in garbled versions" or "mothballed in Harvard"? The poem then presents Dickinson doing daily tasks, but she is also one "for whom the word was more/ than a symptom—/ a condition of being." The final definition of Dickinson is that she "chose to have it out at last/ on [her] own premises," a woman who resisted the usual roles and was willing to face condemnation in order to create her self through her art.

The title poem, "The Necessities of Life," traces the different stages of growth of the speaker. She moves from her earliest existence as a "dot" to such roles as "Jonah" and "Mary Wollstonecraft." In order to preserve herself, she has made herself "unappetizing." Leaving those days and roles behind, however, she can now "dare to inhabit the world/ trenchant in motion as an eel, solid/ as a cabbage-head." The contrasting similes of motion and stasis suggest something of the power the speaker has found. The last few lines show her coming into her own as houses call to her "like old women knitting, breathless/ to tell their tales."

"To Judith, Taking Leave" is a poem that speaks of love between women. The poem begins in separation, with only a letter to link them. The speaker then describes and praises the woman to whom the poem is dedicated. Their love is described as something emerging from earlier roles, when they were "shared out in pieces/ to men, children, memories." They will no longer be "cramped sharers/ of a bitter mutual secret," but will have a higher and fuller union that is described in an effective simile as "two eyes in one brow."

"Women" is another poem on the roles of women. The first two women are in a familiar female role, sewing. The first sews "for the procession," in which she will reveal "all her nerves"; everything she is will be visible before the world. The second sews "a seam over her heart which has never healed entirely." These two are clearly victims. Yet the third sister is not sewing, and "her stockings are torn." She does not play any assigned feminine role but is "gazing" at the possibilities of life "spreading westward far out on the sea," and she "is beautiful." The proper role of a woman is, then, to be a visionary instead of a victim and to refuse the trap of roles defined by society.

"Planetarium," in "The Will to Change," uses an historical figure, Caroline Herschel (1750-1848), to speak powerfully of women's oppression and creativity. In her ninety-eight years, Herschel discovered eight comets. The stars that she is exploring are described, however, as monsters—a common appellation for women, since any woman who attempted to be a scientist could only be a monster in the eyes of a male-dominated society. The last part of the poem shows the speaker affirming her self and her place in the universe. The art of the astronomer is now metaphorically linked to the art of poetry. "I am an instrument in the shape/ of a woman trying to translate pulsations/ into images   for the relief of the body/ and the reconstruction of the mind." Rich describes her role to be that of a prophet and healer. This feminist stance is very different from that of the psychological seeker of the first two sections. Furthermore, Rich no longer follows such models as W. H. Auden, W. B. Yeats, and Robert Frost. She announces her place as a truly independent poet and spokesperson for all who would open themselves to a reconstruction of the mind and body.

Collected Early Poems is likely to find a large audience, since it includes both elegant and powerful poems. In addition, Rich's poetic odyssey from well-crafted poems to direct social statements reflects the history of contemporary poetry. She moves from exploring the conflict between the ideal and the real to dealing with the problem of living more fully while acknowledging "the necessities of life." She seems to have abandoned most overt poetic techniques, such as regular meter, retaining only the simile. Yet the later poems in this collection have a directness and power that can be claimed by few contemporary poets.

James Sullivan

Sources for Further Study

Booklist. LXXXIX, December 1, 1992, p. 645.
Houston Post. April 25, 1993, p. C4.
Library Journal. CXVII, December, 1992, p. 144.
The New Republic. CCIX, November 8, 1993, p. 33.
The New York Times Book Review. XCVIII, November 7, 1993, p. 7.
Publishers Weekly. CCXXXIX, December 28, 1992, p. 61.
San Francisco Chronicle. April 18, 1993, p. REV3.

COLLECTED POEMS
1930-1993

Author: May Sarton (1912-   )
Publisher: W. W. Norton (New York). 542 pp. $27.50
Type of work: Poetry

> *This rich collection of poems, culled from six decades, marks the lifetime achievement of one of America's most noted writers*

May Sarton has authored over fifteen volumes of poetry, nineteen novels, several children's books, and a number of journals. Yet it is perhaps as a poet that she wishes to be remembered. Her *Collected Poems: 1930-1993* is a stunning testament to a lifetime achievement in a genre Sarton has always found "so much more a true work of the soul than prose" precisely because a "poem is primarily a dialogue with the self" (*Journal of a Solitude*, 1973). Containing close to three hundred poems, Sarton's *Collected Poems*, appearing in her eighty-first year, marks a lifetime devoted to this "dialogue with the self." Here Sarton explores her major themes and concerns: love and the vicissitudes of passion, the need for solitude and work, the art of poetry and the search for order it embodies, the psychological struggles of the solitary, and the necessary restoration of the self. An adroit metrist, Sarton writes most often in rhymed verse and traditional forms—iambic pentameter quatrains, heroic couplets, tercets, the ballad, and occasionally the villanelle. Yet in many of her travel poems she illustrates an ease with open form as well. While Sarton occasionally writes of national matters, particularly in her later work, domestic subjects and everyday details characterize the core of her poems, testifying to the importance of observation and awareness to a worthwhile solitary life.

Only three selections from Sarton's earliest book of poetry, *Encounter in April* (1937), find their way into the *Collected Poems*, yet each sets forth a tone and a style, a voice, typical of Sarton's later work. "First Snow," a seemingly simple, carefully metered and rhymed poem, parallels snow, a natural image, to a spiritual and emotional state, here both despair and desperate passion. "She Shall Be Called Woman" illustrates Sarton's feminist themes. A ten-part free-verse form, the poem focuses on the creation of woman and her awakening body, which links her to the curve of the earth. Passion and pride in all parts of her body—her nails, her hands, her breasts—mark the female consciousness. "Strangers" returns to traditional form—alternate-rhyme quatrains—and depicts the brief coupling of two people, introducing to Sarton's work the theme of love and separation, a recurring concern.

Of Sarton's early work, perhaps her best can be found in *The Lion and the Rose* (1948), represented by thirty-eight selections. Many of these are travel poems, focused on various sites in North America: Monticello, Charleston, Texas, the Colorado mountains, Boulder Dam. Some of these are landscape poems that reach toward transcendent meaning, exploring the inner self in relation to what the landscape symbolizes and discovering places of joy and solitude. One of these is "Of the

Seasons," capturing the beauty of the Sangre de Cristo Mountains in Santa Fe, New Mexico. Finding "the bronze and the violet" of the mountains in different seasons exhilarating, the poet evokes a spiritual experience at the end of the poem when in winter "the mountains iced/ Are burned again," representing "The Blood of Christ." Similarly, "The Lion and the Rose" draws rich natural images to symbolize physical passion (the lion) and spiritual love (the rose). With its short lines and two to three rhymes, the first stanza has a staccato effect, the end of passion. Midway in the poem a religious meaning emerges, and with it greater peace. The poet yields to "God of the empty room," repeating "Thy will be done" as a signal of her surrender. In the end, she finds "unearthly peace" and transcendent love: "The spiritual rose/ Flower among the snows."

While such spiritually rich meanings symbolized by landscape and natural elements are characteristic of Sarton's work, so also are feminist themes and the search for purity and order. Two other important selections with the latter concerns are the frequently anthologized: "My Sisters, O My Sisters" and "The Lady and the Unicorn," a poem based on the Cluny tapestries. "My Sisters, O My Sisters" comprises four parts. The first, in rhymed hexameter couplets, celebrates the struggle of women poets and writers: Dorothy Wordsworth, Emily Dickinson, Christina Rossetti, Sappho, and George Sand, among others. Freed from traditional female roles, the many writers named here each sacrificed some important experience in order to create. Sarton writes, "—they all know it,/ Something is lost, strained, unforgiven in the poet." Such women may be poor lovers, though good grandmothers; they may be "too powerful for men . . . too sensitive."

In part 2 Sarton explores the nurturing female roles of lover, mother, feeder, while part 3 introduces female archetypal figures, Eve and Mary, the creative that is countered by the destructive, the woman who loves "an only son/ As a lover loves, binding the free hands." In the final section of the poem, Sarton writes of the universal quest of women to find themselves, to join together and to "ask men's greatness back from men," the greatness given them by women's nurturing. Interestingly, parts 2 through 4 move away from the hexameter couplets to varied forms, including free verse.

Significantly different in tone and style, "The Lady and the Unicorn" is important for introducing themes that recur in Sarton's later poetry. An allegory of the quest for artistic expression and purity, "The Lady and the Unicorn" employs several incremental refrains and resembles a French rondel. The speaker is the unicorn, who bows his head to lie in the bed of "the lady woven into history"—that is, he is the mythical creature who succumbs to the real woman, in this case the poet. A poem using similar images is "Song Without Music," found in *The Leaves of the Tree* (1950), a selection of thirteen largely allegorical poems. There, however, what the unicorn seeks is pure, innocent love rather than artistic expression.

The title poem of *The Land of Silence* (1953) introduces a series of poems about spiritual quest. "Letter to an Indian Friend," which questions the friend on wisdom, evokes images of planting and harvesting silence, the peace that comes with meditation and stillness. "Of Prayer" follows this theme but links spiritual nourishment with creativity, the creative act with prayer. The "Prince of the Imagination" mentioned in the poem seems an echo of Percy B. Shelley's Spirit of Intellectual Beauty. Indeed, as in Shelley's "Hymn to Intellectual Beauty," the poet turns to a Platonic concept. The last lines speak of the

> Pure Idea that cannot break apart,
> Creator of children or the work of art.

"Because What I Want Most Is Permanence" echoes William Butler Yeats's "Sailing to Byzantium" in the poet's desire for the intensity and permanence of art, here expressed in the domestic image of building a fire "to bank the blaze within." In contrast to these spiritual and aesthetic concerns, a sonnet sequence near the end of *The Land of Silence* treats the stages of love from its narrow beginnings in fervid passion and longing to its erotic flowering and eventual dissolution or maturation. Entitled "These Images Remain," the sequence is noteworthy for its use of architectural images that reflect an attempt to abstract love into some essence or, at least, to see the growth and demise of passion framed as through an arch or a window.

In Time like Air (1958), *Cloud, Stone, Sun, Vine* (1961), and *A Private Mythology* (1966) form a midlife core in the *Collected Poems*. Most noteworthy from the first are "The Metaphysical Garden," a philosophical poem dedicated to the poet's father, George Sarton, an eminent scholar, and "The Frog, That Naked Creature," another landscape poem that parallels the humble, naked frog to the human soul that has yielded pride. The title poem raises metaphysical questions about the soul's suspension in the body. The central metaphor is that of sea salt, dissolved in water yet appearing again when the water dries. In contrast to such metaphysical concerns, "A Divorce of Lovers," a twenty-sonnet sequence that comprises most of the selections from *Cloud, Stone, Sun, Vine*, is rooted in the painful and earthy experience of love and heartbreak, what Sarton calls "love at the bone." The poet's journey here is from harshness and desperation through the storm of accusations and childish psychological games that mark the "divorce" to eventual solitude and peace. The images are domestic and personal. In "Moving In," which follows the sonnet sequence, the poet focuses on her new house, a symbol of her new life, and "that one fly buzzing on the air," an allusion to her still active pain and to Emily Dickinson's "I heard a Fly buzz—when I died—," which also links the mundane and the serious.

Of the poems in the middle segment of the *Collected Poems*, however, those of *A Private Mythology* are the most expansive. Travel poems abound, many in free verse; the poet's vision has clearly expanded through her travels to Japan, India, and Greece. Most stunning are the Japanese poems: "A Child's Japan," "A Country House," "Kyoko," "Japanese Prints," "Inn at Kyoto," "An Exchange of Gifts," and "Wood, Paper, Stone." Through vivid imagery and detail, these capture the ceremony of a tea ritual, the grace and beauty of sparse furnishings of Japanese houses. Changed by her experiences, the poet sees beauty now in details:

                    Neither a house,
                    Nor a garden
                    Nor a rock, nor a tree
                    Would ever look the same again.

While the selections from *As Does New Hampshire* (1967) are all short lyrics, grief and experiences of a "dark night" are reflected in several poems in *A Grain of Mustard Seed* (1971). "A Hard Death" calls for compassion and the wisdom to see God in others because death detaches us and makes us strangers. The poem probably originated in the death of Sarton's mother (regret in the poet's embattled relationship with her mother is alluded to in later poems). "The Silence" returns to the existential theme of life's emptiness, while "Annunciation" offers images of futility and death and has the Virgin Mary abandoned by God and the archangel after the announcement of her impregnating. "At Chartres" and "Once at Chartres" seek the comfort prayer and the church provide; the poet finds the church a mother that comforts in death. Perhaps the most important poem in this segment is "The Muse as Medusa," a powerful aesthetic and psychological statement about the cold, stony muse who nevertheless grants the poet creative power. Seen as a shadow self, Medusa is the dark, unfeeling self that the poet must confront in the creative act. Like other feminist poets, Sarton redefines myth for her own purposes, using the mythical figure of Medusa in a context that reclaims the Gorgon's power.

The dark imagery in such poems as "The Waves," "Beyond the Question," and "Invocation" in *A Grain of Mustard Seed* represents the poet's attempt to find expression for the shadow self, the force hidden in creative love and the creative act itself. *A Durable Fire* (1972) returns to images of light and green, life reborn in the soul after a struggle and a ten-year solitude. Love reappears, now a mature, autumn love celebrated in such poems as "A Chinese Landscape" and "Reeds and Water." The tree symbol, in earlier poems representing the self, recurs, now nourished from within. Angels as ministering symbols appear, one celebrated in the long sequence entitled "Letters to a Psychiatrist." "The Autumn Sonnets" explore new love and its growth.

Halfway to Silence (1980), *Letters from Maine* (1984), and *The Silence Now* (1988) come from Sarton's later years. Love remains a central theme, and Medusa returns, but now as a celebrated figure. Sarton's strong lyrical gift remains, despite her fear that winter (old age) is a "fallow time." Indeed, the later poems have a rich, ripe quality, partly emerging from the autumnal imagery but also found in the poet's willingness to strip away inessentials and write simple poems of love and loss, poems less embedded in allegory and metaphor. One of the most poignant is "The Cosset Lamb," where a lamb's innocence stuns the poet and leads her to offer a simple prayer:

                    For all that is so dear
                    And may be mauled,
                    For terror and despair
                    And for help near,
                    I weep, I am undone.

Such tenderness embodies a longing for meaning, a caring for order and nature, that strikes the reader throughout the *Collected Poems*. Indeed, this volume offers a testament to Sarton's maturing art, the wealth of her experiences, and the growth of her insight and wisdom. The reader who seeks a poetic guidebook to a remarkable solitary life spanning most of the twentieth century will find May Sarton's *Collected Poems* an important and rewarding volume.

Stella Nesanovich

Sources for Further Study

St. Louis Post-Dispatch. August 15, 1993, p. C5.
Seattle Times. January 9, 1994, p. E2.

COLLECTED POEMS, 1935-1992

Author: F. T. Prince (1912-   )
Publisher: The Sheep Meadow Press (Riverdale-on-Hudson, New York). 319 pp. Paperback
$13.95
Type of work: Poetry

An undervalued English poet, who ranks with W. H. Auden and Stephen Spender as a major poet of their generation, presents his collected works

Praised by T. S. Eliot, who published F. T. Prince's first long poem, "An Epistle to a Patron," in *The Criterion* late in 1935; encouraged by William Butler Yeats, whom he met in Dublin in 1937, to trust in happy thoughts and influenced by Yeats to cultivate a lifelong grasp of speech rhythms and a sense for the conversational logic of the verse paragraph; inspired by the works of modern French poets such as Arthur Rimbaud, Paul Valéry, Paul Verlaine, and St.-John Perse as well as the fiction of American writer Henry James; fortified with first-class honors in English at the University of Oxford; and, studious thinker and teacher that he became, committed to long intervals between publications—F. T. Prince slowly and gradually developed his lyrical talent and metrical genius. Today he stands as the last living poet of the greatest generation of English poets since the Romantics.

Whereas other poets of the 1930's such as Auden, Spender, and Christopher Isherwood were attracted to the political left, Prince converted to Catholicism. His poetry did not take on a doctrinal cast, however, even though the exotic aestheticism of his earliest poems cooled somewhat. The resulting seriousness and intensity benefits from this interesting mix of sensuous diction and moral gravity. For example, in "An Epistle to a Patron" the poet speaker addresses his "patron" as "A donor of laurel and of grapes, a font of profuse intoxicants." This kind of aesthetic paganism yields to the passionate religious feeling of "Soldiers Bathing":

> I feel a strange delight that fills me full
> Strange gratitude, as if evil itself were beautiful,
> And kiss the wound in thought, while in the west
> I watch a streak of red that might have issued from Christ's breast.

Although the modern reader will detect touches of late Pre-Raphaelite sensual religiosity in these lines, a second look will also evoke the tragic joy of Gerard Manley Hopkins at his most intense. The opposites of sense and spirit never cease to dance their all-consuming rhythms in Prince's verse.

Perhaps this is most evident in his "Apollo and the Sibyl," one of the last poems in a collection first published in 1954. This poem is based on the myth involving Apollo and the Sibyl of Cumae. The god granted her "as many years as there were grains in a certain heap of dust." She, however, forgot to ask for enduring youth. Had she accepted Apollo's love, eternal youth would have been hers. Refusing the god's desire, she lived on to become a prophetess, and at last "only a voice, haunting her sea cave at Cumae." In a brilliant dramatization, Prince has the disembodied voice of the Sibyl resonate in the "cave" of his poem, which echoes rhythms, cadences, and metrical patterns in a long tidal lament. The effect is both deeply sensuous and probingly spiritual. The waters lap ceaselessly as consciousness yearns for spiritual deliverance:

> —Questions of hope, despair, changes of mind. . . .
> Acceptance of the changeless mind!
> And now I sit and hide my face;
> And know that where the soft and rough tide hurries,
> The tide will rise and wash the rocks tomorrow;
> That cloud of an angelic dignity
> Will form and melt tomorrow—and tomorrow,
>
> While far out in the milky straits
> The black shape of a boat sits,
> And drags itself. . . .
> Wet flashes on dipped oars.

The Sibyl's endless vigil evokes Romantic echoes such as Percy Bysshe Shelley's famous closing stanza in *Prometheus Unbound* (1820), "To love, and bear; to hope, till Hope creates/ From its own wreck the thing it contemplates" and the late Romantic pathos of Alfred, Lord Tennyson's "The Lady of Shalott," "There she weaves by night and day/ A magic web with colors gay." But finally, there is a distinctly modern urgency in the tension between suffering and redemption in Prince's sonorous closing stanzas:

> I remain in my pain that is
> A golden distance endlessly,
>
> . . . .
> Outrageously more beautiful,
> The burning young tumescent sea,
>
> . . . .
> —And the sky opens
> Like a fan its vault of violent light, unfolding
> A wide and wingless path to the impossible.

Opposites are a dialectical challenge to Prince. They do not deconstruct into a deferred meaning that is food only for skeptical detachment. The voice of the Sibyl is historicized in the monologue, "The Old Age of Michelangelo." The great artist speaks for Prince's own struggle with the opposites of desire and faith that have rages in unabated confrontation:

> And now I have grown old,
> It is my own life, my long life I see
> As a combat against nature, nature that is our enemy
> Holding the soul a prisoner by the heel;
> And my whole anxious life I see
> As a combat with myself, that I do violence to myself,

> To bruise and beat and batter
> And bring under
> My own being,
> Which is an infinite savage sea of love.

Prince has his lighter vein and delights in the play of verse as well as its passion. In a collection of 1963, *The Doors of Stone*, he experimented with an Italian stanza first introduced to English poetry by Sir Thomas Wyatt. These stanzas, "Strambotti," enable Prince to exercise his dialectical imagination in a poised, cerebral dance of witty argument and rhyme. At the same time, the intensity of love hovers over the wit like a protective vapor:

> I am not lodged in such and such a street,
> But live in banishment with dust and stones.
> I wear these clothes you see for cold and heat,
> And yet I burn and shiver in my bones.
> Apparently I live, and work to eat,
> But inwardly I die of wounds and groans.
> And you know well that you can bring me balm,
> My pearl, to whom I pray with open palm.

F. T. Prince was born in South Africa of English parents. His love of the South African landscape of his childhood never left him and may account for his wanderlust, his lifelong wandering. He studied at Princeton University and served with British intelligence in Cairo during World War II; he has taught in English departments in Halifax and Jamaica, for one year at Washington University in St. Louis, and for two years at Brandeis University in Boston. His cosmopolitan life is reflected in his poetry, perhaps most impressively in "Drypoints of the Hasidim" (1975), a late and long poem of some four hundred lines. It is a measure of Prince's devotion to religious experience that he, a devout Catholic, should have been drawn to the intense inwardness of Jewish mysticism. It is also expressive of his interest in the other, his fascination with the exotic, the different, and demonstrates the commitment of his art to transcendent imagination.

On one level, the remoteness of the Hasidic Jews of Eastern Europe is conveyed with haunting imagery: "Dark hollow faces under caps/ in days and lands of exile." On another level, Prince is identifying his own life in exile, outward and inward: "To believe is above all to be in love,/ And suffer as men do who are in love." Critics have remarked that there are unspoken allusions to the Church in this "Jewish" poem, but the connections between Christianity and Judaism in this poem are not a matter of doctrinal counterpoint. What intrigues Prince is the closeness of that which appears remote, of the mysterious power of the religious impulse to raise and level all humankind ("The same in us, the same in them") and steel human beings "To endure and be silent,/ Reason, rejoice and pray;/ Die if you must."

There is a certain irony that this poet, one of the last of the moderns, should be so clearly identified with traditional values of high craft, religious transcendence, and historical continuity. His career reminds us that we do not stand in relation to the past exclusively in a landscape of revolutionary change. On the contrary, it is in our very experience of difference that we are finally reassured of our common humanity in time and thought.

Peter Brier

Sources for Further Study

Choice. XXXI, October, 1993, p. 293.
Library Journal. CXVIII, May 15, 1993, p. 72.
The Observer. April 25, 1993, p. 62.
The Spectator. CCLXXI, November 27, 1993, p. 36.
The Times Literary Supplement. August 27, 1993, p. 8.
The Virginia Quarterly Review. LXIX, Autumn, 1993, p. SS137.

COLLECTED POEMS, 1953-1993

Author: John Updike (1932-   )
Publisher: Alfred A. Knopf (New York). 387 pp. $27.50
Type of work: Poetry

John Updike brings together more than 350 of his poems, nearly 20 percent hitherto unpublished, exploring a variety of everyday subjects and demonstrating his mastery of poetic form

Most readers of contemporary highbrow literature are familiar with John Updike as the author of fifteen novels and several collections of short stories. Some may have run across his nonfiction as well in such prestigious periodicals as *The New Yorker* and *The Atlantic*, or perused his essays in collections such as *Hugging the Shore* (1983) and *Odd Jobs* (1991). Genuine devotees know that Updike has been a prolific poet as well, taking time out from his duties as a chronicler of American domestic and intellectual life to produce what he calls in the introduction to *Collected Poems, 1953-1993* the "beloved waifs" of his life's work as a writer. The aggregate of four decades spent playing with language, trying to give shape to stray observations of the world around him and the people who inhabit it, is brought together in a single handsomely constructed volume which shows throughout the author's loving touch.

Since 1953, Updike has been sending out his poetry to magazine editors for inclusion in both popular and scholarly journals. His work has appeared in such diverse places as *The American Scholar, Harper's, The Nation, Ladies' Home Journal, Poetry Review, Punch, Shenandoah, The Harvard Lampoon*, and *Scientific American*. He has seen fit on five previous occasions to collect his poetic creations, in *The Carpentered Hen and Other Poems* (1954), *Telephone Poles* (1958), *Midpoint and Other Poems* (1963), *Tossing and Turning* (1968), and *Facing Nature* (1985). Over the years, he has published more than a dozen chapbooks or special editions of individual works, usually occasional and celebratory in nature. *Collected Poems, 1953-1993* brings together more than 350 of Updike's works; in the volume Updike includes not only almost all that had appeared in other places but also nearly six dozen previously unpublished poems.

The significance of the collection should not, therefore, be underestimated. As a minimum, it serves as an introduction for readers unfamiliar with Updike's talents as a versifier to the multifarious nature of his poetic gifts. For those who have already encountered Updike's poetry in the earlier volumes, reading this volume will be like renewing acquaintances with old friends. For lifelong fans, the collection will probably replace the yellowing copies of paperback editions of *Telephone Poles*, *The Carpentered Hen and other Poems*, and *Midpoint and Other Poems*, volumes whose spines have probably cracked from old age and frequent perusal. *Collected Poems, 1953-1993* is Updike's alternative résumé, a reminder that he has had a choice of writing professions. While he has made his reputation (and his fortune) in prose, it has been a matter of authorial preference; for as this volume indicates, he could have achieved a measure of fame by his verse as well.

The collection of forty years' work reveals much about Updike's enduring interests: domestic relationships, sexuality, theological issues, the everyday world around him, and the not-so-everyday world encountered in travels. Even the world of science is transformed into poetry. Some may find his frank discussion of sexual matters offensive; Updike would likely reply that humanity is made up of body as well as mind, and that the flesh is something to be loved and celebrated, not ignored or written of as if it were an object of shame. Indeed, nothing seems taboo for Updike, but it is in his identification of the sacred in the everyday that he is especially gifted. In his poetry as in his fiction, Updike looks to isolate those things from the everyday world that suggest for humankind the way to happiness and salvation.

If there are overriding distinguishing characteristics to be identified in Updike's poetry, they are humor and style. The hundred-plus pages of light verse will make even the most cynical or sentimental reader smile often and occasionally laugh outright. Updike is a master of the sight rhyme and quick to take advantage of the oddities of the everyday world; it seems that almost anything can prompt him to dash off a few verses. As an example, his casual notice that someone named V. B. Wigglesworth had been named the Quick Professor of Biology at the University of Cambridge elicits an outrageous comparison to the hero of the nursery rhyme "Jack Be Nimble, Jack Be Quick"; the result is "V. B. Nimble, V. B. Quick," a lighthearted look at a professor who scurries about performing scientific experiments and delivering lectures about them. The experience of a luxury cruise—something most readers think of as exotic and exciting—is transformed into a lyric about the monotony of life at sea, titled with ironic appropriateness "Shipbored." A flyer inviting him to become a member of the Swingers Life Club spurs him to write a lengthy (and at times erotic) ode on the physical aspects of female sexuality. Even the serious poems contain humorous elements, and a genuine comic spirit pervades the author's view of the world about him.

Updike understands how a poem works, and he is a skilled technician. He has a firm grasp of the literary tradition and is one of the best mimics of poetic form and matter, turning the great writers on their heads to elicit a laugh or a tear from his own readers. To delve into Updike's poetry is to engage in a luxuriating experience of intertextuality. In *Midpoint and Other Poems*, his lengthy autobiographical examination of the human condition in the twentieth century, Updike models the four major sections of the poem successively on Dante's *Divine Comedy*, Edmund Spenser's *The Faerie Queene*, Walt Whitman's "Song of Myself," and Alexander Pope's *An Essay on Man*.

Widely read and capable of retaining just the right phrase from works as diverse as the Bible, English and American literary masters, and popular magazines, Updike continually surprises the educated reader by providing a phrase or a line or an offhanded allusion that calls to mind some other work whose theme, suddenly recalled, gives resonance to what may appear to be a rather slight poem. Again, selections from the light verse can serve as apt illustrations. A phlegmatic romantic pass at an usherette ("To an Usherette") is cast in the form of Ben Jonson's "Come, My Celia," a seventeenth century love poem. A line in a film review in *Life* magazine noting how the film ending is different from the novel on which it is based prompts Updike to write "In Memoriam." While his verse is a cynical comment on the way crass Hollywood producers take liberties with novels, the title of the work recalls Alfred, Lord Tennyson's serious elegy on the death of his friend Arthur Henry Hallam, and Updike's final line, "Say, Does he wake, or sleep?" is a parody of the close of John Keats's "Ode: To a Nightingale." What Updike means by this latter comparison is not clear, but the parallels suggest there is more to his verse than one might imagine by a casual reading.

With the exception of *Midpoint and Other Poems*, Updike has confined himself to lyric or short narrative verse. Most of his poems tend toward the descriptive rather than the analytic; readers will no doubt find that they are asked to see more than they are forced to think. Updike's special strength lies in his ability to see things around him and his capacity to describe the physical world in minute detail. The volume is filled with poems of cities and landscapes, the best ones being those describing the terrain of Updike's childhood and the New England region where he has made his adult life. A small collection could be made featuring places that have captured Updike's imagination, sites as varied as Pompeii, Nassau, Tulsa, Seattle, Indianapolis, Rio de Janeiro, and São Paulo. A lengthy, rather despondent ode to Washington, D.C., reflects the author's love for a country that has many problems that government cannot solve. Scattered throughout the volume are dozens of sonnets, a form for which Updike appears to have a particular predilection. His sonnets are more like those of Robert Frost, however, than those of William Shakespeare; Updike chooses to keep the form open rather than to adhere to strict conventions of rhyme scheme and stanzaic patterning.

Updike has tried hard to make this volume a "scholarly" edition. He has taken great care to arrange the works both chronologically and thematically, dividing his collected assemblage into "poems" and "light verse" so readers can distinguish between serious efforts and their more lighthearted compatriots. He has been a careful editor, excising eighteen poems that appeared in earlier collections (and providing a list of those works in an appendix). Fifteen pages of notes are provided to identify obscure allusions or explain the significance of passages readers might misinterpret. An alphabetical index of titles lists the date of composition or first publication and the collection in which the work previously appeared.

Such information is commonplace in collections edited by university professors, but not in those by practicing poets. Updike offers a reason for the textual apparatus in his preface: "I feared that if I did not perform the elementary bibliographical decencies for [my poems] no one else would." There is no reason to believe that he is being disingenuous about his motives, but one might wonder why Updike has gone to all this trouble. Certainly someone, someday would have done the task; libraries are filled with scholarly editions of juvenilia, ephemera, or insignificant poetry written by literary giants famous for works in other genres. Since Updike's poetry has already received attention from academic critics, the odds are quite good that his poetry would have been collected and edited—perhaps even more extensively than he has done. No stranger to the academic world, Updike surely would know that his beloved waifs would not remain orphans for long.

One might reasonably conclude, therefore, that, like much of the verse, Updike's scholarly apparatus means more than it appears to on first glance. Updike may simply not want his poems to be edited by others, because the final shape of such an edition might misrepresent his intentions. By producing *Collected Poems, 1953-1993* himself, Updike has given the world an approved view of "Updike as Poet." Readers should not be surprised at what might seem at first to be a rather arrogant and self-serving gesture. In a study of four influential literary figures, *Testamentary Acts* (1992), Michael Millgate explains how in the years before their deaths Alfred, Lord Tennyson, Robert Browning, Thomas Hardy, and Henry James took extraordinary measures to shape the image of themselves they wished to leave for posterity. Entering the seventh decade of life, Updike may simply be trying to do the same thing. How successful he has been will no doubt be the subject of scholarly discussion long after the best of his poetry has passed into the canon of American literary masterpieces, while the remainder languishes between the covers of this useful and revelatory collection.

Laurence W. Mazzeno

Sources for Further Study

America. CLXIX, November 13, 1993, p. 22.
Atlanta Journal Constitution. June 13, 1993, p. N8.
Booklist. LXXXIX, March 15, 1993, p. 1274.
Boston Globe. April 25, 1993, p. 37.
The Christian Century. CX, December 1, 1993, p. 1215.
Houston Post. April 25, 1993, p. C4.
Library Journal. CXVIII, April 15, 1993, p. 94.
The New Criterion. XI, April, 1993, p. 6.
The New Yorker. LXIX, December 27, 1993, p. 161.
Publishers Weekly. CCXL, March 1, 1993, p. 43.
Washington Times. May 2, 1993, p. B8.

THE COLLECTED STORIES

Author: Reynolds Price (1933-   )
Publisher: Atheneum (New York). 625 pp. $25.00
Type of work: Short stories
Time: Mainly the twentieth century
Locale: The American South, Europe, Israel

In stories from five decades displaying a wide range of subject and an elegant prose style, Reynolds Price has established himself as a major voice in American short fiction

The Collected Stories brings together fifty short stories Reynolds Price has written over five decades, from "Michael Egerton" in 1954 to "An Evening Meal" in 1992. Half of the stories are reprinted from Price's two earlier collections, *The Names and Faces of Heroes* (1963) and *Permanent Errors* (1970); and most of these stories, as well as the previously uncollected other half in the book, have actually seen print before, in *Esquire, Harper's, Playboy, Encounter, The Paris Review, The Southern Review, The New Yorker,* and a dozen other major vehicles for short fiction.

Yet Price is not one of the best-known practitioners of the genre. Perhaps because these stories have been spread over almost forty years and half of them appeared before 1970, Price is not known primarily as a short-story writer. Rather, he is familiar to many readers as an author of twenty-five books and as a poet, playwright, and, most notably, a novelist. Yet as these stories reveal, he is also one of the best practitioners of the short-fiction genre at work in the United States, particularly in the great Southern prose tradition of James Agee and Eudora Welty, Truman Capote and Josephine Humphreys.

In a short preface, "To the Reader," Price explains the publishing history of the stories in this collection and gives something of his theory of fiction. What defines short fiction, he argues, is its intensity, and thus "the story's technical and emotional demands are more strenuous in some ways than the novel's." While the novel covers a broader space of time, "the story has charted briefer stretches of concentrated feeling, and it always speaks an intimate language." What marks a story is "its single-minded intent and the narrow ground from which it looks." Short fiction, Price concludes, is "the prose narrator's nearest approach to music . . . the lean lament or ballad of hunger, delight, revulsion or praise."

Price has not revised his earlier stories here, but he presents them in an interesting way. Rather than collect the stories chronologically, he has arranged them in a new order, by mood and theme, which suggests "an alteration of voices, echoes, lengths and concerns." This order juxtaposes stories in such a way as to throw fresh light on their subtle and complex concerns. Older stories are seen anew when placed between more recent examples; newer stories gain some depth by being placed next to similar stories decades older. "The Warrior Princess Ozimba," for example—collected in *The Names and Faces of Heroes* in 1970 but first published in the *Virginia Quarterly Review* in 1961—follows the more recent opening story "Full Day" in the book. Both, however, concern caring for older people, and in their order here they cast revealing shadows on each other.

The range of Price's stories is remarkable: stories of European travel, of Christmas on the West Bank in Israel, of a visit to an American Indian reservation. The best of Price's fiction, however, taps his family history, the rich Southern roots of his North Carolina childhood. Like Eudora Welty—*Permanent Errors* was dedicated to her—and other Southern writers he admires and emulates, Price has found within his own family history a well from which he can draw endlessly for his fiction.

Often, in fact, he has disguised his characters very little. A boy protagonist may be called Reynolds, and his father Buck Price; other characters are various aunts, uncles, and grandparents on several sides of his family, and the black families who have worked for these relatives for generations. Price knows these lives so well that he can render them in rich detail, and his mainly rural Southern characters come alive through the intimate detail he gives so effortlessly—food and flowers, gossip and language, work and religion. Price burst on the American literary scene in 1962 with the novel *A Long and Happy Life*, a brilliant re-creation of the sexual and religious experiences of several young people in rural North Carolina, and in some ways he has been writing about that experience ever since.

If Price has an overriding theme within this setting, it is adolescence, particularly for the young boy of eleven or twelve whose fictional experiences are propelling him toward adulthood. Like James Agee, Carson McCullers, and a whole raft of twentieth century American writers, Price has a peculiar feel for the difficulties of the young person navigating the shoals of adolescence. What distinguishes his version of the American growing-up story is a dual focus on sexuality on the one hand and spirituality, even mysticism, on the other.

In "The Enormous Door," the third story in this collection, for example, a twelve-year-old boy narrates his encounter with adult sexuality. The burning question in his adolescent mind is *"What are grown men like, truly, in secret?"* He miraculously gets his answer when, in a boarding house where he and his parents live, he is able to observe Simon Fentriss, the new high school math and science teacher, through a hole in the door. What he sees is both a sexual and a mystical experience. As he says at the end, "I'm the last man alive . . . to whom a god unquestionably came and showed the sacred joy that waits in any human body."

Many of Reynolds Price's stories echo these sexual and spiritual initiation experiences in one way or another. In "Deeds of Light" a boy gets to share his life briefly with a young soldier in the summer of 1942. *"Don't let this end,"* the boy says to himself. *"Let it teach me everything I need."* His momentary friendship with the older male has all the joy and homosexual tension such an experience can possibly carry. Yet the Price adolescent learns about more than sex; in "Watching Her Die," for example, the young narrator discovers the mystery of death. Such an experience can even be humorous: in "The Company of the Dead," two boys are hired as "setters" to stay by the corpse for the night, and their adventures (especially after they discover that "Miss Georgie was blowing a sizable bubble") may remind readers of the works of other Southern writers from William Faulkner to Fannie Flagg.

It would be a mistake to say, however, that Price is best only when he stays in his family's South. Some of his most powerful fiction breaks those boundaries. "Endless Mountains" is a long account of a soldier wounded in the Civil War and nursed to health by a young girl and boy. "An Early Christmas" is a religious allegory using both Old and New Testament terms and taking place in 1980 in the Old City of Jerusalem in Israel's West Bank. "The Last of a Long Correspondence" is the letter to a woman from her dying godfather recounting the weekend of the Cuban missile crisis some thirty years earlier, when he took her into the mountains for safekeeping.

It would not be unfair to say, however, that Price's weaker fiction nearly always takes place somewhere outside the South. He has several stories of American couples wandering aimlessly around Europe and suffering from some angst that readers cannot identify and the characters will not talk about (as in "Waiting at Dachau," from *Permanent Errors*). There is also a strong strain of sentimentality in Price; controlled, it creates a tension that is reminiscent of such writers as Truman Capote and James Agee. Yet occasionally, as with all writers, the author's control is lost, and the sentimentality sweeps readers away on its flood. ("Walking Lessons," for example, the longest story here, never recovers from its opening line: "My wife killed herself two weeks ago, her twenty-sixth birthday.")

Put another way, Price is often writing intimate family stories; their tragedies and triumphs are poignant but can quickly slip over the edge into the maudlin. "Uncle Grant" is a good example. This story of an old black family retainer could easily become mawkish; Price controls it by focusing not only on this wonderful old character but on the growth of the narrator within Uncle Grant's sight and love. A similar case is "Bess Waters," the story of generations of a black family in all their sadness and sorrow. This is in fact where Price is at his best, describing his own Southern history, and in a metaphorical language matched by none. "Buckeye Price's son, Reynolds," asks the one-hundred-year-old Bess to tell her story.

> And honest to God, Bess tries to tell it. Her dry lips work and her mind sends words—she only recalls these scattered hours—but what comes out is dark shine and power from her banked old heart and the quick of her bones, dark but hot as a furnace blast with a high blue roar. It burns the boy first. Bess sees him blown back and starting to scorch; then it whips round and folds her into the light till both of them sit in a grate of embers, purified by the tale itself, the visible trace of one long life too hard to tell.

Price's best prose, like this, is the poetry of detail and metaphor. Few American writers can match it.

Price's prose is also perfectly appropriate to his themes, for a strain of spirituality runs through many of these stories, a thinly veiled mysticism that may remind readers of much in Native American literature. Price's characters are constantly discovering the mysteries of the human and natural worlds, of the spiritual heart residing within life, and the power humans have of achieving that spirituality by caring for one another and achieving true intimacy. For Price's characters, and his adolescents in particular, the lessons of this world are full of aching joy and sadness. Like the fiction he defines in his preface, Reynolds Price's short fiction often achieves an intensity close to music.

David Peck

Sources for Further Study

Booklist. LXXXIX, April 15, 1993, p. 1495.
Chicago Tribune. May 16, 1993, XIV, p. 1.
Choice. XXXI, October, 1993, p. 293.
Commonweal. CXX, December 3, 1993, p. 22.
Library Journal. CXVIII, May 1, 1993, p. 120.
National Review. XLV, June 7, 1993, p. 68.
The New York Times Book Review. XCVIII, July 4, 1993, p. 8.
Publishers Weekly. CCXL, April 19, 1993, p. 49.
San Francisco Chronicle. June 27, 1993, p. REV5.
USA Today. June 18, 1993, p. D4.

COME TO ME

Author: Amy Bloom (1953-   )
Publisher: Aaron Asher Books/HarperCollins (New York). 175 pp. $20.00
Type of work: Short stories

The twelve stories in this collection—a psychotherapist's first work of fiction—focus mainly on the forces which pull people suddenly and passionately toward one another

Perhaps the most refreshing thing about Amy Bloom's short stories is that she examines the hidden contours of her characters' lives without presenting them as unsavory. Though she frequently focuses on sex and sexuality in relationships that may be adulterous, incestuous, or simply painful, her focus is not on presenting them voyeuristically or moralistically. Instead, her focus is usually on what her main character finds uplifting or renewing about a relationship that defies conventional expectations, and secondarily, what in this relationship is too painful for words.

The first and most big-hearted of the stories in this collection is "Love is Not a Pie," and is the story which most explicitly explores the underlying views of love which tie the various stories together. Told from the point of view of Ellen Spencer, a law school student, on the day of her mother's funeral, the story explores Ellen's memories of one particular summer spent at a lake house with her parents, her sister Lizzie, a friend of her parents, Mr. DeCuervo, and his daughter Gisela. As the summer develops, Ellen begins to realize first that her mother is having an affair with Mr. DeCuervo, and later, that her father has full knowledge of and is probably a full participant in this affair. How such a three-way relationship developed, and how her mother was able to remain close to both men while keeping her family life stable, are questions that Ellen lives with until after her mother's death, when, at her funeral, Ellen learns that her sister Lizzie had known for years about their mother's affair with Mr. DeCuervo.

The story's title comes from the mother's explanation of how she was able to handle such a situation. "Love is not a pie," she told Lizzie, meaning that giving love out to different people does not mean that there is less love for each; their mother loved each person in different ways. Ellen imagines trying to explain all of this to John, the man she is engaged to marry, and believes that he would never understand; certainly she could never explain it to him. Deciding that love should not necessarily be "normal," and that she is not ready to marry a man whose expectations would be of a normal home life, she resolves not to marry John, and calls him to tell him so. When he responds by pointing out that they have already ordered the invitations, she knows she has made the right decision. Love, for her, as it was for her mother, and as it is for many of the characters of this story, is too important and too amorphous to confine only to a preestablished, socially established view of a normal marriage.

The dilemma that many of Amy Bloom's characters face is that they associate sexual desire with transcendence. Wanting either sex or transcendence, they go looking for the other as well. Though they meet with only limited degrees of success, the author is clearly sympathetic to their quest. Thus, two of the stories, "Song of Solomon" and "Faultlines," bring us to the point where a deep, yearning passion is beginning to be fulfilled. "Song of Solomon," the more tender and spare of the two, follows a young single mother who is sinking into the gloom of a depression and tracks down her baby doctor on his way into a temple. The author presents us with the moment of mutual recognition, attraction, need, and fear that passes between the two, but ends the story perfectly and sweetly with the gesture of communication which will take the man and woman into the future together at least for a short time. "Faultlines" follows Henry DiMartino through an evening when he has invited the woman he has been fantasizing about over to his house, so that he can meet her boyfriend, and she can meet his wife. Despite the social tangle, Henry and the woman, Mary, do find themselves wrapped together in what the author describes as "a perfect kiss," and the sexual affair that they were both hoping for but also hoping to avoid is off and running; all the complications that have previously been hinted at are certain to follow.

"Faultlines" is actually one of two connected stories in a section titled "Henry and Marie," and those stories are loosely connected to a trilogy grouped under the title "Three Stories." Marie is Henry's wife, and her story, "Only You," tells of her unhappy slide into middle age, brightened by an unexpected sexual awakening thanks to her hairdresser, Alvin Myerson. Though sensitive in its portrayal of Marie, the story is written in an occasionally awkward present tense, and has an unnecessary glibness of tone in its opening ("Marie, who is not a very sexual person . . . gets almost all her needs met at The Cut Above, Alvin Myerson's beauty salon") and at other points throughout the story.

More successful as a series are the stories which feature David Silverstein, a psychotherapist, his wife and former client, Galen, and their two daughters, Rose and Violet. David's story, "Hyacinths," focuses on a childhood accident in which his cousin Willie was shot in the chest while the two boys were playing in a barn. The accident pushes his father into a pitch of fervent, vengeful Christianity, and David reacts by deciding to adopt the Judaism of the relatives with whom he is sent to live. As an adult, David marries Galen, a woman of higher and lighter spirits than his own, and tries to come to terms with his own impulse to control people and situations close to him, though he is only partially successful.

Galen's story, "The Sight of You," tells of her affair with Henry DiMartino (of "Henry and Marie"), an affair which takes them to the edge of leaving their respective spouses before Galen draws back. Henry is a construction worker and owner of his own business; Galen sees him as physical and impulsive, in many ways the opposite of her husband, and she cherishes the sense of power he allows her to experience. Galen, a musician, has never craved nor identified herself with the type of normality that life with David represents. Running off with Henry appeals to her as a change from the life she has settled into, until she realizes that Henry has no desire to leave his old life behind, but would be bringing every bit of it he could with him. The story succeeds in making a character who could be easily maligned likable because we see that she is a round peg tired of trying to fit into a square hole; while she does things which might be hurtful, she means no one harm, and she deeply considers the feelings of others.

The trilogy of stories comes to an effective close in "Silver Water," which tells of the descent into schizophrenia by David and Galen's daughter, Rose. Told from the point of view of Rose's sister, Violet, "Silver Water" shows the courage, pain, and humor of the family as they learn to accept Rose in her madness, but also reveals Rose's ultimate inability to accept herself.

The topic of a sudden and apparently arbitrary descent into madness comes up again in "When the Year Grows Old." This time the focus is on a high school girl, Kay Feldman, who comes home to discover that her mother, Laura, has retreated to the basement to work on an ambitious literary project. Kay is thrilled by these signs of strength and rebellion in her mother, whom she had previously seen as kowtowing to the demands of middle-class respectability and her controlling husband, Martin, Kay's father. Not only is Laura's new life of living in the basement, smoking cigarettes, and feeding her newly adopted cat, Blake, a new excitement, but to Kay's way of thinking, it is also more sane, at least at first. Quickly, though, Laura's condition deteriorates, and Martin steps in to have her institutionalized. When Laura returns several weeks later, she has returned to her previously "normal" state. From Kay's point of view, she and her mother have lost, and her cold, distant, and manipulative father has won, though Kay still has the memory of her mother's rebellion.

Amy Bloom has a fondness for openings which grab the reader's attention like a hook. Sometimes, as in the aforementioned "Only You," such an opening can overshadow and overdetermine the story which follows. Sometimes it can be more effective, as in the story, "Light Breaks Where No Sun Shines," which begins "I didn't expect to find myself in the back of Mr. Klein's store, wearing only my undershirt and panties, surrounded by sable," an opening which works less because of any "shock value" than because it captures the defiance and disbelief of the narrator, Susan. It also works, however, because after presenting the basic dramatic conflict up front, the story has the good sense to switch gears into the much more subtle form of character presentation which begins in the third paragraph: "No one except Mr. Klein had ever suggested that my appearance was pleasing." The provocative beginning in this case, however, has the unfortunate effect of inviting an equally provocative ending when we learn that, after Mr. Klein ended their sessions in the back of his store, Susan turned her affections to a piano teacher. The final line, "I loved him, too," is both too suggestive and too ambiguous, and undercuts the sensitively written story it ends.

A story which presents many dramatic possibilities, and two engaging main characters, but which ultimately does not find a clear direction is "Psychoanalysis Changed My Life." Again, Bloom begins with a gripping beginning—Marianne Loewe's dreams of naked fat women, which she has been describing to her psychotherapist, Dr. Zurner—but neither the dreams nor the psychoanalysis of Marianne Loewe (herself a psychotherapist) turns out to be the heart of the story. Instead, the story focuses on the change in these two women's relationship as Dr. Zurner becomes increasingly ill and unable to continue as a therapist. Marianne herself never comes sharply into focus, and the glimpses we get are almost too suggestive. The story as a whole provides too many distractions, including an unfortunately flippant title, though it explores characters and situations which are themselves interesting.

A story which navigates sure-footedly past many potential wrong turns is *"Semper Fidelis."* The story of a younger woman married to an older man who is dying, it focuses on her loneliness, her grief, her resentments, and her flights into fantasy—and her courage as well, as she continues to love him. Her husband Max, being significantly older, tries to exercise an implicit license to understand his wife, joking suggestively about the future lovers she must surely be rehearsing even now. It is clear, however, to both that the love between them is deeper than either can easily understand, and that any future lovers will be no replacement for Max once he dies.

Perhaps the single strongest story in the collection is "Sleepwalking," which tells the story of a widow's brief incestuous encounter with her stepson, Lion, after her husband, Lionel, a jazz performer, has died. Handled with sensitivity and understanding, the story puts this encounter into the grief-filled frame of mind through which the protagonist is sleepwalking. Life goes on, and the stepson shows all the signs of bouncing back from their encounter, which he has in no way yet understood; in contrast, his stepmother's recovery from grief is only beginning.

It is much to the credit of the writer that there is a recognizable voice and a powerful vision uniting these various stories. Amy Bloom has a deep understanding of the power of love, as well as of the faith and suspicion that her characters feel toward that power. The author well understands that love is not in every instance healing or restorative or transcendent, but that the need to view it in all of those ways is very strong, and that at times it can be all of those things for people.

Thomas J. Cassidy

Sources for Further Study

Booklist. LXXXIX, May 15, 1993, p. 1672.
Houston Post. August 29, 1993, p. C4.
Kirkus Reviews. LXI, April 1, 1993, p. 388.
Library Journal. CXVIII, May 1, 1993, p. 119.
Los Angeles Times Book Review. June 13, 1993, p. 3.
The New York Times Book Review. XCVIII, July 18, 1993, p. 16.
Publishers Weekly. CCXL, May 3, 1993, p. 293.
San Francisco Chronicle. October 17, 1993, p. REV5.
The Washington Post. July 29, 1993, p. C2.

CONDUCT UNBECOMING
Lesbians and Gays in the U.S. Military, Vietnam to the Persian Gulf

Author: Randy Shilts (1952-1994)
Publisher: St. Martin's Press (New York). 784 pp. $27.95
Type of work: History
Time: 1778 to the 1990's
Locale: The United States, Europe, and Asia

This massive study provides an exhaustive historical overview of the presence of lesbians and gays in the U.S. military and their continuing contributions to the defense of a nation that has ignored and even reviled them

Appearing in the middle of a heated debate over the inclusion of lesbians and gays in the United States armed services, *Conduct Unbecoming: Lesbians and Gays in the U.S. Military, Vietnam to the Persian Gulf* argues forcefully that homosexuals have always served in the U.S. military, for the most part honorably, and have become targets of inquiry and active persecution only during peacetime or when politicians and military leaders have needed a convenient scapegoat. Randy Shilts's work demonstrates exhaustive research conducted over five years and recounts hundreds of case histories gleaned from eleven hundred interviews with military personnel and civilians. It tells a complex story of individual bravery and institutional hypocrisy and paranoia, as it narrates the tales of patriotic gays and lesbians who have served their country only to be repudiated and harassed when their services have not met the immediate needs of the military. Throughout, Shilts makes a compelling case for social tolerance and for full civil rights for homosexuals.

Like Shilts's previous works, *The Mayor of Castro Street: The Life and Times of Harvey Milk* (1982) and *And the Band Played On: Politics, People, and the AIDS Epidemic* (1987), *Conduct Unbecoming* humanizes history, portraying personal dramas against a backdrop of social conflict and changing attitudes. While it consists primarily of interconnected personal narratives, this study returns time and again to a strong central thesis: that homosexuals have played and continue to play key roles in all levels of the military in spite of persistent, though admittedly fluctuating, institutional hostility to them. In the 1980's alone, Shilts estimates, the cost of investigating and replacing gay personnel ran into the hundreds of millions of dollars. During wartime, however, gays with areas of expertise that were in short supply have often been accepted and even actively recruited by the military.

Such institutional hypocrisy dates back to the very beginnings of U.S. history. Benjamin Franklin engaged the services of a Prussian captain, Baron Frederich Wilhelm von Steuben, to provide much-needed training to American revolutionaries serving under George Washington, even though it was widely known that Steuben had a male lover and was a protégé of the flamboyant King Frederick II of Prussia. Even though Steuben served the Americans honorably and perhaps provided the training necessary for the revolutionaries to defeat the British, his service coincided with the first recorded dismissal from the U.S. military for homosexual activity. Lieutenant

Gotthold Enslin was court-martialed on March 10, 1778, for sodomy after being discovered in bed with a private; he was discharged in disgrace by George Washington. Such schizophrenic treatment of gays continued and intensified through the nineteenth and twentieth centuries.

It was not until 1916, however, that homosexuality was explicitly condemned by American military (rather than civilian) law. Following Sigmund Freud's now thoroughly discredited theories, the homosexual man came to be seen in the early decades of the twentieth century as a weak and dangerously unstable individual. No longer were specific sexual acts alone punished; instead, individuals were rendered suspect and even punishable for desires that they may never have acted upon. This evolution from the perception of homosexuality as simply condemnable sexual activity to homosexuality as identity led to numerous purges of suspected gays and lesbians.

The vast bulk of Shilts's book is concerned with recounting the details of such periodic purges from the 1950's through the early 1990's, as lives and careers were destroyed because of innuendo and paranoia. Tom Dooley, the bestselling author of *Deliver Us from Evil* (1956), was less than honorably discharged from the Navy in the 1950's for "homosexual tendencies and activities" even though he performed heroically as a medical officer in Vietnam. As Shilts makes clear, Dooley's discharge came before the beginning of full American involvement in the Vietnam conflict and before the armed services recognized that they desperately needed *any* individuals whom they could find to fill the ranks of the troops in Southeast Asia.

During the war itself, gays were often tolerated because of necessity. Shilts tells how one officer briefing Marines on where they could find prostitutes included information on engaging the services of young men. Scores of gay veterans report uninhibited sexual activity among soldiers in Vietnam; in times of stress and isolation, barriers seemed to fall quickly and easily. The draft situation also mandated a certain tolerance; so many young men were claiming to be homosexual to avoid military service that the excuse was rarely accepted. In 1966 the Pentagon directed draft boards to ignore all claims of homosexuality unless the draftee could offer incontrovertible "evidence." This meant that few individuals were excused or barred.

Such hypocrisy is reflected in hard statistical and factual evidence. Shilts reports that from 1963 to 1966, the Navy expelled around seventeen hundred individuals a year for homosexuality. Yet as the Vietnam War intensified, these numbers dropped dramatically, to around eleven hundred in 1967, eight hundred in 1968, and six hundred in 1969. The fluctuations of such numbers stand in direct conflict with the explicit policy of the Department of Defense: "The presence of homosexuals would seriously impair discipline, good order, morals and the security of our armed forces."

Conduct Unbecoming makes clear, however, that unlike gay men, lesbians have been rarely tolerated, even during times of dire staffing needs. Organized around principles of masculinity and power, the military has always had a problematic relationship with its female personnel. Shilts does a superb job in tracing the interconnections between sexism and homophobia, and recounts ample testimony proving the extreme constraints under which both heterosexual women and lesbians have attempted to serve their country. In a nation where women are seen as signifiers of weakness and as sexual property, lesbians are often perceived as the most threatening affront imaginable to patriarchal values. Historically, they have been targeted for vicious attacks and investigations by the armed services.

Penny Rand, for example, was not only sexually harassed but also, like other women in the services, ordered to make herself more attractive to men by wearing makeup and shaving her legs. When she complained, her superiors suspected that she had been "infected" by the terrible illness that they feared was spreading among the women on her base: lesbianism. In a typically confused and erroneous rationale for their investigation, they claimed that lesbians were harassing other women, when in truth it was heterosexual men who were constantly harassing the female personnel. Rand could not live with this hypocrisy; she joined antiwar protesters at her base, defied direct orders from superiors, and was finally discharged from the service, after which she went to work for the antiwar movement full time. In a way, Rand was lucky; other suspected lesbians were physically assaulted, locked in closets for days on end, and even imprisoned for years.

In the 1970's, with the end of the Vietnam War, the witch-hunts of lesbians and gays intensified, even though the larger American culture seemed to be growing more tolerant of homosexuals. The Civil Service was forced to open its 2.6 million jobs to gays and lesbians in 1975, when it could not prove that there was a job-related rationale for excluding them. Yet the military continued to react paranoically and hypocritically. Men who had been decorated for service in Vietnam were expelled less than honorably after the war. Some dischargees, however, became willing to fight their superior officers in court. With the birth of the gay rights movement in the late 1960's, lawyers and activists started looking for clear-cut cases of discrimination with which to challenge government policy. They found many.

Leonard Matlovich's story is worth repeating here. Matlovich received the Bronze Star, a Purple Heart, two Air Force commendation medals, and an Air Force Meritorious Service Medal during three tours in Vietnam. On March 6, 1975, he directly challenged the Air Force policy excluding homosexuals by writing a letter to the Secretary of the Air Force in which he disclosed his sexual orientation and asked to be allowed to continue to serve. When no evidence of poor conduct and service by Matlovich could be unearthed, Air Force officers simply changed records. They carefully chose members of the panel hearing Matlovich's case to make sure that no tolerant individuals were included. He received death threats and was placed in embarrassing situations with nude airmen in an attempt to manufacture evidence that he had harassed other personnel. Finally Matlovich was less than honorably discharged; the only career that he ever desired was denied to him. When he died of acquired immune deficiency syndrome (AIDS) in 1988, the Air Force would not even allow an American flag to be draped over his coffin, though they could not deny him a space in a military cemetery. His grave marker reads, "When I was in the military, they gave me a medal for killing two men, and a discharge for loving one."

Through the 1980's the gay civil rights movement was inextricably tied to the AIDS crisis, and so was the plight of gay men in the military. AIDS added fuel to social homophobia even as it galvanized gay leaders and provided a rallying point for political activism. The military's response to the AIDS crisis was predictable. Just as Ronald Reagan was slow to react to a disease that many interpreted as divine retribution against homosexuals, so too did the military ignore the possibility that sexually active troops were at risk for HIV infection. When the Defense Department did finally take notice, it did so slowly and without regard for truth. HIV-positive soldiers were harassed and summarily discharged in the early 1980's. Later, when the military agreed to stop discharging them, infected military personnel were still treated as pariahs, often beaten and scorned as they were summarily assumed to be gay by their peers. Yet when the military conducted the first survey of HIV's prevalence among enlisted men in the mid-1980's, it doctored the results so that almost all the soldiers were said to have contracted the disease heterosexually; this allowed the Department of Defense to continue to claim that homosexuality was practically nonexistent in the military, even as it continued its witch-hunts to locate lesbians and gays. Later, when questioned by nonmilitary personnel, most of the soldiers who had claimed to be heterosexual were found to be gay. The AIDS crisis in the military has proved to be hopelessly complicated and muddled because of the military's intransigence and prejudice.

Conduct Unbecoming takes the reader up to the early 1990's. During the war in the Persian Gulf, the military actively recruited previously discharged gay servicemen because there was a shortage of translators of Arabic. Even so, for those with less essential skills, the story was one of ongoing misery. In 1989 and 1990, Sergeant Dan Bell of the Air Force was repeatedly locked inside bare closets in order to coerce from him the names of other homosexuals. In 1990, the Supreme Court let stand two federal appeal rulings that allowed the discharge of Army Reservist Miriam Ben-Shalom and Navy Ensign James Woodward. The military even started demanding that gays and lesbians repay all ROTC (Reserve Officer Training Corps) scholarship money that they received. This decision, however, worked to galvanize groups and individuals opposed to the military ban.

In the early 1990's, colleges and universities across the nation responded to the new recoupment policy by expelling ROTC programs, stating that the military's continued discrimination on the basis of sexual orientation violated their own campus policies. In 1990, several leading college organizations wrote to Secretary of Defense Richard Cheney asking him to rescind the military ban; Cheney, who was known to view the ban as outdated and impractical, nevertheless refused. He did, however, order the Joint Chiefs of Staff to stop the vindictive attempt to recover tuition money and to halt massive purges of gay servicemen and women. The tide seemed to be turning as the military establishment came face to face with changing social beliefs and the political power of the gay and lesbian rights movement.

Shilts's book cannot provide a real conclusion. Published just as President Bill Clinton was taking office, it cannot tell the reader what will happen finally to the military ban. The court cases that it traces in its last chapters were still subject to being appealed or overruled, and the careers of many individuals questioned were in limbo. Even so, *Conduct Unbecoming* is a powerful and rich narrative of social discrimination and institutional hypocrisy. Shilts completed the book while hospitalized with AIDS. His death in 1994, at the age of forty-two, brought an end to a distinguished journalistic career characterized by first-rate reporting and a passionate commitment to gay issues.

Donald E. Hall

Sources for Further Study

Chicago Tribune. May 30, 1993, XIV, p. 5.
Los Angeles Times Book Review. September 5, 1993, p. 7.
The Nation. CCLVI, June 7, 1993, p. 806.
National Review. XLV, April 26, 1993, p. 12.
The New York Review of Books. XL, September 23, 1993, p. 18.
The New York Times Book Review. XCVIII, May 30, 1993, p. 2.
Publishers Weekly. CCXL, July 5, 1993, p. 35.
Time. CXLI, May 24, 1993, p. 76.
The Wall Street Journal. May 18, 1993, p. A16.
The Washington Post Book World. XXIII, April 25, 1993, p. 1.

CONSIDER THIS, SEÑORA

Author: Harriet Doerr (1910-   )
Publisher: Harcourt Brace (New York). 241 pp. $21.95
Type of work: Novel
Time: Approximately 1962-1968
Locale: Amapolas, Mexico

In this exquisitely nuanced drama, four expatriate Americans take up residence for a short time in a remote Mexican village, where they get to know one another as well as the Mexican villagers

> *Principal characters:*
> SUSANNA (SUE) AMES, a beautiful, recently divorced woman in her late twenties who enjoys solitude and painting
> BUD LOOMIS, a short, red-faced land speculator fleeing tax-evasion charges in Arizona
> FRANCES (FRAN) BOWLES, a forty-something twice-divorced woman, working on a travel book of Mexico
> URSULA BOWLES, Frances' seventy-nine-year-old mother, who was born in Mexico and moved to the United States as a child
> ENRIQUE ORTIZ DE LEÓN, a local dignitary, who sells his family's ancestral estate to Bud and Sue
> PADRE MIGUEL, the local priest
> PEPE GÓMEZ, an elderly man, the grandson of Don Enrique's great-grand-father's majordomo
> PATRICIO GÓMEZ, Pepe's great-grandson, a resourceful young man whom Sue hires to watch her house and run errands
> ALTAGRACIA GÓMEZ, Patricio's adolescent sister, who works for Sue and the others as a maid
> FRANCISCO (PACO) ALVARADO TORRES, Fran Bowles's Harvard-educated lover, twice a widower
> OTTO VON SCHRAMM, an Austrian expatriate musician who speaks no Spanish
> MADAME ANNA, Herr Otto's sister
> CHARLES MACLAIN, an American who has a brief affair with Sue
> CARTER RILEY, Fran's next love interest after Paco

Consider This, Señora is the second novel by Harriet Doerr, who won the American Book Award in 1984 for *Stones for Ibarra*. Like the earlier work, *Consider This, Señora* centers on several expatriate Americans in a small village in Mexico in the 1960's and their interactions with the local people. Also like her earlier novel, several chapters of *Consider This, Señora* appeared before publication in various journals. Although the chapters can stand on their own as individual short stories, they fit neatly together to form a cohesive whole.

In her typically clear, precise prose, Doerr depicts approximately six years in the lives of four Americans who settle temporarily in the tiny village of Amapolas from 1962 to 1968. Each of her ten chapters describes an episode in the life of one or more of the Americans, whimsically contrasting them and their actions with Mexico and its people. Her flashes of insight into what the Mexicans think of these Americans who have invaded their shores speak volumes, especially considering the language barrier. Her descriptions of the downside of Mexican culture—the corruption, the senseless deaths, the poverty, even the major detours and time-consuming delays that accompany efforts to travel, all these things that the Mexicans accept so blithely as a part of everyday life and that the Americans constantly rail against—combine to form a very complete, detailed picture that is more perceptive than tragic.

The story begins with Susanna Ames, a beautiful divorcée in her late twenties who decides to buy a house in Mexico. At the real estate office, she meets fellow American Bud Loomis, a land speculator who persuades her to back him in his latest venture. He has his heart set on Don Enrique Ortiz de León's ancestral home, which he wants to subdivide into smaller lots for resale. Ever the gentleman, Don Enrique invites the two on a picnic to the property to make certain they really want to buy it. It is remote, barren, and dry, and will get drier yet before the rains. The once-beautiful mansion of the Ortiz de Leóns has become a crumbling ruin since the Revolution of 1910. Thus, on the ruins of a once-illustrious Spanish estate will be built the modern homes of foreigners seeking peace, beauty, and, most important, escape.

The other two Americans who join Sue and Bud are Fran Bowles, whom Sue meets in Santa Prisca over Easter weekend, and her aging mother, Ursula Bowles. Because of her age and because she is the most fully realized character, Ursula is perhaps the character with whom the author most identifies. Ursula, apparently, was born not far from Amapolas, in a small mining village. She has, in essence, come home to die. Fran, however, who is twice divorced, wants a remote retreat where she can entertain the latest love of her life—the handsome and distinguished Francisco Alvarado, or Paco, as she calls him. Fran is currently writing a travel book on Mexico to be published in the United States. Although the reader can only assume that she bought the two lots in order to be closer to her mother, Fran is rarely in residence, as she is too busy pursuing her elusive dreams—in other words, Paco—to spend time with her mother.

As Bud sells the lots and oversees the construction of the houses, the four Americans are eventually joined by others. One of these is Herr Otto von Schramm, a seventy-five-year-old expatriate Austrian musician, who is heard day after day pounding a single note on his Steinway concert grand piano. Until his sister, Madame Anna, comes to join him, he is rarely seen. Despite Bud's rosy prognosis, however, the lots prove difficult to sell, and so the project never reaches full occupancy.

Although set in the 1960's, *Consider This, Señora* could have as easily been set in the 1990's; there is nothing to ground the themes or characters in that particular time period. In fact, in Amapolas one day is much like the next, a fact best illustrated by Don Enrique's forgetting to cross dates off his calendar: They tend to slip by "unnoticed." Sue, too, falls victim to the lethargy of the place as she lets the letters from her former husband pile up, unanswered. The setting and characters reinforce this sense of timelessness. The elderly Pepe Gómez, the oldest man Sue "had ever seen," recalls an earlier, more glorious time. As the grandson of Don Enrique's great-grandfather's majordomo, Pepe is an aging reminder of a time before the Revolution of 1910, when the ancestral home was a prosperous estate—echoed in the name of the nearby village: Amapolas, meaning "poppies." Now Amapolas is dry and barren, as Pepe is old and bent. A certain continuity is established via Patricio and Altagracia Gómez, Pepe's great-grandchildren, who now serve the Americans living on the former estate just as Pepe's grandfather served Don Enrique's family.

The other Mexican characters, too, continually evoke the past. Don Enrique maintains connections with Pepe because of their ancestors' mutual bond. Further, Don Enrique's description of his ancestral home to prospective buyers Bud and Sue necessarily prompts reminiscences of his illustrious ancestors: "On my father's side, . . . a governor, a conductor of the national symphony, a rector of the university. On my mother's, a foreign minister and two bishops." Furthermore, Patricio and Altagracia fall naturally into positions of servitude to the Americans who come to inhabit the land formerly served by their ancestor. Even the woman in the village post office, Carmen, inherited her post following the retirement of her mother, Old Carmen. The Mexicans have a long memory and sense of tradition.

In contrast, the Americans exist solely in and for the present. Literally as well as symbolically, they are fleeing their pasts. Bud, unbeknown to the others, has fled tax-evasion charges in Arizona. For her part, Sue desires a place to think following her divorce, away from well-meaning family and friends. Fran hopes to find a secluded spot, away from the city and other ties, to draw her beloved Paco to her, to fan the fading flames of their passion. Ursula is escaping old age by returning to the land of her youth. Even Herr Otto has a mysterious past, only hinted at, which may include flight from Germany and its concentration camps of World War II.

Most interesting, perhaps, is the way each of the protagonists views their retreat, Mexico. Sue sees the country through the eyes of a painter. She fills canvases with the endless sky; she paints the faces of the children. She continually seeks to interpret what she sees and experiences, and travels endlessly in her pursuit of subjects. Watching her sketch the property as she and Bud are preparing to buy it, Don Enrique is a bit alarmed: "Consider this, señora. . . . You are transforming Amapolas into something more beautiful than it is."

Sue's delusion at the outset foreshadows that of all the other Americans as well— they make their retreat out to be more than it is. Granted, the wealthy Americans bring a certain prosperity to the area, best symbolized perhaps by Sue's taking the young and gawky Altagracia under her wing, fitting her with braces, and buying her new clothes. They mingle in local affairs and shop in the local markets, becoming known for the profusion of flowers they purchase. Unfortunately, certain things they cannot change: the poverty, the disease, the continual droughts. By the end of the novel, the foreigners are gone, to seek their dreams somewhere else.

Their self-delusion is further symbolized by Fran's travel book. Her descriptions of Mexican cities, hotels, and restaurants ignore the truth—the bad food and lousy service—in favor of painting a rosy picture of the country. Her delusion is also mirrored in her affair with Paco, who is handsome, wealthy, and Harvard-educated;

Fran glamorizes him and ignores his philandering. The publication of her book coincides with the end of their affair.

Ursula too sees Mexico in her own way. As death draws near, she reminisces on her childhood. She recalls riding her horse, Rosi, down a steeply winding road to the nuns' school accompanied by the gardener, Manuel. She delighted in trying to teach the illiterate Manuel how to read and write. A month before her death, Ursula persuades Patricio to drive her to the village where she grew up.

Despite her sketchy memory, the two, through trial and error, navigate unmarked roads until they at last reach the nuns' school, which is in ruins, and the road, now closed, that led to her home. From a cluster of adobe huts emerge some twenty people, obviously very poor and curious about their unusual visitors. The bleak reality of the present clashes with the fond remembrances of the past. In a last romantic gesture, Ursula stubbornly shoves thousand-peso bills into the hands of anyone claiming to be related to Manuel, despite Patricio's warning that they may be claiming to be related to her friend only in order to get the money.

Most enigmatic of the four Americans is Bud. He, too, sees in Mexico opportunity, but of a baser kind. He is driven by money. When he haggles with Don Enrique over price for the land, he has "no interest in the colonial towns of Mexico or in the saints who protected them." He sees only the possibility of making a profit, ignoring the area's remoteness and lack of reliable water supply. Yet Bud is the one most influenced by his stay in Mexico, and is in fact the only one of the four who remains by book's end. Once a thorn in Sue's side, discouraging her interference in the lives of the Mexicans, he begins a relationship with Altagracia, who becomes over the course of the novel a mature and beautiful young woman. When Altagracia's aunt is being cheated out of her absent husband's paychecks, which are being stolen from the mail, Bud tracks down the thief and takes care of her family. His love for Altagracia engenders his love for Mexico, brings to him a certain humanity, and ultimately wins the sympathy of the reader.

The book's setting is essential to Doerr's quietly perceptive tale of life and death, of escape and self-discovery. Mexico's people, landscape, and sense of history are interwoven to form the rich tapestry against which Doerr's characters are brought to life.

> Sue Ames had noticed Mexican excess as soon as she drove across the border. First, the plethora of junkyards lining the road south. . . . Then a hundred miles of desert. Then a hundred miles of grazing land. Then the sudden green of fields where corn and chiles shared the furrows under steep mountainsides of darkening blue.
>
> The Mexican sky was excessive too, she believed. Wider than others, it stretched over people who appeared no fonder of life than death, as they darted on bicycles between trailer trucks and buses and hurried hand in hand, whole families strong, across divided freeways.

In the end, each protagonist comes to some sort of resolution. Bud overshoots his budget and loses the property, but marries Altagracia and starts yet another property development. Sue is reconciled with her former husband, and they leave Amapolas forever. Fran loses Paco but finds Carter Riley, an archaeologist, and leaves Mexico to travel with her new love. Even Ursula, though dead, leaves Mexico, as her ashes are taken back to the United States to be spread near those of her husband.

The Mexicans, with their quiet tolerance, watch the Americans come and watch them go. The Americans' mass exodus prompts the very perceptive remark of Don Enrique at book's end that the reason for the Americans' short stay and eventual departure was that they "had moved too far from the dwellings and graves of their ancestors.... 'Their roots are shallow from frequent transplanting.'" In fact, Sue alone among the Americans has planted an extensive garden during her stay, and she alone retains possession of her house, although she never returns to Amapolas. In essence, she has put down roots, of both a physical and symbolic kind. Doerr ends with Patricio's letters to her, in which he keeps her informed about Amapolas and her house. He writes of the extremes of the weather, the vagaries of the public officials, the projects started that through miscommunication and poor planning are never completed—in other words, business as usual.

Consider This, Señora is a well-written, frequently amusing take on the lives of its four protagonists, as well as the Mexican-North American dynamic. Having spent time in Mexico, Doerr has absorbed the essence of the land and its people and puts her chosen setting to good use, allowing the recurring themes of Catholicism, death, time, and self-discovery to resurface continually. Although the stories themselves are simple, her vivid imagery gives them substance and brings them to life in the mind of the reader.

Cynthia K. Breckenridge

Sources for Further Study

Booklist. LXXXIX, June 1, 1993, p. 1734.
Boston Globe. August 15, 1993, p. 14.
Chicago Tribune. August 22, 1993, XIV, p. 5.
The Christian Science Monitor. September 1, 1993, p. 13.
Los Angeles Times Book Review. August 22, 1993, p. 1.
The New York Times Book Review. XCVIII, August 15, 1993, p. 12.
The New Yorker. LXIX, November 8, 1993, p. 139.
Publishers Weekly. CCXL, June 21, 1993, p. 84.
USA Today. August 27, 1993, p. D5.
The Washington Post Book World. XXIII, August 8, 1993, p. 4.

THE CREATION OF FEMINIST CONSCIOUSNESS
From the Middle Ages to Eighteen-seventy

Author: Gerda Lerner (1920-   )
Publisher: Oxford University Press (New York). 395 pp. $27.50
Type of work: History
Time: The seventh century to 1870
Locale: Western Europe and the United States

The second volume in Gerda Lerner's Women and History *chronicles the twelve-hundred-year development of women's understanding of their own subordination and the genesis of strategies for change*

Principal personages:
> HROSVITHA OF GANDERSHEIM (932-1002?), the first woman dramatist and historian
> HILDEGARD OF BINGEN (1098-1179), an abbess, visionary, writer, preacher, scientist, and musician
> CHRISTINE DE PIZAN (1365-c. 1430), the writer of an allegorical history of women
> MARGERY KEMPE (1373-1438), a mystic and pilgrim; the first woman autobiographer in English
> ANNA VETTER (fl. 1663), a German pietist and visionary
> BETTINA BRENTANO VON ARNIM (1785-1859), a writer, salonnière, and reformer in the German Romantic movement
> RACHEL MORPURGO (1790-1870), a Jewish poet from Trieste
> SARAH GRIMKÉ (1792-1873), the abolitionist daughter of a Charleston slave-owner; a feminist theorist
> REBECCA JACKSON (1795-1871), an African-American mystic, evangelist, and Shaker
> EMILY DICKINSON (1830-1870), the poet-recluse

With *The Creation of Feminist Consciousness: From the Middle Ages to Eighteen-seventy* Gerda Lerner has completed her two-volume magnum opus *Women and History*, which she began in 1986 with *The Creation of Patriarchy*. Ranging over the whole of Western history from prehistory to the late nineteenth century, Lerner has theorized how and why the system of patriarchy originated (in the first volume) and the long process by which women began to "think their way out" of that systematic subordination (in the present volume). Unlike many historians, Lerner is undaunted by the task of working in many areas—sources in medieval Latin, Middle English, and Old High German; meditations of medieval mystics and Reformation visionaries; Jewish Romantic poetry; and medieval drama. Such a broad view is refreshing in an age of narrow specialization and makes the book particularly useful for the general reader and teacher. This "long history" view (the term—a favorite of Lerner—is from historian Mary Beard) enables Lerner to speculate and generalize about women in history, over varied epochs and cultures.

Lerner could be called the mother of modern women's history. Her books, especially *The Majority Finds Its Past: Placing Women in History* (1979), have nourished a whole generation of women's history scholars, helping them to ask new questions and use new sources in order to resurrect and restore women to history, to find the lost women, and to put women at the center of the analysis. Lerner insists that historians see with *both* eyes (traditional [men's] history and women's history) in order to correct for blind spots, gaining peripheral vision and depth perception. Recalling Galileo Galilei's whispered "And still, it moves" after his forced retraction of the heliocentric view of the universe, Lerner concludes: "Once the basic fallacy of patriarchal thought—the assumption that a half of humankind can adequately represent the whole—has been exposed and explained, it can no more be undone than was the insight that the earth is round, not flat."

Lerner's book is courageous not only because she does "long history" but also because she takes on many whose work has already been the subject of much historical and literary work—from Christine de Pizan and Hildegard of Bingen to Emily Dickinson. She also challenges traditional assumptions about women's intellectual prowess. Lerner is not cowed by the task, simply noting that women have not been system-builders in the past because they lacked access to education and their own history. Her own background as a short fiction and screenplay writer (in New York in the 1940's, before she returned to academe) undoubtedly helps with her exegesis of poets and dramatists and with her superb translations of such German poets as Anna Louisa Karsch (1722-1791).

She rigorously examines disparate sources to help answer her central question: How and when did feminist consciousness develop? Feminist consciousness, according to Lerner, is a five-step process:

(1) the awareness of women that they belong to a subordinate group and that, as members of such a group, they have suffered wrongs; (2) the recognition that their condition of subordination is not natural, but societally determined; (3) the development of a sense of sisterhood; (4) the autonomous definition by women of their goals and strategies for changing their condition; and (5) the development of an alternate vision of the future.

This process could come to fruition only once there was the possibility of autonomous women's organizations and a knowledge of women's history—so that women could build on what women before them had done.

Lerner points out how, time after time, a perceptive woman discovers important arguments to combat women's supposed inferiority—yet she will not have known or used the work of her predecessor a generation or several hundred years before. This is particularly true of feminist interpretations of biblical passages. Even more critical, that woman did not have the encouragement and mentoring of her foremothers but believed that she was the "only" woman to tackle the problem. Even into the twentieth century, Virginia Woolf in *A Room of One's Own* (1929) and Simone de Beauvoir in *The Second Sex* (1949) made erroneous assumptions about women writers and women's history. Lerner's great insight here is that women's subordination cannot be changed as long as history is obscured.

Reviewing the patriarchal assumptions that she had analyzed at length in the first volume, Lerner uses Aristotle's *Politics* and the debate over the U.S. Constitution two thousand years later to show how such assumptions continued to deny women membership in the polity. Both Aristotle and the Framers of the U.S. Constitution framers debated the rights of slaves but not of women. The notion of women's rights lingered below the threshold of the conceivable. Men had the power to define, and women were not a part of the discussion.

In the rest of the volume, Lerner analyzes women's struggle for education ("The Educational Disadvantaging of Women"); the importance of mysticism, biblical criticism, and religious thought for women's autonomous being; how the concept of motherhood gave women authority; the uses of female creativity; the beginnings of female spaces and networks; and the development of women's history. Two generalizations are made about women's education: Women are almost always less well educated than their brothers, and any education is a privilege of class. When education became institutionalized (instead of being handled by the family and apprenticeships), the disparity between male and female education became obvious: Women were not prepared for university education by being taught Latin and Greek unless they were of nobility and in line for rule. Nevertheless, there were islands of possibility for some women to be well educated at different times in history: the double monasteries (presided over by an abbess) and nunneries of the Middle Ages, the lay women's religious communities in the cities of Holland and the Rhineland in the twelfth century, some Renaissance courts in Italy and France, and centers of the Protestant Reformation. Still, "learned women" are estimated by Lerner to have been fewer than three hundred in all of Western Europe up to 1700.

Fully a third of the book is taken up with discussion of the importance of religion in women's quest for autonomy. The mode of mystical revelation has been essential for women. Christianity teaches that the Holy Spirit is no respecter of persons and that neither class nor gender is of qualifying importance. A sudden revelation of knowledge can come to anyone, and the "way of the mystics" is honored in church tradition—but it is particularly available to the unlettered and women. While only 20 percent of all saints are female (according to one study), a much larger proportion (40-52 percent) of saints known for "mystic contemplation, visions and communication with the supernatural" were women.

Lerner carefully analyzes Hildegard von Bingen and her works—visions, letters, sermons, biographies, biblical commentary, medical texts. Lerner believes that Hildegard was the first woman who derived her authority from God and convinced others (both her contemporaries and those who followed) that she had this authority. Her visions were the basis for her remarkable public role as abbess of the Rupertsberg convent. In this capacity she became a kind of Billy Graham or Ann Landers to whom everyone wrote for advice and answers to religious questions. She also traveled, visited, and preached—to emperors and popes as well as to common people. Her "sapiental theology" (Divine Wisdom) and her use of female symbolism and iconography, derived from her visions, are unique. Eve, for example, is shown not as a person but as a seashell filled with stars.

There are other fascinating sections on Margery Kempe, mystic and pilgrim, the writer of the first autobiography in English; on the Cathar and Beguine religious communities, which gave women leadership roles; on women in the left-wing sects of the Protestant Reformation—women such as German Pietist Anna Vetter, who prophesied redemption through the female, Quaker Margaret Fell, and "Mother" Ann Lee, the founder of the Shakers. In the nineteenth century a number of African American women became known for their mystical visions, preaching, and evangelistic fervor. A luminous example is Rebecca Jackson, who set up a Shaker community in Philadelphia for black women. The very rare Jewish women mystics (since women are specifically barred from these religious leadership roles in orthodox Judaism) are also examined in this section.

Another chapter chronicles the thousand-year history of women's biblical exegesis. Looking at three key texts—the Creation and the Fall from Genesis and the Pauline passages on women in the New Testament—Lerner shows that women commentators have developed a consistent form of argumentation for the female side of the Creator, against the culpability of Eve, and for women's leadership in the early Church. Yet these scholars have not been aware of their foremothers' work, arguing always against the church fathers and having to rediscover the same points. Sarah Grimké, a Southern Quaker abolitionist, stressed translation in her biblical commentary, noting readings based on the original language and insisting on her right to interpret meaning. Given Lerner's own Jewish background, her work on Christianity is especially interesting. Her theological explanations are very clear, even for a reader with little religious knowledge.

Women had to find some way of authorizing themselves to speak and write in the public world. Lerner examines the history of three modes of self-authorization: mystical experience (using the example of Hildegard of Bingen), the experience of motherhood, and independent creativity, especially poetry. Her extended discussion of Emily Dickinson is particularly illuminating.

She ends with two chapters designed to counterbalance the weight of the negative stories of the rest of the book. In a chapter on "female affinitive clusters and female networks," Lerner chronicles women's support groups from the medieval religious communities through the salons and "bluestockings" of the eighteenth century; she ends with an analysis of the German Romantic women, especially Bettina Brentano von Arnim. The chapter on women's history reiterates Lerner's belief that only with the development of women's history and an active women's movement have women been able to get beyond the repetition of individuals working in a vacuum.

Far-reaching and well written, *The Creation of Feminist Consciousness* will function as an excellent general text for the nonspecialist in women's history, but there is plenty of new detail and insight for the professional historian as well. The bibliography is very helpful, arranged topically, chronologically, and by individual.

Lerner has managed to negotiate the inevitable tradeoff a scholar must make between the narration of galvanizing stories and the scholarly and exhaustive evidence for analysis. Still, one wants more detail about all these notable women. Inevitably, she has shortchanged nineteenth century women, probably because of the more detailed knowledge already available of their movements, organizations, and lives. More is needed on networks in the eighteenth and nineteenth centuries. Medieval scholars may quarrel with some of her interpretations, as may Emily Dickinson specialists. Still, in telling these stories and in arguing that women must have both knowledge of their own history and a viable collective movement in order to come to feminist consciousness, Lerner creates a believable alternative to patriarchal history.

Margaret McFadden

Sources for Further Study

Belles Lettres. VIII, Summer, 1993, p. 60.
Booklist. LXXXIX, March 1, 1993, p. 1139.
Choice. XXXI, September, 1993, p. 194.
Kirkus Reviews. LXI, February 15, 1993, p. 205.
Library Journal. CXVIII, April 15, 1993, p. 104.
Ms. III, March, 1993, p. 63.
The New York Times Book Review. XCVIII, May 2, 1993, p. 12.
Publishers Weekly. CCXL, February 15, 1992, p. 227.
San Francisco Chronicle. September 26, 1993, p. REV8.
Women's Review of Books. XI, October, 1993, p. 19.

CRIME AND PUNISHMENT IN AMERICAN HISTORY

Author: Lawrence M. Friedman (1930-   )
Publisher: BasicBooks (New York). 577 pp. $30.00
Type of work: History
Time: 1619 to the twentieth century
Locale: The United States

A thorough account, scholarly but entertaining, of changes in the American criminal-justice system since Colonial times

> *Principal personages:*
> CHARLES GUITEAU, the assassin of President James A. Garfield
> ANTHONY COMSTOCK, an activist against pornography
> LIZZIE BORDEN, an accused ax-murderer
> BRUNO HAUPTMANN, a defendant in the Lindbergh kidnapping case
> ALFRED KINSEY, an Indiana University sexologist
> BILLY SOL ESTES, a Texas wheeler-dealer
> GEORGE WICKERSHAM, who headed a commission on police enforcement

About three and a half centuries ago, there was a stir in the colony of New Haven, Connecticut. A sow had given birth to a "monstrous" piglet. In the minds of the colonists, this was no accident. Surely the misbirth was some sort of omen. Specifically, it had to be a sign of sin, a sign of a revolting, deadly crime: carnal intercourse with the mother pig.

Thus commences one of the best books of 1993, a provocative, riveting tour de force, broad in scope, deep in substance, and written in a witty, urbane style by a mature social historian of the law at the top of his craft. The content encompasses both theory and practice, with the emphasis being on how America's criminal-justice system has responded over time to such "felt necessities" as politics, economics, and most of all the cultural mores of the American people. Lawrence M. Friedman demonstrates the malleability of the criminal-justice system in adjusting to power shifts in race, class, and gender in American society. Tracing the changing nature not only of crime but also of the justice system, urban police forces, and penitentiaries over three distinct epochs, the author makes profound observations about the shaping of the American character and its effect on society's treatment of antisocial elements.

Friedman asserts that during America's Colonial period, hierarchical village theocracies ("tight little islands") had little need for paid constables and punished evildoers in ways that stressed repentance and ultimate acceptance back into the community. The exception was for capital offenses, of which there were many. In bestiality cases, such as happened in New Haven, even the poor animal was executed. Punishment was public, communal, and frequently humiliating, such as spending time in the stocks or the pillory. In matters pertaining to religion and public morals, sentences could be as severe as banishment or death (although the Salem witchcraft trials were certainly an aberration) or as mild as a warning or a fine.

Social and geographic mobility characterized the nineteenth century (at least for free, white, adult males), giving rise to the need for laws relating to bigamists and swindlers, duelists and vigilantes. In the wake of rapid industrialization, immigration, and urbanization, epidemics and threats to the sanctity of the marketplace gave rise to public-health laws. In a chapter entitled "Power and Its Victims," Friedman shows how such laws were sometimes manipulated to impede religious and racial minorities from playing by the so-called laissez-faire rules of the game. Attempts were made to force the Chinese out of the laundry business, Catholics out of having convents, and free blacks out of antebellum cities. When resort to nuisance ordinances failed, vigilantes sometimes took the law into their own hands. Victims had little recourse.

Riots against blacks, Catholics, and Chinese were one thing; attacks on the property of the elite quite another. As cities teemed with unruly newcomers, professional police forces were formed amid hot debates over whether the crime fighters should be outfitted with uniforms and side arms.

In terms of abject institutional brutality, no antebellum practice matched the horror of the New South's convict-lease system, where life expectancy was measured in months rather than years. The Georgia chain gang lasted well into the twentieth century, although revulsion against whipping, branding, and hanging led to the gradual elimination of these practices, at least as public spectacles. It is disquieting to read Friedman's accounts of the morbid interest in executions. When one took place inside New York City's Tombs, the neighboring buildings, according to a contemporary observer, were "black with people, seeking to look down over the prison walls and witness the death agonies of the poor wretch who is paying the penalty of the law."

The functions of nineteenth century police forces supposedly were to uphold the law and preserve order. In truth the "men in blue" were unprofessional and often partook in rampant corruption as allies of political machines. Frequently headquartered in the heart of ghetto slums, such as Mulberry Bend on the Lower East Side of New York's Manhattan Island, they carried out rudimentary welfare functions as an arm of the big-city political machines. "New York's Finest," for example, cared for lost children and sheltered the homeless in lodginghouses. Philadelphia police provided such transients with tea and crackers. In times of depression these quarters became so overcrowded and filthy as to incur the wrath of progressive reformers, leading to their abolition.

By the turn of the century, lay justice and class control were giving way to crime control and incarceration of felons by professionals less susceptible to corruption but still susceptible to brutality. The precursor to the Federal Bureau of Investigation (FBI) was being set up under orders from President Theodore Roosevelt by a descendant of Napoleon, Attorney General Charles J. Bonaparte. During the course of the twentieth century, the FBI would grow tremendously in power and influence, coming to enjoy a reputation (probably undeserved), under Director J. Edgar Hoover, for integrity. The 1931 indictment of lawless city police forces by the Wickersham Commission, set up by President Herbert Hoover to assess prohibition enforcement, led to demands for a new professionalism at the local level. The commission described "Third Degree" weapons ranging from brass knuckles to rubber hoses (favored because they left fewer incriminating marks).

The Earl Warren court widened the scope of civil liberties, but the later proliferation of violent crime, which Friedman attributes to America's ethos of rampant individualism combined with profitable drug trafficking by macho youth gangs, has shifted the pendulum of public opinion away from law and toward order. The Warren Burger court, for example, brought back the death penalty after it had apparently been proscribed as cruel and unusual punishment. Insanity defenses have come under attack and have become more difficult to sustain; Friedman shows that juries tend to accept insanity defenses in cases where they sympathize with the defendant and tend to reject them in cases where the crime is especially heinous, regardless of the defendant's state of mind. To cite two nineteenth century examples, a jury convicted an obviously deranged Charles Guiteau for killing President James A. Garfield, yet another jury accepted the temporary insanity plea of Congressman Daniel Sickles, who killed his wife's lover.

Despite little or no evidence that they are a deterrent, drug laws have become more punitive, engulfing America's prison system in a population explosion of unprecedented proportions. No other Western industrialized country incarcerates so many of its citizens. More violent crime takes place in New York City daily, however, than in a year in Scandinavian cities. A gun-toting society obsessed with the cash nexus, the United States has allowed heavily armed drug lords to become the new *mafiosi*. Drug laws are the great exception to the trend toward decriminalizing "victimless" crimes or morals offenses. As Friedman mentions, triple-X video boutiques, government-financed abortions, or state lotteries would have been unimaginable to the Founding Fathers or to nineteenth century antipornographer Anthony Comstock.

Alfred C. Kinsey, the Indiana University sexologist, did as much to change public attitudes toward sex as Sigmund Freud or Hugh Hefner. Kinsey, writes Friedman, "had at one time been an expert on gall wasps. This may seem an obscure subject, but human sex life was so taboo that it was just as obscure, if not more so. Kinsey set about to rectify this situation." Friedman mentions the subsequent liberalization of fornication and sodomy laws, although he points out that the Supreme Court has refused to go as far as some states on this matter.

Crime and Punishment in American History covers everything from white-collar crime to treason and infanticide, from libel law to mail fraud. Since popular culture has played such a central role in how American society has defined criminal behavior, however, Friedman might well have discussed the influence of the automobile (one subject he virtually ignores is the rise of state police forces and highway patrols) and of television and cinema on the criminal-justice system. He does have some pithy things to say about the news media. Such circus trials as the 1926 Hall-Mills case and the 1935 Bruno Hauptmann case showed the deleterious effects of media publicity on justice. During the 1960's the high court even tossed out convictions in the Billy Sol Estes fraud case and the Sam Sheppard murder case because of juries' having been compromised by publicity.

Regarding famous trials as cultural sideshows rather than normative (plea bargaining being the common form of legal resolution), the author nevertheless demonstrates an impressive familiarity with the extensive literature on such celebrated and notorious defendants as Lizzie Borden (who probably wielded the ax that killed her father and stepmother, even though a jury found her not guilty) and Nicola Sacco and Bartolomeo Vanzetti (one of whom may have played a part in the crime—still, their trial, taking place during the Red Scare, was patently unfair). Friedman's treatment of women and the criminal-justice system (mostly as victims, since the overwhelming preponderance of crimes are committed by males) deserves high praise. The reader learns that women prisoners are nearly all of lower-class origin or former battered wives. To really have brought the book up to date, Friedman might have included material about stalking laws. Jack Kevorkian is nowhere to be found in the book either; as America's population ages, issues raised by the "suicide doctor" will grow in importance.

Friedman's book ends on a fatalistic note. He attributes the contemporary "siege of crime" not to Americans' frontier roots but to their present freedom-loving social fabric. It is "the price we pay," he concludes, "for a brash, self-loving, relatively free and open society." He doubts that the country will commit the resources to adopt his one practical proposal: a "full-employment program for young men with nothing to do." His final chapter, entitled "A Nation Besieged," ends with these words: "For now, at least, there may be nothing to do but grit our teeth and pay the price."

James B. Lane

Sources for Further Study

Chicago Daily Law Bulletin. CXXXIX, October 12, 1993, p. 2.
Chicago Tribune. September 5, 1993, XIV, p. 5.
Choice. XXXI, February, 1994, p. 1003.
The Economist. CCCXXVIII, September 25, 1993, p. 106.
Library Journal. CXVIII, August, 1993, p. 127.
Los Angeles Daily Journal. CVI, December 3, 1993, p. 7.
Los Angeles Times Book Review. September 19, 1993, p. 6.
National Review. XLV, November 1, 1993, p. 68.
The New York Times Book Review. XCVIII, September 26, 1993, p. 11.
Publishers Weekly. CCXL, June 28, 1993, p. 65.
The Washington Post Book World. XXIII, August 29, 1993, p. 11.

CRUELTY AND SILENCE
War, Tyranny, Uprising and the Arab World

Author: Kanan Makiya
Publisher: W. W. Norton (New York). 367 pp. $22.95
Type of work: Current history
Time: 1990-1993
Locale: Iraq, Kuwait, and other Arab countries

A pretentious, self-serving polemic on contemporary Middle Eastern politics by the author of a best-selling attack on the Iraqi regime of Saddam Hussein

> *Principal personages:*
> ABU HAYDAR, an anonymous Iraqi soldier
> KHALIL, A Kuwaiti in his early thirties
> OMAR, a young engineer from Baghdad
> MUSTAFA, a Kurd from northern Iraq
> TAIMOUR, a young Kurdish boy
> SADDAM HUSSEIN, president of Iraq
> EDWARD SAID, a prominent Palestinian American literary and cultural critic

Kanan Makiya made his name, or rather his pen name, Samir al-Khalil, with a book originally published in 1989 with little hope of finding a wide audience. *Republic of Fear*, which Makiya published under the pseudonym Samir al-Khalil, became a widely lauded best-seller in the wake of the 1990-1991 Persian Gulf crisis and war. *The Times Literary Supplement* called it "A sophisticated and brilliantly savage denunciation of Arab populist politics." *The New York Review of Books* praised it as "An extremely subtle and erudite analysis of the way [the Baath regime of Saddam Hussein] actually thinks and functions." *Republic of Fear* may deserve such praise; it is hard for someone who has not read it to judge. *Cruelty and Silence*, unfortunately, is another matter.

Several of Samir al-Khalil's essays, and a review of his short book on Baathist Iraqi architecture, *The Monument* (1991), were published in the centrist *New York Review of Books* in the wake of the Gulf War. Readers received the (surely accurate) impression that the writer used a pseudonym for reasons of personal safety. Yet the pseudonym—and Makiya's later dramatic abandonment of it—became a controversial part of his mystique and celebrity as a commentator on Arab and Iraqi politics. Lawrence Weschler's long, helpful profile of Makiya and his architect father Mohamed Makiya appeared in the January 6, 1992, issue of *The New Yorker*.

Cruelty and Silence must not be read without reference to the controversy its author's postures and opinions have aroused. By no means should it be a first source for readers seeking greater knowledge of Arab politics. To Makiya's discredit, he has published what amounts to a confused diatribe against other Arab intellectuals; most unfortunately, he squandered a good opportunity to write a book that would interest and educate the general Western reader. One wonders why it was published in English. Is it uncharitable speculation to suggest that the book's author and/or publisher wanted to profit financially from the name recognition of Samir al-Khalil and the possibly well-deserved success of *Republic of Fear*?

The introduction of the book under review begins by telling how the invasion of Kuwait and the Gulf War made *Republic of Fear*, as Makiya puts it, "something as close to a best-seller as a specialist book on one country of the Middle East (barring Israel) can be in the English language." He writes (self-servingly): "Strange as it may seem now, only a short while ago very few people were willing to believe that things were that bad inside Iraq. Many a reader or editor found the manuscript 'biased and one-sided,' not scholarly enough, or excessively polemical." He dismisses the notion, widespread in some circles, that the United States is to blame for the Gulf War. "The Gulf Crisis was never simply a matter of foreign manipulation or of the evil man playing the demagogue; it was at bottom an Arab moral failure of historic proportions." In *Cruelty and Silence* he does not "claim to have fully explained what went wrong; my purpose is to acknowledge and describe it."

Though it usually is not appropriate to fault an author for something he does not attempt, one must ask wherein might lie the value of a book such as *Cruelty and Silence*, especially for an English-speaking readership, if it does not explain. "The first part of the book . . . is by far the most important; it is a journey through that cruelty told in words of individuals who experienced it at first hand," Makiya writes. "My role was to turn the words of the heroes of this book—Khalil, Abu Haydar, Omar, Mustafa, and Taimour—into stories, tales of the otherwise impossible-to-believe things that we human beings are capable of doing to one another."

An admirable sentiment. Yet Makiya's treatment of such searing material is aesthetically and intellectually sloppy. Disputing a harsh critic of *Republic of Fear* he writes:

> How important is the fact that at least 100,000 innocent Iraqi men, women, and children were trucked from their villages to their deaths over a six-month period in 1988? How important is it that since 1975, no less than 3,500 Kurdish villages have been demolished by the Iraqi government in the name of Arabism?

The answer, to put it brutally, is: no more or less important than that Hitler slaughtered six million Jews in the name of racial purity, or that Burma's military junta slaughters and enslaves its citizens in the name of central control over ethnic minorities, or that the United States destroyed villages in Vietnam in the name of democracy. Few dispute that Saddam Hussein is murderous. But Makiya, by clumsily retelling a few horror stories from the war, makes an offensively proprietorial claim to awareness of and concern about the regime's atrocities. Indeed, that is the point of the book's second section, whose title, "Silence," refers to Arab intellectuals who he believes should have responded differently to the invasion of Kuwait. "While the cruelties that are talked about in Part One were going on, the Arab intellectuals who could have made a difference if they had put their minds to it were silent. . . . The main point of this book is that the collective Arab silence toward the cruelties that are so often perpetrated in the name of all Arabs originates from many years of thinking in a certain way . . . it is *a politics of silence*" (Makiya's emphasis).

The basic theme of Makiya's attack seems to be that Arab intellectuals have failed to speak out frankly and concretely on the *Arab* sources of Arab misery and oppression. Prominent among his targets is the well-known literary and cultural critic Edward Said. Makiya writes of Said's book *Orientalism* (1978) that it "makes Arabs feel contented with the way they are, instead of making them rethink fundamental assumptions which so clearly haven't worked. . . . [Young Arabs] desperately need to unlearn ideas such as that 'every European' in what he or she has to say about their world is or was a 'racist.' " He goes on: "The very adoption of the book in academic institutions of learning in the West—at a time when empires had long since collapsed (Britain and France) or were in a state of terminal decline (the United States)—suggests the irrelevance of its guiding thesis to modern Western scholarship on the Middle East."

Makiya's point seems to be that Arabs, notably Arab intellectuals, need to look lucidly at their own culture and take responsibility for its faults and cruelties. This surely is true. Yet many would argue that imperialism is far from dead, and in any case a less splenetic, less hurriedly composed book could have made Makiya's point much more effectively. The poor quality of his storytelling; his frequent resort to facile *pensées* ("No one can know what tomorrow will bring, and so everything and nothing are always possibilities in moments of great crisis"); his verbosity ("But political positions are not what I am trying to grapple with here; they will be considered in the second half of this book"); his sloppy grammar ("Khaled grew angry and bitter toward Palestinians resident in Kuwait *whom*, he felt, supported the Iraqi occupation" [emphasis added]); his vastly excessive quoting of long extracts from interviews—all these, along with the book's poorly conceived structural conceit, combine to undermine the reader's confidence in Makiya as a reporter or a thinker.

One begins to assume his adversaries are right, which may be unfortunate, since surely they are at least partly wrong. It is just that from Makiya's account it is so difficult to tell. Certainly it is important for different camps of Arab intellectuals to argue with each other, in pursuit of an understanding of the Gulf War's implications. Certainly Makiya has at least a few good points. By publishing such an undisciplined, mean-spirited rant, though, he does his own cause little good.

Cruelty and Silence was published simultaneously in English, Arabic, and Kurdish. Confused and poorly written though it is, it surely is a contribution of sorts to an important debate among Arabs. For readers interested in that debate, a very good starting point is Eqbal Ahmad's review of *Cruelty and Silence* in *The Nation* of August 9, 1993. Ahmad, a MacArthur Foundation fellow and teacher at Hampshire College (and, as he acknowledges in his review, a friend of Edward Said), scathingly dissects Makiya's book, finding in it factual errors, unprofessional interviewing methods, and offensive attitudes. Makiya's "libels against Islam and Arab culture are far too sophomoric—and tasteless—to be recounted here," writes Ahmad. "He has not a positive thing to say about the values and traditions—tribal, communal, spiritual or aesthetic—that bind the peoples of the Middle East. The world he sees is engulfed in 'cruelty and silence.' "

If *Cruelty and Silence* were not such an unremittingly bad book, Makiya's attitudes and claims might invite interesting comparisons to V. S. Naipaul, particularly Naipaul's travel book about four (non-Arab) Muslim countries, *Among the Believers: An Islamic Journey* (1981). Naipaul was thoroughly an outsider to the countries he wrote about (Iran, Pakistan, Malaysia, and Indonesia), while Makiya is an Arab writing about his own culture. Yet one hears Naipaul's concerns echoed throughout *Cruelty and Silence*. "The answer to the question that haunts all Arabs—Who am I?—has . . . increasingly taken on the form of a move toward tradition—Islam—or, as in the case of [poet Nizar] Qabbani, a revolt against facts," writes Makiya. And Naipaul's book, like Makiya's, was mostly praised by the establishment literary press and vilified by those outside the mainstream. Charles Michener in *Newsweek* (November 16, 1981) called *Among the Believers* "a brilliant report of social illness." Auberon Waugh in the *Daily Mail* called it "beautifully written and almost impossible to put down." Pakistani novelist Bapsi Sidhwa called it "such a superficial little book" and told an interviewer: "But what does that book amount to, written in any language? It could be condensed into a feature article on a tour into Pakistan, Iran, etc., etc. There's nothing creative in it. But it may be only in the West that these writers are considered so important."

Geraldine Brooks in *The Wall Street Journal* (April 7, 1993) called *Cruelty and Silence* "one of the most important books ever written on the modern Middle East." Eqbal Ahmad asserts that

> With his rationalizations, dual lives, pseudonymous pretensions, ill-founded hates and self-absorption, Makiya is a mess, just the type the media would find suited to personify the good Arab. . . . The media award and extol him because he serves their purpose: He confirms their stereotypes about Arabs and Muslims, argues that imperialism exists only as an alibi for Third World tyranny, calls for an activist American role in remaking the Middle East and bashes the *betes noires*—Edward Said and Noam Chomsky—of the Western right and center. Above all, after Communism's demise a book like this can be pressed into demonizing Islam as the latest menace to Western civilization.

Ahmad's review should not be read uncritically. For a reader serious about studying the modern Middle East, though, it is a very good starting point—far better than Makiya's book itself.

Ethan Casey

Sources for Further Study

Foreign Affairs. LXXII, Summer, 1993, p. 208.
The Nation. CCLVII, August 9, 1993, p. 178.
National Review. XLV, July 5, 1993, p. 51.
The New Republic. CCIX, July 19, 1993, p. 37.
New Statesman and Society. VI, May 14, 1993, p. 34.
The New York Review of Books. XLI, May 27, 1993, p. 3.
The New York Times Book Review. XCVIII, June 27, 1993, p. 7.
The New Yorker. LXIX, April 26, 1993, p. 114.
Publishers Weekly. CCXL, March 1, 1993, p. 46.
The Times Literary Supplement. June 11, 1993, p. 14.

CULTURE AND IMPERIALISM

Author: Edward W. Said (1935-   )
Publisher: Alfred A. Knopf (New York). 380 pp. $25.00
Type of work: Literary and cultural criticism; history
Time: Primarily the nineteenth and twentieth centuries
Locale: Great Britain, France, and the United States; Africa, the Caribbean, India, Ireland, and the Middle East

> *In this successor to* Orientalism, *one of the most influential texts in contemporary criticism, Edward Said argues that culture and empire have been inextricably intertwined under the aegis of Western arrogance*

Edward Said's ambitious new book reconsiders a historical experience the nature of which, on a factual level, is not subject to debate. In the course of the nineteenth century, the European powers—preeminently Great Britain—gained control of an enormous proportion of the earth's surface. By 1914, Said writes, "Europe held a grand total of roughly 85 percent of the earth as colonies, protectorates, dependencies, dominions, and commonwealths." If that figure seems high (Said refers us to Harry Magdoff's *Imperialism: From the Colonial Age to the Present,* 1978), no one will question the general scope of European colonialism. By the same token, while there is more room for debate about the nature of American imperialism, the policies of the United States in the Philippines, in Central America, and in many other regions have undeniably revealed the arrogance of power that characterized European colonialism.

This record of Western imperialism (still a virulently potent presence, many would argue) is familiar enough, the subject of exhaustive historical investigation. Said's central claim, however, is that even while acknowledging the brutal realities of empire as earlier generations could not, we have failed to grasp the impact of imperialism not only on the colonized but also on the colonizers.

Said regards the relationship between imperial powers—his focus is on Great Britain, France, and the United States—and the distant lands they dominated or continue to dominate as "constitutively significant to the culture of the modern West." By repeated emphasis on what he calls "the all-pervasive, unavoidable imperial setting," Said asserts that the imperial relationship—with its oppositions between superior and inferior, civilized and primitive, white and colored, domestic and exotic, its perverse assurance that certain peoples were destined to be ruled by others—was absolutely fundamental: "No area of experience was spared the unrelenting application of these hierarchies." While he explicitly disavows a crude determinism, à la Marxism-Leninism, he is particularly interested in exploring the intricate cultural manifestations of imperialism, not only in unashamedly racist and jingoistic pronouncements such as one finds in the writings of Thomas Carlyle but also in oblique form in such unlikely sources as the novels of Jane Austen. At the same time, Said wants to read Carlyle and Austen and Rudyard Kipling and Joseph Conrad side by side with "the enormously exciting, varied post-colonial literature produced in resistance to the imperialist expansion of Europe and the United States in the past two centuries. To read Austen without also reading [Frantz] Fanon and [Amílcar] Cabral—and so on and on—is to disaffiliate modern culture from its engagements and attachments."

That is the thrust of *Culture and Imperialism*, but such a summary hardly suggests the achievements or the failures of this complex, frequently maddening book. A Palestinian American born in Jerusalem, educated at Cairo's elite Victoria College and at Harvard University, Said is steeped in English literature and the Western cultural tradition (he has written widely on music in addition to the literary and polemical pieces for which he is best known), yet he also shares the intense anger that animates many writers from the Third World. In *Culture and Imperialism* he seeks to define a stance that is true both to his experience of literature and of art more generally and to his enforced awareness of imperialism. Rather than being anomalous, he suggests, his in-betweenness is exemplary: "No one today is purely *one* thing. Labels like Indian, or woman, or Muslim, or American are not more than starting-points, which if followed into actual experience for only a moment are quickly left behind."

That stance offers a welcome contrast to the increasingly strident voices of identity politics (whose targets have included Said himself). Much of Said's argument, however, does not so readily command assent. Most obviously questionable is the way in which he presents his project in relation to other work being done in literary studies.

A reader who had to depend on *Culture and Imperialism* as a guide to the current critical scene would be grossly misinformed. First, in insisting on the connection between culture and empire, Said repeatedly invokes an opposing view, one that he claims is dominant in the humanities, according to which works of art are seen as inhabiting "an isolated cultural sphere, believed to be freely and unconditionally available to weightless theoretical speculation." This opposing view insists on the autonomy of art, cut off entirely from history. To anyone who is familiar with contemporary criticism (and especially criticism devoted to the novel, the form to which Said's attention is largely restricted), this characterization will be simply baffling. While there are critics (and novelists) who affirm the autonomy of art in the terms outlined by Said, they are far from dominating critical discourse.

Even more baffling is Said's failure to acknowledge the extent to which the very approach he advocates has become one of the most fashionable—perhaps *the* most fashionable—in contemporary criticism. Again and again he insists that critics have ignored the connection between culture and empire. While he notes that "a new group of often younger scholars and critics—here, in the Third World, in Europe—are beginning to embark" on the course he proposes in *Culture and Imperialism* (he adds that "the efforts so far made are only slightly more than rudimentary"), and while he generously acknowledges the work of several former students in his introduction, the reader would never guess from Said's account that academic publishers' lists are positively crowded with titles such as Rob Nixon's *London Calling: V. S. Naipaul, Postcolonial Mandarin* (Oxford University Press, 1991; Nixon is one of the former students whom Said acknowledges), Zohrah T. Sullivan's *Narratives of Empire: The Fictions of Rudyard Kipling* (Cambridge University Press, 1993), Nigel Leask's

British Romantic Writers and The East: Anxieties of Empire (Cambridge University Press, 1993), and Annie E. Coombes's *Reinventing Africa: Museums, Material Culture, and Popular Imagination in Late Victorian and Edwardian England* (Yale University Press, 1994). It won't do to object that these are all very recent titles; this highly selective list is representative of a scholarly outpouring dating to the late 1980's. Aggressively marketed by publishers under such headings as "postcolonial studies" and "cultural studies," books in this vein are ubiquitous in the 1990's, and a look at the leading scholarly journals will reveal the same pattern.

The discrepancy between actual critical practice and Said's description of it really is striking. Thus, for example, Said writes:

> there is no way that I know of apprehending the world from within American culture (with a whole history of exterminism and incorporation behind it) without also apprehending the imperial contest itself. This, I would say, is a cultural fact of extraordinary political as well as interpretative importance, yet it has not been recognized as such in cultural and literary theory. . . .

But the perspective that Said outlines here is right in the mainstream of "cultural and literary theory" today; see for example the volumes published in Duke University Press's New Americanists series, under the general editorship of Donald E. Pease, such as *Cultures of United States Imperialism* (1994) and *National Identities and Post-Americanist Narratives* (1994).

In itself the fact that "postcolonial theory" has been adopted and applied by many academics says nothing about its validity. On one hand, the theory's popularity could be a tribute to its great explanatory power. On the other hand, there is always reason for skepticism when a theory is taken up whole instead of undergoing sustained critical examination. Suddenly a great many critics are using the same language: "The proliferation of oriental settings in British Romantic literature was not fortuitous, but linked in important ways with Britain's emergence as a global imperial power." Key terms recur with dizzying frequency: "representations," "metropolitan center," "construction of national identity." A criticism that specializes in ideological vigilance rarely turns its suspicions on itself.

This leads to the most problematic aspect of *Culture and Imperialism*. Throughout the book, Said refers to what he calls "contrapuntal reading" or "contrapuntal analysis." Reading contrapuntally means "extending our reading of texts to include what was once forcibly excluded—in *L'Etranger*, for example, the whole previous history of France's colonialism and its destruction of the Algerian state, and the later emergence of an independent Algeria (which Camus opposed)." Given this emphasis ("contrapuntal analysis" even has its own entry in the index, with seventeen page references), it is surprising that Said never attempts to step outside his own argument to imagine how a critic might read the key assumptions and inferences of *Culture and Imperialism* contrapuntally.

Consider one of Said's central themes: the way in which the Western imperial powers, "permeated with ideas about unequal races and cultures," were utterly complacent in their sense of superiority. Said returns to this fact again and again, as if it were remarkable, in need of elaborate analysis. He says that we must "comprehend how the great European realistic novel accomplished one of its principal purposes— almost unnoticeably sustaining the society's consent in overseas expansion"—as if, without the prop of the novel, those once-complacent imperialists might suddenly begin to question what they were doing.

In fact, however, as even a cursory study of history or anthropology will confirm, "ideas about unequal races and cultures" are not distinctive to modern Western societies. Said knows this, of course, and must acknowledge it, but he does so in a most peculiar way:

> All cultures tend to make representations of foreign cultures the better to master or in some way control them. Yet not all cultures make representations of foreign cultures *and* in fact master or control them. This is the distinction, I believe, of modern Western cultures.

One does not know where to begin to refute this, so remote is it from historical reality. Were the Arab rulers of Spain not mastering or controlling a foreign culture? Were the Chinese who conquered the indigenous peoples of Southeast Asia not mastering or controlling foreign cultures?

In ancient China, Frank Dikötter writes (*The Discourse of Race in Modern China*, 1992),

> The border between man and animal was blurred. "The Rong are birds and beasts." This was not simply a derogatory description: it was part of a mentality that integrated the concept of civilization with the idea of humanity, picturing the alien groups living outside the pale of Chinese society as distant savages hovering on the edge of bestiality. The names of the outgroups were written in characters with an animal radical, a habit that persisted until the 1930s. . . .

How does the Chinese attitude toward non-Chinese differ fundamentally from the European attitude toward non-Europeans? If it is true that similarly ethnocentric attitudes have characterized virtually all peoples, why is it remarkable that these attitudes were characteristic of Great Britain and France in their colonial heyday, and too often of the United States? Is it not more remarkable that today there is also a strong public critique of ethnocentrism, especially in the United States?

Said's argument depends on the premise that Western imperialism is unique—a premise that he hedges now and then, only to reassert it with renewed force. Once that assumption is questioned, the notion of a special link between culture and empire is thrown into doubt as well. Take for example Said's proposed reading of Camus' *The Stranger* (1942), which should include "the whole previous history of French colonialism and its destruction of the Algerian state." Why stop there? Why not extend the reading to an earlier epoch of imperialist advance, when Islamic armies from Arabia conquered North Africa, the homeland of St. Augustine, and effaced the Christian culture there so thoroughly that the average Bible-reading American has no idea that it was one of the flourishing centers of the early church? That would indeed be a contrapuntal reading, a "comparative literature of imperialism," but it is doubtful how much it would enrich our understanding of Camus.

John Wilson

Sources for Further Study

Commentary. XCVI, July, 1993, p. 60.
Foreign Affairs. LXXII, Summer, 1993, p. 194.
Journal of Historical Geography. XIX, July, 1993, p. 339.
London Review of Books. XV, April 8, 1993, p. 11.
Los Angeles Times Book Review. February 28, 1993, p. 3.
The Nation. CCLVI, March 22, 1993, p. 383.
The New York Times Book Review. XCVIII, February 28, 1993, p. 11.
Publishers Weekly. CCXXXIX, December 28, 1992, p. 51.
The Times Literary Supplement. February 19, 1993, p. 3.
The Washington Post Book World. XXIII, February 28, 1993, p. 1.

CULTURE OF COMPLAINT
The Fraying of America

Author: Robert Hughes (1938-   )
Publisher: Oxford University Press (New York). 210 pp. $19.95
Type of work: Current affairs

Reflections on the State of the Union by the Australian-born art critic and historian

Robert Hughes's new book is engaging, quotably witty, never dull; it can easily be read in an evening. As an analysis of what divides Americans, it is less than satisfactory, symptomatic of the moral confusion that it purports to anatomize.

Born in Australia but long resident in the United States, Hughes has been the art critic for *Time* magazine since 1970 and has written more than half a dozen books of criticism and art history. In addition, he is the author of *The Fatal Shore* (1987), a history of the early colonial period in Australia, and *Barcelona* (1992).

Culture of Complaint: The Fraying of America had its origin in a series of three lectures given by Hughes at New York Public Library in January, 1992. As Hughes explains in his introduction, the first two lectures appeared in condensed form as a *Time* cover story, "The Fraying of America" (February 3, 1992). Later, in preparing the lectures for publication in book form, he expanded them significantly and added references to events through the presidential election of November, 1992.

What does Hughes mean by "culture of complaint"? The phrase follows a formula that has become increasingly popular since Oscar Lewis wrote of "the culture of poverty" in the 1960's and Christopher Lasch of "the culture of narcissism" in the 1970's (see Stephen Carter's *The Culture of Disbelief: How American Law and Politics Trivialize Religious Devotion*, reviewed in this volume). Hughes's title suggests that he will attribute the "fraying of America" to an excessive readiness to complain on all sides, that he will trace the evolution of a culture in which people are climbing over one another to claim victim-status and in which a pervasive sense of entitlement persistently frustrates initiatives for the common good. Hughes makes sporadic gestures in this direction, finding affinities, for example, between "the rise of cult therapies which teach that we are all victims of our parents," the radical feminist image of "woman as helpless victim of male oppressor," and the notion that "the idea of 'quality' in aesthetics is little more than a paternalist fiction" contrived to exclude women and minorities. For the most part, though, Hughes's title turns out to be merely a gimmick, and for long stretches he abandons the theme of "complaint" altogether.

What then is Hughes's real subject? In the introduction he promises to address "the clouded issues of 'political correctness,' 'multiculturalism,' and the politicization of the arts," and indeed he does. The explanatory framework in which he treats these issues is neatly laid out in the dust-jacket copy:

> PC censoriousness and 'family-values' rhetoric . . . are only two sides of the same character, extrusions of America's puritan heritage into the present—and, at root, signs of America's difficulty in seeing past the end of the Us-versus-Them mentality implanted by four decades of the Cold War.

There, in a nutshell, is what Hughes's book is about.

The pattern is established early in lecture 1, "Culture and the Broken Polity" (the longest of the three by a good margin). After deftly dissecting several egregious examples of political correctness, Hughes makes a swift transition. One moment asserting that "the right is as corroded by bankrupt ideology as the academic left" (note that his critique of the left is modified by "academic," while the right is simply "the right"), the next he is saying that "The loss of reality by euphemism and lies was twenty times worse and more influential in the utterances of the last two Presidents and their aides than among *bien-pensant* academics." A page later, Hughes assures us that "The right has its own form of PC—Patriotic Correctness, if you like—equally designed to veil unwelcome truths. It, too, has a vested interest in keeping America divided, a strategy that bodes worse for the country's polity than anything the weak, constricted American left can be blamed for."

Repeatedly in the course of these lectures Hughes follows this pattern. Yes, political correctness is bad, yes, some proponents of multiculturalism distort history and promote separatism—but the "right" is just as bad; twenty times worse, in fact. After all, Hughes says, Reaganism was responsible for the Savings and Loan scandal that cost thousands of people their life savings. Indeed, Reagan's maleficent power knew no bounds; "his style of image-presentation cut the connective tissue of argument between ideas and hence fostered the defeat of thought itself." (Really? Whose thought? Perhaps some were more strongly affected than others.)

That the Savings and Loan scandal involved a widespread betrayal of public trust is clear, but what does it have to do with Hughes's thesis about the symmetry between left and right, political correctness and the phantom "Patriotic Correctness"? How does it relate to the "polarization" which left and right thrive on, their "vested interest in keeping America divided"? Let us take a specific case. Under the editorship of Hilton Kramer, *The New Criterion* (which Hughes refers to with scorn) has consistently and forcefully criticized what Jonathan Rauch calls "the new assault on free thought." Is Hughes suggesting that the validity of *The New Criterion*'s critique of campus speech codes, or of the theft of virtually the entire print run of a campus newspaper by black students who objected to an editorial therein, is in some way compromised by the Savings and Loan scandal? For the purposes of argument, let us suppose that President Bill Clinton and Hillary Rodham Clinton were culpable in the Whitewater scandal. Then, by Hughes's logic, would left-of-center critiques of Patrick Buchanan's divisive rhetoric concerning immigration somehow be invalidated?

Equally suspect is the logic of Hughes's claim that the polarization of contemporary American society is best understood in the context of the Puritan heritage and the aftermath of the Cold War. Throughout these lectures, Hughes uses the term "Puritan" as others might say "fascist." (This makes for some perplexity when, in his last lecture, "Art and the Therapeutic Fallacy," he tells us that to understand the current controversy over the arts "we have to go back to the very foundations of Protestant America, and not in some facile spirit of ridiculing the Puritans either.") He gives no evidence of knowledge of the Puritans beyond the familiar caricature, nor does he substantiate his assertion that political correctness is rooted in Puritanism. (Some commentators, such as the Slavist Gary Morson, have been struck instead by parallels between political correctness in American universities in the early 1990's and practices that flourished in the Soviet Union and its satellites for decades.)

Still, if it is difficult to establish the distant antecedents of this or that contemporary phenomenon in Puritanism, it is almost as difficult to disprove conclusively their existence—which is one reason that the Puritans remain such a popular scapegoat. With the Cold War, though, we are in the realm of recent history—so recent that we may be brought up short when we read: "Meanwhile the sense of common citizenship dissolved in a welter of issues that enable Americans to take unnegotiable stands on smaller things, now that they can no longer define themselves against the Big Thing of the Cold War." Meanwhile? Since all the issues that Hughes discusses were being hotly debated well before the Cold War ended, it is hard to know what he is talking about.

Before long, Hughes provides some examples: "With Communism gone, the politics of division needs other 'outsider' and 'deviant' groups to batten on, such as homosexuals. It also needs people or symbols to idealize. Hence . . . the bizarre politics and imagery of the new Sacrificed Body of American conservatism, the fetus." Here Hughes displays a notion of causality and a sense of chronology that merit his own appellation, "bizarre." Is there a shred of evidence to connect the intensity of public debate over abortion with the end of the Cold War?

Hughes goes on to make the same point in regard to multiculturalism ("There is no Marx left to fight, so forth we go in knightly array against the vague and hydra-headed Multi") and controversies over obscenity and public funding of the arts. Is it necessary to note that Allan Bloom's *The Closing of the American Mind* and E. D. Hirsch's *Cultural Literacy*, two of the most-often-cited titles in the multiculturalism debate, were published in 1987, well before the end of the Cold War?

Indeed, there is an incoherence at the heart of Hughes's vision of what ails America and how it might be fixed. "America," he writes, "is a collective work of the imagination whose making never ends"—a powerful image!—"and once that sense of collectivity and mutual respect is broken the possibilities of Americanness begin to unravel. If they are fraying now, it is because the politics of ideology has for the last twenty years weakened and in some areas broken the traditional American genius for consensus." This is the classic liberal response. The problem, Hughes would have us believe, lies with extremists, those purveyors of the "politics of ideology," the "politics of division."

Alasdair MacIntyre has observed that "Where the standpoint of a tradition involves an acknowledgment that fundamental debate is between competing and conflicting understandings of rationality, the standpoint of the forums of modern liberal culture presupposes the fiction of shared, even if unformulable, universal standards of rationality" (*Whose Justice? Which Rationality?*, 1988). This describes Hughes's stance perfectly. He positions himself as a bluff, no-nonsense man of the Enlightenment (and not an academic, but rather a "practising writer"). From this standpoint he slashes about, making short work of fools and knaves. But when he is done, who is left standing?

That is why something rings hollow about Hughes's invocation of "the traditional American genius for consensus." A gloss on what Hughes means by "consensus" is provided by an op-ed piece by the historian George Marsden, "Religious Professors Are the Last Taboo" (*The Wall Street Journal*, December 27, 1993). Marsden notes that in the academy today it is generally deemed unacceptable for a professor who practices a particular religion to teach about it. "We might think of some analogies," Marsden muses. "Perhaps no feminist should teach the history of women, or no political liberal should teach American political history." Indeed, the "compromise" which professors with religious convictions are expected to make is quite simple: In exchange for the privilege of teaching at the university, they are expected to give up freedoms which their colleagues enjoy as a matter of course.

While ideologues often exaggerate and exploit conflict to their own advantage, the "fraying of America" so vividly described by Hughes cannot—contrary to his repeated assertions—be attributed primarily to such manipulative strategies. Rather, it reflects genuine disagreement across a wide spectrum of issues.

Precisely because the divisions between Americans are real and often fundamental, men and women of good will must seek common ground wherever they can find it. Here is where a "sense of collectivity and mutual respect" must come into play. Hughes pays lip service to this principle, but he does not practice it very well. Consider his contemptuous treatment of Charles Colson, "one of the minor Washington villains of the Watergate years." Hughes recalls his skepticism when "Colson announced at the very gate of the minimum-security prison that he had seen the light of Christ and been born again. Surely Americans won't swallow this? But they did."

In the midst of this bit of good fun (the quoted passage is followed immediately by a reference to David Duke), Hughes never pauses to ask the question that would seem to be required of anyone presuming to judge the genuineness of another's conversion: what has Colson been doing in the twenty years since? During that time, Colson has devoted himself to Prison Fellowship, a ministry to prisoners that he directs. In 1993, this organization had more than fifty thousand volunteers visiting prisons throughout the United States. Colson has called for a total overhaul of the American correctional system, with an emphasis on restitution rather than incarceration except in the case of dangerous criminals. For his work with Prison Fellowship, Colson received the 1993 Templeton Prize for Progress in Religion—the equivalent of a Nobel Prize.

Prison Fellowship provides a model for the kind of limited consensus-building that is badly needed in our increasingly divided society. Colson's recommendations for prison reform are endorsed by other activists who do not share his religious convictions but who agree that the present system is inhumane and utterly counterproductive. Here is a real example of what Václav Havel, in a passage approvingly cited by Hughes, calls "politics as practical morality, as service to the truth, as essentially human and humanly measured care for our fellow humans."

John Wilson

Sources for Further Study

Artforum. XXXI, Summer, 1993, p. 100.
Business and Society Review. Spring, 1993, p. 67.
Los Angeles Times Book Review. March 28, 1993, p. 6.
The New York Review of Books. XL, April 22, 1993, p. 3.
The New York Times Book Review. XCVIII, April 11, 1993, p. 1.
The New Yorker. LXIX, April 19, 1993, p. 113.
Newsweek. CXXI, April 26, 1993, p. 67.
Publishers Weekly. CCXL, February 15, 1993, p. 220.
The Times Literary Supplement. May 21, 1993, p. 8.
The Washington Post Book World. XXIII, April 4, 1993, p. 3.

THE CULTURE OF DISBELIEF
How American Law and Politics Trivialize Religious Devotion

Author: Stephen L. Carter (1954-   )
Publisher: BasicBooks (New York). 328 pp. $25.00
Type of work: Current affairs

Arguing that strong religious communities strengthen American democracy, Carter contends that the nation's political and legal culture tends to treat religious believers with disdain, a result that he seeks to correct by showing how American religious life provides a needed bulwark against the intrusive power of the state

In his nineteenth century classic, *Democracy in America*, Alexis de Tocqueville, that astute French observer of the young nation's life, emphasized that "the religious atmosphere of the country was the first thing that struck me on arrival in the United States." Religion's importance in the United States, he added, was that it did so much to teach Americans what Tocqueville called "the art of being free."

A century and a half after the publication of *Democracy in America*, Stephen L. Carter, a leading legal scholar at Yale University, amplifies key parts of Tocqueville's understanding of religion in the United States. American religion, Carter affirms, still has much to teach about "the art of being free," but today the religious atmosphere of the United States tends to hinder that instruction. It does so because the atmosphere is dominated by a political and legal culture that leans toward trivializing religious devotion. If that trend continues, Carter fears that the result will be a culture of disbelief. Such a culture will undercut the diversity of religious commitment and perspective that helps to ensure the vitality of democratic life.

Carter's persuasive book combines theoretical and practical interpretation. Drawing on his impressive mastery of law and jurisprudence, as well as his perceptive religious understanding, he clarifies reflection about contemporary issues such as school prayer, abortion, euthanasia, and capital punishment. An additional virtue of the book is that Carter's scholarly analysis never obscures where the author stands.

As a legal scholar, he believes that the dominant legal and political forces in contemporary American life have interpreted the U.S. Constitution's First Amendment in ways that rob religious belief of its importance. Determined to safeguard the wall of separation between religion and the state, those forces have placed too little emphasis on the fact that the First Amendment's primary purpose is to provide protection for the "free exercise" of religious life. In Carter's judgment, the effect of First Amendment interpretations has too often promoted indifference, if not hostility, toward religion.

The "free exercise" of religion has been needlessly restricted, Carter argues, and the country is worse, not better, for it. Those philosophical views do not mean that Carter ends up with predictable public policy positions that reflect conventional conservative or liberal outlooks. He does think that the courts have properly proscribed formal prayer in the schools, and he is opposed to capital punishment. Although he would not deny women the right to abortion, he has strong "pro-life" sympathies as well. But his book is primarily an inquiry—not a set of public policy pronouncements—that reasons its way to views that he wants to be part of a wide-ranging national conversation about the state of the nation's union.

Carter's judgments are informed not only by his study of the law but also by his religious commitments and his ethnic heritage. A dedicated Christian of Episcopalian persuasion, Carter is also an African American who firmly believes that the free exercise of religion had much to do with civil rights advances in American society. He knows, of course, that religion has never been an unmitigated force for justice. Many of history's most destructive chapters have been written in blood spilled by and for religiously inspired causes. Even in the United States, the "free exercise" of religion is rightly checked and balanced by sound legal restraints to ensure that it does not become an instrument of oppression. Nevertheless, Carter affirms, religion remains overall a great force for good. "In recent history," he writes,

> we have seen religious witness against oppression around the world, which tyrannical governments have often met with antireligious slaughter. In America, we have seen religious witness against slavery and segregation, against the war in Vietnam, and against poverty. Witness of this kind will be most effective in a nation that truly celebrates its diverse religious traditions, valuing them instead of trying to hide them.

Carter carries no brief for every religious belief and practice, but he is deeply sympathetic when American religion plays a resisting, independent, minority role. When religious expressions work in that way, Carter insists, they "promote freedom and reduce the likelihood of democratic tyranny by splitting the allegiance of citizens and pressing on their members points of view that are often radically different from the preferences of the state."

A key strength of religion is its power to dissent not only from state power but also from the tyranny that cultural conformity and other forms of "majority rule" are tempted to enforce. Following Tocqueville, then, Carter upholds a tradition affirming the importance of religion as source of moral understanding that checks the tendencies of a secular state and culture to dominate tyrannically. Religion's proclivity to be unfashionable, its refusal to go along with what most people may find expedient, politically correct, or even rational—in short, the very dissenting aspect of religion that many of its critics most fear—is precisely religion's great strength and gift to a democratic republic.

Contemporary American society, however, is in danger of diminishing religion's strength, if not of rejecting its gift outright. Irony permeates that prospect because an overwhelming majority of Americans identify themselves as religious. Polls cited by Carter indicate, for example, that nine out of ten Americans believe in God and four out of five pray regularly. Americans are much more likely to attend worship services regularly than any other people in the Western world. Overwhelming numbers of them also report that religious faith is a crucial factor in their moral decisions. Granted, not all of these reportedly religious Americans take religion very seriously, but in Carter's view that fact has a lot to do with what he calls the trivialization of religious devotion. Religion has been trivialized in the United States not only because many people fail to take it seriously but also because secular authority—especially in our legal interpretations—often makes it impossible for religion to be, in Carter's words, little more than a private hobby that neither governs an individual's life decisively nor intrudes on anyone else's.

To see more of what Carter means, notice first that the United States is one of the most religious nations on earth, at least in the sense of having a deeply religious citizenry, but Americans are also wary when people are too zealous about their religious commitments. In particular, Americans are vigilant about guarding public institutions against explicit religious control. That vigilance certainly has its place, for religion is not without oppressive tendencies, and if any religious tradition dominates public institutional life, the outcome can be tyrannical. In contemporary American life, however, Carter thinks that this vigilance has lost its balance. A legitimate concern has reached too far and turned punitive toward religious influence on public life. Public expressions of religion are silenced, even punished, and the religiously devout are disabled "from working seriously in the realm of policy." One effect of this imbalance is that it is fine to be religious in private but religion is cast in a far more dubious light when private beliefs are publicly expressed and become the basis for public action.

There are exceptions to this rule. When restricted to the confines of generally accepted, official places of worship, religion is no bother. When its voice simply echoes sentiments or values held by the dominant culture, religion is no threat. But when religion reaches beyond these boundaries, cries about imposing religious values or undue political involvement are bound to be heard.

"Our public culture," writes Carter, "more and more prefers religion as something without political significance, less an independent moral force than a quietly irrelevant moralizer, never heard, rarely seen." In zealously preventing the imposition of religion, Carter believes, Americans have silenced public expression of religion too much for their own good. It is wrong, he argues, to think that religious impulses to public action should be prejudged as oppressive or even wicked. History, especially American history, cannot sustain such judgments. In history's long run, at least in the West, religion has had a liberalizing, democratizing effect that has undergirded human freedom and equality and that has resisted their enemies. Nor, according to Carter, can such restrictive attitudes toward religion in contemporary American life do justice to what religion actually is and entails, a point that should not be overlooked in a nation with such a long-standing commitment to defend religious liberty.

As Carter understands religion, it finds its primary location in traditions of group worship. Religion is essentially a social and public activity, not just a private and individualistic matter. Religion assumes the existence of a reality—most, but not all, Americans would call that reality God—which is more than human. In Carter's view, this reality is not bounded by the observed principles and limits of natural science. Even more important, this reality and the traditions it inspires make demands on their adherents.

Religious belief and practice require acting in some ways and not in others; they entail convictions about right and wrong, good and evil, that must find public expression. Those convictions must do so because no person's life is ever a purely private affair—we all live in public—and because the demands that religion enjoins rarely, if ever, are purely private matters, either. Thus, Carter fears trends that he sees: Americans endanger both religion and the ideal of democratic liberty to the extent that their suspicions about imposing religion escalate into positions that restrict American religion from informing and influencing the public dialogue on which the health of democracy depends.

Naturally, Carter's concerns direct his attention to the U.S. Constitution and its central role in establishing boundaries and protections for American expressions of religion. His jurisprudence underscores that "the metaphorical separation of church and state originated in an effort to protect religion from the state, not the state from religion. The religion clauses of the First Amendment were crafted to permit maximum freedom to the religious."

The American government can neither require sectarian observances nor favor one religion over another. Yet Carter holds that other considerations are equally valid: The government cannot bring sanctions against anyone's religious persuasion without a compelling reason to do so. Neither is it the government's place to ban religiously motivated people from influencing public policy. Nor is the government banned from listening to and being affected by such voices.

"The principal task of the separation of church and state," says Carter, "is to secure religious liberty." Thus, the state properly forbids the imposition of religious belief. But *imposing* religious belief must not be confused, and certainly not equated, with *acting* from religious motivation. Granted, the practices and programs that are advocated when people act from religious motivations may rightly be found wanting, but Carter's position is that it will not do to discriminate against them simply because those practices and programs arise from religious motivations. Instead, as Carter celebrates the separation of church and state as one of the greatest insights that American political philosophy has given to the world, he stresses that the state must avoid imposing religious belief so that people are free to express themselves religiously in public as well as in private.

But there is the rub: In contemporary American culture the difference between imposing religious belief and acting from religious motivation is not discerned clearly enough. Carter is concerned that American culture too readily equates the latter with the former, ignoring a crucial difference in the process. If people say publicly that they must do this or refrain from that, or that they advocate this and deplore that, because their religious persuasion requires it, they may be regarded as odd, irrational, scary, or worse—especially if their religious persuasion entails dissent from what the majority of society believes is right. According to Carter, however, religion's tendency to "thumb its nose at what the rest of the society believes is right" is invaluable for democratic life. To be sure, a society may need to protect itself from dissent that goes well beyond nose-thumbing, but Carter contends that the autonomy of religion should be upheld unless the reasons to check it are truly clear and compelling.

Taking different paths from those of the dominant culture is at the heart of religious life that affirms "the authority of God as *superior to* the authority of the state." Such autonomy for religion can help the nation to think more deeply, critically, sensitively, freely, and fairly about what is good, right, and just. A healthy democracy, Carter concludes, will not want religion to *impose* its particular values on society, but it should want religion to *influence* public life, because that is how religion helps to teach the art of being free.

John K. Roth

Sources for Further Study

ABA Journal. LXXIX, October, 1993, p. 114.
The Christian Science Monitor. October 15, 1993, p. 13.
Commonweal. CXX, October 8, 1993, p. 22.
The New Republic. CCIX, September 13, 1993, p. 4.
The New York Times Book Review. XCVIII, September 19, 1993, p. 15.
The New Yorker. LXIX, October 18, 1993, p. 127.
Newsweek. CXXII, September 20, 1993, p. 56.
Publishers Weekly. CCXL, July 26, 1993, p. 55.
U. S. News and World Report. CXV, September 20, 1993, p. 20.
The Washington Post Book World. XXIII, October 3, 1993, p. 8.

CURRICULUM VITAE
Autobiography

Author: Muriel Spark (1918-   )
First published: 1992, in Great Britain
Publisher: Houghton Mifflin (Boston). 213 pp. $22.95
Type of work: Autobiography
Time: 1918-1957
Locale: Edinburgh, Scotland; Africa; and London

A lively and engaging, though somewhat incomplete, memoir of Muriel Spark's first thirty-nine years

> *Principal personages:*
> MURIEL CAMBERG SPARK, a Scottish novelist, poet, and editor
> BERNARD CAMBERG, her father
> SARAH ELIZABETH MAUDE UEZZELL CAMBERG, her mother
> PHILIP CAMBERG, her older brother
> SYDNEY OSWALD SPARK, her first husband
> ROBIN SPARK, her son
> CHRISTINA KAY, a teacher at James Gillespie's High School for Girls and the model for Miss Jean Brodie
> DEREK STANFORD, a onetime collaborator with Muriel Spark who later perpetrated falsehoods about her

If American biographers and autobiographers offend good taste and decorum by publishing works that are too often ponderous in detail and embarrassingly personal, British autobiographers too often frustrate their admirers by producing memoirs that are sketchy in detail and evasive about personal matters. This is certainly the case with Muriel Spark's *Curriculum Vitae: Autobiography*, which lives up to its title by being a brief overview of the first thirty-nine years of her life. Though another volume is promised, presumably picking up where this one leaves off, many readers will put down this book with mixed feelings of desire and gratitude: desire for additional personal information, gratitude for the liveliness and charm of what they have been given.

In a brief introduction, Spark admits that since the 1940's she has been a fanatical hoarder of documents and acknowledges that this habit—and this book—is calculated to set the record straight. She is appalled, from a personal and scholarly point of view, that much of what passes for fact about her is incorrect and that as a consequence scholars of her work form erroneous conclusions. This is an admirable motive for autobiography, and presumably Spark has fulfilled her intention regarding those parts of her life covered by the present volume. Whenever necessary, she quotes at length from relevant documents to expose error and substitute fact.

It is not until the sixth chapter of this seven-chapter book, however, that the documentary evidence is available. The first five chapters are built of less rigid stuff—memories, often corroborated by friends or relatives. These chapters are, not surprisingly, the warmest, most charming, and most intimate in the book. They are also, and again not surprisingly, the most sketchy, although one suspects that the sketchiness is often deliberate.

The book opens with a succession of brief vignettes with enticing titles: "Bread, Butter, and Florrie Forde," "Tea," "Mrs. Rule, Fish Jean, and the Kaiser," and the like. In these are evoked the life of Edinburgh in the early 1920's, when Muriel was a young girl. Her father, a Jew, was an engineer; her mother, more embarrassingly, English. They enjoyed a rich home life, with frequent calls from interesting people, such as Professor and Mrs. Rule, an American couple brought there by his theological studies, and Mrs. Kerr, whose daughter Jean was training her voice for a career on the stage. From her earliest years, Muriel was a watcher of people, a child who found that by keeping quiet and listening carefully she could eavesdrop on the mysterious adult world. Such memories are often wonderfully sharp and evocative, recalling a way of life that seems foreign now. Was it really as rich with sights and smells, with dialect expressions and interesting characters, as Ms. Spark remembers? It does not really matter. What does matter is the verisimilitude of the picture she draws, the sense of stability, warmth, and peace that pervades those early memories. Hers was a rich and privileged childhood, not in material possessions but in liveliness and security.

Chapter 2 begins the account of the most formative years of the writer's life. Thanks to the foresight of successful Scots, Edinburgh afforded talented girls of modest means such as Muriel the opportunity for a first-class education. James Gillespie's High School for Girls was Muriel's school for twelve years, from 1923 onward. Scholarships relieved her parents of school fees for the last six years of her stay there. It was there, at age eleven, that she met Christina Kay, the model for her most famous creation, Miss Jean Brodie. In the most extended commentary this book gives on her own writing, Spark compares the real and fictional characters in some detail, providing a rare glimpse into the creative process. The tone of this chapter is warm and tactful; teachers are remembered more for their good qualities than for their failings, and Spark's own memories are reinforced or corrected by the recollections of her classmates. With characteristic ironic detachment, she tells of being awarded a poetry prize and crowned "Queen of Poetry" at a ceremony commemorating Sir Walter Scott.

James Gillespie's school was not a boarding institution, and consequently Muriel was spared the horrors often reported in British autobiographies. Instead, she enjoyed a rich "parallel life," recorded in chapter 3. Here the reader learns of the family's annual holidays with Muriel's maternal grandparents and the resulting genesis of her story "The Gentile Jewesses." Her earliest attempts at poetry, the influence of the Scottish border ballads, the "social nervousness" of Depression-era Edinburgh, and the crisis of what to do after graduation are detailed. As it happened, the young school-leaver and budding poet made an unusual but influential decision: She took a course in précis writing at a vocational school, and her writing style has reflected its influence ever since. This was followed by secretarial training, a job in a department store, and finally her disastrous engagement and marriage to Sydney Spark in 1937.

Chapter 4 will be for many readers the most disappointing of the book. Covering Spark's seven years in Southern Rhodesia, the period during which, she claims, she "learned to cope with life," this chapter is frustratingly short on detail. During this period she witnessed the horrifying events that led to the story "Curtain Blown by the Breeze," gave birth to her son, watched her husband descend into mental illness, and experienced the outbreak of World War II from an unusual position. She also suffered the trials of a divorce made difficult by existing law, survived economically and emotionally as a single mother, and made the perilous journey from Africa to England during wartime. These and other events are discussed only briefly. Foremost among the questions left unanswered in these pages are "What sustained her during these traumatic times?" and "How did these events influence or shape the works that she began writing a few years later?" It is helpful to be told that "The Seraph and the Zambesi" resulted from memories of a trip to Victoria Falls and that "The Go-Away Bird" was a reaction to the call of the gray-crested laurie, but both the ordinary reader and the scholar are more likely to be frustrated than satisfied by these tantalizing hints. What is missing is not simply the literary detail that helps readers understand the writer's work but also the kinds of personal revelations that illuminate the essential character of the person and the writer.

Chapter 5 reads almost like an excerpt from a spy novel, for Spark's war work was in the Foreign Office as a secretary to Sefton Delmer, who masterminded an ingenious radio station that broadcast subtly subversive messages to German civilians and troops. This is fascinating reading, including the unlikely incident of her spending the night in the home of Louis MacNiece, an experience that she later turned to fiction in "The House of the Famous Poet."

Chapters 6 and 7 constitute the "record-straightening" part of the autobiography and mark a significant change in the book's tone. Abruptly, the chatty, informal manner of the first five chapters gives way to a sharp, at times abrasive, self-defense. Her first literary job as a subeditor with the *Argentor*, a jewellers' trade magazine, is described with pleasure, but in chronicling her frustrating experience as the editor of *Poetry Review*, a journal she transformed from a haven for bad Georgian poets into a respectable outlet for original verse, she becomes defensive. The petty but juicy quarrels of the *Poetry Review*'s board are recorded in some detail, and Spark's account makes entertaining reading. Nevertheless, the very pettiness of these conflicts suggests that a lighter hand would have been more appropriate. One wishes here for the satirical side of Spark's talent. She scores her best point with a droll bit of humor directed at Marie Stopes, the birth-control advocate: "Up to his death three years earlier she had been living with Lord Alfred Douglas, the fatal lover of Oscar Wilde, an arrangement which I imagine would satisfy any woman's craving for birth control." Here, too, is the beginning of *Forum*, which she founded with other poets, and the ending of her relationship with Howard Sergeant, her boyfriend for eighteen months. Following this came the unfortunate collaboration with Derek Stanford on a book about William Wordsworth, which eventually resulted in his vindictively inaccurate memoir about her. This was another formative period, during which she transformed herself from an editor and journalist into a creative writer, but again the relevant details are sadly missing. Even her crucial conversion to Roman Catholicism is passed over rather quickly, as are her very genuine sufferings from undernourishment and Benzedrine dependence as she pursued too single-mindedly her literary ambitions. The reader does learn of Graham Greene's generous financial support during difficult times. This section ends with the publication of her first novel, *The Comforters* (1957), and the promise of another volume to come.

Spark's accomplishments as a writer are many and significant. She will probably be best remembered as a novelist with a gift for macabre humor and devastating social satire, but her short stories are of equally high merit and deserve far more attention than they have received. She considers herself primarily a poet.

Curriculum Vitae is thus a work of more than passing interest. Like Spark's fiction, it is elegantly written and in places wonderfully observed. The hand of a master is clearly at work. At the same time, one cannot help but wish that Spark had been able to overcome the traditional British reticence that mars so many literary autobiographies. It is not lurid sexual detail one longs for, nor tedious self-analysis, nor even name-dropping. What is wanted is personal revelation and the kind of biographical detail that enables one to see how life became transformed into fiction. Except for the revelations about Miss Brodie, most references to Spark's published work are too brief to reveal much of value. Readers who value Spark's fiction will treasure this book for its very real strengths, but they will also wish that it were significantly longer and more revealing of the fascinating woman who lives behind that fiction.

Dean Baldwin

Sources for Further Study

Belles Lettres. XI, Fall, 1993, p. 26.
Chicago Tribune. May 16, 1993, XIV, p. 3.
Choice. XXXI, September, 1993, p. 124.
The Christian Science Monitor. May 18, 1993, p. 14.
Commonweal. CXX, May 21, 1993, p. 13.
Los Angeles Times Book Review. May 16, 1993, p. 2.
The New York Times Book Review. XCVIII, May 16, 1993, p. 13.
Publishers Weekly. CCXL, March 22, 1993, p. 62.
The Wall Street Journal. May 19, 1993, p. A12.
The Washington Post Book World. XXIII, June 6, 1993, p. 5.

DAKOTA
A Spiritual Geography

Author: Kathleen Norris (1947-   )
Publisher: Ticknor & Fields (New York). 225 pp. $19.95
Type of work: Autobiography
Time: The early 1970's to the present
Locale: Lemmon, South Dakota

A poetic and often surprising first-person nonfiction account of one woman's experiences on the modern South Dakota plains, a land in which she discovers not only her ancestral roots but her spiritual roots as well

> *Principal personage:*
> KATHLEEN NORRIS, an American poet

Kathleen Norris' transcendent nonfiction work opens with a quotation taken from the Spanish philosopher José Ortega y Gassett: "Tell me the landscape in which you live, and I will tell you who you are." In *Dakota: A Spiritual Geography*, Norris does just that, describing for the reader her starkly beautiful Dakota plains home—the physical world—as a means of revealing her own inner landscape, the topography of her very soul. In clear, richly imagistic prose, Norris presents disparate bits of information—weather reports, geographic and historical facts, quotations, lines of poetry, religious references—and skillfully weaves a story from the resulting mix, a story not only of one place and one life, Norris's own life in her adopted home of Lemmon, South Dakota, but the more universal tale of how each and every one of us comes to call a certain place "home."

The story of how Norris, a poet (*Falling Off*, 1971; *The Middle of the World*, 1981; *The Year of Common Things*, 1988), came to call the Great Plains her own is nothing short of remarkable. From the very beginning, Norris speaks of her life in Dakota (a term she uses for both North and South Dakota) as one of destiny. "This is my spiritual geography," she writes, "the place where I've wrestled my story out of the circumstances of landscape and inheritance." Norris and her husband, also a poet, both left successful careers in New York City in the early 1970's to take over Norris's ancestral home in Lemmon. "We expected to be in Dakota for just a few years," Norris writes. Yet luckily for the reader, Norris and her husband remained in Lemmon permanently, supporting themselves through a series of odd jobs (Norris worked for a time as a poet-in-the-schools), stubbornly clinging to a land that often seemed to reject all attempts to claim it, all the while fighting to explain their move to baffled city friends, to curious native Dakotans, whose innate distrust of outsiders might be enough to scare anyone away, and to themselves.

Norris recognizes others' bewilderment at her decision to remain in such a seemingly desolate environment, and much of *Dakota* is taken up with her reflections on what it means to give up the trappings of outward success—steady jobs, a supportive artistic community, dinners out, even television—in order to find inner peace. What makes her story so engaging is her ability at one moment to share in others' bafflement at her monastic Plains existence—"Where I am is a place where the human fabric is worn thin, farms and ranches and little towns scattered over miles of seemingly endless, empty grassland"—and the next moment to celebrate with a poet's keen eye the striking beauty of a land stripped to all save for vast stretches of earth and sky. It is not as if Dakota is easy to like. It is, after all, a land abandoned by 80 percent of its homesteaders within the first twenty years of its settlement, Norris tells us. To carve a life out of such unforgiving territory it takes a certain faith (which Norris possesses in abundance) and a love for all that is not simple or obvious or even, finally, of this world. By breaking down her life and her land into their most simple elements—reflected in chapter titles such as "Dust," "Frontier," "In the Open," and "Weather Report"—Norris charts the path she has followed in her journey from city skeptic to Plains believer.

First and foremost in Norris' inner pilgrimage is the land itself. Dakota is a desert—literal and in some ways cultural—and in exploring the link between self-identification and place, Norris writes of inheriting country so barren and at times so foreboding—dust storms, little rainfall, bitter cold, and baking heat are the norm—that often it is a struggle simply to survive. Instead of giving up or becoming disillusioned in the face of such adversity, she rises to the challenge not only of meeting the land and its inhabitants (in some areas, not even two per square mile) on their own terms but also of coming to the realization that she must completely change her perceptions of what has value and meaning in her life. Dakota pushes its inhabitants to both test and question what they are made of: "A person is forced inward by the spareness of what is outward and visible in all this land and sky." For Norris, this means a gradual spiritual conversion, a search for what she calls the desert within the desert. Faced with the seemingly endless emptiness of prairie, she chooses not to fill her life with things or other people, but to create an imaginative and spiritual life so perfectly and devoutly realized that she makes the reader want to pack up and head for the High Plains: "Pelicans rise noisily from a lake; an antelope stands stock-still, its tattooed neck like a message in unbreakable code; columbines, their long stems beaten down by hail, bloom in the mud." Moments of such wistful poetry are frequently observed in *Dakota* as Norris turns her attention to the seasons, plains animals and inhabitants, and the minutiae of prairie existence with equal success.

From these close examinations of the natural world, a church of air and light, Norris is inspired to rediscover her own religious roots. A Protestant "with a decidedly ecumenical bent," she becomes an "oblate" or an associate to a community of monks, spending periods of time in prayer and seclusion in their monastery. She also fills in for several months as a pastor at a local Presbyterian church, winning over its congregation despite the fact that she is both a woman and an outsider. It is at this point in *Dakota* that the two threads of the story—Norris' faith in the spirit of place and her faith in a larger spirit, a religious devotion—come together to form one seamless and unbroken cord. She makes many comparisons between the lives of the monks, their chosen existence of relinquishment, denial, and quiet prayer, and her own life of solitude, with its long hours spent watching the unshifting horizon, reflecting on all she has given up and all she has gained. Norris comes to see that simple acts such as hanging out the wash in a clover-scented breeze, taking a walk along a dirt road at dawn, finding beauty where others see only desolation are in themselves acts of devotion, a natural form of prayer. "The silence of the Plains, this great unpeopled landscape of earth and sky," she writes, "is much like the silence one finds in a monastery, an unfathomable silence that has the power to re-form you."

Re-form it does. As Norris' love for her adopted home grows, so does her sense of self and her place in the world. Like the monks she studies and worships with, she learns to love order, the repetition of days, one barely imperceptible from the next, the vast sweep of grass where, through luck and fate, she has landed. Dakota becomes her religion, her discipline, her teacher. Norris is not afraid to reveal the mystical side in this course of wondrous self-discovery, yet she never falls into the traps so common to writing that stems from religious experience. This material, a mystical and religious awakening, might have been both leaden and tedious in another's hands. It is difficult to record a spiritual conversion of any sort without coming across as self-righteous, sanctimonious, smug, or just plain silly. Yet here Norris triumphs once again, not only transcending her material but surprising even the most agnostic and skeptical readers with the restrained and calm style with which she conveys her beliefs. "I think of it as the quantum effect: here time flows back and forth, in and out of both past and future, and I, too, am changed." Through such gentle turns of phrase she allows the reader to discover her faith along with her, to feel brief flashes of the elation that must come with such mystical discoveries. Yet she never forces her beliefs too strongly or even requires that the reader take her at her word. Without fanfare or inflated prose, Norris simply presents the material necessary for one's own awakening. Her tale is a testament to what is possible in the world.

Others have explored the Great Plains in recent nonfiction works, most notably Ian Frazier in his wonderfully adroit *Great Plains* (1989) and William Least Heat-Moon's sprawling *PrairyErth* (1991). What distinguishes *Dakota* from these and other works about life in what has been referred to as America's outback is Norris' use of both the very personal and the very public, her ability to knit together everyday observations of a church potluck supper or a conversation with a local rancher with her private longings and secrets. She is not afraid to reveal the map of her own windswept heart: "Maybe the desert wisdom of the Dakotas can teach us to love anyway, to love what is dying, in the face of death, and not to pretend that things are other than they are." By the time Norris arrives at the point in her story at which she confides such deeply felt perceptions, she has already proved herself to be such a careful guide to her literal and metaphoric landscapes—the Dakotas of both her home and her soul—that the reader fully trusts and believes her. Norris earns her moments of quiet revelation with every beautifully rendered dust storm, with each flattened Plains horizon across which she makes readers feel as if they too might see forever.

The Great Plains were once a vast inland sea. In a land practically devoid of water, a land in which rain might fall only once or twice over a period of months, even years,

Norris hears echoes of this long-forgotten ocean and sees in the unbroken grasslands the means to float slowly away from the trappings of modern existence. It takes a sensitive soul—a poet, perhaps a mystic—to put an ear to the flat, dry earth and hear waves, but Norris has just such a talent. "Like all who choose life in the slow lane—sailors, monks, farmers," she writes, "I partake of a contemplative reality." In *Dakota: A Spiritual Geography* this reality takes the shape of a beautifully realized narrative, a love story for a place and a way of life. In the end, Kathleen Norris discovers water in the desert and brings beauty to a forbidding land.

Liesel Litzenburger

Sources for Further Study

America. CLXIX, August 14, 1993, p. 23.
Belles Lettres. VIII, Summer, 1993, p. 37.
Chicago Tribune. January 10, 1993, XIV, p. 3.
The Christian Science Monitor. April 27, 1993, p. 11.
Los Angeles Times. December 31, 1992, p. E8.
The New York Times Book Review. XCVIII, February 14, 1993, p. 8.
The New Yorker. LXIX, March 15, 1993, p. 123.
Publishers Weekly. CCXXXIX, December 7, 1992, p. 52.
Utne Reader. May, 1993, p. 113.
The Washington Post Book World. XXIII, January 24, 1993, p. 3.
Women's Review of Books. X, May, 1993, p. 20.

DAPHNE DU MAURIER
The Secret Life of the Renowned Storyteller

Author: Margaret Forster (1938-   )
Publisher: Doubleday (New York). 457 pp. $25.00
Type of work: Biography
Time: 1907-1989
Locale: Great Britain

The life story of a famous writer, revealing the emotional turmoil that found expression in her works

Principal personages:
DAPHNE DU MAURIER, an English novelist
GERALD DU MAURIER, her father, a famous actor
MURIEL BEAUMONT DU MAURIER, her mother
FERNANDE "FERDY" YVON, her teacher and friend, a lesbian
FREDERICK ARTHUR MONTAGUE "TOMMY" BROWNING, her husband, who attained the rank of lieutenant-general in the British army and a knighthood
ELLEN DOUBLEDAY, a publisher's wife, her friend and at one time the object of her love
GERTRUDE LAWRENCE, an actress, her lover

As the author of four previous biographical works, Margaret Forster is no stranger to research. When she undertook a biography of Daphne du Maurier, however, she found herself in a unique situation. On one hand, there was no dearth of documents or of recollections about the writer, and her children, who held much of the source material, had expressed their intention of cooperating in every way on what was meant to be the official biography of their mother. On the other hand, as her research proceeded, Forster began to make some discoveries that she realized might well disturb du Maurier's family, in particular accounts of her lesbian involvements. Fortunately, as the acknowledgments indicate, du Maurier, who herself had written several biographies, had made her opinions on the subject quite clear. While she did not wish to see her own biography published during her lifetime, she felt very strongly that such works were worthless unless they were totally truthful. By allowing Forster to see and to use all the source materials in their possession, du Maurier's children made it possible for her to turn out a book that meets their mother's high standards.

When she subtitled her volume *The Secret Life of the Renowned Storyteller*, the biographer indicated what she sees as the central truth of Daphne du Maurier's life: that she habitually concealed her real identity by assuming the personality that others expected or demanded. As a result, du Maurier's fiction became not only a way to achieve financial independence but also, by admitting her to the only world in which she could feel perfectly free, a necessity of her existence.

Du Maurier's problem with identity had its source early in her childhood. She was born on May 12, 1907, the second daughter of the highly successful actor Gerald du Maurier and his wife, Muriel Beaumont du Maurier, a former actress. Of the du Mauriers' three girls, Daphne was the one most like Gerald and, perhaps for that reason, most troubled by her father's desire for a son. Forster quotes a poem that Gerald du Maurier wrote for Daphne in which he expresses his love for her but reiterates his belief that she should have been a boy, whether to fulfill his needs or to realize her true nature is not clear. In a theatrical family, it was perhaps not surprising that an imaginative little girl would invent an alternate identity for herself, dressing as a boy and pretending that she was the daring "Eric Avon" instead of the pretty and feminine Daphne.

Certainly in her adolescence Daphne du Maurier behaved like a girl, falling violently and obviously in love with a married thirty-six-year-old cousin. Forster points out, however, that Daphne continued to think of herself as a boy in a girl's body. These feelings, Forster suggests, may have been more than a wish to please her father; they may also have been Daphne's response to her father's well-known infidelities, which were one more example of the freedom afforded to men and denied to women. At any rate, when at eighteen Daphne was sent to school in France, she soon found herself attached to Fernande "Ferdy" Yvon, a lesbian teacher. In letters to her former governess describing Ferdy's advances to her, what Daphne seemed most concerned about was her own responsiveness. She could not imagine having her homophobic father discover that she was a lesbian, or a "Venetian," in the term used by the family. Moreover, Daphne was convinced that any woman who desired another woman must in fact be a man in a woman's body, as she feared was the case with her. Breaking off her physical intimacy, though not her friendship, with Ferdy, Daphne now limited herself to heterosexual relationships. She also found some release for her frustrations by throwing herself into full-time writing. In 1931, when her first novel was published, she had the satisfaction of seeing it become a bestseller.

Having established a firm basis for her theory about the nature of du Maurier's inner conflicts, Forster can offer new insights into her works. It is significant, for example, that the protagonist of du Maurier's first novel, *The Loving Spirit* (1931), often bemoans the fact that she was born a woman, not a man, and hopes after her death somehow to live on through her beloved son. In the realistic novel that followed, *I'll Never Be Young Again* (1932), the author explores sexual passion through the eyes of her protagonist, who is a male. The autobiographical implications of du Maurier's third novel are also unmistakable. In *The Progress of Julius* (1933), a self-made millionaire adores his daughter to the point of nearly suffocating her, and finally strangles her rather than let any other man take his place in her life. In her examination of the rough drafts of this novel, Forster found that du Maurier had initially modeled her villain much more closely on Gerald than she did in the final version, clearly referring to the jealousy that her father exhibited whenever she went out with a young man.

By 1932, however, du Maurier seemed to have settled down to a conventional life. Almost as soon as she saw Major Frederick Arthur Montague Browning, or "Tommy," a handsome, highly decorated military officer and a fun-loving, adventurous yachts-man, Daphne fell in love with him, and he was just as enamored of her. After their marriage on July 19, 1932, they formed a bond that outlasted not only passing affairs but even the end of their physical intimacy after World War II. Their three children, Tessa, Flavia, and Christian ("Kits"), were admittedly troublesome for a writer to deal with, but du Maurier was a gentle mother who could utilize her imagination in playing with her children as well as in her work. Although she showed scant affection to her little girls, evidently saving any expression of love for her son, in later years du Maurier become very close to her daughters. In choosing her illustrations for the biography, Forster clearly tried to include pictures of everyone whom Daphne du Maurier had ever loved. Those of the author with her children and her grandchildren reveal what a source of joy they were for her.

Another source of pleasure was the home in which du Maurier spent much of her life. In 1926, when she first came upon the secluded house in Cornwall named Menabilly, du Maurier found it enchanting. The place so stimulated her imagination that it became the setting for her most famous book, *Rebecca* (1938), in which, as "Manderley," Menabilly becomes the house where the second Mrs. de Winter fights her battle with the ghost of the first. Interestingly, Forster sees a close connection between the sense of isolation felt by du Maurier's embattled protagonist and du Maurier's own misery in Egypt, where she had begun writing the novel while she was attempting to function as a military wife and feeling very much an outsider in her husband's milieu. Appropriately, it was the financial success of *Rebecca* that enabled du Maurier to lease Menabilly and thus to establish a home that would be hers, wherever her husband chose to live.

Menabilly was important to du Maurier in many ways. Not only did the house and its surroundings suggest settings for later novels, but it also provided an environment where the children could roam almost at will while their mother hid away and wrote. Menabilly was also the symbol of du Maurier's cherished independence. Admittedly, at a time when a wife's subservience to her husband was firmly based on the fact that most women had no money of their own, du Maurier's attitude probably did no good to her marriage. When Tommy returned after World War II, bringing not only the haunting memories but the habit of command, problems were perhaps inevitable. It is unclear, however, why neither Tommy nor Daphne took steps to renew their physical intimacy. At any rate, in 1946, this aspect of the marriage ceased forever, and the long, tragic years of politeness and public pretense began.

The last two sections of Forster's biography are entitled "The Breaking Point, 1946-1960" and "Death of the Writer, 1960-1989." The dates attached to these sections are particularly interesting because in each case, what would ordinarily be thought of as occurring at one point is described as occurring over a period of years. What Forster seems to imply is that du Maurier's psychological and creative decline was a very gradual process. On the surface, her later years seemed to be filled with fulfillment. After making the decision not to move to London with her husband, du Maurier remained in the place she loved, writing and publishing regularly and with every book achieving more of the financial security she craved. Moreover, she now felt free to admit that she was physically attracted to women as well as to men. Although she was not able to persuade Ellen Doubleday, the publisher's wife, to be more than a friend to her, she had more success with the accomplished actress Gertrude Lawrence, who, ironically, had been cast as the character modeled on Ellen Doubleday in du Maurier's play *September Tide* (1949).

Yet this relatively happy period in du Maurier's life did not last long. In 1952, Lawrence died very suddenly, leaving du Maurier devastated. In 1958, another blow fell. Although Tommy had been delighted to serve as treasurer to the Duke of Edinburgh, he had never recovered from the stresses of the war. It was now obvious that he must retire and live with his wife at Menabilly. While du Maurier never questioned her duty, she wondered whether she could possibly continue writing without the peace and privacy that she so desperately needed.

It may seem peculiar that Forster describes the final twenty-nine years of du Maurier's life, which saw the publication of fifteen of her books, as the "death of the writer." The answer to this question lies in the nature of the books she was writing. Many of them were biographies and reminiscences, others collections of short stories, most written at an earlier time. In fact, after the failure of her last novel, the satirical *Rule Britannia* (1972), du Maurier concluded that she would probably never again find a work of fiction shaping itself in her imagination, with characters demanding to be brought to life on the printed page. Without her creative powers, Forster believes, du Maurier had no reason to live, and therefore from the late 1970's she was merely marking time, willing herself to die with ever-increasing fervor. The end came during the night of April 18, 1989.

In this poignant account of her last years, one can see another aspect of the identity issue that was of central importance throughout du Maurier's life. While she may have remained ambivalent about her own sexuality and even her own gender, and while she certainly resented experiencing the conflicts between the demands of the self and the demands of the family to which women are subjected, in one respect du Maurier attained certainty: Whatever or whoever else she might be, she knew that, above all, she was a writer.

The author of *Rebecca* deserved a biography as thoroughly researched, as meticulously crafted, and as beautifully written as this one. With the same degree of skill that du Maurier used to keep her readers mystified until the final pages of a novel, Margaret Forster has unriddled the author's own life story and, as a result, has revealed new dimensions in her fiction.

Rosemary M. Canfield Reisman

Sources for Further Study

Booklist. XC, October 1, 1993, p. 246.
Boston Globe. October 3, 1993, p. 38.
Library Journal. CXVIII, November 1, 1993, p. 92.

The New York Times Book Review. XCVIII, October 17, 1993, p. 37.
The New Yorker. LXIX, November 8, 1993, p. 127.
The Observer. March 28, 1993, p. 61.
Publishers Weekly. CCXL, September 13, 1993, p. 114.
Sight and Sound. III, June, 1993, p. 45.
The Times Literary Supplement. April 9, 1993, p. 23.
The Washington Post Book World. XXIII, October 3, 1993, p. 3.

DARK HARBOR

Author: Mark Strand (1934-   )
Publisher: Alfred A. Knopf (New York). 51 pp. $19.00
Type of work: Poetry

Mark Strand projects an eerie interiority without ever seeming unnaturally self-absorbed; he writes less of a self than of a condition

Dark Harbor is a poetic sequence made up of forty-five numbered parts introduced by a "Proem." The parts, which can be read as individual poems, are cast in loose, three-line stanzas (a few end in couplets) in which neither sound nor sentence abets the shape on the page. The shortest poem is two stanzas in length, the longest nine, with the average being six or seven. Thus each, with the exception of the longest ("XXXVIII"), fits on a single page, as if the printed page were a unit of composition. Across this popular typographical medium, with its vague nod to Dante's terza rima, Mark Strand threads a graceful, somber meditation on loss, dislocation, and the general unease of a mind and spirit strangely alienated from all that it attends to and even accepts. Either too decorous or too numb to celebrate or rebel, Strand's persona charts a quiet, restrained course in which a mood of seeming passivity or resignation nevertheless gains tension and ambiguity.

The collection (or long poem) is perfectly titled. Whether one imagines the harbor as a place of departure or destination or return (or all three), it is a protected region whose depths make anchorage possible. Yet it is not a happy, sunlit domain of comfort. Strand's region of sensibility is uncomfortable with its very comfort, anxiously becalmed, darkened by the presence of human limitation, death, pain, foreboding. Vaguely dissatisfied in a world that offers humans so much of what they need and desire, Strand sings a song at once melancholic and absurd: Something is always missing. With him, readers vainly and halfheartedly try to locate it, name it, but they come up empty.

If it were not for the fact that Strand has been conjuring this mood for over thirty years, one might conclude that he has captured the angst of his own late middle age. More than likely, however, he has recorded the late middle age of Western experience.

As ever Strand's diction is simple, his manner direct, his style uncluttered. Now less obviously a writer influenced by Surrealism (though perhaps the Surrealist label was always specious), he is still capable of the unexpected juxtaposition, and there is a dreamlike quality as well as dream logic in many sections of *Dark Harbor*. Strand's images and metaphors remain basic and general, if not abstract: aspects of sun, moon, stars, and water. These link poem to poem, although there is nothing inevitable about the order of Strand's units. Because Strand's poems have something like a setting without being specifically localized (with a few exceptions), and because of the mythic resonance of his repeated images, the dark harbor and its surrounding landscapes become a place within. Strand projects an eerie interiority without ever seeming unnaturally self-absorbed; he writes less of a self than of a condition.

"Proem" matter-of-factly establishes the sequence as the journey or quest of a wandering bard who would distinguish, assess, and respond to the songs (natural and otherwise) met on his travels. In this way, Strand creates a link between his aspirations in *Dark Harbor* and such American spatial epics as Walt Whitman's *Leaves of Grass* (1855; final authorial edition 1892) and Hart Crane's *The Bridge* (1930)—both also sequences rather than extended narratives. In fact, Strand's "Proem" functions in the same way as the introductory "Song of the Open Road" does in later editions of Whitman's text. Moreover, as the projection of an everyman self, the whole of *Dark Harbor* echoes "Song of Myself" (1855), which also (in its later versions) is presented as a series of numbered parts. Affinities to *The Bridge* are less obvious, except for the fact that Crane's sequence also begins with a formally labeled "Proem: To Brooklyn Bridge" and evokes a similar malaise.

In looking for Strand's paradigms or historical inspiration, one need not be claiming for Strand a bold, competitive intention, merely an almost unavoidable attachment to traditions that are in the lifeblood of American poetry. Moreover, Whitman and Crane are most likely distant influences. It is not Strand's way to approach the lyric or dramatic intensity of these writers. Nor does he programmatically map his vision of America. Strand's work is more brooding and ruminative. It stays on the accessible side of the more heady meditative sequences of such poets as Wallace Stevens and Charles Olson, particularly the Stevens of *The Auroras of Autumn* (1950)— to which *Dark Harbor* bears some formal resemblance, even though *The Auroras of Autumn* does not have the same kind of epic sweep of experience. Indeed, one could call Strand's effort the sequence-epic for minimalists.

Though there is no announced division and the shift is not abrupt or absolute, the second half of this book has greater particularity and narrative dimension than the first. This gradual movement toward specificity and definite action gives the entire sequence its own kind of perceptual movement and low-key drama. It reads—and one must with Strand accept metaphors from the visual arts—like a series of lens adjustments, a coming into focus. Yet poems of relative concreteness can be found among the earlier parts of the book as well.

Though there is no question that in *Dark Harbor* the whole is greater than the sum of its parts, many of the parts are fine poems that will stand tall in anthologies. It is unfortunate that their titles will remain numbers or first-line references (though this problem has not hurt Emily Dickinson). Particularly powerful is "III," a study of the mixed emotions of homecoming to a typical American town deadened by the accumulation of shops carrying useless goods that have become necessities, the "luminous cones" that fall from the street lamps, the "icy green from TVs." In a setting reminiscent of the futuristic nightscape of Ray Bradbury's story "The Pedestrian," Strand's speaker wonders whether "this coming back is a failure/ Or a sign of success, a sign that the time has come/ To embrace your origins as you would yourself." The flat ending makes this home a dark harbor indeed: "look, there in the kitchen are Mom and Dad,/ He's reading the paper, she's killing a fly."

Dark Harbor is not a condition of unmitigated dismay. Interim pleasures keep one alert to the possibilities of redemptive delight, though maybe this hope is only the stubborn human resistance to the blackest moods, the acceptance of purposelessness. Poem "VIII" is an illustration of Strand's momentary upbeat swing, but its flat tone brings ironic deflation even before the painful conclusion. It begins:

> If dawn breaks the heart, and the moon is a horror,
> And the sun is nothing but the source of torpor,
> Then of course I would have been silent all these years
>
> And would not have chosen to go out tonight
> In my new dark blue double-breasted suit
> And to sit in a restaurant with a bowl
>
> Of soup before me to celebrate how good life
> Has been and how it has culminated in this instant.

The poem concludes with a wish to Strand's "partner, my beautiful death,/ My black paradise, . . . My symbolist muse," for assurances that "I have not lived in vain" and that "what I have said has not been said for me." If poetry itself is Strand's act of faith, if the harbor is a harbor of words, then purpose lies in the projection of an individual will and a distinctive vision and voice.

Another remarkable piece is "XVI," which reminds us that in "a world without heaven all is farewell," no matter what our mood or behavior. Life, we are told, is a series of moments in which "the end/ is enacted again and again. And we feel it/ In the temptations of sleep, in the moon's ripening,/ In the wine as it waits in the glass." Does this awareness flatten or heighten the discrete beauties, voices, motions, or stillnesses? Strand seems to say that it does both.

In "XXVIII," Strand posits that "the world is altered for the better . . . only while Orpheus sings. When the song is over/ The world resumes its old flaws." The poet can temporarily change the world, "but he cannot save it." Knowing this, Orpheus' song, like Strand's, is troubled, and yet that sad song makes of the world the best that can be made—that is, if anyone is listening. This slippery second-guessing about vocation, purpose, and the efficacy of hope pervades *Dark Harbor*, enriching it tonally and intellectually while simultaneously narrowing the emotional scope and the reader's chance of avoiding bitter truths. Variety in this sequence comes from language-making, saying it a bit differently each time out. Fortunately, Strand is up to the task: "The day has made a fabulous cage of cold around/ my face. Whenever I take a breath I hear cracking" (from "XXX").

Dark Harbor does its work with very few historical or geographical allusions. "XXX" is an exception, with its references to the atrocities of Adolf Hitler and Joseph Stalin, and there is the occasional Canadian placename that reminds readers of Strand's country of birth. The passing references to material culture (television, stereo, and the Calvin Klein suit in "XXXI") only emphasize how little Strand depends on this kind of imagery and context. Allusions to mythology and art are somewhat more frequent, especially in the later poems, but even here Strand is constrained.

Strand's interests in painting and photography (about which he has written extensively) are reflected hardly at all by way of name-dropping. Yet the visual framing of
scenes and the keen rendering of gradations of light and dark are hallmarks of his art.
He works with a painter's eye for composition and illumination. Poem "XXXVI"
begins with imagining a stroll into

> the somber garden where the grass in the shade
> Is silver and frozen and where the general green
>
> Of the rest of the garden is dark except
> For a luminous patch made by the light of a window.

In passages like this one, Strand simply and directly registers simultaneous physical
and psychological settings or conditions.

All in all, *Dark Harbor* is an impressive achievement. Strand's immaculate poetic
manners certainly deserve the acclaim they have received. Yet this very mannerliness
might be his limitation. There is an absence of fire in this work, an absence of necessity.
It is hard to find the rough edges that reveal the difficulty overcome, the urgency to
share. Still, if a sense of absence, of exile, is one of his century's main themes, Strand
is one of its important poets.

Philip K. Jason

Sources for Further Study

Boston Globe. March 21, 1993, p. 14.
Chicago Tribune. August 1, 1993, XIV, p. 4.
Los Angeles Times Book Review. May 9, 1993, p. 11.
The New Republic. CCVIII, March 8, 1993, p. 34.
The New York Times Book Review. XCVIII, April 18, 1993, p. 15.
St. Louis Post-Dispatch. May 30, 1993, p. C5.
The Virginia Quarterly Review. LXIX, Autumn, 1993, p. SS136.
The Yale Review. LXXXI, July, 1993, p. 134.

DAYS OF GRACE
A Memoir

Authors: Arthur Ashe (1943-1993) and Arnold Rampersad (1941-   )
Publisher: Alfred A. Knopf (New York). Illustrated. 304 pp. $24.00
Type of work: Memoir
Time: 1943-1993
Locale: Primarily the United States

A unique memoir of a star athlete's spiritual journey through racism, international politics, heart disease, and AIDS

> *Principal personages:*
> ARTHUR ROBERT ASHE, JR., a tennis champion who became an influential
>   public figure in the African American community
> JEANNE MOUTOUSSAMY-ASHE, his wife, a photographer
> CAMERA, their daughter

Tennis champion, role model, black celebrity, heart patient, and AIDS victim, Arthur Robert Ashe, Jr., managed to record his third and final memoir with matchless integrity. Coauthor Arnold Rampersad, the distinguished biographer of Langston Hughes, helped to bring Ashe's voice to the reader with great clarity. Arranged loosely by topic, the eleven chapters of *Days of Grace* focus not on the deterioration of Ashe's body but rather on the evolution of his spirit. While typically reserved in tone, the book reveals Ashe's deeply personal journey leading up to his death from AIDS on February 6, 1993. The details of his struggle toward altruism are related so simply that the reader loses sympathy for Ashe, finding it replaced by profound empathy. Assessing the material nature of modern living from the threshold of spiritual clarity, Ashe unifies his essays with pragmatic piety and intelligent faith.

The first chapter, "My Outing," begins with the central turning point of Ashe's last years: The threat that *USA Today* was about to reveal that he had AIDS. Mortified by the prospect of negative publicity, Ashe felt his most prized earthly possession—his reputation—threatened. Ashe's roots in African American spirituality led him to believe that his ancestors (including his mother, who died when he was six) as well as his living relatives would share the shame of his potential ostracism. It is an idea which bookends the memoir; Ashe's closing chapter reassures his own six-year-old daughter, Camera, that he will be "watching and smiling and cheering [her] on" from beyond the great divide. Deciding to hold a news conference before the story broke, Ashe had the benefit of following Earvin "Magic" Johnson, the first "prominent heterosexual" to reveal that he had contracted AIDS. Well-acquainted with international travel, Ashe feared many doors would become closed to him and recalled lying about his infectious disease in order to enter South Africa in November, 1991. He was relieved to discover that his golden reputation, intimate friendships, health-care coverage, and financial support by sponsors were not reversed by the turn of that one day's proclamation.

In hindsight, Ashe's proactive announcement proved cathartic, unburdening Ashe and freeing him to serve a new cause under the "Arthur Ashe Foundation for the Defeat of AIDS," with half of its proceeds going outside the United States. Public speaking invitations (including an address to the United Nations) tripled following the briefing, and especially after *Sports Illustrated* named Ashe "Sportsman of the Year" in 1992. Having been "sacrificed to the fervent American mass media, Ashe's HIV status provided an ironic contrast to that of earlier AIDS victims (gays and IV-drug users) who felt that the media failed to cover their stories adequately. Despite letters from U.S. presidents, flowers from Elizabeth Taylor, and a tremendous amount of contact from other AIDS sufferers, Ashe was keenly aware of the political backlash his disease could bring especially regarding race and sexuality. In his memoir, Ashe allies himself with a "guiltless" band of AIDS victims, obsessively stressing—more than a dozen times—that his own case of AIDS could be definitively traced to a second blood transfusion following his 1983 double bypass surgery. Yet Ashe once surprised reporters who wondered whether heart disease or AIDS had proven to be his worst cross to bear, responding that race was "a grave burden, one that outweighs all others in my life."

The second chapter of *Days of Grace*, titled "Middle Passage," opens with Ashe's early retirement from tennis due to quadruple coronary bypass surgery in December, 1979. As the chapter's title suggests, the complex issue of race complicated Ashe's middle years and proved his greatest hardship. Rejecting black militancy, Ashe took the high road of trying to love an imperfect humanity. Though he had once dated a white woman (whose mother was appalled when she first saw Ashe on television and discovered that he was black), Ashe married Jeanne-Marie Moutoussamy, a black professional photographer, in 1977, and felt a strong paternal instinct shortly thereafter. Though reared primarily by his father, Ashe agrees in principle with a two-parent system.

Ashe's middle chapters explore racism in sports, politics, the black community, and education. At times cumbersome, the section on sports is primarily for tennis fans, centering on a tedious account of Ashe's reign as captain of the U.S. Davis Cup team. Ashe is uncharacteristically petty in his portrayal of John McEnroe and Jimmy Connors; here, atypically, Ashe himself is an all-too-human figure whose revulsion at profanity and disreputable behavior finds a target or two.

The double rejection of Ashe's applications for the South Africa Open in 1969 and 1970 fired his political conscience, as would his AIDS "outing" later. Although Ashe was able to enter the segregated competition in 1973, his ethical fuse was lit, and he sought to compensate for his lack of racial leadership during the Civil Rights movement. While some blacks in Africa and America castigated Ashe as an "Uncle Tom" for playing in an apartheid country, Ashe was gratified that others were inspired by his march through a "whites' only" sport. One adolescent African boy was astounded by the very presence of Arthur Ashe, the first free black man he had ever beheld.

An early speech by Ashe blamed poverty on "laziness" as much as white oppression, a comment which, like many of Ashe's public statements, drew the ire of black radicals. Painfully reminded that he represented more than himself, Ashe recalls taking a white doll away from his daughter at a benefit in order to avert black criticism.

Politically, he could be described as a conservative left-wing Democrat.

Ashe argues that blacks have a lower quality of life in the 1990's than they did in the 1960's, attributing the decline in part to lack of education and morality. Shocked by the contemporary rage of black youth out for vengeance rather than justice, Ashe feels "as if spirits from another planet had come to earth and invaded black bodies." Ashe's *New York Times* essay, "Coddling Black Athletes" described cultural bias as a myth to justify entitlement and did nothing to help endear Ashe to his black critics. Expressing gratitude to the Jewish community for its stance on racism, Ashe boldly asserts that, despite the advantages of fame and wealth, he reserves a right to comment on the black experience. Many readers will learn for the first time of Ashe's many charitable projects in the black community. *Days of Grace* also shares his failed venture; while Ashe overspent $300,000 of his own money on the three-volume *A Hard Road to Glory: A History of the African-American Athlete, 1619-1985* (1988), it remained one of his proudest investments.

Regarding sexual politics, Ashe denies any gay inclinations in a chapter ironically called "The Beast in the Jungle," the title of a story by Henry James about a character blind to his own repressed homosexuality. Having discovered his HIV-status via diagnosis of a brain infection, toxoplasmosis, Ashe's most immediate concern was for his wife and daughter, who tested HIV-negative. Ashe weighs the pros and cons of the drug AZT and of herbalists and then discloses that his annual drug bill ran to $18,000. Ashe acknowledges the national disgrace of health care inequity and homophobia in America. Apparently unaware of Nelson Mandela's rejection of civil rights for homosexuals, Ashe retained a blindspot for his hero, who in Ashe's eyes seemed to be "free of the prejudices that prevent many political leaders from confronting [AIDS]." While Ashe has the dignity to refute the idea that AIDS is divine punishment for gays and drug addicts, he admits "I find its elements and properties peculiarly appropriate to our age." Ashe speaks more about the inappropriate response to the disease, however, and although Ashe's moral sense seems impossibly idealistic, it is always fair. Ashe hopes his daughter will grow up tolerant of gays, expresses dismay at exclusive practices of some churches, and supports the boycott against Colorado's anti-gay "Amendment 2."

In a controversial chapter titled "Sex and Sports in the Age of AIDS," Ashe criticizes black role models Wilt Chamberlain (for his boast of 20,000 sexual conquests) and Magic Johnson (who claims a modest 2,500 partners), as creating "racial embarrass-ment" and doing "their best to reinforce the stereotype." By contrast, Ashe praises Billie Jean King for fighting sexism and homophobia, which cost her significant endorsement monies. (King once quipped that she possessed a blacker attitude than Arthur, who ponders whether he should have beaten her to assert his racial identity!) Ashe notes that professional skating seems as disproportionately gay as tennis does lesbian and then provides an account of his own loss of heterosexual virginity. Recalling his own naïveté, Ashe condemns then-President George Bush's censorship of explicit sexual language in AIDS education for youth. As if doing his part to counter the destructive ignorance, Ashe provides a graphic and fascinating catalog of HIV-transmission including the risks of women during menstruation and insertive partners during anal intercourse. Ashe points out that the global majority of cases has always been, and remains, heterosexually transmitted.

Ashe recounts his final battle with Pneumocystis Carinii Pneumonia (PCP) in a room at New York Hospital where John F. Kennedy, then a senator, was once treated. It is an appropriate setting from which Ashe watches Bill Clinton's inauguration. At age fifty, Ashe notes that for the first time in his life a man younger than himself is president, and his optimism for a new era runs high as Maya Angelou reads the inaugural poem. Meditations at this solitary phase are rich as Ashe envisions himself a citizen of the world indebted to other cultures.

Days of Grace closes with a letter addressed to Ashe's daughter, which is reminiscent of an earlier dialogue in which he first explained his AIDS diagnosis to her. Profound in its simplicity, controlled in its emotion, the epistle poignantly instructs his daughter on the essential principles of life by using the African American folklore symbols of the river and tree. Passing on genealogy, Ashe explains the ongoing consequences of slavery and warns Camera that "because of the color of your skin and the fact that you are a girl, not a boy, your credibility and competence will constantly be questioned no matter how educated or wealthy you are." Ashe bids her to rise above excuses for failure and to mingle with a variety of peoples, warning her against the extremes represented by Patrick Buchanan on the one hand and "black demagogues" on the other. Money, time, alcohol, and romance are to be treated with prudence, as the means rather than the end of one's search for happiness. Assuring his child that poetry and the arts are not frivolous but divine gifts, Ashe reminds Camera of the golden rule and teaches her to pray not for favors but for the will to accomplish good work even while anticipating occasional setbacks. Asking only not to be pitied or hated for dying prematurely, Ashe reminds her that he will be with her in spirit. The compassion expressed transcends parental concern and speaks to adult readers who must also live in a world wherein humanity is overcast by "the shadow [which] is always there; only death will free me, and blacks like me, from its pall."

John W. M. Hallock

Sources for Further Study

Chicago Tribune. June 13, 1993, XIV, p. 1.
The Christian Science Monitor. June 29, 1993, p. 14.
Ebony. XLVIII, September, 1993, p. 18.
Los Angeles Times Book Review. July 4, 1993, p. 3.
The New York Times Book Review. XCVIII, June 13, 1993, p. 1.
Tennis. XXIX, September, 1993, p. 30.
Time. CXLI, June 21, 1993, p. 70.
The Times Literary Supplement. July 30, 1993, p. 28.
The Washington Post Book World. XXIII, June 27, 1993, p. 3.

THE DEATH OF BERNADETTE LEFTHAND

Author: Ron Querry (1943-   )
Publisher: Red Crane Books (Santa Fe, New Mexico). 218 pp. $22.95; paperback $12.95
Type of work: Novel
Time: The late twentieth century
Locale: Northwestern New Mexico and northeastern Arizona

A beautiful young Indian woman's life is snuffed out by a vengeful former suitor who involves himself in witchcraft

Principal characters:
> BERNADETTE LEFTHAND, a beautiful young woman, part Jicarilla Apache, part Taos Pueblo Indian, who is a champion fancy dancer at powwows
> GRACIE LEFTHAND, her younger, homely sister and devoted admirer
> ANDERSON GEORGE, a young Navajo rodeo rider, her boyfriend and later her husband
> TOM GEORGE, his brother
> EMMETT TAKE HORSE, a young Navajo who was once Bernadette's suitor
> STARR STUBBS, a rich Anglo woman who is Bernadette's employer and friend

Ron Querry's first novel joins the increasing number of stories and novels written by American Indians dealing with life on reservations or in small Indian towns. Querry, whose heritage is Choctaw, has chosen to tell the story of the murder of a beautiful young woman who lived in Dulce, center of the Jicarilla Apache reservation in New Mexico. Bernadette and her younger sister, Gracie, are the children of a Jicarilla man and a woman from the Taos Pueblo; most of Bernadette's story is told by Gracie.

Bernadette's death is reported to her father and sister in the novel's opening pages, so there is little mystery about that fact—although it is not clear for some time that she did not die as so many young Indians do, in an automobile wreck, but was murdered. Almost the entire novel is devoted to the story of the last year or two of Bernadette's life, including trips to rodeos where Anderson George, her Navajo fiancé and later her husband, is a not-very successful bronco rider. Gracie goes along on these trips and is able to report on Anderson's increasing dependence on alcohol, a tendency that also disturbs Tom George, Anderson's brother. Gracie also reports on Bernadette's popularity as a fancy dancer at powwows all over Indian country; she often wins prizes and money.

Querry adds two more layers of narration to Gracie's. One is that of Starr Stubbs, the bored wife of a popular country-western singer who has chosen to build a large house near Dulce as a kind of refuge, a place where he can rest from the frantic pace of life on the road. Starr is intelligent and well-intentioned; she has read widely about Indians and has befriended Bernadette, who works for her as a kind of housekeeper. Starr goes so far as to hire Anderson to care for her horses as a way to provide more money for Bernadette's family. Querry uses Starr, however, as a means of showing that even caring and informed Anglos do not understand Indian ways. Unintentionally

Starr offends Bernadette by laughing at a plan to take Anderson to a Navajo "trembler" to diagnose his vague illness; Starr offers to pay for a trip to Albuquerque so that a "real" physician can examine him. Clearly, she fails to recognize that witches and healers are very much part of Navajo reality.

The third level of narration is in the third person and is used on occasion by Querry to show the George brothers when Gracie could not possibly observe them, and later on to show the character, at first unidentified, who visits an ancient Navajo witch in order to become initiated into witchcraft. Eventually it becomes clear that this character is Emmett Take Horse, who hates Anderson and Bernadette. Once their schoolmate at the school for Indians in Santa Fe, Emmett was a successful jockey in informal horse races among the Indians until an accident left him scarred and crippled in an arm, a hand, and a leg.

Gracie's admiration and love for her sister make her a somewhat naïve narrator, but even in her reports there is a gathering sense of menace as Emmett appears more often. When the two brothers and two sisters go to Gallup after a rodeo and stay in a famous old hotel, Anderson leaves the others to go drinking with an old acquaintance. Despite promises to return soon, he does not reappear until the next morning, having spent the night in the drunk tank in the Gallup jail and having lost his hat, boots, and quite a bit of cash. He tells the others of a terrible dream he has had in which he was pursued by a coyote—a traditional symbol of warning to Navajos. Increasingly, even after his son is born, Anderson neglects Bernadette and takes refuge in drinking. His skills as a bronco rider diminish. He takes a small prize at one rodeo because most of the contestants have withdrawn, but at another, at a village on the Navajo reservation, he is thrown before the horse even emerges from the chute.

Bernadette seems to accept Anderson's problems with equanimity and strength. If she is troubled by the increasing amount of time he spends with Emmett Take Horse and by his drinking, she does not complain either to Gracie or to Starr. After her child is born, both sisters derive pleasure from taking care of the infant, Anthony. To support her family, Bernadette returns to her job with Starr, although Gracie now takes over some of that work.

The climax of the novel comes on a night when a powwow is held in Dulce to benefit Jicarilla children. Bernadette goes with Gracie and is honored by the chairman for her past accomplishments as a dancer; the money given to her she turns back to the fund for the local children. Anderson is not there, but he shows up with Emmett and causes a disturbance before being convinced to leave. He goes on drinking, and Bernadette returns to the dance. Eventually Gracie leaves, taking little Anthony with her. That night, after leaving the powwow, Bernadette is savagely hacked to death.

In the final pages it becomes clear that in the end Emmett did not rely on witchcraft. Although he had apparently planned to bewitch Anderson so that his rival would kill Bernadette, he made sure that Anderson was too drunk to know what he was doing when Emmett himself slashed and killed Bernadette, later arranging matters so that Anderson is the only possible suspect. Consumed by grief and guilt, Anderson manages to hang himself in his prison cell.

By opening the novel with the news of Bernadette Lefthand's death, Querry forfeits one opportunity for suspense, but there are other kinds of suspense in *The Death of Bernadette Lefthand*. The reasons for her murder and the way in which the murderer prepared for it are not clear for a long time. Querry also shows real skill in the gradual intrusion of Emmett Take Horse into the novel as he makes himself more a part of the other characters' lives, and the author saves until the very end the revelation of who actually committed the crime. The use of several levels of narration is occasionally somewhat awkward, but the construction of the novel is otherwise quite skillful.

Despite the importance of a brutal murder to the plot, one of the principal virtues of *The Death of Bernadette Lefthand* is its relatively mild description of Indian life, less gloomy than such predecessors as Leslie Marmon Silko's classic novel *Ceremony* (1977) and James Welch's *Winter in the Blood* (1974). While Querry does not ignore or attempt to ameliorate the problems of alcoholism, poverty, and exploitation among American Indians, he shows that for at least some young Indians, much of day-to-day life is interesting and enjoyable. On the one hand, Gracie Lefthand's description of the desertlike poverty of the ironically named Navajo town of Many Farms is pungent and dispiriting. On the other hand, Gracie clearly comes from a family in which there is warmth and love. Trips to visit her mother's sister in Taos, contacts with her paternal aunts in Dulce, and the widowed father's care for his daughters are all factors in making her life more than tolerable and in allowing her to feel that she is loved.

A trip taken by the two George brothers and the Lefthand sisters to Second Mesa on the Hopi reservation is another manifestation of this sense of caring. Despite the tribal enmity between Hopi and Navajo, the George brothers are made to feel welcome by the family of Bernadette's Hopi friend, Mae Lomayaktewa. There is for Gracie the fun of meeting new people, there are dances, there is the sometimes cruel mischief of the clowns, which keeps Gracie in a nervous state during the ceremonial dances. There is also the enjoyment of preparing for the feast and the greater enjoyment Gracie takes in the feast itself.

Unfortunately, there is considerable awkwardness in Querry's use of Gracie to impart information about Indian customs and Indian country. Tidbits of information about such things as Navajo belief in witchcraft, the Navajo attitude toward death, and the construction of the traditional hogans are planted here and there, as are descriptions of Canyon de Chelly, Window Rock, and other parts of the reservation landscape. Some of Gracie's comments on Navajo customs seem designed not to advance the plot but to demonstrate that beliefs and what some regard as superstitions vary among Indians as much as they do among other Americans. Except for the information about witchcraft, none of this material is integral to the story; the visit to the Hopi reservation is especially noteworthy for its irrelevance to the rest of the narrative. Tony Hillerman's Jim Chee/Joe Leaphorn novels provide better models of how this kind of information can be smoothly integrated into fictional material.

There is also an ambiguity about Querry's use of Navajo witchcraft. Emmett Take Horse is an interesting character, an outcast who thirsts for revenge on people who have done nothing to harm him but who are simply better off than he is. Emmett is terrified in the early stages of his venture into witchcraft, but he persists. The problem for the novel is that Querry seems to vacillate in his view of witchcraft, at first presenting it as a powerful active force but in the end having Emmett carry out the murder himself instead of taking revenge through his powers. The murder and the frame-up of Anderson George do not partake of anything peculiar to witchcraft. Louis Owens' *The Sharpest Sight* (1992), which also deals with murder and the supernatural among Indians, is more sure-handed in its use of such material.

Despite these difficulties, *The Death of Bernadette Lefthand* is an impressive first novel. If Starr Stubbs is a stock character, the major Indian characters are clearly delineated: Bernadette, the beauty who is also talented and genuinely kind; Anderson George, the handsome young man who turns to alcohol when he is overwhelmed by his failure to live up to his own expectations and by the reality of adult life in a society that has no place for him; Gracie, the dumpy, homely younger sister, forever in the shadow of Bernadette but feeling no resentment of her status, always pleased to be taken along on trips and to be allowed to help rear Anthony; Emmett Take Horse, scarred brutally by another's action, resentful of what has happened to him but fearful of his own powers. The styles in which the characters are presented are appropriate to the different narrators, and Querry has provided a wealth of information on how American Indians regard themselves, one another, and their world.

John M. Muste

Sources for Further Study

Library Journal. CXVIII, July, 1993, p. 122.
The New York Times Book Review. XCVIII, November 28, 1993, p. 31.
Publishers Weekly. CCXL, June 28, 1993, p. 68.
Star Tribune. November 14, 1993, p. F17.

DEEP POLITICS AND THE DEATH OF JFK

Author: Peter Dale Scott (1929-   )
Publisher: University of California Press (Berkeley). 413 pp. $25.00
Type of work: Current history
Time: 1935 to 1990, especially the 1960's
Locale: Dallas, Washington, D.C., and Chicago

This challenge to the Warren Commission's one-man, one-gun finding suggests a Byzantine, transnational organized-crime involvement in the assassination of John F. Kennedy

Principal personages:
JOHN F. KENNEDY, thirty-fifth president of the United States, 1961-1963
ROBERT F. KENNEDY, his brother, attorney general of the United States, 1961-1964
LEE HARVEY OSWALD, the accused gunman in Kennedy's assassination
JACK RUBY, Lee Harvey Oswald's assassin
J. EDGAR HOOVER, the director of the Federal Bureau of Investigation (FBI), 1924-1972
MEYER LANSKY, a leading figure in organized crime
JIMMY HOFFA, the president of the Teamsters' Union, 1957-1971
ALLEN DULLES, the director of the Central Intelligence Agency, 1953-1961

Deep Politics and the Death of JFK is a book that one studies and keeps returning to rather than merely reads at a sitting and forgets. It is an extraordinarily complex book that traces in dogged detail the Byzantine links between organized crime and the government of the United States. These links, in Peter Dale Scott's view, resulted in the assassination of John Fitzgerald Kennedy (JFK) and led to an ensuing coverup in which the Federal Bureau of Investigation (FBI) and the Central Intelligence Agency (CIA) misled and withheld relevant information from the Warren Commission (in 1964) and the House Select Committee on Assassinations (in 1979). These investigative bodies were themselves full of members who had vested interests in cloaking the truth of the assassination in secrecy.

Scott, Canadian member of the United Nations General Assembly from 1957 to 1961 and currently professor of English at the University of California's Berkeley campus, has written or collaborated on six other investigative books that focus on the Kennedy assassination or on related topics, such as the war in Indochina. He has also produced two volumes of politically oriented poetry, part of a projected autobiographical trilogy in verse, *Coming to Jakarta: A Poem About Terror* (1989) and *Listening to the Candle: A Poem on Impulse* (1992).

In his poetry and prose, Scott consistently penetrates far beneath surface appearances to unearth the details and true nature of what he sees. In doing so, he reveals conspiratorial patterns; in *Coming to Jakarta*, for example, he uncovers the CIA's conspiratorial role in the Indonesian massacre of 1965. He presents his findings, often discomfiting and sometimes alarming, in exceptional detail and interprets them with profound psychological insight.

Although Scott is neither hysterical nor paranoid, reading his revelations will promote hysteria and paranoia among some of his readers. His investigations, nevertheless, are, in the case of John F. Kennedy's assassination, among the most well documented, clearly reasoned presentations in any of the more than two thousand studies that have addressed the topic since Kennedy's death.

Crucial to a full understanding of this book and its basic arguments are a number of propositions that Scott articulates at various points in his highly lucid discourse. Perhaps the most important of these, if readers are to understand some of the dynamics of what happened following the Kennedy assassination as well as many of the factors that led up to the killing in Dallas, is Scott's revelation that in the eyes of some, the FBI's major focus under the directorship of J. Edgar Hoover was the surveillance and repression of political dissidence rather than the prosecution of crime.

If such a contention is accurate, it may stem in part from the fact that Meyer Lansky, a kingpin of organized crime, had, in the mid-1930's, come into possession of incontrovertible evidence of Hoover's now well documented homosexual activities. Through the years, Lansky had gathered similar embarrassing information about other prominent people in government, who became willing to overlook many of Lansky's nefarious activities in Las Vegas casinos—from which he illegally skimmed millions of dollars every year—and to focus their attention on less threatening subjects, such as Alger Hiss and Dalton Trumbo.

Scott also documents the collusion of the CIA, the FBI, and metropolitan law-enforcement agencies in the shootings during the 1960's of such political dissidents as Malcolm X (his bodyguard was an undercover officer of the New York Police Department), Fred Hampton, and Mark Clark. Curt Gentry has documented in his *J. Edgar Hoover: The Man and the Secrets* (1991) Hoover's knowledge of the dangers that lurked in Dallas weeks before the president's trip there and his failure to act on this information.

In his attempt to divine patterns in the enormous body of material he has been studying, Scott concludes that each decade since the end of World War II has been marked by some major political crisis. The first of these crises occurred in the late 1940's and early 1950's, when McCarthyism hobbled much governmental activity, terrorized intellectual America, and led to the unjust ruin of many American citizens who were loyal to their country but not blindly so. Scott prefers to call the activities of this period "Hooverism" rather than "McCarthyism" because they reflect so accurately Hoover's priorities for his agency.

The second major crisis resulted in the assassination of John F. Kennedy. Immediately before his death, Kennedy announced publicly that one thousand troops would be withdrawn from Southeast Asia by year's end—December 31, 1963—signaling the start of the winding down of the American engagement in Vietnam.

Two days following the assassination—even before Kennedy's funeral—the new president, Lyndon B. Johnson, rescinded his predecessor's mandate, ordering an escalation of the Vietnamese conflict quite in line with what the American Security Council, such influential anti-Communists as William Pawley, Robert Morris, and General Charles Willoughby, and such defense corporations as General Dynamics,

Lockheed, General Electric, Honeywell, and Motorola had been urging. Clearly, the "deep politics" to which Scott refers in his title were alive and extremely active.

The third major crisis was Watergate. Scott shows that many of the forces at work in plotting the Kennedy assassination were also behind Watergate. He calls Richard Nixon not so much a guilty perpetrator as a guilty victim of the Watergate scandal, but points out that it is perhaps more than coincidental that news of Watergate broke only days after Nixon had announced plans to wind down the Vietnamese conflict. His decision had broad implications for the deep political forces mentioned above, particularly for the military establishment, major corporations that supplied armaments and other goods to the military, and drug traffickers, much of whose raw material came from Southeast Asia's Golden Triangle. Watergate brought about results similar to what had shaken Dallas and the nation in 1963: A president who threatened the deep political structure was handily deposed.

Iran-Contra, the scandal of the 1980's, broke a month after President Ronald Reagan returned from a conference with Mikhail Gorbachev in Reykjavik at which an end to the Cold War was envisioned as a distinct possibility—one that many players in the games of the deep political community viewed with alarm. Iran-Contra threatened to discredit Reagan's "Teflon" presidency as no other event had. The banking scandals that came to light as a result of Iran-Contra had far-reaching effects and implications and helped bring to public attention the savings and loan scandals of the late 1980's.

Considered in this total context, the Kennedy assassination becomes part of a fabric much broader than the isolated tragedy—whether viewed officially as a conspiracy or not—that it was. In the context Scott patiently pieces together, the assassination fits into a pattern related to the vested interests of the military-industrial complex and of organized crime.

Scott does not ask his readers to take much on faith. He spends fifty pages demonstrating how Lee Harvey Oswald was manipulated by the deep political forces he has identified—in Oswald's case, particularly the CIA—and another seventy establishing Jack Ruby's close association over thirty years with organized crime and the FBI's calculated suppression of information about this association in its reports to the Warren Commission.

Oswald's checkered past included service in the United States Marine Corps, where he was trained in intelligence. He was later assigned to the naval air station at Atsugi, Japan, a major base for U-2 reconnaissance flights over the Soviet Union, and to Operation Strongback in the Philippines, where CIA influence was strong. In 1959, Oswald defected to the Soviet Union, but he was not alone; a large number of former military men trained in intelligence defected at about the same time, a fact that suggests the CIA was using them to infiltrate the Soviet Union.

Oswald's subsequent activities, detailed carefully by Scott, suggest further direct connections to the CIA, particularly during the months preceding the assassination, and also reveal indirect links between Lee Harvey Oswald and Jack Ruby. Information about this Oswald-Ruby connection was not reported to the Warren Commission, nor were crucial files about Oswald's military service provided to the commission. These files, shockingly, were ultimately destroyed.

Scott's investigation of Ruby reveals that although the assassination of Oswald had all the earmarks of a mob killing, little was said of Ruby's long association with the Chicago underworld before he moved south. He was well known in Dallas as a petty player in a much larger, transnational game that included drug trafficking, gambling, and prostitution.

Ruby and his brother grew up in Chicago, members of a gang that was part of the political machine of the notorious Jake Arvey of the Twenty-fourth Ward. Scott has uncovered evidence of Ruby's longtime informant status in narcotics. Although he played both ends against the middle, Ruby was useful to the FBI and to organized crime alike, so his duplicitous game went unchecked. The Warren Commission, in repudiating any suggestion that Ruby had a connection with organized crime, was clearly covering up information that even the most incompetent neophyte investigators could not have failed to uncover. Scott makes it clear that here the Warren Commission flagrantly and knowingly deceived the public. Evidence of Ruby's mob connections is so substantial that it would not have been possible for any investigative body to be unaware of it.

In his revelations about the postassassination investigations of Ruby, Scott provides his most damning evidence against the Warren Commission and the subsequent House Select Committee on Assassinations. In this part of his investigation, Scott eliminates any lingering doubt concerning his central thesis: that the assassination of John F. Kennedy was, despite the government's official findings to the contrary, the result of a shocking conspiracy that involved the FBI, the CIA, the military-industrial complex, and organized crime.

Scott demands that the full archive on the Kennedy assassination be made available to the American public. Until such access is granted, the full story of Kennedy's death cannot be known. What is at stake, according to Scott, has to do not merely with the brutal murder of one man but with the entire moral fiber of the United States.

If deep politics determines the nation's future, the United States risks going down in destruction—as, Scott recalls in his epilogue, the Roman Empire did a century after the assassination of the reform-minded Tiberius Gracchus. The parallels are indisputable. The ruthlessness of the deep political forces about which Scott writes, however, is so colossal that one questions whether they can ever be controlled.

R. Baird Shuman

Sources for Further Study

Booklist. XC, September 15, 1993, p. 107.
Kirkus Reviews. LXI, August 15, 1993, p. 1059.
Library Journal. CXVIII, October 15, 1993, p. 76.
San Francisco Chronicle. November 18, 1993, p. E1.
The Washington Post Book World. XXIII, October 31, 1993, p. 4.

DIARY
Volume III: 1961-1966

Author: Witold Gombrowicz (1904-1969)
First published: Dziennik 1961-66, 1966, in France (sections from *Kultura* for 1967-1969 added
   to English-language edition)
Translated from the Polish by Lillian Vallee
Edited by Jan Kott
Publisher: Northwestern University Press (Evanston, Illinois). 220 pp. $29.95; paperback
   $12.95
Type of work: Diary and essays
Time: 1961-1966
Locale: Argentina, Paris, Berlin, and the French Riviera

The final volume of Witold Gombrowicz's Diary *covers his return to Europe after a quarter
century in Argentina and offers provocative, often amusing appraisals of writing and society*

Principal personage:
WITOLD GOMBROWICZ, an émigré Polish writer

At the very end of August, 1939, Witold Gombrowicz landed in Buenos Aires and
immediately found himself stranded because of the German invasion of Poland, his
homeland. His literary career disrupted by history, Gombrowicz started life anew in a
foreign country without benefit of either a secure income or knowledge of the
language. Yet without ever returning to Poland or even setting foot in his beloved
Europe until 1963, he established a place in the top ranks of Polish writers after World
War II.

This remarkable achievement becomes more so when one considers Gombrowicz's
talent for making things difficult for himself—and everyone else. Reported to be
sickly, secretive, and self-centered, he was never easy to get along with. Proud and
insecure, he defied labels and critical explication of his work, resenting all attempts
to tie him to any group or movement.

Wanting to express himself fully, but never finally, he took naturally to the diary
form. Not surprisingly, however, the *Diary* reveals no single, essential Gombrowicz,
but a syndrome, a constellation of symptoms surrounding an ungraspable center. Part
fact, part fiction, the Gombrowicz of the *Diary* is an outrageous creation, self-involved
and self-indulgent, vicious and resentful, misogynistic and misanthropic, as withering
as Louis-Ferdinand Céline in his disdain. Possessed by an unfailing sense of the
absurd, however, Gombrowicz is never dreary. To the contrary, iconoclast and gadfly,
provocateur and malcontent, Gombrowicz entertains like a jester of the old school,
sparing no one's pretensions, his own least of all.

A scion of the doomed landed gentry, Gombrowicz felt at home neither with
aristocrats nor with writers: "I was in between worlds. Being in-between is not a bad
way to elevate yourself." This ironic (often melancholy) superiority pervades the
Diary, with Gombrowicz wielding his rough edges ruthlessly to cut both ways.
Ultimately, he commands the reader's sympathy and respect because, on the page at
least, his bilious bluster reflects the torment of a human soul revealing, and reveling

in, its painfully tenuous identity.

In Argentina, with friends and admirers ready to help him, he refused the burden of obligation or expectations. Too competitive, even combative, to ingratiate himself with the Polish colony, he isolated himself, eking out a livelihood on loans and irregular journalism, even checkers. In keeping with a lifelong fascination with self-degradation, he frequented the notorious sections of Buenos Aires where he picked up lower-class boys and sailors (simultaneously pursuing affairs with women).

Despite such distractions, his literary career was resumed with the publication of his fiction in Spanish translation. After the war, he secured a job that gave him the freedom to finish a novel, later serialized in *Kultura*, a Paris-based Polish émigré magazine. His irreverent debunking of received opinions about the war and Polish politics and literature attracted ever-increasing attention in Europe—and made him enemies.

The resulting controversies run throughout the *Diary*, published in *Kultura* from 1953 to 1969. In this last volume, however, they have degenerated to mere squabbles, perhaps because his cynicism has come into vogue and few any longer take seriously the attacks instigated by Poland's Communist government. Still, to a surprising extent the axis of his career remains tilted toward the same Warsaw circle that he had left in 1939. Not one to pull punches in the literary free-for-all, Gombrowicz never takes sides permanently, preferring to discomfort everyone.

"My truth and my strength rely on my endless spoiling of the game . . . for myself and others," he says, proceeding to overturn many an apple cart in the pursuit of a new game. "Artificially candid and candidly artificial," his works are innovative but rooted firmly in the Polish literary tradition that he parodies and prods toward its future. Repetitive, digressive, vulgar, his neo-baroque style interweaves slang and dialect, adjectives and colorful expressions in an elaborate, even musical fabric. Though this is hard to capture in translation, the range of styles in this volume is impressive.

One moment uncompromising and categorical, Gombrowicz oozes despair the next, often making a face behind his prose, twisting his seriousness into a joke on himself. What others deny he runs wild with, like a dog chasing his tail, his rhetoric so convoluted that he often ends by collapsing, but usually with a canine satisfaction in the mundane—as if after everything is said and done, all that really matters is what one ate for lunch. Then he is up and running again, breathlessly exuberant, almost out of control in pursuit of that eternally elusive goal: "to be myself, myself, not an artist or an idea or any of my works—just myself."

Yet all writing is fiction that can never possibly re-create experience or identity. Unable to pretend otherwise, Gombrowicz foregrounds and lampoons literary devices in the vain hope that somehow this will weaken their stranglehold on his reality. He carries on imaginary conversations, relates his actions in third person, paints obviously fictitious accounts of events, and skewers his pretensions with self-commentary in italics.

Often Gombrowicz works a surrealistic vein deep into his imagination, making the most extraordinary statements and observations with a deadpan tone that induces the discomforting dislocation of a nightmare. In his world, objects terrorize consciousness; for example, in Berlin he cannot shake off the vision of a hook in the wall, emblematic of Nazi war crimes. Sometimes the invention is whimsical, as when his ship back to Europe passes his ship bound to Argentina. On that same voyage, however, a human eye lies unexplained on the deck, and throughout Gombrowicz's work people are reduced to body parts, as if the whole world were ready to collapse into some horrible messy pile.

In fact, that mess underlies all experience, out of which people can construct a self only because of the human genius for imposing form on the chaotic flux of reality. As an artist, Gombrowicz hungers for form, but wars against it, too, because form imposes itself on the person, distorting and destroying identity.

He fights especially hard because he cannot win. Form is institutionalized in conventions and mores. Conformity is so crucial that the group molds each member to its purpose, mostly in a superficial way, stamping on a face but leaving the soul merely deformed (the source of torment and hope in Gombrowicz's universe). Existentialist in his belief that every act and interaction defines identity, Gombrowicz denies freedom the primacy Jean-Paul Sartre gives it because each act is too conditioned by the situation ever to be free.

Still, if never free, Gombrowicz is always the rebel. When society does its best to give each individual a happy face, his "proud humanity" refuses to falsify its nature by smiling. Rejecting the perfect God for Adam fresh from the clay, Gombrowicz opts for self-creation (if only negatively), challenging anything laid down strictly.

Consequently, even before reaching Paris, Gombrowicz knows, "I will not be able to exist if they do not perceive me as their enemy." He soon finds opportunity enough to hate Paris, where fashion has replaced beauty—the most diabolical sort of victory of form because it cloaks the human body, which is the basis for all true beauty. Worse, culture denies beauty's frightening source: immaturity, inferiority, stupidity—in a word, youth.

In Gombrowicz's universe, wedded pairs of opposites—predominantly youth and age—create force fields of mutual attraction and repulsion so strong that they paralyze identity unless resisted and exposed. Just as Gombrowicz the aristocrat dallied with lower-class boys, Gombrowicz the writer bends like Narcissus over his lost youth. Determined to see himself clearly, not to prettify with fashion, he exposes his divided nature. He delineates the web of erotic obsessions created by the interplay of opposites, not to titillate, since there is no explicit sexuality, but to shock his readers back into a connection with the reality of the body underlying their imposed identities.

With people locked into combat with everyone else in the struggle for identity, radical individuality is Gombrowicz's recurrent war cry. He attacks intellectuals whose empty talk enhances social control and maintains their place in the hierarchy. Already most are in so cozy a position that they end up as mere "spiritual functionaries" who assist as "all of Europe seems like a horse that steps into a horse collar voluntarily."

In particular, Gombrowicz dreads society's too-willing submission to the yoke of science, which reduces the person to an object. This criticism extends to Marxism and Sartre's existentialism, which deny the painfully messy quality of human existence. Unfortunately, no theory ever makes imposed social roles natural, but to avoid painful uncertainty, people become more rigidly conformist, not less.

In Gombrowicz's Berlin (and he is very careful to stress that this Berlin is his creation, but he offended his first readers anyway), a new generation is traumatized by the guilt of its Nazi parents. He is fixated on the hands of these young people, like overdetermined dream symbols, both bloody hangman's hands and dead weights dragging the young to a new damnation. Through work, through their hands, they seek to reconstruct a heritage too compromised to endure. As fiercely as their Nazi forebears, they strive to create new lives, proving that humankind strengthens its barbarity by pretending to have conquered it. Gombrowicz sees the children marching forward as resolutely and as ignorantly as the parents had, hands raised in salute.

Published in *Kultura*, the Berlin entries caused great offense, but Gombrowicz objects in return: He was not there as a guest, but as himself. Everywhere he wants to be himself, defiantly. This is hardest for him among his literary colleagues, for he craves their acceptance while expecting himself to rise above such vanity. This ambivalence emerges clearly in his hyperbolic, hysterical account of a conference of PEN (International Association of Poets, Playwrights, Editors, Essayists, and Novelists) in Buenos Aires. Riddled by self-doubt and self-loathing, he mocks himself for taking a seat among the armchairs of his fellow writers, both one of them and not.

He fits in no better in Europe. He recounts, and no doubt elaborates, an incident in Paris when his inquiry about a certain writer elicits pabulum about literary schools and prizes. "I shouted that I was neither a writer nor a member of anything, neither a metaphysician nor an essayist. I was me—free, unencumbered, living. . . . Ah, yes, they said, so you are an existentialist." Frustrated, Gombrowicz starts undressing and clears out the restaurant—proving to his own satisfaction that no one really wants to know anyone else as he truly is.

Most of his literary encounters are equally farcical, but there is bitterness and resentment, too. Writing by its very nature has no dignity; at first the writer struggles to have anyone listen, and then suddenly everyone feels free to judge him or her without regard to truth. Moreover, Gombrowicz cannot even claim to enjoy writing. There has been obsessiveness at times, he says, but no joy—and always nagging uncertainty. Yet he cannot moan without making fun of himself for being such a "saint" of art. He further undermines his lamentations by admitting that his thoughts are now consumed with the progress of his translations. It is with an almost contented sigh that he concedes defeat: "My rebellion will find publishers, commentators, readers, and will be smoothly absorbed by the mechanism."

Of course, there are rewards. He mocks his greed for literary prizes, asserting that art should not cause personal gain, but he appreciates the spoils of success: a house on the Riviera, a fairly normal life, even a wife (though her existence is hardly mentioned). He is gratified, too, by the endurance of *Ferdydurke*, his 1937 surrealistic satire of modernism.

Nevertheless, he says, something always "knocks the plate out of my hands at the very moment it nears my lips." Returning to Europe, he says, he returns to his death. Troubled since 1958 by asthma, he becomes very ill in Berlin in 1964. Succumbing slowly thereafter to heart and respiratory problems, Gombrowicz remains the man in-between. Having left Argentina, but unable to return to Poland because of the Communists, he has no homeland. With death's shadow lengthening over the *Diary*, even his self-deprecation cannot render less poignant the definite elegiac tone.

> You strive for many long years to be somebody—and what do you become? A river of events in the present, a turbulent stream of facts, happening now, at this cold moment that you are experiencing and you can relate to nothing else. Confusion—only this is yours. You can't even say good-bye.

Philip McDermott

Sources for Further Study

Chicago Tribune. August 8, 1993, XIV, p. 6.
Publishers Weekly. CCXL, April 19, 1993, p. 56.

A DIFFERENT MIRROR
A History of Multicultural America

Author: Ronald Takaki (1939-   )
Publisher: Little, Brown (Boston). Illustrated. 508 pp. $27.95
Type of work: History
Time: The 1400's to the late twentieth century
Locale: The United States

This revisionist history of the United States features the experiences of various immigrant and minority groups who are often excluded from traditional histories

Near the end of this multicultural history of the United States, historian Ronald Takaki articulates the thesis and the goal of his book. Citing Gloria Anzaldúa's concept of a borderland, "a place where 'two or more cultures edge each other,'" he concurs with her that an "inner struggle" to understand the American cultural heritage must take place before Americans can change their troubled society. This understanding "must ultimately be ground in 'unlearning' much of what we have been told about America's past and substituting a more inclusive and accurate history of all the peoples of America." Takaki's contribution to this goal is a retelling of American history from the point of view of the various ethnic and racial groups who settled here, attempting to see all the "different shores" from which they came as "equal points of departure" in the building of American culture.

What could have become a loose, baggy monster of a project is given form by several structuring elements. The first is an extended metaphor that compares the New World to the wilderness in William Shakespeare's *The Tempest*, a play that opened in 1611 and was based on a contemporary incident involving an English ship that was heading for Virginia but ran aground in the Bermudas. Takaki speculates that the play represented English expansion into the Americas. Caliban, the quasi-human native of the island to which Prospero is exiled and over which he claims sovereignty, becomes a figure for the natives of the New World and later for the Africans brought as slaves. Takaki uses this image to illustrate what he refers to as the "racialization of savagery," the tendency on the part of white Americans to associate barbarism with dark skin, an attitude that would determine the treatment of black slaves as well as Native American tribes. The image of Caliban is used throughout Takaki's study to describe the struggles especially of those immigrant groups, including the Chinese as well as African Americans and Native Americans, that could not assimilate into mainstream American society because of racial differences. They were often denigrated in the same terms (savage, lazy, dirty, inferior, treacherous) in order to justify harsh policies toward them, whether of slavery, removal from their land, or restrictions of their immigration and civil rights. This pattern, first established when the English met the Indians, thus repeated itself throughout the next two centuries.

A Different Mirror: A History of Multicultural America is also structured, though loosely, in a rough historical sequence consisting of four main sections: "Boundlessness," from discovery through slavery; "Borders," covering the Market Revolution and western expansion; "Distances," treating European and Asian immigration; and "Crossings," a contemplation of America's dilemmas in the twenty-first century, with the changes in the racial composition of U.S. population and the accompanying questions about who is "American."

Who is American? In the book's first section, to trace the English colonists' attempts to grapple with this question Takaki examines the policies they developed to deal with blacks and indigenous peoples during a time when the country seemed boundless. Questions of race and racism were particularly acute at this time, as the English tried to define themselves in contrast to the indigenous peoples they found in the New World. Yet much of the rhetoric used against the Indians, Takaki shows, was not based on color, at least not initially; it was similar to that being used against the Irish in the period when the English were colonizing Ireland, and for similar reasons of land acquisition. The pattern Takaki establishes in this first section has social, political, and economic ramifications for the rest of the book, for the pattern repeated itself in different forms with each new immigrant group that arrived in the new country.

Takaki cites letters and contemporary English accounts that found parallels between the Indians and the Irish. Both groups were seen as uncivilized because they were unchristian and unlettered and failed to bring their land under cultivation and make it more productive. Capitalist patterns of ownership and productivity were integrated into the English definitions of civility and morality, as Takaki has shown in an earlier work, *Iron Cages: Race and Culture in Nineteenth-Century America* (1979). The English idea that the Irish and the Indians were immoral savages was difficult to separate from their idea that they, the English, had both a right and a moral obligation to take the land from them because they could better exploit it economically. Much of Takaki's focus in the rest of the book is to show how this theme is repeated, with variations, in the settling of the rest of the continent.

In another important early chapter, Takaki takes up the development of black-white racism. Africans brought to North America shared roughly the status of the white indentured servants from the British Isles, some of whom were sold or stolen into servitude. Takaki traces the slow but steady codification of laws based on skin color, including laws against racial intermarriage and laws making only blacks and their offspring slaves for life, in an effort to keep indentured whites and blacks from making common cause with each other to improve their lot. For them to do so would undermine the South's developing plantation economy, which depended on cheap labor. In addition, Takaki asserts,

> this division based on race helped to delineate the border between savagery and civilization. In the wilderness, the English colonists felt a great urgency to destroy what historian [Winthrop] Jordan described as "the living image of primitive aggressions which they said was the Negro but was really their own." Far away from the security and surveillance of society in England, the colonists feared the possibility of losing self-control over their passions. . . . Thus, they projected their hidden and rejected instinctual parts of human nature onto blacks. . . . Internal boundaries of control were required, or else whites would be swept away by the boundlessness of the wilderness.

The seeds of race consciousness and economic domination that were sown in the early history of the republic make many of the experiences Takaki documents of Mexicans, Chinese, Japanese, Jewish, and Irish immigrants unsurprising, though painful and often tragic. Takaki uses sources ranging from government documents to popular songs to describe not only the events but also the attitudes and feelings accompanying immigrant experience in the United States. Often the rhetoric of barbarity was leveled at the newest group to arrive, but just as often, the reason beneath this apparent hatred of difference was economic fear and fierce competition for jobs. To a large extent, Takaki's book is a history of American labor. He chronicles the divide-and-conquer strategies of white leaders, such as the importation of Chinese laborers to work on plantations and on the railroads, and of Mexican migrant laborers to pick crops. They were brought to compete with white laborers and to foil union organizing, but often their arrival was followed by racially based fears that America was being "overrun" by the group in question, and subsequently restrictions were placed on their entry into the country or their movements. The underlying ideology that made this possible was, Takaki asserts, that America is a homogeneous society, that Americans are white, and that everyone else is not really American, is somehow here on sufferance.

Takaki's purpose, then, is to call attention to this ideology and to counter it with stories not only of the experiences but also of the contributions of the various ethnic and racial groups who built America in ways that are just as real and important as those of the dominant white culture. For example, he credits the Japanese with teaching California farmers how to raise fruit commercially. The end result is to demonstrate that the United States never was racially homogeneous. His hope is that the more Americans know about one another's experiences, the more tolerant they will become as a society.

Takaki's range in this book is very wide, his research extensive and detailed. He has a readable narrative style that makes complex issues clear to the nonhistorian. The use of popular source materials such as songs and letters often adds special poignancy to the stories he tells. As Paul Boyer noted in his review in *The Washington Post*, however, the treatment of various ethnic groups is uneven, and Takaki tends to focus on the struggles between whites and nonwhites with insufficient attention either to distinctions among whites or to those whites who resisted discrimination and injustice. He seems to use the Irish and the Jews as representative of the European immigrant experience, for no others are discussed. To some extent, constraints of time and space would serve as understandable explanations for these omissions, but they should be noted, for otherwise he seems to reduce the complexity of the history of whites in America even as he clarifies the histories of peoples of color; this in turn could interfere with his ultimate purpose.

Students of American ethnic history should also be aware of the difference in depth of treatment of minorities in *A Different Mirror*. African Americans, Asians, and Mexicans are represented in greater detail and more often in their own voices than are the Native Americans. One limitation of the discussion of Indians is that Takaki often represents them through the eyes of white people—from Thomas Jefferson and Andrew Jackson to Francis Amasa Walker and John Collier—who were trying to eliminate or control them. While that ironic treatment of white leaders has its own powerful effect in showing their racism and the unreasonableness of their positions, once the reader rejects their portrayal of Indians, a gap remains. How do Native Americans see themselves? Takaki answers this question insufficiently. He leaves their story with the failure of the stock reduction program of the 1930's and misses an opportunity to discuss the revival of Indian culture and political activism in the 1970's, 1980's, and 1990's, including the activities of the American Indian Movement. In fact, in the cases of all the racial minorities he discusses, recognition of the significant literary flowering they have experienced during the latter decades of the twentieth century would not only offset the bleakness of the economic and social conditions Takaki so eloquently traces in his last section, "Through a Glass Darkly," but also, perhaps, provide a starting point for the intergroup communication he seeks.

Nevertheless, Takaki has written a fascinating, informative multicultural history of the United States which provides an important corrective to most Americans' understanding of their culture's roots. Furthermore, he writes with energy and a sense of commitment that enhances the telling of these stories, which become all our stories.

Elizabeth Zanichkowsky

Sources for Further Study

American Heritage. XLIV, September, 1993, p. 10.
The Christian Science Monitor. August 10, 1993, p. 11.
Commentary. XCVI, September, 1993, p. 64.
The Economist. CCCXXVII, June 26, 1993, p. 97.
National Review. XLV, October 4, 1993, p. 57.
New Leader. LXXVI, May 17, 1993, p. 32.
The New York Review of Books. XL, October 7, 1993, p. 21.
The New York Times Book Review. XCVIII, August 22, 1993, p. 17.
Publishers Weekly. CCXL, April 19, 1993, p. 41.
The Washington Post Book World. XXIII, June 20, 1993, p. 3.

A DIFFERENT PERSON
A Memoir

Author: James Merrill (1926-   )
Publisher: Alfred A. Knopf (New York). 271 pp. $25.00
Type of work: Autobiography
Time: Mostly 1950-1952
Locale: Europe and the United States

A lyrical account of a two-year stay in Europe, during which a young poet underwent psychoanalysis and came to understand better both himself and his relationship with his parents

Principal personages:
    JAMES MERRILL, a poet
    CHARLES MERRILL, his father, a wealthy stockbroker
    HELLEN PLUMMER, his mother, who was divorced from his father and
        remarried
    CLAUDE FREDERICKS, his lover, a printer
    DR. DETRE, his psychoanalyst

James Merrill is one of America's most critically acclaimed living poets, having received, among many other honors, two National Book Awards, for *Nights and Days* (1966) and *Mirabell* (1978), the Bollingen Prize in Poetry, for *Braving the Elements* (1972), and the Pulitzer Prize, for *Divine Comedies* (1976). His prodigious literary output has also included fiction, drama, and essays. With *A Different Person: A Memoir*, Merrill turns to yet another genre, and with remarkable success. His first strictly autobiographical work, *A Different Person* is a lyrical, insightful portrait of a young writer's struggles with his own desires and the expectations of his parents. Much like James Joyce's *A Portrait of the Artist as a Young Man* (1916), it takes the reader inside the consciousness of a confused, sensitive individual, capturing in its free-flowing style a process of discovery, both of the writer's "self" and of his ties to others. Unlike Joyce's work, however, this memoir focuses on a young adulthood rendered even more difficult by homosexual yearnings and the fractures these cause in a homophobic family and culture.

Merrill's memoir focuses primarily on two crucial years in his development as a writer and a person. From 1950 to 1952, Merrill traveled widely in Europe, underwent psychoanalysis, and gained remarkable insight not only into his own life but also into those of his lover, friends, and parents. Merrill's narrative proceeds chronologically in twenty-one sections devoted to journeys through numerous European cities, but he ends each chapter with italicized musings, some recounting real events, others transcribing imaginary conversations, dreams, and hidden fears. Merrill captures brilliantly the complexity of an individual consciousness, tracing the many ties linking the swirling, amorphous present to a fixed, unchangeable past, as well as a future over which one has some control. In scrutinizing so intensely a brief period of time, Merrill avoids the appearance of name-dropping or chattiness; in opening up his narrative with brief excursions through time and consciousness, he deepens his analysis of how dramatically and fortuitously one's life can evolve over a two-year period.

In early 1950, the twenty-three-year-old Merrill was a young poet whose first book was about to be published and who had just met the man whom he thought would be his partner for life. As the narrative opens, however, an older, wiser Merrill, who is narrating and reflecting on his past, reveals just how deluded and pompous he was at the time. Isolated and insecure, the young writer was creating poetry that was verbally brilliant but lifeless. His social existence was equally shallow, rich in conversation and aesthetic texture but virtually emotionless. The prodigious wealth of his family allowed him a cushion of comfort that was productive, in that it allowed him the leisure to pursue his calling, but that also had unfortunate consequences, for it encouraged his diffidence and dilettantish behavior. In preparing to set sail for Europe, the young Merrill was making a conscious effort to disentangle himself from his past, to search out his own essence, to find his own voice.

Numerous interpersonal problems and childhood legacies had contributed to a static life in the United States. In particular, his troubled relationship with his father, Charles Merrill, intruded on his equanimity and sense of selfhood. The elder Merrill, one of the founding partners of the highly successful brokerage firm Merrill Lynch, was a no-nonsense businessman and reserved father whose early attempts to mold his offspring in his own image led to feelings of estrangement and mistrust on both sides. Profound guilt was added to this combustive mixture, for Merrill at the beginning of his narrative is unsure whether his father even knows of his homosexuality. The elderly Merrill is in uncertain health, and the son has been warned explicitly by his mother that knowledge of his sexual orientation would "kill" his father. In escaping to Europe, the young writer hopes to reevaluate this relationship and perhaps redefine it, for his father will meet him for a brief time on the Continent.

Merrill's relationship with his mother is equally unhappy. She knows of her son's sexuality and disapproves highly. More persistently than his father, Merrill's mother attempts to remake her son, opening letters and consulting doctors as she searches for a way to "cure" his homosexuality. While Merrill does not feel at ease with his father, he actually has running battles with his mother, both real and imagined, as he attempts simultaneously to shock her and to gain her acceptance. A narrow notion of propriety leads Merrill's parents to dread any hint of social scandal that sexual abnormality in their son might instigate. Merrill's portrait of his parents is one of an entire generation, one that had survived the Depression and clung to conformity and rigid standards of behavior as forms of security against social and economic chaos.

As he begins his journey, Merrill senses that something is lacking in himself, or, more precisely, in his knowledge of himself. He feels emotionally dead, unable to love. While moderately happy in the company of friends, he is terrified of being alone. Even his new relationship, with Claude Fredericks, a successful printer of fine limited-edition books, seems stifled by the distracting social life he has created in New York. Yet Merrill's relationship with Claude is also one of mistaken knowledge. Desperately wishing to find "love," he has hastily chosen to commit himself to someone whom he hardly knows. In arranging to meet Claude in Europe, Merrill hopes to deepen what has been so far a shallow sexual liaison, one that has had only the trappings of a deeper emotional commitment.

Travel does provide the impetus for change, but not travel alone. Taking up temporary residence in Rome, Merrill commits to a yearlong course of psychoanalysis. Dr. Detre, whose distance and reserve mirror that of the elder Merrill, helps the young poet confront his feelings of anger and inadequacy. In doing so Merrill will recover— or, more precisely, discover—an identity and a poetic voice. Part of this process is coming to terms with his feelings of abandonment as a child; ignored by his wealthy parents, passed along to servants for primary care, he became suspicious, withdrawn, unable to love. Venting his emotions on his analyst, he begins to heal. The older, narrating Merrill reflects often on the efficacy of the psychoanalytic process, but rarely does he do so in the simplistic terms of a convert. In his italicized musings, Merrill fully allows that if he had sought assistance from a different analyst or during a different time period, the mechanism for self-exploration would have been far different. His point is that psychoanalysis can aid analysands in searches for which they must take primary responsibility. Responsibility is key, for the process Merrill under- goes is that of taking responsibility for his own life; as he does so, his relationships change dramatically and irrevocably.

As all maturing individuals must, Merrill comes to see his parents as human and flawed people, ones who have made terrible mistakes in the past, but who were acting with their own psychic and cognitive limitations. In discussions with his father, whose health continues to fail, Merrill recognizes a humane spirit at the core of the bluff businessman. During a visit by his mother, he uncovers the fear that accounts for her oppressive notions of propriety and that is manifested in her offensive racism and homophobia. Never coming to agree with their opinions or treatment of him, Merrill does come to forgive his parents, and through that forgiveness to heal. Taking responsibility for his own life, he strives to incorporate into his personality his own humanistic ideals—generosity, honesty, forthrightness—instead of simply replicating the traits of his parents and living out his life in anger and emotional isolation.

This, of course, means reevaluating his relationship with Claude, who joins him in Rome and who also undergoes psychoanalysis with Dr. Detre. Slowly they drift apart and then break permanently. Merrill finds Claude's "bookish airs" too confining and lifeless. Searching for a new expressiveness and engagement with life, Merrill drifts in and out of relationships with men who possess vitality and openness. While the reader does not notice many immediate, positive results of Merrill's determination to "love" more fully, Merrill's italicized mental wanderings move forward in time to recount the long-term consequences of his efforts to become a "different person," consequences that include a successful, stable, and fulfilling partnership with another man.

As the commentary above indicates, *A Different Person* relates a psychic journey, but that is only one of its many features. Merrill renders vivid this extraordinary two-year period by relating his personal narrative of growth and reconciliation against a changing backdrop of European scenery and encounters with fascinating figures. In his wanderings around the continent, Merrill befriends and converses with Alice B.

Toklas, Gertrude Stein's "widow," whose attachment to her former partner becomes a model for the love that Merrill wishes to express and receive. W. H. Auden and Alison Lurie also enter the narrative and play key roles in the changing perceptions of both the young Merrill and the narrating, older Merrill. The reader finds a rich emotional and descriptive texture in this work, for Merrill describes the Italian, Greek, and Turkish landscapes with remarkable sensitivity and power. In its variety, energy, and intelligence, this narrative never fails to engage even as it instructs.

The didactic aspect of Merrill's narrative is never heavy-handed, but certainly represents a primary impetus for its writing. Merrill challenges readers to move beyond anger, to avoid the pitfall of unproductive struggles with the unchangeable past. In allowing readers to eavesdrop on his most private thoughts and view some of his most painful personal experiences, Merrill invites them to muse similarly on their own lives, to formulate their own ideals about the people they would like to become. In his last paragraphs Merrill speaks of "retrieval," literally that of a passport or wallet that he has left behind in Rome, but symbolically of his repossession of self and recovery of poetic voice. Yet his voice has changed and matured. In his creative efforts after his return from Europe, Merrill no longer imitated others; he came to terms with and moved beyond the past. His memoir asks readers to do the same, not simply in terms of poetic creation, for not all are gifted writers, but rather in the sense of creating oneself anew. The Merrill of the end of the narrative is not only a poet; in a sense, he is a poem as well, a conscious and successful creation of himself, a living testament to honesty in perception and self-critique.

The relative smoothness of Merrill's transition and the overall optimism of his narrative represent the only aspects of this work that may strike some readers as overly simplistic. While he does a superb job of linking his main narrative of growth to aspects of both his past and his future, Merrill does suggest that lives are fully reconstitutable, that psychoanalysis and hard work can lead to selves so different that one in fact becomes a "different" person. This may be too easy, for unproductive behavior patterns, suspicion of others, and a general aloofness would certainly resurface at odd times, and the struggle to maintain the "new" self would continue throughout life. Perhaps his efforts in this regard will be explored in future volumes of his memoirs, for as it stands, this works seems a bit too tidy in its resolution of profound life conflicts in the space of 271 pages.

Even so, *A Different Person* is a graceful, memorable work of autobiography. Its candor and lyricism place it in the same category as 1992's National Book Award winner *Becoming a Man*, by Paul Monette. Linking these narratives is the acuity with which their writers trace the hardships of growing up gay in a homophobic climate, of coming to voice in a world that seeks to deny atypical voices. The brilliance of these memoirs also lies in their accessibility and universality, for Merrill's struggle to become a different person and Monette's process of becoming a man are journeys all individuals must take if they are to claim proprietorship over their lives and discover the unique visions that are their own.

Donald E. Hall

Sources for Further Study

Booklist. XC, October 1, 1993, p. 244.
Boston Globe. September 5, 1993, p. 14.
Chicago Tribune. September 26, 1993, XIV, p. 3.
Library Journal. CXVIII, October 15, 1993, p. 66.
Los Angeles Times Book Review. September 5, 1993, p. 3.
The New Republic. CCIX, September 20, 1993, p. 49.
The New York Review of Books. XL, November 4, 1993, p. 31.
Publishers Weekly. CCXL, August 16, 1993, p. 96.
The Wall Street Journal. October 14, 1993, p. A15.
The Washington Post Book World. XXIII, September 12, 1993, p. 4.

DISRAELI
A Biography

Author: Stanley Weintraub (1929-)
Publisher: Truman Talley Books/E. P. Dutton (New York). Illustrated. 707 pp. $30.00
Type of work: Biography
Time: 1804-1881
Locale: England

A social biography of the great Conservative prime minister, which emphasizes his Jewish background and the autobiographical nature of his novels

> Principal personages:
> BENJAMIN DISRAELI, a Conservative member of Parliament and prime minister of Great Britain (1868, 1874-1880)
> ISAAC D'ISRAELI, his father, a man of letters and religious skeptic
> MARY ANNE DISRAELI, his wife
> LORD GEORGE BENTINCK, a Conservative member of parliament who was his patron
> WILLIAM GLADSTONE, a Liberal prime minister of Great Britain (1868-1874, 1880-1885), his chief political antagonist
> MONTAGU CORRY, his private secretary and trusted friend
> SIR ROBERT PEEL, a Conservative prime minister of Great Britain (1834-1835, 1841-1846)

Stanley Weintraub betrays his profession in this important biography of Benjamin Disraeli. Weintraub, Evan Pugh Professor of Arts and Humanities at Pennsylvania State University, is clearly no historian, but then Disraeli has been well served by historians. His politics have been widely treated by Maurice Cowling, Paul Smith, Peter Ghosh, F. B. Smith, E. J. Feuchtwanger, and others; his writing by John Vincent, Daniel Schwartz, and Sheila Smith; his life in Robert Blake's political classic *Disraeli* (1966). Yet until now, no one had attempted a life as Disraeli himself might have sensed it. In this respect, Weintraub's expertise as a cultural historian enables him to bring a fresh perspective to one of the great political figures of the nineteenth century.

Benjamin Disraeli was culturally the most unusual of Victoria's prime ministers. In 1748, his Jewish grandfather had emigrated from Italy to England, where he established himself in business and trade. His father, Isaac, was a confirmed skeptic and noted man of letters who, according to a biographer, "lived exclusively for literature." In 1829, Isaac D'Israeli became a country gentleman, taking a long-term lease on Bradenham, a venerable manor house surrounded by more than thirteen hundred acres of Buckinghamshire woodland. Benjamin Disraeli was thus born into a family of comfortable means, ethnically Jewish but perfectly willing to encourage their son to convert to Anglicanism at the age of thirteen in order to further his chances in the narrow world of English high society.

Weintraub begins in 1837, with Disraeli's fourth attempt to enter Parliament. As he spoke from the platform of the Maidstone Corn Exchange, resplendent in canary waistcoat and green trousers, chains glistening and pomaded black curls falling to his cheeks, the stereotypical anti-Semitic clichés of "Shylock" and "old clo's" (that is, "old clothes"; as Weintraub observes, "Selling second-hand clothes was the cliché occupation of the Jewish underclass") resounded from the milling crowd. Thus were Maidstone's conservative voters reminded that no one with such a name could be, as he claimed, "an uncompromising adherent to that ancient Constitution which was once the boast of our Fathers, and is still the Blessing of their Children." Nevertheless, Disraeli's magnificent oratory and the financial patronage of Wyndham Lewis finally propelled him onto the stage of national politics which would make him internationally famous.

A careful examination of the Maidstone election reveals a number of the suggestive ironies that characterize most lives and validate the quality of this biography. When the call for elections came upon the death of King William IV, Disraeli was diverted from the writing of his second novel, an avocation that had first gained him notoriety and that he pursued fitfully throughout his life. Prejudiced listeners at Maidstone shouted "Ol' clo's" and "Shylock" at a dandy who was already some twenty thousand pounds in debt. According to a reliable political broadsheet, Disraeli's list of lenders included "Tailors, Hosiers, Upholsterers, Jew Money Lenders (for this Child of Israel was not satisfied with merely spoiling the Egyptians), Spunging Housekeepers and, in short, persons of every denomination who were foolish enough to trust him." He would not dispose of the last of his debts until the late 1870's. In a darkly fortunate circumstance, Disraeli's Maidstone patron, to whom he owed five thousand pounds, died in 1838. Disraeli married Mary Anne Wyndham a year later. By 1839, the defining features of his life were clear. The question for observers was, what would Disraeli make of his political ambition, his literary pretensions, his Jewishness, his debt, and a pretty wife twelve years older than himself?

Weintraub has added little to an understanding of Disraeli's politics. His review of Disraeli's rise to prominence, culminating in the risky challenge of 1846 over Sir Robert Peel's renunciation of the traditional Conservative policy of protection, is sound but unexceptional and understates the value of his subject's skill in debate. Too often in Weintraub's account the politics are incidental to the "life." In reviewing Disraeli's limited role in the development of Conservative legislation in 1874-1875, for example, Weintraub simply leaves one with "However Disraeli's Parliamentary accomplishments came about, they did come," a nonexplanation that necessarily contributes to nebulous explanations of later failures. In an odd way, there is some justice in this confusion. Disraeli had so long been interested in achieving power for its own sake and upon such general principles that he was uncertain of how it might be put to use. Robert Browning had noticed this in the 1840's, writing to Elizabeth Barrett that Disraeli and his followers "hold that 'belief' is the admirable point—*in what*, they judge comparatively immaterial!"

In a number of cases, Weintraub is positively misleading, taking almost at face value his subject's own valuation of people and events. In no meaningful sense were Disraeli's legislative programs "gestating" since his Young England novels of the 1840's. Furthermore, Weintraub is consistently ungenerous to those who thwarted

Disraeli, including the fifteenth Earl of Derby, onetime Conservative ally, and William Gladstone, longtime Liberal enemy. Throughout, Disraeli's sexual affairs, lying, and self-serving are discussed matter-of-factly, as the necessary means of making a place for oneself, while Gladstone's sexual temptations, convictions, and self-deceptions are judged by a more rigorous standard, leading not to political success but to "blatantly bigoted" statements and "manic intensity." Disraeli and a host of others may have been convinced that Gladstone was "the greatest Tartuffe of his age," but there were just as many who considered him the greatest statesman of his age. Given that history has largely confirmed the latter judgment, it seems odd that a modern biography of Disraeli should so minimize the strength of the competition. Weintraub scarcely mentions Robert Blake's *Disraeli*, a superior political biography and one that must still be read to understand the place of politics in Disraeli's life.

Nevertheless, Weintraub is superb at re-creating the imprint of less overtly political concerns. While Blake's approach to issues such as Disraeli's literary career, his marriage, and his debt is largely topical, Weintraub skillfully weaves these factors into the unfolding portrait of an aspiring politician, gifted but constantly harassed and never certain of success. The reader is not allowed to forget that Disraeli as a young man was frequently on the verge of arrest for failing to pay his debts and that a regular and significant portion of his days was spent in putting off, cajoling, and avoiding creditors. As Disraeli himself observed, one of the greatest stimulants in the world was debt, and in his own case, he had to be successful simply to remain ahead of the legal tidal wave; as a Member of Parliament he was safe from arrest.

Disraeli's relationship with his wife, Mary Anne Wyndham, was less rosy than Blake imagined, but the truth is far from clear. She had some money, though not a great fortune—certainly not enough to bail him out of financial difficulty. She was a good hostess, a devoted wife, and a firm believer in her husband's genius, but was ill educated—she could never remember which came first, the Greeks or the Romans—and prone to gaffes. They clearly cared for one another and took great pains to express it in many ways, but one suspects that their good relations had more to do with commitment and affection than with that inexplicable thing called love. In Weintraub's portrait, their occasional rows, Disraeli's secrecy, and the lack of complete intimacy represent the tensions that seldom surface outside the home in any relationship. Then there is the circumstantial evidence, far from persuasive, that Disraeli fathered at least two children with lovers during the 1860's. Yet no matter what tensions existed between Benjamin and Mary Anne during their thirty-three years of wedded life, it seems fair to say that they had a happy marriage. One is reminded of Disraeli's retort to George Smythe's incredulity at the match: "George, there is one word in the English language, of which you are ignorant . . . gratitude." For all his faults, Disraeli was not ungrateful, and had always remembered the personal debts he owed to others. He had many reasons for appreciating Mary Anne.

It has long been recognized that Disraeli's first writing efforts were vehicles for ambition, for he had no other way to pay his debts or to gain entrée into the society of the well-connected. If he had written sixteen books of propaganda and bad romance before he published his first piece of good literature in *Coningsby* (1844), he had nevertheless attracted quite a bit of attention from prominent people who liked to be entertained. Disraeli's wit and romantic imagination, together with great eloquence on the hustings, proved an unbeatable combination in securing wealthy patrons, frequently older women. This irresistible combination of charm, affairs, and letters attracted his first public lover, Henrietta Sykes, and his most generous benefactor, Sara Brydges Willyams, who left him thirty thousand pounds upon her death in 1863.

As Weintraub shows, however, there was more to Disraeli's writing than this. The potential power of print could also be used to spread political ideas. Disraeli's Young England trilogy is famous, *Coningsby* (1844), *Sybil* (1845), and *Tancred* (1847) marking the advent of the political novel. Yet they are today famous precisely because Disraeli applied his wit to the overriding political concern of the day—the condition of England. In doing so he foreshadowed his challenge to Peel's leadership. Although *Coningsby* was superficially anti-Whig, its theme was in fact, according to one critic, "venomously anti-Tory." Throughout the trilogy, Disraeli subtly fashioned a new Tory orthodoxy based upon a modern, progressive attitude toward society. Written at a time when he had been spurned by the Tory leadership and seemed to have no political future, he was creating a new avenue for himself, at the head of a younger conservative movement. More directly, he wrote scores of pamphlets and articles, many of which spoke to contemporary economic and political questions, and a good political biography of Lord George Bentinck (1852). His participation in the short-lived conservative newspapers *The Representative* (1826) and *The Press* (1853-1856) shows that his craft was linked to larger political purposes. As this biography demonstrates, Disraeli was a writer, not simply a politician who wrote.

The most notable feature of Weintraub's biography is its emphasis upon the Jewish factor. More than anyone else, he re-creates the formidable cultural impact of Disraeli's ethnicity. If the elaborate description of Disraeli's rite of circumcision is suspect owing to his subject's limited awareness at eight days of age, it evokes the compact society that Orthodox, worldly, and secular Jews all understood, regardless of their commitment to its "Truths." Though Disraeli had never been religiously Jewish, throughout his career he made a virtue of his Jewish past. Unlike the vast majority of Britons, who saw the Jews as culturally backward, Disraeli portrayed them in his novels as a great and heroic race, whose achievements had *made* Christianity—and, by extension, English society. It was indeed a "curious flattery" to remind a large Manchester audience in 1844 that the Eastern Mediterranean had boasted "a brilliant civilization developed by a gifted race" when "the manufacturers of Manchester, who now clothe the world, were themselves covered with skins and tattoos like the red men of the wilderness."

The nature of Disraeli's Jewishness has long been debated. Blake presents an Anglicized portrait, with his subject's eccentricities more Italianate than Levantine. One of Weintraub's principal goals in this work is to revive Disraeli's sense of his own Jewishness, and in this he has been remarkably successful. It is no small point, for Disraeli's sense of ethnicity was pervasive. It is hardly surprising that an enormous gap of sensibility would yawn between someone such as Disraeli, who as a very young man had already come to deplore the Greeks, and Gladstone, who saw them as the very fountainhead of all great cultural achievements. This underlying lack of sympathy had far more to do with their political differences than is usually recognized.

Weintraub's biography is not whole. The complex interplay of high politics is glossed, sometimes beyond recognition. He declares that Disraeli is "difficult to love" but in fact portrays him always in the most sympathetic light. His narrative too frequently suggests the transcription of "one damn notecard after another." Nevertheless, *Disraeli: A Biography* must be read. The progress of Disraeli's life has never been presented in so compelling a fashion. What Weintraub lacks in analysis, he repays in fidelity to that mystical procession and admixture of the enormously variegated gifts, circumstances, and challenges that make a human being. It is perhaps the highest praise to say that many of the faults that exist in this biography are suggested by the standards of a historical discipline. Life is never as neat as it ought to be.

John Powell

Sources for Further Study

Booklist. XC, September 15, 1993, p. 125.
The Christian Science Monitor. October 4, 1993, p. 13.
Library Journal. CXVIII, September 1, 1993, p. 194.
The New York Times Book Review. XCVIII, October 17, 1993, p. 14.
Publishers Weekly. CCXL, August 9, 1993, p. 428.
San Francisco Chronicle. December 5, 1993, p. REV5.
The Spectator. CCLXXI, November 13, 1993, p. 33.
The Times Literary Supplement. November 26, 1993, p. 3.
The Wall Street Journal. September 30, 1993, p. A16.
The Washington Post Book World. XXIII, November 21, 1993, p. 6.

THE DOOR IN THE WALL

Author: Charles Tomlinson (1927-   )
Publisher: Oxford University Press (New York). 62 pp. Paperback $10.95
Type of work: Poetry

Fifty new poems from an English poet whose skill in the observation of nature, brilliance of imagination, and metrical authority promise him a place that may rival the assumed ascendancy of Philip Larkin and Ted Hughes in later twentieth century English poetry

Charles Tomlinson's poetry, including *Collected Poems* (rev. ed., 1987), *The Return* (1987), and *Annunciations* (1989), reveals his powers of natural observation, the transforming magic of his imagination, and the aesthetic shine of his sound. A painter and film writer in his youth, Tomlinson brings to his poetry a richness of visual and aural awareness that remains true to the "mutability" and "interdependency" of the human experience of nature without relinquishing the poet's natural right to assert the shaping powers of his voice, imagery, and metaphoric wit.

Harold Bloom, Wallace Stevens' best interpreter, writes that for Stevens, like William Wordsworth, nature "was enough." What Bloom means is that Stevens found sufficient stimulation and verification of his own philosophical flights in nature; it was unnecessary for him to go anywhere else. Tomlinson admits to a heavy influence by the great modern American poets, particularly Ezra Pound and Wallace Stevens. Like Stevens, Tomlinson luxuriates in nature, and like Stevens he can transform the landscapes of nature into landscapes of the mind.

> only a little snow
> has chalked in everywhere,
> as if a whole landscape might be unrolled
> out of the atmosphere.

What becomes clear in *The Door in the Wall* is that Tomlinson is settling into a deeply felt but increasingly ordinary sense of the poet's craft. To be sure, this is the ordinary in a sublime mode; nevertheless, again and again the reader is introduced to a conception of the making of poetry that is at home in the world as it is, that trusts the natural and the ordinary to inspire the mind and heart, to underwrite its capacities for joy and pain.

The opening poem, "The Operation," is a detailed pastoral describing the aesthetic intuition of a tree trimmer as he lops and saws his way through the trees, "giving thought to the size and shape/ Of what he must do"; "Painting not pruning: he is as much/ Making a tree as taking a tree apart." The tree trimmer is Tomlinson's alter ego, the poet observing the vicissitudes of nature and through his imagination and craft giving nature form and identity. While celebrating the power of the tree-trimmer-poet, Tomlinson avoids hubris and is careful to maintain the autonomy of nature. Nature has the last "word" (in this case, an engraver's mark) so that he can continue to spin his own in future poems. The detritus of the tree trimmer's work, all those cut branches, must be piled up and burned. The haze of the fire alters "as it flows into the twilight,/ The million burin strokes of branches/ To soft charcoal lines, the incense/ Leaving the senses open to the night."

Should the senses close to the night, the imagination would cease to function—and function it must, as continually and prosaically as perception itself. Human beings cannot trust teleological or apocalyptic thinking to supply ideas or loyalties that justify life. Musing on the politics of their youth, Tomlinson reminds his lifelong friend the Mexican poet Octavio Paz, "What matters in the end (it never comes)/ Is what is seen along the way." Like the New Zealand sheep shearers, cousins to the tree trimmer, who travel around the world with their "wild" women to shear sheep in Gloucestershire, Tomlinson travels in these poems from Germany to the Caribbean, from the Susquehanna to the coast of Ireland. "Shearsmen and poets travel far these days."

To build support for his notion that the poet's imagination is central to the needs of ordinary perception, Tomlinson pursues an interesting strategy of intertextual statement. By implication, echo, and sometimes explicit reference, he questions the Romantic fascination with the mysterious and unconscious in order to rediscover the ordinary at the heart of Romantic naturalism. Perhaps the key poem here is "The House on the Susquehanna." A cat listens to the grass along the riverbank. The river itself "flows with no more show of movement/ Than the swamps that feed it—yet/ Can take possession of house and town/ In one rising sweep." This poem is in ironic dialogue with one of the most sensational poems in all of English Romanticism: Samuel Taylor Coleridge's "Kubla Khan: Or, A Vision In a Dream." Tomlinson writes:

> You can tell
> The current by the slight swell at the tips
> Of the reflected trees—it scarcely ruffles
> Their riding image. The gleam on the surface
> Might almost rekindle that dream
> Of pantisocracy in this spacious place
> The dreamers never saw.

He adds a footnote (the only one in this collection) to make sure that readers understand the obscure allusion to Coleridge: "Pantisocracy: this utopian community on the Susquehanna, where all should rule equally, was the dream of Coleridge and Southey." This was Coleridge's political dream, somewhat analogous to the dream of "Paris in Sixty-nine" which Tomlinson shared with Paz but which ultimately deferred to the more personal dreams of their lives and work: "Do you, too, *work* when walking?"

In Coleridge's case the dream of social deliverance gave way to the chimerical and fantastic pursuit of abstruse ideas and subconscious mysteries, both of which are powerfully but, in a sense, self-destructively displayed in "Kubla Khan":

> A savage place! as holy and enchanted
> As e'er beneath a waning moon was haunted
> By woman wailing for her demon lover!

In Tomlinson's poem the "woman wailing for her demon lover" has become the "cat . . . treading/ From tie to tie of the railroad track"; at poem's end, the cat "has its mouse." Coleridge's "forced" and "flung" river has become that "silent immensity of still water/ That flows with no more show of movement/ Than the swamps that feed it." Coleridge's eerie shadow floating "midway on the waves" is now the "riding image" of reflected treetops. This is the only utopia humankind can experience: nature's gradual passing. The floods of tragedy—"one rising sweep"—are inevitable and cannot be oversimplified to "ancestral voices prophesying war." Finally, Kubla's palace is not "five miles of fertile ground/ With walls and towers . . . girdled round" but a simple house "on the shore . . . foursquare and of brick." Coleridge has his prophet-poet build "that dome in air." Tomlinson is committed to building his poems on the ground. In "Hacienda" he celebrates the channeling of a river into three streams: one to drive a turbine, the next a grist mill, and the last to fill the planter's "open-air Jacuzzi." All three streams eventually rejoin the natural river in the valley floor. No "caverns measureless to man" here—and, even more to the point, no severe distinction between worldly and poetic power. A pacific Kubla Khan and a demystified poet are joined in the practical planter and river of "Hacienda."

The tragic reminder of "the rising sweep"—nature is no beneficent Witch of the North—is reflected throughout these poems. Observing the social tensions in a New York restaurant, where recent immigrants from all over the world constitute "a sweating ballet of waiters and waitresses," Tomlinson sees that in their affectation and acting these insecure young people are coping creatively with their condition ("At Hanratty's"). Their floundering is sweaty, but a thing of grace (ballet); they are "working" while "walking"; their "end" is unclear, but they are "seeing along the way." The subtext is Walt Whitman. Tomlinson has grown American roots. "Ode to San Francisco" is a dark poem about acquired immune deficiency syndrome (AIDS): "The city/ has an air of medieval fatality," while those who are dying come up with euphemistic explanations: "a caring relationship . . . a tropical infection." This human frailty and deception is primarily the result of the union between Venus and Eros ("Hesiod/ calls him the son of Chaos"), a marriage defined by nature but certainly not made in heaven.

Poets cannot be expected to defer to nature's sense of itself; indeed, they are empowered by imagination to go beyond nature's performance when that performance is wanting. In "On a Dutch Picture" (Tomlinson commiserates with the realist painter who could not remain content with the flat skies of his flat land and "preferred/ To fill his upper air with shapes/ Wholly imaginary, that scale the canvas space/ Like his tentative painter's mind." This would seem an embrace, after all, of Coleridge's poet as a builder of domes in air. Not quite. The painter remains rooted in landscape; his imagination is directed toward trimming the tree, shearing the sheep, bringing out what is under the surface in nature as a whole and not only in his own mind. The poet who fails to take nature along when he puts his imagination to work runs the risk of confusing mind with end, life with death, and the serene *and* tumultuous rivers of experience with dammed-up reservoirs of closed-off memory.

Tomlinson muses of Thomas Hardy ("On a Passage from Hardy's *Life*):

> You were a poet who put on the manners of ghosts,
> Thinking of life not as passing away but past . . .
> One Stygian current buoying up gravestone on gravestone.

Hardy's mistake was to drown in abstractions of fate and cosmic indifference. His was another version of Coleridge's error.

Tomlinson has learned from John Keats the wisdom of "negative capability," the capacity to refrain from seeking absolutes and rational explanations to deal with all life's questions. There are simply too many questions, too many things to notice.

> But let be the garden, too,
> as you tread and travel
> this broken pathway
> where the sun does not dazzle
> but claims company with
> all these half-hidden things
> and raising their gaze
>
> does not ask of them wings.

Peter Brier

Sources for Further Study

Poetry Review. LXXXII, Winter, 1993, p. 63.
Stand Magazine. XXXIV, Spring, 1993, p. 69.
The Times Literary Supplement. December 18, 1992, p. 19.
World Literature Today. LXVII, Autumn, 1993, p. 829.

THE DOWNING STREET YEARS

Author: Margaret Thatcher (1925-   )
Publisher: HarperCollins (New York). Illustrated. 914 pp. $30.00
Type of work: Memoir
Time: 1979-1990
Locale: London

A political memoir of Margaret Thatcher's years as prime minister of Great Britain

> *Principal personages:*
> MARGARET THATCHER, the prime minister of Great Britain, 1979-1990
> GEOFFREY HOWE, the British foreign secretary, 1983-1989
> NIGEL LAWSON, the chancellor of the Exchequer, 1983-1989
> FRANÇOIS MITTERRAND, the president of France, 1981-
> RONALD REAGAN, the fortieth president of the United States, 1981-1989
> GEORGE BUSH, the forty-first president of the United States, 1989-1993

Margaret Thatcher was prime minister of Great Britain for eleven years, serving in that position longer than any previous prime minster since the early nineteenth century. In November 1990, however, her own party forced her out of office, even though she had not been rejected by the voters and, indeed, had never lost a general election. *The Downing Street Years* is her memoir of this period and provides her view of why her tenure as prime minister came to such a sudden and unexpected end.

Thatcher suggests that when she became prime minister she found it difficult to assert her authority over other prominent Conservatives because she was an outsider in two important respects: She was a female and from a lower social class than most Conservative Party leaders. The clash within the cabinet over the 1981 budget provided an early test of her ability to overcome these handicaps. Thatcher portrays the cabinet members who opposed her over the budget as men who could not accept working for a woman, men who could interact with women only if the latter played the role of the "weaker sex" and accepted male advice. By her account, some of her cabinet opponents assumed that she should defer to their opinions because they were from a higher social class than she. When she eventually dropped Christopher Soames from the cabinet for resisting her views, she claims, he reacted as if he had been dismissed by his housemaid.

The crisis over the 1981 budget was one of the first great turning points in Thatcher's tenure as prime minister. Great Britain was in a recession at the time, with high unemployment, which led many cabinet members to advocate a policy of increased government spending. Thatcher had taken office convinced of the desirability of substantially reducing government spending, however, and she urged this policy despite the depressed economy. She states that she felt so strongly about this issue that she was determined to resign if the cabinet did not accept her position. There was an angry confrontation when the cabinet discussed the budget, and the majority of the cabinet opposed her. She did not forget or forgive those whose views conflicted with hers, and after her budget proposals were approved, she removed most of these persons from the cabinet.

There seems little doubt that the war with Argentina over the Falkland Islands (Islas Malvinas) was another great turning point in Thatcher's tenure. In 1982, when Argentina seized the islands, the Conservative Government was unpopular, and public-opinion polls indicated that it was unlikely to be reelected. Great Britain's victory in that war has been credited with restoring the government's popularity and enabling it to win the 1983 general election. Some critics have suggested that the war was unnecessary and occurred because the British government had not made it clear to the Argentines that it would fight to defend the Falklands. Thatcher, however, rejects this view, claiming that the British had no inkling of Argentina's intention to invade the islands.

Once the invasion took place, Thatcher seemed to be imitating Winston Churchill's 1940 stance against Nazi Germany. Her minister of defense, John Nott, informed her privately that Great Britain was not militarily capable of removing the Argentinians from the Falklands by force. Despite Thatcher's opposition, Foreign Secretary Francis Pym urged the War cabinet to accept an American proposal for a negotiated settlement that would not have restored the islands to Great Britain. Conflict over the issue was avoided when the cabinet agreed to put the U.S. peace proposals to the Argentine government under the assumption—which proved accurate—that they would be rejected. If they had not, it would have placed Thatcher in a dangerous position, for Pym, backed by other cabinet members, would have resigned if his proposal had been rejected, whereas Thatcher states that she would have resigned rather than accept it.

Thatcher's style of governing resulted in an unusually high turnover among cabinet ministers. Her conviction that politics was a matter of principle not only made it difficult for her to see any merits in the views of political opponents from other parties but also encouraged the perception that fellow Conservatives who disagreed with her were enemies. This intolerance led to the dismissal of powerful Conservatives, such as Geoffrey Howe and Nigel Lawson, who eventually contributed to her downfall. Thatcher's uncompromising style of governing contributed to her reputation as the "Iron Lady," but it tended to conceal the reality that on several occasions she did make significant political compromises.

Thatcher believed that the reestablishment of a "special relationship" with the United States was a cornerstone of her foreign policy, and while Ronald Reagan was president of the United States she had considerable success. Although she did not think Reagan very intelligent, his views on most issues coincided with hers, and she drew maximum advantage from this. There are hints that she used her femininity to encourage Reagan to move in the direction she wished him to go. She refers to herself, for example, as Reagan's "principal cheerleader" within the North Atlantic Treaty Organization (NATO). Thatcher states that the only issue on which she and Reagan continued to disagree was that of the high and rising U.S government deficit.

Thatcher acknowledges that Great Britain's "special relationship" with the United States ceased after George Bush was elected president. Her description of Bush draws attention to his limitations. She claims that it was apparent that he had never had to think through his views on issues before he became president, and she implies that she regarded him as her intellectual inferior. She indicates that Bush seemed uncomfortable with intelligent women who dominated a conversation. In order to improve relations with him, she found it necessary to defer to him in conversation and to praise him constantly. Although she concedes that following Iraq's invasion of Kuwait Bush displayed a sense of confidence, she notes that this was in sharp contrast to his previous hesitation and indecisiveness.

Thatcher's opposition to closer links with the European Community brought her into conflict with powerful members of the Conservative Party, including Nigel Lawson, her chancellor of the exchequer, and eventually led to his resignation. In one of the more curious episodes during her final years, Thatcher claims that beginning in March, 1987, Lawson secretly followed an economic policy of which she was unaware and to which she would have been opposed if informed. Lawson's policy of "shadowing" the deutschmark—that is, maintaining the pound at a fixed relationship to the deutschmark—was intended to demonstrate that Britain could safely participate in the European rate mechanism of the European Monetary Union (EMU) without harm to the pound and thus to undermine Thatcher's opposition to British EMU membership. Thatcher states that at one point Lawson and the foreign secretary, Geoffrey Howe, threatened to resign unless she agreed to British participation in the European rate mechanism, but she refused to give in to what she considered blackmail. Thatcher's unwillingness to move toward closer links with the European Community eventually resulted in the resignations of both Lawson and Howe and contributed to the pressure from Conservative members of Parliament for her removal from office.

Thatcher's ill-feeling toward John Major, who succeeded her as prime minister, emerges very clearly in her portrayal of him as ambitious but inept and disloyal. She states that when Lawson resigned as chancellor of the exchequer, she appointed Major to replace him because she was already thinking of the latter as someone she might wish to succeed her, and she wanted to give him the experience he would need to do so. She claims that his performance as chancellor was disappointing, however, because he was more concerned with maintaining party unity on British participation in the European exchange-rate mechanism than with following correct economic principles, as Thatcher suggests she would have done. She claims to have been deeply disturbed by Major's support for full British participation in the EMU. She attributes Major's behavior to a willingness to flow with the tide and says that he lacked any sense of direction. Here, as in other character assessments, Thatcher uses her memoirs as a means of gaining revenge against persons whom she thinks betrayed her.

The manner in which Thatcher ceased to be prime minister is bizarre, for it is highly unusual for a prime minister to be removed from office by her own party without first being rejected by the electorate. Thatcher's memoirs display no awareness that it was her policies on the poll tax and the European Community that stimulated a revolt within her own party against her. Instead, her downfall is attributed to the failings of others: the treachery and ineptitude of those whom she had considered her allies. This tendency to view herself as blameless when things went wrong but deserving of credit when successes occurred is echoed elsewhere in the volume.

Thatcher's account of her final days as prime minister is related as a moving story of intrigue and betrayal, an approach that is entirely consistent with her view throughout the volume. She suggests that the Conservative Party establishment wanted her removed from office and that cabinet ministers conspired to persuade her to withdraw from the party leadership contest. Even Major, who owed his promotion to high political office to her, is described as betraying her at the final moment when she asked him for support. When the members of her cabinet, with few exceptions, informed her privately that she could not win and stressed that if she persisted it would result in victory for Michael Heseltine, Thatcher agreed to resign.

The Downing Street Years is an important account of Thatcher's tenure as prime minister but is decidedly her view of events. The validity of her version has already been challenged by others who had firsthand knowledge. Furthermore, the book is almost entirely the record of her public life; readers who wish to know more about Thatcher's private life and her thoughts on matters other than public issues will be disappointed. Although some sections of the book—especially the chapters on the Falklands War—are vividly written, long sections of it consist of dry summaries of government documents. While *The Downing Street Years* will be an important source for historians seeking to reconstruct what happened during a crucial period of British history, it should not be mistaken for an objective record of those years.

Harold L. Smith

Sources for Further Study

Chicago Tribune. November 7, 1993, XIV, p. 5.
The Christian Science Monitor. December 15, 1993, p. 17.
Commentary. XCVII, January, 1994, p. 56.
Foreign Affairs. LXXIII, Winter, 1994, p. 155.
The New Republic. CCIX, December 20, 1993, p. 37.
New Statesman and Society. VI, November 5, 1993, p. 39.
The New York Review of Books. XL, December 2, 1993, p. 7.
The New York Times Book Review. XCVIII, November 14, 1993, p. 1.
Newsweek. CXXII, November 1, 1993, p. 41.
The Observer. October 24, 1993, p. 17.
The Spectator. CCLXXI, November 6, 1993, p. 46.
The Times Literary Supplement. October 29, 1993, p. 28.
The Wall Street Journal. October 29, 1993, p. A12.
The Washington Post Book World. XXIII, October 31, 1993, p. 1.

DREAM MAKERS, DREAM BREAKERS
The World of Justice Thurgood Marshall

Author: Carl T. Rowan (1925-   )
Publisher: Little, Brown (Boston). Illustrated. 475 pp. $24.95
Type of work: Biography
Time: 1908-1991
Locale: The United States

This biography of the first African American Supreme Court justice explores the life and times of the man who became known as "Mr. Civil Rights"

Principal personages:
THURGOOD MARSHALL, a U.S. Supreme Court Justice, 1967-1991
J. EDGAR HOOVER, the Director of the Federal Bureau of Investigation from 1924 to 1972
CHARLES H. HOUSTON, the Dean of Howard Law School when Marshall attended; Marshall's mentor and champion
LYNDON B. JOHNSON, the thirty-sixth President of the United States, 1963-1969
RICHARD M. NIXON, the thirty-seventh President of the United States, 1969-1974
ELEANOR ROOSEVELT, a former First Lady who advocated human and civil rights
GEORGE WALLACE, the Governor of Alabama from 1963 to 1966 and again from 1971 to 1979
EARL WARREN, the fourteenth Chief Justice of the Supreme Court, 1953-1969

Thurgood Marshall, who was born to a primary school teacher and a club steward in Baltimore, Maryland, in 1908, and who died in 1993, arguably had the most formidable credentials in civil rights activism of any American who has ever lived. The Reverend Martin Luther King, Jr., with whose campaign of nonviolent resistance Marshall did not always agree, is certainly the only individual who could challenge Marshall's reputation in that arena. Marshall's attitude toward other black leaders of his time varied from reverence for his mentor Charles H. Houston to contempt for such militants as Stokely Carmichael. About King he was more ambiguous, at once admiring and resentful, even jealous. About the 1955 Montgomery bus boycott King helped organize, Marshall snorted, "All that walking for nothing. They might as well have waited for the Court decision."

Marshall unquestionably believed that the best, most direct path to equality for American blacks started at the courthouse door. His unshakable belief in the power of the judicial system to change the lives of the nation's underprivileged was rooted in his own experience. When he was a young lawyer, nothing preoccupied Marshall more than the rejection he had suffered from the University of Maryland Law School, which had refused to admit him in 1930 simply because of his race. His strategy for avenging himself, a successful lawsuit in 1935 mandating that the law school admit qualified black applicants, set the tone not only for his most celebrated victory, *Brown v. Board of Education* (1954), but for his entire career.

The University of Maryland litigation occurred early in Marshall's tenure as an attorney at the National Association for the Advancement of Colored People (NAACP). Marshall began his career with the NAACP after he was graduated first in his class at Howard University Law School in 1933. His victory in the case against the University of Maryland was followed by a number of similar lawsuits challenging the doctrine of "separate but equal" in the educational arena, among them such landmark cases as *Gaines v. Canada* (1938).

Gaines v. Canada was only one of thirty-two cases—twenty-nine of them victories—that Marshall argued before the United States Supreme Court during his NAACP years. In 1940 he became head of the newly formed NAACP Legal Defense and Education Fund, a position he held for more than twenty years. During this time, Marshall's legal activity was prodigious, as he took on such diverse issues as the admissibility of murder confessions, equal pay for black schoolteachers, the rights of blacks to vote in primary elections, and courts-martial of black soldiers during the Korean War. Such activity required him to work long hours and to travel the country, and the world, on a shoestring budget—often at great personal risk. Carl Rowan documents not only Marshall's frequent illnesses but also his brush with death when he was almost lynched in Columbia, Tennessee, in 1946 after defending two accused murderers there.

The high point of Marshall's career as a litigator, however, doubtless was *Brown v. Board of Education*, when Marshall and the NAACP took on the issue of school integration, challenging not only the "separate but equal" doctrine the Supreme Court had sanctioned in *Plessy v. Ferguson* in 1896 but also what was euphemistically called "the Southern way of life." Although he would later express great frustration at the slow pace of change set by the high court in *Brown II* in 1955, Marshall's reaction on hearing the Court's initial decision was entirely accurate: "We hit the jackpot." The ramifications of the decision would affect every American.

The history of the case itself is long and tortured, beginning in 1950, when Oliver Brown's seven-year-old daughter was not permitted to enroll in the local elementary school, and not concluding until five years later, when the Court delivered its ruling on the mechanics of school desegregation. *Brown I* was argued twice, apparently because the Court was deadlocked. The hiatus between oral arguments, however, saw the death of Chief Justice Fred M. Vinson and his replacement by Earl Warren, who was able to secure a unanimous decision. No outsider is privy to internal debates among the justices, but Rowan provides one clue as to how Warren was able to realign the Court. Early in 1954, President Dwight Eisenhower invited the chief justice to the White House for dinner, during which the president performed some overt lobbying on behalf of "separate but equal." Disparaging this breach of ethics and violation of the separation of powers, Rowan speculates that Warren was deeply offended by Eisenhower's gaffe and used it to convince his colleagues of the necessity for social change.

It was Marshall's fate that he would serve a significant role in integrating not only the educational system but also the American judicial system. President John F. Kennedy wanted to be the first president to put a black person on the Supreme Court. After rejecting Judge William Hastie, the first black named to any federal judgeship, Kennedy settled on Marshall. He knew, however, that appointing Marshall would be extremely controversial, so he decided as an opening gambit to nominate Marshall in 1961 to the U.S. Court of Appeal for the Second Circuit. That appointment, too, was controversial, but despite a prolonged rejection campaign mounted in the Senate by Strom Thurmond of South Carolina, in 1962 Marshall became only the second black person ever to serve on any federal appellate court.

Marshall sat on the Second Circuit bench less than three years when President Lyndon B. Johnson announced that Marshall would be the government's new solicitor general. Thanks to Johnson's political skills, this time the confirmation was not an ordeal, and the earthy Marshall wryly, but gladly, put on the uniform of striped pants and swallowtail coat to act as the government's chief advocate before the Supreme Court. Marshall's record as solicitor general—winning fourteen of nineteen cases— was only slightly shy of what it had been when he appeared before the Court for the NAACP. He did not always agree with the positions he had to argue for government, but often he did. When Marshall assumed the office of solicitor general, the nation was already beginning to see the fruits of his previous labors, and he was able to advance the government's—and his own—agenda by winning Supreme Court ap- proval for such advances as the 1965 Voting Rights Act.

When President Johnson nominated Marshall to be the Supreme Court's first black justice in 1967, Marshall joined a Court still dominated by liberal, activist members, including Hugo L. Black, William O. Douglas, William J. Brennan, Abe Fortas, and Chief Justice Warren (more conservative members included John Marshall Harlan, Potter Stewart, and Byron R. White). By the next year, however, all had changed: Warren tendered his resignation, Johnson withdrew his nomination of Fortas as Warren's replacement, and Johnson himself withdrew from the presidential race. In 1969 a conservative Republican president, Richard Nixon, was sworn into office after campaigning against the Warren Court's "coddling" of criminals. Later that year, Nixon nominated Warren E. Burger as chief justice.

Although the Court would soon take a sharp turn toward the right, its activist days were not yet over, and Marshall still had a considerable role to play as civil libertarian. Rowan details, for example, Marshall's crucial contribution to *Roe v. Wade* (1973), insisting that a woman's right to abortion be protected into the second trimester, when the fetus becomes viable. Marshall was also influential in persuading the Court effectively to abrogate—if only temporarily—all state capital-punishment statutes in the landmark case *Furman v. Georgia* (1972).

Increasingly, however, Marshall's voice was raised in dissent. By the 1980's, he said, he was in the majority on only one issue, "breaking for lunch." Despite recurrent and increasingly serious health problems, though, Marshall remained on the Court to speak out in support of the expansion of individual rights. The decision that finally broke his spirit, according to Rowan, was *Payne v. Tennessee*, decided June 27, 1991, in which the Court reversed its own recent precedents by declaring victim-impact statements during criminal trials to be constitutional. The same day, citing his age and ill health, Marshall tendered his resignation to President George Bush.

Carl Rowan, a journalist and syndicated columnist, knew Marshall for forty years, and his book reads more like a memoir than a biography. On the plus side, Rowan's approach to chronicling this legendary figure often gives the reader Marshall in his own words. On the minus side, Rowan devotes too much time to Marshall's "world"— especially Rowan's own place in it. Two whole chapters are devoted to Rowan's—not Marshall's—interactions with Eleanor Roosevelt and George Wallace, with little attempt to demonstrate how these associations impinge on Marshall's life. Moreover, although it is certainly proper that Rowan's focus should be on Marshall's legal career (in particular the years 1936 to 1961, when Marshall was most active as a civil rights lawyer and strategist), the book could have revealed more about other aspects of Marshall's life. For example, the prolonged illness and death of Buster, Marshall's wife of twenty-five years, in the midst of his involvement with the *Brown* cases is little explored (apparently because Rowan never met her). Marshall's marriage to his second wife, Cissy, receives little more attention, and Rowan says nothing about the two sons born to them.

Dream Makers, Dream Breakers: The World of Justice Thurgood Marshall is graced by the author's long association with his subject. This long association also leads, unfortunately, to an unequivocal endorsement of Marshall, perhaps most evident in Rowan's ready dismissal of rumors of Marshall's laziness and penchant for delegating most of his work to law clerks. It is doubtless Rowan's closeness to Marshall that leads him to attempt to rebut these rumors with a contrived exercise: comparing casual remarks Marshall made on various legal subjects over the years with his written opinions in order to demonstrate substantive similarities.

Despite its faults, however, *Dream Makers, Dream Breakers* presents readers with an indelible portrait of a complicated man whose intelligence, wit, compassion, and drive made him a legend worthy of the title "Mr. Civil Rights."

Lisa Paddock

Sources for Further Study

ABA Journal. LXXIX, March, 1993, p. 90.
America. CLXVIII, March 20, 1993, p. 15.
Choice. XXX, June, 1993, p. 1707.
The Christian Science Monitor. January 28, 1993, p. 14.
Human Rights. XX, Spring, 1993, p. 8.
Los Angeles Times Book Review. March 7, 1993, p. 4.
National Review. XLV, March 1, 1993, p. 56.
The New York Times Book Review. XCVIII, February 7, 1993, p. 14.
The Washington Post Book World. XXIII, January 24, 1993, p. 1.

EINSTEIN'S DREAMS

Author: Alan Lightman (1948-   )
Publisher: Pantheon Books (New York). Illustrated. 179 pp. $17.00
Type of work: Novel
Time: April 14 to June 28, 1905
Locale: Berne, Switzerland

In 1905, twenty-six-year-old patent clerk Albert Einstein ponders the various faces of time as he nears the publication of his Theory of Special Relativity

> *Principal personages:*
> ALBERT EINSTEIN, age twenty-six, a clerk in the patent office in Berne, Switzerland
> MICHELE ANGELO BESSO, his professional associate, friend, and confidant
> MILEVA MARIČ, his wife since 1903, who does not appear but is discussed

Albert Einstein was a patent clerk and young father in 1905, the time setting of *Einstein's Dreams*. He comes early to the patent office one morning toward the end of June because he has a manuscript to deliver to the secretary, who types for him in her off hours. His research on magnetism and electricity has made him realize that he must try to understand time in its many dimensions. He is moving rapidly toward articulating his important Theory of Special Relativity, whose formula, $E = mc^2$, is possibly the scientific formula now best known by laypersons throughout the world.

Alan Lightman's book—Lightman calls it a novel, although it takes a broad definition to fit the work into that genre—is a fanciful musing based on hard scientific data of which the author, a professor of physics and writing at the Massachusetts Institute of Technology, is in excellent command. Presented in diary form comprising thirty entries or intervals, *Einstein's Dreams* is printed in an appealing Lilliputian format, so that the volume is little larger than a pack of cigarettes. It begins with a prologue and ends with an epilogue.

Following entries 8, 16, and 24 are interludes in which Einstein talks with his lifelong friend and scientific associate, Michele Angelo Besso (1873-1955). Their conversations revolve around Einstein's work, health, and unhappy marriage to Mileva Marič, who at this point has borne Hans Albert, the first of their two children.

The heart of this splendidly lucid, highly imaginative book is the thirty intervals, in which Lightman presents various aspects of time to which Einstein was forced to give serious consideration as he worked toward unraveling the mystery of relativity, whose major dimensions are time and space. Breaking from an entrenched Newtonian physics that viewed space as three-dimensional and time as one-dimensional, Einstein viewed time-space as a coordinated, four-dimensional system.

To arrive at such an insight, Einstein passed through various speculative stages that Lightman explores in his crisply presented text, written with an ease and lucidity that make it accessible to general readers. The book, while scientifically factual, is surrealistic in the way that *Alice in Wonderland* (1865) and *Through the Looking Glass*

(1872) by Lewis Carroll (pseudonym of mathematician Charles Lutwidge Dodgson, 1832-1898) are. The May 14 entry in *Einstein's Dreams*, which deals with approaching and achieving the center of time, is particularly evocative of these two works by Carroll, who, like Lightman, had a strong scientific orientation. Upon arriving at the center of time, everyone and everything is frozen—presumably for eternity—in a given instant.

Early in the book, Lightman deals with mechanical time versus body time. He divides people into two general types according to which of these two times they naturally follow. The person who follows body time might say something like "I am tired, so I am going to sleep," while the person who follows mechanical time looks at the clock and says, "It is midnight, so I must go to bed." The first group of people live according to bodily needs, the second according to external mechanisms.

One is reminded on reading this entry of the Lilliputians' conclusion in Jonathan Swift's *Gulliver's Travels* (1726) when they emptied Gulliver's pockets. Finding his timepiece they presumed that this strange mechanism was a sort of god to whom Gulliver was beholden. Lightman ends this April 24 entry by saying that both bodily and mechanical times are true, but their truths are different from each other.

The next entry (April 26) deals with the hypothesis that time passes more slowly as one's distance from Earth's surface increases. In this whimsical entry, people live as close to the tops of mountains as they can. The very rich ascend the tallest peaks, on which they have their houses built on stilts that extend far up into the sky. Lightman, at his satirical acme, points out that the rich have become so conditioned to living at high altitudes that they have, through the years, forgotten their reasons for living at these heights. They live their elevated lives, prejudiced against those who dwell beneath them, forbidding their offspring to play—and, heaven forfend, to inter-marry—with anyone from the lower levels. They endure the cold, perversely reveling in its discomfort for the stoic satisfaction it imparts. Ironically, their lifestyle results in their becoming a scrawny, bony populace that grows old prematurely, thereby defeating the compelling reasons for which their ancestors originally ascended to and settled in the heights.

Lightman considers the moral dimensions of time, which impinges forever upon people in industrialized cultures. Clocks abound, and punctuality is considered virtu-ous. For some people, time, because of its absolute nature, offers convincing evidence of the existence of God: It takes a Creator (with a capital *C*) to design and produce anything as intricate and symmetrical as time, which is observably in perfect balance. Lightman realizes how comforting it is to know that in a world in which people may be erratic and unpredictable, time is dependably ordered and predictable. Devices to measure time—calendars, clocks, sundials—have always been a mark of humankind's passage from a primitive to a more developed state, as one can observe in the ancient Indian cultures of Latin America or in the early cultures of the Middle and Far East.

The May 15 entry is one of the most artistically satisfying passages in *Einstein's Dreams*. It considers what a world would be like devoid of time. It would consist of objects in space, but the objects would have little meaning outside the temporal context in which people have grown used to observing the objective world. Lightman presents catalogs of things one might expect to see in such a state. These lists match up to some of the best catalogs in Walt Whitman's *Leaves of Grass* (1855) and in John Dos Passos' *U.S.A.* trilogy (1930-1938). Still, Lightman himself cannot escape sufficiently from the temporal context in which he exists to write outside it. He tells of a child spellbound by its *first* glimpse of the ocean. He writes of a boat on the water at *night*. He mentions a leaf in *autumn*. He talks about the soft rain on a *spring day*. All these allusions involve time and its passage. They demonstrate—quite calculatedly, one must assume, in anything produced by as meticulous a writer as Lightman—that a world without time is inconceivable.

The June 17 entry deals with discontinuous time. Suddenly time stops and all activity within it is frozen, but for a barely perceptible second. When the lapse ends, everything returns to where it was, remaining there until the next such lapse. Yet within such a context, one is forced to dissect the smallest segments of time (as physicists like Einstein have had to do) in order to realize and understand the discontinuities. The changes that occur because of such discontinuities are so subtle as to be virtually nonexistent. In Lightman's example, however, two people who are contemplating a budding romance are affected by the discontinuity as a "gossamer vacancy" crosses the smile of one of the two.

If change is the major characteristic of discontinuous time, lack of change characterizes the kind of time Einstein dreams of in the April 14 entry. This entry examines the Nietzschean concept of eternal recurrence—a concept thought to have contributed in part to Friedrich Nietzsche's suicide in 1900: People live all the days of their lives only to die and be reborn to relive each day exactly as they lived it in the life that went before. Time seemingly goes on forever in such a context; like Sisyphus, all participants in life repeat and repeat and repeat their life's activities ad infinitum.

This antiprogressive, continuously recurrent view of life offers humankind the promise of rebirth and eternal life, but at a price so great as to make it seem less attractive than the complete, timeless void one encounters in nihilism. Humankind's inextricable linkage with time, however, places this void outside the ken of most humans. People cannot envision total vacancy, absolute nothingness, for by their very imagining they obliterate nothingness; it is a sense of "somethingness" that time contributes to space when one thinks in relativistic terms.

The three interludes in this book—each preceded by one of Chris Costello's black-and-white illustrations of a scene from Berne—supply the human dimension that perhaps permits the book legitimately to be called a novel even though it can be so identified only in a most unconventional sense. The conversations that make up these interludes are with Besso, for half a century Einstein's close friend and confidant. The two exchanged hundreds of letters, of which over two hundred survive.

In the first of the interludes, Einstein and Besso walk slowly down Berne's Speichergasse in the late afternoon. Einstein, who has already confided to Besso his need to understand time, now reveals why he is pursuing this elusive study: "I want to understand time because I want to get close to The Old One." Until his death,

Einstein continued to seek the elusive unified field theory that would explain creation to him.

Besso listens patiently and points out the difficulties. Then, in the manner of the skeptical deist he probably was, he suggests that The Old One, should such a being exist, might not wish to get close to Its creations in any case.

The second interlude occurs nearly four weeks later. Besso is concerned because Einstein, who has been losing sleep and forgetting to eat as he moves ahead with his study of time, does not look well. Besso's exceptional concern for Einstein's welfare is explained in part by Lightman's revealing a side of Einstein of which many people are unaware: When Einstein and Besso were students together, Besso's father, with whom Michele had never gotten along, died suddenly. Besso was overwhelmed with guilt and grief. Einstein took the young man into his lodgings for a month and nurtured him.

Besso also reveals in this interlude how Einstein, in reviewing patent applications, often altered them slightly to strengthen them technologically, seeking neither remuneration nor credit for his improvements. Such was Einstein's giving nature.

In this interlude also is revealed Einstein's discontent with his wife, Mileva (from whom he was finally divorced in 1919). He questions why he married her in the first place, saying that he at least expected that she would do the housework, but their house is a chaos of unmade beds, unwashed dishes, and unswept floors.

In the final brief interlude, Besso joins Einstein on a Sunday afternoon to fish on the river Aare. As usual, Einstein catches nothing, but, resorting to fable, Lightman makes clear that Einstein is nearing the culmination of his theory of time. Besso suggests that when he has worked it through to its conclusion, they come fishing again so that Einstein can explain it to his friend, who can then say that he was the first to hear it.

R. Baird Shuman

Sources for Further Study

The Economist. CCCXXVI, January 16, 1993, p. 90.
Los Angeles Times Book Review. January 10, 1993, p. 3.
Nature. CCCLXII, March 4, 1993, p. 28.
New Scientist. CXXXVII, March 20, 1993, p. 41.
The New York Times Book Review. XCVIII, January 3, 1993, p. 10.
The New Yorker. LXVIII, January 18, 1993, p. 111.
Publishers Weekly. CCXXXIX, October 19, 1992, p. 57.
Time. CXLI, January 18, 1993, p. 65.
The Times Literary Supplement. January 22, 1993, p. 19.
The Wall Street Journal. February 1, 1993, p. A8.
The Washington Post Book World. XXIII, February 7, 1993, p. 4.

THE ELEPHANT VANISHES

Author: Haruki Murakami (1949-   )
Translated from the Japanese by Alfred Birnbaum and Jay Rubin
Publisher: Alfred A. Knopf (New York). 328 pp. $21.00
Type of work: Short Stories

A collection of seventeen short stories which presents comic, witty, and surrealistic portrayals of Japanese urbanites who are in their twenties and thirties

Haruki Murakami is acclaimed as the "voice of a generation" in Japan. His first two novels to appear in English, *A Wild Sheep Chase* (1989) and *Hard-Boiled Wonderland and the End of the World* (1991), won high praise from American critics. *The Elephant Vanishes*, his first collection of short stories, again demonstrates that Murakami's is, indeed, one of the most exciting voices in international literature.

In *The Elephant Vanishes*, Murakami intermingles reality with fantasy, memory with illusion, and the physical world with metaphysical contemplation. His characters are ordinary people. They are homemakers, store clerks, paraprofessionals, business people, and college students. Many of these characters suffer from the modern syndrome of angst, ennui, emptiness, and loneliness. Their ontological relationship with reality appears to be defined by their ability to create unreality. For some of these characters, the ability "to be in two places at once" is what compensates for an otherwise boring, stressful, and monotonous life and what helps create meaning for an otherwise meaningless existence.

In "The Wind-Up Bird and Tuesday's Women," reality convolutes into fantasy. The narrator quit his longtime job in a law firm, partly because he did not find the job challenging enough and partly because the job did not allow him to be who he wanted to be. After being unemployed for three months, however, he becomes bored with the domestic duties he has to perform at home. A woman's harassing telephone call on a Tuesday ushers him into a world where the distinction between reality and fantasy is blurred. In his search for the family cat, he passes through an alley that looks like "some abandoned canal." At the end of the alley, he meets a high school girl whose smile is as seductive as the woman's voice on the telephone. When the narrator closes his eyes, he is thrown into an Orphean trance in which history and fantasy are made possible to converge with reality.

"The Little Green Monster" is another fantasy story. The narrator is a lonely housewife. After her husband leaves for work, she cannot think of anything to do but stare at and talk to an oak tree in the garden. One day, she sees a small green monster crawling out of the ground near the base of the tree. The monster is very cordial and friendly. In fact, he has come to the narrator to propose marriage. After discovering that the monster can read her mind, however, she uses her telepathic power to torture and eventually slay him.

"The Little Green Monster" portrays a very complex situation: Even though the narrator's relationship with her fantasy world is more intimate than her relationship with reality, accepting the monster's proposal would finalize her situation of loneliness and make it permanent. It is therefore not hard to understand why she fights the monster so resolutely and vehemently.

Some of Murakami's stories are "memory stories"; they study the paradoxical relationship between fiction and memory and between the past and the present. The narrator in "The Last Lawn of the Afternoon," for example, does not believe that there is a difference between memory and fiction:

> Memory is like fiction; or else it's fiction that's like memory. . . . Either way, no matter how hard you try to put everything neatly into shape, the context wanders this way and that, until finally the context isn't even there anymore. You're left with this pile of kittens lolling all over one another. Warm with life, hopelessly unstable.

Where the distinction between memory and fiction fades, imagination comes alive. "The Last Lawn of the Afternoon" starts as a story about the narrator's breaking up with his girlfriend but turns into a moving description of two lonely-hearts' search for understanding and companionship. After the narrator finishes mowing the lawn for a stranger, he is offered a drink by the host. A visit to a well-preserved room of the host's absent daughter reminds the narrator of his relationship with his former girlfriend. The visit makes him realize that a person can shape memory the same way he mows lawns, for both involve deliberate and highly subjective choices: "All I wanted, it came to me, was to mow a good lawn. To give it a once-over with the lawn mower, rake up the clippings, and then trim it nice and even with clippers—that's all. And that, I can do. Because that's the way I feel it ought to be done."

"Barn Burning" portrays a man's struggle with a piece of a memory that has left an indelible impact on his life. The narrator is married, but that did not stop him from falling in love with an advertising model. The model was also a pantomime student; she told him that the trick behind doing the pantomime of peeling an imaginary mandarin orange was "not a question of making yourself believe there *is* an orange there, you have to forget there *isn't* one." Through the model, the narrator met her new boyfriend, who announced that soon he was going to burn a barn in the narrator's neighborhood. Failing to grasp the significance of the person's talk about the possibility of simultaneity—being able to be at two places at the same time—the narrator became very excited about barn burning. He actually bought a map and studied which barns were most likely to be burned down in the area. In his imagination, the narrator envisioned himself striking the match several times. At the end of the story, although he finally realizes that no barns will be burned where he lives, he confesses: "Just now and then, in the depths of the night, I'll think about barns burning to the ground."

In several of Murakami's stories, his characters express a wish to be able to live in two worlds. The "barn burning specialist" in "Barn Burning," for example, believes in "simultaneity." He explains it thus to the narrator of the story:

> I'm here, and I'm there. I'm in Tokyo, and at the same time I'm in Tunis. I'm the one to blame, and I'm also the one to forgive. Just as a for instance. It's that level of balance. Without such balance, I don't think we could go on living. It's like the linchpin to everything. Lose it and we'd literally go to pieces.

The narrator in "The Kangaroo Communiqué" also yearns "to be able to be in two places at once." He is a bored store clerk; his job is to check the merchandise to prevent collusion between the purchasing section and the suppliers and to respond to customer complaints. A visit to the local zoo inspires him to write a letter to a female customer who complained about a record she bought from his store. His reply deteriorates, however, into an interior monologue that reveals both his confessional impulse and his ability to fantasize. He admits that his work is boring and he is not happy with being who he is. In the theory of the Nobility of Imperfection, however, he finds both an answer to the customer's complaint and an excuse to console himself. The theory gives the narrator the illusion of having choice. "To be able to be in two places at once" thus remains a dream that can be fulfilled only by his fantasy.

Murakami's use of surrealism in *The Elephant Vanishes* is especially effective, bridging the parallel worlds of the visible and the invisible, the permanent and the impermanent, reality and fantasy. It enables the writer to make comprehensible what otherwise appears incongruous and thus turn the ordinary into the extraordinary. Both "Sleep" and "TV People" epitomize how effective surrealism works with Murakami's thematic concerns. "Sleep" follows a long line of literary tradition that challenges the conventional distinctions between night and day, life and death, reality and fantasy. The narrator was an avid reader of literature in both high school and college. After she was graduated from college, however, her family could not afford to send her to graduate school. In her search for financial security, she ended up marrying a dentist whose pet phrase was "It's not my fault I'm so good-looking." Everything looks normal in the family until the narrator discovers one day that she has lost the ability to sleep. To kill time, she starts reading Lev Tolstoy's *Anna Karenina* (1875-1877). Instead of making sleep come more easily, however, reading turns things upside-down: It turns the narrator's day into night and night into day, and it turns her husband and son into "strangers."

Yet reading also renews the narrator's old passion for books, revitalizes her, expands her, and gives her a new perspective on reality and life: "After I gave up sleeping, it occurred to me what a simple thing reality is, how easy it is to make it work. It's just reality. Just housework. Just a home. Like running a simple machine. Once you learn to run it, it's just a matter of repetition."

At the end of "Sleep," however, exhaustion has taken its toll. Under the influence of alcohol, Russian novels, and lack of sleep, the narrator starts to hallucinate. Her belief in her ability to work both day and night without sleep proves to be an illusion, and her relationship with her fantasy world becomes as mentally and physically detrimental to her as her relationship with reality.

In "TV People," Murakami again uses surrealism to portray a person's confusion about illusion and reality. The narrator works in the advertising department of an electrical-appliance manufacturer. He enjoys reading and does not own a television or a videocassette recorder. Yet he can feel the omnipresence and omnipotence of television. Under the pressure of work and his strained relationship with his wife, he starts to hallucinate about the invasion of TV People, a group of people whose surrealistic existence is more existentially meaningful to him than reality is.

Several American reviewers and critics, including Bruce Sterling and Jay McInerney, have pointed out that the appeal of *The Elephant Vanishes* to American readers lies in its recognizable landscape and in the universal significance of its thematic preoccupations. While *The Elephant Vanishes* indeed "captures the common ache of the contemporary heart and head," as McInerney puts it, it also introduces American readers to conflicts and struggles that are indigenous to Japanese culture specifically and to Asian cultures in general. The conflict between a character's aspiration for self-fulfillment and his or her sense of social and familial responsibility, for example, results from the enforcement of communitarian standards that require individuals to forfeit their claim to personal freedom in exchange for harmony. Murakami's stories, therefore, revolve as much around the dialectical relationship between reality and fantasy as around issues such as the freedom of choice and having control of one's life.

Qun Wang

Sources for Further Study

Booklist. LXXXIX, February 1, 1993, p. 955.
Boston Globe. March 28, 1993, p. 39.
Chicago Tribune. March 28, 1993, XIV, p. 6.
Library Journal. CXVIII, March 1, 1993, p. 111.
Los Angeles Times Book Review. April 4, 1993, p. 3.
The New York Times Book Review. XCVIII, March 28, 1993, p. 10.
Publishers Weekly. CXL, February 1, 1993, p. 74.
The Virginia Quarterly Review. LXIX, Autumn, 1993, p. SS130.
The Wall Street Journal. May 5, 1993, p. A20.
The Washington Post. May 28, 1993, p. G5.

ELIZABETH BISHOP
Life and the Memory of It

Author: Brett C. Millier (1958-   )
Publisher: University of California Press (Berkeley). 602 pp. $28.00
Type of work: Biography
Time: 1911-1979
Locale: Nova Scotia, Massachusetts, Key West, Brazil, and New York City

A carefully researched and sensitive biography of a major poet

> *Principal personages:*
> ELIZABETH BISHOP, an American poet
> MARGARET MILLER, her college roommate and traveling companion
> LOUISE CRANE, her friend and traveling companion
> MARIANNE MOORE, her mentor
> MARJORIE STEVENS, one of her lovers
> ROBERT LOWELL, her fellow poet and lifelong friend
> LOTA SOARES, her long-term lover and companion in Brazil
> SUZANNE BOWEN, her student at the University of Washington, later her
>   lover
> ALICE METHFESSEL, her friend at Harvard University

Readers unfamiliar with Elizabeth Bishop's poetry may find the first chapter of this biography slow going. Since Brett Millier is writing a literary biography and believes that discussion of a writer's work is integral to understanding the life, she almost immediately begins by analyzing the autobiographical content of Bishop's stories and poems. This works well for readers already familiar with Bishop's *oeuvre*, but to the uninitiated it may prove frustrating that the analysis precedes the narrative. If the reverse were the case and the autobiographical content of the stories were rendered in the biographer's narrative voice, the biography would stand a chance of winning many new readers for Bishop. Then the biographer would be free to introduce significant analysis of Bishop's writing, showing how a master stylist developed the autobiographical elements already told, in story fashion, by the biographer.

Millier began her work on Bishop in graduate school, and occasionally her biography shows signs of a thesis mentality—not in the sense of emphasizing a single approach to the poet but in assuming, once again, more knowledge of the poet than can be expected from a general audience. Most readers may have read a few anthologized poems by Bishop but are unlikely to appreciate the way Millier links one title to another in her text before (in some cases) providing a narrative foundation for such linkage.

Once these criticisms of biographical technique are put aside—and they can be jettisoned after the early chapters—Millier emerges with a clear, sensitive, and compelling narrative presentation of her subject's life. One of the pleasures of reading the biography is to observe the biographer growing in confidence: As she gets to know her subject better, she begins to provide a deeper sense of Bishop as a person and earns the reader's confidence by carefully evaluating the evidence. Millier is never quick to judge Bishop, but she is not chary of making judgments when they are needed to advance her interpretation of Bishop's life and work.

The overwhelming impression conveyed by the biography is of a very lonely person and a gifted writer who took extraordinary pains over her prose and verse, often spending twenty years to finish a piece and refusing to release any work of which she was not absolutely certain. Bishop's courage and tenacity are awe-inspiring. She would experience dry spells. It was not unusual for her to go two years without completing a single poem, and it was not remarkable for her to put a poem through as many as fifteen drafts. She wanted to write more quickly and produce a great volume of verse, but her way of cultivating the imagination simply took years and years of labor, and she could not force herself to be prolific, though she often vowed to do so.

Bishop often reacted to her loneliness as if it were a curse, but it seems, in retrospect, to have been necessary to the kind of poet she became. Sometimes she chose loneliness over the hectic demands of full-time work and of urban existence, but her childhood experience suggests that a feeling of isolation was thrust upon her and could not be shaken off, no matter how much she tried to change her lifestyle in later years.

Bishop's earliest years were spent in Great Village, Nova Scotia, though she was born in Massachusetts. Her father died eight months after she was born, and her mother had a mental breakdown from which she never recovered. Bishop spent her childhood with uncomprehending relatives, first in Nova Scotia and then in Massachusetts. Though she eventually found family members who tolerated her precociousness, she was never at ease in any home and, except for fifteen years in Brazil, never really settled down anywhere. Her travels were extensive: all over the United States, Spain, France, Mallorca, England, Morocco, Mexico, Haiti, Brazil, Italy, Greece, Finland, and the Soviet Union.

At Vassar College, Bishop certainly made close friends and began to find outlets for her literary talent. Still, several things about her made her stand apart from her generation. This was the 1930's, a time when poets such as W. H. Auden were writing political poetry and inspiring a generation of writers to believe that art had to be concerned with social change. Bishop had virtually no interest in politics. Her favorite poet was Wallace Stevens, and she found his allegories about the nature of existence just the kind of philosophical and metaphorical poetry she wanted to write. Her poems were rooted in reality, but the idea of making political points—of assigning oneself, so to speak, to the right or to the left—appalled her when it did not bore her.

There was also the fact that Bishop was a lesbian in an age when an open avowal of anything but a conventional heterosexual orientation would have been difficult for a struggling poet who wanted to be considered simply a poet—not a woman poet and certainly not a lesbian poet. Bishop seems to have been well into her thirties before she clearly recognized that she was a lesbian. It is somewhat difficult to tell from Millier's biography, probably because the biographer has no clear-cut evidence of exactly when Bishop saw that her sexual needs were best fulfilled by women. At least one man, Robert Seaver, proposed to her; he committed suicide shortly after she rejected him. Robert Lowell was strongly attracted to Bishop (as she was to him) and told friends in the late 1940's that he had meant to marry her—though he did not admit as much to her until several years later.

Another isolating factor was Bishop's rejection of the kind of confessional poetry that came in vogue in the 1960's. Although she thought that a genius such as Lowell could manage to create beautiful poetic forms in autobiographical poetry, she dismissed most of the genre as merely self-indulgent and out of control. Bishop had almost a classicist's belief in form—that the poet must submit herself to the meter of poetry, which disciplines what she has to say. For her the freedom to express the self and to be original had to emerge out of a craft one learned from one's forebears. One did not simply emote—as she saw all too many students do in her poetry classes at the University of Washington and Harvard University.

The closest Bishop came to being in harmony with herself and with others was in her fifteen-year sojourn in Brazil. She found there a companion, Lota Soares, of tremendous ability and energy, involved in developing her beloved Brazil, but also a woman of great literary sensibility who provided the security and nurturing that Bishop rarely was able to provide for herself. Living in Brazil was also much cheaper for Bishop, who lived in Soares' house and could make do with the small income from her father's estate.

Soares, in fact, was one of several women on whom Bishop would rely in her later years for psychic and economic support. Bishop held no full-time job until she was thirty-eight, and that was only for a year, as poetry consultant in the Library of Congress. Later she taught, but teaching was an ordeal she never really mastered, for she had little interest in it—or in the whole business of being a poet, for that matter. She disliked public readings, promoting herself, or writing to deadlines for money. She worked best in tropical lands where she could spend days and days pondering a single poem, uninterrupted by the frenetic pace of cities. She dreaded going to New York and other large cities.

A lifelong alcoholic, Bishop never really got her drinking under control. She had periods of sobriety, but almost anything could bring on a bout of binge drinking: writer's block, the onset of holidays that would remind her of her isolation, the departure or illness of lovers. After Soares died at fifty-seven, Bishop found that she could no longer tolerate Brazil on her own and was never again to find peace, even though the last ten years of her life were marked by growing recognition, magnificent reviews of her poetry, and a large circle of devoted friends. Nothing seemed able to relieve her fundamental sense of isolation—which she kept to herself, except when alcohol got the best of her and her friends received her ranting late-night calls (always followed up by an apologetic letter). As Millier observes, alcohol was at best a temporary anodyne for her suffering. Her constant breakdowns, mental and physical— like many alcoholics, she became accident-prone in her sixties—led to several hospitalizations. These enforced rests were often to her liking because she was fussed over and always attended to—precisely what she had lacked in her painful childhood years.

It is telling that one of her greatest poems is a retelling of the Robinson Crusoe story, for she was clearly drawn to the individual on his own, creating his own world. This is what she had done in her poetry without ever conceding to the fashions of her day or worrying about her place in the cutthroat literary world of her contemporaries. Yet she was not an escapist, at least not in terms of her writing. Poetry was a way of understanding, not evading, reality. In fact, poetry was primary; it was what she knew as reality: "Tomorrow, we shall have to invent,/ once more,/ the reality of the world." Creating poetry was a way of remaining sane—a vital belief for Bishop, who saw not only her mother but also three of her lovers succumb to mental illness: Robert Seaver, Lota Soares, and Suzanne Bowen.

Some of Bishop's best lines combine her travel quests and sense of geography with her sexual yearning and search for knowledge. Thus she suggests that the sea is

> like what we imagine knowledge to be:
> dark, salt, clear, moving, utterly free,
> drawn from the cold hard mouth
> of the world, derived from rocky breasts
> forever, flowing and drawn, and since
> our knowledge is historical, flowing, and flown.

Millier notes that Bishop was often happiest when aboard ship. It did not matter whether it was a freighter or a luxury liner. She was literally and psychically buoyed up by water and wanted always to live by the sea and skirt the edges of the shore like the sandpiper—the subject of one of her best poems. What is extraordinary about Bishop is how well she knew herself. She was almost never self-deluded, and her superb self-criticism prevented her from producing the reams of work less important poets publish without embarrassment.

Bishop made enormous demands on her friends, especially in her last years, when she was particularly needy (for affection and for money), but it is a tribute to the quality of friendship she offered that so many first-rate writers were willing to help her. She was a very giving person and almost totally devoid of the jealousy and backbiting that often spoil friendships between writers. The words she wanted put on her tombstone sound a little facetious, yet they do sum up a complex person who was never sentimental about herself or about the world: "Awful, but cheerful."

Carl Rollyson

Sources for Further Study

Belles Lettres. IX, Fall, 1993, p. 49.
The Christian Science Monitor. September 8, 1993, p. 15.
London Review of Books. XV, March 11, 1993, p. 6.
The Nation. CCLVI, April 19, 1993, p. 530.

New Directions for Women. XXII, May, 1993, p. 27.
The New York Times Book Review. XCVIII, April 4, 1993, p. 15.
The New Yorker. LXIX, March 29, 1993, p. 107.
Publishers Weekly. CCXL, January 11, 1993, p. 45.
The Washington Post Book World. XXIII, March 21, 1993, p. 9.
Women's Review of Books. X, June, 1993, p. 7.

AN EYE FOR DARK PLACES

Author: Norma Marder
Publisher: Little, Brown (Boston). 296 pp. $19.95
Type of work: Novel
Time: The first half of the twenty-first century
Locale: London and the English countryside

Sephony Berg-Benson, middle-aged, socially straitjacketed, is transported for a time to an alternative world, Domino, where she discovers the seeds of her ultimate liberation

> *Principal characters:*
> SEPHONY BERG-BENSON, age forty-seven, a student of ancient history
> MAREK, her husband, an engineer
> ROLF,
> SIMON,
> DOTE, and
> MELANI, their children
> MUMS, Sephony's mother
> MUGS, her brother
> ARI, her sister
> AARON LIMORRZ, her first love, a biologist
> MO, a hologram artist who follows the winds
> JOANNE, a medical seer
> REB NACHT, a mystical rabbi
> CLARO, Sephony's guide in Domino

An appreciative reading of *An Eye for Dark Places* demands the willing suspension of disbelief that Samuel Taylor Coleridge called for in *Biographia Literaria* (1817). Having once transcended the credibility barrier, readers who value such novels as Ursula K. Le Guin's *A Wizard of Earthsea* (1968) and *Tehanu: The Last Book of Earthsea* (1990), Doris Lessing's Canopus in Argus series of the 1980's, and Margaret Atwood's *The Handmaid's Tale* (1985) are ready for the apocalyptic adventure Norma Marder has concocted.

Her story explores the midlife concerns of a wife, bored with her loveless marriage, and mother, faced with the permanent departure of her children from home. Sephony feels disconfirmed in her marriage. Her first independent act—studying ancient history—alienates her from her family.

Upper-middle-class and conventional in many ways, Sephony lives a generation or two beyond the last years of the twentieth century. She pilots her own futuristic flying machine, commuting between the farm where she lives with her family and graduate school in London, half an hour's flying time away, where she is working toward a degree in ancient history. Her marriage, a quarter-century old, was passionless from the start. It shows every sign of continuing for no better reason than that it has endured this long.

Genuine passion once consumed Sephony, but Aaron, her first love, did not pass muster with her well-to-do parents. They knew that his great-grandparents had been exposed during some long-past cataclysm in Norwich to minoxine, whose genetic side effects they feared would affect his offspring. Ever the compliant daughter, Sephony did her parents' bidding, turned from Aaron, and married the more acceptable Marek, a humorless, passionless engineer with little sensitivity and less imagination. Sephony and Marek occupy the same physical space; the mental space they inhabit is in different continents—or should one say "hemispheres"?

Early in the novel, Sephony is severely stressed. Her university work presses; important examinations loom. She takes the great risk of turning the "brainer," to which she attaches herself, to a dangerous calibration of four in a desperate effort to enhance her learning speed. A minor emotional breakdown ensues.

In *An Eye for Dark Places* Marder shapes a world of futuristic trappings: brainers, hovercraft, memory bands, robots, currency cards. This is a world of Triangle-mandated space migration, one in which unions between two people are renewed every seven years or, at the wish of either, "severed," as the operant parlance antiseptically calls divorce.

Great Britain has become a Huxleyan jumble of genetically engineered humans including Dulls, whose fulfillment comes from performing lifetimes of repetitive, menial tasks, and Bristers, brighter than the Dulls but far from independent, always traveling in groups and, like the Chinese, limited to having one child per couple. Their labors are supplemented by the services of robots, sparking memories of Karel Čapek's *R. U. R.* (pr. 1921, with Josef Čapek; English translation, 1923).

Sephony's brave new world is administered by the Triangle, a lurking, totalitarian oligarchy, an overpower that handles regulation better than maintenance: The infrastructure it oversees is disintegrating. Marder establishes a despairing tone on page 1, where birds limp and government billboards peel.

Seeking some escape from her unrewarding routine, Sephony drags an unenthusiastic Marek to a retreat run by Reb Nacht, a rabbi with mystical leanings whose sessions draw the disenchanted. This is an early attempt of Sephony to seize more than life now offers her. Little can she foretell what Fate is about to toss upon her path.

As she works in her kitchen, preparing dinner for a pair of tiresome guests, the Whatleys, Sephony espies a man coming up the walk carrying dead chickens. She dubs him "Chicken Man." Claro, as he is more commonly known, comes into her kitchen; the next thing she knows, Sephony is following him through a passage that has fantastically opened in the floor of her larder, terminating in his world, Domino—a world "out there," a world with its own morality, its unique social codes.

Claro is enticing rather than threatening. With Sephony plastered to his back, Claro flies around, her arms clutching his neck. In Domino, Sephony meets Claro's wives (who, like him, can fly under their own power), sees their world, and temporarily becomes part of it. The people Sephony encounters during her through-the-looking-glass escapade are innocent of jealousy, rancor, and other red-blooded human emotions that, ironically, contribute to defining one's place in conventional, civilized human society.

Sephony's unanticipated outvoyaging has left dinner uncooked, with dinner guests imminent. Marek lacks the imagination to deal with the situation as well even as the unimaginative, image-conscious Edward does in T. S. Eliot's *The Cocktail Party* (pr. 1949, pb. 1950). Marek levels with his guests, who help search for Sephony; he dismisses them, dinnerless, when the search proves futile.

For a British matron with a husband and four children, however, self-indulgent adventuring in Domino cannot last indefinitely. Sephony returns, emerging not in the larder from which Claro transported her but in the Jungle, formerly London's zoo, which had been abandoned some forty years earlier when the Triangle killed the animals during the Great Drought. In this preserve lurks some undefined evil.

Trapped behind the unclimbable wall that encloses the Jungle, a disoriented Sephony tries to attract attention and get somebody on the other side to help her. People hear her cries but quite ignore her, as society typically ignores middle-aged women in bleak—even threatening—situations. Marder's sharpest feminist commentary resonates in this section of the novel.

Finally Lela, a woman outside the wall, rescues Sephony by throwing her a rope ladder. Back on familiar turf, Sephony remembers like a Wordsworthian infant that baffling yet enticing world, Domino, in which some regions are constantly wet, others unrelentingly dry, a world where everyone dresses similarly in loose-fitting tunics (good for flying), one in which unconditional, nonjudgmental love, total openness, and honesty prevail—quite opposite to the conventions of the British society Marder is satirizing.

An Eye for Dark Places has several subplots, the most important of which is the Aaron-Sephony romance. Having had their hopes of marriage scuttled by Sephony's parents, the two did what duty (and society) dictated: Sephony married Marek; Aaron married Sibyl. Neither marriage is happy, yet neither is dramatically or unbearably unhappy. Rather, Aaron and Sephony have settled into conventional relationships with spouses for whom they have little feeling—a fate not unusual even in contemporary contexts.

Both might have muddled through this way for the rest of their lives had Sephony not spied Aaron across the room at her mother's seventy-fifth birthday party. Furious to find that Aaron and Sibyl have been invited, Mums upbraids Sephony for including them. Later she discovers that it was Sephony's sister Ari who had sent the couple their invitation, an act that is to change forever the dynamics of the two families.

The Aaron-Sephony meeting unnerves the pair, yet it is unlikely that, save for Sephony's trip to Domino, their lives would have been turned inside-out by it. This journey, presented as actual, is clearly fraught with underlying meanings that permit Marder to hold the mirror to the absurdity of the social conventions most people— particularly the British—embrace under the guise of civilized propriety.

An Eye for Dark Places, akin in many ways to Aldous Huxley's *Brave New World* (1932) and George Orwell's *1984* (1949), is a spiritual heir, certainly, of Sir Thomas More's *Utopia* (1516). Its flights of fancy, so necessary to the development of Marder's controlling metaphor, evoke, however, the strongest comparison to Lewis Carroll's *Alice's Adventures in Wonderland* (1865) and, more particularly, *Through the Looking-Glass* (1872).

Sephony's excursion into a world of surreal fantasy with Claro, an androgynous surrogate parent, makes Marder's novel work and enables her to communicate pointed and evocative feminist sentiments. Marder's feminism, however, is more patient and resigned than that of some more militant feminists. It resembles the feminism that lurks near the surface in the Virginia Woolf of *Mrs. Dalloway* (1925) and *To the Lighthouse* (1927) more than that of Le Guin's novels or Gloria Steinem's outpourings. Marder's approach to domesticity raises the inevitable question of what has happened to the feminist advances of the late twentieth century. Has the status of women not changed basically in the light of these advances?

The author seems more distressed by the conventions society imposes upon people, particularly women, than she is by women's continuing roles, even in the twenty-first century, as cooks, housekeepers, and child-bearers. If Sephony represents the "new woman," she differs from her earlier counterparts mainly by having taken on more work and responsibility for no additional recompense. She is married to a male chauvinist who defines male-female roles by earlier, conventional standards.

Sephony is a curious character. She adored her father yet was clearly not his favorite. Upon his death, she learned that he had bequeathed less to her than he had to her siblings, Mugs and Ari. This discovery, however, does not diminish Sephony's love for him: "Reject a daughter," Marder writes, "and she adores you forever."

Open, long-term enmity exists between Sephony and Mums. Mums is a thoroughly interesting character. At seventy-five, she has an old family friend as lover. Witty and bright, Mums is incapable of treating Sephony as anything but the child she was, reducing her even now to a trembling infant simply by shooting her a disapproving glance.

The novel and Sephony's marriage both end quietly. Sephony leaves Marek and goes to work as a medical seer in a clinic, caring for Dulls injured at work. In the end, Melani, about to enter her last year of secondary school, spends her birthday weekend with Sephony and Aaron at a coworker's cottage in the Lake District. Arrangements have been made for Melani to board out the following year, but she asks whether she might instead live with her mother and Aaron. Neither objects. Sephony suggests that Aaron's daughter Gretta might live with them too, but Aaron vetoes the idea, realizing that Melani far outshines Gretta intellectually.

The big question is whether, in the end, Aaron will bring himself to leave his family. Meanwhile, Marek, hurt as only the insensitive can be hurt—hurt because his routine is disrupted, his ego lacerated—works overtime at muddling through, all the while expunging Sephony's memory from his household. He digs up her garden and replaces her prizewinning roses with pear trees.

Melani displays promising signs of youthful rebellion, a behavior rarely observed in Triangle-programmed children. She even espouses the subversive notion that space migration should be discontinued, but Aaron calls her notion unrealistic. He suggests that Melani pursue a career in biology. Perhaps she will have some part in genetically engineering the citizens of the future.

R. Baird Shuman

Sources for Further Study

Booklist. LXXXIX, July, 1993, p. 1950.
Boston Globe. August 15, 1993, p. 15.
Kirkus Reviews. LXI, April 15, 1993, p. 480.
Library Journal. CXVIII, May 15, 1993, p. 97
Locus. XXXI, September, 1993, p. 72.
Publishers Weekly. CCXL, May 24, 1993, p. 68.

FAITH IN A SEED
The Dispersion of Seeds and Other Late Natural History Writings

Author: Henry David Thoreau (1817-1862)
Edited by Bradley P. Dean
Foreword by Gary Paul Nabhan
Introduction by Robert D. Richardson, Jr.
Publisher: Island Press/Shearwater Books (Washington, D.C.). Illustrated. 283 pp. $25.00
Type of work: Natural history
Time: The mid-nineteenth century
Locale: Principally Concord, Massachusetts

The first collection and edition of a number of articles on natural history, unfinished and drafted in the last years of Henry David Thoreau's life, which demonstrate his genius as a writer-scientist

This publication of Henry David Thoreau's late writings will prompt thoughtful readers to reconsider their places in both the natural and the intellectual world. In the introduction, Robert D. Richardson, Jr., contrasts the poet-naturalist author of *Walden: Or, Life in the Woods* (1854) with the later Thoreau, the writer-scientist. While there is merit in considering such phases in Thoreau's career, the distinction is a fine one. He was always both naturalist and philosopher, and no amount of scientific observation could obscure the larger issues that he always found orbiting the trajectories of nature.

Faith in a Seed: The Dispersion of Seeds and Other Late Natural History Writings may at one level serve as a guide to Thoreau's status as a cult figure, for few authors have had their rough drafts so elegantly produced. Throughout adulthood Thoreau was a prescient observer of nature. Between 1852 and 1862, he recorded enormous amounts of primary material, principally in three sets of notebooks—a journal, notes on aboriginal North America, and a pair of large notebooks containing extracts from and annotations to a wide variety of writings on natural history. In the late 1850's, he began rereading these materials in preparation for production of a vast statistical survey of the natural world of Concord. Exactly what form this was to take is unclear. Thoreau himself, shortly before his death, did not consider that he had made much progress toward the goal. As a result, earlier scholars found little of worth in Thoreau's "technical writing." It is clear, however, that the articles included in *Faith in a Seed* were at least initial attempts to narrate the statistical record of the natural life of his home within a broadly philosophic base.

The composition of this volume is in spirit a reflection of Thoreau's philosophy. There is no thesis, no authority, no authoritative form, but rather a loose collection from which one may randomly be edified. The personal and ecologically informed foreword was written by Gary Paul Nabhan, cofounder and research director of Native Seeds/SEARCH and vice president of the international Seed Savers Exchange. The biographical introduction was penned by Richardson, professor at Wesleyan College and author of *Henry Thoreau: A Life of the Mind* (1986). The volume is graced with illustrations from Thoreau's notes and with Abigail Rorer's line art, the latter so subdued, tasteful, and perfectly suited to its subject as to suggest perfection.

The main course around which this eclectic array of supplemental material is drawn is the collection of Thoreau's writing, selected and expertly annotated by Bradley P. Dean, secretary of the Thoreau Society and editor of the *Thoreau Society Bulletin* and the *Thoreau Research Newsletter*. The focal point of the collection is "The Dispersion of Seeds," the most finished of the pieces, which makes up some seventy percent of the space devoted to Thoreau's works. Twenty-five pages of "Wild Fruits" was the beginning of a book-length manuscript that he put aside in 1861 in order to work full-time on "The Dispersion of Seeds." "Weeds and Grasses" and "Forest Trees" are tiny fragments that might in time have been incorporated into a finished product.

The meticulous care given to the preservation and dissemination of these pieces should not obscure the fact that this is a collection built around "a very early draft" of a book-length study. For Nabhan, Richardson, and Dean, the master's voice is clear, even in draft, and deserves the widest audience. The question is, does the content warrant such devotion?

Thoreau's work must be considered at several levels. First, as a work of scientific inquiry, it is a remarkably thorough and acute piece of mid-nineteenth century observation. Thoreau's goal was to refute the popular notion that trees "spontaneously" regenerate themselves, and in this he brilliantly succeeded. First, he developed an unprecedented knowledge of his Concord laboratory, which enabled him to elucidate "most of the dominant patterns of seed dispersal" there. Between 1852 and 1862, he kept lists—the dates of fruit's ripening, the first appearances of birds, recorded sightings of many mammals, reptiles, fish, and insects. By 1862, he had prepared large tabular charts, indicating, for example, the first appearance of April flowers over ten years, or the leafing patterns of Concord forests for a similar period. This intimate knowledge of Concord's natural history enabled him to deduce patterns in a variety of ways—by measuring distances between trees of the same species; by observing the effects of wind, water, and seasons on seeds; by noticing where and when seeds accumulated; by noting the interaction between seed-bearing animals and their treasure.

Careful observation of his own "wilderness" then enabled Thoreau to assess and incorporate the judgments of a wide variety of naturalists, from Pliny to Charles Darwin. Thoreau was in fact one of the earliest exponents of Darwin's theories of dissemination. He read *On the Origin of Species by Means of Natural Selection* (1859) in January 1860, carefully tracing Darwin's arguments and applying them to his mountain of inductive data. Yet even in the midst of such scientific applications, Thoreau was philosophizing. He was certainly right in saying that "one receives only what he is ready to receive, whether physically or intellectually or morally. . . . We hear and apprehend only what we already half know." Darwin's influence was acknowledged and undeniable, but was part of a great chain to which Thoreau's work of the 1850's was already linked. As he read authorities such as Darwin, Augustin-Pyrame de Candolle, Theophrastus, and John James Audubon, Thoreau mined hundreds of relevant extracts. During the late 1850's, as he began to compile his charts and prepare the articles that make up this book, he systematically reviewed the observations and study of a decade in order to produce a work of both science and moral philosophy.

As a work of science, Thoreau's project was both ambitious and ahead of its time. Calendrical histories of nature were not unusual, but none for New England was so thoroughly based upon careful and extended observations or so thoroughly grounded in scholarship. This volume certainly enhances understanding of the state of the natural sciences in the middle of the last century. Ultimately, however, it becomes clear that Thoreau's work was not principally scientific.

As art, the value of these articles is problematic. There are flashes of brilliance reminiscent of *Walden*, but on the whole too little craft. The passage on willows is suggestive, however, of where Thoreau's observations on natural history were heading. After a lengthy series of scientific observations, he laments the emblematic attachment of the willow to despairing love. "It is rather," he heroically suggests, "the emblem of triumphant love and sympathy with all Nature." To ground this surprising conclusion, he then alludes to the Bible, Greek history and myth, and English etymology and biography. It is clear at which point Thoreau returned to his compilation of scientific notes in order to develop the willow's world role.

Leaving the physical world of sixteen-inch twigs two-thirds buried in a sandy shore, for the metaphysical, he writes that he would gladly hang his "harp on such a willow. . . . Sitting down by the shore of the Concord, I could almost have wept for joy at the discovery of it"; later he remarks that the "willow of Babylon blooms not the less hopefully here. . . . It droops not to commemorate David's tears, but rather to remind us how on the Euphrates once it snatched the crown from Alexander's head." Thoreau was fashioning a moral economy for an audience steeped in the Bible and knowledge of the classical Mediterranean world. By alluding to its moral examples, he sought to establish for his readers a similar identity for the plants he was discussing. As precise and scientific as Thoreau undoubtedly intended to be, he was always thinking in larger terms, seeking implications for every observation. Unfortunately, there are no similar portraits for the pitch pine, the saw-leaved alder, or the maple. There is, however, enough craft herein to cause one to lament Thoreau's early death.

It is perhaps unfair to criticize the author for a draft that he was not yet prepared to publish, but the reader should be aware that the very real merits of this work are almost always embryonic, suggestive of what the finished product might have been. Thus some sections are little more than compilations of notes or a string of observations set out roughly in narrative prose. This becomes all the more important as one considers Thoreau's indifference as a taxonomist, the validity of whose work depended upon a transcendental insight usually thought alien to an arid scientific environment. Having been forewarned, however, no aspiring naturalist will be sorry to have spent some time with Thoreau in the rough. One will hardly be able to read "The Dispersion of Seeds" without a heightened awareness, both aesthetic and scientific, of the fragile rhythms of life that are too often taken for granted. Thoreau's careful observation of the ubiquitous squirrel, for example, gives meaning to a common observed activity and elevates one's sense of the earth's wholeness.

Richardson is right to distinguish between the "fable of freedom" embodied in *Walden* and the "fable of dissemination" that is prominent in "The Dispersion of Seeds." Yet the two works are more similar than a glance might suggest. If "The Dispersion of Seeds" seems to celebrate "fertility, fecundity, and interconnectedness" while *Walden* is about "the sweet freedom" of a life that is "single, unattached, and uncommitted," one must remember that it was the same unattached Thoreau reporting on both scenes. He could hardly refrain from such observations, and he almost certainly would have produced a more finished philosophical reflection had he lived to complete his study. Thoreau's gift to humanity was a subtle but irresistible warning to slow down, to observe, to take pleasure in the rich complexity of the garden in which one grows. Even unfinished, *Faith in a Seed* is an important part of that legacy.

John Powell

Sources for Further Study

American Horticulturalist. LXXII, July, 1993, p. 26.

The Economist. CCCXXVII, May 1, 1993, p. 97.

Library Journal. CXVIII, May 15, 1993, p. 93.

Los Angeles Times Book Review. April 18, 1993, p. 1.

The Nation. CCLVI, June 7, 1993, p. 768.

Natural History. CII, October, 1993, p. 36.

Nature. CCCLXIII, June 10, 1993, p. 507.

The New York Times Book Review. XCVIII, May 23, 1993, p. 12.

Publishers Weekly. CCXL, March 15, 1993, p. 79.

The Washington Post Book World. XXIII, April 4, 1993, p. 11.

FDR
Into the Storm, 1937-1940

Author: Kenneth S. Davis (1912-   )
Publisher: Random House (New York). 692 pp. $35.00
Type of work: Biography
Time: 1937-1940
Locale: Washington, D.C.

An account of Franklin D. Roosevelt's stormy second term, featuring the so-called court-packing fight and the coming of World War II

> *Principal personages:*
> FRANKLIN D. ROOSEVELT, thirty-second President of the United States
> ELEANOR ROOSEVELT, his wife
> HARRY HOPKINS, head of the Works Progress Administration, 1935-1938, and Secretary of Commerce, 1938-1940
> JOHN NANCE GARNER, Vice President of the United States, 1933-1941
> CORDELL HULL, Secretary of State, 1933-1944
> HENRY A. WALLACE, Secretary of Agriculture, 1933-1940, and Roosevelt's running mate in 1940
> WENDELL WILLKIE, the Republican candidate for U.S. President in 1940
> JOSEPH P. KENNEDY, U.S. Ambassador to Great Britain, 1937-1940
> CHARLES LINDBERGH, an isolationist critic of Roosevelt
> CHARLES EVANS HUGHES, Chief Justice of the U.S. Supreme Court, 1930-1941

At the annual Gridiron Dinner of the National Press Association in December 1939, the backdrop for one of the spoofing skits was a papier-mâché sphinx eight feet tall, its face that of a wide-smiling Franklin Roosevelt with a long-stemmed cigarette holder clamped at a jaunty angle between his teeth. Roosevelt promptly arranged to have it stored for exhibit in the museum of the a-building Roosevelt library.

This is, on the surface, an intimate, old-fashioned biography of the sphinxlike Franklin Delano Roosevelt, without a doubt the most beloved, and most deeply despised, of our modern presidents. It is replete with portentous weather reports and parenthetical asides. Here is the unflappable thirty-second President of the United States in the White House, mixing evening cocktails at what was called "Children's Hour" for Missy LeHand and other staff intimates; or reading Charles Dickens' *A Christmas Carol* (1843) around the fire and distributing presents to assorted toddlers; or laughing so hard at a joke made at an enemy's expense that he nearly falls out of his wheelchair. Here he is at his beloved Hyde Park estate, entertaining the British royal family at a time when he more than anyone was aware of the need for a symbolic display of Anglo-American amity; or supervising construction of his dream house nearby, separate from his mother's and his wife's; or poring over ticker-tape election returns and briefly fearing that he has lost the 1940 contest before addressing well-wishing neighbors. There he goes on oceanic cruises and transcontinental campaign train trips, intermixed with ceremonial dedications of New Deal edifices, before retreating for recuperative rest at Warm Springs, Georgia.

While *FDR: Into the Storm, 1937-1940*, (the fourth of a projected five-volume series) pays homage to the twentieth century's consummate politician, its central theme is drift, the disquieting equivocation of a pragmatic democrat who freely put himself at the mercy of the tide of circumstance. Amid a sea of self-interested sharks, Roosevelt was unable to restrain giant corporations for long. Insufficiently dedicated to either national planning or vigorous antitrust prosecution, he failed to check the accelerating growth of technological tyranny that eventually would imperil the planet. Convinced that he needed corporate support to mobilize effectively against the threat of Axis aggression, the president started steering his administration to the right. Author Kenneth S. Davis challenges Roosevelt's assumption that he needed to woo big-business leaders and adds that, in any case, most were implacable enemies of the New Deal. As Davis puts it, foxes were "being called to the capital to guard the chicken coop and fatten up the chickens in preparation for their own hearty repast."

Book 1, titled "The End of the New Deal," opens with Roosevelt squandering his sweeping 1936 personal mandate by proposing to expand the Supreme Court with up to six additional members. As much as the high court had done to thwart the New Deal, Davis believes that the constitutional crisis was more one of appearances than of actuality. What was required was patience and good timing. Uncharacteristically, FDR exhibited neither when he sprang his so-called court-packing plan on Congress. Most of his advisers had also been kept in the dark and were distressed to learn of the plan. They tended to favor, if anything, a constitutional amendment allowing congressional review of court decisions touching on the constitutionality of legislation. Roosevelt was delighted at Attorney General Homer Cummings' discovery that reactionary justice James C. McReynolds had proposed a measure similar to his own two decades previously. Titling one chapter "Tragic Error Is Compounded by a Stubborn Persistence in It," Davis compares Roosevelt's act of hubris in prolonging the fight to Stephen Douglas' Kansas-Nebraska proposal of the 1850's and Woodrow Wilson's mishandling of the Versailles Treaty after World War I. Roosevelt's closest adviser, Louis Howe, had died (he would after a time be inadequately replaced by the president's son James), and Roosevelt was not sensitive enough to realize how duplicitous his rationale for the plan (merely an efficiency measure, he claimed) would seem or how insulting it would be to "Old Isaiah," the octogenarian Louis D. Brandeis, who suggested through a third party that Chief Justice Charles Evans Hughes rebut the president's explanation of the situation. Davis goes on to describe how ill-advised and controversial was the judicial appointment of Alabama Senator and former Klansman Hugo L. Black. (Ironically, Black turned out to be one of the Court's leading liberals, while so-called liberal Felix Frankfurter, a 1940 nominee, turned out to be much more conservative.)

Second presidential terms are rarely successful. Amazingly resilient, Roosevelt did not suffer the ruinous fate of his Democratic predecessor Woodrow Wilson. Like Dwight D. Eisenhower and Ronald Reagan, he remained personally popular even as his governing coalition waned. After his ill-considered court-packing fight and rash attempt to "purge" (a word more apropos to the methods of Joseph Stalin and Adolf Hitler) disloyal Democrats in the 1938 primaries, Roosevelt became palpably timid in matters foreign and domestic (such as the Spanish Civil War and the antilynching bill). Bent on conserving his political capital for matters pertaining to national security, he tolerated paralytic internecine feuds (such as between Secretary of War Harry Woodring and Assistant Secretary Louis A. Johnson) and rebuffed, with tragic consequences, efforts to relax immigration laws for victims of Nazism. Even his few second-term legislative accomplishments, such as governmental reorganization and minimum-wage laws, represented compromises that would have been unnecessary had it not been for the court-packing fight. Roosevelt even backed away from a battle to cut funds from the House Un-American Activities Committee, thereby allowing that vehicle for mindless anti-Communism to grow like a cancer. Davis writes:

> Roosevelt hesitated. He procrastinated. The indirection, the secretive deviousness which he had practiced intermittently in more prosperous times, often, it seemed, for the sheer fun of dramatic surprise and role-playing, was now practiced by him almost continuously out of, clearly, a felt grim necessity. On occasion, his reluctance to meet opposing forces head-on became extreme to the point of cowardice.

One dispute Roosevelt was forced to resolve featured Tennessee Valley Authority directors Arthur E. Morgan and David E. Lilienthal. The former was an unorthodox visionary whose refusal to abide by the wishes of his colleagues eventually cost him his job, despite the president's efforts at mediation. At one point Morgan's rival was summoned to the White House bedroom to meet the president, clad only in his underwear. Lilienthal noted in his journal his impression of FDR's "amazing assurance and nonchalance and complete lack of self-consciousness that made it seem appropriate to be discussing matters of high priority with a gentleman in his B.V.D.'s, and particularly a man whose legs are shrivelled up."

Based almost totally on secondary sources, *FDR: Into the Storm, 1937-1940* is thin on new revelations but rich in character development, not only of the buoyant president and his inner circle but also of such adversaries as isolationists Burton K. Wheeler, Joseph P. Kennedy, and Charles Lindbergh ("I am absolutely convinced Lindbergh is a Nazi," FDR told Henry Morgenthau) and charismatic 1940 Republican challenger Wendell Willkie. The Hoosier lobbyist (Harold Ickes dubbed Willkie "the barefoot boy from Wall Street") was a cut more liberal than the rank-and-file of the Republican Party, which, according to Davis, had become a morally bankrupt, single-interest (big business, of course) party unworthy of founders Abraham Lincoln, Charles Sumner, and William Seward. Senate Republicans, for example, would not support cloture to allow a vote on the antilynching bill, which had been approved by the House of Representatives after two African Americans were chained to trees and tortured to death with blow torches.

Davis describes the 1940 Republican convention as one of the GOP's few dramatic ones, most being spectacles "having as their main purpose the packaging in attractive disguise of candidates and programs which, frankly exposed to public view, would be seen to serve very few at the expense of very many." Despite delivering an acceptance speech that Socialist Party leader Norman Thomas characterized as "a synthesis of Guffey's First Reader, the Genealogy of Indiana, the collected speeches of Tom Girdler, and the *New Republic*," Willkie started the campaign on a somewhat high road, accepting most of the legislative accomplishments of the New Deal and agreeing with Roosevelt's aid-short-of-war policies toward Great Britain. As the campaign heated up, however, Willkie became more demagogic in claiming that a third term for Roosevelt would lead to war and one-man rule. Stooping to conquer, the president agreed to tell the mothers of America that their sons would not be sent off to war.

By the time of the 1940 Democratic convention, Roosevelt had broken with Vice President John Nance Garner and political operative James A. Farley, who had thrown their hats into the ring. Although they were unable to deny him a chance at a third term, there was near rebellion at Roosevelt's choice of Henry A. Wallace as his running mate. At one point the president actually drafted a message declining the nomination when it looked as though the delegates might nominate House Speaker William B. Bankhead, a conservative Alabaman whose daughter Tallulah would become more famous than he. A speech by Eleanor Roosevelt helped carry the day for Wallace. In an endnote located at the rear of the book is mention of friction between the staffs of the president and the first lady. One presidential adviser, Samuel Rosenman, neglected to mention Eleanor's role in the matter in his otherwise extensive recollections of the convention.

Other nuggets found in the endnotes are the fact that Willkie's eccentric, strong-willed mother (shades of Sara Roosevelt) wore French high heels into her eighty-first (and final) year and information about the secret recording of White House press conferences and meetings. One such conversation dealt with how to counteract Republican campaign strategists who had gotten possession of letters to a religious cult leader from Wallace addressed "Dear Guru." Secretly recorded was Roosevelt's suggestion of threatening retaliation by bringing up Willkie's alleged affair with New York *Herald Tribune* book reviewer Irita Van Doran.

One wishes Davis would have concentrated more on the social consequences of the New Deal and less on the coming in Europe of World War II. There is almost nothing about the Good Neighbor policy in Latin America; and the resolution of the Mexican crisis, precipitated when Lázaro Cárdenas threatened to seize foreign oil holdings, deserves fuller treatment (this was one of the few times when Roosevelt did not slavishly follow the desires of the politically potent Catholic hierarchy). Sloppy editing has left one chapter's endnotes misnumbered and several dates in error (such as the 1933 London Economic Conference). Quibbling aside, however, this is a thought-provoking liberal critique of modern America's premier president as the United States entered the storm of the twentieth century's most important event.

James B. Lane

Sources for Further Study

Campaigns and Elections. XIV, June, 1993, p. 60.
Chicago Tribune. January 3, 1993, V, p. 1.
Choice. XXXI, September, 1993, p. 199.
The Christian Science Monitor. March 26, 1993, p. 13.
Foreign Affairs. LXXII, Summer, 1993, p. 199.
Library Journal. CXVIII, February 1, 1993, p. 90
The New York Times Book Review. XCVIII, March 21, 1993, p. 9.
Publishers Weekly. CXL, January 11, 1993, p. 45.
The Wall Street Journal. March 24, 1993, p. A12.
The Washington Post Book World. XXIII, March 28, 1993, p. 3.

FEATHER CROWNS

Author: Bobbie Ann Mason (1940-   )
Publisher: HarperCollins (New York). 454 pp. $23.00
Type of work: Novel
Time: 1900, 1937, 1963
Locale: Western Kentucky

An uneducated country woman gives birth to the first set of quintuplets in North America and must find a way to cope with the fame that results

> *Principal characters:*
> CHRISTIANNA "CHRISTIE" WHEELER, a young mother of quintuplets
> JAMES WHEELER, her husband, a farmer
> WAD WHEELER, James's uncle, to whom the couple owe money
> AMANDA WHEELER, Wad's wife, Christianna's best friend
> ALMA WHEELER, Wad's sister
> MITTENS DOWDY, an African American nursemaid to the quints
> GREENBERRY MCCAIN, the lecturer for the tour of the quints

Bobbie Ann Mason's first collection of short stories, *Shiloh and Other Stories* (1982), made critically famous what has been called Kmart realism and received good reviews, and her novella *In Country* (1985), about the personal aftermath of the Vietnam War, was made into a topically interesting film. Short fiction has always seemed ideal for Mason, given her perceptive eye for the symbolically telling detail and her carefully controlled language. What she has done with her first long work, *Feather Crowns*, is to write what might be called a textbook example of the novel form, with all the conventional characteristics of that genre explored and foregrounded.

Instead of focusing, as she has in the past, on the late twentieth century cultural milieu of lower-middle-class Kentucky characters, Mason has chosen the traditional historical novel as her format, creating a period piece evoking the authentic look and feel of Kentucky farm life in the symbolically significant year of 1900. What ties all this local color together is the character Christianna Wheeler, a farm wife who gives birth to the first recorded set of quintuplets in North America. In an interview after the book was published, Mason, who is herself from a small town in western Kentucky, said that she set the novel in 1900 instead of the present because she was trying to imagine what life was like for her grandparents; it helped her understand who she was and where she came from.

In the cultural world that Mason tries to capture in this novel, every natural event means something, whether a change in the weather, the way the crops grow, or the way the body reacts. Thus, the momentous event of the birth of five children to one woman at one time is not merely an accident of nature; it has some secret significance. Similarly, something so pivotal as the turning of the century must be meaningful and marked by some grand event, and indeed a great earthquake is predicted for New Year's of the beginning of the new century. This focus on the symbolic significance of events is a central thematic strand of *Feather Crowns*, for Christianna undergoes considerable anguished soul-searching trying to understand why she, of all women, has been so chosen and what it all means. Although Christianna is named for Mason's own mother, the word "Christ" in her name takes on symbolic significance in the story, for the birth of her children is compared to the "borning" of Jesus, and all the people who come to see them are compared to the Wise Men bearing gifts.

The transforming power of fame is the most emphatic theme in Mason's novel. Once word gets out about the miraculous birth, people begin to come from all over the South to see the children and to take away a memento of the event, as if they were paying homage to a religious manifestation of great magnitude. Although Mason tells her story in the third person, she stays very close to the perspective of Christie. There are no discursive discussions of the thematic implications of the focus on the spiritual meaning of physical events; rather, the events are presented from the point of view of a believer in their significance.

Mason describes in some detail the hordes of people that descend on the Wheeler home after the press hears of the birth of the children. They range from the merely curious to those who lament their own childlessness in the face of such fecundity and come as if visiting Lourdes to gain some magical spiritual influence. The women look longingly and the men look admiringly at Christie's husband James as a symbol of masculine power for his ability to father such a miraculous brood. Gradually, the onlookers begin to consider it their right to invade the private life of Christie and her babies, for by their birth both she and they have been transformed into public property, elevated above the ordinary into the realm of transcendent significance. The fact that Christie's in-laws begin charging admission and selling souvenirs does not seem so much ignorant greed as the inevitable result of such a momentous occasion—just as Christmas has become the center of the commercial year even though its origin lies in a sacred event.

The death of the five infants within a few months of their birth is the occasion of more soul-searching by the young mother, as she wonders whether she is being punished for enjoying too much the sex act that brought them into being. As is often the case with such seeming manifestations of the spiritual at work in the physical world, the infants become even more mysteriously meaningful after their death. Preserved in airtight containers by the local undertaker, they are put on display as if they were religious relics to be worshiped by true believers. The babies never come alive in the book as real human beings, but instead remain frozen as symbolic objects.

The title of the book derives from little woven pockets of feathers in the mattress that the babies slept on. Made by parasites among the feathers, these "feather crowns" were usually taken by the folk to be a sign of imminent death if they were found in someone's bedding. Christie sees them as celestial tokens and believes that they mean her babies are in heaven; an angel has left the crowns, she imagines, the way the good fairy leaves money for a lost tooth.

Christie's decision to allow the dead infants to be taken on tour stems from her belief that the world killed them and that she must force the world to face her indignation.

Her decision to accompany the infants on the tour derives from both her unwillingness to let them go and her desire to leave the isolated town in which she was born and see something of the world. The tour begins respectably enough, as a scientific and educational presentation accompanied by a restrained lecture about the miracle of the quintuplets' birth. In a parable of the gradual and inevitable degeneration of fame, however, as the fickle public begins to lose interest in this latest phenomenon, the tour begins to decline from restrained lecture to carnival come-on, from dignified exhibit hall to sideshow tent. Gradually, the quintuplets come to seem much like the other freaks on exhibit in the carnival—the snake woman, the fat lady, the sword-swallower—a motif that allows Mason to indulge in some implicit theorizing through the perspective of Christie about all fame as essentially freakish.

The simple plot of *Feather Crowns* can be summarized in a few sentences, for as fantastic as the central event of the book is, it is not complexities of plot that make it a full-length novel. Rather, it is the character of Christie, a young woman caught in something bigger than herself and tormented by her efforts to understand the meaning of the event. In one subsection of the novel, entitled "Desire," Mason focuses on Christie's attitude toward the sex act, which she and her husband call "plowing" and about which she feels guilt because she enjoys it greatly. Sex is considered by Christie to be a part of a deeply secret life, but at a revival meeting her desire becomes identified with religious passion, and she is puzzled at the public display of the same kind of rapture that characterizes her secret life with James.

What also makes *Feather Crowns* a novel rather than a short story, what makes it blossom into some 450 pages, is the fact that Mason fills it with every turn-of-the-century rural folkway and saying that she can either remember or research. Given its thematic centrality, the significance of secret signs is a large part of the novel's voluminous detail. For example, finding the sign of a fork inside a persimmon seed means a hard winter. Placing an ax under the bed of a woman in childbirth will cut the pain. If Christie's husband strokes her pregnant belly sensuously, the child may be born with unwholesome thoughts. Everything means something in Christie's world; nothing happens without some secret purpose.

A large number of earthy idioms fill the book. Someone will warn a disobedient child, "I'll jerk a knot in your tail." To someone who refuses to answer a question, one might say, "Speak butt. Mouth won't." Milk is called "sweet milk" to distinguish it from buttermilk; sliced white bread is called "light bread" to distinguish it from cornbread. One is said to be "eating high on the hog" when things are good. A piece of rag filled with sugar for a baby to suck is called a "sugar tit." Since the book is told primarily from Christie's perspective, even the comparisons made by the narrator are drawn from folk sources. The fingers of the infants are said to be as tiny and new as green beans setting on the vine when the bloom starts to shrivel away. At one point when Christie keeps her feelings to herself, Mason describes it as her "stoppering up her feelings the way her mother bottled grape juice with her mail-order bottle-capper."

At the end of the degenerated tour of the quints, Christie decides to give the bodies of the babies to an organization called the Institute of Man in Washington, D.C., for scientific research, where they will no longer be subjected to the gaze of the curious masses. When she and James then return home to resume their ordinary lives in the symbolically named town of Hopewell, the novel is over except for two postscript sections. In the first one—a description of Christie's visit to Canada to see the Dionne quintuplets—Mason focuses on what happens when the state takes over such a phenomenon. The Dionnes become wards of King George. A strict schedule of their activities is maintained, and they are kept highly controlled. Although Christie has come to visit with the mother of the Dionne quintuplets, after seeing their public and controlled lives she leaves without talking to her.

The final chapter, which takes place in 1963, is a tape-recorded monologue by Christie as a ninety-year-old woman, in which she tidies up all the loose ends of the book and compares her own experience to that of Elvis Presley, another simple country person taken over by a public that has transformed him into something beyond his control. This transforming nature of fame, by which something unique and treasured becomes ultimately distorted into a parody of itself, is the central theme of the book. Yet this theme could have been treated in much less space than it is in *Feather Crowns*, and the novel could have been much shorter if Mason had not felt the novelistic need to create a complete sense of the cultural world in which the story takes place. Mason pads the novel with so much small folksy detail that it becomes more dependent on local color for its interest than on its exploration of character, culture, or idea.

Charles E. May

Sources for Further Study

Booklist. LXXXIX, August, 1993, p. 2012.
Boston Globe. September 12, 1993, p. 45.
Chicago Tribune. September 12, 1993, XIV, p. 1.
Library Journal. CXVIII, November 1, 1993, p. 148.
Los Angeles Times Book Review. October 24, 1993, p. 2.
The New York Times Book Review. XCVIII, September 26, 1993, p. 7.
Publishers Weekly. CCXL, July 12, 1993, p. 68.
The Times Literary Supplement. October 15, 1993, p. 20.
USA Today. September 17, 1993, p. D6.
The Washington Post Book World. XXIII, September 5, 1993, p. 5.

FIDEL CASTRO

Author: Robert E. Quirk (1918-   )
Publisher: W. W. Norton (New York). 898 pp. $35.00
Type of work: Biography
Time: 1927 to the 1990's
Locale: Havana, Oriente Province, and cities around the world

Fidel Castro emerges from this biography as a man obsessed with a lust for personal power, willing to use any means to gain his ends

Principal personages:
FIDEL CASTRO, the dictator of Cuba
RAÚL CASTRO, his younger brother
ERNESTO "CHE" GUEVARA, his friend and fellow revolutionary
DWIGHT D. EISENHOWER, the thirty-fourth president of the United States, 1953-1961
JOHN F. KENNEDY, the thirty-fifth president of the United States, 1961-1963
RICHARD M. NIXON, the thirty-seventh president of the United States, 1969-1974
NIKITA KHRUSHCHEV, the premier of the Soviet Union, 1958-1964
LEONID BREZHNEV, the premier of the Soviet Union, 1964-1982
CELIA SÁNCHEZ MANDULY, Castro's most trusted confidante and some-time mistress
JAMES EARL "JIMMY" CARTER, the thirty-ninth president of the United States, 1977-1981
RONALD REAGAN, the fortieth president of the United States, 1981-1989
GEORGE BUSH, the forty-first president of the United States, 1989-1993

This massive biography of Fidel Castro presents an unremittingly critical account of the Cuban dictator's life from his birth to the date of the book's publication. Relying primarily on published sources, author Robert E. Quirk concentrates most of his attention to the period after Castro overthrew the regime of Fulgencio Batista in 1959. The author presents only a perfunctory account of his subject's antecedents, childhood, and education. Even Castro's revolutionary exploits receive relatively little space. Quirk's coverage of Castro's career after his appearance on the world stage, however, is remarkably comprehensive.

Quirk adds nothing to the information concerning Castro's parents contained in the many biographies of the Cuban dictator which preceded his. Although his account of Castro's childhood draws exclusively on published sources, Quirk does add one new dimension to the familiar story of the spoiled rich boy who became a revolutionary. Quirk shows his subject as a bully, determined to force his will on everyone around him through whatever means necessary. Departing from several previous accounts of Castro's life, Quirk argues persuasively that Castro never developed a real social conscience or any true sympathy for the underprivileged masses of Cuba during his adolescence or his college years. The young Castro in Quirk's book is a bully who displays contempt for the rights and desires of anyone other than himself.

According to Quirk, when Castro matriculated at the University of Havana in 1945, he displayed none of the characteristics of the charismatic natural leader often commented on by his admirers. Most of the other students regarded him as a pushy bumpkin and something of a clown. Although Castro tried desperately to bully his way to the top of campus politics, his peers usually laughed at his often-bizarre antics and his simplistic political positions. Castro's speeches during his college years bitterly criticized the corrupt political regimes of Ramón Grau San Martín and Carlos Prío Socarrás. His own political views, however, remained relatively conservative. Despite Castro's later pronouncements, the future dictator almost certainly never even read the works of Karl Marx during this period, much less converted to Marxist ideology.

Quirk does not comment, as some of his predecessors have done, on two characteristics Castro displayed during his college days that help explain his eventual rise to power: his seemingly superhuman energy when engaged in a project that interested him and his almost photographic memory, which enabled him to cram a year's worth of studying into a few days. This last ability allowed Castro to pass his university examinations even though he was a poor student. Quirk also says very little about Castro's marriage to Mirta Díaz Balart in 1948.

Castro's first sojourn into revolutionary activity, according to Quirk and most previous biographies, resulted from his frustration at being unable to break into Cuban politics legally. After Batista's coup d'etat in 1952, Castro began to conspire with other young people in Havana to overthrow the dictatorship. Quirk argues that Castro's antigovernment activity derived from his desire to aggrandize himself, not from any real concern for the Cuban people. Castro and his small band of conspirators subsequently attacked the government military installation at Moncada in Oriente Province. Quirk portrays the attack as a poorly conceived fiasco in which Castro's actions were less than heroic. Quirk gives only a brief account of Castro's trial for his part in the failed attack. Although other accounts of his life have made much of Castro's famous political manifesto *La Historia me absolverá* (1953; *History Will Absolve Me*, 1959) that resulted from a long statement during the trial, Quirk dismisses it as of relatively little importance.

Castro's real education came during his subsequent imprisonment on the Isle of Pines. During several years of forced inactivity, Castro read widely from the works of philosophers and political ideologists, including Marx. Nevertheless, according to Quirk, Castro remained politically conservative. His letters and conversations from the Isle of Pines period offer no evidence that his readings had converted him to radical political or socioeconomic views. He emerged from prison determined to overthrow Fulgencio Batista, but only as a means of catapulting himself to national power. Quirk finds no indication that Castro had developed any real concern for the poor and downtrodden masses that Castro in his marathon speeches repeatedly pledged to "save" from the evil machinations of the capitalists and the imperialist United States government.

Quirk even denigrates Castro's role in the revolution that brought him to power. In Quirk's account, the success of Castro's movement resulted more from the Batista regime's ineptitude than from Castro's leadership. The author also points out the indispensable role played in Batista's deposal by a number of revolutionary groups whose only tie to Castro was their common hatred of Batista. According to Quirk, Castro's role in the success of the revolution was only nominal.

Along with most of Castro's other biographers, Quirk identifies Castro's cold reception in Washington, D.C., as a crucial incident in his career. Castro felt humiliated when President Dwight D. Eisenhower declined to meet with him. He developed an instant dislike for then Vice President Richard M. Nixon during a brief meeting which escalated into perpetual animosity toward the U.S. government. Nixon's distrust of and distaste for Castro led the U.S. government into repressive trade policies toward Cuba and attempts to assassinate the dictator. Quirk is almost as critical of U.S. government officials and their policies toward Cuba as he is of Castro. The U.S. attitude toward Castro and his regime, according to Quirk, pushed him into the camp of the Soviet Union during the then intense Cold War. Documented plots by several U.S. agencies sanctioned by the White House to assassinate Castro came to his attention and accelerated his growing hatred of the United States. The abortive U.S.-financed invasion of Cuba at the Bay of Pigs perhaps convinced him that any reconciliation with the United States was impossible.

Castro's embracing of Marxism-Leninism had nothing to do with personal philosophy. Quirk writes that Castro's conversion to Marxist principle and the subsequent socialization of the Cuban economy represented Castro's expedient to further his self-aggrandizement and repay the insult he believed to have been inflicted on him by the U.S. government. The alliance with the Soviet government that followed his announced conversion was always a marriage of convenience. Castro continually chafed at the control over his freedom of action exercised by Nikita Khruschev and his successors in the Kremlin. Castro's continued insistence on maintaining socialist institutions in Cuba despite considerable criticism from his countrymen derives from his realization that Marxist-Leninist dogma provided him with an excuse for maximizing his personal power over everyone around him.

Quirk portrays Castro as having been willing to plunge the world into nuclear holocaust during the Cuban Missile Crisis rather than surrender personal power. He sees Castro's foreign policy as having been designed to elevate the Cuban dictator to international prominence rather than to free what Castro called the "oppressed people of the world." Castro's dispatch of Cuban troops to "wars of liberation" in Latin America and Africa was prompted by his lifelong fascination with weapons and violence and his desire to humiliate the U.S. government. Even when Castro became an eloquent spokesman for the Third World, according to Quirk, he did not develop any genuine concern for the general welfare of the human race. His advocacy represented, in Quirk's view, merely another ploy to elevate his status in the international community.

U.S. leaders fare little better than Castro in Quirk's account of U.S.-Cuban relations, which dominates the biography. Jimmy Carter blundered as much as Nixon, especially in Quirk's recounting of the Mariel incident. Quirk saves his most telling sarcasm for

Ronald Reagan, who appears as a bumbling incompetent who exacerbated animosities between Cuba and the United States at a time when proper handling would perhaps have resulted in Castro's fall from power. Quirk's account of Reagan's faux pas in the exchange of invectives between him and Castro are often hilarious.

Quirk shows Castro's willingness to sacrifice long-time friends in order to keep himself in power. General Arnoldo Ochoa Sánchez, a highly decorated soldier and personal friend of Castro, found himself charged with drug trafficking and money laundering. He meekly confessed to the charges while specifically exonerating Castro from any knowledge of his crimes. Quirk argues that Castro had to have known about Ochoa's activities, and that he must have sanctioned them in an effort to secure hard currency to meet Cuba's pressing economic problems. This episode demonstrates, in Quirk's view, Castro's utter disregard for international law and his determination to use any means to hold on to the power he desperately craves.

The picture Quirk paints of contemporary Cuba is almost as bleak as his predictions for its future. Using accounts of recent visitors to the island and his own observations there, Quirk portrays Castro's workers' paradise as a Malthusian/Orwellian nightmare. Since the collapse of the Soviet Union and the end of massive aid from that country, Cuba's economy has fallen into chaos. The destruction of the Cuban economy has accelerated because of the conversion of Cuba's former socialist trading partners in Eastern Europe to market economies. Cuba's population increased dramatically under Castro, while food production increased only marginally. Now that the Cuban govern-ment no longer receives subsidies from the Soviet Union and cannot trade for needed foodstuffs, the island's people suffer shortages of almost everything, including neces-sary food and medicine. One of the most visible results of those shortages is a "neuropathic" epidemic that affects eyesight and motor abilities, probably caused by vitamin deficiency that has affected "hundreds of thousands" of people. The island's population also suffers from shortages of fuel and electricity that have shut down many factories and caused power outages throughout the country. The cities are cockroach-infested and decaying, perhaps beyond repair. Housing in the cities is inadequate. At least 40 percent of what are perhaps the best-educated people in the world cannot find work. The morale of the people has dipped to an all-time low. Most Cubans openly despair of the future under socialism.

Despite the obvious failure of Castro's policies, Quirk believes that the dictator will desperately cling to power as long as he lives. He will tolerate no criticism of himself or his regime. In one of his most revealing quotes from the mountains of printed words culled from Castro's speeches, Quirk shows the dictator's refusal to acknowledge his own failures or even entertain any efforts toward reform: "All criticism [to my regime] is opposition and all opposition is counterrevolutionary." As his country sinks into poverty and despair, Castro will steadfastly refuse to adopt any course other than socialism. Quirk believes that this inflexibility results not from any true ideological conviction on Castro's part, but out of his belief that it is the only way he can cling to the power that has obsessed him throughout his life.

Paul Madden

Sources for Further Study

Booklist. LXXXIX, August, 1993, p. 2011.
Boston Globe. September 26, 1993, p. 16.
Chicago Tribune. October 10, 1993, XIV, p. 5.
Foreign Affairs. LXXII, September, 1993, p. 164.
Library Journal. CXVIII, August, 1993, p. 114.
The New York Times Book Review. XCVIII, September 19, 1993, p. 3.
Publishers Weekly. CCXL, July 5, 1993, p. 57.
The Spectator. CCLXXI, November 27, 1993, p. 35.
The Virginia Quarterly Review. LXX, Winter, 1994, p. SS16.
The Washington Post Book World. XXIII, November 7, 1993, p. 5.

THE FIFTIES

Author: David Halberstam (1934-   )
Publisher: Villard Books (New York). 800 pp. $27.50
Type of work: History
Time: The 1950's
Locale: The United States

This social, political, economic, and cultural history focuses on the significant events and influential personages of the decade of the 1950's in the United States

Postwar American society is David Halberstam's own special historical turf. In his trilogy on power in America, he focused on U.S. involvement in Vietnam in *The Best and the Brightest* (1972), the omnipresence of American media in *The Powers That Be* (1979), and the American automobile industry in *The Reckoning* (1986). In a lighter and more personal mood, he took on the great symbolic sport of baseball in *Summer of '49* (1989), spotlighting the American League pennant race between the New York Yankees and the Boston Red Sox in 1949. *The Fifties* combines some of the sober gravity of his highly respected trilogy with a bit of the nostalgic levity of his baseball book. Such a combination is inevitable for the 1950's—on the one hand, a decade that saw the apocalyptic advance of the hydrogen bomb and the righteous rise of the Civil Rights movement is not to be taken lightly; on the other hand, how can one take seriously a decade whose best-known figures were Lucille Ball and Milton Berle?

Indeed, the period of the 1950's has not always been taken seriously. Sometimes dubbed the "placid decade," the era is best remembered as a time of postwar enthusiasm, when the only war was a "cold" one and both the economy and babies were booming. It was the era of President Dwight D. Eisenhower, that grandfatherly soldier who "won" the war and would protect a society yearning for a new isolationism from all attacks, foreign and domestic. It has been characterized in nostalgic novels and films as a time of innocence—before drugs, before gangs, before the sexual revolution—when Father knew best, Mother was best at baking cookies, girls wore poodle skirts, and boys wanted to be like Ricky Nelson. Compared to the sometimes fearful and always riotous and free-wheeling 1960's, the 1950's was alternately delightful and downright dull.

Yet as Halberstam tells the story of the era when the baby-boomers were still babies, behind all this naïveté and innocence was a hovering darkness, for beyond the joy of victory over the Japanese lurked the potential holocaust of "the bomb." Moreover, trailing after the triumph over the Nazis was the fear of the "Commies," an anxiety that led to the "Red-baiting" of the McCarthy hearings. As Halberstam narrates the details of the most important events of the period, he always pauses to provide the background of the era's most important figures. He knows that the real meaning of McCarthyism lay in the person of Joseph McCarthy himself and that the underlying significance of the nuclear arms race lay in the conflict between the personalities of scientist J. Robert Oppenheimer and Edward Teller, father of the hydrogen bomb.

The structure of Halberstam's account is primarily anecdotal and chronological, for he seems simply to move from one event and one character to another. In fact, each of the book's forty-six chapters could be read independently of the others. Nevertheless, an underlying theme runs implicitly throughout the book. It is first announced in the account of General Douglas MacArthur, a larger-than-life figure who, as Halberstam says, worked long and hard to create and perpetuate his own legend. With his dark glasses, rakishly placed cap, and well-crafted dramatic lines, he was the complete narcissist—more rhetoric than real.

With the rise of television, the most influential technological means of communication not only of the decade but indeed of the twentieth century, the difficulty of perceiving the difference between what was actuality and what was drama became more pronounced. The first real example of the power of the new medium was manifested the week of March 12, 1951: During the Kefauver hearings on organized crime, millions of Americans watched on small black-and-white screens the nervous drumming fingers of gang leader Frank Costello. Dramatic gesture dominated over mere language. According to *Life* magazine, the United States and the world had never witnessed anything like it, for never had the attention of the nation been so centered on a single event. The power of the media to focus more on image than on content was to become apparent also at the end of the decade, when a cool, smooth John F. Kennedy faced the sweaty, exhausted Richard Nixon, whose five-o'clock shadow was partially responsible for his losing the presidential election of 1960.

Some of the best-known television performers of the decade purposely confused drama with reality, and audiences loved it. In 1951, Lucille Ball and Desi Arnaz, married in real life, debuted in a show in which they portrayed husband and wife; *I Love Lucy* became so popular that the large Chicago department store Marshall Field's closed on Monday nights when the show aired. By the mid-fifties, Ozzie and Harriet Nelson, with their real sons, David and Ricky, were playing a make-believe family living an idealized family life in which the kids got into only occasional mischief and Mom and Dad never got angry. In spite of the audience's nagging feeling that all of this was too good to be true, there was the lingering fact that the Nelsons were a "real" family, so how could it not be true?

The confusion about the "truth" of reality on television was scandalously laid bare in the mid-fifties, when quiz shows giving away such fabulous sums as sixty-four thousand dollars became highly popular. It was the ultimate American dream that an ordinary person could win a considerable amount of money merely by knowing the right answers. The dream was shattered when it was discovered that a good-looking, personable young English instructor, Charles Van Doren, who had won more than one hundred thousand dollars on the quiz show *Twenty-one* had been given answers in advance. What made the scandal so symbolic of television's confusion between fantasy and reality was the fact that the producers of the show could not understand what all the fuss was about. After all, it was entertainment.

Yet it was not only television that made imagery dominate over reality in the 1950's. There were also industry, business, and advertising, all of which rapidly became synonymous with television. How much reality was involved in major American cars that became bigger and more powerful? With bumper guards that looked like Jayne Mansfield's breasts and fins that looked ready to lift off into space, automobiles became more than merely a means to move from place to place; they became symbols of status and the achievement of desire. How much reality underlay the American tobacco companies' drive to make cigarette smoking the ultimate in sophistication and rugged individuality? What teenage boy didn't want to be the Marlboro man? Then there was the building of Levittown, the prototypical American subdivision, with houses mass-produced the way Henry Ford had created assembly-line cars. The development of fast-food restaurants made the fat-filled hamburger the basis of economic empires. Nothing is a clearer testimony to the power of images created by advertising in the 1950's than the fact that an ordinary woman named Betty Furness, whose main talent was opening a refrigerator door with a flourish, became as well known a national figure as the politicians who were charged with running the country.

Perhaps the central symbolic figures of the era were Marilyn Monroe and Elvis Presley. Destined to be recognized forever by their first names only, Marilyn and Elvis seemed to sum up the ambiguous mixture of innocence and power that characterized the decade. Childlike and naïve, but at the same time a magnet for sexual desire, Marilyn was, like the 1950's itself, both silly and savvy. Her marriage to baseball hero Joe DiMaggio seemed more scripted than real, as did, in her search for cultural respectability, her second marriage to playwright Arthur Miller. Elvis was a similar combination of disparate elements. On the one hand, he was rustic boyishness, with a shy smile and an "aw-shucks" attitude; on the other, he was a dynamo of sexual suggestiveness. Ironically, Elvis' main claim to immortality may be the fact that he was indirectly responsible for the emergence of African American music as a cultural force to be reckoned with. When songs like "Heartbreak Hotel" hit jukeboxes in the mid-1950's, the music of black blues, formerly restricted to little-known singers such as Muddy Waters and Jimmy Reed, began to echo in high-school gymnasiums and soda joints throughout the country. It was the beginning of a long-overdue recognition of America's only original musical art form.

One of the strongest aspects of Halberstam's history of the 1950's is the fact that he packs it full of men and women who had a major impact on the political, social, and cultural life of the United States—from the alleged Communist conspirator Alger Hiss to the sociologist C. Wright Mills; from the highly visible J. Edgar Hoover, largely responsible for American Cold War paranoia, to the less visible professorial Alfred Kinsey, primarily responsible for the impending sexual revolution; from Hugh Hefner, the creator of the Playboy image and empire, to the most important advocate of sexual freedom for women, Margaret Sanger; from the dynamic voice of Martin Luther King, Jr., to the simple but powerful gesture of Rosa Parks; from Allan Dulles, director of the Central Intelligence Agency, to Gary Powers, U-2 spy-plane pilot.

If there is any weakness in *The Fifties*, it is its failure to focus on any aspect of American culture that cannot be called "pop culture." Although Halberstam does devote brief sections to the writers of the Beat Generation, such as Jack Kerouac and

Allen Ginsberg, the most important literary works of the period, according to Halberstam, were Mickey Spillane's hard-boiled detective novels and *Peyton Place* (1956). As far as Halberstam is concerned, there was no Norman Mailer, no Bernard Malamud, no John Updike, not even a J. D. Salinger. As far as drama is concerned, the only significant figures are those who were as much image as substance—the posturing Marlon Brando and his sulking act-alike, James Dean. As for music, the only sound with an impact was rock and roll; not even master showman Leonard Bernstein is mentioned. Television in the period, suggests Halberstam, was primarily Uncle Miltie and *I Love Lucy*; conspicuously absent from his account is Rod Serling, *Playhouse 90*, and the marvelous world of live television drama. Whether this oversight is attributable to Halberstam's devotion to his implicit thesis—that image rather than substance dominated the decade—or to his primary focus on the popular rather than the serious arts is never quite clear, but the effect is to create an overall impression of insubstantiality insofar as the arts are concerned in the 1950's.

As the decade winds down and the reader moves exhaustedly toward the end of this very big book, the 1950's begin to look more and more like the high-tension decade that was to follow. The last few chapters focus on the beginnings of the Civil Rights movement in Little Rock, Arkansas—which helped trigger an era of political and social confrontation; the U-2 spy-plane revelations, which initiated an era of public distrust of American intelligence activity; Betty Friedan and her book *The Feminine Mystique* (1963), which inaugurated the women's movement; and the Nixon-Kennedy debates, which marked the dawning of the Camelot era. The so-called placid decade did not so much end as it indiscernibly blended into the riotous upheaval of the 1960's.

Charles E. May

Sources for Further Study

Chicago Tribune. June 20, 1993, XIV, p. 3.
The Christian Science Monitor. July 16, 1993, p. 14.
Los Angeles Times Book Review. June 20, 1993, p. 4.
The Nation. CCLVII, September 20, 1993, p. 287.
The New York Times Book Review. XCVIII, June 20, 1993, p. 12.
Newsweek. CXXI, June 7, 1993, p. 65.
Publishers Weekly. CCXL, April 26, 1993, p. 63.
Time CXLII, July 19, 1993, p. 63.
The Wall Street Journal. June 23, 1993, p. A12.
The Washington Post Book World. XXIII, May 23, 1993, p. 1.

FIMA

Author: Amos Oz (1939-   )
First published: Ha-Matsav Ha-Shelishi, 1991, in Israel
Translated from the Hebrew by Nicholas de Lange
Publisher: Harcourt Brace/Helen and Kurt Wolff (New York). 322 pp. $22.95
Type of work: Novel
Time: February, 1989
Locale: Jerusalem

During five February days in Jerusalem, a fifty-four-year-old Israeli takes stock of a life richer in dreams than accomplishments

> *Principal characters:*
> EFRAIM "FIMA" NISAN, a fifty-four-year-old dreamer
> YAEL, his former wife, an aeronautical engineer
> TED TOBIAS, her second husband, an American engineer
> DIMI TOBIAS, the ten-year-old son of Yael and Ted Tobias
> BARUCH NOMBERG, Fima's eighty-two-year-old father, a successful cosmetics manufacturer
> ALFRED WAHRHAFTIG, a senior gynecologist at the clinic where Fima works
> GAD EITAN, a gynecologist at the same clinic, Wahrhaftig's former son-in-law
> TAMAR GREENWICH, a nurse at the clinic
> ANNETTE TADMOR, a patient at the clinic and one of Fima's lovers
> URI GEFEN, Fima's friend, a former pilot, an importer
> NINA GEFEN, Uri's wife, a lawyer, and Fima's occasional lover
> TSVI KROPOTKIN, a history professor, Fima's friend

Efraim Nisan—"Fima"—is a fifty-four-year-old *luftmensch* whose dreams exceed his accomplishments. Working as a receptionist in a gynecology clinic in Jerusalem, Fima has never fulfilled the promise that his talents seemed to everyone to manifest. Forever taking stock of where he stands, he notes:

> In the course of his life he had had several love affairs, several ideas, wrote a book of poems that aroused some expectations, thought about the purpose of the universe and where the country had lost its way, spun a detailed fantasy about founding a new political movement, felt longings of one sort or another, and the constant yearning to open a new chapter.

The thirty short chapters of *Fima* follow its title character through five wintry days in February. Except for a chapter that reprints his former wife's farewell letter, and except for Annette Tadmor's long, aggrieved account of her unhappy marriage, the point of view is Fima's.

Fima awakens from uneasy dreams, reads the newspapers, and spends time at his job, but what he does primarily, incessantly, is think: about personal relationships, Israeli politics, the corruption of language, international tensions, and an absent God. He is forever convening and presiding over imaginary cabinet meetings and composing but never sending letters and articles on the sorry state of the planet. He begins but never completes ambitious essays on creeping insensitivity and on the Christian origins of anti-Semitism. Fima envisions a student, whom he names Yoezer, occupying his Jerusalem apartment in 2089, a distant future that he is sure will differ quite dramatically from the present, but he often overlooks actual people alive around him. Acutely mindful of the sufferings of Palestinians and stray pets, Fima is so absent-minded that his telephone service is suspended because he forgets to pay the bill. His compassion extends to the cockroaches that overrun his messy kitchen. Fima is so preoccupied with solving the problems of the world that he neglects to button his shirt. His relationship to money is casual and oblivious.

Less a narrative of extraordinary events than the study of an exasperating yet engaging personality, *Fima* manages to make the reader care about a man who is a "unique combination of wit and absent-mindedness, of melancholy and enthusiasm, of sensitivity and helplessness, of profundity and buffoonery." The novel's title character is kin to ineffectual or irresolute figures in Russian fiction such as Ivan Goncharov's Oblomov, Ivan Turgenev's Bazarov, and Fyodor Dostoevski's Underground Man. Nina Gefen, his best friend's wife and his own occasional lover, likens Fima to a Pushkin antihero transposed to a Jerusalem neighborhood: "You're the Eugene Onegin of Kiryat Yovel," she tells him. In American literature, Fima recalls James Thurber's Walter Mitty in his absorption in fantasy and Saul Bellow's Moses Herzog in his imaginary exchanges with eminent men. Like Hamlet, who is "sicklied o'er with the pale cast of thought," Fima is paralyzed by ceaseless cogitation. "That's the whole of your problem," explains his former wife, Yael. "You don't do anything. You just read the papers and get worked up." Yael, who, after aborting his baby, left Fima almost twenty-five years ago, is an aeronautical engineer; in striking contrast to her immobile former spouse, she specializes in jet propulsion. "What have you done with life's treasure? What good have you done?" Fima asks himself, and the questions haunt him and the book to which he gives his name.

It was not always so. What his friends call his "tortoise years" have followed Fima's "billy-goat year." In 1960, newly graduated from Hebrew University with an honors degree in history, Fima fell madly in love with a French tour guide and pursued her to her home in Lyons. He eventually found himself penniless in Gibraltar and deported to a military prison in Israel. Released after six weeks, Fima impregnated the wife of a prominent official and then bolted to Malta, where he married the owner of the cheap hotel in which he stayed. Less than two months after the wedding, he fled to Greece, where he fell in love with three young Israeli women who were backpacking around the country. It was Yael, the most reserved of the three, whom Fima ended up marrying and with whom he set up housekeeping in a two-room flat that his father purchased for them in Jerusalem.

"How come there are still people who can stand me?" wonders Fima, who botches his connections to virtually everyone he respects. Some critics, unable to answer that question, have faulted Oz for focusing his story on a figure so ostensibly devoid of laudable traits. Yet, despite his fecklessness and sloth, Fima does inspire affection among a devoted circle of friends that includes Uri Geffen, a retired fighter pilot, his lawyer wife Nina, and Tsvi Kropotkin, an eminent historian. Though Fima exasperates them with lengthy, tendentious telephonic treatises at all hours of the day and though they patronize him as the "clown" of the group, they are genuinely fond of their eccentric underachiever. Even Yael maintains frequent contact with the ne'er-do-well she divorced long ago, and her current husband, an American engineer named Ted Tobias, is remarkably tolerant of Fima's frequent visits to their apartment. Nina occasionally sleeps with him, more out of solicitude than lust. For all his frailties and follies, there will still be readers who can stand him because they recognize in Oz's darkly comic portrait the shared absurdity of being human.

Fima, in turn, becomes ardently attached to Dimi, the ten-year-old son of Yael and Ted Tobias. He fantasizes a paternal bond to the boy, on whom he lavishes much unsolicited attention. An albino, Dimi is the butt of childish cruelty, and Fima feels protective toward the young pariah, psychologically if not genetically a kindred creature.

Fima's own father, Baruch Nomberg, is a formidable figure who has dominated his son's life since a cerebral hemorrhage killed his wife when the boy was Dimi's current age. He continues to underwrite his impractical, unproductive son. An immigrant from Kharkov who founded a prosperous cosmetics company, Baruch is a forceful representative of the pioneering generation that created the Israeli state and that stands in marked contrast to its equivocating offspring. At eighty-two, Baruch is still an imposing presence, a spirited and digressive conversationalist whose oral legacy is apparent in what Yael calls Fima's "verbal diarrhea." Father, a vehement Likudnik, and son, a leftist skeptical of nationalistic sentiments, clash over politics without diminishing their mutual affection. Yet Fima is only fully assertive after the death of his father, in the final pages of the book. Even then, he sneaks away from the mourning rituals in order to see a comedy starring Jean Gabin; inept to the last, Fima sits through another film after realizing that the one he wanted to see has already ended its run.

The Death of Augustine and His Resurrection in the Arms of Dulcinea, a precocious book of poetry that he published in 1962, augured an illustrious career for Fima. His muse soon went silent, however, and Fima undertook a job rather than a profession—as the receptionist in a gynecology clinic. Working for Alfred Wahrhaftig and Gad Eitan, whose practice is largely devoted to performing abortions, Fima, who is forever finding himself entangled with several women simultaneously, witnesses the agonies of the feminine fate. He arouses the interest of the clinic's nurse, Tamar Greenwich, and the passion of a distraught patient, Annette Tadmor.

Set entirely in its author's native city, *Fima* is a tender evocation of the sinuous streets and residents of Jerusalem. Though he characterizes the Israeli capital as "less like a city than a lunatic asylum," its inmate Fima is loath to follow Yael to Seattle or, after the *Wanderjahr* of his billy-goat year, to abandon Jerusalem for anyplace else. A long, run-on sentence toward the end of the novel captures the fascinating complexities of the ancient city on the eve of a February sabbath in 1989.

First published in Hebrew in 1991, before Israel's accord with the Palestine Liberation Organization, and set in 1989, before the fall of the right-wing Likud government, *Fima* takes the pulse of a troubled character and nation. A leader of the

Israeli Peace Now movement, author Amos Oz has been outspoken in his criticism of Jewish militarism and in support of efforts toward reconciliation of Arabs and Jews, and it is difficult not to read his latest novel, like *In the Land of Israel*, his 1983 nonfiction study, as a diagnosis of national malaise. Fima is troubled by the contradictions, disappointments, and dangers of life in contemporary Jerusalem, even as he himself represents the impasse of a native generation who find themselves devoid of the idealism, energy, and initiative of their pioneering predecessors.

Originally published under the Hebrew title *Ha-Matsav Ha-Shelishi* (the third state), *Fima* contemplates a luminous reality beyond sleeping and waking, a condition that transcends immediate confusion and pain. Though he is a fervent atheist and both a shlemiel and a shlemazel ("the shlemiel spills his tea and it always lands on the shlemazel," explains Baruch), Fima longs for the "supernal radiance" that he imagines is the Third State.

> All suffering Fima said to himself, everything that is ridiculous or obscene, is purely the consequence of missing the Third State, or of that vague nagging feeling that reminds us from time to time that there is, outside and inside, almost within reach, something fundamental that you always seem on the way to yet you always lose your way to.

A report card on the state of Fima and of the Jewish state, *Fima* also offers radiant intimations of a third, transcendent state. Beyond and through the indecision and ineptitude of the clumsy Fima, it holds out the promise of grace.

Since the enthusiastic reception of his second book, *My Michael* (1968), Amos Oz has, in *Unto Death* (1970), *A Perfect Peace* (1982), *Black Box* (1987), *To Know a Woman* (1990), and other novels, established himself internationally as one of the most accomplished authors writing in Hebrew. *Fima*, the thirteenth book by its Israeli author to be translated into English, demonstrates again the wizardry of Oz.

Steven G. Kellman

Sources for Further Study

Booklist. XC, October 15, 1993, p. 418.
Boston Globe. October 31, 1993, p. 105.
Chicago Tribune. November 14, 1993, XIV, p. 3.
The Christian Science Monitor. October 28, 1993, p. 13.
Library Journal. CXVIII, October 15, 1993, p. 90.
New Statesman and Society. VI, September 17, 1993, p. 38.
The New York Times Book Review. XCVIII, October 24, 1993, p. 12.
San Francisco Chronicle. November 28, 1993, p. REV6.
The Times Educational Supplement. October 1, 1993, p. A10.
The Times Literary Supplement. October 8, 1993, p. 28.
The Washington Post Book World. XXIII, November 28, 1993, p. 6.

FLAUBERT-SAND
The Correspondence

Authors: Gustave Flaubert (1821-1880) and George Sand (1804-1876)
First published: Correspondence Flaubert-Sand, 1981, in France
Translated from the French by Francis Steegmuller and Barbara Bray
Edited by Alphonse Jacobs with additional notes by Francis Steegmuller
Foreword by Francis Steegmuller
Publisher: Alfred A. Knopf (New York). 428 pp. $35.00
Type of work: Letters
Time: 1863-1876
Locale: France

These letters chronicle the evolution of an undying friendship between Gustave Flaubert and George Sand, unique literary figures of nineteenth century France

When Gustave Flaubert and George Sand began their thirteen-year friendship in the early 1860's, both had acquired controversial reputations in France's literary and social circles. Sand was born Amandine-Aurore-Lucile Dupin in 1804 to Maurice Dupin, an officer in Napoléon I's *armée d'Italie* and Sophie Delaborde, a young proletarian woman; when she and Flaubert first met, she had already acquired the status of an accomplished writer of plays, novels, and articles. Married in 1822 to Casimer Dudevant and renowned for her tumultuous affairs with Alfred de Musset, novelist, playwright, and poet, and the composer Frédéric Chopin, Sand played an active role in France's social and political evolution. She was a frequent contributor to *Le Figaro*, *La Revue de Paris* and *La Revue des Deux Mondes*. After breaking with the latter, whose editor was uncomfortable with her socialistic tendencies, Sand cofounded *La Revue Indépendante* in 1841. Her early works, autobiographical in inspiration, evoke a quest for love and happiness. In such lyrical novels as *Indiana* (1832) and *Lélia* (1833), Sand recounts the torments experienced by women who must struggle against their passions. In the last twenty-five years of her life, Sand lived tranquilly, and her works written during this time communicate a humanitarian view of existence and her love of nature and of rustic life.

Seventeen years younger than she, Flaubert was born in 1821 to Achille-Cléophas Flaubert, the chief surgeon of Rouen's municipal hospital, and Caroline Fleuriot, daughter of a physician. Afflicted with a nerve-related illness, Flaubert abandoned his law studies in Paris in 1844 and devoted himself exclusively to his writing. In 1838 he had written his first novel, *Mémoires d'un fou*, an autobiographical piece describing an unfulfilled passion (for Mme. Schlésinger, wife of a music publisher) that would serve later as a preliminary sketch for *L'Éducation sentimentale*, to be published in 1869. In 1856, *La Revue de Paris* published in serial form *Madame Bovary*, subsequently to appear in its entirety in 1857. The work, which depicts the illicit involvements of Emma Bovary, torn between a life of illusory romance and the reality of her brutish husband, caused an extreme furor among most critics, who condemned vehemently the immorality of the main character. Indeed, the French government undertook unsuccessful legal action against Flaubert in an attempt to halt the publication of the work. Although Sand defended *Madame Bovary* in an article for *Courrier de Paris*, she and Flaubert would not establish contact, apart from a brief introduction in 1857 at the Théâtre de l'Odéon in Paris, until 1863, when she wrote to him, mentioning an article she had written on *Salammbô*, his Carthaginian novel published in 1862. Thus began their friendship, which was characterized by extreme warmth, sharing, and support that would last until Sand's death in 1876.

It is possible to see this correspondence as one of the most noteworthy of the nineteenth century, for despite distinct differences in the aesthetics and literary attitudes of Flaubert and Sand, it reveals an evolution from a cordial friendship built on respect to a relationship of profound intimacy, intellectual honesty, and mutual support. That two creative temperaments with such opposing literary ideals could be so accepting and at ease with each other is remarkable. Flaubert's unfailing desire for authorial detachment and impersonal style was in some ways a burden; it led to a certain loss of freedom. A genetic study of *Madame Bovary*, for example, reveals that during revisions to the manuscript Flaubert conscientiously removed narrative elements that in traditional realistic works are intended to guide the reader, such as in Honoré de Balzac's monumental work *La Comédie humaine* (1829-1848). Flaubert strove to constrain any authorial lyricism, and endeavored, for the most part, to produce a uniformly sober style devoid of excessively descriptive details. On the other hand, in *Consuelo* (1842-1843) Sand created a turgid and effusive style, not uncharacteristic of her other works. In a letter to Louise Colet on November 16, 1852, Flaubert assesses Sand's work: "In G. Sand, one smells the 'white flowers': everything oozes, and ideas trickle between words as though between slack thighs." However divergent their vision of literary creation, Sand and Flaubert shared with each other their commitment to literature, their creative struggles and aspirations.

The initial period of their correspondence, which began in January, 1863, and ended in March, 1864, and which includes only five letters, reveals a tone of respect and admiration, present especially in Flaubert's letters, which soon develops into a restrained intimacy. Throughout their relationship, there was never any indication of romantic involvement between the two. Their bond was platonic and offered each a confidant as well as a cordial companion. It is evident from the first letter Flaubert wrote to Sand, in which he asked for a portrait of her to hang in his study in the country, that their friendship was to be based on understanding, deep affection, and esteem.

Sand and Flaubert became better acquainted at weekly gatherings of writers and artists at a private dining room of the Restaurant Magny in Paris's Latin Quarter, organized by such notables as the writer Charles-Augustin Sainte-Beuve, the artist Paul Gavarni, and the Goncourt brothers, Edmond and Jules, historians and writers. Sand was the only woman to attend such dinners as a member of the group. Flaubert and Sand met on numerous other social occasions. Many of the subsequent letters contained references to evenings spent with each other, social gatherings or plays attended together. Much of the correspondence served for finalizing future plans both in Paris and in the country.

Other passages reveal two individuals who contemplate the nature and objective of their art. Sand wrote to Flaubert in October 1886: "One writes for everyone, for all those who need to be initiated. If one's not understood, one resigns oneself to it and tries again. That's the whole secret of our unremitting labours and our love of art. What is art without the hearts and minds into which we pour it?" In the spring of 1866, Flaubert introduced into a letter an idiosyncratic use of the feminine adjective *chère* with which he modified the masculine noun *maître* or master, as he referred to Sand. This usage was continued throughout the remaining correspondence. In the same year, for her part, Sand began using the familiar *tu* when addressing Flaubert, and she did so consistently as of early 1867, while he retained throughout the correspondence the formal *vous* out of respect for a woman who was also his senior.

In one of the most poetic passages in the entire collection, dated June 14, 1867, Sand recounts a visit she once made to Tamaris, a village near Toulon on France's southern coast. Here, while botanizing, she encountered a small group of maritime gypsies who lived off their catch, spoke not French nor Italian nor the local dialect but rather a language the local people could not understand, intermarried, and were reputedly descendants of the Moors who had invaded this area in the ninth and tenth centuries. Wondering why they were held in such contempt by the local inhabitants, Sand could conclude only that once again those who are different are condemned by the majority.

In his letter of February 23-24, 1869 (which he wrote until four o'clock in the morning), Flaubert expressed his belief that sensitivity in children cannot be fostered or repressed, that basic human character cannot be altered. This statement is in opposition to one earlier made by Sand that children should be exposed only to good until reason can assist them in accepting or challenging evil. Flaubert believed that this would lead to a terrible disillusionment and that, since life is an unceasing education, everything from talking to dying must be learned. In the same letter, he indicated that he was suffering from an abominable grippe, that winter was approaching, that *L'Éducation sentimentale* was half-completed, that *Don Quixote* (1605-1615), which he was rereading, was a splendid book, that Sainte-Beuve, a rich and talented writer, should curtail his newspaper writing for the more serious writing of books. Such a letter is typical of Flaubert's expressiveness to Sand. Thoughts are expressed, are briefly outlined, and inevitably lead to others, somewhat disparate, as he attempts to inform Sand of his recent activities, both creative and mundane.

As completion of *L'Éducation sentimentale* drew near, much of the correspondence of 1869 dealt with various aspects relating to the manuscript, from the choice of the title to the reception accorded the novel by the press and critics. At this time also, Sand intervened on behalf of Flaubert to secure a higher payment for his future novel, *Salammbô*, from the publisher Michel Lévy. The publication of *L'Éducation sentimentale* brought unflattering assessments from many critics, who berated Flaubert for a perceived lack of originality and excessive descriptions. Though others such as the novelist Émile Zola praised Flaubert, the reception was sufficiently negative for Flaubert to request that Sand, who believed the novel to be original and powerful, write an article on the work; her piece was published shortly thereafter in *La Liberté*.

Her support was reciprocated in 1870, when the second installment of her novel *Malgrétout*, appearing in *La Revue des Deux Mondes*, greatly offended Empress Eugénie, wife of Napoléon III, who believed herself alluded to in a brief passage underlining the conniving ambition of the character Mlle. d'Ortosa. (The Spanish-born empress had been known as Mlle. de Montijo before her marriage to the emperor.) Flaubert was urgently contacted by Sébastien Cornu, who acted as spokesperson for the empress; she was assured by Flaubert, and later in written form by Sand herself, that the character depicted was purely imaginary. The furor that arose is less surprising, perhaps, if one considers the precarious nature of sociopolitical life at that time.

A volatile political situation had thrown confusion into French writers' lives. Expanding Prussian power and extreme tension between the two countries resulted in a declaration of war in July, 1870. Both Sand and Flaubert unequivocally condemned war, in general, seeing in it humankind's disposition to savagery. Moreover, Flaubert perceived in war an inherent mystical element that enraptures the masses. Troubled by his powerlessness to assist his country, he offered his services as a nurse at the Hôtel-Dieu in Rouen. In September, the Prussian forces were victorious at Sedan in the Ardennes; more than eighty thousand French troops, and the emperor, surrendered and became prisoners of war. Soon thereafter, the Third Republic was proclaimed in Paris. In a curious letter dated September 10, 1870, Flaubert informed Sand that he had become lieutenant of the Croisset company of the National Guard and offered a misogynistic pronouncement: "I curse women: they are the cause of all our woes." This is the most glaring of such comments, several in number, contained in his letters to Sand. The context explaining this remark is unclear. A possible explanation is that Eugénie, blamed for having encouraged her husband to follow prowar advisers, fled to England days after the French defeat in the Ardennes. Crowds in Paris were demanding her head.

A wartime disruption of postal services curtailed correspondence between the two friends until February 1871. During these few months, the war was drawing to an end. When peace was restored, Alsace and part of Lorraine were ceded to Prussia. Both Sand and Flaubert were shaken by the war; their idealism, now shattered, was not regenerated in the remainder of their correspondence. Ill health among themselves, friends, and family came to occupy much of their thoughts. Flaubert was especially preoccupied by the failing health of his mother, who died in 1872. Sand immediately offered maternal support and consolation at the loss of the person Flaubert most loved.

It is obvious from the latter portion of Sand's correspondence that her nurturing and praising nature as well as her genuine affection for Flaubert provided him needed emotional stability at a time when he was becoming more anguished, reclusive, and misanthropic. Sand, for her part, acquired a serenity that bespoke her inner peace, a spirituality that colored her view of existence as her life drew to an end. Her death, in 1876 from an inoperable intestinal blockage, devastated Flaubert, who felt that he had lost his mother a second time.

Flaubert-Sand: The Correspondence, while chronicling the social and historical evolution of nineteenth century France, offers a probing look at two complementary artistic temperaments. Sand was a constant source of consolation and reassurance to Flaubert. She openly expressed to him her belief that his work would occupy one of the most influential places in French literature, while hers would in all probability be denigrated fifty years after her death. She also acknowledged his somewhat misanthropic nature, but one is perplexed that she did not attempt to counter directly his overt misogyny. It is all the more puzzling that he should have felt comfortable expressing to her such attitudes. Given her choice of pseudonym and the nonsexual nature of their friendship, perhaps he viewed her more as a male confidant and thus felt free to make disparaging remarks about women. It is also evident from the correspondence that Flaubert needed to reveal his most personal thoughts and ideals to Sand, just as she saw herself as a nurturing influence on him. Ultimately, their relationship is testimony to their common ideal of a humanitarian life, guided by principles of truth and justice.

Kenneth W. Meadwell

Sources for Further Study

Belles Lettres. VIII, Summer, 1993, p. 48.
London Review of Books. XV, May 27, 1993, p. 9.
Los Angeles Times. February 4, 1993, p. E2.
The New Republic. CCVIII, March 29, 1993, p. 46.
The New York Review of Books. XL, June 10, 1993, p. 5.
The New York Times Book Review. XCVIII, February 21, 1993, p. 3.
The New Yorker. LXIX, July 26, 1993, p. 32.
Publishers Weekly. CCXL, January 18, 1993, p. 460.
The Times Literary Supplement. March 26, 1993, p. 5.
The Wall Street Journal. March 26, 1993, p. A8.

FOR LOVE

Author: Sue Miller (1943-   )
Publisher: HarperCollins (New York). 301 pp. $23.00
Type of work: Novel
Time: The 1990's
Locale: New England and Chicago

In this intimate novel, bestselling author Sue Miller explores the various permutations of love between siblings, friends, lovers, parents, and children, exposing subtle connections between love, pain, and death through a female writer's midlife crisis

Principal characters:
> CHARLOTTE "LOTTIE" GARDNER, the protagonist, a journalist who reaffirms her need for love during her forty-fifth summer
> CAMERON REED, her younger brother, a bookstore owner
> ELIZABETH HARBOUR BUTTERFIELD, her childhood rival and Cameron's high school sweetheart
> RYAN GARDNER, her college-bound son
> DEREK GARDNER, her first husband and Ryan's father
> JACK, her new husband, an oncologist
> JESSICA LAVER, the nineteen-year-old summer nanny to Elizabeth's children
> EVELYN, Jack's first wife, now deceased
> MEGAN, Jack's teenage daughter
> LARRY BUTTERFIELD, Elizabeth's husband

The third of Sue Miller's novels to explore love's permutations, *For Love* seems more blatant in its examination of this universal emotion through personal metaphors while also more intimate in following its heroine's journey to self-understanding than *The Good Mother* (1986) or *Family Pictures* (1990). Through discovering what she and those around her are willing to do "for love," Lottie Gardner's life is radically transformed over the course of her forty-fifth summer. Unable to remain distant from her brother's obsessive affair with a neighbor—his former high school sweetheart who is newly estranged from her philandering husband—Lottie evolves from interested observer to reluctant coconspirator in their doomed romance.

A series of unexpected events and revelations erode Lottie's own emotional armor, finally propelling her to fight to save her troubled marriage. After a freak car accident erases the separations between love, pain, and even death in her superficially secure world, Lottie comes to understand that she has avoided intimacy out of fear—as have the people she cares for most deeply—and that one cannot truly be open to love without also risking pain.

When the reader meets Lottie, she is a successful journalist who has survived a battle with breast cancer, has recently married Jack—a Chicago oncologist she met while researching an article about cancer—and is taking a summer sabbatical from her life to prepare her aging mother's Cambridge house for sale. Newly installed in a nursing home, Lottie's mother suffers from senility and liver damage, and Lottie finds it difficult to relate to the withdrawn woman whose alcoholism and anger pervaded her painful childhood. Lottie's younger brother Cameron, the unmarried owner of a

Boston bookshop, is more forgiving of their mother's flaws, so his relationship with Lottie is supportive but strained. As Lottie attempts to assuage her familial guilt by replacing the wallpaper and sanding her mother's hardwood floors with the help of her college-bound son Ryan—the primary focus of Lottie's affections since her divorce from his father during Ryan's infancy—she is forced to examine her past and make some hard choices about her future. She also suffers a mild writer's block and avoids work on her latest article, ironically an essay exploring love from societal and historical perspectives.

Things change irrevocably, however, when Lottie's emotional solitude is pierced by Cameron's renewed affair with Elizabeth Butterfield (née Harbour), who grew up across the street and whose "perfection" still proves a painful mirror to Lottie's self-doubts. Cameron has pined for Elizabeth since she married someone else, and Elizabeth's return to her mother's home with her two young children to escape her philandering husband, Larry, miraculously provides Cameron with an opportunity to win her back. Elizabeth allows herself to become involved with Cameron as much to assuage her wounded ego as out of genuine affection for him. Yet when Larry arrives to mend their rift, she chooses him over Cameron once again, understanding "what's best" in the long run for her children and herself. Her desire for a clean break from Cameron's smothering love is prevented by a freak accident that occurs when Cameron rushes to fight for Elizabeth's love—his car hits young nanny Jessica as she glides down a dark driveway to head him off at Elizabeth's frantic request. After a shocked and grief-stricken Cameron disappears the next day, Elizabeth turns to Lottie for moral support and asks her to confirm to Larry that she and Cameron were "just friends."

As Lottie discovers the obsessive nature of Cameron's love for Elizabeth, she also gains a new perspective of their shared childhood. During their adolescence Elizabeth had evolved from best friend to nemesis as the economic, social, and intellectual gaps between them widened. Secure at last in her own talent as a writer, Lottie comes to see that she and Elizabeth have long envied each other—Lottie desirous of Elizabeth's "perfection" and popularity, Elizabeth coveting Lottie's creative gifts as she fled from Cameron into a financially comfortable marriage that has proved painful.

In usual Miller style, however, Lottie's inner demons erupt to the surface as her troubled marriage receives close examination under her emotional microscope. Lottie met Jack after her battle with cancer, and they easily became secret lovers as Jack's first wife, Evelyn, paralyzed and unable to communicate after a serious heart attack, continued to deteriorate. While Jack blossomed in Lottie's love, his devotion to Evelyn's memory as a vital woman shadowed their relationship, yet heightened the tension of their furtive romantic encounters.

When Evelyn passed away at last, leaving Jack "free" to marry Lottie, the chemistry between them could not sustain this dramatic change. Unable to let go of the past, Jack has stifled Lottie's efforts to create a new intimacy between them. In Jack and Evelyn's sprawling and impersonal house, Lottie feels like an unwelcome visitor. Jack's teenage daughter Megan, who still grieves for her mother, has had trouble relating to her new stepmother, adding to Lottie's sense of being a usurper in Jack's world. Thus the return to her childhood home catalyzes both old and fresh wounds, helping clarify her real feelings for Jack and the potential for their future together. Lottie has doubts about both of these upon arriving in Cambridge, but her doubts turn to hopes when Jack arrives for a weekend visit. After their initial lust deteriorates into disagreement once again, Jack returns abruptly to Chicago, and divorce seems inevitable.

As Lottie is thrust into the midst of Cameron and Elizabeth's affair, however, she sees how precious her marriage really is. Spontaneously she decides to go home to solidify her future with Jack. Despite a debilitating toothache from a badly filled cavity, Lottie drives through the night from Cambridge to Chicago. She collapses painfully in Jack's silent house while he is at work. She is eager for him to return and discover this tangible evidence of her love; fortunately, his own hard feelings have softened since their Cambridge reunion, and he is grateful that she is also willing to work things out. Thus the specter of death overshadowing Lottie's marriage is transformed through the rebirth of love in the end.

The subtle connections Miller draws between death and life and love are summed up poignantly in a conversation between Lottie and Ryan as they drive home from Jessica Laver's funeral. Ryan is reminded of a freshman biochemistry course he took the previous year at Yale:

> And there was this section called Sex and Death. The point being that where you have partheno-genesis, you know, before you have sex, animals don't ever die. They just go on splitting forever. They're immortal. But once you get two different sexes coming together to make a third creature—to make life—there's also death.

While Miller chooses to guide the reader through Lottie's journey to love via the winding and often shadowy scenic route rather than the expressway, the final destination wherein her love is renewed and human foibles are forgiven proves worth the trip. Lottie Gardner's realistic yet hopeful discoveries about what people do for love cannot help but prompt exploration of the reader's own relationships.

Barbara Elman Schiffman

Sources for Further Study

Chicago Tribune. April 11, 1993, XIV, p. 3.
The Christian Science Monitor. June 17, 1993, p. 14.
Los Angeles Times. April 2, 1993, p. E6.
The New York Times Book Review. XCVIII, April 11, 1993, p. 7.
Newsweek. CXXI, April 19, 1993, p. 63.
Publishers Weekly. CCXL, January 11, 1993, p. 51.
Time. CXLI, May 3, 1993, p. 79.
The Wall Street Journal. May 10, 1993, p. A9.
The Washington Post Book World. XXIII, April 4, 1993, p. 4.
Women's Review of Books. X, July, 1993, p. 33.

THE FOURTEEN SISTERS OF EMILIO MONTEZ O'BRIEN

Author: Oscar Hijuelos (1951-   )
Publisher: Farrar, Straus & Giroux (New York). 484 pp. $22.00
Type of work: Novel
Time: The 1890's to the 1990's
Locale: Pennsylvania, Cuba, and Ireland

Oscar Hijuelos' panoramic chronicle of the marriage and children of Nelson O'Brien and
Mariela Montez spans a century of historic and social changes that affect the family members

Principal characters:
NELSON O'BRIEN, an Irish photographer who immigrates to Pennsylvania
MARIELA MONTEZ, his Cuban wife
MARGARITA MONTEZ O'BRIEN, the eldest of their daughters
EMILIO MONTEZ O'BRIEN, their fifteenth child and only son

Oscar Hijuelos' third novel is a wide-ranging chronicle of the lives, loves, struggles, and interrelationships of the fifteen children of an Irish man, Nelson O'Brien, and a Cuban woman, Mariela Montez, who have settled in a small town in Pennsylvania. *The Fourteen Sisters of Emilio Montez O'Brien* is presented in the form of an album of continuous memories, verbal photographs, and nostalgic images, clustered around major events in the lives of the family members. It is recounted in associative rather than chronological order, and it deliberately creates the effect of sorting through a century of family photographs, while a variety of voices comment on the images and recall their different versions of how events fitted together. Both Nelson and his only son, Emilio, are photographers, and emphasis is placed on both visual images and the importance of these pictures through time. The novel reflects on how these images, like the images of memory, represent and reconfigure past events.

The Fourteen Sisters of Emilio Montez O'Brien is told in third-person narrative, primarily from the perspective of Margarita, the book's central and most fully explored character. Margarita is the first of the fourteen daughters of Nelson and Mariela, and it is her life span and her perceptions that define the story. The novel begins with Margarita's first romantic passion as she fantasizes about a young aviator whose Sopwith Camel has made a forced landing in a nearby hayfield, in 1921, and the story immediately folds back to the moment of her birth, on the ship that was bringing her parents from Cuba to the United States in 1902. When the novel concludes, Margarita is quite elderly and bedridden, and she recalls resigning from her last library job in 1994. Her dreams and memories fuse as she rereads her mother's notebooks and floats "back like a moth through time," recalling scenes from all the eras of her life, her parents' memories as well as her own, and concluding finally with an image of her long-dead father in his own old age, holding his old-fashioned camera with its folding bellows-type canopy, as he focuses the lens on a springtime rose in a field. From beginning to end, the novel is a series of collages of roselike memories, sweet-smelling and heavy with petals of sentiment and nostalgia, like the letters Mariela receives from her beloved Cuba, "always scented with the tropics and the perfume of blossoms."

Unlike Hijuelos' first two novels, *Our House in the Last World* (1983) and the Pulitzer Prize-winning *The Mambo Kings Play Songs of Love* (1989), which center on pain, loss, and cultural displacement following the central characters' moves to the United States from Cuba, *The Fourteen Sisters of Emilio Montez O'Brien* is a sunny book, crammed with the largely successful life stories of Nelson, Mariela, and their fifteen children. Margarita, in her role as the eldest child, has known them all well. She inherits her mother's notebooks filled with a lifetime's poems and musings, visits both Cuba and Ireland to retrace her parents' footsteps, and intermittently nurtures and listens to her fourteen siblings. Margarita's awakening sexuality opens the novel, which closes with description of her extraordinarily vigorous old age, with its open and energetic sexuality, her last marriage at the age of ninety with all of her siblings present, and her thrill when she first pilots a plane at this advanced age: She is delighted that "late in life she seemed to be experiencing yet another moment of unexpected earthly pleasure." Symbolically she has progressed from falling in love with a pilot who spurns her as the book opens to flying a plane herself as well as marrying its pilot-owner.

The fifth and last section of the book, "A Few Moments of Earthly Happiness," weaves together the strands of the seventeen lives that have been described intermittently in the first four sections, in which their various life trajectories are discussed within clusters of memories that eventually fall into chronological sequence. In the last section, the family becomes more closely united after decades of pursuing separate careers and paths. The fifteen children of Nelson and Mariela all represent different forms of success and achievement. They are engaged in the musical world, in fashion modeling, in photography, in acting, in feeding the hungry, in marriages, and in parenting.

Like *Our House in the Last World* and *The Mambo Kings Play Songs of Love*, *The Fourteen Sisters of Emilio Montez O'Brien* is a family saga that examines Cuban identity in exile. All three novels provide moving and vivid portrayals of immigrant family life. Nelson O'Brien comes from Ireland with his beloved sister Kate with the intention of settling permanently in Pennsylvania, and it is mere chance that Kate's early death leads him to travel to Cuba as a photographer with the First New York Infantry Brigade during the Spanish-American War. When he returns to Pennsylvania years later with his Cuban bride, it seems a familiar place to him, but it is difficult for her to adapt to her new surroundings. Mariela's insistent, continued Cubanness is portrayed in affectionate detail throughout the novel. Mariela's few close friends share her Spanish language, and her kitchen is full of the aromas of green plaintains, black beans, suckling pig, and chicken stews. Her "absolute determination to remain Cuban in an all-American town" and her inability to learn English are accepted by her family as lovable eccentricities. Only the older children learn to speak Spanish well, but the others, including Emilio, make efforts to learn it later in life. As children all of them are steeped in their mother's sentimental idealizations of Cuba and her memories of a tropical paradise—which contrasts with the real Cuba many of them experience on later visits. Their mother's verbal photographs are vivid, and as children

sometimes at night they would think about their mother's Cuba and they would have the sensation
that the rooms of the house had been turned into a rain forest, that orchids were budding out of the
walls, that lianas were hanging off the ceiling beams, that one could hear in the distance the ocean
and smell the sea foam. . . . Cuba in the air, the atmosphere of a house in the tropics.

Hijuelos' earlier novels are predominantly about male Cuban immigrant experience
and perspective, but *The Fourteen Sisters of Emilio Montez O'Brien* focuses primarily
on women: on Mariela and her preservation of her Cuban heritage, on Margarita,
inheritor of her mother's notebooks and nostalgia, and, to a lesser extent, on Margarita's thirteen younger sisters, each made remarkably distinctive. It is Margarita who
keeps everyone in touch with the rest of the family, and Margarita whose memories
and curiosity and strength of will keep all the intertwined stories in order. In the
dominant metaphor of the book, she is the one who sorts and labels the masses of
family pictures and arranges them into a verbal scrapbook that records and reveals
their lives. After Margarita, Isabel is born, blonde and Irish-looking; she becomes the
only sister to marry and settle in Cuba. Maria, Olga, and Jacqueline pursue success in
musical careers and manage to stay together, while beautiful Helen becomes a model,
marries wealth, and becomes the most neurotic of them all. Clairvoyant Patricia ends
up living contentedly in a community of psychics, and Marta and Carmen work at
Disneyland before settling into marriages. Sensual Violeta unexpectedly becomes a
minister's wife, and the last daughter, Gloria, who struggles with her excessive and
incestuous love for her brother Emilio, finally marries a coworker who is unnaturally
attached to his mother. The other sisters, too, lead roller-coaster lives of hopes,
disappointments, and celebrations. All the sisters' afflictions and talents, mishaps and
successes, are as melodramatic as soap opera plots, yet in this gently rolling cyclical
account of alternating memories, dreams, projections, and sensuous fantasies, the
stories fuse together as inclusive of all aspects of life and seem both plausible and
engaging.

Although the novel is in large part the account of the developing lives of the houseful
of women, the sisters are grouped, as in the title, *The Fourteen Sisters of Emilio Montez
O'Brien*, in relationship to Nelson and Mariela's fifteenth and last child, Emilio. For
Emilio, this all-pervasive female presence immerses him from the beginning in
sensuality. As a child

in his sisters' company, he'd experience a sensation of pure happiness and it would seem that
everything around them emanated from those females, the world itself a fertile living thing, the earth
beneath them humming with its unseen life: roots and stems and burrowing insects and worms
aerating the soil, and flowers striving to reach the light, and the soft grass surrounding them reaching
up toward the sun, in the way that his hands would reach toward his sisters' faces.

His struggle to define himself as a man, as a soldier, as an actor, and later as a
husband and a father is made more difficult by the ease and comfort of his childhood,
when it seemed to him that "the world and everything in it emanated from a female
source" and that therefore "what was ugly in life, he thought male." To a great extent,
the fourteen sisters and their mother, Mariela, are portrayed as variants of a sensual

earth mother, fecund and imperturbable, physical and attuned to the odors of fields and kitchens and the rhythms of the sea and of sex. Hijuelos' is a very male view of femininity, and it is this male fantasy perception of women as sex, perfume, and food that Emilio feels is alternately cradling and strangling him. His father's "good and honest though confused nature" is no help to him in his effort to distinguish his individual capabilities from the collective family personality of image and legend where (as Margarita perceives) "the family's history seemed to repeat itself." Eventually Emilio seems to find comfort in becoming a photographer like his father, just as Margarita finds peace by floating through her memories of a century of family history.

In addition to photographs, a web of associations with their readings connects the family members. Nelson immigrates to the United States with his head filled with images from cowboy novels about Jesse James and Wild Bill Hickok. One of Mariela's childhood books from Cuba, *La vida en el planeta marte* (life on the planet Mars), figures in her daughters' notion of reality as well as her own. The world of *Ivanhoe* (1819) is as real to Margarita at nineteen as the Pennsylvania fields, and when she sees the young aviator, he seems to her just "like a character out of a Sir Walter Scott novel." The family saga is interwoven with re-creations of the past based on other images. Trying to imagine her father as a youth in Ireland, Margarita speculates that "perhaps he resembled those earnest Cockney boys from the Rank Organization film versions of Dickens' novels." The Montez O'Brien children have all grown up helping to run the town theater, owned by their father, and they are steeped in cinema lore from the days of silent films through the popular films of subsequent decades.

The history of motion pictures and changes in film technology are part of the book's continuous background, the social and historical settings of the events portrayed. Beginning with descriptions of Ireland, and of Cuba during the Spanish-American War, the family saga includes constant references to changing technology: the first Model T's, the Sopwith Camel, the products Nelson sells as a door-to-door salesman, and the gradual spread of electricity and modern plumbing. The course of twentieth century history in Cuba is discussed frequently, as various members of the family visit and write.

No startling events occur in *The Fourteen Sisters of Emilio Montez O'Brien*, nor is heroic action portrayed. Rather than emphasizing exceptional individuals, the novel recounts the stories of quite ordinary people who live out their lives as best they can, helping one another through the difficult moments and enjoying their times of earthly happiness. It is a novel that celebrates love, sensual pleasures, and human relationships.

Mary G. Berg

Sources for Further Study

Chicago Tribune. January 3, 1993, V, p. 6.
Library Journal. CXVIII, March 1, 1993, p. 107.

Los Angeles Times Book Review. March 14, 1993, p. 3.
The New Republic. CCVIII, March 22, 1993, p. 38.
New Statesman and Society. VI, July 30, 1993, p. 39.
The New York Times Book Review. XCVIII, March 7, 1993, p. 6.
The New Yorker. LXIX, March 29, 1993, p. 107.
Publishers Weekly. CCXL, February 1, 1993, p. 74.
Time. CXLI, March 29, 1993, p. 63.
The Washington Post Book World. XXIII, March 14, 1993, p. 1.

FOXFIRE
Confessions of a Girl Gang

Author: Joyce Carol Oates (1938-   )
Publisher: E. P. Dutton (New York). 328 pp. $21.00
Type of work: Novel
Time: 1952-1956
Locale: "Hammond," a small upstate New York city near Lake Ontario

Thirty-five years after their violent exploits, a member of a 1950's girl gang transcribes her notebooks of the teenage gang and its legendary leader, Legs Sadovsky

Principal characters:
> MADELEINE FAITH "MADDY" WIRTZ, the historian of the gang and the devoted follower of its leader
> MARGARET ANN "LEGS" SADOVSKY, the gang's first-in-command and the inspiration for most of its exploits
> BETTY "GOLDIE" SIEFRIED, the first lieutenant of FOXFIRE
> ELIZABETH "RITA" O'HAGAN, a slightly overweight young girl in the gang
> VIOLET "SNOW WHITE" KAHN, the most beautiful girl in the gang, whose beauty is used in some of its worst crimes

Foxfire: Confessions of a Girl Gang tells of girls lost in the bland, male 1950s, but girls who band together to work out a revenge for what has happened to women before and since. *Foxfire* is thus a novel about crimes against women and about what happens to the young women who unite to fight the people and the system that perpetuate those crimes.

The novel begins on November 12, 1952, when sixteen-year-old Legs Sadovsky escapes from her grandmother's house in Plattsburgh, New York—where the State Department of Human Welfare Services has sent her to get her away from her "unsuitable" Hammond home—and shows up at the home of Maddy Wirtz. That "is how FOXFIRE will come to be born." On New Year's Day, 1953, five Hammond high-school girls tattoo each other with the gang's sacred emblem—a tall, erect flame—and sign their allegiance to FOXFIRE (it is always capitalized in Maddy's chronicles). All outsiders, poor white teenagers from broken homes, they find in FOXFIRE the identity they never had in their dysfunctional families. Maddy's father, for example, is dead, her mother not available; Legs's mother is dead, and Ab Sadovsky, with his various girlfriends, may not be her real father. Under the leadership of Legs Sadovsky, the girls find love and purpose, and that purpose is aimed directly at men and at sexual exploitation.

Their first act of revenge is against Mr. Buttinger, the ninth-grade mathematics teacher who humiliates Rita O'Hagan, an insecure, overweight girl, and who also manages to touch her inappropriately whenever he gets the chance. They paint his car with his crime ("IM A DIRTY OLD MAN") and their motto ("FOXFIRE RE-VENGE!"). Buttinger never returns to school after his humiliation, and FOXFIRE has learned the power that it holds; this power will be used throughout the novel to defend women against exploitative men. "Oh Maddy-Monkey," Legs explains to her favorite, "*we're all Rita*."

Maddy finds out how true this is when she tries to retrieve an Underwood typewriter that her uncle, the owner of a men's store in Hammond, is discarding. Uncle Wimpy, seeing her, wants money for it—worse, he intimates that the thirteen-year-old Maddy can get it free for certain sexual favors. The gang sends Maddy back as a lure, and they beat up Wimpy Wirtz when he exposes himself. Maddy knows the "certain talismanic power . . . *in knowing how to write*," and the old Underwood will give it to her. More important, she has learned the power that women have in union, and that FOXFIRE gives each of its members. As she writes, "It was a time of violence against girls and women but we didn't have the language to talk about it then." *Foxfire* the novel is about the discovery of that language, as FOXFIRE the gang is about the revenge for the violence.

Yet, as in so many Joyce Carol Oates novels, less is more. Legs has befriended an old, alcoholic priest named Father Theriault, who gives the gang a semi-Marxist analysis of the class structure of history. Their initiation ceremony mixes this language of the "Revolution of the Proletariat" with biblical terminology—"Valley of the Shadow of Death." One of their first acts is a protest against a pet store that is mistreating its animals, and from which they rescue Toby, their loyal Husky.

The enemy is thus not only men but also the institutionalized ideology of the 1950's. The authorities assume that FOXFIRE is the auxiliary of some male gang, but male gangs are themselves threatened by FOXFIRE. One day, on the school grounds, Legs pulls a knife to defend a member of her gang; she is thereupon expelled from school. She steals a car, crashes it into a bridge (in a foreshadowing of the final scene of the novel), and is sent to the Red Bank Correctional Facility for Girls for fourteen months. In prison, her purpose is solidified. The truth she learns in Red Bank, she tells Maddy on her release, is "that we do have enemies, yeah men are the enemy but not just men, the shock of it is that girls and women are our enemies too sometimes." Yet the 1950's ideology is not only sexist; at the celebration party for her release, the gang shuns the two black girls Legs has invited. FOXFIRE the gang is thus a part of the very ideological structure it is trying to fight.

Legs finds a house outside Hammond where the gang can live together, as well as a car ("Lightning Bolt"), and FOXFIRE HOMESTEAD begins. The gang's purpose stays the same: When Legs finds a dwarf tied up outside another rural dwelling who is being used for sexual purposes, she burns down the house. It is hard to come up with the money for their new responsibilities, however, and "FOXFIRE HOOKING" begins; girls from the gang are used as bait to trap predatory men.

When still more money is needed, Legs proposes "the final solution." In prison, she has met the daughter of a Hammond steel magnate on a visit of charity. Invited to their mansion after her release, Legs takes the beautiful Violet, and the two lure Whitney Kellogg, Jr., into his own kidnapping. The plan goes awry, however, when Kellogg finds Christ and refuses to cooperate at all, and when his wife is so emotional that the gang is unable to relay their demands over the phone. By mistake, Kellogg is shot, the plot unravels, the gang scatters, and Legs and the girl who shot Kellogg are chased by the state police. In an accident resembling the earlier one, they slide off the road into a river and disappear.

In the epilogue, a fifty-year-old Maddy returns to Hammond, from a successful life away, and meets Rita. They reminisce about Legs, and Rita shows Maddy a 1961 newspaper photograph of Legs—with Fidel Castro. Nevertheless, what has happened to her will always remain a mystery. What remains is the devotion the other girls have for this now-legendary heroine, love that has a certain sexual tension to it. The confessions that Maddy is transcribing here from the old notebooks are her gift to Legs, their adolescent larger-than-life leader.

Foxfire explores the 1950's from the peculiar perspective of a member of a gang of girls, and in that sense it is distinctive. The narrative, broken into five parts, slips easily from first person into third and back, as Maddy describes her own feelings at the same time that she is chronicling the gang's exploits or getting into the head of Legs in prison. As with many other Oates works, readers are carried into a historical moment and into the minds of younger people experiencing it.

Yet *Foxfire* is also a 1990's novel looking backward, for its subject and its perspective clearly reveal a contemporary understanding of exploitation and sexual violence against women. In this sense, *Foxfire* resembles E. L. Doctorow's *Ragtime* (1975), which takes place at the turn of the century but has at its center a violent black gang (like the Black Panthers of the 1970's). *Foxfire* is a novel of the 1950's written with a 1990's feminist consciousness. "Rebel Without a Cause" has become "Rebels with One," Laverne and Shirley have become Thelma and Louise, as women in the novel are working out their revenge against men. "It's true as I stated at the outset of these Confessions, FOXFIRE was an outlaw gang, and became even more so as time passed. And we were pledged not to feel remorse—FOXFIRE NEVER LOOKS BACK!"

Foxfire contains many recognizable Joyce Carol Oates trademarks. In work after work, Oates has probed the situation of a naïve young woman seduced by some powerful male figure. In her classic 1970 story "Where Are You Going, Where Have You Been?" for example, the demonic Arnold Friend lures Connie to her death. In the novel *Black Water* (1992), the powerful unnamed "Senator" drives the naïve Kelly Kelleher to her death (in a car accident that anticipates the two in *Foxfire*). Oates has often depicted this power struggle from the perspective of the victim, and her psychological realism is usually overwhelming. Here, in *Foxfire*, the perspective is the same: that of members of some white underclass who are looking up at their personal and institutional exploitation. What is different is that the women in this novel have gained power against men, and gained the knowledge that language can give them to act in their power. *Foxfire* is a novel of 1950's life written with a 1990's feminist and linguistic consciousness.

David Peck

Sources for Further Study

Booklist. LXXXIX, March 15, 1993, p. 1275.
Boston Globe. August 1, 1993, p. 35.
Chicago Tribune. August 8, 1993, XIV, p. 3.
Library Journal. CXVIII, April 15, 1993, p. 127.
Los Angeles Times Book Review. August 22, 1993, p. 3.
New Statesman and Society. VI, August 6, 1993, p. 38.
The New York Times Book Review. XCVIII, August 15, 1993, p. 6.
Publishers Weekly. CCXL, May 31, 1993, p. 40.
The Times Literary Supplement. August 13, 1993, p. 19.
The Washington Post. July 30, 1993, p. G2.

FRAUD

Author: Anita Brookner (1938-   )
First published: 1992, in Great Britain
Publisher: Random House (New York). 262 pp. $21.00
Type of work: Novel
Time: The 1990's
Locale: London and Paris

A middle-aged woman who has been dedicated to serving her mother confronts life on her own and finds fulfillment

> *Principal characters:*
> ANNA DURRANT, the fifty-year-old heroine
> AMY DURRANT, her weak, demanding mother
> LAWRENCE HALLIDAY, their family doctor and Anna's former "suitor"
> VICKI HALLIDAY, his loud, vulgar wife
> MRS. MARSH, a friend of Amy Durrant
> NICK MARSH, her divorced, disillusioned son
> PHILIPPA BARNARD, her widowed daughter
> MARIE-FRANCE FORESTIER, Anna's lifelong friend and confidante, devoted to her imperious father

Fraud is Anita Brookner's twelfth novel in as many years. The last three of these might almost be considered a trilogy on the dilemma faced by docile, obedient women trying to find an authentic life in a social system that little values their strength of character, modest demeanor, and physical plainness. *Fraud* differs from *Brief Lives* (1991) and *A Closed Eye* (1992) in ending "happily"; if the three novels do form a loose trilogy, then, Brookner is suggesting that a measure of happiness is possible for the woman who finds her own way on her own terms, with or without a man.

Like Harriet Lytton in *A Closed Eye*, Anna Durrant has dedicated almost the whole of her adult life to serving others, in particular her widowed and weak mother, who suffered from a heart condition in both senses of the word. Selfishly, Amy Durrant used her daughter, exacting from her an excessive level of devotion. Moreover, Amy flaunted her own success with men by entering a new marriage late in life, to a Belgian who proved to be a bigamist and who abandoned her after extracting a considerable amount of her money. When Amy finally dies, Anna finds herself burdened with a habit of service, an almost anorexic condition, no obviously marketable skills, and the disappointment of having seen Lawrence Halliday marry a flashy, flirtatious, shallow woman rather than herself.

Also like *A Closed Eye*, *Fraud* opens with a mystery, for Anna has been missing for four months and has left no clue as to her whereabouts. The fact that she could disappear for so long and be missed only by her doctor is itself a poignant comment on her isolation. The police are called in to investigate, but they learn very little. The novel seems to be bracketed by the mystery formula, with a disappearance in the first chapter and a reappearance in the final one, yet the material in between owes more to Henry James than to Agatha Christie. Most episodes are seen either through Mrs.

Marsh or through Anna—the latter is an interesting novelistic sleight of hand, since technically Anna is a missing person. There is also an omniscient narrator who at times shades into other consciousnesses, notably Lawrence's. These shifting perspectives provide contrasting points of view but nothing that could be called kaleidoscopic or indeterminate. This is not a postmodernist exercise in the elusiveness of truth but a Jamesian foray into the recesses of the human heart and the clash of various points of view.

The basic structure of the novel, then, is a series of contrasts and dramatic scenes, some of which are presented from more than one point of view. The chief confrontations are between Anna and her mother, and Anna and Mrs. Marsh. These three form a triangle, with Anna at the apex, torn between the alternatives represented by the other two. Amy is weak, silly, dependent, mildly hypochondriacal. She exploits her daughter's desire to serve while paradoxically wanting her to find her own life and become married. Mrs. Marsh, an eighty-one-year-old widow, prides herself on her independence and dislikes Anna's meddling ministrations, even though she is happy enough to receive them when she falls ill. Moreover, Mrs. Marsh enjoys the company and services of her daughter Philippa, at whose house she spends an enjoyable and relaxing summer. If there is a streak of Amy in Mrs. Marsh, however, there is also a streak of Anna, for when her son Nick comes down with the flu, she finds the first real happiness she has known in years by nursing him as she did when he was a boy.

There are only two men of consequence in the novel, Nick Marsh and Lawrence Halliday. Nick is disillusioned; his wife had an affair and thereby "forced" him to divorce her. Since then he has hardened, defending himself against further emotional injury. His relations with women are condescending and predatory, though he is capable of sacrificing for his mother. Lawrence is very different from Nick. Reared from age ten by his widowed mother, he worked his way up, first by delivering papers and working in the family's news-agent's shop, later through university and medical school. When his doting mother died, he became excessively serious and entered a practice where much of his time has been spent on elderly women. In this way he met Amy Durrant and then Anna, and between him and Anna there arose an unspoken but genuine respect and affection. Although he and Anna never courted, both she and her mother expected an eventual proposal. When he met Vickie, however, he was immediately attracted by her looks, vivacity, and transparent sexuality. After five years, he finds himself in an incomplete marriage and acknowledges that turning away from Anna was "a monstrous wrong-doing."

As the novel progresses, then, the reader sees Anna's encounters with these and other characters and what appears to be the gradual closing down of choices she can make. Mrs. Marsh, she quickly perceives, does not want to become the object of Anna's need to serve, nor does anyone else. As a young woman, Anna studied design and decoration, but she has never seriously pursued her research into turn-of-the-century fashion, nor does she harbor ambitions to write. The business of seeing to her late mother's estate and finding a new apartment is quickly settled. During Christmas, she reflects that she is relatively wealthy and completely independent, so she visits her friend Marie-France in Paris, only to learn that at sixty Marie has become engaged. Their friendship cannot continue on its former level, therefore, and Anna is thrown back on her own meager resources. She consults Lawrence, asking for more sleeping pills, and though he tries to show concern, their interview is a disappointment to both. He is now attached to his wife much as Anna was to her mother; she looks to him for some magic word that he cannot speak. Both come away from the interview with the unspoken insight that each could have made the other happy.

The novel climaxes in a comic-tragic scene that could have come from the pen of Jane Austen. Vickie Halliday, responding to her husband's concern for Anna's health and to her own instinctive fear that Anna represents a threat, insists on inviting her to dinner. Anna knows in advance that the occasion will not succeed, that Vickie is arranging it to dismiss her, that Lawrence is too docile to prevent or salvage it. Still, she goes, having no excuse to refuse, and it turns out to be worse than anything she could have imagined. Vickie, "for whom marriage had been easily accomplished, so easily that she regarded the unmarried with contempt," shows not only contempt for Anna but malice as well, humiliating Lawrence in the process. Nevertheless, by the evening's end, Anna feels sorry for the Hallidays and stronger in herself: "Some kind of plateau had been reached."

The denouement comes in one swift chapter, during which Mrs. Marsh visits Philippa, unknowingly interrupting her affair with her art teacher, a married man. Philippa joins his class trip to Paris, where, by chance, she runs into Anna. Anna is amused to learn that she has been missed and that Lawrence reported her absence. She has been designing clothes for Marie-France and has found enough self-confidence and sense of direction to tell Philippa, "Fraud was what was perpetrated on me by the expectation of others," and to warn her, "Don't be too obedient. . . . Don't be like me." Philippa takes her advice immediately, breaking off the furtive affair with her lover.

In spite of this upbeat ending, *Fraud* is a disturbing and in many ways pessimistic look at contemporary mores. Brookner's characters and scenes often resemble Barbara Pym's; they both deal in "excellent women" who need to serve and be useful, but Brookner lacks Pym's humor and eye for satire. Brookner is evidently highly suspicious of happiness in any form, particularly in the relations—or perhaps the battle— between the sexes. Amy, Philippa, and Lawrence's mother were happily married, but all were widowed early. Nick's marriage ended in divorce; Lawrence will continue in his marriage because he lacks the courage and a good reason to divorce his wife. The suggestion emerges that a marriage can be happy only if it is relatively brief—and not always then. On the subject of parent-child relations Brookner is more sanguine. Mrs. Marsh has a healthy love for both her children, but she knows them well. Nick, especially, bothers her: His divorce was unnecessary, his treatment of women is now shabby. She loves him without liking him much.

The relationship between Amy and Anna is even more complex and problematic. On the surface, it appears that Amy simply exploited her daughter's docility, but Anna is not resentful. The rift between them resulted from Amy's unseemly second marriage, for it broke the bond of trust and eventually made them fearful. What Anna must do is not reject her mother but break "the habit of affection, rather than affection itself: she was puzzled when it was refused or denied and tended to persist in its quest, not being quite adept at reading the signals." In other words, Anna's problem is the larger one of finding authenticity, her true self, in a society that overwhelmingly defines a woman's selfhood through marriage or at least sexuality. In this respect, Brookner has made a significant change in the fictional cliché of the dedicated daughter who has sacrificed her life for an aging parent. In magazine fiction, the daughter resents her parent's demands and longs to be free. The parent's death presents the long-awaited opportunity, and the question to be answered is whether the daughter can find happiness (a man) so late in life. This set of expectations may underlie many readers' responses to the book, which is one reason that the reversal at the end comes as something of a surprise. The surprise ending may also be something of a structural flaw: The need to keep the mystery unresolved and to provide a rapid denouement conflicts with the novel's careful psychology, so that while readers see the elements of Anna's reformation, they do not see the final steps in the process. The ending may thus seem cobbled together rather than inevitable.

Yet Anita Brookner is an accomplished novelist, blessed with an acute sense of people's inner lives and a fresh, lucid style. Unlike her master, Henry James, she can deal in complexity without prolixity, in subtlety without tendentiousness. She is, then, a serious novelist who enjoys playing with the conventions of popular fiction. Brookner has much light to shed on how people live day by day, and there are many new subjects waiting for her intelligent analysis and clarity of vision.

Dean Baldwin

Sources for Further Study

The Christian Science Monitor. February 8, 1993, p. 14.
Contemporary Review. CCLXII, January, 1993, p. 48.
London Review of Books. XIV, October 8, 1992, p. 12.
Los Angeles Times. January 12, 1993, p. E2.
The New York Times Book Review. XCVIII, January 10, 1993, p. 7.
The New Yorker. LXIX, February 22, 1993, p. 183.
Publishers Weekly. CCXXXIX, October 5, 1992, p. 50.
Time. CXLI, February 8, 1993, p. 83.
The Wall Street Journal. January 20, 1993, p. A10.
The Washington Post Book World. XXIII, January 31, 1993, p. 3.

THE FURIES

Author: Janet Hobhouse (1948-1991)
Publisher: Doubleday (New York). 293 pp. $22.95
Type of work: Novel
Time: The late twentieth century
Locale: The eastern United States and Great Britain

Helen, the first-person narrator of the novel, relates her conflicts and struggles, many of which are continuations of patterns seen in the women of the previous three generations in her family

Principal characters:
> HELEN, the narrator, who tells her life story
> MIRABEL "ANGEL," her great-grandmother, matriarch of the clan
> ELIZABETH "SHRIMP," Mirabel's "good" daughter
> EMMA "GOGI," Mirabel's "bad" daughter, Helen's grandmother
> BETT, Emma's "good" daughter, Helen's lovely but severely depressed mother
> CONSTANCE, Emma's "bad" daughter, Helen's aunt
> FRANCIS LOWELL, Helen's father, whom she never knew as a child but later meets in London
> HUGH GRUNWALD, an Oxford student, Helen's fiancé and first significant lover
> EDWARD "NED," the Oxford student who becomes Helen's husband

"Photographs are not memories," says the narrator in the opening line of *The Furies*, for as Helen studies old family photographs she cannot make them mesh with her own realities and remembrances. "For a long time my mother and I lived such a solitary life, city-trapped and economically precarious, so isolated from everything resembling family or stability," Helen says, that the faded photographs of her ancestors seem "even now a kind of fairy tale." Yet familial patterns influence and shape Helen not only in her formative childhood but also in her adult relationships. The Furies of Greek mythology are avenging spirits—older even than Zeus or any of the other Olympians—who hound their victims relentlessly from place to place; here it is Helen's family background that pursues her and dominates her image of herself. In this autobiographical novel Janet Hobhouse, through her narrator Helen, richly portrays loves that cannot translate into practical help, loves that—however intense—prove unworkable, inadequate. Yet ultimately Helen believes that it is only the continuing spirit of love that matters or redeems.

In the poetic opening section of the novel, titled "Prologue," Helen relates her family lineage. Ancestors emigrated from Germany to New York and became prosperous with a Japanese import business that continued for decades, providing exotic foreign travel, pleasant summers in Upstate New York, and secure jobs for family members and additions through marriage. The business collapsed, however, with the death of Mirabel, Helen's great-grandmother, the respected matriarch who had managed it for many years after the death of her husband Samuel. Mirabel, called Angel, was "no beauty"; Helen says, "I, who did not know her long enough to fall in with the adulation,

I am the one to tell you: she was downright ugly." Mirabel and all the family seem to have believed that her looks predetermined her fate. Since she could not be a beauty like her mother, Elizabeth Woolf, she "agreed to be clever." From Mirabel on, offspring are seen as "good" or "bad" depending on looks and personality, the qualities that determine their chances for marriage, success, happiness.

As a young woman Mirabel dropped her hopes for a career and agreed to marry as her parents dictated, though it cost her a nervous breakdown. At twenty-six she wed a Tennessee widower several years her senior, and they quickly had two daughters, Elizabeth and Emma. Tennessee, as the family called him, joined the family business but had little presence in the household.

Of the two daughters, Elizabeth (named for her grandmother Elizabeth Woolf but called "Shrimp") is the "good" one—obedient, marrying properly, giving up career for family. This socially acceptable scenario is shattered, however, when her handsome husband runs off with "a peroxide starlet" and Shrimp, like her mother, suffers a nervous breakdown (though this time over the divorce rather than over marrying). Shrimp then returns home to live with her mother and later in an apartment "in stoical solitude."

The slightly younger daughter, Emma, is judged by the family as hard, daring, and rebellious. At seventeen she runs off with an older art teacher. In the first few days with Vergil she realizes that he is not the right partner for her adventures, but her parents track her down and insist that she must now marry him. Emma gives up her dream to become an artist and marries Vergil, who joins the family firm. They quickly have two daughters, Bett and Constance. Vergil is a religious fanatic who fills the household with tension, fear, and abuse. By the time Emma is thirty-two she is divorced and living as a poor would-be artist in Greenwich Village. Bett and Constance bounce between her and their grandmother Mirabel, "simultaneously motherless and overmothered."

Bett and Constance, one dark and one fair, repeat the dualities and oppositions seen in Shrimp and Emma. "Bad" Constance is a placid blonde, egotistical and self-absorbed. "Good" Bett (named for her Aunt Elizabeth) is exceptionally beautiful and graceful but chronically nervous and prone to "panics." The sisters quarrel steadily. Bett marries a tall Englishman, Francis Lowell, but finds living with him in England terrifying; within two years she suffers a nervous breakdown and comes home to New York without a husband but with a baby girl. Although originally named Constance, for her aunt, after Bett and her sister again quarrel, the baby is renamed Helen.

At the end of this extended prologue opening the novel, the six females of the family, from Mirabel to Helen herself, are summed up as "four generations of almost mystical Manichaean symmetry and Mendelian simplicity, an unassailable oval, an egg shape of female solitude."

When the elderly Mirabel dies (the year is now 1951), "bad" Emma and Constance depart on separate travels, "good" Shrimp retreats to a solitary apartment, and Bett is left with a child whom she is unable to support either financially or emotionally. Although as a child Helen knows nothing of this family background, she will be marked by it forever.

Part 1, "Women," traces Helen's history through her graduation from high school. This section of the novel is written in a simpler and more direct style suited to the discussion of the childhood and adolescent years. For Helen these are years of confusion and frustration. From age five to ten, she is parked in a dismal boarding school, her only bright moments the occasional, unpredictable visits from her beautiful and beloved mother and the summer weeks she can live with her. These fractured years follow cycles of desperate hopes, overemotional reunions, and betrayals when her mother again deserts her. Bett has similar feelings. As intensely as she wishes to be with her daughter, something seems to conspire against fulfillment. With her beauty and charm, Bett is readily hired, but she is unable to overcome her nervous attacks and cannot retain jobs. With a naïve optimism she believes that things will get better, yet she finds herself in a succession of cheaper and cheaper apartments. Helen learns to make excuses for her mother and to lie about her strangeness and poverty.

When Helen is ten, Emma returns to New York with a new husband, Bill, and Helen begins to spend much of her time with her grandmother. When Emma dies of cancer, this too seems like abandonment. Later Helen develops some friendship with her aunt Constance, but all such connections seem implicitly to betray her mother. Throughout all these years Helen's dominant emotional relationship is with Bett, the mother who loves her but is too depressed to cope. Helen, in turn, senses that it must somehow be her own fault that they cannot be together and happy.

Part 2, "Men," shows how these patterns of seduction and abandonment undermine Helen's adult relationships with men. After high school she goes to England to find the father she has never known. Francis Lowell is remarried and not eager to parent or befriend Helen. He is quick to quarrel with, lecture, and belittle Helen, though he treats her with slightly more respect when she becomes engaged.

Helen's fiancé and first significant lover, Hugh Grunwald, is a fellow student at the University of Oxford. Their love is passionate and distracting, but it ends after Hugh moves away and Helen becomes absorbed with Edward, "Ned," a poor but brilliant fellow literature scholar who has his own family problems. They are eventually married, but theirs is a stormy and tenuous connection with endless leavings and returnings, clearly following the enthrallments and heartbreaks of Helen's love for her mother. A weary tone pervades the entire section. The marriage finally ends just after Bett, the ever-depressive mother, commits suicide.

Part 3, "The Furies," in prose like a collapsing black hole, concerns the losses weighing heavily on Helen. In this section the Furies appear full-blown as disasters culminate. Helen goes again to England but becomes even more cut off and confounded. It seems no more than can be expected that her house goes up in flames, destroying all of her possessions including some of her writing, and that a man who woos her admits that he carries a sexually transmitted disease. She returns to the United States and, with desperate hope of self-repair, rents a little house on Cape Cod. The months she spends there alone are at first demon-ridden, a descent into darkness. With perseverance and numerous changes in attitude and action, however, including immersion in work, she begins a healing process. In this much-improved state she decides to go to New York at Christmas to see her friends.

The short final section, "Alone," opens with Helen seeing a doctor when she arrives in New York City. The doctor shatters her newfound glimpse of peace by announcing that she has ovarian cancer. An immediate operation indicates that the cancer is undoubtedly fatal.

In her shock and fear while she is in the hospital, Helen is surprised to hear herself say to the relatives of another patient, "You know in your hearts, don't you, that no one really dies, ever, because their spirit lives always." As she anxiously reviews her life, she concludes, "I'd loved a lot and I'd been loved, and in the end, which this seemed to be, that was all that mattered." That Helen can understand this despite the tormented loves she has known is a tribute to her and to that sense of the undying human spirit.

Janet Hobhouse was still working on *The Furies* at the time of her death from cancer in 1991, and this last section includes some fragments, which is remarkably appropriate to Helen's situation. A final paragraph-long coda shows Helen still surviving a year after her cancer treatments. Such was not the case for Hobhouse. Yet in a very real sense she too survives through her writings. Each of her previous three novels was loosely autobiographical, but none as much as this one published posthumously. *The Furies* is a captivating record of a dark life lightened by courage and a commitment to love even in the stark acknowledgment of love's limitations. The writing styles with which Hobhouse tells this story deftly connect prose form and narrative content, from the lush fantasylike re-creation of a family past to the crisp, realistic closing section which refuses to indulge in cliché or sentimentality. *The Furies* is a compelling and memorable novel.

Lois A. Marchino

Sources for Further Study

Kirkus Reviews. LX, November 1, 1992, p. 1326.
Library Journal. CXVIII, January, 1993, p. 165.
London Review of Books. XV, March 11, 1993, p. 19.
Los Angeles Times Book Review. April 25, 1993, p. 2.
The New York Review of Books. XL, May 13, 1993, p. 47.
The New York Times Book Review. XCVIII, January 10, 1993, p. 11.
Publishers Weekly. CCXXXIX, November 2, 1992, p. 48.
The Times Literary Supplement. October 16, 1992, p. 23.
The Wall Street Journal. February 23, 1993, p. A18.
The Washington Post Book World. XXIII, February 7, 1993, p. 8.

GABRIEL'S REBELLION
The Virginia Slave Conspiracies of 1800 and 1802

Author: Douglas R. Egerton
Publisher: University of North Carolina Press (Chapel Hill). Illustrated. 262 pp. $45.00; paperback $14.95
Type of work: History
Time: 1798-1802
Locale: Richmond, Virginia, tidewater Virginia, and North Carolina

Based on exemplary research and analysis, Egerton's study argues that the leaders of slave conspiracies in Virginia in 1800 and 1802 were inspired by a radical strain of urban republicanism which emphasized egalitarianism and the primacy of labor and mistakenly believed that many more whites would support their action than did

> *Principal personages:*
> GABRIEL (Prosser), an enslaved African American blacksmith who spearheaded the conspiracy in Richmond in 1800
> BEN (Prosser),
> SOLOMON (Prosser),
> JACK DITCHER,
> SAM BYRD, and
> BEN WOOLFOLK, coconspirators with Gabriel
> JAMES MONROE, governor of Virginia at the time of the rebellions
> SANCHO, a leading figure in the slave conspiracies in North Carolina and Virginia in 1801 and 1802

On August 30, 1800, Gabriel Prosser, an enslaved African American blacksmith who lived near Richmond, Virginia, planned to mass with well over one hundred of his supporters at a bridge outside Richmond, march on the city, fire and seize it, and proclaim an end to slavery in Virginia. Counting on recruits from as far away as Norfolk, Petersburg, and surrounding rural counties to strike toward Richmond at the same moment, Gabriel hoped to so disrupt and terrify the state that its leading politicians and merchants would choose to sit with him and negotiate an end to slavery rather than continue on with this bloody mayhem. If not abolition, undoubtedly more than enough mayhem would have ensued and forced white Virginians to grapple with the frightening consequences of their brutal labor system. While all the cells of rebels were coordinated, the capricious forces of nature refused to cooperate: Late in the afternoon of August 30, one of the most torrential rainstorms ever witnessed in Virginia broke forth, washing out rivers, bridges, and the hopes of Gabriel and his compatriots. Confused, scattered, and soon informed upon, the rebels were quickly apprehended; many, including Gabriel, were executed as terror gripped the whites of tidewater Virginia.

By the next year a handful of slaves who were inspired by Gabriel hoped to rekindle the rebellion. The locus of this plot shifted to the south of Richmond and was centered among the numerous black boatmen who ferried the agricultural products of southeastern Virginia down its numerous rivers to Norfolk. Plotting soon spread to northeastern North Carolina as the boatmen moved word of it down rivers flowing to the Albemarle Sound. But they were no more to realize an end to slavery than was Gabriel. As more and more people along the rivers were alerted to the plot, it became more difficult to coordinate and the chances of discovery by white authorities multiplied. By late 1801, Virginia officials began moving against the conspirators while the cover of the North Carolina action was ruined by Easter, 1802. By the summer, after numerous hangings, an anxious peace was restored.

The details and significance of these key incidents in the history of slavery in the American South are explored in detail in Douglas Egerton's new book, *Gabriel's Rebellion: The Virginia Slave Conspiracies of 1800 and 1802*. Egerton has so thoroughly combed governmental records, private papers and correspondence, and newspapers for every shred of evidence pertaining to these conspiracies that one leaves this work with a strong sense that he has uncovered it all. Egerton's excavation of covert slave communication networks—a little understood but vital part of slave culture—employed by Gabriel and the boatmen of the 1801-1802 conspiracy is breathtaking. Through a meticulous use of contemporary records, Egerton traces the ventures of such key conspirators as Sam Byrd into Petersburg and as far west as Charlottesville in the piedmont counties to organize slaves for the 1800 uprising. No one has ever delineated the world of the black boatmen who dominated the carrying trade on such rivers as the Appomattox, James, and Roanoke as Egerton has done. He reveals how these mobile laborers formed the most vital link in orchestrating wide-reaching plans of resistance in 1801 and 1802. Moreover, Egerton's treatment of the much neglected debate over colonization and gradual abolition in the Virginia legislature from 1801-1805 is the best we have and shows how that debate actually had a greater potential to end slavery than did the more celebrated Virginia debate of 1831-1832. Finally, his work is a major new exploration of the ways in which whites and blacks joined forces in specific acts of resistance against slavery in the antebellum South.

Egerton opens with a summary of how the era of the American Revolution undermined the fairly stable world of slavery that had existed in Virginia under the rule of such firm patriarchs as William Byrd, Robert "King" Carter, and Thompson Mason. Volatile tobacco prices plunged in the second half of the century and many concerned planters began shifting to less labor intensive grain production, rendering many slaves superfluous. Owners increasingly looked to manumission and the hiring-out of their slave artisans as ways to dispense of or profit from excess laborers, thus creating a caste of free and nearly free blacks who offered a dangerous example to the tens of thousands of remaining bondsmen. The religious upheaval born in New England in the late 1730's was firing Virginia by the 1760's with "New Light" Baptist preachers wandering the countryside, challenging the authority of the Anglican ministry and their gentry patrons. They disregarded racial mores and exhorted mixed groups of blacks and whites about the equality of all before God, welcoming converts from all races and stations into their congregations. The Revolution itself filled the air with talk of universal liberty and fraternal equality and the right to fight for them if they were denied by a tyrannical authority. Despite futile efforts to confine this message to whites alone, slaves too were inspired by these verities and used the social disruptions of the era to plot against bondage and to run away on an unparalleled scale. Indeed, many white patriots in Virginia were finding slavery incongruent with republican virtues and openly questioned its continued existence in the state. By the end of the century, the slaves of Virginia were laxly regulated by their overlords, excited by the vision of revolutionary freedom, and alert to doubts among whites about the viability of bondage.

Egerton's chief task and triumph has been to describe the social milieu and tensions fostered by these conditions. Since the Revolution the role of towns in the tidewater economy had expanded dramatically. By 1800, Richmond and Petersburg had become bustling commercial centers, and their demand for artisans of various skills soared. Lacking enough white artisans, merchants in these towns turned to neighboring planters whose slave artisans were often underemployed. One such planter was the young and ambitious Thomas Prosser, who in 1798 inherited about fifty slaves from his father. Seeking new ways to profit from them, he allowed a number of them to find employment in and around Richmond as artisans and return a stipulated sum to him. Among them was an energetic young blacksmith named Gabriel.

Egerton vividly re-creates the world of these urban black artisans. Although slaves, they negotiated labor contracts, supplied their own room and board, and largely controlled their leisure time. Their sense of pride in their craft and the near independence it had won them threatened the abiding bond between them and their owners. Egerton also argues that close bonds developed between white and black artisans who often labored side by side in large shops controlled by local merchants. These bonds were further cemented by interracial congeniality after work in illicit grog shops.

Urban blacks also quickly came to learn of conflicts existing between whites. White craftsmen worked with blacks for the large, powerful merchants of the towns, who controlled the assignment of work. Resentment ran high among whites against such employers, who often squeezed them by arbitrarily lowering wages or simply refusing to pay. In response, these urban white artisans developed a brand of republicanism which celebrated the fraternity of laborers and the value which labor alone imparted to products. It also disparaged the merchants, who merely marketed and profited from the labor of other people's hands.

As blacks shared work and rum with whites, they also came to imbibe this republicanism of the artisans—an ideology which suggested that not all whites were their enemies, only those who sought to steal the fruits of labor from black and white alike. Thus, when Gabriel decided to organize a mass action against slavery, he targeted the white merchants alone as his enemy and expected not only the mass of white laborers to see the slaves' struggle as theirs but also thousands of white rural Republicans.

By the summer of 1800, Gabriel witnessed another source of tension between whites: Federalists and Republicans were locked in a bitter political battle for control of the nation. Gabriel heard both rural and urban wings of Virginia's Republican party crying out against such repressive measures as the Alien and Sedition Acts, used by the Federalist administration of President John Adams to silence Republican dissent. He also saw the administration's hated efforts to close the Democratic clubs favored by urban artisans. As the national election neared in the fall of 1800, Virginia seemed veering toward civil strife as the two parties' invective and threats toward each other mounted. This deep rift in white society helped Gabriel conclude that now was an auspicious time to strike against slavery.

According to Egerton, Gabriel fatally misunderstood the character of republicanism in Virginia. Steeped only in its urban variant, he believed that the white rural Republicans shared essentially the same political principles as their presumed urban artisan brethren. This belief was fostered because the parties muted internal disputes in order to close ranks during the bitter election. In fact, however, a large gulf separated urban from rural Republicans: Urban Republicans, grounded in the experience of artisans and working people, were far more radical and egalitarian than were the rural Republicans, who represented the slaveholding elite.

This complex evaluation of Gabriel's life, ideology, and motivations is not without problems. Foremost are what exactly were the experiences Gabriel and other black urban artisans had and what was their impact upon them. Writing the history of African Americans for this period can be extremely difficult because of the paucity of documents. Egerton, aided especially by trial transcripts from both Gabriel's plot and those of 1801-1802, has done a remarkable job working with very limited resources. A license for judicious conjecture must be tolerated in writing this sort of history or else much of it might not be written at all. Egerton, however, comes close to overstepping this boundary. No evidence remains on Gabriel's specific work environment in Richmond, yet Egerton moves very close to assigning to him as actual lived experience such general characterizations as those described above from the world of artisans and blacks in Richmond. Egerton writes that "[i]t was natural that Gabriel was influenced by the bold words of the white workers he encountered in the forge and the tavern." Elsewhere he asserts that "[t]he artisans he sweated beside in the city, with their talk of a laboring brotherhood, were another [source of strength]." Perhaps Gabriel was much more likely to have had these experiences than not, but we must also bear in mind that he may not have and, even if he did, that they may not have affected him in the ways Egerton suggests.

As these judicious conjectures are treated more and more as fact, they are then used as the basis for attributing to Gabriel a mindset which the available evidence simply does not support as definitely as Egerton asserts it. The author describes Gabriel as readily aligning with white artisans after his urban education and as far more preoccupied with matters of class than of race. Egerton's relentless digging has shown that a few white laborers did seem to have offered to help, or at least listened sympathetically to, the conspirators. He has also made an important contribution by uncovering the roles of two mysterious Frenchmen—Alexander Beddenhurst and Charles Quersey—in the conspiracy. Yet it is equally true that the state's chief witness against the rebels, Ben Woolfolk, stated that "all the whites were to be massacred, except the Quakers, the Methodists, and the Frenchmen" and that numerous other rebels were quite eager to kill whites, including one who stated that "I could slay the white people like sheep." Egerton downplays the likely racial animus of the rebels in order to have them more nearly conform with his model of the secular, urban artisan who was driven far more by class analysis than racism. Egerton makes the reader recognize that racial barriers were more permeable in the socially unsettled world of the postrevolutionary tidewater and that some—both black and white—may have surmounted them. But until he can supply us with much more evidence than probably exists to establish that the rebels abandoned deep-seated racial animosities and suspicions, what we know about the divisive force of racism in Virginian and American history will force us to question this sort of neat, large-scale alliance between white and black laborers, regardless of the depth of their exposure to republicanism.

Egerton draws too sharp a dichotomy between the worlds of African Americans in the countryside and those in the towns. According to the author, rural slaves were communal, religious, and Africa-influenced, while their urban counterparts had been transformed by mobility and town life into independent, secular, and republican individuals. This distinction is drawn not only to once again force Gabriel to conform with Egerton's model of republican urban artisans; it is also intended to show why Gabriel was unable to communicate effectively with rural slaves and thus largely failed to enlist their support for the plot. Gabriel's "association with politicized white artisans pulled him away from the religious traditions of the quarters," both evangelical Christian and African. Unable to merge his political aspirations with the rural slaves' deepest religious hopes, he could not rally them to opt for rebellion. Yet this ignores the degree to which these slaves who hired out their time in towns regularly moved between the towns and the countryside and had spent most of their lives there. Gabriel hired himself out both in and outside Richmond and regularly visited his wife, Nanny, and other kin in and around Prosser's farm. Save for two years or so, all of Gabriel's life had been spent on Prosser's rural plantation. Why should some time in a town intimately interwoven with the surrounding hinterlands totally void Gabriel's memory of the ways of the people he had lived among for most of his life, leaving him unable to communicate in those terms? Even if he had decided to reject those ways—and there is no evidence that he had—he should still have been able to apply them. Indeed Gabriel's brother, Martin, used powerful Christian imagery to sanction resistance at a "preachment" attended by Gabriel and many other conspirators, and one set of the condemned rebels spent the night before their execution singing hymns and worshiping. One might viably argue that Gabriel did wield religious imagery in the countryside and with some favorable response. Yet Egerton adheres to the position that Gabriel and his closest associates eschewed all religion because his rigid rural-urban dichotomy confines religious beliefs and less political thinking to rural blacks and can thus help explain apparent failures in rural recruiting.

This dichotomy also leads Egerton to overstate the extent to which Gabriel believed white rural Republicans would assist him. Most of Gabriel's exposure to the conflicts between the Republicans and the Federalists occurred in Richmond, and perhaps the favorable experiences that he may have had there with white Republicans led him to review his attitudes on those in the countryside. But it stretches credulity to imagine that Gabriel was so altered by his urban experience as to believe that rural Republicans, whose continued commitment to slaveholding could not have escaped him, would suddenly assist his conspiracy. The failure of Gabriel's Conspiracy did not lie here but rather in the weather and foremost in the frightening impediments to organizing slave resistance over a broad area.

These comments on Egerton's use of evidence are extensive because they address the linchpin of his argument—the role mobility and town life played in shaping the Virginia rebels of 1800 and 1802. But they are offered as an adjustment to that argument, not as a dismissal of it. Egerton's emphasis on the impact of urban artisan republicanism on Gabriel is thoroughly appropriate. That experience probably was what led Gabriel to conceive the extensive plot he did. Egerton, however, tends to ignore or downplay the impact of other equally important experiences whose influence the evidence suggests continued to operate upon Gabriel. Nevertheless, this is a compelling and pioneering book which will challenge all scholars of slavery to duplicate its high standards of research and analysis.

Peter P. Hinks

Sources for Further Study

Choice. XXXI, February, 1994, p. 987.
Publishers Weekly. CCXL, September 6, 1993, p. 89.
Richmond Times-Dispatch. October 31, 1993, p. F5.
Virginian Pilot. November 14, 1993, p. C3.

GARBAGE

Author: A. R. Ammons (1926-   )
Publisher: W. W. Norton (New York). 121 pp. $17.95
Type of work: Poetry
Time: The 1980's and 1990's
Locale: Florida

Garbage *is a long poem that attempts to place garbage, nature, and humankind into a tenuous and provisional order*

Garbage is A. R. Ammons' attempt to write a long poem, the modern equivalent of the ancient genre of the epic. The modern long poem may have a unifying theme, but it is, as Northrop Frye has suggested, a "discontinuous epic." It relies on short lyrical sections rather than an overall narrative. It is, as Alfred, Lord Tennyson said in *In Memoriam* (1850), "short swallow flights of song."

The style that Ammons chose for the poem is significant as a structuring principle. It is written in long free-verse lines. The structural unit is the couplet, but these are not heroic couplets that rhyme and are separate units in themselves. These couplets run on; they do not rhyme, and there is minimal punctuation. The couplets give the reader a sense of order, while the lines run beyond the confines of the couplet. The run-on couplets mirror the movement of the poem's affirmation and disavowal of order.

Garbage begins not with an invocation to the muse, as the epic does, but with a message being sent down the poet's back by "creepy little creepers" to tell him that it is time to write "that great poem/ the world is waiting for." He cites William Carlos Williams on the importance of producing such a poem, since "someone somewhere may be . . . dying" because it has not appeared. Yet the poet is resistant. He may now be "wasting" his life in teaching poetry, but he is settled; he can live on social security and does not need the challenge of the great enterprise that the long poem would represent. Furthermore, who would the long poem be for? Who would be the audience? Are "fuzzy/ philosophy's abstruse failed reasonings" needed? Yet he does agree to answer the call and write the poem, although he is still filled with doubts. Humankind may be in a "crusty world, heading nowhere, doorless," but will the poem overcome that emptiness? The purpose of the poem, it is clear, is to move the reader to some emotional change. It cannot and will not rely on argument or try to persuade the reader.

The second section of the poem announces the theme: "garbage has to be the poem of our time because/ garbage is spiritual, believable enough// to get our attention." Ammons describes landfills as "ziggurats," the modern equivalent of Egyptian pyramids, so garbage takes on an ancient form. In the tradition of Walt Whitman, Ammons attempts to unify all the diversity of the world, including elements that are unpoetic. Nature is his subject in nearly all of his poems, and he insists here that "nature models values." He announces that this work will be a "scientific poem." His "science," however, contains idealism that overcomes decay; matter may be destroyed but spirit remains: "in the abiding where/ mind but nothing else abides, eternal." He ends the section by speaking of his dead: his mother, his father, his dogs. They too are subject to a transforming process: "what/ were they then that are what they are now." This is an ambiguous statement that does not affirm transcendence. There seem to be many claims of universal transcendence in the poem, but Ammons questions his own affirmations, balancing the optimism with moments of pessimism or doubt. The movement of the poem, then, is a dynamic struggle between these two views; it is not a clear and logical process or even a dialectical one.

Once Ammons has accepted the challenge of the long poem and announced its subject, he structures the poem in eighteen sections that are filled with affirmations and denials; he even contradicts his own assertions. It is a loose and nonlogical but finally dramatic process that both defines the place of garbage in the modern world and affirms what humanity's ultimate fate is. The poem can best be discussed by tracing some of Ammons' major themes in all of their complexity and contradictions to see how he arrives at a resolution of opposites.

The first of these oppositions is order and disorder. Ammons tries out a number of descriptions of the nature of order and disorder. For example, he comments on the flaws in his students' writing that can lead to discoveries. Errors will be cured as "all motion is/ translated into form." The third section ends by commenting that shape will be given to "false matter." Some form and order will finally come out of all elements, even garbage, which is the decay of those elements. Ammons uses an image of decay, "hamburger meat left out." Yet even that is part of the shaping order and the "renewing change."

Ammons then invokes the "high assimilations" as he continues to insist on the assurance that there will be a beneficial transformation to all apparent misshapen and disordered things, especially garbage. So the most significant design of the poem is to affirm again and again not stasis but change, transforming processes that Ammons sees constantly at work. "Everlasting fire" is a central image in the poem, as it embodies and aids the transforming process. The section ends with a traditional affirmation: "all is one and one is all." This would seem to be the final answer that Ammons has been seeking. Yet the poem must confront the negative side more fully before it can find any true or lasting resolution.

The seventh section confronts the problem more deeply. Ammons first affirms that everything will return and nothing is truly lost. Yet he sees the immediate future as disease and delays, obstacles to renewal: "strokes, hip replacements,/ insulin shots." There may be pain and "pathology," but "wonder" will go on in the midst of the negative elements. Ammons sees "wonder" and "miracle" in nature, and these balance or drive out the pessimism when he is overcome by the garbage of the world. He closes the section, however, by indicting the very instrument he is using: words. Words get in the way. He knows the language of the song of the bluejay, but "grooming does for/ baboons what words do for us." Words only inflate; they do not give the vision humans need to overcome despair.

The ninth and tenth sections confront evil more directly than before. Ammons acknowledges the law of the jungle that exists in the natural world, where animals prey on each other. Nevertheless, the fear that such a view would create must be overcome. First, one must not try to avoid risk, since that in itself is more "risky." He ends by asserting: "being alive/ means being alive to mischance's chances." Ammons celebrates an openness to the world and its changes. He accepts the lack of order while finding order in local areas and moments of insight. He refuses the closure of either a positive or a negative finality.

The poem continues to question the concept of benign order as Ammons summons up humankind's ancestor, the Neanderthal. He seems to be questioning what is called "human" nature, since humankind's ancestor is a predator and it has not left those traits behind. Apparently, there is no evolution of morals in humanity. The end of the tenth section reverses the usual affirmation by seeing a different sort of process: Everything people eat eventually becomes garbage. Ammons momentarily sees garbage as an end rather than an element that is subject to the refining processes. This moment of doubt, however, is later rejected.

The eleventh section of the poem begins the turn from the negative view. According to Ammons, everything must be seen under the "aspect of eternity." He now sees miracles rather than predators in nature. Still, he will assert no beliefs, since they would leave him with a static view. He is, however, willing "to sit with us." This moment of quietness and openness does lead finally to the perception of a design. "I can think of nothing I'd/ rather do than think of skateboard loops out/ of skateboard bowls, the various designs in the/ momenta: the rising up in rounds over the rims." It is a local and temporary order, an Ammons way of seeing order in the midst of disorder.

The twelfth section indicts words once more, as Ammons compares them to garbage. Here, however, he changes "saying" to "singing" and asserts a principle: "rights consistent with/ other rights." This sounds more like saying than singing, and Ammons admits that it "says little." Yet it is meant to be the only belief he is willing to stand by, simplistic as it may be. The section ends with one of Ammons' central themes, "departure and return." People die, but along with all other things, including garbage, they return. Such a promise of renewal and change is necessary to free humans from the finality of death.

Ammons revises this assertion in the fourteenth section. He states that people will not be "forever in forever." He is now willing to accept the finality of death and to be "glad that I was here." After asserting this finality, however, Ammons claims that everything is "awash in/ ideality, ideal meaningless, ideal absurdity,/ ideal ideas." Ammons wishes to affirm the "ideal" nature of the world, but he will not do so by denying the negative elements.

The fifteenth section begins by acknowledging the presence of "waste" in nature and humankind. The seeds of a leaf may be crushed on the highway and never become a tree; a man may sing into alcohol and drugs and be dead "at 32." Ammons' wailing "at loss" is displaced, however, by an image of light. Nature renews itself, and there are "furrows of definition." There is another moment of doubt as Ammons notes the pain and dying of his father, but he asserts that there is order: "the sequences having become/ right because that is the way they had to run." Still, the certainty of unity and order remains "always beyond." Order is affirmed although it can be explained.

The next section of the poem attempts to resolve some of the opposites. "Life" comes from each person as he or she supports lice and other creatures. What is "real is spiritual." People may prey on others, as all animals do, but they are also "praying." The law of the jungle does not dominate; people are spiritual beings. There are no "blank walls." The poem began with a "doorless" world, but now Ammons affirms that all directions lead to the spirit; there are no dead ends.

In the seventeenth section, Ammons accepts all apparently discordant elements in the world because "we do not want a world without a bitter aftertaste." All things will not "degrade," but will become "light," an image of transformation from the material to the spiritual. "True matter" has no "matter," which he exemplifies with "sound," something that is present but is not weighted down by substance. He closes this section with a paradox: "reticence is fullness in emptiness." Words are necessary to convey the vision, but they can impede its discovery.

The last section of the poem affirms most fully the order in the universe, although Ammons does qualify that assertion. He first speaks of an "outer design" that stands for the local orders he sees. There is a "divinity in all of us," and "all is holy even garbage." There are "completion" and "miracles," but the poetry that deals with those contains, as it must, tension rather than "resolution." The poem then closes with an image rather than an assertion. As he reaps "the peripheries," Ammons asks, will his "hardweed seed and dried roughage" flower? Will they be found "above snow . . . in a painted hold"? It is an image of life returning and resting above the obliterating power of the snow. It is seen in a perfect moment of beauty, sufficient to itself. This is the best and only vision one can have in this world. Ammons' epic may contain philosophical ideas, but it gives the reader, finally, images of reality, not answers.

Garbage is structured as a journey through affirmation and reticence to arrive, finally, at an image of unity that is beyond logic. Ammons has consciously chosen garbage as a subject so he can show how it is a part of the harmonious universe. In the American tradition of Walt Whitman and Ralph Waldo Emerson, he maintains an optimistic view of nature and humankind. Yet he gives full representation to the voices of disorder, so that he can more truly affirm the spiritual essence of the world.

James Sullivan

Sources for Further Study

Booklist. LXXXIX, August, 1993, p. 2032.
Boston Globe. October 17, 1993, p. 17.
The Christian Science Monitor. December 30, 1993, p. 13.
The Chronicle of Higher Education. XL, December 1, 1993, p. A6.
Library Journal. CXVIII, August, 1993, p. 108.
The New York Times Book Review. XCVIII, December 12, 1993, p. 30.
Publishers Weekly. CCXL, July 19, 1993, p. 239.
The Virginia Quarterly Review. LXX, Winter, 1994, p. SS31.

GATES
How Microsoft's Mogul Reinvented an Industry—and Made Himself the Richest Man in America

Authors: Stephen Manes (1949-   ) and Paul Andrews (1949-   )
Publisher: Doubleday (New York). Illustrated. 534 pp. $22.50
Type of work: Biography
Time: 1955-1992
Locale: Seattle and Redmond, Washington, and Albuquerque, New Mexico

This biography traces the career of William H. Gates III, head of Microsoft Corporation, and his relationship to the growth of the personal computer industry

> *Principal personages:*
> WILLIAM GATES, cofounder and chairman of Microsoft
> PAUL ALLEN, cofounder of Microsoft
> JOHN SHIRLEY, president of Microsoft from 1983 to 1990
> MICHAEL HALLMAN, president of Microsoft from 1990 to 1992

The subtitle of this new biography of William H. Gates, chief executive officer of Microsoft Corporation, may be long and cumbersome, but it accurately describes the book's dual direction. Although in biographies of most famous people—and Bill Gates has indeed become famous—readers may be interested in the personal life behind the public persona, what inquiring readers really want to know about Gates is how he became a billionaire while still in his thirties. The answer lies in the other half of the subtitle: Gates has become so identified with the meteoric rise of the personal computer (PC) industry that to talk about the industry is to talk about him, and to talk about him is to talk about the industry. Microsoft Corporation's disk operating system MS-DOS has always been the software brains behind IBM and IBM-compatible computers, and its graphic user interface, Microsoft Windows, is quickly becoming the favorite "look and feel" of those same computers.

Although many may think it is unusual that Gates became so wealthy so young, the fact of the matter is that in the beginning of the volatile computer industry, youthful millionaires were the norm. This business enterprise began as a boy's passion—technologically oriented Tom Swifts tinkering with parts from Radio Shack. Yet while other boy millionaires, such as Apple computer originators Steve Jobs and Steve Wozniak, were playing around with soldering irons, young Bill Gates—only in the eighth grade at the time—was learning how to speak the first primitive language of the new machines: Beginner's All-Purpose Symbolic Instruction Code, or BASIC. For Gates, as for many other young hackers, what began as a fascination with a new toy quickly became an all-consuming passion.

Gates and other computer enthusiasts initiated not only an industry but also a lifestyle. With his freckled face, shock of unruly hair, oversized glasses, and unkempt appearance, Gates practically invented the stereotype of the computer nerd. Not only has he graced the cover of *People* and of *Time*, but he became as familiar a figure of parody in the Sunday comic section as he is in the business section—his greasy hair as recognizable as the protruding ears of Ross Perot. Despite his youthful, awkward appearance, Gates has proved himself a consummate, sometimes cutthroat, executive. Even when he had to order Shirley Temples at businessmen's power lunches, he was able to take the starch out of the button-down collar professionals at powerful IBM.

Gates learned to program on large time-sharing mainframes when he was still in junior high in Seattle, Washington. Consequently, when the Altair 8800—the forerunner of all small personal computers—was introduced in the January, 1975, issue of *Popular Electronics*, Gates was ready for it. He and his friend Paul Allen contacted MITS, the small company assembling and selling the Altair in Albuquerque, New Mexico, and brashly informed its people that they had developed a full-blown BASIC program that would run on the primitive machine. It was the first, but not the last, time that Gates would promise something he did not have and then pressure himself and those around him to deliver it.

For those familiar with computers, Stephen Manes and Paul Andrews' account of the origins of Microsoft is the stuff that hackers' dreams are made of. Staying up all night repeatedly, filling yellow legal pads with assembly-language code, spending hundreds of hours at a keyboard, Gates and Allen finally put together a program that they could take to Albuquerque. Computer enthusiasts will appreciate the tension-filled moment in New Mexico when Allen typed in the memory size for the program—an impressive seven kilobytes—and the primitive teletype machine typed out "READY." Stunned that the program actually worked, Allen typed "PRINT 2+2." When the machine clacked out the remarkable response "4," the meteoric rise of Bill Gates from unknown nerd to best-known nerd in America had begun.

During Microsoft's Albuquerque period, Gates, a mere twenty, hired programmers who were as obsessive as he was—willing to work overtime, live on pizzas and cokes, and compete with the boss himself; in short, he learned how to run what has become the most powerful software company in the world. In the late 1970's and early 1980's, as new personal computers were developed—many of which have since become outdated museum pieces—all of them needed a programming language, a set of instructions, to be of any value. Developing programs for Commodore, Apple, Tandy Corporation, and Texas Instruments, Microsoft grew fast enough that it was able to break away from the poorly run MITS, whose persistent hobbyist orientation made it unable to keep up with the rapid changes in the industry.

By the time Gates moved to Bellevue, Washington, a suburb of Seattle, Microsoft had already had its first million-dollar sales year. Yet selling computer languages such as BASIC and FORTRAN for microprocessors was only the beginning. The next important phase of Gates's rise to fame and fortune was his frequently rocky relationship with mainframe computer giant IBM, which, in response to the small desktop challengers, was working on its own PC and looking for an operating system to run on it. The story of Gates's meeting with IBM executives in Boca Raton, Florida, in a suit too big for him and a tie he bought at the last minute on the way to the meeting, has become one of the minor legends of the computer industry. The deal to make Microsoft DOS the essential system on those original IBM PCs—a deal that transformed a child's hobby into an indispensable part of American business—simultaneously marked the reinvention of the computer industry and the most important step in the rise of Bill Gates to his status of richest man in America. Since August 12, 1981, when the IBM PC was announced, computers and the software that makes them useful have leapfrogged each other in ever-increasing speed and sophistication.

Even as this second phase of Gates's career was getting under way, the groundwork for the third phase was already being laid. During the same summer as the release of the IBM PC, Steve Jobs, Chairman of Apple Computer, rightfully concerned at the new competition IBM posed for the Apple II, discovered a new way to interact with computers that had been developed at Xerox PARC's think tank in California's Silicon Valley—something that was to be called a GUI, or graphic user interface. Making use of pictures instead of text and a point-and-click device, breezily called a mouse, instead of esoteric commands, the new interface promised to take computers out of the hands of the "nerds" and "tekkies" and put them in the hands of "the rest of us." Both Jobs and Gates saw the possibilities. In the hands of Jobs and his colleagues at Apple, the new interface became the Macintosh computer, which would take the place of the old Apple II technology displaced in the marketplace by IBM. In the hands of Gates and his "smart guys" at Microsoft, it became, after a number of false starts, Windows.

As Manes and Andrews tell the story, the decade of the 1980's was for Microsoft an era of transformation from a developer of low-profit operating systems to a factory for high-profit applications. With the rise of the Macintosh, or Mac, Gates's word-processing program Microsoft Word soon became the program of choice for the platform, displacing Apple's own less-powerful MacWrite. The company also developed a spreadsheet and a database management program for the Mac, as well as similar programs for computers running DOS. Gates's real passion, however, was the development of a graphic user interface that would forever guarantee Microsoft's indispensability to the users of IBM-compatible machines. As early as 1983, in an interoffice directive, he announced his plan to discontinue investment of resources in character-based IBM PC applications and to implement products for the Mac that could be ported to Windows. As the authors put it, Gates was "betting the company on GUIs."

Yet over the next eight years, Gates's grand plan for Windows did not materialize; the early versions of the product were slow, confusing, awkward, and downright clunky. In spite of these failures, thanks to Gates's energetic business tactics, a bit of luck, and the staying power of the company's mainstay DOS, Microsoft grew bigger and Gates grew richer. When the company went public in March 1986, a number of Microsoft executives became instant millionaires.

The final section of this book details Gates's many battles—the fight with charismatic Philippe Kahn of Borland over who would dominate the development of programming languages (Borland practically outprogrammed and underpriced Microsoft out of business), the extended court case with Apple over Gates's having stolen the "look and feel" of the Macintosh interface (Apple lost, the judge ruling that it had borrowed the whole thing from Xerox PARC in the first place), the competition with IBM over whether IBM's OS/2 operating system or Microsoft's Windows would dominate the GUI field (Windows eventually pulled out ahead), and continuing investigations into Microsoft's supposed violation of antitrust laws by monopolizing the market for computer operating systems, operating environments, computer software, and computer peripherals.

In spite of all the conflicts and roadblocks, the 1990's began with even greater success for Microsoft. In a highly publicized New York rollout show on May 22, 1990, a day his mother called the "happiest day of Bill's life," Windows 3 was announced, and many computer commentators agreed that Microsoft had finally gotten it right, at least for the most part. Under the banner "Witness the Transformation," after the biggest software party ever held, Windows began to sell at the rate of eleven thousand copies a day. After DOS 5.0 was released on June 11, 1991, with a great deal of fanfare and marketing savvy, even though it was the same cumbersome DOS that it had always been, more than one million units were shipped in the first six weeks. By the end of the year, eight million copies of the old standby were in circulation.

What does the reader know about Bill Gates the man after reading this book? One knows fairly little: that he likes to drive fast, that he is absent-minded, that he abhors what he calls "decadence" or "big spending," that he does not suffer a fool gladly, that he has a highly inflated sense of self, that he still does not wash his hair enough, and that he never did gain a sophisticated look. Yet this book is not about Gates the personal man, but Gates the businessman, a man whose life has followed the course of the computer industry. Although it is true that much of his success is owed to his being in the right place at the right time—especially for the original deal with IBM—the real secret of his prosperity is probably the same secret of all highly successful people: obsession. For Gates his life is his work. Since his work is the most highly influential industry in the world today, he has become a central icon in American culture, a driving force, a man to be reckoned with. Although the world of computers changes faster than any other enterprise in the United States in the late twentieth century, there is every indication that Bill Gates will continue to be at the center of that industry for a long time to come.

Charles E. May

Sources for Further Study

Business Week. February 15, 1993, p. 20.
Byte. XVIII, February, 1993, p. 222.
The Christian Science Monitor. February 4, 1993, p. 9.
Fortune. CXXVII, February 8, 1993, p. 138.
The New York Times. January 10, 1993, p. C8.
Newsweek. CXXI, February 1, 1993, p. 72.
Publishers Weekly. CCXXXIX, December 29, 1992, p. 56.
The Wall Street Journal. January 27, 1993, p. A14.
The Washington Post Book World. XXIII, February 14, 1993, p. 3.

GENET
A Biography

Author: Edmund White (1940-   )
Publisher: Alfred A. Knopf (New York). Illustrated. 728 pp. $35.00
Type of work: Literary biography
Time: 1910-1986
Locale: Primarily France; also Africa and the United States

A trailblazing, painstakingly researched but unduly detailed life of France's brilliant outlaw-author

> *Principal personages:*
> JEAN GENET, a French writer
> CAMILLE GABRIELLE GENET, his mother, who abandoned him to a foundling home
> EUGÉNIE REGNIER, his foster mother
> JEAN COCTEAU, a distinguished writer who became his most important literary patron
> JEAN-PAUL SARTRE, France's most famous post-World War II philosopher, who wrote an important study of Genet
> JEAN DECARNIN,
> LUCIEN SÉNÉMAUD,
> DECIMO,
> MOHAMMED EL KATRANI,
> TACKY MAGLIA, and
> ABDALLAH BENTAGA, his leading lovers
> BERNARD FRECHTMAN, his English translator and agent
> MARC and OLGA BARBEZAT, his publishers and friends

In 1952, the world-renowned Jean-Paul Sartre, at the height of his career, published a critical disquisition, more than six hundred pages long, on a comparatively unknown homosexual writer-thief, Jean Genet. This remarkable work, *Saint Genêt: Comédien et Martyr* (*Saint Genet: Actor and Martyr*, 1963), accepted and celebrated many exaggerated, half-true claims that Genet had made about his past: that he had "chosen" to become a prostitute and a thief, that he had "chosen" to be homosexual, that he had been socially alienated by having been abandoned by his mother, unloved by his foster parents, poorly educated, and generally cast out of bourgeois society, and that he had pursued an alternative, depraved lifestyle in order that, by doing evil, he would discover the evil that he had been told possessed him. According to Sartre, Genet's counterculture experiences made him the perfect existentialist hero, for he decided to play the role into which life had already placed him. Sartre was delighted to publicize his version of Genet as someone who, born in a meaningless and hostile world, willed the existence he had been given. It was as if Jean-Jacques Rousseau had come across a live Noble Savage who would confirm his views of primitivism.

Edmund White, American-born but a long-term resident of France, himself a novelist, essayist, and declared homosexual, devoted six years of research and writing to producing this first full-scale life of one of the twentieth century's most gifted, complex, and baffling writers. Winner of the National Book Critics Circle Award for biography, White's study is candid, comprehensive, balanced, stately, and sympathetic but by no means sycophantic. Unfortunately, it is also cluttered by too many lengthy quotations and the often pointless appearances and disappearances of a multitude of minor characters. White asserts a goal for his work that he fails to achieve: "Few people may think a sexual and social deviate . . . can provide an example to others, but this biography shows how such a transformation can be wrought." It does not. The moral or aesthetic example of Genet's life and letters eludes White's—perhaps anyone's— understanding. To be sure, White's book is indispensable as a repository of information about Genet. It constitutes, however, only a stepping-stone toward more perceptive interpretations that future scholar-critics will devise.

Little can be discovered about Camille Gabrielle Genet, who listed her occupation as "governess," age as twenty-two, and status as single when she signed in at a public welfare clinic and gave birth to Jean on December 19, 1910. In French, *genet* is the name of a common broom plant, frequently growing in the countryside, and Genet often fantasized about his name as establishing his roots with French soil and history. His shadowy mother kept him for seven months, then abandoned him to the French state, which classified him as Public Assistance Ward Number 192.102 and placed him with a carpenter and his wife, Charles and Eugénie Regnier, in the small town of Alligny-en-Morvan, 150 miles southeast of Paris.

Genet passed a placid, Catholic childhood in dull and dreary Alligny, with his kind, gentle, and indulgent foster parents. He read everything in the school library, became a choirboy, and scored first in the primary-school leaving examinations when he was twelve. In consequence he escaped the fate of the vast majority of welfare boys, who ended up as farm workers. Instead, he was sent as an apprentice to a printing shop near Paris, one of Public Welfare's best educational centers. Eugénie Regnier had died in April, 1922.

When did Genet begin his lifelong habit of stealing? In his autobiographical *Journal du voleur* (1948; *The Thief's Journal*, 1954), Genet states that he began pilfering from his foster family when he was ten, felt no remorse, but was deeply wounded when he was found out, "enough to make me want, deliberately, to be what other people made me blush about being." Was Genet accurately representing his feelings? Sartre thought so. As for his homosexuality, which Genet acknowledged about the same time he started to steal, he explicitly rejected Sartre's notion that he had voluntarily decided to be gay. The attraction to males came first, then the determination to act out his sexual nature.

Only two weeks after he had enrolled in trade school, Genet ran away from it. This began a lifelong habit of taking flight when he felt insecure or threatened. He escaped school repeatedly until he was sentenced to a notoriously repressive agricultural reformatory, Mettray, near Tours. Genet fictionalized Mettray's harsh discipline and homosexual ambience in the confessional novel *Miracle de la rose* (1946; *Miracle of the Rose*, 1966). He spent two and a half years there, and despite—perhaps because of—the colony's cruelty and severity, he came to regard Mettray as an extended family.

Confinement there taught Genet to value conflicts that he would dramatize in his novels and plays; honor versus treason, domination versus submission, authenticity versus dishonesty, fidelity versus disloyalty, piety versus blasphemy, love versus abandonment. In his sexual affairs Genet was a passive, "femme" partner, the most sought-after in the colony.

In March, 1929, he left Mettray to enroll in the army, doing various periods of service in Syria and Morocco and taking the opportunity to read extensively, particularly in Stendhal, Fyodor Dostoevski, and André Gide, identifying strongly with the outsider-criminal Raskolnikov in *Prestupleniye i nakazoniye* (1866; *Crime and Punishment*, 1886). Between service tours Genet traveled widely in Spain and Eastern Europe, stole frequently, lived as a prostitute, beggar, and chronic vagabond, and established a lifelong appetite for reciprocal power relationships, both in his own conduct and in his books: robber-robbed, executioner-victim, judge-accused, guard-convict, officer-enlisted man. During the 1930's, he was arrested numerous times, was tried for desertion from the army or for stealing, and was given prison terms of two to five months.

When the German army humiliated France in the spring of 1940, Genet was serving his eighth sentence; he was freed the June day that German troops entered Paris. He found his political sympathies divided: His hatred of France's Third Republic and admiration of physical violence and domination inclined him toward Fascism. His empathy with the dispossessed, however, disposed him to the Left. The scales were decisively tipped leftward by his first long-term lover, Jean Decarnin, who became a Resistance member.

Between December of 1940 and March of 1944, Genet spent a total of twenty-one months behind bars, using his confinements to compose several books. By 1947 he had written his quartet of novels: *Notre-Dame des Fleurs* (1944; *Our Lady of the Flowers*, 1949); the previously cited *Miracle de la rose*; *Pompes funèbres* (1947; *Funeral Rites*, 1968); *Querelle de Brest* (1947, revised 1953; *Querelle of Brest*, 1966). He had also done a direct autobiography, the *Journal du Voleur*, and a long, boldly erotic poem, *Le condamné à mort* (1942; *The Man Condemned to Death*, 1965).

Jean Cocteau read this poem, admired it, asked to meet Genet, and became his most influential literary patron for some years—but never his lover. Cocteau urged Genet to stop stealing: "You are a bad thief, you get caught." Genet ignored the advice and was once more arrested for theft: books, as usual. By this time he was facing his twelfth conviction, and with it confinement for life as an incorrigible offender. Cocteau hired a top-flight attorney in Genet's behalf and testified in court that he considered Genet "the greatest writer of the modern era." The judge gave Genet a three-month sentence; had he added one more day, Genet would have spent the rest of his life behind bars.

Perversely, Genet kept on stealing books and selling them to bookstores. When the French courts discovered, in 1948, that he had failed to serve all of one of his sentences, he again faced life imprisonment. This time Cocteau and Sartre wrote a public letter to the president of France, Vincent Auriol, asking him to pardon Genet and declaring that "the example of Villon and of Verlaine convinces us to ask you for your aid for this very great poet." Additionally, a manifesto for Genet was signed by more than forty artists, including Colette, Paul Claudel, and Pablo Picasso. As a result, the President of the Republic proclaimed a pardon for Genet in August, 1949—provided he stayed out of legal trouble for the next five years. This time Genet did—or, at least, was not apprehended. White writes that Genet's reputation for theft had become "picturesque" by the late 1940's, with society hostesses hoping that he would pilfer some of their possessions when he was their guest.

Genet met Sartre and his companion, Simone de Beauvoir, for the first time in May, 1944. Beauvoir was amazed that, though self-taught, Genet had the unselfconscious poise of people who are highly educated and cultured. Sartre's childhood and youth had been comfortably privileged—all the more reason for him to be fascinated by what he considered Genet's victimization by society, his lonely status as an outcast. He and Genet spent many hours together in intense conversations for several years, as a result of which Sartre wrote his immense homage. Genet refused to be blinded by Sartre's dazzling brilliance, insisting that he had far more literary talent; as for Beauvoir, he dismissed her as having "the sensitivity of a fork." In 1947, Sartre arranged to have Genet win a literary prize awarded by France's most distinguished literary jury. One juror who opposed the award was Albert Camus, who disliked Genet's sumptuous prose style, disapproved of his conduct, and found his increasingly hard-left politics increasingly distasteful.

By 1948, Genet had completed his fiction, his sparse production of poetry, and his first play, *Les Bonnes* (1947; *The Maids*, 1954). White points out that his very success had robbed him of the marginal status on which his autobiographical works depended. In 1949, the most prestigious French publishing house, Gallimard, began to publish him. He was no longer society's scabrous scourge; he was in danger of becoming its darling.

Yet Genet insisted on remaining solitary, anarchic, antisocial, inassimilable, and often disloyal. A young American living in France, Bernard Frechtman, became his English-language translator, sometime agent, and good friend. His renditions were generally regarded as excellent. Yet Genet ignored fifteen years of Frechtman's extraordinary devotion by harshly breaking with him in 1961. Genet told an interviewer that, were either Frechtman or Sartre to die tomorrow, he would not think about them twice. In 1952, he ruptured his friendship with Cocteau, writing him, "I have owed you a great deal. But I no longer owe you anything." In the early 1940's, Genet was befriended by Marc and Olga Barbezat, who comforted him during his prison stays, published his work, encouraged him during his frequent spells of depression, and lent him money when he needed it. Even though Genet purloined some of their rarest books when he was their house guest, they never reproached him. Since the Barbezats treated him as a family member, he eventually felt compelled to rupture the intimacy. In 1956, he signed a contract to have one of his plays published by Marc Barbezat. Later Barbezat discovered that Genet was planning to have Gallimard issue the same work. They exchanged sharp letters. Several years later, Genet threatened Barbezat with a thrashing because he had issued a new edition of one of his books without Genet's approval. Barbezat insisted that Genet *had* given him permission. Their friendship ended.

In the years 1955-1957 Genet wrote his three most famous plays: *Le Balcon* (1956; *The Balcony*, 1957), *Les Nègres* (1958; *The Blacks*, 1960); and *Les Paravents* (1961; *The Screens*, 1962). He reworked his old obsession with power relations into taunting parables about race, social caste, and colonialism. His drama suited the frenzied theoretician Antonin Artaud's notion of a "theatre of cruelty," fashioning rites of sacrifice and exorcism, sadism and masochism, revolt, conquest and submission, seeking to strip away the lies and impostures of the respectable world.

After this burst of creativity, Genet's artistic imagination lay fallow most of the remainder of his life. He entered, serially, into a number of long-term liaisons, of which the most intense was with Abdallah Bentaga, who was eighteen when he encountered the forty-six-year-old writer. Bentaga was an Algerian acrobat for whose high-wire lessons Genet paid; he also supported Bentaga's widowed mother for years. In 1959, Bentaga fell from the wire and irremediably injured his knee. Genet bought a small circus for his lover. When Genet eventually became interested in another man, Bentaga committed suicide by slitting his wrists. Genet took a vow, which he nearly kept, never to write again. He was to publish only occasional essays, as well as one last major work, *Un captif amoureux* (1986; *Prisoner of Love*, 1992): part memoir, part dialogue, part tract, part epic.

Genet's interests turned to radical politics as he sought to alleviate the depression that increasingly engulfed him. He cheered on the French student revolt of May, 1968, then covered, for *Esquire*, the turbulent U.S. Democratic National Convention that summer, even though he had virtually no English. In his *Esquire* article Genet, while supporting the hippies and Yippies, shocked his readers by praising the superbly muscular thighs of Chicago police. In 1970, he published an essay hailing the German Red Army Faction, a terrorist group headed by Andreas Baader and Ulrike Meinhof. Yet his longest and deepest allegiance went to the Palestinians, whom he befriended for eighteen years and to whom he devoted most of the content of his last book. Genet was aware that his sympathies for the Palestinians arose from their disinherited status. He told an interviewer in 1984, "The day the Palestinians become a nation like other nations, I will no longer be there."

Genet worked feverishly to finish *Prisoner of Love* in 1985-1986, knowing that throat cancer was killing him. He died April 15, 1986, after having corrected the book's second set of proofs. His body was transported from Paris to a cemetery in Lavache, Morocco, near Bentaga's remains.

Gerhard Brand

Sources for Further Study

London Review of Books. XV, June 10, 1993, p. 3.
Los Angeles Times Book Review. November 21, 1993, p. 1.

New Statesman and Society. VI, June 25, 1993, p. 41.
The New York Review of Books. XL, October 21, 1993, p. 8.
The New York Times Book Review. XCVIII, November 7, 1993, p. 1.
Newsweek. CXXII, November 29, 1993, p. 74.
Publishers Weekly. CCXL, September 20, 1993, p. 54.
The Times Literary Supplement. June 11, 1993, p. 7.
The Wall Street Journal. November 10, 1993, p. A18.
The Washington Post Book World. XXIII, November 14, 1993, p. 1.

GENIE
An Abused Child's Flight from Silence

Author: Russ Rymer
Publisher: HarperCollins (New York). 221 pp. $20.00
Type of work: Psychology
Time: 1970-1984
Locale: Los Angeles County, California

> Genie *recounts the history of an abused child rescued from twelve years of extreme isolation, and the scientific excitement and controversy surrounding her treatment*

> *Principal personages:*
> GENIE, an abused child
> IRENE, her mother
> CLARK, her father
> SUSAN CURTISS, the author of a dissertation about her
> DAVID RIGLER, a psychologist, her foster father
> JEAN BUTLER RUCH, her teacher
> NOAM CHOMSKY, a well-known psycholinguist

In November of 1970, a stooped young girl, led by her nearly blind mother, shuffled into a Los Angeles County welfare office. Since that day, the unfortunate child has found her way into the pages of countless textbooks of linguistics. Russ Rymer's *Genie: An Abused Child's Flight from Silence* tells the story of that tortuous and extraordinary journey. At once a fascinating piece of investigative journalism, a lively presentation of important ideas in the field of linguistics, and a serious study of the ethics of human research, Rymer's highly readable narrative weaves together three threads: the child's sad personal history, the fascinating questions about language and human nature that scientists hoped she might answer, and the intense and bitter controversy that arose over her treatment and scientists' right to study her.

Genie, as she is called in the textbooks to protect her real identity, was the fourth child born to Clark and Irene, a couple living in Temple City, California, fifteen miles from Hollywood. Clark did not want children, in part because of his extreme intolerance for noise. When their first child was born, Clark was infuriated by her crying and put the baby in the garage, where the two-month-old infant soon died. A second infant died shortly after birth because of the incompatibility with the Rh factors in Irene's blood. The third child, a boy, survived intact.

Born in April, 1957, Genie, too, had Rh disease. Although she received a blood transfusion soon after birth, her pediatrician noted that she had kernicterus, a condition resulting from Rh incompatibility in which bile pigments deposited in the brain and spinal cord cause degeneration of nerve cells. How much the Rh disease may have affected Genie's nervous system will never be known, because Clark's abuse soon compounded the damage.

Convinced that the child would be profoundly retarded, Clark believed that she needed his "protection" from an evil world. He sewed a harness with which to fasten

Genie, twenty months old, to a potty seat in a small bedroom. She was sometimes removed from the potty chair at night and placed in a restraining sleeping bag inside a cagelike crib. Alone and naked except for her harness, Genie was to remain in her tiny room day after day, month after month, for almost twelve years. She heard few sounds except distant traffic, saw little but the walls, the crib, the potty chair, and two plastic raincoats hung on the wall. Her mother was forbidden to have any contact with her except for feeding her baby food in silent haste. Genie heard no human speech except her father's occasional curses when he beat her for making a sound.

Irene, imprisoned in her own home, lost her sight during these years. When Genie was thirteen and a half, Irene finally left her husband after a violent argument. Seeking services for the blind, she happened into the Los Angeles County welfare office with Genie in tow. She and Clark were promptly arrested and charged with child abuse. Clark soon shot and killed himself; Irene was later acquitted. Genie, meanwhile, was admitted to Children's Hospital of Los Angeles.

At age thirteen, Genie weighed only fifty-nine pounds. She was incontinent and could not chew or fully extend her limbs. She could speak only three or four words and understood fewer than twenty. It was her lack of language that was to embroil her in scientific controversy.

The intellectual history of the struggle to understand the nature and significance of human language is both long and complex. Rymer does an admirable job of presenting this history with a vitality not found in any textbook. The history of language study goes back at least twenty-seven hundred years, to King Psamtik I of Egypt, who isolated two infants in a shepherd's hut, forbade the shepherd to speak to them, and waited for their speech to reveal the original human tongue. Ever since, students of human nature and human language have been excited by the rare occurrence of "natural experiments" that echo King Psamtik's experiment—"wild children" who, through some accident, have grown up isolated from human language. Until Genie, the most famous of these was Victor, the Wild Boy of Aveyron, discovered in France in 1800.

As Rymer points out in some detail, Victor's history and Genie's show uncanny parallels. Both unfortunate children were burdened with the high hopes of scientists looking for answers to fundamental questions. Is language an innate, built-in, biological function like digestion? Or does one learn it from one's environment? This question reflects a deeper, more fundamental question concerning human nature itself: Are the attributes of humanity (language among them) innate? Are we born with them? Or are we born "blank slates" to be molded by our environment into more or less human creatures?

In 1970, when Genie stumbled on the scene, these age-old questions were very much in the air, thanks in large part to the recent work of psycholinguist Noam Chomsky. Chomsky's work focused on syntax, the rule systems that govern all languages. He proposed that all languages, despite their superficial differences, share a deeper, universal grammar and that knowledge of this rule system is innate, built into the human brain. He and other students of child language acquisition pointed out numerous examples of the subtle and complex linguistic rules that very young children follow flawlessly—rules of which even adults rarely have explicit knowledge. Other linguists were arguing with equal force for the importance of the environment in children's acquisition of language. At about the same time that Chomsky's ideas were creating an unprecedented stir among linguists, neuropsychologist Eric Lenneberg proposed the critical-period hypothesis—the idea that children can acquire a first language only up to the age of puberty, but no later. Like Chomsky, Lenneberg tied language closely to biology.

Rymer devotes a large part of his book to fascinating and informative discussion of these issues in linguistics. His discussion is based on his interviews with Chomsky and with several other distinguished linguists, including Susan Curtiss, whose dissertation was to become the single most significant published research concerning Genie. Rymer's discussion is enlivened by his ability to capture, with a novelist's skill, the personalities behind the theories. As an outsider to the field of linguistics, he succeeds in presenting complex scientific arguments in straightforward language.

Into the controversy over the nature of language and how and when children acquire it stumbled Genie—essentially without language and at the very end of the supposed critical period for its acquisition. Could she provide answers? There was great excitement in the scientific community—and bitter debate. Researchers eager for the chance to make a scientific coup competed vigorously for access to the child and the right to carry out their research. No one could agree on what was ethical treatment and what was exploitation. Incredibly, there was serious debate over whether Genie's own needs should take precedence over the needs of those who wished to investigate her.

The viewpoints of the principal actors in this drama are irreconcilably different. Rymer does not attempt to draw conclusions but allows each person involved to speak for himself or herself. What emerges is a complicated tale driven by the mixed motives common to human beings everywhere—ambition, jealousy, compassion, curiosity, anger, love.

After eight months in the hospital, Genie lived for two months with Jean Butler Ruch, a special education teacher associated with the hospital, who resented the intrusions of scientists into her home and was embittered by her failure to be appointed Genie's foster parent though the child was attached to her and had thrived in her care. Instead, Genie lived for the next four years in the home of David Rigler, a psychologist at the hospital and administrator of several research grants to study Genie's development.

When the grants were not renewed, because of the lack of substantive research coming out of the project, Genie went home to Irene, who had remained on the periphery of her daughter's life for five years. Unable to cope, Irene soon placed Genie in foster care, in a situation that unfortunately turned out to be abusive. Of the fifteen scientists who had been involved in studying Genie, only Curtiss maintained contact with her and worked vigorously to get her removed from the abusive foster home.

Ruch, meanwhile, launched a vituperative letter-writing campaign against the Riglers, with whose treatment of Genie she vigorously disagreed. She eventually encouraged Irene to sue the researchers and Children's Hospital for breaches of patient confidentiality and unethical treatment of Genie. The legal wrangling, including skirmishes over control of Genie's pathetically small financial resources, occupied five years. Irene eventually placed Genie in a home for retarded adults, and the scientists lost contact with her. The few who saw or heard of her reported that she had regressed, becoming more withdrawn, disturbed, and uncommunicative.

What, finally, emerged from the bitter struggle over rights to research Genie? Did Genie help to answer the question of the origin of language? Genie's mental abilities grew by leaps and bounds after her release from her prison, demonstrating that she was not, in fact, retarded. She acquired an extensive vocabulary and demonstrated an uncanny ability to communicate nonverbally. Yet she failed to acquire the rules of syntax, and her speech retained the condensed and truncated style of a telegram with the words strangely ordered. Neurological testing showed that she was processing language entirely in the right hemisphere of her brain, unlike most people, in whom the left hemisphere is dominant for language. Curtiss suggested that perhaps language input from the environment is necessary for normal development of the left hemisphere, which, when it does develop normally, has a unique, innate capacity for grasping syntactic rules. This implies that at least the syntactic aspect of language may have an innate component, but that it requires an environmental trigger for its development.

Yet there are too many unknowns in Genie's history to allow any clear conclusions to be drawn. It is not known what effect Rh disease and kernicterus may have had on Genie's brain early in her life. It is not known how much exposure to language she may have had before she was confined at twenty months of age—an age by which most normal children are already talking in two-word "sentences." It is not known how language development—and brain development—is affected by extreme social isolation and emotional abuse. Of the many scientists invited to study Genie, only Lenneberg wisely declined, observing that the waters were too muddy for good science.

Rymer interviewed several prominent scientists involved in later research on language and the brain. Much of this research has looked at deaf children, deprived of language from birth but not, like Genie, of the social and emotional context for its use. Scientists would probably have arrived at much of their current understanding of human language even if Genie had never fallen into their midst.

Looking back, those who studied Genie agree that her greatest impact on their lives was finally personal, not scientific. Although she remained profoundly disturbed, Genie was immensely lovable, a human being of great courage and charm who used the parts of language she did learn to share her unbearably painful history, her mind and heart, herself.

Rymer's disturbing tale makes clear that the most significant lessons arising from Genie's "case" do not finally concern language at all, but an even more fundamental aspect of human nature: the age-old conflict between self-interest and compassion, the continuing uncertainty over what it means to treat human beings humanely. While

Genie will be of especial interest to students of language, the ethical and human questions Rymer raises are of universal concern.

Jennifer Ward Angyal

Sources for Further Study

Boston Globe. April 27, 1993, p. 61.
Choice. XXXI, October, 1993, p. 369.
Kirkus Reviews. LXI, March 1, 1993, p. 288.
Lancet. CCCXLII, August 7, 1993, p. 355.
Library Journal. CXVIII, April 15, 1993, p. 114.
Los Angeles Times Book Review. July 4, 1993, p. 11
New Statesman and Society. VI, May 14, 1993, p. 33.
The New York Times Book Review. XCVIII, April 25, 1993, p. 12.
Publishers Weekly. CCXL, April 5, 1993, p. 60.
The Times Literary Supplement. August 6, 1993, p. 27.

GERALD BRENAN
The Interior Castle

Author: Jonathan Gathorne-Hardy (1931-   )
First published: 1992, in Great Britain
Publisher: W. W. Norton (New York). Illustrated. 660 pp. $35.00
Type of work: Literary biography
Time: 1894-1987
Locale: England and southern Spain

Jonathan Gathorne-Hardy's detailed biography of Gerald Brenan is an intimate portrait of this English writer who spent much of his long life in Spain

> *Principal personages:*
> GERALD BRENAN, an English writer and student of Spanish culture
> GAMEL WOOLSEY, the South Carolina-born writer who became his wife
> DORA CARRINGTON, a disturbed young woman who was his obsessive love interest in his youth
> RALPH PARTRIDGE, his closest friend
> MIRANDA CORRÉ, his daughter by Juliana Martín Pelagrina, a Spanish peasant girl
> JOHN HOPE-JOHNSTONE, an eccentric Englishman
> LYNDA PRICE, a talented young art student who became his companion

Gerald Brenan will be best known to Americans as the author of three excellent books on Spain: *The Spanish Labyrinth: An Account of the Social and Political Background of the Civil War* (1943), *The Literature of the Spanish People, from Roman Times to the Present Day* (1951), and *South from Granada* (1957). He had one close tie to America in his wife of thirty-eight years, Gamel Woolsey, a poet from Aiken, South Carolina, who was a half-sister to John Woolsey, the federal judge who in 1933 declared that James Joyce's *Ulysses* (1922) was not obscene.

Brenan's father, Hugh Brenan, was a British army officer who had to retire early because of deafness. He was an irascible husband and father and a lifelong worrier about money who tried to control Gerald by parceling out funds in small amounts. Gerald's mother, Helen Graham, came from a *nouveau riche* family near Belfast. She was married to Hugh in 1892, and Gerald was born in 1894 in Malta. The difficult birth left Helen Brenan so ill that Gerald was nursed for five months on the milk of two Maltese she-asses. The Brenans were to have one other child, Blair (1901-1980).

Before his discharge for deafness, Hugh Brenan's military career took his family to South Africa and to India; part of Gerald Brenan's childhood was spent at these outposts and part in Ireland. In 1902 the Brenans rented a house in Miserden, a small village near Cirencester in south-central England, and they lived there for fifteen years. Gerald entered Winton House prep school in 1903, and five years later (with the lists being full at Harrow) he moved up to Radley, where he probably read the Hispanophile George Borrow's *The Bible in Spain* (1842) and *Wild Wales: Its People, Language, and Scenery* (1862). It seems likely that the sexual inhibitions that troubled Brenan all of his life were rooted in these years at Radley.

Hugh Brenan was a difficult husband, and he was not the most liberal of fathers. His firm intention was that Gerald was to forgo an Oxbridge education and train at Sandhurst for a military career. Gerald, however, had other ideas. Under the spell of the freethinking poet Percy Bysshe Shelley, he concocted with John Hope-Johnstone, "one of those delinquent upper-class Bohemians who leaven the English class system" and eleven years Gerald's senior, a mad walking tour that they planned would take them to central Asia. The whole undertaking had to be kept secret.

The two adventurers escaped on August 26, 1912, Brenan absurdly disguised in a gas-fitter's suit under a bulky military overcoat and wearing a slather of dye on his hair. He threw away a futile fake mustache and buried his clothes with a trowel. The trip more or less lived up to the comic note of this beginning. Hope-Johnstone decided to winter in Italy, and on December 23, Brenan started on foot from Venice with two pounds in his pocket, two blankets, a blue umbrella, a cake of soap, a Bible, and William Blake's poems. He was headed for the Pamir Mountains, three thousand miles somewhere to the east. In January, lost in Bosnia in a snowstorm, he gave up, and a month later he was in Venice, waiting to be rescued by a greatly annoyed father. The experience, a failure in the literal sense, as it had to be, nevertheless stiffened the young Brenan's faith in himself, and he was to be an indefatigable walker all of his life.

Hugh Brenan's next plan for his rebellious son was service in the Indian police, but Gerald was saved from that career by the outbreak of World War I and service as a commissioned officer. His distinguished combat career was interrupted by a severe shrapnel wound that hospitalized him for three months. Seven months later he was back at the front and served so valiantly in France that he was awarded two medals, including the Croix de Guerre.

During his service Brenan met two people who were to influence his life powerfully. The first was Ralph Partridge, a fellow officer, a University of Oxford graduate, and a handsome man whose ease around women Brenan envied greatly. Partridge was to remain Brenan's most intimate friend for forty-five years and a correspondent to whom Brenan—a tireless letter writer—wrote many long, fluent dispatches about his work and his personal entanglements.

A second, and exceptionally distracting, force that came into Brenan's life was a young woman named Dora Carrington, whom he first heard of in 1915 from Hope-Johnstone. Carrington stuck in Brenan's imagination from Hope-Johnstone's description, and in 1919 at an inn in Oxford, she appeared—with Partridge. She was a year older than Brenan, an art student and a bisexual. She evolved a compatible liaison with the homosexual Lytton Strachey and through an odd chemistry was to obsess Brenan for a decade. When Strachey died in 1932, Carrington killed herself with a shotgun.

Brenan went to Spain in 1919 and for nineteen months lived in the small Berber village of Yegen, in the southern mountains near Málaga. The conditions were primitive—no running water, and a lavatory that consisted of a hole in a plank spanning the chicken run—but demanding physical circumstances always suited Brenan. He was to be back and forth to Yegen until 1924, when he left for five years, and his dogged pursuit of Spanish history and literature got its start in Yegen's grand setting.

Brenan finally freed himself from Carrington in 1929, and after a brief period of living with and caring for a beautiful prostitute named Lily Holder, he made directly for Yegen and what became the great sexual experience of his life. Juliana Martín Pelagrina came from a destitute family, and Brenan hired the fifteen-year-old girl as a maid. Despite comic episodes with his jealous housekeeper, Brenan seduced Juliana and for eight months enjoyed a passionate affair that astonished him. In April, 1925, however, Brenan gave her a gramophone and seven hundred pesetas, dumped her on Paco, a more than willing local replacement, and returned to England without knowing that she was pregnant.

Back in England, living at East Chaldon, Brenan met Gamel Woolsey in 1930. Woolsey was born on Breeze Hill plantation in Aiken, South Carolina, in 1895, and by 1921 she had gravitated to New York's Greenwich Village. She soon married an irresponsible New Zealand journalist, Rex Hunter; she lived with him in bohemian poverty in Patchin Place and associated with writers such as E. E. Cummings and Theodore Dreiser. When Brenan met her, Woolsey was in the fifth year of an emotionally draining menage-à-trois with the writer Llewelyn Powys and his wife, Alyse Gregory; the circumstances were right for both Brenan and Woolsey to begin a new undertaking together. Although they were not formally married until 1947, their thirty-eight years together until her death in 1968 were a great satisfaction to both of them.

In 1934, the two returned to southern Spain, this time to Churriana, where they settled in and began to raise Brenan's three-and-a-half-year-old daughter—renamed Miranda Woolsey Brenan. The Spanish Civil War forced the family's return in 1936 to England, where they took up residence at Bell Court, Aldbourne, Wiltshire. When the Blitz began, Brenan joined the Home Guard and got his first major book, *The Spanish Labyrinth*, ready to publish.

By 1949, still at Bell Court and with both parents dead, Brenan suffered an agony of lust for his eighteen-year-old daughter and personally conceived and supervised her deflowering by a young Spanish friend. Brenan was a lifelong unabashed voyeur, resorting to telescopes and stealth. On one occasion he excitedly called Partridge to watch a beautiful girl taking a bath next door. Partridge's view through Brenan's telescope was a letdown: "Gradually, the steam cleared [on the girl's bathroom window] and there emerged a rather fat middle-aged man drying himself."

The next two decades were eventful and generally happy. Miranda married a young doctor, Xavier Corré, in 1951, *The Literature of the Spanish People* was published to high praise in 1951, and on January 7, 1953, Brenan and Woolsey arrived once more at their home in Churriana. Brenan worked hard at his writing and was known as a serious Hispanist, and visitors such as Cyril Connolly and Bertrand Russell (who made determined advances to Gamel) came and went.

Brenan's escapades in search of love continued unabated, as he became infatuated in 1957 with another Carrington, Joanna, niece of his earlier obsession. A manipulative young woman, Hetty MacGee, who came with the standard hippy baggage—art school, jazz musicians, drugs, sexual adventuresomeness, and a heroin-addicted husband—enlivened his life. In 1959, when Brenan was sixty-five, he ended up in Tangier with MacGee dressed like a demented harem outcast, hitchhiking to the Atlas Mountains. At one point they rode 130 miles in a taxi with seven Berbers and a ram. Brenan became violently ill with influenza and finally collapsed with a high temperature after he was offered a sheep carcass to eat at a Berber dance. He got back to Churriana barely alive. (Whatever one thinks of the propriety of such activities, they cannot go unnoticed in the life of a man of sixty-five.)

Woolsey was diagnosed with breast cancer in 1967, and she died the next year at Churriana. Brenan's grief at her death was genuine, but before the year was out he had taken into his home as his companion a beautiful twenty-five-year old art student named Lynda Price. Price did her duty faithfully by Brenan, and for the next sixteen years he was mostly happy. In 1969 they sold the house in Churriana and built a new house not far away, near Alhaurín el Grande; a year later they bought a car, and Brenan learned to drive at age seventy-five.

Although Brenan could only yearn impotently for Price, it was difficult for him to accept Lars Pranger, the thirty-seven-year-old Swedish painter with whom she began an affair in 1973. The two artists were married five years later. Brenan worked his way through that crisis, and Price managed to divide her time between him and her husband. Inevitably, by 1984, aged ninety and beset by all the expected infirmities, Brenan became too much for her to cope with, and friends in England arranged that he leave Spain for Greenways Residential Home in the London suburb of Pinner.

The denouement would have been difficult to invent. A young Spanish poet and admirer of Brenan, Eduardo Castro, came to believe that Brenan had been more or less kidnapped back to England; with several Spanish officials who wanted the eminent scholar to live out his days in Spain, Castro had the exhausted nonagenarian whisked back to Madrid. Brenan was so confused that he thought he had been to China and had returned to Spain speaking Chinese. Back at Alhaurín, in the house he and Price had built, Brenan died on January 19, 1987. As he had requested, his body went to the medical faculty at Málaga.

Frank Day

Sources for Further Study

The American Scholar. LXII, Autumn, 1993, p. 626.
Booklist. LXXXIX, March 15, 1993, p. 1289.
The Guardian Weekly. CXLVII, July 26, 1992, p. 28.
Kirkus Reviews. LXI, February 15, 1993, p. 196.
Library Journal. CXVIII, March 15, 1993, p. 84.
London Review of Books. XIV, August 20, 1992, p. 17.
Los Angeles Times Book Review. May 2, 1993, p. 3.
New Statesman and Society. V, July 17, 1992, p. 47.

The New York Times Book Review. XCVIII, May 16, 1993, p. 12.
The Observer. July 12, 1992, p. 57.
Publishers Weekly. CXL, February 22, 1993, p. 79.
The Spectator. CCLXIX, November 21, 1992, p. 43.
The Times Literary Supplement. July 31, 1992, p. 5.

GHOSTS

Author: John Banville (1945-   )
Publisher: Alfred A. Knopf (New York). 245 pp. $21.00
Type of work: Novel
Time: The late twentieth century
Locale: An unnamed island

A postmodern mystery that raises questions it has no intention of answering, most intriguingly on the reality of works of the imagination

> *Principal characters:*
> THE NARRATOR, formerly a convict, now assistant to Professor Kreutznaer
> PROFESSOR SILAS KREUTZNAER, an art expert
> LICHT, the Professor's typist
> FELIX,
> FLORA,
> SOPHIE, and
> CROKE, four of the seven castaways who stay briefly on the island
> VAUBLIN, an eighteenth century Dutch painter

Is it that Anthony Hopkins has become so powerful and pervasive an icon of contemporary culture that it is no longer possible to see the world that stretches from *The Silence of the Lambs* (1991) through *Howards End* (1992) and *The Remains of the Day* (1993) to *Shadowlands* (1993) except through his, which is to say his characters', eyes? Or is it, rather, that the repression for which Hopkins is surely cinema's modern master has become so pronounced an element of postmodern culture, the flip side as it were of late capitalism and carnival excess, the "haunted ashen look" on the faces of the characters in Don DeLillo's paradigmatic postmodern fictions? Whatever the answer, *Ghosts*, Irish writer John Banville's ninth novel, is surely a work with a role or two for Hopkins, though the repression here is just as certainly of a different order, less a mask for the psychologically perverse than an occasion for the stylistically and intertextually dazzling. No less intricate in design than intriguing in its "coagulating" plot, and no less lyrical in its language than ludic in its structure, *Ghosts* is a work not of supernatural chills but instead of comic terror, at once painterly, theatrical, dreamlike, learned, and mad (the madness not of Edgar Allan Poe but of Vincent Price playing Poe). Its subject—to the degree that it has one—is the relationship between the real and the imagined, the old art-versus-life business done up in postmodern drag.

The complications start early. The novel begins on an island with the arrival of seven castaways whose day's outing came to a sudden end when their drunken captain sailed their boat onto a sandbank. There is Sophie, the black-clad, "mildly famous" photographer whose work-in-progress, on various ruins, is entitled *Tableaux morts*. Then there is the beautiful Flora, "like one of Modigliani's girls," who claims to be twenty-one but who may be two or three years younger and whose job it is to care for the three children, Alice, Pound, and Hatch "with his pixie's face, violet eyes and pale little clawlike hands." Finally there are the two men, the aged Croke and the enigmatic Felix, "a thin, lithe sallow man with bad teeth and hair dyed black and a darkly watchful eye." Those already on the island prove no less curious and no less literary in their lineage. There is the once-famous art expert Professor Silas Kreutznaer; his typist, Licht, a man of indeterminate age who has a wonderfully improbable penchant for self-improvement schemes and who, as it turns out, owns the house in which he seems little more than a servant; and the novel's unnamed narrator.

Echoes of William Shakespeare's *The Tempest* can be heard throughout Banville's novel (as it can through so many postmodern, postcolonial, and postmasculinist texts—Peter Greenaway's *Prospero's Books* [1991], John Edgar Wideman's *Philadelphia Fire* [1990], and Angela Carter's *Wise Children* [1991], to name only three). As clearly discernible as they are self-consciously situated, these echoes are just as deliberately complicated and compromised in various ways. The Professor, for example, ought to be the novel's Prospero figure but is not—is in fact connected by patronymic not with Shakespeare's master magician at all but instead with that far more prosaic Prospero, Robinson Crusoe, whose name before it was anglicized had been Kreutznaer. Similarly, the seven visitors derive not only from *The Tempest* but from the American television series *Gilligan's Island* (1964-1967, itself a retelling of *Robinson Crusoe* [1719]), from Luigi Pirandello's absurdist play *Six Characters in Search of an Author* (1921), and figures from various paintings, including one entitled *Le monde d'or* which exists only in Banville's fiction. The island itself, for all its barrenness, appears just as semantically and intertextually overrich and overdetermined as the characters. Prospero's island is also Devil's Island, Hades, Thomas Mann's Magic Mountain, William Butler Yeats's Innisfree, Oscar Wilde's Reading Gaol, the Count of Monte Cristo's Chateau d'If, and the destination noted in the title of Jean Antoine Watteau's famous painting *Embarkation for Cythera* (1717). The island is also a painting in its own right, framed by water.

Ghosts resists the reader's, like the narrator's, efforts "to understand things, in however rudimentary a fashion. Small things, of course, simple things." It resists these efforts because, as the narrator understands and the reader must learn, "there are no simple things":

> The object splits, flips, doubles back, becomes something else. Under the slightest pressure the seeming unit falls into a million pieces and every piece into a million more. I was myself no unitary thing. I was like nothing so much as a pack of cards, shuffling into other and yet other versions of myself. . . . Nor did it seem possible to speak simply. I would open my mouth and a babble would come pouring out, a hopeless glossolalia. The most elementary bit of speech was a cacophony. . . . When I tried to mean one thing the buzz of a myriad other possible meanings mocked my efforts. . . . I wanted to be simple, candid, natural—I wanted to be, yes, I shall risk it: I wanted to be *honest*—but all my striving provoked only general hoots of merriment and rich scorn.

The narrator's, as well as the Professor's, interest in the painter Vaublin is in this respect especially instructive (not least because Vaublin is himself a fiction, a pastiche based upon a number of eighteenth century Dutch painters). Vaublin's very name is uncertain, his early career and works (if any) unknown, his merit and importance not at all clear, and the attributions questionable. The narrator is nevertheless strongly attracted to Vaublin's work, to their "brilliant" and impenetrable surfaces and the "reticence that lends his pictures their particular power."

> Even in *Le monde d'or* ["the last and most enigmatic of his masterpieces"], apparently so chaste, so ethereal, a certain hectic air of expectancy bespeaks excesses remembered or to come. The figure of Pierrot is suggestively androgynous, the blonde woman walking away on the arm of the old man—who himself has a touch of the roué—wears a wearily knowing air, while the two boys, those pallid, slightly ravaged putti, seem to have seen more things than they should. Even the little girl with the braided hair who leads the lady by the hand has the air of a fledgling Justine or Juliette, a potential victim in whom old men might repose dark dreams of tender abuse. And then there is that smirking Harlequin astride his anthropomorphic donkey: what sights he seems to have seen, what things he knows!

The narrator's description of *Le monde d'or* is disturbing for two quite different reasons. (It is also, however, comically portentous.) One is the whiff of decadence, the strong implication of some already existing evil beyond every semblance of inno-cence. The other reason, however, proves far more troubling, for it suggests that what the reader assumes to be the very basis of the narrator's tale, the arrival of the seven castaways on the island, is nothing more than a fiction—nothing more, that is, than the narrator's turning Vaublin's painting (if it is Vaublin's painting, one later comes to ask) into a fiction in which characters previously frozen in paint are given a more expansive verbal reality. (This possibility has been there from the very first: "Who speaks? I do. Little god.")

A means out of this predicament is provided at the very end of the novel's first, and longest, section. There the narrator and Flora talk about

> how the present feeds on the past, or versions of the past. How pieces of lost time surface suddenly in the murky sea of memory, bright and clear and fantastically detailed, complete little islands where it seems it might be possible to live, even if only for a moment.

As they talk, however, Flora—"Our Lady of Enigmas"—is suddenly transfigured into "a girl, just a girl," who in the process of becoming just herself permits the things around her to become just what they are, relieved, for the moment at least, of the signifying process. Significantly, however, the very process by which Flora has become more real is rendered in purely artistic terms. "It is as if she had dropped a condensed drop of colour into the centre of the world and the colour had spread and the outlines of things had sprung into bright relief."

In the second of the novel's four parts, the narrator sidesteps entirely the what-is-real, what-is-imagined issue by telling the story of how he came to seek refuge on the island as Professor Kreutznaer's assistant. "Let us regress" begins the narrator's account of his release from prison after serving ten years of a life sentence, his meeting Billy, a prison friend, and his subsequent trip to the island, where he has been ever since. The narrator is careful not to "regress" too far—careful, that is, not to mention his crime. For that, the reader will have to consult Banville's previous novel *The Book of Evidence* (1990) or extrapolate from the "hypothetical case" briefly described in part 1. Either way, the reader will learn that the narrator fell in love with a painting, which he stole, only to be caught in the act by a servant whom he murdered, and for whom he came to care more than he did for the painting.

That small irony seems to bear a special significance in the light of the novel's next (and shortest) section, a brief historical description and explanation of the Pierrot figure, from the *commedia dell'arte* tradition, in Vaublin's *Le monde d'or*. Just as Vaublin presumably modeled his clown on one of the actors at the Comédie-Française, the narrator seems to have modeled his life on Vaublin's art (or what may well be someone's, perhaps the Professor's, imitation of Vaublin's art). Before any of the novel's numerous enigmas can be cleared up, however, the tide rises, the boat that had previously run aground floats free, and the visitors—including Flora, who had said that she would stay—depart for the world whence they came, a mainland that must forever remain offstage, or at least off the page. As for all the loose ends, they, like the Professor, Licht, and the narrator, must remain. "No: no riddance" the novel enigmatically (and playfully) concludes.

There is certainly "no riddance" to *Ghosts*, a novel that is content to remain silent on the many mysteries it teasingly raises, a novel content to be its own brilliantly crafted self and not the key for unlocking some moral or metaphysical conundrum, a novel content to be real without feeling under the obligation to be somehow about reality (other than the reality of the reading experience itself). *Ghosts* offers no special insight into the Jeffrey Dahmers and Hannibal Lecters of the world. Then again, it does not pretend to. Perhaps the reader might say of *Ghosts* what the narrator says of *Le monde d'or*:

> Evidently there is an allegory here, and symbols seem to abound, yet the scene carries a weight of unaccountable significance that is disproportionate to any possible programme or hidden discourse. It is first of all a masterpiece of pure composition.

Yet it is also a masterpiece that may be a fake, a possibility that leads the narrator, and subsequently the reader, to this more dizzying possibility: "If this is a fake, what then would be the genuine thing?" What would, indeed?

Robert A. Morace

Sources for Further Study

Australian Book Review. XXXI, May, 1993, p. 53.
Booklist. XC, November 15, 1993, p. 601.
Chicago Tribune. December 12, 1993, XIV, p. 1.
Library Journal. CXVIII, September 15, 1993, p. 102.

London Review of Books. XV, April 22, 1993, p. 10
Los Angeles Times Book Review. November 7, 1993, p. 3.
New Statesman and Society. VI, April 16, 1993, p. 41.
The New York Times Book Review. XCVIII, November 28, 1993, p. 1.
Publishers Weekly. CCXL, August 23, 1993, p. 57.
The Times Literary Supplement. April 9, 1993, p. 20.

GIRL, INTERRUPTED

Author: Susanna Kaysen (1948-   )
Publisher: Turtle Bay Books/Random House (New York). 168 pp. $17.00
Type of work: Memoir
Time: 1967-1969
Locale: McLean Hospital, Belmont, Massachusetts

Girl, Interrupted *is Susanna Kaysen's account of the nearly two years she spent in a mental institution, after she was "interrupted in the music of being seventeen"*

> *Principal personages:*
> SUSANNA KAYSEN, a creative young woman
> ALICE,
> DAISY,
> GEORGINA,
> LISA, and
> POLLY, her fellow inmates
> VALERIE, the head nurse at McLean Hospital, an honest, straightforward
> woman

In 1967, having been interviewed briefly by a physician she had never seen before who told her that she needed a rest, eighteen-year-old Susanna Kaysen was put in a taxi and sent to McLean Hospital, a private residential psychiatric treatment center outside Cambridge, Massachusetts. The case for her commitment seemed to have been based on a failed—and fainthearted—suicide attempt involving fifty aspirins, along with her failure to measure up to her parents' expectations. Kaysen was not committed to McLean by her parents, but the depression that landed her there seems to have resulted from her inability to measure up to their image of what she should be. As Kaysen memorably puts it in *Girl, Interrupted*, "Lunatics are designated hitters. Often an entire family is crazy, but since an entire family can't go into the hospital, one person is designated as crazy and goes inside."

Kaysen does not know whether she was crazy in 1967, and she does not know whether she is crazy still. As she has said about that period of her life, "I was desperately unhappy, but I'm not sure it's the same thing [as being crazy]." After a year and eight months of treatment, she was released not because she was cured, but essentially because she had received a marriage proposal, a socially acceptable resolution to her term in an alternative institution that, Kaysen says, supplied her with the equivalent of a college education. Indeed, Kaysen's diagnosis, something called "borderline personality disorder," partakes more of a sense of social maladjustment than of a mental disorder. The symptoms of this malady seem to consist of "uncertainty about several life issues," such as self-image, sexual orientation, and long-term goals, which manifest themselves as promiscuity and excessive shopping. As one of her psychiatrists tells her, a "borderline personality" is "what they call people whose lifestyles bother them."

Kaysen argues that most young people caught up in the turbulence of the late 1960's suffered from what the larger society perceived as personality disorders. She makes the case for the general craziness of the times most compellingly in a chapter called "Politics," which features a young McLean inmate named Brad Barker, who is her roommate's boyfriend. Brad has been committed because he has delusions that his father is a Central Intelligence Agency operative who works with two individuals named Liddy and Hunt, "guys who will do anything." As Kaysen notes, what happens in the parallel world of the loony bin is a tryout for the great world: Years later Bernard Barker, G. Gordon Liddy, and E. Howard Hunt would be connected with the break-in at the Democratic Party headquarters in the Watergate Hotel in Washington, D.C.

Although she conveys her story of her tenure at McLean with a great deal of irony, Kaysen does not deride her experience there. She seems to have valued, above all things, the sense of protection it afforded her at a time in her life when she was feeling extraordinarily vulnerable. This protection did not come without a price—the room checks every five, fifteen, thirty minutes, the barred windows that could only be opened by the staff—but it provided a framework, a sense of stability around which to organize the chaos that raged within her. In a chapter titled "Velocity vs. Viscosity," Kaysen describes with unforgettable acuity some of the thought patterns that constitute insanity:

> First, break down the sentence: *I'm tired*—well, are you really tired, exactly? Is that like sleepy? You have to check all your body parts for sleepiness, and while you're doing that, there's a bombardment of images of sleepiness, along these lines: head falling onto pillow, head hitting pillow, Wynken, Blynken, and Nod. . . . Uh-oh, a sea monster.

Kaysen structures her memoir by interspersing brief chapters devoted to discrete incidents with pages taken directly from her McLean medical records, which she secured with the aid of a lawyer twenty-five years after she was discharged. The effect of this juxtaposition is jarring. The official language of craziness, the dry, matter-of-fact way in which the details of her incarceration are recorded—for example, the episode in which she bites her hand until it bleeds in order to find the bones within is labeled one of "depersonalization"—is entirely at odds with the graceful simplicity Kaysen employs in describing her state. As she points out, madness, the madness of those incarcerated at McLean Hospital in particular, has powerful artistic connotations; at various times McLean housed Ray Charles, James, Kate, and Livingston Taylor, Robert Lowell, and Sylvia Plath. Kaysen does not dwell overmuch on the nexus between her diagnosis and her own creative gifts, instead saying wryly:

> My parents and teachers did not share my self-image. Their image of me was unstable, since it was out of kilter with reality and based on their needs and wishes. They did not put much value on my capacities, which were admittedly few, but genuine. I read everything, I wrote constantly, and I had boyfriends by the barrelful. . . . Boyfriends and literature: How can you make a life out of those two things? As it turned out, I did.

Kaysen is today a writer with published novels to her credit. Her gifts as a writer show themselves in *Girl, Interrupted* not only in her philosophic explorations of the meaning of madness but also in her portraits of those who shared her parallel world in McLean. Kaysen has admitted that she had to invent dialogue for her memoir, adding, "My argument is that it's true even if it might not be the facts." Similarly, even though insanity might be said to have its own paradigms and patterns, Kaysen has surely added shape to the experiences of her fellow inmates. While her roommate Georgina may have "lacked affect" after Kaysen poured hot melted sugar over her hand, it is Kaysen the writer who makes the connection between Georgina's lack of reaction to being burned and G. Gordon Liddy's nightly ritual of holding his palm over a candle flame as a rehearsal for torture. While Daisy's father may have purchased an apartment for his daughter in a building surmounted with a sign reading "If you lived here, you'd be home now," Kaysen's deft and subtle touch underscores the irony of Daisy's subsequent suicide in a space presided over by such an epigraph.

Kaysen's portrayals of those on the other side of reality, her keepers at McLean, are no less vivid and no less artfully drawn. The straight-talking, fearless head nurse, Valerie, is contrasted with Dr. Wick, the head of Kaysen's ward, who uses words like "attachment" when referring to sexual relations, and Mrs. McWeeney, the night head nurse, who speaks only in clichés. Kaysen devotes a chapter to Melvin, her therapist, later her analyst at McLean, a seemingly simple-minded individual who takes a literal approach to psychiatry. When, after a night filled with fighting and noise on her ward, Kaysen falls asleep during a session with Melvin, he tells her that she is manifesting a desire to sleep with him. Later, after making the transition to analyst (Kaysen was his first analytic patient), he entirely misses her interpretation of the appeal of the maze of underground tunnels connecting the McLean complex, insisting that she sees them as a womb, when Kaysen in fact has something more sophisticated in mind: Plato's cave.

Kaysen is at her drollest when describing her encounters with those at the head of the psychiatric universe. The doctor who originally strong-armed her into McLean, for example, did so because during his twenty-minute interview with her he observed that she had been picking at a blemish. Similarly, in brief encounters with residents at McLean, a patient's claim to have a headache is interpreted as "hypochondria," and her denial of the accuracy of a nurse's report about her behavior is officially (and officiously) labeled "hostility." These people have power over commitment and incarceration; why, Kaysen seems to be asking, are they playing games?

As Kaysen makes clear, those who have crossed over into madness can never come back entirely. Getting there is easy—"most people pass over incrementally, making a series of perforations in the membrane between here and there until an opening exists"—but because of the fear her stigma of craziness engenders in others, and in herself, Kaysen realizes that she never will get entirely free of the alternative world she inhabited in her youth. In a memorable and moving coda to her memoir, Kaysen explains its title, taken from a Jan Vermeer portrait titled *Girl Interrupted at Her Music*, which features a young girl with her music teacher. Kaysen contrasts this painting with two others by Vermeer housed with it in the Frick Collection in New York City. When she first saw Vermeer's girl, Kaysen herself had been seventeen, and she did not notice the other two paintings, having been distracted by a warning that she felt the girl was trying to deliver. Sixteen years later, when she revisited the painting, it filled her with sadness, for she saw that, as had happened to her, one moment of the girl's life had been made to stand for all the others. As Kaysen asks rhetorically, "What life can recover from that?" Today Kaysen contrasts the girl at her music, who "sits in . . . the fitful, overcast light of life" with the subjects of the other Vermeers, self-contained paintings illuminated by unreal light. Life is not, Kaysen implies, a sunny affair for anyone, sane or insane, and no one can accurately judge others or even oneself. The division between the parallel worlds, both of which Kaysen has inhabited, is a matter of perception.

Lisa Paddock

Sources for Further Study

Booklist. LXXXIX, April 1, 1993, p. 1396.
Kirkus Reviews. LXI, March 15, 1993, p. 351.
Library Journal. CXVIII, March 15, 1993, p. 95.
Los Angeles Times Book Review. July 4, 1993, p. 6.
The New York Times Book Review. XCVIII, June 20, 1993, p. 1.
Newsweek. CXXII, July 5, 1993, p. 56.
Publishers Weekly. CCXL, June 14, 1993, p. 51.
Utne Reader. September, 1993, p. 120.
The Washington Post Book World. XXII, July 25, 1993, p. 9.
Women's Review of Books. X, September, 1993, p. 7.

THE GOD OF INDETERMINACY

Author: Sandra McPherson (1943-   )
Publisher: University of Illinois Press (Urbana). 90 pp. $11.95
Type of work: Poetry

Sandra McPherson's tenth collection of poetry focuses on quilting and blues singing in its attempt to reach toward a new metaphysic

The God of Indeterminacy is Sandra McPherson's tenth full-length collection of poems. A well-recognized California poet, McPherson has won three National Endowment for the Arts grants as well as a number of other prestigious awards over the years, including a Guggenheim Foundation grant. The trademarks of her style have become well known to her readers, and looking at the cover of a tenth book (there are even more, if you count chapbooks) one might justifiably wonder: Can such a prolific poet do anything new?

The answer in this case is yes. These poems do represent a departure, although the change is in focus rather than in style, and the many readers who appreciated her earlier work will be neither puzzled nor disappointed. Once again McPherson crafts her poems with the scientific exactness, the precise terminology, that caused commentators to compare her work with that of both Marianne Moore and Elizabeth Bishop. McPherson's earlier works, however, are more nature-based, more in the school of Moore and Bishop; the natural world provides the analogue for the human. Romantic and naturalist meet warily in these poems. In *The God of Indeterminacy*, the focus is more on cultural likenesses and sharings, and an intriguing metaphysic lurks beneath the surface. The element of the romantic has increased, perhaps, although it is still held in check by the discipline of precision.

This collection is particularly satisfying to read, because the poems do not simply sit there and ask for one's admiration, but they do something. Action, not dizzying frenetic action but repetitious meaningful activity, is at the core of this poetry. These poems explore certain societal rituals in what McPherson describes as "often unlooked-at *corners* of culture in America and more distant places," rituals of quiltmaking and of singing the blues, of handicrafts, of dancing. These are both art forms and culture-defining rituals, and in them McPherson searches for a "center," a center that is "indeed in the corner or elsewhere, the indeterminate godly place without a name."

McPherson's special skill has always been the blending of two actions or events into one so that each becomes a comment on the other and so that the surface of the poem crackles with the unexpected intersections between the two. Often the technical vocabulary of one action serves also to describe the other. "Collapsars," from her 1973 collection *Radiation*, is an example of this technique; she uses information about black holes taken from a scientific journal to describe the death of a neighbor in a fire, so that the reader experiences this death as a black-hole phenomenon:

> *The matter*
> *in such stars*
> *has been squashed together*

like a victim
of a fire
carried down in a bag,
half size,
but then again and again,
fire after fire,

> *into forms*
> *unknown on earth.*

The coldness of the scientific description lends emphasis to the human vulnerability to disaster and the indifference of the natural world. The poems in The God of Indeterminacy tend instead to blend two human activities, and the result might be described as a kinder, gentler poetry.

In this collection, the main presence is a series of quilts. McPherson researched the subject by serving as curator of a quilt show, and the descriptive tags of the quilts sometimes appear as epigraphs. The quilts, sometimes anonymous, sometimes attached to names, reflect the lives and times of their makers and comment on the values of their cultures. A second motif is blues-singing and blues singers. These two major cultural expressions comment on each other, so that quilt-making is seen as a way of singing the blues. Other "corners of culture" turn up—dancers, people gardening, a mentally unstable daughter who constructs her own world from discarded bits and pieces of reality. In all these overlooked areas there is activity, motion and grace, a way of recording history and personal identity through sound, pictures, and gestures rather than through words alone. Each art is a way of defining the relationship between the artist and the world, and through this definition, of securing and affirming it. The gestures are forms of worship, and the forms reflect the god.

The modes of spirituality that practitioners of these arts demonstrate point toward a new definition of the divine presence. Reenvisioning godhead warps old expectations out of shape, like the way the quilt in "Mysterious-Shape Quilt Top, Anonymous, Oklahoma" twists the news from the daily paper the unknown maker used as a base. The woman who made this quilt followed the pattern in her head to approximate her vision in cloth, while the events of the world crumpled beneath her fingers:

> and behind one sea-snail shape—
>
> Mrs. Walter Pounds served refreshments
>
> and behind one laurel leaf—
>
> the underground to Lond
> the Nazi begins to suspect
> true love, the Commando, is
> her little Norwegian village
>
> and behind another leaf-eye soul-shape—
> the amazing
>
> —dispatches from the world she didn't create.

The anonymous quilt-maker is a positive figure, following her own coherent vision while the world from which she is more or less excluded carries on its dubious business. It is significant that the scenes the quilter is twisting into her work are of war and leisure, both alien to her. She creates a comforting world from scraps of a hostile one.

Quilting and blues are paralleled in one of the most memorable poems of the collection, "Designating Duet." Its two parts, "Putting Your Name in Your Blues" and "Names Not on Quilts," show how the creative act itself names and identifies the creator—regardless of whether the maker's name is woven into the creation. The maker of the blues song may put his or her name into the work to achieve immortality through the many voices that will sing the song. This is the power of the naming, says the poem's speaker, that "When you write the song with your name in it,/ you give yourself that name . . ."

> So that the vibrations of your sung name
> are distinguished from anyone's
> stone-cold name in the rain,
> even one that is climbed by wild rose
>
> So that nothing corrodes your name in time.

The maker of the blues song thus defines the identity of self and work for the future. The mostly anonymous quilt-makers in the second part of the poem have only colors as signatures, as their creations are "Unsigned/ but orange, blue, pink,/ if those are signs." This part of the poem weaves the wonderful names of forgotten quilters into meditations on the meaning of signing or not signing the quilts:

> Your mother didn't
> name you Fame.
> But your name, a scrap.
> Your name, bright orange.
>
>   Birdaree Williams
>   Wonderose Lewis

Thus the artifact is signed in one sense merely by being made; the maker's mark is in the weave of it.

Another memorable poem, "Appliqué Tulip Quilt from Kansas," shows the means by which the quilt-maker puts her world into the quilt by providing a double focus on the quilt and on the garden and other elements of the quilter's world. As in other poems, the reader has the impression of looking through binoculars with different images in each lens—here the illusion is of looking through the quilt into the actual 1930's garden that was its subject. Close one eye—there is the quilt; close the other—there is the garden. When one has both eyes open, however, the illusion is maintained, and one looks at not only the garden-quilt and the quilt-garden but at the mystical point at which gardening and quilting converge.

The title poem links all the strands of the collection. The real appeal of these poems is the attempt to define a feminine—not so much a feminist—metaphysic through the detailed analysis of what quilting and blues-singing have to say about the nature of the creative act. It is not so much the quilts' symmetries that interest the poet as their quirks, their deviances; individual characteristics of the blues makers, their idiosyncrasies, interest her too. In these personality-linked elements of creativity she looks for a creative force, a divinity. "Ode for the God of Indeterminacy" describes a distant corner "outside a Yoruba village" where a chicken is being sacrificed to a mound of raw earth.

> The mud is a shrine—to Eshu, the god
> of indeterminacy, odd numbers, asymmetry,
> occurrences so singular
> you cannot entice them again.

This odd worship parallels her own search for the force behind quilting and the blues, and she describes it in terms that suggest the quilting imagery that dominates the book:

> If you spread all your beliefs
> crossways to your disbeliefs
> the square where they intersect
> is holy ground.
>
> Though it is struck from all sides,
> it is your hearth, your patch, your junction of amends.

The poems in the collection all tend to affirm that there is a luminousness in the human actions McPherson describes. Her poems may suggest Wallace Stevens' work in their combination of exaltation and elegy, and in their search for a metaphysics of flux. As his poems do, McPherson's seek a new definition of divinity, not as the basis for some eternal order but as a volatile spirit that informs human creativity. The speaker in "Ode for the God of Indeterminacy" longs for this revelation: "O god as migratory as a swan or a goose,/ be mine."

Janet McCann

Sources for Further Study

Booklist. LXXXIX, April 1, 1993, p. 1403.
Publishers Weekly. CCXL, March 22, 1993, p. 75.
The Yale Review. LXXXI, October, 1993, p. 138.

THE GONNE-YEATS LETTERS 1893-1938

Authors: Maud Gonne (1866-1953) and William Butler Yeats (1865-1939)
Edited, with an introduction, by Anna MacBride White and A. Norman Jeffares
Publisher: W. W. Norton (New York). Illustrated. 544 pp. $35.00
Type of work: Letters
Time: 1893-1938
Locale: Ireland

The correspondence between the impassioned revolutionary Maud Gonne and her poet admirer William Butler Yeats reveals much about their common interests in Celtic mythology, the occult, Ireland, and the theater

Principal personages:
WILLIAM BUTLER YEATS, Irish poet, playwright, parliamentarian
MAUD GONNE, Irish beauty, revolutionary, muse of Yeats

What a revealing, humiliating, finally fascinating correspondence this is: W. B. Yeats, the Irish poet of the Mask that both hides and expresses the person, stands in a unique way naked here, in the hastily written letters his beloved Maud Gonne sent him, replete with their occult and paranormal events, rich in his implicit sadness. (Most of the letters Yeats wrote back were destroyed by the Free Staters when they pillaged Gonne's home in Dublin, but hers to him survive; this volume contains only thirty of his letters, as against 373 of hers, and the majority of Yeats's letters are from the later years of their relationship.)

The critic George Steiner notes in *The New Yorker* (February 8, 1993) that his correspondence is, "on almost every page," a chronicle of the occult—of ectoplasm and clairvoyance, table-rappings and Rosicrucianism, Celtic witchcraft and incense—but that "it was from this mumbo-jumbo that Yeats drew and fashioned some of the most powerful, coherent poetry in the language." Steiner is plainly dismayed at this material: he calls it "puerile or repellent . . . hard going." And yet he persists, for "it is from the mauve flimflam and tea-leaf mendacities of the occult, of the medium's parlor tricks, that Yeats hammered out verse of a marmoreal, uncannily lit, and tranquil authority."

Yeats himself has left us not only the poems—"All Soul's Night," to give one towering example—but also his prose meditations on occult matters, in such volumes as *A Vision* (1925, 1937, based on what a later generation would term "channeled" material received through his wife) and *Per Amica Silentia Lunae* (1918). But even granted that *A Vision* is hard to follow (in somewhat the way that Yeats's hero William Blake's private myth is hard to follow through his Prophetic Books, or Yeats's contemporary the psychiatrist Carl Jung hard to follow in his first major work, *Psychology of the Unconscious*), these are wrought works, the result of Yeats's own arduous synthesis of many strange (that is, paranormal) experiences. Thus we can see this "mumbo-jumbo" and "flimflam" not simply as the raw material of a thousand idiocies—which it also can be and often is—but also as rubble from a stone which the builders of contemporary civilization rejected, and which Yeats made the cornerstone of his own building.

In Gonne's letters to Yeats, then, we can witness with a freshness that Yeats's own more mannered pieces deny us, the sort of quest that he was on, the sort of rubble he sifted through to build his grand edifice. That is, in the end, the primary reason to read this correspondence.

There is more. Maud Gonne was a fascinating woman in her own right, and it is well to draw her out from behind Yeats's shadow and come to know her in greater depth: her love affair with the French politician Lucien Millevoye, by whom she bore two children; her passionate Irish Republicanism, which drew her into the Irish Republican Brotherhood; her hatred of the British and their Empire; her imprisonments and hunger strike; her love of theater, her acting, her involvement in the National Theatre Society and the Abbey Theatre.

These letters also tell us much about Yeats's love for her: their "spiritual marriage," her prayer "that we may gain spiritual union stronger than earthly union could ever be" and its effect on Yeats, her almost discarnate comment that "Our children were your poems of which I was the Father sowing the unrest & storm which made them possible," and his horror at her brief but real—and brutal—marriage to John MacBride, hero of the Irish fighting against the British in the Boer War.

Yet it is to that shadowy realm, the occult, that these letters lead time and again. And what is to be made of it? For Yeats, quite literally, the poems. For Maud Gonne, equally literally, Irish nationalism. "We need this communion with the Gods increased & strengthened," she writes, "& then we shall have new Cuchulains and Dermotts who will free us [from] the hideous tyranny of English materialism." Yeats's and Gonne's Celtic mysticism, with all its theosophic and occult appurtenances, then, is not something peripheral to their lives, as some of the earlier biographers of Yeats would have liked to suppose: it is central.

All this may seem strange, uncanny even. It may conflict with religious belief or realistic ideology. It may appear dangerous, or merely silly. Yet it is central to Yeats and Gonne, it is the very fabric of their politics, their theater, their poetry, their love. It is their reality; it cannot be avoided.

At one point, Gonne sends Yeats a letter she received from her cousin discussing color symbolism, with her comments: "Mercury being in a way air & the messenger of the gods it is natural she [the cousin] should see the divine blue with him." She asks Yeats to keep her cousin's letter, for "it will prove that we took no other [symbolic] system but that the Celtic Gods sent us."

The Celtic Gods are real for Gonne and Yeats, real in the sense that they can be communicated with, and that their communications are worth receiving. This is an affront to the orthodox religious mind, no less than to the irreligious—and yet perhaps the greatest poet of the century, and his muse, hold them as truths. And poets are, in Shelley's phrase, "the unacknowledged legislators of the world."

If poetry is more than a pretty arrangement of words, if it is indeed a way of ascent, a means to the highest human goals, Yeats and Gonne are legislating a reality that includes more things than are commonly dreamt of in philosophy. There are Gods, gods, discarnate spirits, trances, mediums, symbols, coincidences, leadings. Prayer is efficacious, work is worship, poetry is prayer.

Yeats will speak "at Monday's Concert on the art of chanting." Mundane philosophy would suggest that chanting is at best monotonous, at worst a charlatan affair. Yeats would see it as a magical use of words to influence deep levels of being. Yet his mysticism of the word is no simple mumbling of phrases: "It is by sorrow and labour," he writes in a pamphlet of 1901, "by love of all living things, and by a heart that humbles itself before the Ancestral Light, and by a mind its power and beauty and quiet flow through without end, that men come to Adeptship and not by the multiplication of petty formulae."

Gonne asks Yeats to bring his tarot cards on Sunday. Mundane philosophy would see in the tarot more charlatanry, at best a crutch to allow the intuitive mind to formulate itself. Yeats would see the tarot—as Kathleen Raine has sufficiently documented in her *Yeats, the Tarot and the Golden Dawn*—as the Sephirotic Tree of the Cabala in visual form, a sequence of images again of great power to move mind and emotions upward towards what Plato called *anamnesis*, the remembering of our original, Paradisal body: "Beloved, gaze in thine own heart,/ The holy tree is growing there."

Is it syncretism, eclecticism, to think at one moment in terms of Celtic gods, and at another of images from an Italian card game grafted onto a Jewish cabalistic tree and decked out with questionable "Egyptian" symbolisms as the "Book of Thoth"? As Raine points out, eclecticism may be poor scholarship, but it enriches the imagination, and imagination—the very word is cognate with image, magic, mage—is the heart of poetry; indeed, "moments of impassioned syncretism have (as at the time of the Renaissance) often accompanied vital movements of the arts."

"I believe more than ever in some terrible upheaval in Europe in the near future," Gonne wrote presciently in 1898.

> The other night here I saw the most extraordinary sight I ever witnessed. I was lying on the grass in the garden in the evening when all of a sudden I saw curious lines of light across the sky, at first I thought it must be some huge fire somewhere, & I got up & went out on the hill to see it. It was about 9.30 in the evening & the sky was wonderfully clear but there was no moon [indecipherable]. Across the Northern and Western half of the heavens rose great rays of light at first faint & then gradually brighter and brighter, several times they faded & brightened, then in the middle of one of the largest rays for a moment there flashed a spear of light, then the ray gradually turned from white into a dull red & faded . . . It was so wonderful I felt a sort of awe I am sure it presaged terrible events.

It matters little whether what Gonne saw was a vision or a phenomenon (the Northern Lights, perhaps, seen unfashionably far south?). What matters is her way of seeing it: the spear of light, the sense of awe, the presentiment of "terrible events." Not many in Europe at that time had so keen a grasp of the trouble that was even then brewing, and which would spill out in the Great War. And her insight is of a piece with Yeats's own later, more celebrated observation in "The Second Coming":

> Things fall apart; the center cannot hold;
> Mere anarchy is loosed upon the world,
> The blood-dimmed tide is loosed . . .

Yeats's and Gonne's occultism, then, is symbolic, imaginative, and prophetic. It proposes a worldview, a reality, which includes intuitions, correspondences, magical acts, synchronicities, and mystical attainments. It is the reality proposed also by that other great visionary occultist of the early twentieth century, Carl Gustav Jung. Indeed, Yeats's words describing (in *Anima Mundi*) his theory of vision and the reality his vision apprehended could—in every detail—have been penned by Jung:

> Before the mind's eye whether in sleep or waking, came images that one was to discover presently in some book one had never read, and after looking in vain for explanation to the current theory of forgotten personal memory, I came to believe in a great memory passing on from generation to generation. But that was not enough, for these images showed intention and choice. . . . If no mind was there, why should I suddenly come upon salt and antimony, upon the liquefaction of the gold, as they were understood by the alchemists, or upon some detail of cabalistic symbolism verified at last by a learned scholar from his never-published manuscripts. . . .

This is the heart of Yeats's occultism: an alchemical relationship with that which is both more intelligent and wiser than oneself—a reality which is "occult" only in the sense in which that much-abused term means simply "hidden"—as one may speak of the moon being occulted by clouds.

What is reality? The correspondence between Gonne and Yeats raises this painful question—painful only because of the lingering assumption that the answer is already apparent, obvious, already known. It raises this question because Yeats and Gonne—in their political strivings, their theatrical work, and in what, yes, may now properly be termed their poetry—live out the possibility that there is more to reality than meets the eye.

There is that which meets vision.

Charles Cameron

Sources for Further Study

The Antioch Review. LI, Spring, 1993, p. 301.
Choice. XXX, May, 1993, p. 1466.
The Christian Science Monitor. January 19, 1993, p. 13.
Commonweal. CXX, August 13, 1993, p. 24.
Contemporary Review. CCLXI, October, 1992, p. 219.
The New York Times Book Review. XCVIII, January 10, 1993, p. 13.
The New Yorker. LXVIII, February 8, 1993, p. 109.
Publishers Weekly. CCXXXIX, October 15, 1992, p. 65.
The Times Literary Supplement. April 24, 1993, p. 5.
The Washington Post Book World. XXIII, February 14, 1993, p. 1.

HAUNTS OF THE BLACK MASSEUR
The Swimmer as Hero

Author: Charles Sprawson
First published: 1992, in Great Britain
Publisher: Pantheon Books (New York). Illustrated. 307 pp. $23.00
Type of work: Cultural history

A detailed, anecdotal exploration of the meaning of swimming and the psychology of the swimmer in Western literary history

The seeds for Charles Sprawson's *Haunts of the Black Masseur: The Swimmer as Hero* were sown, the author tells us, in the four years he taught classical literature in what is identified only as "an Arab university." Deprived of the refreshing pleasure of recreational swimming in a parched climate, the young Englishman spent long afternoons in his shadowy quarters and nights on the rooftop beneath the stars tracking down and making extensive notes on references to springs, pools, and bathing in the books that came his way. In the "strange, unnatural climate" in which he lived, he explains, "novels and poetry seemed to revolve around water and swimming, in a way that was quite out of proportion to the author's intentions." From this temporary obsession arose a curiosity about the psychology of the swimmer, and about what 1956 Olympic Champion Murray Rose described to Sprawson as the "feel for water" that motivates humans to immerse themselves in a medium that is simultaneously threatening, soothing, and seductive.

The somewhat sinister overtones of Sprawson's title are as misleading as the academic implications of the subtitle and colon. In fact, *Haunts of the Black Masseur*—the phrase comes from a Tennessee Williams story—is the kind of informal and personal rumination over a subject that only a nonacademic Englishman could write. It is more like a travel book than a history, as the author moves through time and across geographical borders, pausing to explore anecdotal byways and amusing biographical side roads, dipping in a rock-strewn pool here and splashing there beneath a waterfall. The dominant tone is far from ghoulish: The book is as cool and refreshing as its subject.

Swimmers, Sprawson argues, are solitaries. The great swimmers, those who have been described and remembered, have engaged in a Homeric endeavor that is fueled as much by the mind as by the body. The long and lonely hours of training induce meditation and dreams. "So intense and concentrated are his conditions that he becomes prey to delusions and neuroses beyond the experience of other athletes." It is not clear whether or not a lonely person is particularly prone to this sport above others, but Sprawson sees in literary culture the evolution of a symbolic swimmer, a figure who has come to represent "characters with a heightened sensitivity to the promises of life." The book thus simultaneously presents the reader with a somewhat arbitrary but fascinating history of swimming and its development as an international sport and an imaginative analysis of the idea of the swimmer as it has appeared in fiction and poetry.

Wherever one turns, it seems, there are swimmers. Although he later delves into the classics for references to the bathers of secular mythology, Sprawson begins with "The English Ascendancy"—his chapter heading—in the nineteenth century. In this period pools and floating baths were spread like cerulean carpets about England. Swimming galas were held in coastal towns. The winners of international races—most of them English—were greeted as national heroes. Contrary to popular beliefs about the period, swimming naked was the rule rather than the exception, and only the breast-stroke was deemed acceptable. People were drawn by the thousands to the seaside, and mermaids captured the popular imagination, as did such strenuous performers as Annette Kellerman, an Australian who swam up the Thames, the Seine, and the Danube while spectators lined the banks and who in 1911 was the second person to swim the English Channel. The first, Captain Matthew Webb, swam it thirty-six years earlier, continued his career performing public feats of endurance, and died in a futile attempt to cross the Niagara River three miles below the falls.

It was to the Romans and the Norsemen that the English looked for examples of their new national pastime. The Greeks may have peopled their springs and waterways with deities, but the Romans built baths, sometimes of enormous size, created vast fountains and water gardens, created grottos around wilderness pools, and embraced all things having to do with water with a previously unknown voluptuousness. To the Christians who followed, this was abhorrent: Swimming was associated with deca-dence, water regained its older meaning as a means of purification, and the swimmer, no longer a hero, became dependent for survival on divine grace rather than skill.

Benjamin Franklin, who invented attachable paddles to assist the swimmer, consid-ered the establishment of a swimming school in London in the middle of the eighteenth century, but it was not until 1828 that England's first such club was founded by a group of old Etonians who had learned to swim at school. There the notorious Eton style had been perfected: The feet alone were used to propel the water, and in the dive, the famous "Eton plunge," the swimmer disturbed the water as little as possible and the head had to reappear before the feet had broken the surface. The Romantics embraced the sport as passionately as their Roman ancestors had, but Sprawson sees a telling contrast between the sensual, erotic fascination with water associated with Percy Bysshe Shelley—who could not himself swim—and later Algernon Charles Swin-burne, Gustave Flaubert, and Paul Valéry, and the view of the swimmer as muscular hero associated with George Gordon, Lord Byron. In an effort to immerse himself—literally—in the experiences of the latter, Sprawson tries his own crossing of both the Hellespont and the Tagus estuary in Portugal, which turn out to be vastly amusing exercises in frustration.

Among the now scarcely modern English modern authors—still inspired, in Sprawson's view, by their school reading of classical texts—the author devotes time to John Cooper Powys, Frederick Rolfe ("Baron Corvo"), Denton Welch, D. H. Lawrence, and Rupert Brooke. The importance of British swimming seems to have declined, however, with the demise of empire. German, American, and Japanese swimmers gained preeminence, and with the cult of the healthy body that followed the reestablishment of the Olympic Games, the swimmer entered new domains of the imagination. Although, for example, Johann Wolfgang von Goethe's bathing experiences had a profound impact on the themes and images of his texts, and thus on generations of German-speaking readers, it was not until the advent of such powerful swimmers as Johnny Weissmuller that Germans began to dominate the field. The Nordic hero as swimmer served as a model for the Aryan athlete idealized by Nazi Germany, and Sprawson wonders whether the diving figures that brought to a close Leni Riefenstahl's film of the 1936 Olympics were "less expressions of celestial aspiration, more a premonition of those German eagles and Condor legions that were soon to sweep down and devastate Guernica and Poland."

American Indians, like the natives of the South Sea islands, had an ease in the water lacked entirely by their European brethren, several of whom Sprawson depicts as tying frogs to threads in order to observe their strokes. Yet the Indians themselves figure less prominently in the book than the images of their water frolickings depicted by Henry Wadsworth Longfellow and the painter George Catlin. Thomas Eakins' waterhole paintings and Walt Whitman's declared preference for loafing by the waterside reinforced the American view of bathing as both arcadian and democratic. Through such water lovers as Jack London and Zelda Fitzgerald, who once dove naked into the fountain in Union Square in Manhattan, Sprawson moves to Florida, where two of the fabulous pools of the 1920's survive in Coral Gables, and to Hollywood. Famous pools, like William Randolph Hearst's magnificent series at San Simeon, and famous swimmers, like Esther Williams, lead to descriptions of movies, actors, artists, and directors. In *Sunset Boulevard* (1950), William Holden is found floating in Gloria Swanson's pool. In Val Lewton's creepy *Cat People* (1942), a swimming pool becomes the locale of atavistic fantasy. In David Hockney's paintings, the glittering waters of California pools become images of narcissism and the self-absorption of the artist.

Japan emerged as an Olympic swimming power in the 1930's, and it is with the Japanese author Yukio Mishima that Sprawson brings his book back to the image of mystical renewal. Mishima found in seas and rivers not simply the opponent worthy of the hero but also the source of purity, strength, and beauty. In their pollution and stagnation he saw the measure of human decay. From Mishima's suicide, Sprawson moves on to his own attempt to follow the path of André Gide in Northern Africa, discovering, appropriately enough, that the great Roman baths at Gafsa, once bubbling and medicinal, had become filthy and littered, stinking of decay.

It is not easy to convey the relaxed, leisurely, and certainly eccentric quality of *Haunts of the Black Masseur*. Anyone seeking a straightforward history of the sport would certainly be disappointed—although there is certainly a wealth of factual information scattered here and there among the pages. The lack of footnotes and index suggests that such a demand would in any case be inappropriate. What the book does supply in abundance is intelligent speculation and anecdotes, which are served up at the pleasure of the author (and the reader) without apparent attention to their relative importance or significance. Thus one may learn much about the works of Baron Corvo, the introduction of Jantzen bathing suits, the novels of Jack London. The reader learns that Orson Welles had a local chemist develop a colorless chemical that would turn red in the presence of urine and then stood about dismayed as his guests found themselves swimming in "raspberry-colored clouds," and that Hart Crane did a swan dive when he committed suicide by plunging off the deck of a steamer in the Bay of Mexico. The Swedes, the reader is told, introduced diving as an international sport. Esther Williams, according to Sprawson, modeled bathing suits but refused to wear a bikini. Although the organization of the book is nominally chronological, the author's unwillingness to be bound by rigid structure gives *Haunts of the Black Masseur* a refreshing charm as a meditation on one particular manifestation of cultural history.

The illustrations are an enticing enhancement to the text. Another author might have chosen to include conventional line drawings and reproductions to document the pre-Dauguerrean era; Sprawson instead limited his pre-twentieth century images to reproductions of a handful of paintings and a famous erotic print of a female Japanese pearl diver. The rest of the images are extremely handsome photographs, ranging from Riefenstahl's soaring fliers to a Busby Berkeley still from *Footlight Parade* (1933). The pictures are less illustrations than complements to the written word.

Jean Ashton

Sources for Further Study

The Atlantic. CCLXXI, March, 1993, p. 130.
Booklist. LXXXIX, January 15, 1993, p. 872.
Library Journal. CXVIII, February 15, 1993, p. 171.
The New Republic. CCIX, October 25, 1993, p. 37.
The New York Review of Books. XL, March 4, 1993, p. 3.
The New York Times Book Review. XCVIII, March 7, 1993, p. 27.
The New Yorker. LXIX, April 5, 1993, p. 104.
Publishers Weekly. CCXL, January 4, 1993, p. 64.
The Times Literary Supplement. July 17, 1992, p. 28
The Washington Post. February 24, 1993, p. B2.

THE HEATHER BLAZING

Author: Colm Tóibín (1955-   )
First published: 1992, in Great Britain
Publisher: Viking (New York). 245 pp. $20.00
Type of work: Novel
Time: The early 1940's to the 1990's
Locale: Dublin and the east coast of Ireland

A chronicle of a judge's legal and family life

> *Principal characters:*
> EAMON REDMOND, the protagonist, a judge
> MICHAEL REDMOND, his father, a teacher
> CARMEL O'BRIEN, his wife
> NIAMH, his daughter

Colm Tóibín's interest in describing landscape is clear in *The Heather Blazing*, as it is in his previous novel *The South* (1990) and in his travel books *Homage to Barcelona* (1990) and *Walking Along the Border* (1987). To the main character of *The Heather Blazing*, Eamon Redmond, whose point of view structures the novel, the physical presence of nature is a continual lure to his attention, especially in Cush on Ireland's east coast, where he goes with his wife, Carmel, every summer to vacation when the term of the High Court in Dublin is over. Once in Cush, Eamon spends his time reading up on the law, walking on the strand, and swimming in the sea.

The novel is in three parts. Each begins with a legal proceeding on which Eamon must make a judgment and ends with an event that elicits his personal feelings. The chapters alternate between Eamon's current and past life.

The first case concerns whether a mentally disabled child has the right to indefinite free hospital treatment. Eamon rules no, deciding in favor of the state over the individual in accordance with the Irish constitution as he sees it. Then he and Carmel drive to Cush for their summer vacation. On the way, Carmel tells him that their unmarried daughter, Niamh, is pregnant.

Thus the first chapter shows Eamon with little sympathy for the child whose case he judges and indifferent to the child his daughter is carrying. Chapter two shows Eamon himself as a child. Here one begins to see why he becomes "so hard to talk to," as Carmel tells him. He is an only child, and his mother dies before he knows her. In secondary school, as a student in the class his father teaches, he learns "to wait, to be quiet, to sit still." In Enniscorthy, the town they live in, his father writes for the local newspaper and is a political organizer for the Fianna Fáil Party. Finding himself constantly on the outskirts of his father's life, young Eamon becomes extremely studious. World War II throws a kind of shadow over his existence: It is on people's minds much more than he is.

The house in which the adult Eamon spends his summer vacations goes back to this period of his life. At first it belongs to the Cullen family, but later Eamon buys it, and over the years the sea gradually encroaches on the cliff on which it stands. Nearby, his cousin Mike's house has lost its entire front to the eroding cliff.

Like the sea, death eats away at one's family and other things one cherishes. Young Eamon first experiences this kind of death at the end of part 1. His grandfather's death is followed almost immediately by that of Eamon's Uncle Stephen, a victim of tuberculosis. The boy is not allowed to see either corpse; when his father comes to comfort him, Eamon keeps his grief to himself.

Throughout his life, Eamon is surrounded by family and friends, yet remains deeply isolated. Carmel keeps—and keeps him—in touch with his aged Aunt Margaret, informs him about their daughter, and is a warm companion to him, but though he responds to her and listens to his aunt, he holds himself in reserve rather than flowing out on any tide of emotion. As a child, he plays cards in the Cullens' busy house in the summer and is immersed in family activities at his grandparents' house at Christmas. Yet playing cards well is a mental exercise that calls for secrecy, and this is what he likes about it.

During summers in Cush, Carmel reads novels because they express feeling, but Eamon reads law reports because they exercise his mind, his interest in history. He is following the pattern of his father, who graded examinations during vacations. The men in the novel, in fact, pursue the secrets of politics while the women tell the secrets of family. The men tend to be guarded and the women outgoing.

That Eamon is all but insufferably cautious and distant is especially brought out by the case he judges at the beginning of part 2. A pregnant girl has been dismissed by the Catholic school she attended, and Eamon rules in favor of the school, arguing that the Irish constitution is based on the idea of God, which means that institutions based on this idea have rights that supersede an individual's. Though the concept of family is also basic to the constitution, the plaintiff cannot claim this concept in her defense, since the father of her child is unstated and the law has not updated its concept of family.

Meanwhile, Niamh has given birth to a son, Michael, and she and her baby accompany Eamon and Carmel to Cush after the judgment. Carmel and Niamh disagree with Eamon's recent ruling, as do his son Donal (who works for the Irish Council for Civil Liberties) and Donal's girlfriend Cathy, a lawyer. Then Carmel has a stroke.

All this hostility and misfortune drive Eamon into his past again. The memories are mostly unpleasant: After his father's stroke, Eamon is abandoned by everyone for a whole day. He is sent to live with his Aunt Kitty's family and feels out of place among its unstudious farmers. He is fourteen at the time, and during his stay his passions are stirred by novels and by Anne Walsh, the niece of a neighbor, with whom he has his first sex and because of whom he starts to masturbate. He feels guilty, depressed by the thought of the cold emptiness of his house, and afraid that his disabled father will make a fool of himself when he returns to teaching.

The end of this part of the novel turns on Eamon's relationship with Carmel. Before her stroke, she accommodates his need for sex; after her stroke, she soils herself, and he must clean her and clean up after her.

A note of compromise enters the judgment that Eamon, with two colleagues, hands down at the beginning of part 3. The Special Criminal Court, established to deal with terrorist offenders like the Irish Republican Army, hears the case of three men accused of membership in the IRA and of using guns against the Garda (police). One of the men is cleared of attempted murder, though not of "intent to endanger life," and the other two are found guilty only of belonging to the IRA. After this the reader finds out that Carmel has died the preceding winter. Eamon seems to have become more humane. When he returns to Cush, however, the house there repels him; to avoid it he goes for very long walks and even sleeps in his car.

Once again, the present—in this case, Carmel's absence—stimulates his memory. He recalls their lovemaking during Carmel's pregnancy and her reproaches for his remoteness. He remembers how before they were married he condemned a rapist-murderer to hanging, and how Carmel avoided him for a long time afterward. He also looks back on his father's death, which pained him a great deal. His desolation is made worse by his disbelief in the Church's vision of an afterlife—in fact, in any afterlife. To him, those he loved and who died are nothing, despite the tears he shed for his father and the tears he sheds every day for Carmel.

It is neither his thoughts nor his long walks that save him, but his children. After he finally calls his son, Niamh, Michael, Donal, and Cathy visit him and in short order bring life back to the house in Cush. At first his grandson is terrified of him, but gradually Eamon wins him over by giving him a basin of water to play with and not looking straight at him. Later, while Niamh swims in the sea, Eamon carries the boy into the water on his shoulders, as his own father did him. When the boy is frightened, Eamon brings him back to shore. Thus in the sea, as in life, one must be cautious yet relaxed if one is to survive.

The title *The Heather Blazing* is a phrase in a song that Uncle Tom sings after the Christmas dinner that Eamon remembers from his childhood. The song is about those who rose up in the Irish Rebellion, and it serves as a counterpoint to Eamon's character, for though he belongs to a world of feeling, he is distant from it, never rebels, and never loses control. Yet life does bear him up like the sea, and it does make him burn with longing, for his father and for Carmel, and burn with the loss of them.

The minimalist style of *The Heather Blazing* certainly fits the point of view of a protagonist as controlled as Eamon Redmond, but it tends to flatten out every gesture and event in the novel. For example, when Carmel returns from the hospital after her stroke, she and Eamon have the following conversation:

"Did I rave a lot when I was in Vincent's, or did I sleep?"
"You tried to talk to me, but the nurse said it wasn't good for you."
"What did I say?"
"I couldn't make it out."
"I wonder what it was."

Tóibín's forte is description, and *The Heather Blazing* describes many scenes in detail. Scenes like the following draw the reader in:

> They were close to the soft edge of the cliff, the damp, marly soil which was eaten away each year. He listened for the sound of the sea, but heard nothing except the rooks in a nearby field and the sound of a tractor in the distance, and coming from the house, the swells of the music. . . . The grass was wet now with a heavy dew, but the air was still as though the day had been held back for a few moments while night approached.

Passages like this, and the accumulating pathos of an Irish Catholic intellectual hurt by the loss of those whom he loves and by his inability to connect openly with them, make this novel well worth reading.

Mark McCloskey

Sources for Further Study

Booklist. LXXXIX, January 15, 1993, p. 879.
Chicago Tribune. February 14, 1993, XIV, p. 1.
The Christian Science Monitor. March 17, 1993, p. 13.
Library Journal. CXVIII, February 1, 1993, p. 114.
Los Angeles Times Book Review. June 13, 1993, p. 2.
The New York Times Book Review. XCVIII, March 14, 1993, p. 9.
Publishers Weekly. CCXXXIX, November 23, 1992, p. 51.
The Times Literary Supplement. September 4, 1992, p. 19.
US Catholic. LVIII, September, 1993, p. 48.
The Washington Post Book World. XXIII, January 31, 1993, p. 1.

HEISENBERG'S WAR
The Secret History of the German Bomb

Author: Thomas Powers (1940-   )
Publisher: Alfred A. Knopf (New York). Illustrated. 609 pp. $27.50
Type of work: History, biography, and science
Time: 1939-1945
Locale: Germany, Switzerland, and the United States

The definitive account of the activities of Germany's top atomic scientist during World War II, explaining why Germany never developed the bomb

> *Principal personages:*
> WERNER HEISENBERG, a German physicist, winner of the Nobel Prize in 1932
> ADOLF HITLER, the chancellor and political leader of Germany
> MORRIS "MOE" BERG, a professional baseball player, linguist, and American spy
> J. ROBERT OPPENHEIMER, the chief physicist of the U.S. Manhattan Project
> NIELS BOHR, a Danish physicist, winner of the Nobel Prize in 1922

There are many kinds of hero. Werner Heisenberg was a man of heroic thought: a physicist of the first water, inventor of quantum mechanics and of the Uncertainty Principle that bears his name, 1932 Nobel laureate—and the one man in Hitler's Germany who could conceivably have put together a project to build a German atomic bomb.

Hitler himself, in his utterly perverse way, was another kind of hero to those who adored him: an intensely charismatic leader with an uncanny knack for saying and doing whatever would feed on the deepest hatreds and unspeakable fears of the German people, a Wotan-clone preaching his own Wagnerian Twilight of the Gods.

Morris "Moe" Berg—Princeton-educated cum laude, attorney, fluent speaker of a fistful of languages including Japanese, catcher for the Boston Red Sox, and spy for the United States as an agent of the wartime Office of Strategic Services—was yet another kind of hero.

The grand sweep of the story of Heisenberg's war has to do with the question of whether Heisenberg actually tried to build a bomb for Hitler; if so, why he failed; and if not, why not. But this story becomes most personal and thus most fascinating in the meeting between Heisenberg and Berg in neutral Switzerland in 1944. According to Powers' account, which has been skeptically received in some quarters—see, for example, the review by Arnold Kramish, *American Scientist* 81 (September-October 1993): 479-480—Heisenberg was lecturing on physics in Zurich, and Berg was in his audience, with a loaded pistol in his pocket. Berg, not to put too fine a point on it, had been authorized to assassinate the physicist if he caught even a hint that Heisenberg was on the way to building Hitler a bomb.

David Cassidy's *Uncertainty: The Life and Science of Werner Heisenberg* (1992) and David Irving's *The German Atomic Bomb* (1967) explore aspects of the story, and

Moe Berg has two biographies: Louis Kaufman, Barbara Fitzgerald, and Tom Sewell's *Moe Berg: Athlete, Scholar . . . Spy* (1974) and Nicholas Dawidoff's *The Catcher Was a Spy: The Mysterious Life of Moe Berg* (1994). But it is to Thomas Powers' massive book, *Heisenberg's War: The Secret History of the German Bomb* that one must turn for the fullest account of a pivotal point in history—the German quest for a bomb.

Germany was the birthplace of modern physics, the place where the breakthrough in physics that made the atomic fission bomb possible had occurred just before the outbreak of war—and Hitler was boasting of possessing a secret weapon. It was the Allies' justifiable fear of a Nazi bomb that prompted President Franklin D. Roosevelt to authorize the creation of the massive Manhattan Project that led first to the successful test at Alamogordo (July, 1945) and then to the dropping of atomic weapons on Hiroshima and Nagasaki (August, 1945). Yet at war's end, it was clear that Germany had no bomb, and was not even close to getting one. What had happened? And in particular, what had happened to Heisenberg?

These are not easy questions to answer, because the collapse of Hitler's Thousand Year Reich at the end of World War II created a special kind of intellectual and moral backlash: Many Nazi sympathizers were happy to remain silent about their participation in the Nazi regime, glossing it over or denying it outright; many more German patriots who had hoped for their country's military success while despising (and in some cases even attempting to assassinate) Hitler found themselves holding opinions that their non-German colleagues could hardly understand; and even those who had worked consciously against the regime had of necessity often done so under cover, and in some cases had little or no documentation to prove their stories.

The tide of the world's judgment on Hitler swept aside all subtleties in its path, and personal histories were frequently rewritten to ensure survival in the postwar world— even in some instances by the Allies themselves, eager to convert Nazi scientists into British, French, Russian, or American wizards. Wernher von Braun, director of Hitler's Peenemünde rocket research program and builder of the V-2 rockets that Hitler finally launched against Britain, was thus remade into Wernher von Braun, director of the U.S. Army's Ballistic Missile Agency and later chief architect of the 1958 launching of the first American scientific satellite. So what had happened to Heisenberg? What kind of a hero was he?

Heisenberg was in America on a lecture tour in 1939, and never brought up the topic of war with his host in Berkeley, J. Robert Oppenheimer. At the University of Rochester, however, he told physicists Hans Bethe and Victor Weisskopf that he "believed" Nazi Germany would win the coming war. Pressed by his many friends to remain in America, he declined, saying there were few enough positions available to Jewish physicists who were forced to emigrate from Germany, and he did not wish to take a job away from one of them. He also told Victor Weisskopf that he still hoped to be able to help create "islands of decency" in Germany by remaining.

It was not a position that Heisenberg's emigrant friends in the United States were happy with. Indeed, Powers' portrait shows us a man misunderstood by his many friends, and the most important of the misunderstandings seems to have been that between Heisenberg and his mentor, the physicist Niels Bohr.

Bohr was the grandfather of quantum physics, a Danish scientist of impeccable integrity. He had taken an interest in Heisenberg as far back as 1924, inviting his young colleague to join him on a walking tour of North Zeeland, showing him Hamlet's castle and telling him his beloved Norse sagas. These were signs of affection that other brilliant colleagues did not receive. Together, and not without their late-night disagreements, Bohr and Heisenberg formulated what came to be known as the Copenhagen Interpretation in quantum physics—the view against which Einstein argued in his celebrated phrase, "God does not play dice with the universe."

Bohr and Heisenberg, then, had long been good friends of a sort that can hardly be imagined outside the arena of some momentous movement in science or the arts. They were both men of diverse interests and wide reading, as well as co-conspirators in one of the more arcane dimensions of thought.

When war broke out, fission had just been discovered in Germany. Bohr visited Britain at the time and assured Winston Churchill via a common friend that an atomic bomb was unworkable, but others were not convinced. The physicist Leo Szilard, in particular, fully believed that Heisenberg would be capable of creating such a weapon. And Heisenberg? Naturally, he would be the chief scientist in any German team that attempted to build a bomb. Naturally, the German military was interested. Yet it would appear that Heisenberg himself, for his own complex reasons, did not wish the project to succeed. "Heisenberg . . . tries to delay the work as much as possible." That was the message that came out of wartime Germany. But not everyone believed it.

On September 14, 1941, Heisenberg arrived in Copenhagen to see Bohr. The visit had been arranged on the pretext that Heisenberg would deliver a lecture at the German Scientific Institute, but it was Heisenberg's intention to discuss the bomb with Bohr, to gain the advice of a wiser and older head about a problem of epic magnitude: how to prevent Hitler from getting the bomb. Things had to be done in a roundabout way, however. Even the fact that Heisenberg had spoken at the German Institute outraged most Danish scientists, and his comments at dinner with Bohr were likely to be reported back to the German authorities, so no doubt he was circumspect in his speech.

After dinner, the two men took a stroll through the streets of Copenhagen, and their talk turned first to politics. Heisenberg infuriated Bohr by suggesting that Stalin was worse even than Hitler: How could a man like Heisenberg draw such subtle distinctions after the invasion of France? And so, by the time the moment arrived for Heisenberg to seek Bohr's advice, Bohr was already disgusted and furious with his friend.

Heisenberg wanted to know if Bohr would join him in asking a core of scientists— Heisenberg himself had said earlier that twelve key people would be enough—to agree, worldwide, not to cooperate with their governments in building atomic bombs. Bohr apparently interpreted this request as an attempt to persuade the Allies to abandon their bomb development—while the Germans quietly went ahead. It was a fateful misunderstanding, and it left Niels Bohr horrified at Heisenberg in a way that was never satisfactorily cleared up while the two men both lived.

Heisenberg's work on the development of the German bomb seems to have been held back not only by Heisenberg's own willingness to delay the project but also by his sense that such a project would need to be very large indeed—as the Manhattan Project was—and the inability of the German bureaucracy to envision undertaking a project of this size while the duration of the war was still unknown.

Powers describes the work in some detail: Heisenberg's encounters with the bureaucrats, and also with those physicists such as the Nobel laureates Philipp Lenard and Johannes Stark, who rejected Einstein's theories as "Jewish Physics" and sought a "German" or "Aryan" physics with which to replace them, his own labors to design a crude atomic energy plant, his complete failure to attempt a bomb. Powers contrasts this at best slow progress with the Allied fears that Heisenberg was heading a marathon secret effort to build a German bomb, and the resulting rush to make the American bomb first.

The dramatic high point of the story comes, however, when the Americans, terrified of Heisenberg's undoubted genius, suspect—as a result of his misunderstanding with Bohr and the misplacement of almost every other piece of intelligence favorable to him—that Heisenberg is in fact hot in pursuit of the bomb. Their response is to teach the scholar-catcher-spy Moe Berg just enough physics to make an informed guess as to whether or not Heisenberg is doing just that, and smuggle Berg into Switzerland to listen to Heisenberg lecture—and assassinate him if necessary.

Berg was no fool, and the prospect of killing one of the giants of modern scientific thought cannot have appealed to him. In the event, he felt that Heisenberg presented no real threat, and his gun remained in his jacket pocket.

The end of Powers' story deals with the various Allied attempts to get to important scientists in the now crumbling Reich in time to scoop them up before the Russians could; powerful eyes were set on the prizes these scientists would make in postwar economic terms. Heisenberg himself cycled for three nights from Hechingen across country through the chaos of defeated Germany, sleeping in the hedgerows by day—and at one point bribing a stray officer with a pack of American cigarettes to allow him to proceed—before finally arriving at his home in Urfeld. When the radio announced the news of Hitler's death, Heisenberg and his wife celebrated with a bottle of wine. On May 3, 1945, U.S. officers of the ALSOS mission located him and began their courteous interrogation.

To the end of his life, Werner Heisenberg's name was always under a cloud of suspicion, and the old, easy friendship with Niels Bohr never returned. A collaborator, or a brilliant procrastinator? A man of genius whose patriotism blinded him to the worst of the Nazi regime? Or a man of perhaps greater genius who managed to avoid giving Hitler the bomb, when it was in his power to give or to refuse it? What kind of hero was he?

Heisenberg's greatest contribution to physics was his Uncertainty Principle. Denuded of its mathematics and stripped from its specific context, it argues this: There are simply certain things that we can never know.

Charles Cameron

Sources for Further Study

American Scientist. LXXXI, September-October, 1993, p. 479.
Los Angeles Times Book Review. March 14, 1993, p. 1.
Nature. CCCLXIII, May 27, 1993, p. 311.
The New York Review of Books. XL, April 22, 1993, p.6.
The New York Times Book Review. XCVIII, March 14, 1993, p. 3.
Publishers Weekly. CCXL, January 25, 1993, p. 69.
Science. CCLIX, March 26, 1993, p. 1923.
Time. CXLI, March 15, 1993, p. 72.
The Times Literary Supplement. May 28, 1993, p. 3.
The Wall Street Journal. March 25, 1993, p. A12.
The Washington Post Book World. XXIII, February 14, 1993, p. 1.

HER OWN PLACE

Author: Dori Sanders (1934-   )
Publisher: Algonquin Books of Chapel Hill (Chapel Hill, North Carolina). 243 pp. $16.95
Type of work: Novel
Time: 1941-1992
Locale: Rising Ridge, South Carolina

A deserted mother of five struggles to become a successful, happy, and universally respected member of her Southern hometown

Principal characters:
> MAE LEE HUDSON BARNES, the protagonist, a black woman of great determination and energy
> ELLABELLE JENKINS ELLIS, her best friend
> DALLACE,
> TAYLOR,
> ANNIE RUTH,
> NELLIE GRACE, and
> AMBERLEE, her children
> JEFF BARNES, her husband
> SAM and VERGIE HUDSON, her father and mother
> HOOKER and MAYCIE JONES, sharecroppers who farm her land
> FLETCHER OWENS, the second love in her life
> CHURCH GRANGER, a kindly white landowner
> BETHEL "THE PROFESSOR" PETTY, the most difficult of her white coworkers at the hospital

In *Her Own Place*, Dori Sanders tells the compelling story of a determined and incredibly resourceful young black woman who rises out of appalling poverty by means of an indomitable inner strength, a sense of humor, a loyal family, and close friends. Mae Lee Barnes, Sanders' central character, is a fine study in what it takes to succeed against all odds and overcome the economic, personal, and social hurdles faced by a black woman growing up in the Deep South during the second half of the twentieth century. With great skill, Mae Lee's struggles and triumphs are set against the larger historical background of the often painfully slow changes in rural South Carolina after World War II.

Mae Lee's own life quickly turns tumultuous when she is still a teenager. The outbreak of the war both speeds up and slows down her relatively sheltered life as the sole child of a family that occupies a special place in the black community of Rising Ridge. Sam and Vergie Hudson own the land that they farm; they are no sharecroppers tilling for a white landlord. Worried that all the good men will enlist and soon be gone, Mae Lee marries her high school sweetheart, Jeff Barnes, the day before his departure to an army camp.

Because the war lasts four years, during which Jeff must remain abroad, Mae Lee does not need to assume immediately the expected traditional role of being a housewife and a mother. Thus, as Sanders' story shows convincingly, the war gives her an unexpected break from the time-consuming chores life normally would hold in store.

With her characteristic determination, which the reader soon comes to admire, Mae Lee puts her free time to good use. Like her beloved mother, another of Sanders' well-drawn, sympathetic characters, Mae Lee begins to work in a munitions factory. Through her work, she slowly gains economic power and matures as a person. Suddenly, she sees a wider world than she could have hoped for.

Saving her wages with an iron discipline is an act handsomely rewarded when Mae Lee is able to buy her own farmland from the white landowner Church Granger, thus laying further foundation for her economic empowerment. With great sense for the importance of the situation, Sanders sensitively describes Mae Lee's emotional roller coaster attendant to the transaction. After deciding to enter through the Grangers' front door, as befits a person ready for business, Mae Lee is nevertheless shy and worried that Church Granger, as his father Jay was wont to do, will cheat her. Suspense is built up carefully, until the reader shares Mae Lee's relief when she sees how the figures add up correctly on the land purchase document.

After this momentous step forward, Mae Lee's life becomes less happy when she is reunited with her husband. Initially pleased with Mae Lee's gift of the land, Jeff is unwilling to become a farmer, or even a true husband. Each time one of his five children is born (in almost as many years), Jeff goes away on a binge, only to return when his money has run out. He tells his wife that he has been trying to find work in the city and insists that he would take her with him if it were not for their little children. After the birth of Amberlee, the last of them, Mae Lee calls Jeff's bluff. Instead of gathering the family to leave Rising Ridge together as he had promised, Jeff drives away alone, never to return.

Far from becoming depressing or turning to an indiscriminate bashing of the black male, *Her Own Place* uses Jeff's departure to highlight Mae Lee's remarkable mastery of her life and shows how other men help rather than hurt her. Through characters such as Hooker Jones, who works alongside Mae Lee on her land and aids her in buying a quality used tractor, and her son Taylor, whose love for his mother shows through his occasional aloofness, Sanders is very careful to assure the reader that Jeff Barnes does not represent all males. Until Mae Lee is retired from farming, however, she is too busy to find romance again, and she rejects various offers by unsuitable suitors.

With Jeff gone for good, the narrative focuses energetically on the next stage in Mae Lee's life, her struggles to rear her five children and farm her land. Here, *Her Own Place* works well on three different levels. First, individual events such as Taylor's futile quest for his father are told as well as are passages that beautifully chronicle the daily routine of the Barnes family. On a second level, their experience operates to display some aspects of Southern black culture. Third, Sanders' tale interweaves larger political events such as the insidious flare-up of lynchings in North Carolina in 1955 and forced school integration in 1963, and her characters react to these historic moments. Without any dryness or oversimplification, *Her Own Place* depicts here what America's recent history looks like from the point of view of a rural black family led by an indomitable young mother.

The fashionable garden wedding of Annie Ruth, the second oldest daughter, turns into a festive affair that reunites all children but Taylor, who is recuperating in San Francisco after having been wounded in Vietnam. Yet more comforting than the return of Mae Lee's children, who have successfully reached adulthood, is the return to Rising Ridge of Ellabelle Ellis, her best friend in high school. By bringing back Ellabelle, whose husband has died in the war, Sanders provides her protagonist with a close friend who alleviates some of the loneliness Mae Lee begins to feel as her children embark on their successful careers.

Although their lives take different directions and include both happiness and sorrow, Mae Lee's children share a commitment to getting educated and becoming professionals. In what is perhaps their strongest common bond apart from the love they all bear toward their mother, all five are graduated from college, and none becomes a real failure at life. The importance of education is stressed with great subtlety; the reader does not feel preached at, but rather rejoices with these well-drawn and genuinely likable characters as they receive their hard-earned degrees.

In their personal lives, however, there is ample conflict, and Sanders imagines very realistic lives. No matter how deeply they are hurt, however, all five, like their mother, never give up, and they refuse to wallow in self-pity. Thus, while Dallace's marriage to a fellow psychologist fails and Nellie Grace's breaks down soon after the birth of her baby girl Travenia, both daughters do well in their work and love, if not spoil, their own children.

Even though all four of Mae Lee's daughters are well educated, Sanders' narrative does not prescribe a career as the only valid option for a young and intelligent woman. When Annie Ruth decides to stay at home to rear her family, there is no implied judgment for this choice. What is criticized, through the words of Taylor, is his wife Bettina's passivity. For Sanders, the reader senses, any life that is committed to achieve something good is well worth living.

Once Mae Lee's children are no longer part of her daily life, *Her Own Place* turns its undivided attentions to Mae Lee and tackles head-on the subject of black and white social interactions in the South. Mae Lee retires from farming her land and moves into a new home at the edge of the old town. At the age of sixty-three, she takes Taylor's suggestion and enters the world of whites as she becomes the first black volunteer at the town's hospital. With great insight, Sanders describes Mae Lee and her fellow volunteers' initial difficulties with the evil legacies of segregation, a system designed to preclude exactly such social interchange across the race barrier.

At first, when Mae Lee tells Ellabelle of her work, she cannot bring herself to refer to the whites other than as "Them." The extent of the gulf that separates her from "Them" is skillfully shown through such small but telling details as the rings on the white volunteers' hands, which stand in stark contrast to the callouses on Mae Lee's farmer's fingers and tell her that somebody else is doing the dirty housework for them. Because all the volunteers honestly try to overcome the pain of the past, however, they are rewarded; thus *Her Own Place* reveals hope that a spirit of reconciliation may lead to success.

With a fine storyteller's sense of the appropriate occasion to show how change can be achieved, Sanders uses house parties to display a growing sense of intimacy between her characters. Mae Lee is tested first when she is invited by Sally Jean, and she passes the test when she refutes Ellabelle's argument that she should turn down the invitation. Just as she had entered Church Granger's house through the front door many years ago, Mae Lee does not falter as she steps into the white woman's residence. She soon overcomes her initial discomfort and sets a new standard for interracial social interactions.

Mae Lee's own party, held in her home and featuring her own food, cements this new relationship and helps the black woman to stand her ground with Bethel Petty, a colleague nicknamed "The Professor" for her tendency to display her superior knowledge in an occasionally inconsiderate and overbearing manner. The two clash most strongly over Mae Lee's attempts to find out more about her black heritage on bus trips through the South. Bethel's factual corrections of her somewhat naïve hopes to find traces of her enslaved ancestors are finally put to rest when Mae Lee convinces the other woman that feeling the emotions of the past is as much part of unearthing one's history as is uncovering official documents. Sometimes to stand in a slaves' cemetery is as powerful a connection to the past as finding the "right" tombstone of one's ancestor would be.

Finally returning to matters of the heart, *Her Own Place* concludes dramatically, as another man suddenly enters Mae Lee's life. The story of her second lover, Fletcher Owens, powerfully moves through the stages of hope, despair, and utter relief when the real reason for his sudden departure is revealed.

Born and reared in North Carolina, Dori Sanders writes with a strong ring of authenticity, and her characters and locales breathe a convincing realism. Like Mae Lee's family quilt, which she inherited from her mother, Vergie, and bequeaths to her youngest daughter, Amberlee, *Her Own Place* is woven out of tales of pain suffered, hardships overcome, and joy well earned.

R. C. Lutz

Sources for Further Study

American Visions. VIII, April, 1993, p. 30.
Booklist. LXXXIX, February 15, 1993, p. 1013.
The Christian Science Monitor. June 24, 1993, p. 14.
Essence. XXIV, August, 1993, p. 52.
Kirkus Reviews. LXI, March 1, 1993, p. 255
Library Journal. CXVIII, March 15, 1993, p. 108.
Los Angeles Times Book Review. June 6, 1993, p. 6.
The New York Times. May 3, 1993, p. C11.
Publishers Weekly. CCXL, March 8, 1993, p. 66.
The Washington Post Book World. XXIII, May 9, 1993, p. 12.

THE HIDDEN LAW
The Poetry of W. H. Auden

Author: Anthony Hecht (1923-   )
Publisher: Harvard University Press (Cambridge, Massachusetts). 484 pp. $35.00
Type of work: Literary criticism

In this learned and generously annotated study, poet-critic Anthony Hecht analyzes the poetry of W. H. Auden by highlighting the differences between Auden's public and private works

Wystan Hugh Auden must be ranked with T. S. Eliot, William Butler Yeats, Ezra Pound, Wallace Stevens, and Robert Frost as one of the major voices of twentieth century poetry. Some of his poems, like the justly celebrated "Musée des Beaux Arts," have become mainstays in poetry anthologies and textbooks. Important poets such as James Merrill and John Ashbery—to name only two—are deeply indebted to Auden for both his style and subject matter. Auden acknowledged his own debt to Yeats, Frost, and Eliot in the many essays and articles he composed, especially after moving to the United States in the fateful year of 1939, just a few months before World War II began. Through his close association with Yale University Press, and through teaching positions at Swarthmore College and Bryn Mawr College, he became one of the undisputed arbiters of literary taste, both in his adopted country of America and in his native England, where poets such as Philip Larkin fell under his spell.

Born in York in 1907, Auden grew up in Birmingham and ultimately attended the University of Oxford, where he quickly established himself as a promising young writer. During the late 1920's and the entire decade of the 1930's, he wrote and published at a frenetic pace, often collaborating with playwright Christopher Isherwood. Auden became an American citizen in 1946, but in the late 1960's he moved back to Oxford. He spent his latter years there and in his summer home outside Vienna, where he died in 1973.

Anthony Hecht, a Pulitzer Prize-winning poet and a personal friend of Auden for some thirty years, is in an unusually strong position to write a book on Auden's poetry. Readers will be struck at once by the author's erudition and familiarity with the works of Auden. He almost adopts the role of an old friend, leading the uninitiated reader into the complicated and fascinating landscape of Auden's poetry, beginning with the privately printed *Poems* (1928). Hecht then proceeds to do line-by-line analysis of the key poems in Auden's seven major books of poetry, including *On This Island* (1937), *Letters from Iceland* (1937), a book of poetry and prose which includes the important poem "Letter to Lord Byron," *Another Time* (1940), *The Double Man* (1941), *For the Time Being* (1944), *Nones* (1951), and *The Shield of Achilles* (1955).

Auden's books were often issued in British and American editions with different titles. The British title of *The Double Man*, for example, is *New Year Letter* (1940). A further complication is that Auden made constant revisions, emendations, and even cancellations of his texts. *The Collected Poetry* (1945) contains many such altered texts, and Auden deliberately arranged those poems alphabetically rather than chronologically to forestall any attempt to find an overall theme or direction in his work. For the most part, Hecht wisely defers to Auden's wishes; Hecht's distinction between public and private poems is one that Auden himself made implicitly and explicitly throughout his career. Hecht claims that Auden's greatest poems, such as *For the Time Being*, manage to combine the two realms into one memorable artistic synthesis. Private feelings (grief, loneliness, love) are often juxtaposed to larger facts of history, society, and theology. *For the Time Being* was written as an elegy for Auden's mother: the poem deals as much with his feelings of personal loss as it does with the mystery of Christ's nativity and the cruel stupidity of human governments, dramatically represented by Herod.

Hecht uses few biographical references, even though Auden's literary and personal life is documented in reams of personal letters, notes, and anecdotes. Hecht uses such material sparingly and appropriately, always in support of explication and never as an end in itself. Typically, he will point the reader to the excellent biography by Humphrey Carpenter, *W. H. Auden: A Biography* (1981); occasionally he quotes from Auden's close friends and collaborators. Only twice does Hecht introduce his own reminiscences. His focus, always, is on the poetry.

To read *The Hidden Law: The Poetry of W. H. Auden* is to appreciate Auden on a deeper level and in a complete cultural context because Hecht is a kind of Renaissance man, offering intelligent and literate observations on the sources and references in all the poems under discussion. Auden, like Eliot and Yeats, was brilliantly educated, equally at home in the worlds of literature, art, opera, psychology, history, and politics. He was fluent in most European languages and quite comfortable with classical Latin and Greek. Perhaps the single most useful aspect of the book is Hecht's uncanny ability to pinpoint the precise sources for lines, titles, and imagery in Auden's work, whether Homer, William Shakespeare, Charles Baudelaire, or Theodore Roethke. To read Hecht is to feel intimately connected with that great body of art and writing that constitutes Western civilization. Hecht also refers frequently to the operas of Richard Wagner, the psychological writings of Sigmund Freud (for whom Auden wrote an elegy), and the theological tracts of Martin Buber.

In discussing "Streams," from *The Shield of Achilles*, Hecht makes references to literary figures such as T. S. Eliot, Thomas Campion, and Elizabeth Drew, then proceeds to explain the meaning and context of the words *Homo ludens* and "crankle," which figure prominently in the poem: "To 'crankle' is to zigzag, and the reference to *Homo ludens* (playful man) is both to a Latinate nomenclature descriptive of general human behavior, and to the book of that title by Johan Huizinga." Hecht then quotes a passage from Huizinga's book that applies directly to "Streams." Such learned and appropriate commentary is typical of Hecht's approach throughout *The Hidden Law*.

Hecht regularly points out Auden's unorthodox and occasionally confusing style of punctuation, especially the habit of substituting the colon for the semicolon. He frequently mentions Auden's myopia as a reason for the generalized landscapes that figure so prominently in his work. Auden could not see individual flowers, but he did appreciate the whole panorama of nature, often treating landscapes as symbols of psychological or moral states. These emblematic landscapes are what Hecht calls *paysages moralisées* (moralized landscapes), and they constitute a critical part of his reading of Auden, whom he regards as both a supremely moral poet and a gifted craftsman with an unusually well-tuned ear. Hecht relishes Auden's metrical richness, his use of traditional forms such as the sonnet and rhyme royal as well as his playful limericks and inventive free verse.

Although Auden's homosexuality was an open secret during his lifetime, neither hidden nor advertised, Hecht does not dwell on the sexual identity of his subject except when it bears on the interpretation of particular texts, such as "Uncle Henry," "The Capital," Auden's untitled poem to his companion Chester Kallam (dated Christmas Day, 1941), the privately circulated poem entitled "The Platonic Blow," "Minnelied," and "Pleasure Island," a sardonic description of Fire Island. Hecht prefers to focus on the far greater influences in Auden's literary career, his lifelong preoccupations with European high art and music (particularly opera), his passionate involvement with radical or socialist politics, his abiding curiosity about psychology (especially the work of Sigmund Freud, Carl Jung, Georg Groddeck, and John Layard), and his love-hate relationship with Christianity. Reared in the Anglican church, Auden became an atheist in early life, and then a devout Christian in the later years, as suggested by the profoundly religious books *For the Time Being* and *Nones* (which is based on the traditional canonical hours observed in monasteries).

The dust jacket of *The Hidden Law* features a color reproduction of *Landscape with the Fall of Icarus*, a painting by Pieter Bruegel the Elder that inspired Auden's best known poem, "Musée des Beaux Arts" (1939), a work which most critics interpret as a wry commentary on the deep chasm between the important events of history or mythology (here represented by Icarus) and the dull, predictable nature of day-to-day life (as suggested by the farmer at his plow). As with all of his interpretations, Hecht adds an original slant to this generic reading by noting that Auden firmly believed in the essential frivolity of all art. Auden contended that art should never be taken too seriously, no matter how grand or meaningful it may seem—a rather self-effacing stance for a man who was devoted to poetry all of his adult life, and another clue to his sincere commitment to Christian values, especially the monastic virtues of humility and self-denial.

Hecht touches on all the pivotal works of Auden, but a few of his observations deserve special mention. "September 1, 1939" in *Another Time* is one of Auden's most celebrated poems, not merely because it assesses the horror of World War II and the global spread of Fascism but also because it is a perfect example of Auden's ability to blend the private and public worlds. Hecht places it in the context of two other great poems that Auden wrote in the same period, his elegies on the deaths of his two heroes, Freud and Yeats ("In Memory of Sigmund Freud" and "In Memory of W. B. Yeats"). So Auden's war poem is an elegy, too, a mournful statement on the death of all that was good in Western Europe. As Hecht observes,

He began by feeling the mixed recognition of fellowship with others and the apprehension of having his privacy and individuality invaded by the overpowering forces of history. Throughout the poem there is a dramatic, though unreconciled, oscillation between the corporate, or social, and the individual, or private, life.

For the Time Being, Auden's beautiful book-length poem on the nativity of Christ, represents the height of his Christian artistry; as Hecht points out, however, the poem also relies on numerology, the theories of Carl Jung, and (most important) anachronisms. Auden combines details from the New Testament narrative with artifacts and language of the twentieth century, as in these choral voices from the ninth and final section of the poem, "The Flight into Egypt":

> Come to our jolly desert
> Where even the dolls go whoring;
> Where cigarette-ends
> Become intimate friends,
> And it's always three in the morning.

Hecht closes his analysis with a discussion of "The Shield of Achilles," Auden's great statement on the making of art and on the passing of heroes from the modern world. Auden, like Hephaestus (the artisan-god who fashioned Achilles' shield) has made a magnificent shield to protect him from the world, but nothing could make up for the loss of heroes such as Freud and Yeats. In the closing pages of the book, Hecht borrows Auden's "The Hidden Law" to suggest that a hidden law operates in all the great poems, a kind of poetic justice or classical Greek notion of fate, a balancing force that keeps an imperfect world from destroying itself. For this original insight, and for the abundance of others contained in *The Hidden Law*, readers will be grateful to Anthony Hecht. Like all great critics, he inspires his reader to return to the splendid poems that enchanted him in the first place.

Daniel L. Guillory

Sources for Further Study

The Atlantic. CCLXXI, April, 1993, p. 128.
Boston Globe. April 4, 1993, p. 38.
Choice. XXX, July, 1993, p. 1767.
Commonweal. CXX, December 17, 1993, p. 18.
Library Journal. CXVIII, February 1, 1993, p. 82.
The New York Times Book Review. XCVIII, August 15, 1993, p. 18.
The Times Literary Supplement. April 9, 1993, p. 10.
The Virginia Quarterly Review. LXIX, Summer, 1993, p. SS102.
The Washington Post Book World. XXIII, April 25, 1993, p. 4.
Washington Times. May 2, 1993, p. B8.

HISTORIAN OF THE STRANGE
Pu Songling and the Chinese Classical Tale

Author: Judith T. Zeitlin (1958-   )
Publisher: Stanford University Press (Stanford, California). Illustrated. 322 pp. $39.50
Type of work: Literary history and criticism

   A provocative study of a writer whose tales reveal his fascination with "the crossing of boundaries in human experience"

Those Americans who are not readers of Classical Chinese but already know the work of Pu Songling owe their knowledge to the English translation of the British consular officer and scholarly sinologist Herbert A. Giles (1845-1935). He gave his translation, which was first published in London in two volumes in 1880, the title *Strange Stories in a Chinese Studio*, and he annotated it. A second edition, revised, was published in one volume in Shanghai, in 1908, and later reprinted in New York. If these Americans also learned the work's romanized title, however, they knew it not in the pinyin spelling *Liaozhai zhiyi* (records of the strange in the casual studio) but according to the traditional Wade-Giles system as *Liao-chai chih-i* (meaning the same thing). They also knew its author not as Pu Songling but as P'u Sung-ling. Pu Songling (1640-1715) was a native of Shangdong province and the son of a merchant. Unable to advance via the civil service examination above the level of *xiucai* ("flowering talent," roughly equivalent to a bachelor's degree), he never became a scholar-official but was limited to working as a secretary or teaching children. His leisure was spent in literary writing, especially of short stories written in Classical Chinese. His collection of "strange" tales, *Liaozhai zhiyi*, is the great masterpiece of short fiction of the Qing Dynasty, well worthy of Judith T. Zeitlin's deep critical appraisal.

   Zeitlin's broad study depends basically on Chinese sources but is especially indebted to the modern standard edition of the *Liaozhai* edited by Zhang Yube. Its full title is *Liaozhai zhiyi huijiao hui-zhu huiping ben* (Beijing, 1962; reprinted with a new preface, Shanghai, 1978). This edition is collated and annotated; with its prefaces, colophons, dedicatory verses, and interlinear glosses as well as interpretive commentaries, it is a treasure-trove of information and a model of traditional Chinese discourse. It includes all the commentaries and annotations of previous *Liaozhai* readers and publishers, from Wang Shizhen (1634-1711) to Dan Minglun (fl. 1842). This twelve-*chüan* edition contains 491 tales and anecdotes, sixty more than the popular first printed edition sponsored by Zhao Qigao in 1766, on which Giles had depended. From this springboard Zeitlin dives into her investigation with scholarly aplomb.

   Zeitlin notes the significance of the *hao*, or literary name, which Pu adopted: Yishi shi, or "Historian of the Strange." This *hao* recalled the Herodotus of Chinese history, Sima Qian, who lived 145-86? B.C. and was the author of the famous *Shizhi*, or *Records of the Historian*, the model for all the later dynastic histories of China.

   Thus, any study of Pu's work must consider the relationship of history to fiction, of historiography to the fictive imagination. Why would a writer of fiction call himself a historian? What is the realm of the "strange"? Zeitlin suggests that the "strange" is located "in the changing zone between fiction and history, reality and illusion." Pu's tales blur the distinction between "fictional and historical discourse," promoting ambiguity.

Zeitlin sees Pu Songling's own preface to the *Liaozhai* (prepared in 1679, considerably before his collection was completed) as an important key to the critical understanding of his book. Terming it "a masterpiece of parallel prose and a model of rhetoric and illusion," Zeitlin notes that the preface demonstrates Pu's ability "to infuse a personal voice into the often stilted cadences of Qing formal prose." Zeitlin concludes that in it he was trying to accomplish three things he deemed important to his project: to establish his "authority and credibility" as a "historian of the strange," to reveal his genealogy in order to account for his "affinity with the strange," and to show himself working at night in his cold studio "in the very act of recording the strange." Zeitlin then demonstrates that Pu made these points effectively by placing himself within a literary tradition that included poetry, history, myth, heroic legend, folktales, and tales of the supernatural and miraculous. By linking himself to certain famous writers of the past, he created a literary genealogy for himself that even included the possibility of reincarnation, and by autobiography and confession he showed himself a natural-born connoisseur of the strange and a dedicated beggarly-monk-of-a-writer searching for a "true reader." Having already linked himself to Sima Qian he proceeded to link himself to Qu Yuan (fourth century B.C.) China's first great man of letters; to Gan Bao (fourth century A.D.), a dynastic historian; to Bodhidharma, an Indian monk in China who founded Ch'an (in Japanese, Zen) Buddhism in the sixth century A.D.; to Li Bo and Du Fu, the two greatest poets of the Tang Dynasty; and to Soshi, the great Song Dynasty poet and calligrapher.

Having dealt perspicuously with the preface, Zeitlin turns to an analysis of Pu's tales. For the most part, she observes, they involve the action of crossing certain limits in human experience as a consequence of some boundless desire. The first theme she examines in this context is *pi*, or obsession, a concept that from the Chinese view is wide-ranging, running the gamut from "morbid appetite" in the sense of the Chinese saying "There is no limit to lust and covetousness" to a committed enthusiasm for some hobby such as flower arrangement—of which the learned intellectual Yuan Hong-dao was excessively fond, so that he declared, as Zeitlin quotes him, "Without an obsession, no one is exceptional."

The Chinese early used *pi* as a medical term to indicate *pi shi*, or indigestion, an ailment that could be serious because a *pi* could become hard like stone and then develop an abscess. The wide range of meaning in regard to *pi* in the sense of obsession is shown, according to Zeitlin, in the course of history. By the late Tang, obsession was linked largely to connoisseurship and collection of valued objects both from art and from nature. By the Song, art and nature connoisseurship flourished in the collection not only of paintings and calligraphy but also of various kinds of antiques such as ancient bronzes, carved jades, ink stones, and ceramics as well as natural things such as rocks and flowers. Eventually, people began to worry that an overattachment to objects might court disaster. Despite this concern, various rationalizations and apologies were devised, and by the Ming Dynasty obsession became idealized and glorified. The single-minded attachment of a person to some object or activity was viewed as a "romantic passion." Since the objects of obsessions were usually not human, Zeitlin points out, "this meant anthropomorphizing the object." To illustrate Chinese obsessionism in general and anthropomorphizing in particular, Zeitlin translates and interprets with great skill and insight the Pu story "The Ethereal Rock." It is the tale of an obsessive lover of rocks and his attachment to a rock newly added to his collection. Pu actually managed to endow this rock with a personality of its own. Although a satire involving irony, this tale was not intended, according to Zeitlin, as a put-down or rebuke. To shore up his personal position, Pu also wrote stories in which such obsessions as "gambling, sex, alcohol, geomancy, and chess" were shown in a most unfavorable light.

The second major theme Zeitlin explores is what she calls "dislocations in gender." This theme includes transsexuality, transvestism, and sexual reductionism and elevation. Transsexuality has to do with bodily sex changes, male to female, female to male, and also natural sexual doubling as in androgynes and hermaphrodites, and the sexual switching of roles by homosexuals and lesbians. Transvestism has to do with cross-dressing and sexual mimicry—a male adopting female attire and imitating female behavior, and vice versa. Sexual reductionism has to do with male castration and eunuchism, whether as punishment or for employment, whereas sexual elevation is the assumption by flower or fox spirits of human bodily form and of the appropriation of human feelings and sympathies by animals such as horses and tigers.

Zeitlin cites an anecdote in the *Liaozhai* that illustrates transsexuality. A young maiden, the only child of elderly parents who have no son, is changed into a man one evening when struck by a meteorite as she sits in the family courtyard. Out of filial loyalty, the daughter-cum-son is delighted. Using a remarkable Pu story "The Human Prodigy," which she has translated in its entirety, Zeitlin illustrates transvestism and sexual reductionism. The plot of this tale involves a double dramatic irony. Two sets of characters, a male transvestite named Double Joy, who lives disguised as a girl with an old woman he has deceived, and a Mr. Ma and his wife, Tian, both sexual adventurers, set about acting out a scheme of prospective seduction: Double Joy of Mrs. Ma, Mr. Ma of Double Joy. After Double Joy has gotten into Tian's bed, she skips out of bed immediately so as to allow her husband to substitute himself for her. When Mr. Ma discovers that Double Joy is a man, he castrates him and keeps him in his home as a "maid servant" for years to come. Female cross-dressing is seen in the story "Miss Yan." Miss Yan is an exemplary woman who, having married a husband who possesses no scholarly talent or ambition, decides to disguise herself as a man to pass the civil service examinations and thus serve as a government official. Zeitlin points out that this tale's plot reverses the standard "scholar-beauty" romance.

The third major theme that Zeitlin sees operative in the *Liaozhai* involves dreams and dreaming. Dream images carry narrative themes that are always presented in the present tense. Evidently serving both biological and psychological needs—hopes, fears, sexual desires, intuitive hunches, and creative urges—the dream commands the dreamer's belief during the dreaming process. Although the dreamer's unconscious may contain archetypal images derived from collective experience, one's dreams reflect one's own time and cultural milieu. Because dreams are governed by principles of condensation, displacement, symbolization, allegorization, and projection into the future, their meaning is puzzling. Hence dream interpretation has long been a popular exercise. Writers of poetry and fiction have always been conscious of how closely their creative efforts resemble dreaming and mythopoeia, and Chinese litterateurs are no exception.

About twenty-five of Pu's tales have dream as a principal topic, Zeitlin says, and many others involve dreams. The late Ming and early Qing were fascinated by dream and dream interpretation. The seventeenth century writer Chen Shiyuan not only prepared an elaborate treatise on dream interpretation but also proposed a hermeneutics of dream. Zeitlin enters into an excellent analysis of Pu's dream story "The Goddess of Flowers," in which he is both the first-person narrator and the protagonist.

Zeitlin concludes with translations and analyses of two of Pu's finest stories, in which he gave an entirely new twist to the breaking of boundaries—this time aesthetic limits. "The Painted Wall" is the story of a young scholar who falls in love with a beautiful girl depicted in a painting and who enters into the picture plane in order to marry her. Conversely, "The Painted Horse" is the story of a horse depicted in a painting, which passes outside the picture plane to enter the human world.

Zeitlin's exercise in literary history and criticism is solidly organized, written in clear English, and carried out with impeccable scholarship. If the proper function of criticism is to "promote the understanding and enjoyment of literature" as an art, then Zeitlin has succeeded admirably.

Richard P. Benton

Source for Further Study

Choice. XXXI, November, 1993, p. 464.

A HISTORY OF THE BIBLE AS LITERATURE
Volume I: From Antiquity to 1700
Volume II: From 1700 to the Present

Author: David Norton
Publisher: Cambridge University Press (New York). Illustrated (first volume only). Volume I: 375 pp. $75.00. Volume II: 493 pp. $75.00
Type of work: History of ideas; literary history

An account of "how people have thought about literary aspects of the Bible" from antiquity to the late twentieth century, with a special emphasis on the King James Bible

In January, 1604, several months after his accession to the English throne, James I convened a conference of churchmen and scholars at London's Hampton Court "for the hearing, and for the determining, [of] things pretended to be amiss in the Church." At this conference, John Reynolds, a leading scholar and head of Oxford's Corpus Christi College, proposed a new translation of the Bible. Shortly thereafter, with James's approval, a committee of translators was formed, with a list of fifteen rules to guide their work. The completed translation, published in 1611, is known as the King James Bible (KJB) or (chiefly in Great Britain) the Authorized Version (AV).

In time, the KJB became the version of the Bible with the widest circulation in the English-speaking world (Roman Catholics generally preferred the Rheims-Douai Bible, a translation completed in 1610). Well into the twentieth century it continued to enjoy that status, not only among believers but also in the culture at large. In the words of *The Oxford Companion to the English Language* (1992):

> The KJB has been acclaimed as a landmark in both religious literature and the evolution of the English language, an achievement that comprises all earlier Bible translation and that has set the standard against which all subsequent translation must be judged. Many also consider that its verbal beauty is unsurpassed in the whole of English literature.

This is the received opinion that David Norton wants to correct. The catalyst for *A History of the Bible as Literature* was Norton's discovery that "the cliché of the King James Bible's immediate success as an English classic" was not consistent with the historical evidence. Norton was not seeking to discredit the achievement of the KJB—not at all; rather, he sought to understand the discrepancy between the early reception of the translation (which was by no means universally acclaimed in the seventeenth century) and the exalted reputation which it eventually gained.

What initially seemed to be a modestly scaled project turned into a massive undertaking that occupied Norton for more than ten years. The result is a study not simply of the reputation of the KJB but of "literary ideas of the Bible as they have come into and developed in English culture." Comprising two volumes and more than 850 pages of small print, Norton's history ranges from the third century B.C. to Prince Charles' speech on the 500th anniversary of the birth of Archbishop Thomas Cranmer (December 19, 1989), which included sharp criticism of the New English Bible (NEB;

1961) amid broader reflections on the decline of English usage ("we have arrived at . . . a dismal wasteland of banality, cliché and casual obscenity"). No work of comparable scope to Norton's exists.

Although the range of topics considered matches the work's historical sweep, two themes dominate Norton's narrative. The first concerns a tension implicit in the notion of "biblical eloquence." Many early Christian writers acknowledged a contrast between the refined style of classical literature and the style of the Bible, which did not conform to classical norms. Some Christians saw this contrast as symbolic of the right relation between the Church and secular culture: the simplicity and purity of truth versus the sophisticated untruths of the unredeemed human imagination. For support they could cite Saint Paul's dismissals of eloquence; for example, "As for me, brothers, when I came to you, it was not with any show of oratory or philosophy, but simply to tell you what God had guaranteed" (1 Corinthians 2:1).

At the same time, but more so as the Church became solidly established, other Christians saw genuine eloquence and aesthetic merit in Scripture. Norton shows how Augustine evolved from the first position—emphasizing the opposition between eloquence and truth—to the second, seeing Scripture as eloquent on its own terms, in service to the truth, and thus aesthetically pleasurable as well.

The tension between these approaches runs through the centuries all the way to the present, though in radically different historical contexts. For many nineteenth and twentieth century readers, the language of the KJB seemed particularly appropriate for the Word of God: lofty, rich, distinct from the workaday English of their time. Such readers might have found it difficult to imagine Augustine's first reaction to Scripture, which he encountered in the Old Latin Bible, "notoriously unclassical, even ungrammatical in its language."

From the other side, consider this promotional material for *The Message: The New Testament in Contemporary English* (1993), a translation by Eugene H. Peterson, marketed after Norton's work was completed:

> One of the world's great books might take you by surprise if you knew what it sounded like to its original readers. The New Testament—one of the most revered and respected books of all time—didn't have an official or formal ring to it when it was first read. It was not dry or distant or elevated to some plateau that didn't connect with real life.
>
> No, the New Testament was originally written in the language of the street—an earthy, expressive tongue. And that's exactly what *The Message*—a fresh, contemporary version of the New Testament—recaptures for us.

It is one of the great merits of Norton's study that it provides a historical context for these fundamentally different attitudes toward "biblical eloquence."

Norton's second key theme is the general absence of strictly "literary" considerations when one investigates the explicitly stated motivations and guidelines of the principal translators of the Bible from Jerome (c. 342-420) to the mid-twentieth century. Focusing particularly on the early English translations of John Wyclif and his circle, William Tyndale, and Miles Coverdale; the Geneva Bible (1560) and the

Rheims-Douai Bible; the KJB; and the Revised Version (RV; 1895), Norton repeatedly shows that the translators were guided primarily by a desire to render the text accurately. Literary qualities of these translations—magnificent as they sometimes were—arose as a by-product of that effort, not a consciously sought goal.

In contrast, the committee of British scholars who produced the NEB made literary considerations an "integral part" of the translation process; all the drafts went through a "literary panel," which worked in dialogue with the translators' panels (one panel for the Old Testament and one for the New). In his concluding chapter, Norton recounts the making of the NEB, drawing especially on the account of the scholar Basil Willey, who served on the literary panel. To convey the flavor of their deliberations, Willey included "a few dramatised passages from a typical Old Testament section," from which Norton quotes, remarking that, "Like the very existence of the literary panel whose activity it recreates, it is eloquent testimony to the change in attitude to the nature of the Bible that has taken place. Even if the intention is as narrow as to make the Bible's message 'speak home to our condition,' a literary awareness of the Bible pervades the business of translation."

Ironically, it was precisely the language of the new translation—its manifest lack of literary distinction—that prompted the strongest criticism when the NEB first appeared. Among those whose verdict was unfavorable was T. S. Eliot, who asked "what is happening to the English language?"

Norton's study is so wide-ranging that its extent is only hinted at here. Certainly, as he suggests at the outset, there is enough provocative material to send many readers off in many different directions. That very abundance, however, seems to have overwhelmed him, so that at points there is a failure to stand back and assess the significance of the evidence he has assembled.

That is especially true of Norton's disappointingly perfunctory conclusion. Few will dissent when he writes that "it seems to me likely that no translation will ever become what the KJB has been in the English-speaking world." His next statement, however, is arguable: "I do not suggest this as a judgement on either the quality or the quantity of modern translations, but as a reflection on the decline of Christianity to effective non-existence for the majority of English-speaking people." In fact, there is simply no evidence for "the decline of Christianity to effective non-existence for the majority of English-speaking people." (In Great Britain, yes, but Great Britain hardly contains "the majority of English-speaking people" in the world.) That statement undermines the reader's confidence in Norton's grasp of the actual communities of believers whose lives are centered on the Bible. Moreover, it shifts the discussion to an area outside the scope of his lengthy investigation. Finally, Norton fails to make clear the extent to which the proliferation of contemporary translations reflects the desire of readers for a Bible they can understand and apply to their lives. (He does not mention, for example, the striking growth in the United States of "small groups" meeting for Bible study.) In itself, this requirement could be met by radically different translations; we are not necessarily fated to resign ourselves to the bureaucratic colorlessness or the coercively chummy idiom of the dominant contemporary versions.

Disagreements aside, there is ample reason to be grateful for Norton's work. In addition to the main text, each volume has an appendix which allows the reader to compare different translations of the same biblical passages. Each volume also includes a very selective bibliography and two unusually useful indexes: a general index and a biblical index. Volume 1 includes nineteen black-and-white plates; both volumes are beautifully produced. It is fitting that Cambridge University Press, with their long history of Bible publishing, should have issued this work.

John Wilson

Source for Further Study

Expository Times. CV, November, 1993, p. 33.

THE HOLDER OF THE WORLD

Author: Bharati Mukherjee (1940-   )
Publisher: Alfred A. Knopf (New York). 268 pp. $22.00
Type of work: Novel
Time: The late seventeenth century and the 1990's
Locale: Massachusetts Bay Colony, England, and India; the United States

A complex, engrossing tour de force by Indian-born novelist Bharati Mukherjee, the first naturalized American citizen to win the National Book Critics Circle Award

> *Principal characters:*
> BEIGH MASTERS, a thirtysomething American antiquarian
> VENN IYER, his Indian lover
> HANNAH EASTON, a woman born in Massachusetts in 1670
> HESTER MANNING, Hannah's childhood friend
> GABRIEL LEGGE, Hannah's seafaring husband
> BHAGMATI, Hannah's Indian servant and companion
> RAJA JADAV SINGH, a Hindu ruler in South India
> EMPEROR AURANGZEB, a Muslim conquerer

Much of the best, most provocative, and most commercially successful of serious literary writing of the late twentieth century, on both sides of the Atlantic, has been the work of writers of "minority" ethnic heritage, many of them immigrants. V. S. Naipaul and Kazuo Ishiguro both have won Great Britain's prestigious Booker Prize. The death threat against Salman Rushdie made him famous and brought into the open many of the festering issues about and between "East" and "West" that his and others' writing examines. In the United States, Chinese American author Amy Tan has found an audience, as has Indian-born Vikram Seth. Bharati Mukherjee, born in Calcutta, educated in Iowa, and now teaching in Berkeley, is a major figure in contemporary English-language literature, no matter how one defines the categories. Her story collection *The Middleman and Other Stories* (1988) won the National Book Critics Circle Award, and her novel *Jasmine* (1989) was published to acclaim. *The New York Times Book Review* called *Jasmine* "one of the most suggestive novels we have about what it is to become an American."

Mukherjee is a serious writer who takes on important themes of the contemporary world: rootlessness, the effects of immigration on individuals and a society, and individual versus traditional and communal identities. The protagonists in *The Middleman and Other Stories* are immigrants, legal and illegal, to North America, and the plots deal with their encounters with the liberation it offers as well as the often terrifying demands it makes. Their author clearly has thrown in her own lot with America and has committed herself to using fiction to examine her adopted society in all of its complexity. By making such a commitment, she becomes a target of criticism for "pandering" to a civilization that (as her work does make clear) is not always benign or welcoming.

The Holder of the World is a very bold offering. It is a tour de force, the mature work of a consummate narrative artist. It certainly is both more ambitious and more engrossing than any of Mukherjee's previous work. Not only does it attempt to renarrate in an imaginative, original way the very beginning of the centuries-long (and still continuing) encounter between Britain and India, but it also adds a chapter, perhaps the most trenchant to date, to Mukherjee's ongoing examination of America.

Beigh Masters, the book's narrator, is a thirtysomething "asset-hunter"—a collector and assessor of antiques—who has become obsessed with a diamond called the Emperor's Tear and with the story of a woman from early Colonial New England who became the mistress of a Hindu raja in South India. Ostensibly, the book is the product of Beigh's research and imagination, the fruit of her obsession with reconstructing Hannah Easton's life from scraps of evidence.

Hannah Easton, the protagonist of the tale Beigh reconstructs, was born in the town of Brookfield in the Massachusetts Bay Colony in 1670. When she was very young, her mother, Rebecca, faked her own death to run away to live with her lover, a member of the local community of Nipmuc Indians. Hannah's story suggests a mostly implicit but obvious pun on the word "Indian." The reader is meant to reflect on its misapplication to the native peoples of the New World and to wonder at the scope of the British mercantile and colonial adventure, already in the seventeenth century stretching from New England to India. Beigh finds an artifact of Hannah's at the Museum of Maritime Trade. " 'Looks Indian,' I say [to the curator]. 'Indian-Indian, not wah-wah Indian.' I hate to play stupid for anyone, but I don't want him to suspect me."

Hannah is a curious young woman, not at home in the Puritan world. When shiftless adventurer Gabriel Legge arrives by ship telling lies about his father's wealth, she boldly and calculatingly accepts his offer of marriage, sensing that she needs to see the world and that he can give her the opportunity to do so. She lives in England for several years, during most of which time Gabriel is away at sea. When he accepts employment with the East India Company, she goes with him to the Coromandel Coast.

Hannah settles into a new role as wife of a Company "factor," running a household with servants and tacitly tolerating her husband's "bibi," or mistress, while he goes about his business. Ambition and adventure eventually lead him to leave the Company to become a freelance pirate. When a riot leads to the (figurative and literal) exposure of Gabriel's liaison with his bibi, Hannah resolves to return to England on the next possible ship. (Ironically, in India she is considered English, yet in England she is an outsider, a colonial. She decides to return to a place that is not her "home.") A maritime mishap and another riot, however, cause Gabriel to fake death and become a wanderer. "In December 1700, Hannah became, to her satisfaction, husbandless," relates Beigh. Hannah now is free *not* to return to England.

Hannah and Bhagmati, her servant, are rescued from a storm by Raja Jadav Singh, ruler of a small Hindu state at odds with Emperor Aurangzeb, a mighty Muslim conqueror. She and the raja become passionate lovers. He is nearly killed in an unnecessary battle (rendered in marvelously gory detail) fought with Aurangzeb's soldiers. Hannah's medical skills (learned repairing scalps in Massachusetts) save his life but simultaneously pollute his caste and earn the enmity of the raja's mother. Naïvely, Hannah goes to plead for an end to the war with Aurangzeb, who takes her and Bhagmati prisoner. Beigh's imagined—or reconstructed?—ending to the story reveals the fate and whereabouts of the ostensible object of her search, the Emperor's Tear.

The story—recounted perfunctorily here—is rendered by Mukherjee via the obsessed, modern awareness of Beigh Masters, the narrator. The twin aspects of the novel's complex narrative, Hannah's story and Beigh's deepening awareness and understanding, are governed by an ambitious, perhaps overarching conceit. As Beigh puts it in one of several phrasings: "There are no accidents." Of an important event in Hannah's life she says, "Eventually, because everything in history (as Venn keeps telling me) is as tightly woven as a Kashmiri shawl, Higginbotham's riot changed the course of history." Venn is Beigh's lover, a native of India who is working at the Massachusetts Institute of Technology, researching a computer program to achieve "time-retrieval." "It will be, literally, the mother of all data bases," explains Beigh. "It will be time on a scale of 1:1, with a new concept of real time." Venn's "Big Project" is an obvious but effective ruling metaphor for Beigh's obsession and for the book.

The Holder of the World, like most well-executed, complex novels, is not "about" any one theme or topic. Its theme is the great contemporary topic: the meeting and mixing of peoples. It is an audacious feminist rewriting of Nathaniel Hawthorne's classic novel *The Scarlet Letter* (1850). It is an attempt to narrate early modern history through the (somewhat implausible) reconstructed consciousness of a protomodern protagonist. "Of all the qualities I admire in Hannah Easton that make her entirely our contemporary in mood and sensibility, none is more touching to me than the sheer pleasure she took in the world's variety," comments Beigh.

In a "postmodern" way, the novel also is self-consciously about itself. Beigh is constantly comparing her own attempt to re-create Hannah's life with Venn's project, which involves filing massive amounts of data in the computer to create a facsimile of a few seconds on October 29, 1989. "When I look at all my notes, the five hundred books consulted, the endless paintings, engravings, trade records, journals, the travel and the documentary picture taking, and stack them up in my study, they look impressive," says Beigh. "And when I look at the raw data Venn's program has ingested to create ten seconds from just three years ago, with no character, no narrative, I think, who am I fooling?"

Yet Beigh has something that Venn's program lacks: imagination. Unlike the computer, she can create a narrative. This raises a question that nags the otherwise engrossed reader: Given the constraint the author/narrator has set herself of appearing to be trying to reclaim history from documents and artifacts, how can her vivid, detailed narrative possibly be factually true? The answer, one comes to realize, is that it may well not be, even in the narrator's fictional world. Very late in the book, Beigh comes close to admitting this. Reflecting on the sources she has used, she writes:

Most books take a racy interest in a white divorcee, more rumor than fact, who consorted with a Hindu noble. They call her an adventuress of obscure origins, a pirate's wife who comes off less well than the socially prominent Sarah Bradley, widow of the hanged pirate William Kidd. *Tales from the Coromandel*, it's called, and I've done some borrowing from it here.

So the reader is given to understand that the "Hannah" of the narrative is in large part a quasi-fictional creation of Beigh's obsession. This is clear enough; similar authorial comments are scattered throughout: "Her life is at the crossroads of many worlds. If Thomas Pynchon, perhaps one of the descendants of her failed suitor, had not already written *V.*, I would call her a V., a woman who was everywhere, the encoder of a secret history."

The book's ending rings somewhat false and seems rather self-indulgent, as if the author believed that she had earned the right to satisfy her own desire for a facile closure—which arguably she has.

Finally, *The Holder of the World* raises issues to do with the politics of contemporary literature. Three women are involved in the book's story: Hannah Easton, the protagonist; Beigh Masters, the narrator; and Bharati Mukherjee, the author. Which of the three is responsible for attitudes and depictions in the book surely will spark lively discussion. Mukherjee is an artist with a certain ethnic background writing in a certain country for a certain audience. Fiction is in large degree autobiography, it is true. Yet Mukherjee is attempting—rather boldly—to depict a white American-born woman of the seventeenth century. She writes:

The idea of Hinduism was vaguely frightening and even more vaguely alluring to Hannah. English attitudes saw Islam as a shallow kind of sophistication; Hinduism a profound form of primitivism. Muslims might be cruel, but true obscenity attached itself to Hindus, whose superstitions and wanton disregard of their own kind—burning young widows, denying humanity to those they called untouchable—excited contempt. . . . They worshiped the male sex organ; they worshiped an elephant-headed, fat-boy god. They had more gods than people, and, God knew, they had enough people.

Does Mukherjee "pander" to "stereotypes"? Does she "betray" her own Hindu heritage? Or can she be granted the artist's customary freedom to attempt depictions of people, places and things—and attitudes—quite outside her own experience?

These timely questions aside, *The Holder of the World* is in several ways an impressive achievement, probably the best and most mature work of an important American novelist.

Ethan Casey

Sources for Further Study

Boston Globe. October 17, 1993, p. 15.
Chicago Tribune. October 24, 1993, XIV, p. 5.

Library Journal. CXVIII, October 1, 1993, p. 127.
Los Angeles Times Book Review. October 10, 1993, p. 3.
The New York Times Book Review. XCVIII, October 10, 1993, p. 7.
The New Yorker. LXIX, November 15, 1993, p. 127.
Publishers Weekly. CCXL, July 26, 1993, p. 56.
The Times Literary Supplement. November 12, 1993, p. 23.
The Washington Post Book World. XXIII, October 24, 1993, p. 1.
Women's Review of Books. XI, December, 1993, p. 15.

IN THE EYE OF THE SUN

Author: Ahdaf Soueif
First published: 1992, in Great Britain
Publisher: Pantheon Books (New York). 791 pp. $25.00
Type of work: Novel
Time: 1967-1980
Locale: Cairo, London, northern England, Perugia, and New York

A novel detailing the education, life, and loves of a Europeanized Egyptian woman in Egypt and England just before and following the 1967 war of Egypt and Israel

> *Principal characters:*
> AYSA ULAMA, a young Egyptian woman
> SAIF MAHDI, her husband
> GERALD STONE, her English lover
> CHRISSIE (CARIMA), her best friend

In this voluminous and detail-heavy novel, the Egyptian-born writer Ahdaf Soueif charts the life and loves of her heroine, Aysa Ulama, against a background of Egyptian and Middle East politics from 1967 to 1980. The book opens in London in 1979. Its succeeding chapters move chronologically through Aysa's student days in Cairo and London, with briefer episodes in Perugia and New York. They detail Aysa's interaction with the two principal men in her life, her husband Saif Madi and her English lover Gerald Stone, as well as with women, including her best friend Chrissie, her mother, and her aunt. The book ends with an epilogue in which Aysa, by then installed in London, revisits an Egypt much changed since the late 1960's under Gamal Abdel Nasser's rule.

Aysa is a member of the financially and culturally privileged class in Cairo, and she grows up in what is presented as the end of an era of cultural flowering. Even her name indicates her background, since it means literally "Asia of the learned clerics." Her wealthy family is comfortably cosmopolitan, their household a mixture of European and Egyptian and their life-style defined by products of international luxury, from their cigarettes to their clothing. Though they are Muslim, their adherence to the strictures of Islam seems as comfortably loose as the nominal Christianity of many households in the West. Aysa's family is well educated, especially the women: An aunt is a doctor, and her mother is a university professor. Their closest connection with the vast peasantry of whom most of the Egyptian populace is composed is through a servant, whose nuptial history is rather abruptly interjected into the narrative.

The point seems to be precisely, in fact, that this life of cultured ease was at one point taken for granted in some Egyptian circles and required no justification. Indeed, Aysa's is a story that could be set anywhere in the somewhat sterilized world of airport duty-free luxury. Aysa fits in as well in England as she does in Egypt; in both places she is treated with respect by professors and fellow students as well as by ordinary people.

Nor is there much postcolonial rancor to be found in this book; anti-imperialist sentiment is expressed only in attenuated form and in isolated references. The reading room in the British cultural center, for example, is the former ballroom of the British Embassy, left over—Aysa explains—from when such things were useful. In later years, she interjects in flash-forward, this very room would be used for visa interviews, situations in which the British were to exercise the last shreds of their dominance over a native population. When Aysa has a lengthy affair with Gerald Stone, an Englishman who seems as insensitive to her needs as her husband had been, she asks whether his attraction to her is that of the Westerner to the exotic female held in the bondage of concubinage. No, he says, he is her slave, not the reverse. The topic is dropped.

In Aysa's cultured household, her love of literature is encouraged. Soueif describes in exhaustive detail her heroine's intense interest in the great names of world literature whom she begins studying at Cairo University—where there were, as Aysa remarks, still some standards. One hears at length about one professor who stalks into his classroom and grills the petrified students on the nature of poetry, concluding—before stalking out—only that poetry merely *is*. The story is told from Aysa's breathlessly admiring point of view, with no authorial comment or distancing.

To be sure, the author is not completely oblivious of the world outside of the one through which Aysa moves so confidently. Aysa's mother, for example, comes to chide her in England when she is in the throes of abandoning her coursework. Aysa has received a British Council fellowship for two years, her mother reminds her angrily, and then two years of Egyptian government money on top of that—the latter being badly needed hard currency that the government could have used for other things. Still, Aysa drops her studies, and the question of her relation to a larger society is not further explored.

It is in such moments of friction between Aysa's world and that of others, however slight and fleeting, that most of the book's interest lies. At the end of the book—and in the opening chapters, which serve as a temporal frame for the story of her maturation in Egypt—Aysa has found a job writing birth-control tracts in Arabic that are to be distributed to peasant women back in Egypt. The description of her attempts to write something that is so contrary to the mentality of the simple women who are the intended audience and to make it square with Islam, which defines their lives more than hers, is one of the book's most interesting passages.

Aysa realizes that the average Egyptian male farmer will not countenance the notion of birth control. Furthermore, there is no way to reconcile the secular government's encouragement of it with Islam's command to produce children. At any rate, she reminds herself, both partners in a peasant marriage would be so exhausted at the end of the day that there would be no time for talk about the subject, even if the man were willing to accept the woman's right to bring up topics of this weight to begin with. Yet the perception is simply abandoned and, like other momentary references to the mass of problems facing Egypt in the 1980's and 1990's, disappears into the relentless chronicling of Aysa's clever if ultimately rather superficial mind.

The second main thread of the author's attention, in addition to that of Aysa's education, is her relationship with the two men in her life. As a student, Aysa starts a relationship with Saif Mahdi, a man to whom she is attracted and who respects her need to remain virgin. Once married to him, however, she finds that intercourse with him is physically painful. She becomes pregnant and is less than delighted; her reaction meets with incomprehension by the doctors, who tell her that children are a gift of God. When she has a miscarriage, the doctors assume it to be self-induced. Ultimately her husband exhibits what seems superhuman kindness and tells her that he is willing to live as brother and sister. At any rate, he is frequently out of Egypt, working for the United Nations in Beirut.

Once in England, and after being courted by various men (her beauty is taken for granted, though not dwelt upon), she finds something approaching sexual satisfaction with a man named Gerald Stone. Still, his family name seems to prefigure his ultimate inability to give her what she really wants, though this remains unclear even at the end of the book. At the very least, as a result of this affair sex becomes less than painful for Aysa, though it does not seem to contain any great discoveries. Her husband goes mad with jealousy when he learns of the affair; Saif seems to have renounced living with her on the condition that she not take up with other men. It would be easy for the reader to categorize his reaction as that of a "typical" Mediterranean or Muslim husband, were it not for his very atypical willingness not to force himself on her sexually and to let her lead her own life away from him. What makes him tick? It is never clear.

Indeed, much remains unclear about all the characters besides Aysa, especially the male ones. Though the book is full of dialogue, events are almost unrelentingly presented from Aysa's point of view. Soueif has tried to vary this focus on Aysa's feelings and discoveries with a few interjected episodes in which Aysa is described from Saif's point of view; his reports appear in italics. Still, these are once again accounts of Aysa, and Saif's own world of independent thoughts and feelings is never entered.

The author makes a further attempt to give this relentlessly one-person-centered novel some feel of epic sweep by the rather contrived insertion of headlines from major current events in and around Egypt in the 1960's and 1970's. These, however, are among the most mechanical and least digested episodes in the book, put in as if to anchor it, if only fitfully, to a world outside that of the heroine's jet-set cultural development.

The most perceptible quality of the book, therefore, is its profusion of endless detail regarding all the minutiae of Aysa's life. Much of this, to be sure, is clever and smartly presented. Indeed, this is a clever book, with a number of bright aperçus and telling details. Yet the book shares with a slick autobiography the feel of self-infatuation, of endless talk powered by the belief that such-and-such must be interesting to an outsider because it happened to oneself. Some of this self-absorption seems the result of the heroine's money and social class. Aysa is constantly referred to as "Princess"; the reader wonders whether she might be better termed a spoiled brat.

The novel seems full of missed opportunities to explore the conflicts that should be endemic to the story of a woman caught between two worlds, and between two men from those two worlds. In fact, Aysa is not caught at all. She is too free, too wealthy, too competent, too international, and too self-sufficient. So why should a reader be interested? The book cannot be read as a fable of the postcolonial experience, nor as one of the modern female experience. Though Aysa seems stymied as a woman, one does not know why or how. Does she need to try lesbian sex? Find a better lover? Become celibate? One does not know, and neither does she.

Ultimately, Aysa joins that group of literary creations of the 1970's and 1980's whose problem is precisely that they have had it all—the ne'er-do-wells of plenty whose problem is too many opportunities and no interior direction. Certainly the developing world has as much right to produce characters of this sort as the nominally First World, and perhaps that is the ultimate value of this book. In most such characters, however, the rootlessness and purposelessness of their lives are made clear from the beginning; here the attention paid to Aysa's every tick and quiver and perception is so unrelenting that the reader wonders whether the author realizes that what she has created is pitiable rather than admirable.

The one more intense feeling that lingers on from this book is great veneration for European high culture, whether it is found in Egypt, England, or the United States. The tone of the book with respect to the worldly Cairo of the 1960's is elegiac nostalgia: This was Egypt before the changes following the death of Nasser and the Yom Kippur War, before Egypt's burgeoning population explosion had made Cairo the seething megalopolis paralyzed by gridlock that the first-time visitor experiences in the 1990's. This tone of nostalgia for a vanished Cairene world is given an objective correlate in the heroine's elegy for the great opera house that burned in the early 1970's and has been replaced by a parking lot. This is the nature of alteration in Egypt, it seems: from a building constructed by a Europeanized head of state in the mid-1800's (which saw in its most glorious days the premiere of *Aïda*) to an asphalt slab that retains only the name of the old building—the square is still called "Opera."

Bruce E. Fleming

Sources for Further Study

Boston Globe. June 13, 1993, p. 43.
The Christian Science Monitor. August 3, 1993, p. 11.
Kirkus Reviews. LXI, March 1, 1993, p. 257.
Library Journal. CXVIII, May 1, 1993, p. 118.
Los Angeles Times Book Review. September 26, 1993, p. 15.
New Statesman and Society. V, July 10, 1992, p. 35.
The New York Review of Books. XL, September 23, 1993, p. 28.
Publishers Weekly. CCXL, April 12, 1993, p. 45.
The Times Literary Supplement. June 19, 1992, p. 19.
The Washington Post Book World. XXIII, June 13, 1993, p. 6.

THE INVISIBLE MAN
The Life and Liberties of H. G. Wells

Author: Michael Coren
Publisher: Atheneum (New York). 240 pp. $22.50
Type of work: Biography
Time: 1866-1946
Locale: England

A provocative, succinct biography that raises disturbing questions about the authoritarian and anti-Semitic elements in H. G. Wells's world vision

Principal personages:
HERBERT GEORGE (H. G.) WELLS, a British writer
SARAH WELLS, his mother
JOSEPH WELLS, his father
ISABEL WELLS, his first wife
AMY CATHERINE (JANE) WELLS, his second wife
AMBER REEVES, his mistress
REBECCA WEST, his mistress and literary colleague
HENRY JAMES, a novelist and critic of his fiction
ARNOLD BENNETT, a novelist, his crony
HILLAIRE BELLOC and
G. K. CHESTERTON, Catholic writers who opposed him

H. G. Wells was one of the greatest writers of his age. Before the beginning of the twentieth century, he dominated popular fiction with his science-fiction romances. Novels such as *The Time Machine* (1895), *The Invisible Man* (1897), and *The War of the Worlds* (1898) made him a fortune and established a literary reputation that has endured despite changing fashions and his own uneven output as a writer. Trained as a biologist, Wells gives science fiction a new credibility, making it not merely a tale of wonder but also a serious means of posing questions about the future of humanity.

Not content with success in one field of fiction, however, he soon turned toward novels that engaged the social issues of his time while creating unforgettable characters: *Kipps* (1905), *The History of Mr. Polly* (1910), and the autobiographical *Tono-Bungay* (1909), a vivid recollection of his growing up in the great country home of Uppark, where is mother served as housekeeper. *Ann Veronica* (1909) initiated a series of what he called discussion novels deliberately designed to probe the relationships between men and women and the social conditions that were shaping class structure in Great Britain. Ann Veronica, a science student and an emancipated woman, forsakes her home and family to run away with a middle-aged scientist, defying the conventions of her time and proclaiming the truth of feminism. To Wells's contemporaries, the novel was a scandalous performance, based as it was on his own illicit affair with Amber Reeves, a young woman more than twenty years his junior and the daughter of prominent Fabian socialists—a group, dominated by Bernard Shaw and Sidney and Beatrice Webb, that was intent on gradually transforming the economic and social structure of England. An impatient Wells tried to take over the Fabian Society, rejecting its gradualism and arguing for a much more dynamic assault on the status quo. Thus in both personal and political terms, he made himself into an outcast and yet a thrilling representation to the younger generation of a man not afraid to speak up and act on his own.

Given his own background—he was the son of a servant and was not expected to rise much above his apprenticeship in a draper's shop—Wells was keenly aware of how society was organized to thwart radical change. His own mother, Sarah, a religious zealot, was at a loss as to how to treat her precocious son, who read volume after volume in Uppark's impressive library, including Plato's *Republic*, a utopia that was to have a lifelong influence on Wells's effort to imagine and to promulgate the ideal state. Sarah consented to his career as a teacher only after he ran away from the draper's shop and seemed incapable of serving a conventional apprenticeship. Toward women and family responsibilities Wells had something of his father Joseph's carefree attitude. Joseph was an excellent cricketer and a genial mate, but he possessed a hopeless head for practical affairs. Wells compensated for a similar defect in his own character by making his second wife his business partner, ensuring that she handled the details of his career as a writer.

Wells made his way to late nineteenth century London, studying with the famed scientist Thomas H. Huxley, known as "Darwin's bulldog" because he championed with such vigor the new theory of evolution. Then Wells met his cousin Isabel, with whom he fell in love and to whom he was quickly married. Since he was ignorant about sex and had been tortured by it in his adolescence, marriage seemed a reasonable solution for a young man still bedeviled by the strictures of Victorianism. Yet Wells's ebullient personality chafed at his wife's conventional values, and his own maturing mind and tastes contributed to his estrangement from her. He soon began consorting with other women, abandoning a teaching career for writing and running off with Amy Catherine Robbins, a fellow science student who became his second wife.

After the birth of their two sons, Wells and his second wife apparently ceased their sexual relations. Her attitude toward this change in her marital life has never been successfully explained. Even Wells never knew for sure, calling her an elusive personality. At any rate, he embarked on a series of adventurous liaisons, often with important literary figures and social reformers such as Dorothy Richardson, Violet Hunt, and Margaret Sanger. For Wells, these affairs were more than a diversion; they were part of his search for the perfect mate, what he called his "lover-shadow," and were part of his endless quest for stimulation, which his wife evidently tolerated so long as he returned home and maintained her in an establishment befitting his prominence in public life. Wells tried to be discreet, but his affairs often led to scandal or the threat of scandal, which his wife and his mistresses helped him to cover up.

Wells had a restless personality. No single woman, no one vein of writing satisfied him. He attacked Henry James and his circle for making of fiction a kind of high-church liturgy that squeezed the vitality out of life. He excoriated James's later literary style. He compared its lumbering prose aimed at expressing rarefied but ultimately trivial insights to a hippopotamus straining to pick up a pea. Wells favored writers such as Arnold Bennett, whose precise notation of social detail and concern with the way people lived day-to-day he found fascinating. Bennett also introduced Wells to some of the important opinion-makers of British society and generally made him feel as if he had arrived as an influential figure in his own right.

Not content with fiction, Wells became a world-class journalist, traveling to the United States, the Soviet Union, Australia, and many other parts of the world, endeavoring to report on and to assimilate global developments that contributed to his utopian visions of a future world. He deeply believed that human beings had an opportunity to shape their own destiny even as he despaired of their success in doing so. Hence his attraction to utopias ruled by enlightened intellectual aristocrats (he called them "samurai"), on the one hand, and his attraction to dystopias torn apart by war—as in his novel (1933) and film (1936) *The Shape of Things to Come* which accurately predicted and portrayed the aerial bombing of London in World War II.

Wells was the protean figure of his time, a hero to the younger generation because of his advocacy of a freer relationship between men and women, his jettisoning of Victorian and Edwardian values that ratified the class structure, and his transatlantic— indeed global—vision of a developing world, a vision best exemplified in his ambitious and extraordinarily popular book *The Outline of History* (1920). There he suggested that human beings could digest and surpass the past and build a better future. Yet Wells's grounding in science never allowed him to rest in a facile optimism, and many of his works are cautionary tales—such as *The Island of Doctor Moreau* (1896), where a scientist's experiments on animals, his effort to make them more "human," result in grotesque creatures that mock the human effort at progress. Similarly, Wells's final book, *Mind at the End of Its Tether* (1945), is a bleak reading of human capability.

Wells wrote more than one hundred books and engaged in most of the important public controversies of his time. As a dynamic and sometimes irritable thinker, he often contradicted himself, changed positions, recanted first principles—abruptly dropping his pacifism, for example, to support Great Britain's participation in World War I. Consequently, a biographer must tread very carefully indeed in analyzing what Wells thought. There is room for many different H. G. Wellses in a single biography.

Michael Coren claims to have written an iconoclastic biography overturning the positive judgments about Wells usually made in conventional literary and political history. If his claim seems exaggerated, it is because other biographers have taken note of Wells's dictatorial side but have not made it the focus of their work. Coren has a point, for in many of Wells's novels a distaste for the masses and a skepticism of democratic government are apparent. In his novel *The World of William Clissold* (1926), he spends a chapter attacking Karl Marx and the pretensions of socialists, yet the early Wells championed socialism, and *The World of William Clissold* is no less harsh on individualists. Indeed, in that novel he attacks all system-builders as reductive thinkers who shy away from a complex reality.

Coren is best at conveying the essentials of Wells's life in a shrewd and concise fashion, providing well-balanced accounts of Wells's marriages and affairs. The chapter on Wells and Rebecca West, for example, treats a controversial subject with considerable sensitivity, revealing their prickly personalities and showing how Wells took advantage of the cautious, small nature of his second wife, Amy Catherine, to pursue his sexual affairs. He even renamed his wife Jane and constructed a new identity for her that dutiful biographers tend to accept.

Author of a biography of G. K. Chesterton, who was one of Wells's opponents, Coren is well informed on how Wells stood in relation to his literary and political critics. Although Wells was an expert polemicist, in certain ways he was no match for Hillaire Belloc, and he resorted to a kind of bluster that Coren is good at exposing. As more than one reviewer has remarked, however, Coren seems to give Chesterton the last word, in that Coren seems far more sympathetic to the reasons for Chesterton's anti-Semitism than for the intolerance he believes Wells showed for the Jews. Perhaps Coren's attitude is inevitable, since he seems to have begun as a devotee of Wells and then become dismayed upon discovering the defects in his idol's thinking. Wells, as a man of the future, an advanced thinker, is thus held to a higher standard. More than any other recent biographer, Coren sees Wells's flaws as a man as having influenced his views of women and of race. In this respect, Coren has written what might be called a feminist biography of Wells.

Those who have read the standard Wells biographies will find little that is new in Coren's biography, and they will be dismayed by the rather shoddy scholarship, especially in the inadequate notes. The book's polemical nature makes it unreliable as an introduction to Wells, although it might be selected as a third choice after the standard biographies by Norman and Jean Mackenzie (1973) and David C. Smith (1986).

Carl Rollyson

Sources for Further Study

Booklist. LXXXIX, August, 1993, p. 2029.
Books in Canada. XXII, March 1993, p. 40.
Chicago Tribune. July 21, 1993, V, p. 3.
Choice. XXXI, February, 1994, p. 933.
London Review of Books. XV, April 8, 1993, p. 17.
Nature. CCCLXI, February 4, 1993, p. 413.
New Scientist. CXXXVII, March 20, 1993, p. 46.
New Statesman and Society. VI, January 15, 1993, p. 38.
The Spectator. January 23, 1993, p. 34.
The Times Literary Supplement. January 15, 1993, p. 5.
The Washington Post Book World. XXIII, August 22, 1993, p. 8.

ISLAM AND THE WEST

Author: Bernard Lewis (1916-   )
Publisher: Oxford University Press (New York). 217 pp. $25.00
Type of work: History and current affairs; essays
Time: The seventh century C.E. to the late twentieth century
Locale: Primarily the Middle East and the wider Islamic world

A collection of essays examining various aspects of the interactions of Islam and the West from the inception of Islam to the late twentieth century

In *Islam and the West* Bernard Lewis—one of the grand old men of Middle East scholarship—collects eleven of his erudite and readable essays, written at widely divergent levels of specialization but all having something to do with the relation of the Islamic world and the West. The essays range from a technical consideration of the difficulties of translation from the Arabic and a scholarly treatment of Edward Gibbon's view of Muhammad, Islam's prophet, to an "op-ed" level polemic regarding the current attack on scholars such as Lewis himself, who is proud to call himself by the term coined for those in his discipline in the nineteenth century, "Orientalist." Despite the variety of its topics and scholarly levels, the collection is unified by its consistent tone of Enlightenment confidence in the ultimate power of reasoning to solve problems, as well as by its wide-ranging erudition.

Lewis' main point, reiterated in the various individual essays, is that the currently fashionable disdain for the nineteenth century discipline of Orientalism is illegitimate for a number of reasons. The book builds toward a specific articulation of this point in the second of its three main subsections, which are entitled "Encounters," "Studies and Perceptions," and "Islamic Response and Reaction." In the first section this point is expressed only intermittently, and the reader might almost believe that he or she has bought a book of historical interest alone. The middle section brings the topic out in the open. The book's final section once again becomes more technical, considering the resurgence of Islamic fundamentalism and offering a fascinating characterization of Shiite Islam (the minority sect, and the one in power in Iran) as congenitally prone to revolt because it is intrinsically based on rebellion against the Islamic status quo.

The opening essay in the book's first section offers a historical overview of the interest taken by the Islamic world in the West, and that of the West in the Islamic world. Even here there are hints of Lewis' ultimate point of view and his polemical direction. He makes the point repeatedly that before the twentieth century, interest between the two worlds was radically one-sided, consisting almost exclusively of interest by the West in the Islamic world. This one-sidedness was the result of the fact that the Islamic world was by far the more powerful: It constantly threatened the West, and was in fact enjoying steady expansion. This seems logical to Lewis. Why, he seems to ask, should a world so confident of its own power have been interested in the world of weaklings it expected ultimately to dominate? Even the Crusades that loomed so large in the Christian imagination were nothing but minor skirmishes for the Islamic world, lost in the Islamic imagination among many other military battles of the time.

Here Lewis' vast historical knowledge, worn gratifyingly lightly, comes into play. Sketching for the layperson the Muslim expansion in Russia and across North Africa, he paints a picture of the Christian world at bay, having managed to hang on by the skin of its teeth. Lewis observes that

> in recent years it has become the practice, in both western Europe and the Middle East, to see and present the Crusades as an early exercise in Western imperialism. . . . They were not seen in that light at the time, either by Christians or by Muslims.

Greater historical knowledge provides a different view, in other words, and it is only the impartial scholars of the area such as Lewis—those happy still to call themselves Orientalists—who can provide this historical context.

Even the essay "Legal and Historical Reflections on the Position of Muslim Populations Under Non-Muslim Rule," also in the book's initial section and full of historical arcana, is linked to the late twentieth century intellectual climate of suspicion toward Western considerations of Islam by Lewis' point that Islam has never been able to rationalize a situation that has become more and more common in the West: that of Muslims voluntarily living under non-Islamic governments. It was not supposed to happen, and yet there is virtually no Western city without its population of immigrant Muslims. Islam, Lewis suggests, finds itself without a theoretical explanation for an increasingly important aspect of the international scene. Westerners must consider it.

The theme of the relationship of history to the current intellectual scene breaks to the surface in the essay "The Question of Orientalism," which contains an extended critique of the single most cited attack on Western studies of Islam, Edward Said's *Orientalism* (1978). Lewis sets up his problem by asking the reader to consider how ridiculous one would find it if in ancient Greek studies the demand were made that only those of Greek ancestry talk about Athens, and this only if the scholar were willing to subscribe to currently popular political positions taken by the Greeks, say against their archenemy Turkey in the question of Cyprus. Yet, he suggests, exactly such a situation holds in current Middle East studies, where Arab nationalists and others of radical political persuasions have attacked Western, non-Arab students of the Islamic world.

The charge brought against Orientalism and Orientalists, crystallized in Said's book, is that Western consideration of the Islamic world was the close mate of the nineteenth century Western imperialism that subjugated much of the Islamic world under the colonial control of two nations, France and Great Britain. The discipline of Orientalism is, in Said's view and that of many left-leaning scholars today, a particularly noxious example of the attempt of the powerful to control the less powerful. According to Said, the very images and vocabulary in which the Islamic world are presented in the West are determined by the slanted, power-seeking viewpoints of Westerners. An insufficient sympathy with certain political aspirations of some Arab peoples is also usually asserted by those critical of Western Orientalist studies.

Lewis accuses Said of being little more than an amateur and a simplifier, indeed the creator of what he calls an "alternative universe." Said's book, which has been immensely influential in many Western intellectual circles, is, according to Lewis, simply incorrect and inept. Said, Lewis points out, concentrates on only one part of the Islamic world (while talking of the "Orient"), eliminating any consideration of Persian or Turkish studies. He "rearranges both the geography and the history of Orientalism and . . . places the main development of Arabic studies in Britain and France and dates them after the British and French expansion in the Arab world."

Thus, Lewis says, Said has his chronology wrong: "These studies were well established in Britain and France long before even the erroneously early date that [Said] assigns to British and French expansion." Furthermore, Lewis points out, Said completely ignores essential German contributions to the field—an important omission, given the lack of German colonial aspirations for Muslim lands, and one that should call into question Said's claim that scholarly study was little else but the fifth column of militarily expansionism. Said further emotionalizes the issue, according to Lewis, by consistently using a vocabulary of military attack or sexual domination. All these words seem to suggest, Lewis says, that knowledge is a fixed commodity that can be appropriated and won like sexual favors or booty of war: If the West takes it, then this knowledge is unavailable to Arab scholars.

At this point Lewis' historical contextualization from earlier in the book reemerges, its relevance suddenly clear: "The study of Islam in Europe . . . began in the High Middle Ages and was concerned not with a conquered but a conquering world." It is an unpardonably blinkered view to see the Islamic world as having historically occupied the militarily impotent position it currently does. (Neither side in the debate considers the powerful position of the oil-producing Islamic nations with respect to the West.) Indeed, the remainder of the essay makes clear Lewis' frustration with the lack of context available to politically interested commentators such as Said, most of whom simply lack the scholarly background necessary to put things into context— background such as historical knowledge and expertise in the relevant languages, the strong point of the Orientalists. Here Lewis' fundamentally Enlightenment faith in the power of rationality and of objective knowledge becomes clearest. Knowledge is not something that one side wrests from the other; it leaves unchanged the world that it describes, and is itself neutral.

Lewis is clearly right to point out that Said's view of Orientalism is not so much an argument as a set of presuppositions—what Lewis calls an "epistemology." Furthermore, Lewis at least has the grace to lay out his own epistemology with admirable clarity. The insufficiencies of Said's book notwithstanding (and these have been pointed out by several commentators), it seems unlikely that Said would be convinced by Lewis' refutation—at least not as epistemology goes. It seems likely that he would disagree with just this balanced Newtonian view of knowledge as independent of its object, existing in a metaworld of common discourse. For Said, by contrast—as for his mentor, the French philosopher Michel Foucault, and Foucault's mentor, the German philosopher Friedrich Nietzsche—knowledge does not exist in a metaworld;

instead it is part of the sweaty struggle for domination in the world here below. Lewis scores what seem to be lethal points in showing how Said is wrong in many of his claims; it seems likely, however, that Said would simply try to find other ways of expressing his underlying point, which Lewis has not so much refuted as defined for him.

What the reader ultimately takes home from this book is the tone of voice of an erudite, calm servant of objective knowledge, exasperated at the rebellion of the unschooled and the disfranchised against the shackles and rigors of his discipline. Whether the reader finds this tone of voice soothing or infuriating will clearly be determined by factors other than that knowledge itself.

Bruce E. Fleming

Sources for Further Study

Booklist. LXXXIX, March 1, 1993, p. 1139.
Chicago Tribune. July 7, 1993, V, p. 3.
Commentary. XCVI, December, 1993, p. 57.
Forbes. CLII, October 11, 1993, p. 26.
Library Journal. CXVIII, May 1, 1993, p. 90.
National Review. XLV, August 23, 1993, p. 58.
The New York Review of Books. XL, October 7, 1993, p. 43.
The New York Times Book Review. XCVIII, May 30, 1993, p. 8.
San Francisco Chronicle. July 25, 1993, p. REV.7.
The Times Literary Supplement. July 9, 1993, p. 32.

JAMES JOYCE
The Years of Growth, 1882-1915

Author: Peter Costello
First published: 1992, in Great Britain
Publisher: Pantheon Books (New York). 374 pp. $30.00
Type of work: Biography
Time: 1882-1915
Locale: Dublin, Paris, Trieste, Rome

A biography of the Irish writer James Joyce dealing principally with his formative years in Dublin and Trieste

> *Principal personages:*
> JAMES JOYCE, an Irish writer
> NORA JOYCE, his wife
> JOHN JOYCE, his father
> STANISLAUS JOYCE, his brother

Reading James Joyce, particularly his two great works, *Ulysses* (1922) and *Finnegans Wake* (1939), is a descent into a catacomb for which the correct key, or a well-informed guide, appears indispensable. The key and the guide come in the form of such books as Joseph Campbell's *A Skeleton Key to "Finnegans Wake"* (1947) and Don Gifford's *Joyce Annotated* (1982). Yet armed only with books like these, readers may come away from Joyce sensing that the experience was in some way flat, that between the stones analyzed and annotated lie cracks that seemingly hold the whole thing together, a continuity that eludes the simplistic, fact-by-fact approach of the well-meaning guides. The discovery of this continuity involves the study of Joyce's life itself, to a degree unnecessary to the reading of a less demanding writer. Joyce is the most demanding of writers in the English language, if one dares call "English" his transmogrifications of the language, and not simply insofar as he requires the reader to approach with an air of erudition. Joyce demands to be known, and as is clear from the fervor of the Joyce industry, not a few have acceded to this demand. Shelves and shelves of books have come forth, among them a number of outstanding volumes, and among these at least one biography that, while it is mandatory reading for anyone studying Joyce, can in itself justifiably be called, as Anthony Burgess puts it, "the greatest literary biography of the century"—Richard Ellmann's magnificent *James Joyce* (1965). Yet even as great as this book is, it does not cover certain areas of Joyce's life as fully as possible, and in regard to a few relatively minor facts it is mistaken. Thus it is that Peter Costello's *James Joyce: The Years of Growth, 1882-1915* arrives as a welcome corrective to Ellmann.

Costello's first chapter, "The Dead," is as complete an expedition into the far corners of Joyce's genealogy as one might desire. Costello follows each branch of the family tree, identifying great-granduncles and the like previously passed over by Ellmann. With these identifications come the family anecdotes with which Joyce grew up and of which he later made use in his writings. Famous among these is the anecdote Joyce wove into his story "The Dead" of his grandfather's mill horse Johnny, which became stuck walking round and round a statue in a Dublin park while its rider roared and brandished his whip to no avail. Also, various details regarding the development of Joyce's tastes and mannerisms are provided. For example, "The Yellow Ale," a song that Joyce claimed was the most beautiful in the world and that Ellmann suggests Joyce learned from a 1901 edition of *Irish Homestead*, was actually taught to Joyce as a boy, according to Costello, by his grandfather. Unfortunately, details such as this are often left unreferenced in the scanty endnotes, and the reader is left to wonder how Costello became privy to such interesting and suggestive facts.

A strength of Costello's book is his detailing of Joyce's father's slide into bankruptcy, a story of political backstabbing and deceits not adequately addressed by Ellmann. All of his life John Joyce claimed to have been financially ruined by government bureaucrats who disagreed with his politics, claims that Ellmann largely dismisses as the paranoid delusions of a mind overly pickled in liquor. Costello takes the more sympathetic view that John Joyce's slide into terminal alcoholism resulted from the loss of the means to support his large family, and thus of his self-respect. Costello details the elder Joyce's political entanglements and correlates his initial successes in securing well-salaried government jobs with the successes of the political parties he supported. At the same time, Costello, by a close examination of John Joyce's assets and debits, attempts to show that he was guilty less of living beyond his means than of expecting those means to continue indefinitely. When the winds of politics changed, so did Joyce's fortunes. He lost access to jobs, his pension was unjustly reduced, and the resistance he encountered when making claim to his rights was apparently insurmountable. The effect of the family's fall into poverty on James, not yet in his teens, was profound, establishing in him a permanent sympathy for the poor while at the same time instilling a lifelong obsession with maintaining a semblance, at least, of bourgeois respectability.

At least for the student of Joyce, one of Costello's most interesting achievements is his identifying of the mysterious female character who appears in *A Portrait of the Artist as a Young Man* (1916) by the initials E. C.; in the surviving chapters of the abandoned novel *Stephen Hero* (1944), out of which *A Portrait of the Artist as a Young Man* was developed, the same character goes by the name of Emma Clery. In *Stephen Hero*, Stephen Dedalus, Joyce's name for himself in his novels, approaches Emma on the street and proposes what amounts to a one-night stand; the flustered, astounded young woman turns him down. Research has shown that there was no Emma Clery whom Joyce might have known in the Dublin of his university days. It has been suggested that Mary Sheehy, a friend in Joyce's adolescent years, served as a model for Emma. In later life, however, Sheehy sweetly disavowed any knowledge of Joyce's admiration and even "declined the honor" of such an identification. Ellmann supposed that "Joyce invented most of the romantic episodes in his novels," a possibility that seems quite unlikely given Joyce's compulsive transmutation of his life into art.

Costello has his own candidate whom he persuasively advances. Among the students in Joyce's graduating class was a woman by the name of Mary Elizabeth

Cleary. Costello points out that her initials, M. E., might have suggested to Joyce the name Emma, and the spelling of "Clery" Joyce may have borrowed from his friend Arthur Clery. Costello goes on to paint a portrait of an intelligent, attractive woman who distinguished herself in the political, academic, and social life of Ireland. Her son, a highly regarded professor in Dublin, admitted in conversation with Costello that he had been struck by the coincidence between his mother's name and the character in *Stephen Hero* when it was posthumously published in 1944. He had subsequently learned from his mother that Joyce "had been keen on her" but she had found him a "common, vulgar person" who "told dirty stories and picked his nose." Costello marshals further evidence that makes the connection seem highly likely. He admits that, as with any Joycean character, Emma is a composite of a number of women Joyce might have known, and he indicates who some of these others may have been. Nevertheless, the portrait he draws of Mary Cleary clears what had heretofore been a vague area of Joyce's past and his art, while giving us an amusing and revelatory portrait of the young artist through the eyes of a young woman he admired.

The pinpointing of connections between the Dubliners Joyce knew with the characters that people his books is one of the strengths of this biography. Often, Costello fleshes out these real-life models to a greater degree than does Ellmann, as with the Dublin Presbyterian who one evening helped out the young Joyce, drunk to incoherence, and who was thereby graced with the honor of being transformed into Leopold Bloom in *Ulysses*. Sometimes this wealth of information becomes somewhat overwhelming, and one begins to wish for a quick-reference chart like those provided at the beginning of a Tolstoy novel—a who's who with the web of interconnections made instantly clear. Indeed, it is surprising that Costello did not provide such a chart, given the wealth of addendums already attached. These appendices principally comprise the family trees of four branches of Joyce's pedigree and serve as one of the highlights of the book.

Through his careful research, Costello corrects certain of Ellmann's mistaken assumptions. For example, Ellmann, trusting the report of Joyce's somewhat gullible younger brother Stanislaus, claims that Joyce lost his virginity at the age of fourteen. Yet because the incident occurred following attendance at a play, the first production of which occurred in Dublin when Joyce was already sixteen, Costello suggests that Joyce was not quite so precocious in this area as has been assumed.

One of the major differences between Costello and Ellmann is in the portrait of Joyce that emerges. Ellmann impresses the reader with the complexity of Joyce's character, a man at once timid and fierce, who could be pompous, vengeful, manipulative, and shrewd, acerbic at one time and shy as a lamb at the next. Ellmann does not merely assert his impression of Joyce's character; being a good biographer, he shows the man in action and largely lets the reader draw his or her own conclusions. Costello, on the other hand, fails to bring Joyce to life and especially mutes his strength of character. His willfulness and self-determination dissipate, leaving the impression of a somewhat bland, colorless man who by the by turned literature in the twentieth century topsy-turvy. Perhaps in an attempt to rectify his weakness at portraiture,

Costello includes in his appendices a chart that professes to trace Joyce's character traits through a system of arcane genetic formulas. The theory behind the chart seems fanciful, and the page comes off merely as one of those peculiarities Joyce too often elicits from his admirers, as does the extensive astrological chart that Costello includes.

Another fault of the book lies in the number of errors Costello allows to creep in. While generally the amount of research is impressive, certain points of fact went apparently unchecked. Costello mentions that the boy in the story "An Encounter" finds a priest's "rusted bicycle lamp" when in fact it is the boy in "Araby" who finds the priest's "rusty bicycle-pump," a much more suggestive indication of the priest's sexual perversions. A mistake such as this is perhaps excusable insofar as Costello is not a critic. When names become confused, however, as does that of the Fenian Joyce visited in Paris, Joseph Casey, and when this confusion continues into the index of the book, things seem to be a bit out of hand.

Although Costello claims to have written for the general reader, the wealth of details would bog down such an audience. On the contrary, *James Joyce* seems more of a help to the interested student of Joyce and as such is a worthy supplement to Ellmann's biography.

Peter Crawford

Sources for Further Study

Booklist. LXXXIX, April 15, 1993, p. 1487.
Contemporary Review. CCLXIII, August, 1993, p. 108.
Kirkus Reviews. LXI, February 1, 1993, p. 111.
Library Journal. CXVIII, February 15, 1993, p. 165.
The New York Review of Books. XL, October 21, 1993, p. 28.
The New York Times Book Review. XCVIII, May 2, 1993, p. 18.
The Spectator. CCLXIX, November 28, 1992, p. 37.
The Times Literary Supplement. November 6, 1992, p. 24.
The Wall Street Journal. May 26, 1993, p. A16.
The Washington Post Book World. XXIII, May 23, 1993, p. 9.

JASON THE SAILOR

Author: Diane Wakoski (1937-   )
Publisher: Black Sparrow Press (Santa Rosa, California). 197 pp. $25.00; paperback $13.00
Type of work: Poetry

The second volume in a sequence designated The Archaeology of Movies and Books, *which presents a poetic life through an amalgam of notes, letters, quotations, and poems*

The publication of Diane Wakoski's *Emerald Ice: Selected Poems, 1962-1987* (1988) by Black Sparrow Press marked a point of measure in the life of a very active poet. Since her first book, *Coins & Coffins*, appeared in 1962, Wakoski has seen many volumes of poetry into print. Her singular voice, which incorporates the fusion of pop culture and vernacular language introduced by the Beats, the concern with form characteristic of the Black Mountain poets, and the inquisitive intellectual vision of the San Francisco Renaissance, her protofeminist perspective, her evocative use of deep imagery, and her postmodernist reflexivity would seem to have ensured a prominent place for her in the American poetic galaxy. Yet a maverick spirit has unsettled conventional critics and anthologizers, and consequently Wakoski's work is somewhat less well known and promoted than her accomplishments might suggest.

The crucial components of Wakoski's poetics are also the features that are likely to engender a resistance to her work. Wakoski's version of feminist thinking, for example, tends to elevate women to an equal plane with men but does not support an argument that women are more important and does not offer any examination of the feminine psyche beyond that of the poet herself. While Wakoski's work, from the first, was a rather early expression of a strong feminist position, her persistent interest in men as figures of romantic desire (as in her creation of the semimythical King of Spain) has done as much to limit her audience as to expand it.

In an interview with the *New York Quarterly* that was included in *The Craft of Poetry* (1974), Wakoski claimed, "The Diane who's in my poems is not a real person. . . . The Diane in my poems really is fantasy. . . . no matter what my life is and no matter how it is fulfilled, there are many things that I will not be, and those are the things that I will fantasize." The degree to which Wakoski resembles the "Diane" in her poems has varied through her writing life, but the publication of *Emerald Ice* seems to have altered the relationship so that the two books that follow, *Medea the Sorceress* (1991) and *Jason the Sailor*, offer a writer who has narrowed the apparent distance down to nothing. Consequently, the line she quotes from the poem "Kore" by Robert Creeley, "O Love/ where are you/ leading/ me now?" is as much a motto as a guide, and the direction it sets is through the formative history and current condition of the poet. Using Medea as a construction of the woman as magician, a figure for the shaper of thought through words, and Jason as a figure for an elusive force sometimes sailor, sometimes troubador, sometimes outlaw, sometimes artist, always alluring, Wakoski has established twin poles in a cosmos of shifting realities. The two books can be read separately, just as the poems in each book can stand as separate entities in many cases, but her overarching title for both volumes, *The Archaeology of Movies and Books*, suggests their interlinkage as well as the possibility of future volumes. Wakoski has begun the composition of an epic of the self in conjunction with important cultural features of her time, and its autobiographical attributes are central to her method of organization.

The literal reality of the data is not the essential question here, especially for a poet whose books from Black Sparrow contained, beneath her photograph, the biographical note: "The poems in her published books give all the important information about her life." A map preceding the first poem in *Medea the Sorceress* roughly charts the course of her life (labeled "RIVE EAU DE VIE") in allegorical and actual terms, highlighting her origins on the Pacific coast, her betrayal by the first Jason as lover after her desertion by Jason the Sailor (her father), her life as "Medea the Sorceress in exile" from 1955 to 1975, her return to life's truer course at East Lansing, where she has been writer in residence at Michigan State University and where she currently lives—when at home—with her husband the photographer Robert Turney, whom she celebrates as Steel Man in her poems.

The specificity of this record is sufficient to set a ground of certainty. The method of approach to this record, however, is based on a book by Nick Herbert, *Quantum Reality: Beyond the New Physics* (1985), which is quoted liberally through both volumes. Herbert's main thesis is "There is no deep reality," the Copenhagen inter-pretation that suggests that subatomic particles not only do "not follow classical laws, they do not even follow a classical *kind* of law—that is, a law that governs the motion of real objects." Wakoski uses Herbert's lucid, accessible text to support her implicit contention that the poet, like the quantum theorist, is always examining and creating versions of reality from the available data. The subjectivity of this position is appro-priate for a poet whose romantic capacity for self-creation and self-interpretation depends as much on emotion and instinct as her finely tuned intellect, and who in likening herself to Medea the Sorceress acknowledges the boundary where science and magic (or sorcery) merge. As she says in the poem "The Archaeology of Movies & Books,"

> POETRY BRIDGES THE PRIVATE AND THE PUBLIC,
> no, it is
> both.

Both *Medea the Sorcerer* and *Jason the Sailor* use prose passages extensively, offering both a balance to and an indication of the assembling process behind the poetry. There is a considerable amount of explanation of the poet's contentions as well as arguments with and defenses against various critics, notably feminists who call for a unified position rather than Wakoski's very personal conception growing from her "California youth and adolescence," which she spent "trying to figure out HOW to be perceived as a sexual object," and continuing as "a woman who finally, triumphantly, was able to at least appear sexually desirable." The structure of each book is built around letters to Craig Cotter (described as a former student and a "disciple"), to

Jonathan (described as a troubador/friend receiving her letters at the Ritter Cafe in Vienna), quotes from Herbert, excerpts from a kind of journal signed by the poet to the reader, and the poems themselves. Because of the fairly intricate interlinkage, it is hard to draw single poems from the work as exemplary—there is a complementarity to the collection and an importance to the setting in terms of its preparation for each poem. This does not diminish the force of individual poems but suggests the necessity of reading them within a field of action rather than as single expressions or performances.

Toward the last pages of *Medea the Sorceress*, Wakoski says, "Now that I have finally found a faithful, good husband, I am terrified at the thought of the Jasons who defined my life." This note of candor is characteristic of her efforts to avoid accidental concealment and to confront whatever psychic demons have been hidden during her life. By developing versions of her own identity (signing letters with many shadings of her name, such as "Yr Lady of the Coiling Light," "Yr Lady of the Moon," "Yr (old) California Girl," "Yr Lady of the Silver Foot" in terms of the Medea/Medusa/Media myth, Wakoski has prepared herself for a further journey into the realm of the Jason story/myths. In a variant of Creeley's appeal to love's beckoning, she asks, "Words, words,/ where are you leading me now?" At the heart of her poetic philosophy is a lifelong faith in the revelatory powers of language, as expressed in "The Deer in Me":

> But what if I too
> could make my words, like silver arrows,
> like tinsel, like glittering icicles, like strings of
> water on spider webs or silver finger bowls
> dance and clatter over my body,
> until they draped into soft costume?

Wakoski's ease with her craft, her supple, inventive use of imagery, her mastery of tone and pace, her manipulation of rhythm, remain the sources of her poetic strength. These qualities elevate her work beyond the dangers of sentimental confession, a real possibility when she talks about "all the young troubadours to whom I sing" since they might take "the place of the Jason who left me when I was young." Even her skill with the mythmaking process that converts the personal into an aspect of the general stretching toward the universal might not be sufficient to modulate the kind of yearning almost nakedly presented by the poet who admits, "I continually think of how I have loved men more than myself, and wanted their love, though since I myself do not love women, have never quite understood why men should love me."

The transposition of this desire into a poetry that is more than a record of individual need depends on the success of what Wakoski calls "my lifetime quest for beauty," specifically defined as "the perfect words, the poems, of love and beauty." The limits of the body, changing with age in another act of betrayal, are opposed by the art and act of poetry itself, so that all the Jasons who have failed to satisfy her impossible desire—"I want them to love me more than any/ other woman," as she says in "Hummingbirds, Dazzling in from the Calif. Desert"—might be placed in a more manageable context. She has finally realized that what she wants most is "to be touched with language,/ and the something even more insidious—the mind."

The most effective poems in *Jason the Sailor* engage those questions about love and romance that have always been prominent in Wakoski's work and that here operate beyond the focus of a specific emotion such as anger or hope to include reflective assessments about life and art. As she notes in "Sudden Mendenhall Glacier," her critics say that she has lost "the zest, the bare leg, the cutting/ jag of breath of [her] bohemian youth," but her claim that "wit is all there, condensed into my short frosty hair" indicates her belief that the spry, dancing thrusts of her satirical attacks have modulated into a kind of contentment. The fascination of the natural world— California coastline, Nevada desert, Midwestern forest wilderness, the order of a garden—remains as a source of vitality.

The satisfaction of her relationship with her husband, whose photographs of her appear on her books, has not completely obliterated her agitation concerning the "Jasons." Nevertheless, moments of domestic tranquillity reassure her, as she implies in "The Coffee Brush." That poem closes with an image of "handsome young men" subletting her home, among her intimate objects, "while Steel Man and I are eating/ thin-crusted pizza in Chicago."

The act of thinking and writing about some of the most painful parts of her life has ameliorated some of the most immediate pain, although it will never completely vanish. Wakoski can recognize the complexity of her love/wrath feelings about her father, the primal Jason figure, a sailor who seems to have deserted her family. In "Lotto Night," she acknowledges his gift of the ocean: saying

> I want to live
> by the ocean, I want to look at its silvery lidded cover
> and think about my stout father
> who laughed ghosts with white hair away,
> who reminds me that I have two sets of genes,
> not just the ghostly ones of my moonlit hair,
> but his darker ones, the ones which can stand in the fog
> and do not wince when something invisible,
> like your past
> brushes by.

The capacity to see her life in the cosmos of her work, the deepest "reality" she has reached while driving "Medea's chariot," has continued but to some extent transcended her mythologizing method of extrapolating from the particular to the legendary. Devised as a means of responding to mistreatment, it has always been driven by the fusion of attraction and repulsion, desire mingled with dread. The disparate elements of Wakoski's work—the mix of popular culture with a very refined, highly educated literary sensibility—will probably continue to confound critics, though she wishes that they would admire her work ("Marjorie Perloff, the critic whose praise I have longed for all these years"). Her avowal that "I always felt that I had to be with a man to be complete" guarantees rejection from another entrenched constituency.

Nevertheless, these disappointments will not deter Wakoski from the course she has been following:

> The moon
> in my window tonight
> urging me out of bed
> to go down and look at the orchids.

Wakoski, still in the prime of her poetic life, an endlessly analytic aging romantic, has embarked on the most ambitious of journeys. *Medea the Sorceress* and *Jason the Sailor*, the first two volumes of an unfolding epic of the poetic self, are highly interesting reports from an explorer in what might be called the Cosmos of Reality.

Leon Lewis

Source for Further Study

Library Journal. CXVIII, August, 1993, p. 109.

JESUS' SON

Author: Denis Johnson (1949-   )
Publisher: Farrar Straus Giroux (New York). 160 pp. $19.00
Type of work: Short stories

In Jesus' Son, *Denis Johnson's first book of stories, the poet-novelist takes the reader inside the lives of characters who stagger and fall between states of damnation and grace*

It is no accident that Denis Johnson's *Jesus' Son* opens with a bloody, fatal car wreck on a rainy two-lane highway under a spread of "Midwestern clouds like great grey brains." This incident from "Car Crash While Hitchhiking" sets the stage and the tone for what follows: a series of head-on collisions that Johnson's narrator—an on-the-run junkie—encounters over the course of eleven electrifying stories. Johnson hurls his readers on a shotgunned journey through emergency rooms and dope dens, detoxification wards and rest homes for those whose "impossible deformities . . . made God look like a senseless maniac." The world of *Jesus' Son* is a place, a purgatory of sorts, where "the rapist met his victim, the jilted child discovered its mother. But nothing could be healed." These are the kinds of moments around which Denis Johnson shapes stories that are destined not only to linger but to last, moments that once they are lived through (for to read this book is to live *through* it) will never—can never—be forgotten.

In *Jesus' Son*, Johnson breaks narrative rules and conventions with the candor of a strung-out junkie pawning off his mother's jewelry box in order to cop a quick fix. Standard trademarks of the genre, such as telling a straightforward story (with an Aristotelian beginning, middle, and end), have been tossed aside in favor of a fractured, bullet-holed prose fabric that reflects a man's disjointed hallucinatory memory.

In "Two Men," Johnson begins: "I met the first man as I was going home from a dance at the Veterans of Foreign Wars Hall." The second man never even turns up in this story, although he does show his face in "The Other Man": "But I never finished telling you about the two men. I never even started describing the second one." Johnson's narrator speaks about past events as they randomly reenter his memory. He does not attempt to assemble the mishaps of his life in any kind of chronological order. He is casual about what he tells, as if he were speaking not about himself but about a stranger, someone he met one night at a bar.

Johnson is not the first to write about the criminally drug-driven drifters who inhabit the darker corners of the world, in bars like the Vine, "a long, narrow place, like a train car that wasn't going anywhere," where Johnson's misfits, "people [who] all seemed to have escaped from someplace," converge in a shared sense of malaise, "telling lies to one another, far from God." Norman Mailer, William Burroughs, and even Truman Capote have all written decent empathic books about those who live outside the margins of acceptable behavior. Johnson's prose in *Jesus' Son*, however, is so poetically charged with lines such as "I knew every raindrop by its name" and "When I coughed I saw fireflies" that it is difficult to dislike or to judge the acts of cruel indifference of his narrator. Johnson himself resists condemnation or explanation of his characters' ways. If Johnson's Jesus' son is a junkie, a thief, a man on the run, the reason is simple: He is, period. Johnson deliberately strips his stories of flashback, as if he were simply not interested in how or why a person becomes who or what he may be. Instead, these stories are sprinkled with gear-changing flash-forwards that propel the narrative into a present moment: the time frame from which the narrator is recalling his past—that is, his previous life. In "Dirty Wedding," a story in which the narrator gets his girlfriend pregnant and they opt for an abortion, he explains:

> A man in dark glasses shadowed Michelle right up the big steps to the door, chanting softly in her ear. I guess he was praying. What were the words of his prayer? I wouldn't mind asking her that question. But it's winter, the mountains around me are tall and deep with snow, and I could never find her now.

Since the publication of his debut novel *Angels* in 1983, extending up through *Resuscitation of a Hanged Man* (1991), Johnson, in the words of one critic, "has been carrying on an edgy romance with Catholicism." This romance with religion—a battle between salvation and sacrifice—is the major conflict in Johnson's work. At times, most flagrantly in his third novel, *The Stars at Noon* (1986), Johnson's Christian impulses turn into moments of rhetorical dandruff. Yet in his best work, most notably *Angels* and *Resuscitation of a Hanged Man*, the paradoxical notion of forgiveness in the face of the day-to-day apocalypse sits at the center of Johnson's scarred imaginative landscape.

The world of *Jesus' Son* is one in which the characters, especially the narrator, are nostalgic for a better life, a life with a deeper spiritual meaning, though they would not know how to go about finding a church, let alone what to do once they found one. They are Catholic "wannabes." In "Emergency," perhaps the most unforgettable story in this collection—in any collection—Georgie, who works as an orderly in the emergency room of a hospital, is relaxing with the narrator after a long night spent mopping up blood and "saving lives":

> "I want to go to church," Georgie said.
> "Let's go to the country fair."
> "I'd like to worship. I would."
> "They have these injured hawks and eagles there. From the Humane Society," I said.
> "I need a quiet chapel about now."

A similar note is struck in "Dundun": "It felt like the moment before the Savior comes. And the Savior did come, but we had to wait a long time."

Salvation is on the way, these stories seem to suggest. But it will come on its own terms, in its own sweet time. Until then, there is nothing to do but wait and go along for the ride. That is exactly the state in which Johnson introduces his narrator. In "Car Crash While Hitchhiking," Jesus' son is thumbing his way to a destination that has been left unknown. He is, geographically speaking, exactly in the middle of the United

States, hitchhiking west outside Bethany, Missouri. When "a family from Marshalltown" picks him up out of the pouring rain, he confides to the reader: "I sensed everything before it happened. I knew a certain Oldsmobile would stop for me even before it slowed, and by the sweet voices of the family inside it I knew we'd have an accident in the storm." Jesus' son has been blessed (perhaps cursed) with powers of prescient sight. Later, in the same story, he again realizes the inevitable. Yet he is resigned to do nothing, since there is nothing he can do to stop the tragedy that is about to unfold. "You are the ones, I thought. And I piled my sleeping bag against the left-hand door and slept across it, not caring whether I lived or died."

He confesses that he simply does not care. He lacks the capacity, in this particular instance, to do what is right, to act out of some kind of moral obligation. Consider the facts: His head has been stoked with hashish; he has eaten up a bottle of amphetamines while on the road with a traveling salesman; earlier he had the good fortune of riding in a "Cherokee filled with bourbon." His condition at the time of the accident, which "head-onned and killed forever a man driving west," is not an excuse; it is, instead, simply the truth of one man's life.

Instead of encouraging judgment of his characters' conduct, Johnson forces readers to feel aligned with them. The reader becomes intimates with Jesus' son, becomes his closest kin. One of Johnson's greatest gifts is evident in his ability to seduce readers into believing that he—Jesus' son—is actually one of them.

At the very end of "Car Crash While Hitchhiking," during a flash-forward some years later, after detoxification, the narrator, a man whose actions up to this point have been less than commendable, leans out as if across the threshold of the story itself and addresses the reader directly, thereby luring readers into his world: "And you, you ridiculous people, you expect me to help you."

Such direct addresses resonate especially strongly when they are framed in the context of John Gardner's public outcry in his *On Moral Fiction* (1978) that "true art is moral: it seeks to improve life, not debase it . . . [that it must manifest] a clear positive moral effect, presenting valid models for imitation." It seems ludicrous, if not humanly impossible, for Johnson's narrator (whose Christlike characteristics do exist as much as they do in, say William Faulkner's Joe Christmas) to feel pressured by any other impulse than to tell the truth as he saw it, as he lived it. Johnson does not glorify the fact that toward the end of his telling Jesus' son has successfully lived through "Detox" and is "in a little better physical shape every day," that he is a member of Narcotics Anonymous, that he is holding down a bonafide job.

Instead, Johnson emphasizes how tenuous his narrator's recovery really is, and how it will always be this way: as if he is walking on a tightrope between damnation and grace. As he peeks at a lonely Mennonite woman toweling off after a shower, he confesses,

> I had thoughts of breaking through the glass and raping her. . . . How could I do it, how could a person go that low? And I understand your question, to which I reply, Are you kidding? That's nothing. I'd been much lower than that. And I expected to see myself do worse.

This is true: Johnson has shown just how low a man can go. Yet he has done so without sentimentalizing (as Jean Genet does with his pin-striped deviants) or excusing the sometimes violent tendencies he has explored in the eleven stories (or "Stations of the Cross," as they have been called by James McManus in *The New York Times Book Review*) that make up *Jesus' Son.*

In "Beverly Home," though, the story that closes out this collection, the narrator appears at the beginning of his new life. Jesus' son has come down from the cross, so to speak: he is back from the dead. Yet his faith in God is not nearly as potent or poignant as his devotion to the people—the deranged and grotesquely deformed inhabitants of Beverly Home, "an O-shaped, turquoise-blue hospital for the aged"—he has been hired on to touch. "I walked against the tide . . . greeting everybody and grasping their hands or squeezing their shoulders, because they needed to be touched, and they didn't get much of that."

Johnson himself has "walked against the tide" of trends and tendencies in contemporary fiction. His five books of fiction and four collections of poetry (the third of which, *The Incognito Lounge* was a 1982 National Poetry Series selection) are as strangely diverse and darkly illuminating as any work written today. Those who pick up *Jesus' Son* can expect to be touched. As Raymond Carver once wrote about the poems in *The Incognito Lounge*, the best stories in *Jesus' Son* "bring us closer to ourselves and at the same time put us in touch with something larger." Few writers touch their readers so deeply.

Peter Markus

Sources for Further Study

The Atlantic. CCLXXI, June, 1993, p. 121.
Commonweal. CXX, August 13, 1993, p. 23.
Los Angeles Times Book Review. February 28, 1993, p. 3.
The Nation. CCLVI, February 15, 1993, p. 208.
The New York Times Book Review. XCVII, December 27, 1992, p. 5.
Newsweek. CXXI, February 8, 1993, p. 67.
Publishers Weekly. CCXXXIX, September 28, 1992, p. 63.
Studies in Short Fiction. XXX, Summer, 1993, p. 405.
The Washington Post Book World. XXIII, February 21, 1993, p. 9.
The Yale Review. LXXXI, July, 1993, p. 122.

JUSTICE OLIVER WENDELL HOLMES
The Law and the Inner Self

Author: G. Edward White
Publisher: Oxford University Press (New York). Illustrated. 628 pp. $37.50
Type of work: Biography
Time: 1841-1935
Locale: The United States

An intellectual biography of Oliver Wendell Holmes, one of America's greatest Supreme Court judges

> *Principal personages:*
> OLIVER WENDELL HOLMES, JR., a legal scholar and associate justice of the
> Supreme Court, 1902-1932
> FANNY BOWDITCH DIXWELL, his wife
> OLIVER WENDELL HOLMES, SR., his father, a physician and famous author

Oliver Wendell Holmes, Jr., is probably the most celebrated figure in the history of American law. He continues to be recognized for his early achievements as a legal scholar and his distinguished career as a judge, most notably his long tenure as a justice of the United States Supreme Court.

As biographer G. Edward White points out, there have been many scholarly studies of Holmes's life, yet there has been little attention paid the influence of his private life upon his public career. White's intuition is that the two spheres in which Holmes himself commonly divided his life—"work" and a sphere "outside" his work (as Holmes put it)—were in reality all of one piece. Thus in order to understand Holmes the jurist, one must first understand Holmes the man: his early influences, his traumatic Civil War experiences, his love interests, and his early legal career.

Oliver Wendell Holmes, Jr., was born on March 8, 1841, in Boston, Massachusetts. His father, Oliver Wendell Holmes, Sr., was a Harvard-trained physician and author who gained widespread fame among nineteenth century literary circles for his "Breakfast Table" essays; combining fictional settings and characters with stories and poems, these popular pieces appeared regularly in *The Atlantic Monthly* beginning in 1857. Perhaps his most famous work is the poem "Old Ironsides," written in 1830, after he read that the legendary frigate U.S.S. *Constitution* was about to be destroyed.

Dr. Holmes was clearly the most important figure in his son's early life. By the time he was sixteen, the younger Holmes resolved to formulate his own "life plan" to attain the stature enjoyed by his father. He followed his father's footsteps and enrolled at Harvard in 1857. After being graduated in 1861, Holmes was caught up in the events of the Civil War. Inspired by the Confederate attack on Fort Sumter and the antislavery fervor that was sweeping New England, he enlisted in the Union Army.

Like most young men who joined, Holmes felt that he was embarking upon a great crusade to destroy the "evil institution" of slavery, but soon learned the horror and tragedy of war. He was seriously wounded three times, and his battlefield experiences profoundly affected his thinking about the meaning of his life. He had been motivated to enlist because of a strong moral conviction to fight against slavery, but after being wounded for the third time he came to the realization that it seemed he had survived the fighting almost by chance. Many of his closest comrades were dead, and the ideals of chivalry and duty that had motivated so many young men of his generation to answer the call to arms now seemed to be useless abstractions. Holmes did not believe, however, that these men died in vain; one positive lesson his involvement in the Civil War profoundly communicated to him was that there is virtue in feeling passionately about a noble cause. To act in carrying out that passion was an essential part of living one's life to the fullest.

The war seemed to bring into sharper focus the plan he had outlined for his life. Shortly before leaving for the battlefield, Holmes had written in his diary that he expected to study law as his profession if he survived the war. Once the war was over, he resolved to immerse himself in his chosen career. He entered Harvard Law School in the fall of 1864, but found it to be a tedious experience. Attendance at lectures was not compulsory, and by his second year he stopped attending classes. He chose instead to apprentice himself to a Boston law office. Nevertheless, Harvard awarded him a degree in 1866.

It was during the period between 1866 and 1882 that Holmes would undergo a radical intellectual transformation. From his earliest years as a student he read widely, cultivating interests in literature, philosophy, and natural science. After taking some time off to travel extensively in Europe, Holmes began to come into his own as a legal scholar. It was also during this time that he met his future wife, Fanny Bowditch Dixwell. Married in 1872, Holmes and Fanny remained close companions until her death in 1929.

After passing the Massachusetts bar in 1867, Holmes devoted the next fourteen years to the daily practice of law. He also continued to read widely in the subjects of law, history, and philosophy. His first literary endeavor was an 1873 revision of James Kent's classic *Commentaries on American Law*, and he went on to become a regular contributor to the *American Law Review*.

Holmes's magnum opus was a work entitled *The Common Law* (1881), a compilation of a series of lectures he delivered at the Lowell Institute in 1880. This book was one of the first attempts to analyze American law systematically on a historical and philosophical basis. As such, it was a clear break from earlier German and English traditions, which relied upon ethical and metaphysical foundations for legal theories. Holmes instead argued for an anthropological and evolutionary development of the law (no doubt influenced by Darwin), and an intense pragmatism, which he attributed to his reading of the works of American philosopher William James. In one of the most frequently quoted passages in the history of American legal scholarship, Holmes stated that:

> The life of the law has not been logic: it has been experience. The felt necessities of the time, the prevalent moral and political theories, intuitions of public policy, avowed or unconscious, even the prejudices which judges share with their fellow men, have a good deal more to do than the syllogism in determining the rules by which men should be governed.

The book's appearance in 1881 was greeted by favorable reviews and led to Holmes's appointment as professor of law at Harvard in January of 1882. In December of that year, he was appointed to the Supreme Judicial Court of Massachusetts, a post in which he served with distinction until 1902. During his term on the bench, Holmes handed down nearly 1,300 opinions.

In 1902, when Holmes was sixty years old, President Theodore Roosevelt appointed him associate justice of the U.S. Supreme Court. Holmes joined a Court that contained a conservative majority intent on not interfering with American commerce. Even though he saw himself as a social conservative, he strongly believed that there was no constitutional obstacle that prevented the Court from upholding reasonable economic controls. This viewpoint was the basis for what was perhaps his best-known constitutional opinion, *Lochner v. New York* (1905). A majority of five justices invalidated New York's Bakeshop Act of 1895, which had established a limit of sixty hours per week for bakery employees. (At the time, bakers were often required to work one hundred hours a week or more, often in unhealthful conditions.) The majority ruled that this regulation infringed the plaintiff's "liberty of contract," in violation of the Fourteenth Amendment. In his dissent, Holmes argued that "A constitution is not intended to embody a particular economic theory. It is made for people of fundamentally differing views." Justices, he believed, should properly refrain from injecting their own social or economic preferences into constitutional law.

Holmes was also one of the early twentieth century champions of free expression. In 1919, he dissented from the majority in *Abrams v. United States*, in which an individual was convicted under the Federal Espionage Act of 1917 for publishing a pamphlet bitterly denouncing the American involvement in World War I. It was here that Holmes first introduced his idea of a "free marketplace of ideas" in which he stated that all ideas, even those that are despised by the majority, should be permitted to be heard. He reaffirmed this position in *Gitlow v. New York* (1925), dissenting from the conviction of Benjamin Gitlow for publishing documents advocating the overthrow of the government. Holmes believed that Gitlow's publication presented no "clear and present danger" which the state had a right to prevent.

To some, Holmes had become "the great dissenter" of the Supreme Court, but in reality his dissenting opinions were few in comparison to the number of cases he heard during his thirty years on the bench. To most, Holmes was establishing a reputation as a great judge: a careful thinker, a judicious scholar, and an author of profound and eloquent opinions. He was a legal scholar who was clearly ahead of his time in advocating judicial self-restraint. The Court, he believed, was not to act as a "negative legislature" in areas of law which properly belonged within the province of the legislature.

When Holmes was in his eightieth year, after almost twenty years on the high court, he was universally recognized as a great judge and legal scholar. The recognition and fame he had sought from his earliest years was now a reality. He had reached the pinnacle of his profession and was greatly pleased that legal scholars of whom he thought so highly now regarded him as a "great judge." His last decade on the Court, despite his advanced age and slowly failing health, were, he said, perhaps the most gratifying of his career. His mind remained sharp, his keen legal judgment still very much evident in his written opinions. Chief Justice William Howard Taft remarked in 1926, when Holmes was eight-five, that he was still "an excellent member of the Court . . . [who] may live to bury several of us. In fact, Holmes outlived Taft and continued to serve on the Supreme Court until 1932, retiring at age ninety-one.

In summing up Holmes's long and productive life, White maintains that certain personal characteristics are the key to understanding Holmes's success. He was a man of driving ambition, who grew up in a social circle of nineteenth century Boston intellectuals, which included Ralph Waldo Emerson, Henry Wadsworth Longfellow, and William James, in which it was expected that a young man would strive for achievement and success. White believes that Holmes possessed enormous intellectual and emotional energy, combined with an intense thirst for recognition, and concluded early in his life that to achieve greatness required him to concentrate his intellectual powers on one subject. The study of the law became the area of endeavor that particularly suited his scholarly temperament.

Perhaps his most important characteristic, however, was the passion with which Holmes lived his life. It was this passion which enabled him to survive the horror and personal injuries of the Civil War, drove him to produce quality scholarship while maintaining a busy law practice, and eventually led him to become one of America's greatest judges. Even in old age, he maintained a certain zest for work and life.

What makes White's biography unique among the many works on Oliver Wendell Holmes is his adoption of the style of "intellectual biography"—not merely recounting the events of a person's life, but carefully examining how these events come to shape their thinking. White has shown that in the case of Holmes's life, his childhood, his loves, his fears and disappointments all played significant roles in shaping his public persona. His legal scholarship, for example, can only be understood when seen in the light of the nineteenth century intellectual influences such as Darwinism, liberalism, and laissez-faire economic theories which helped to mold his thinking.

In many ways, therefore, Holmes was a man of his time—a product of the intellectual and social climate in which he lived. Yet the key to his greatness, especially his tenure on the Supreme Court, lies in his role as a legal visionary. Many of the themes which dominate twentieth century American jurisprudence—especially protection of free speech and judicial activism—were areas first championed by Holmes. Indeed, it was Holmes's belief that it was the duty of the government to correct social and economic inequities which set the stage for Franklin Roosevelt's New Deal and such landmark civil rights cases as *Brown v. Board of Education* (1954).

His words have had a lasting influence on the workings of the Court, as evidenced by the numerous times he has been quoted by judges and legal scholars. White's superb biography has succeeded in establishing the connection between Holmes's legal career and his personal life, and it represents a fascinating study, as the subtitle indicates, of the "law and the inner self" of America's greatest jurist.

Raymond Frey

Sources for Further Study

Booklist. XC, October 1, 1993, p. 227.
Boston Globe. December 19, 1993, p. 33.
Chicago Daily Law Bulletin. CXXXIX, November 30, 1993, p. 2.
Kirkus Reviews. LXI, September, 1, 1993, p. 1135.
Library Journal. CXVIII, November 1, 1993, p. 106.
New York Law Journal. CCX, November 26, 1993, p. 2.
The New York Times Book Review. XCVIII, November 21, 1993, p. 22.
Publishers Weekly. CCXL, October, 1993, p. 79.
The Wall Street Journal. December 30, 1993, p. A7.
The Washington Post Book World. XXIV, January 2, 1994, p. 4.

KINDLY INQUISITORS
The New Attacks on Free Thought

Author: Jonathan Rauch (1960-   )
Publisher: University of Chicago Press (Chicago). 178 pp. $17.95
Type of work: Ethics and current affairs

Rauch has written a clear and concise defense of basic elements of the scientific method and applied them to debates in the public arena; whether or not his arguments hold in the end, they provide an important perspective from which one can gain insights into the dynamics of much of modern polemical rhetoric

In an age of information overload, one welcomes a small book, clearly written, with a few points well stated and backed by appropriate examples. It is easy to read and understand, but its ideas are not trivial or unimportant. Indeed, if Rauch is right, they may well be the only hope for modern societies being torn asunder by their own diversity. Unfortunately, he not only must be right but also must persuade others that he is right. And while he is persuasive, he may yet not be right in some important respects.

Rauch's basic case is simple. Liberal science (along with capitalism and democracy) has been built on an intellectual tradition of skepticism, which can be largely encapsulated in two principles: No one gets the final say; no one has personal authority. What this means in fact is that the discussion—any discussion—is really never-ending, and that the best we can ever hope for as far as results, or public knowledge is concerned, is an unsteady consensus, in principle ever open to challenge. There are practical limits to the latter, and while Rauch is aware of these, it is one of the points where his arguments are vulnerable.

Rauch begins his book with a series of mini-case studies, which he uses to pose the problem without doing more than hinting at the solutions he has in mind. He does almost too good a job, leaving the reader at times confused as to where all of this is leading. Rauch is able to bring up a varied set of problems which illustrate his thesis. He lays out the alternatives as he sees them in the form of five competing principles. Over against the liberal principle, which determines who is right by constant and open-ended checking of all interested parties by all others, he names the fundamentalist principle (where those who know what is right determine the right), the simple and radical egalitarian principles (where all sincerely held beliefs have equal claims to respect—with special consideration for those of the historically oppressed), and the humanitarian principle (any of the alternatives to the liberal principle, but with the major stipulation that no hurt be caused in the determination of what is right).

In his second chapter, Rauch traces the philosophical roots of liberal science, as well as its alternatives. He begins with Plato, who comes in for a pretty hard time of it (he was a fundamentalist in Rauch's estimation), moves on to René Descartes, who gets credit for a kind of explicit subjectivism but poor marks for logical follow-through, and finally comes to David Hume, who perhaps goes too far even for Rauch, but who usefully reminds us that any of us may at any point be wrong. This is crucial for Rauch, since upon this mustard seed of doubt he hopes to build the framework for universal tolerance, if not for universal understanding.

It is in chapter 3 that Rauch takes on the hard issue of conflict resolution using the principles of liberal science as he has stated them earlier (no final say, no personal authority). Here he makes his boldest claims for liberal science. He apparently sincerely believes that one of liberal science's major contributions to the public arena is in the area of conflict resolution. Yet the principles he has outlined do not do the job alone, as he at various points hints but does not explicate. What lies only partially examined at this point in Rauch's argument are not the public policy issues, which he knows well and where he is able to present his case (organized society should leave individuals alone insofar as is possible). Rather it is the fact that there is not only real pain, which Rauch can accept, but there are real dangers inherent in opening discussions about fundamentally held values among people who do not even agree on the appropriate methods of resolving personal conflicts. Liberal science is built on much more than radical skepticism. It is also a highly refined rhetorical system, in which not any sort of attack on a person's ideas is considered admissible, but only a carefully reasoned one, and no attack on the person directly (even in verbal form) is admissible at all.

But what if that which is precisely at issue are these deeply held values, including how humans should treat one another and resolve conflict? Rauch is aware of the problem, and prefers to advise taking the high road by ignoring those who would offend us. It would be convenient if it were possible to marginalize people in the way Rauch envisions, but political and economic as well as moral and ethical debates are quite unlike academic ones (though the latter too often degenerate into the former). Only time will tell whether Rauch is right. Science does have a good record in the knowledge area, but Rauch may have fallen into a reductionist trap of believing that at bottom, values are also just another form of knowledge.

Rauch would no doubt answer that many things now generally seen as trivial (as wrong besides) were once considered not only true but "values" as well—that the sun rotated around the earth, which was flat and at the center of the universe, that some peoples were destined to serve others in perpetuity, and so on. Thus what one person considers a realm of irreducible values another considers an untapped source for scientific inquiry. Rauch has been careful to exclude certain experiences from scientific investigation—the private, unrepeatable, often religious experiences of individuals—but what about ideas as to what are proper ways for humans to relate to and to treat one another? Skeptical science cannot take an a priori stand on these matters, but humans must, or risk rejection or worse. Theoretical examination of these kinds of behavioral/emotive spheres of life is possible, and even necessary for things such as cross-cultural communication, but one cannot anymore give up certain deeply held beliefs than convince oneself that $1+1=3$.

In chapters 4 and 5, Rauch attacks conservative fundamentalist appeals to divine authority as well as appeals to moral superiority by the new guardians of political correctness. What he attacks is not the *belief* in this authority or superiority, but the use of it in the public arena to short-circuit the truth-finding, or better put, the error-finding mechanisms of liberal science. In fact, he is harder on the humanitarians than he is on the fundamentalists. Thus he neatly sidesteps the trap of ideological stereotyping, and attempts to get groups traditionally at odds with one another to put aside their private experiential realities for the sake of public discourse. Rauch is willing to settle for this kind of compromise, but he would really like more. He believes that the aforementioned principles are more than just a means for avoiding dangerous conflictual situations. He believes they are the best means we have for achieving the only epistemological goals worth striving for: a never-ending and ever-expanding search for truth.

There are doubtless many people who would agree with Rauch, but even more would like to live in a more certain, well-defined world. This is especially true when it comes to values, to those things held most dearly. It is fine to say that fundamentalism "is the strong disinclination to take seriously the notion that you may be wrong," but it would be hard to find someone who is not a fundamentalist about *something*, if only about the usefulness and correctness of living with a high level of uncertainty, for example. Rauch admits radical skepticism destroys itself, yet he does not spend the necessary ink to show how he has not fallen into that trap, either philosophically or practically. He simply states that things have not fallen apart yet. Some will wonder whether he is right. Put another way, is our present American society, riven with strife and open hostility, really better than the one it replaced, teeming with guilt and repressed anger? Even these questions are hard to ask, since the answers will likely depend on who you are and what your place in the old or new orders was or is. And that is just the problem.

It is interesting to compare what Rauch is doing to Mary Douglas' grid/group analysis, in which she describes cultures as clustering at four corners of a theoretical box, the x-axis of which represents increasing solidarity, and the y-axis of which represents increased limits on freedom. Under this structure, Rauch consistently defends the lower left-hand corner of the box, where entrepreneurs, libertarians, and academics live. Douglas meanwhile feels more comfortable in the upper right-hand corner, with more controls yet more solidarity. Part of the issue is temperamental, but there are strengths and weaknesses to each option, of which Douglas may be even more aware than Rauch.

It comes to this: that when Rauch speaks of all those "unreasonable" people we encounter, it is easy to agree with him, but eventually he gets around to us. There we may be able to broaden our perspective to a certain point, but all questions are not open, not for anyone. And when you finally touch the fundamentalist core of an individual or society, you had better hope that core is either universal or contextually bounded (a specific culture), or conflict and war will inevitably follow.

Robert A. Bascom

Sources for Further Study

Booklist. LXXXIX, March 15, 1993, p. 1281.

Chicago Tribune. March 25, 1993, V, p. 3.

The Economist. CCCXXVII, April 17, 1993, p. 89.

Insight On the News. IX, August 2, 1993, p. 35.

Kirkus Reviews. LXI, March 1, 1993, p. 286.

National Review. XLV, July 19, 1993, p. 68.

The New York Times Book Review. XCVIII, April 11, 1993, p. 1.

Newsweek. CXXI, April 26, 1993, p. 67.

Publishers Weekly. CCXL, March 8, 1993, p. 63.

The Wall Street Journal. March 23, 1993, p. A13.

THE KING OF INVENTORS
A Life of Wilkie Collins

Author: Catherine Peters (1930-   )
First published: 1991, in Great Britain
Publisher: Princeton University Press (Princeton, New Jersey). Illustrated. 502 pp. $29.95
Type of work: Literary biography
Time: The nineteenth century
Locale: England, Italy, and the United States

The story of a professional novelist and man of letters who combined commercial success with a principled interest in women's problems but concealed a secret life of sexual adventure

> *Principal personages:*
> WILKIE COLLINS, a British novelist and playwright
> CHARLEY COLLINS, his unsuccessful artist brother
> CHARLES DICKENS, his older collaborator and employer
> CAROLINE GRAVES, his housekeeper and morganatic wife
> MARTHA RUDD, his mistress and mother of his three children

William Wilkie Collins (1824-1889) is now remembered chiefly as the author of two novels, *The Woman in White* (1860) and *The Moonstone* (1868). The earlier is credited with introducing the popular Victorian genre of the "sensation novel," the novel of incident rather than character, in which violent crime or sexual scandal took place within a solid middle-class setting. The later novel cannot quite claim the credit of being the first English-language detective story, for examples of the genre exist from a few years before its publication; however, it was certainly the first prominent English detective story, and its professional investigator, Sergeant Cuff, became the model for a very long line of successors.

Catherine Peters' biography sets out to expand this limited memory of Wilkie Collins (as he has come to be known) by setting him in two wider contexts: first, that of the professional man of letters who earned his living for decades as the author of more than a dozen novels as well as successful plays, short stories, and continuing journalism; second, the hidden Victorian underworld of sexual repression and sexual politics. The connection between these two fields, Peters suggests, lies in the idea of the double, the *Doppelgänger*, the secret life, the hidden identity. These themes fascinated Collins in fiction and were responsible for much of the spell he exerted on his readers. The reason for his fascination, according to Peters, was that he himself lived a dual life.

Under English law during Collins' lifetime—a law that, for example, forbade a married woman to own property in her own right—it was by no means uncommon for a respectable, middle-aged man to maintain both a wife and a mistress in separate establishments. In such a situation, the wife had little legal or effective recourse. Collins was abnormal even under these circumstances: For much of his adult life he kept two women in different houses, acknowledging the children of one as his own and supporting the child of the other as his stepdaughter, yet he married neither of them. Several mysteries surround these relationships. Why would he never marry? Could it be that he was married already, to some completely unknown person, so that further marriage would have been bigamous and so could have exposed him to blackmail? Did Collins not object when the earlier of his two mistresses eventually married someone else, only to return to living with him as his housekeeper after a couple of years? In the prudish Victorian climate, how far was Collins' behavior an open secret? Perhaps most mysterious of all, what gave him the force necessary to withstand such powerful cultural pressure?

Peters gives an interesting picture of Collins' immediate family background, at first sight (and in the doctored versions of earlier commentary, including Collins' own) unimpeachably respectable. Collins' father and namesake, William Collins (1788-1847), was a successful painter whose work for a while sold at similar prices to those of his now much more famous contemporary John Constable (1776-1837). Accounts of him suggest that his profitable contracts were obtained at the price of extreme deference to the rich and the aristocratic. Wilkie Collins' mother Harriet (1790-1868) appeared to be the entirely respectable partner of a member of the Royal Academy. Her own lightly fictionalized account of her life has survived, however, and been used in Peters' biography for the first time. It indicates how close Harriet Geddes came to dropping out of respectable society entirely, even becoming a professional actress (a career then regarded as little different from prostitution). She and her sister saved themselves from poverty by painting and teaching school. Eventually, and in a somewhat unconventional manner, Geddes met and married William Collins the elder, after which both seem to have been characteristically anxious to conceal former difficulties and present themselves as completely solid members of society.

Against this Wilkie Collins seems to have reacted—very successfully if one compares him with his younger brother Charley, who took up his father's trade, was for a while noted and successful as an associate of the Pre-Raphaelite painters William Holman Hunt and John Everett Millais but slid slowly into depression, ill-health, various forms of phobia (including a fear of drowning so acute that he could not take a bath), and eventual death in his early forties, not having exhibited a painting since the age of twenty-seven. In some views Charley Collins was seriously challenged by the relative artistic success of his wife Kate, daughter of the novelist Charles Dickens. It is probable that some of Charley Collins' problems arose from sexual neurosis: Peter cites a letter from Holman Hunt to Millais about a shared acquaintance (the name has been carefully deleted, but Peters argues that it was Charley Collins) who had become entangled with a prostitute in 1856. It would be typical of him, Peters argues, to feel such guilt at this affair as to ruin his later marriage with Kate Dickens; there were suggestions that he suffered from continuing sexual impotence.

In Wilkie Collins' circle, one can only add, such deep-seated psychological problems seem to have been the rule rather than the exception. Holman Hunt married a model who repeatedly deceived him, and he appears never to have consummated the marriage. Millais married a woman whose earlier marriage to the critic John Ruskin was also not consummated and was eventually annulled. The collapse of Charles

Dickens' marriage in 1858 caused major scandal. In his early twenties, Collins himself gave away a fifteen-year-old bride to a friend in an illegal marriage. The friend, Edward Ward, later cut his own throat. In a macabre prophecy of this, another shared friend of both cut his father's throat and was committed as a criminal lunatic; before being arrested, however, he had made drawings of his friends, Ward included, and painted a red slash across the throat of each. The toll taken by Victorian respectability and repression was, in short, extremely high. Few people, men or women, seemed to have escaped its ill-effects.

Wilkie Collins was, however, arguably one of them. His father's painful conventionality did not prevent him from taking his two sons on a two-year tour of Italy. From this Wilkie at least returned with a sense of liberation and an ability to speak French and Italian; he often went abroad after this time. He was also spared the conventional British middle-class all-male boarding school, a breeding ground for ignorance and fear of women. In later years he would write repeatedly and sympathetically of women's problems, seemingly out of a kind of confidence in his own sexuality. This does not mean that his behavior did not manifest another sort of exploitation.

By contrast to his private life, Collins' professional life was marked by extreme care and even cold-bloodedness. He wrote an early novel of Tahiti, which was never published, and began a second historical novel on a Roman theme. When his father died, however, he turned his attention to a life of his father, for which he could count on certain publication. That written and published, he was able to return to publishers with something of a track record and gained relatively good terms for his Roman novel *Antonina* (1850). Collins also tried his hand at travel writing and had a play produced in 1850, *A Court Duel*. In view of Collins' own later struggles over copyright (American publishers particularly were under no obligation to pay royalties to British authors, no matter how many copies they sold) it is ironic that the play was a translation/plagiarism from the French, a practice then common. Collins, in short, seems to have been looking for an opening. This was provided him by his continuing association with Charles Dickens.

In the 1850's, Dickens was at the height of his fame and influence, though not of his fortune. His journal *Household Words* was a major success, and it was a considerable step for Collins to have his fourth novel, *The Dead Secret* serialized in its pages in 1857, and to have been hired as a paid member of its staff the year before. In 1857, Collins and Dickens also collaborated on a play, *The Frozen Deep*, so successful as to draw a command for a private performance before Queen Victoria. Collins was later to make substantial sums writing for the London stage.

It is nevertheless possible to argue that Collins paid too highly for his relationship with Dickens. There are strong suggestions that Dickens valued Collins as a colleague for nonprofessional reasons, including Collins' relaxed attitudes to sexual escapades. The two men traveled together on the Continent in 1854, and Collins may have returned with Reiter's disease, an illness diagnosed then as "rheumatic gout" but possibly triggered by venereal disease. Charley Collins' marriage to Kate Dickens in 1860 was good for neither of them and caused friction between the two families. Some thought that Collins' novels such as *The Dead Secret* were flattened out by the audience and tastes of *Household Words*.

However that may be, the 1860's saw Collins at the peak of his career. *The Woman in White* was immediately and continuingly successful; its theme, of a woman driven almost to madness and the loss of psychological identity by male plotting and by the use of a double, her half-sister, has become a classic of both feminist and Jungian interpretation. It was believed to be one of the first successful attempts to reach out to the "New Public," the new reading class brought into being by wider education. Collins' follow-ups *No Name* (1862) and *Armadale* (1866) continued to exploit the themes of female vulnerability and of "the self and the shadow," but his next major breakthrough was *The Moonstone*. This tale of a diamond stolen from the East was serialized in *All the Year Round*, the magazine Dickens founded after abandoning *Household Words* in the aftermath of his marital scandal. Both magazine and novel were even more successful than their predecessors, and for some time Collins could take his pick of offers (even breaking into the American market on a paid basis with *Harper's Weekly*).

Nevertheless, serious trouble lay ahead. From about 1860, Collins had maintained Caroline Graves, a beautiful woman of doubtful origins, as his "housekeeper." In 1868, perhaps angered by Collins' setting up of a home with Martha Rudd, a poor woman much younger than either of them, Graves married another man, only to return to Collins two years later. At about the same time, Collins' addiction to laudanum, the alcoholic tincture of opium, grew more severe. A tablespoon of this substance (used by Victorians as a painkiller) is said to be fatal to one not used to it. As his dependence and tolerance increased, Collins was seen to drink as much as a wineglass at a time, more than enough to kill a horse. Comments on his bad health increased. After Dickens' death on June 8, 1870, Collins lost a powerful ally. None of his later works was a success on the same scale as his earlier ones; at least one of his later plays excited ridicule at its overdone and now-familiar "sensational" element. There was a feeling that Collins had lost touch with the audience he helped to create. When he died on September 23, 1889, Collins had been an invalid for some time, and he left surprisingly little for a man so long successful.

An accusation one must finally face about Collins is that in spite of his repeated championing of women's rights to property in marriage, to custody of children after divorce, to being treated with at least no greater severity than their customers if forced into prostitution, he himself seems to have been an exploiter. He acknowledged his children by Rudd legally, yet he never did so publicly. He condemned them to living under false names—his two daughters, who never married, kept this up until their deaths in 1955. The shame he shrugged off was inflicted on them, and the sympathetic language of novels such as *No Name* can seem hypocritical. Against that, Collins was certainly generous financially. To Rudd, one of eight children from a Norfolk village at a time when the wage of a housemaid was sixteen pounds a year, Collins' allowance of twenty-five pounds a month may have seemed a fortune. Yet is that not a reflection only of the immense wage differentials of Victorian society? Morally, as well as in literary terms, Collins remains an enigma. This well-researched biography does, however, provide the reader with uncensored material, much of it entirely new, on which to make a judgment.

T. A. Shippey

Sources for Further Study

Booklist. XC, November 1, 1993, p. 500.
Boston Globe. December 1, 1993, p. 75.
Choice. XXXI, February, 1994, p. 936.
The Guardian. November 21, 1991, p. 26.
New Statesman and Society. IV, October 25, 1991, p. 38.
The New York Times Book Review. XCVIII, November 14, 1993, p. 12.
The Observer. October 28, 1991, p. 60.
The Spectator. CCLXVII, October 19, 1991, p. 37.
The Times Literary Supplement. November 8, 1991, p. 36.
The Wall Street Journal. December 29, 1993, p. A6.
The Washington Post Book World. XXIV, January 9, 1994, p. 4.

KITCHEN

Author: Banana Yoshimoto (1964-   )
First published: Kitchin, 1988, in Japan
Translated from the Japanese by Megan Backus
Publisher: Grove Press (New York). 152 pp. $14.95
Type of work: Novella and short story
Time: The late twentieth century
Locale: Japan

The two pieces in this volume are told from the point of view of young women struggling to mature as they cope with the deaths of loved ones

> *Principal characters:*
> *Kitchen*
> Mikage Sakurai, a young woman
> Yuichi Tanabe, the classmate who befriends her
> Eriko Tanabe, the transsexual mother of Yuichi
>
> "Moonlight Shadow"
> Satsuki, the narrator, a young woman
> Hitoshi, the younger brother of her deceased boyfriend
> Urara, a young woman who befriends her

The first section of this volume is the novella *Kitchen,* which, published in the original Japanese in 1988, sold millions of copies, won prestigious literary prizes, and sparked a cultural phenomenon dubbed "Bananamania" in Japan. The accompanying piece, "Moonlight Shadow," was the author's first story, which won a university prize.

Though the two pieces are similar in themes and narrative devices, the first, approximately twice as long as the second, is clearly the focus of interest in this volume. To non-Japanese readers familiar primarily with translations of the major male authors such as Yukio Mishima, Yasunari Kawabata, and Junichiro Tanizaki, *Kitchen* will come as a fresh addition to twentieth century Japanese literature.

The Japanese fiction available in translation in the latter part of the twentieth century, several reviewers have noted, often rings with allusions to American popular culture. In fact, a certain melancholy tension between traditional Japanese ways and Western influences has been a stock theme of Japanese literature since the first foreigners were allowed into the country.

Banana Yoshimoto's vastly popular stories suggest, however, that some aspects of Western culture have been so thoroughly integrated that the younger, postwar generation finds such references easy and natural. As one reviewer notes, the choice of the word "kitchen" itself is noteworthy: It is "the trendy English loan-word *kitchin* rather than the Japanese term, *daidokoro.*" To be sure, some references can be relatively superficial, such as the mention of Kentucky Fried Chicken in "Moonlight Shadow" or Denny's in *Kitchen.* A reference to the television comedy *Bewitched,* a simile comparing the narrator's calmness to "Joan of Arc before the Dauphin," and an incident from a Brothers Grimm story lightly touch upon a Westernization so seemingly ingrained that it may be remarkable only to non-Japanese readers.

The vignette of a transvestite character "eating soba noodles with fried bits of tempura batter and wearing what is practically the national costume, a two-piece warmup suit" suggests an author capable of sharp observations of a society in subtle transition with which she herself is completely comfortable. Such cultural observations are the lighter, more amusing aspects of these two stories. Much more remarkably modern are the confused but independent young women who narrate both stories. The feminism of Yoshimoto's characters comes through subtly, subsumed in the grim universalities of life that the young female narrators must confront and modulated by a web of communal caretaking.

As *Kitchen* starts, Mikage Sakurai is at a crossroads. Her only relative, a grandmother, has been dead for three days. Both her parents died young, and she was reared by grandparents; her grandfather died while she was in junior high school. Now, on leave from her university studies, she is drifting aimlessly. All that keeps her going is her love of kitchens. In fact, the only place she can fall asleep after her grandmother's death is next to the refrigerator.

In both these stories, recovery from the death of a loved one is the major challenge for the young characters. An important component of the recovery is the struggle to risk connecting to others. Mikage's classmate Yuichi Tanabe is a young man who works in what had been her grandmother's favorite flower shop. Invited to visit his home, Mikage falls in love with the Tanabe kitchen, and, though still in a fog about her emotions and desires, responds to the warmth and charm of the people in the household.

Mikage's adolescent narrative voice is appealing, with its intuitive generalizations about the state of humanity and her open, accepting nature. She is struck dumb with admiration when she meets Yuichi's mother, beautifully made up and dressed and giving "off a marvelous light that seemed to vibrate with life force. She didn't look human. I had never seen anyone like her."

The mother, Eriko, proves to be actually Yuichi's father, who had a sex-change operation when his wife died of cancer. Eriko now owns a gay club and works nights there. She and her son accept Mikage with open arms, and she, having no direction in life, moves in and spends some happy months with them.

Yoshimoto's stories are marked by skillful reversals of gender roles. To the orphaned Mikage, Eriko becomes the fount of female wisdom. One evening, out of the blue, Eriko tells Mikage that it is not easy being a woman and recommends that anyone wanting to be independent should care for and feed something—a child or a houseplant—because it is thus that a person learns her own limitations.

Eriko is a brilliant piece of characterization—warm, loving, fun, though her comments on women can be ambiguous. One day Mikage learns about Eriko's decision to change sex. When he was still a man, visiting his dying wife in the hospital, he took her a pineapple plant. As she got worse, she asked him to take it away. Leaving the hospital on a cold night, he did not take a taxi because he had been crying bitterly; this prompted the realization that he did not like being a man. Somehow, his overwatering that pineapple plant until it died taught him a lesson:

> I realized that the world did not exist for my benefit. It followed that the ratio of pleasant and unpleasant things around me would not change. It wasn't up to me. It was clear that the best thing to do was to adopt a sort of muddled cheerfulness. So I became a woman.

Such pronouncements on the nature of women parallel the ambiguous meaning of kitchen and, by extension, of food and cooking in the story. Mikage may indeed typify "the confusion of young Japanese women, attracted as she is to kitchens and cooking as symbols of comfort and womanliness, yet trying to live independently," as reviewer Elizabeth Hanson notes. On the other hand, kitchens and cooking initially save Mikage from despair and then, in a beautifully simple metaphor, become her means of asserting independence and achieving the strength to return the gift of life to her benefactor.

Having recovered some of her balance in the eccentric Tanabe household, Mikage renews her interest in life by taking up cooking with feverish passion. Learning to cook well is a journey of self-discovery for Mikage. With three books on the fundamentals, theory, and practice of cooking, she teaches herself to cook. Like a frenzied artist determined to grasp the mystery of her art, she pores over her books on the bus, in bed, on the sofa, memorizing caloric content, temperatures, and raw ingredients, pouring all of her earnings into cooking. She discovers a simple lesson, "that dishes turn out badly or well in proportion to one's attention to detail."

Discovering the patience to correct her mistakes coolly in her eagerness to cook well, she lands a perfect job, as assistant to a famous cooking teacher. Because she has experienced despair and loneliness, Mikage is able to feel deep joy in her work, making carrot cakes that include "a bit of my soul" and loving a bright red tomato "for dear life." Her passion distinguishes her from the students, young women from good families who live happily because they are content to stay within their boundaries.

The third part of the story is the most delightful and comic. Mikage has by this time moved into her own apartment and has temporarily lost touch with Eriko and Yuichi. A phone call from Yuichi changes her life again: Eriko has been killed by a man who was infatuated with her and followed her to the gay bar. It is now Mikage's turn to reach out to Yuichi, and the lessons she has learned from cooking stand her in good stead. He has shrunk into despair and loneliness, unable to do much but drink. She spends one night at his house, suddenly understanding how important he is to her. She makes an extravagant dinner, an "international hodge-podge," and they eat for hours: deep-fried tofu, steamed greens, bean thread with chicken, chicken Kiev, sweet-and-sour pork, steamed Chinese dumplings, salad, pie, stew, croquettes. Yuichi suggests that she move back in with him, but Mikage realizes that much as they love and need each other, they are still "two lovers looking over the edge of the cauldron of hell." Their journey toward each other is not complete.

When she is invited to sample the cooking at several inns on the Izu Peninsula, Mikage makes an astute and immediate choice of work over a dangerous relationship. This final section of the story, a picaresque in miniature, shows the modern heroine at her comic best. Repulsed by the vegetarian cooking at the first inn, Mikage sneaks out late at night in search of something heavy and filling. She finds a small, deserted restaurant and orders *katsudon*, deep-fried pork in broth over rice. While waiting for the order, she thinks of Yuichi, who has gone on a monastery retreat. She calls him and commiserates over the boring menu available to him—tofu (bean curd), the simplest of foods. Refraining from gloating about her own rich meal, she has a sudden intuition that the two of them are approaching a decisive moment. Mikage seems to intuit that she owes Yuichi more than a choice between the excess of her "hodge-podge" meal and the meager monastery diet of tofu.

Her discovery exhausts her, leaving her again feeling hopeless, but her professional acumen bolsters her weakness. The *katsudon*, when it arrives, is so good that she orders another to go. Hiring a taxi, she takes the long drive to the monastery, only to find it locked up for the night. Cold and puzzled, she looks around the building and instinctively picks out Yuichi's window. With great difficulty and some pain, she climbs up to his room. Again, in the empathy that has been growing stronger, she senses his nightmare of grief and knows that if she stays she will be lost in it too. Mikage delivers the *katsudon* and her intuition, that he is trying to escape and does not want to return to his life in Tokyo. "But right now," she says, "there's this *katsudon*. Go ahead, eat it." As Yuichi eats, her spirits lift; she has done all she can for him. She returns to her inn and continues on the tour. On the last night she receives a call from Yuichi. He is back in Tokyo, waiting to pick her up.

So it is that Banana Yoshimoto transforms kitchens and cooking from the mundane to the heroic. It is a comic and touching modern twist to an old romantic tale—the confused, intuitive young woman, armed with a bowl of pork and noodles, roaming the countryside and climbing up monastery walls in the dead of night to rescue her young man from despair.

"Moonlight Shadow" explores similarly tragic situations without the humor and whimsy that lighten the tone of *Kitchen*. It is an interesting companion piece, however, because it gives greater emphasis to mystical experiences—sudden flashes of insight, telepathic communication between lovers. Together, these stories establish Banana Yoshimoto as a young writer of considerable achievement and exceptional promise.

Shakuntala Jayaswal

Sources for Further Study

Belles Lettres. VIII, Spring, 1993, p. 43.
Far Eastern Economic Review. CLVI, May 20, 1993, p. 44.
Japan Quarterly. XL, April, 1993, p. 226.
London Review of Books. XV, January 28, 1993, p. 20.
Los Angeles Times Book Review. January 10, 1993, p. 3.
The New York Review of Books. XL, August 12, 1993, p. 29.
The New York Times Book Review. XCVIII, January 17, 1993, p. 18.
The New Yorker. LXVIII, January 25, 1993, p. 109.
The Times Literary Supplement. January 8, 1993, p. 18.
The Washington Post Book World. XXIII, January 10, 1993, p. 8.

THE LAST BEST HOPE OF EARTH
Abraham Lincoln and the Promise of America

Author: Mark E. Neely, Jr. (1944-   )
Publisher: Harvard University Press (Cambridge, Massachusetts). Illustrated. 207 pp. $24.95
Type of work: Biography
Time: 1809-1865
Locale: The United States

Neely offers a carefully researched analysis of Lincoln as a national leader

Principal personage:
ABRAHAM LINCOLN, sixteenth president of the United States, 1861-1865

Mark E. Neely, Jr.'s biography of Abraham Lincoln divides into two distinct portions dependent upon his methodology and approach. In approximately the first fourth of the book, following a traditional approach, he furnishes a straightforward chronological account of Lincoln's life and career before his election to the presidency. In the second, Neely breaks the chronological pattern and devotes four chapters to issues and problems faced by Lincoln during his term of office and provides an additional chapter on the assassination. The resulting text places emphasis upon Lincoln's leadership during the Civil War, the time of the greatest crisis ever faced by the United States.

Even in the initial portion, Neely focuses upon Lincoln's development as a leader, identifying his first love as politics. His Lincoln, a frontiersman, believes strongly in economic development and has confidence in the ability of ordinary Americans to prosper under appropriate conditions. A proponent of Henry Clay's American System, he opposes slavery and maintains a strong sense of the importance of national unity. Even so, he occasionally advocates sectional politics, especially when his distaste of slavery is aroused. Lincoln's character is portrayed as that of an ambitious but patient and honorable political leader, highly pragmatic in his attitudes. As a frontiersman, he views the role of government as assisting economic development through providing infrastructure. He is on the whole optimistic about human nature, and even in early life he inclines toward a long- rather than short-term perspective.

To a remarkable degree, Neely downplays myths and legends based on Lincoln's early life. Myths surround Lincoln to an extraordinary degree and in part account for his stature as a national figure. More shrines and memorials exist to him than any similar national hero, but Neely carefully eschews this rich hagiographic tradition. Nowhere does he mention the story of Lincoln as a boy reading books on the hearth by firelight, an episode that once raised the spirits of struggling schoolboys. Nor does he recount other anecdotes of Lincoln's youth and early manhood, tales calculated to inspire virtue and perseverance.

Although he acknowledges that Lincoln was born in a log cabin, split rails, and worked his way up from poverty, he believes that these facts matter little to the man Lincoln became or to the issues he confronted. Accordingly, Neely points out that Lincoln seemed intent on creating distance between himself and his rural origins, the source of many myths. When first affiliating with a political party, he chose the patrician Whigs over the Jacksonian Democrats—an incongruous choice for an impoverished rural frontiersman. He married into gentility, and his children never met the devoted stepmother who had helped rear him. Although he received little schooling and read for his lawyer's license, he sent his son to Exeter School and Harvard University.

Nor does Neely entertain readers with accounts of Lincoln's wit and humor. In his extensive use of Lincoln's letters and official papers, he selects those that illuminate his role in settling important issues. While he depicts Lincoln's basic honesty and judicious nature, Neely shows that he was not aloof from the realities of politics. This meant that he occasionally resorted to craftiness and guile in political speeches, not avoiding the degree of distortion typical of his times.

Once it reaches the presidential election of 1860, the narrative clarifies the backgrounds of the Civil War and concentrates upon Lincoln's role as leader of the nation, primarily through exploring the major problems that faced the presidency. Of the five chapters in this section, the first concerns Lincoln's role as commander in chief. The second and third explain his handling of the slavery issue and his management of domestic matters during the war. The chapter "Politics as Usual" traces partisan affairs during his term and especially during the 1864 election. The final chapter, "Fate," explores matters relating to Lincoln's assassination.

Although presidents before Lincoln had faced the perils of warfare, no other had dealt with a conflict so long or so destructive as the Civil War. Population growth, industrial development, and sectional rivalry had laid the groundwork for a bitter, prolonged, and costly engagement. In his approach to the role of commander in chief, Neely recounts Lincoln's difficulties with his generals, making clear what lay at the root of his numerous problems. Lincoln himself, eager to end the war quickly, was at times too much inclined to manage the army's moves in detail. When his orders led to costly losses, he became somewhat less specific in his directives.

Yet he possessed a keen understanding of men and soon realized that General George B. McClellan, the best available officer to assemble, equip, and train an army, was the poorest to lead it into battle. Although Neely devotes most of his detailed attention to the Lincoln-McClellan conflict, Lincoln's relationships with his other generals are also carefully analyzed. Lincoln's exasperation with George G. Meade, commander at Gettysburg, for his failure to pursue Robert E. Lee's defeated army and end the war two years sooner looms large in the narrative. Neely makes evident the president's deep displeasure without exploring the situation faced by Meade. A more aggressive commander might have seized the opportunity and launched an attack, but most would probably have regrouped as Meade did, following heavy Union losses. Lincoln eventually found his aggressive commander in Ulysses S. Grant, who had captured Vicksburg during the same week as the Battle of Gettysburg. One notes that Neely's account devotes more attention to Lincoln's failures with his other generals than to his successes with Grant.

In his analysis of the slavery issue, Neely traces the reasons Lincoln delayed issuing the Emancipation Proclamation. He had opposed slavery for most of his life and was elected on a platform of preventing its extension; he desired to see it end—but clearly not at the cost of losing the Union. At the beginning of the war he kept silent for fear that all the border states would secede if he freed the slaves. Neely reminds readers that had all the border states sided with the Confederacy, the Union would probably have been defeated. Following his initial hesitation, Lincoln considered the issue from a legal standpoint, wondering whether as president he could free the slaves on his own authority without an act of Congress. An ultraconservative Supreme Court lent no support, and Lincoln had to choose his own time. During the delay, he found it occasionally necessary to cancel some decrees by overzealous military leaders who had freed slaves in occupied areas. Neely suggests that the military reality was perhaps the most influential factor in prompting Lincoln to act. Thousands of freed African Americans served in the Union Army, and he saw the possibility of recruiting many more with a proclamation of freedom.

In his chapter on domestic policy during the war, Neely points out that the president encountered little success in advancing his ideas for economic development of the frontier, largely because he was preoccupied with winning the war. Lincoln faced a very different domestic situation from that of later war leaders. No one had any concept of marshaling the nation for an all-out effort or of organizing the national economy for victory. Although Lincoln was interested in technological developments affecting weaponry, military leaders of the time believed that the war would have to be won with existing weapons, and the president's personal views had little effect. The war was fought on principles and with weapons developed during the Napoleonic Era. Yet Lincoln does have the unenviable distinction of being the first president to institute national conscription. Previously the draft had been used for state militias but not for the nation as a whole. This effort worked successfully in meeting the need for soldiers, but it met with public opposition in places such as New York, where draft riots occurred.

In Neely's view, Lincoln's most compelling legacy on the domestic scene was negative—the curtailment of civil liberties, notably the right of habeas corpus. Numerous opponents of the war were arrested and held without formal charges, some for only expressing their views. Lincoln knew about these practices and even condoned some of them; in effect, he suspended provisions of the Bill of Rights, if only temporarily.

The chapter titled "Politics as Usual" suggests cynical back-room politics and nineteenth century corruption, yet Neely intends the title as both favorable and unfavorable. Although there was no organized pro- or antiwar propaganda, the commonly used political posters, cartoons, and speeches pilloried opposition in familiar ways. Yet as Neely points out, the Northern Democrats formed a loyal opposition, and Lincoln himself remained aloof from the political conflicts. Rightly, Neely emphasizes that elections were conducted in the normal manner throughout the war, an astonishing achievement considering the perils of the time.

During the election of 1864, the Democrats selected General McClellan as their nominee, and the election was vigorously contested. McClellan, sensing the nation's weariness with the war, spoke vaguely of a negotiated peace, a message that resonated through a large part of the nation. Despite the Gettysburg and Vicksburg victories of 1863, which finally drove Confederate forces from the North and cut the Confederacy in half, the war remained troublesome to most voters. Lincoln believed that he would lose the election and planned for a smooth transition. Typically, he hoped to take steps to secure the Union before McClellan took office, fearing that his opponent would grant either independence or autonomy to the South. During the election campaign, however, the military situation turned decisively in Lincoln's favor. General William T. Sherman's capture of Atlanta convinced many in the North, as well as foreign nations still sympathizing with the South, that the Confederacy could not hold out much longer, and the president was accorded a second term.

In his final chapter, "Fate," Neely discusses the assassination, explaining the remarkable lack of security for nineteenth century presidents. It was widely believed that a president had little need of protection, because assassination had not been a part of the American political experience. Except in unusual circumstances, the president had, by modern standards, a grossly inadequate entourage and practically no protection. The White House staff consisted of two secretaries and two doormen, but no regularly assigned security officers. Neely demonstrates that John Wilkes Booth encountered little difficulty in approaching and mortally wounding the president. Also, Neely sifts prevalent theories concerning Booth's motives and concludes that he was neither insane nor part of a deeper conspiracy, but motivated by genuine fanaticism and hatred of Lincoln's principles.

If one were to read only one biography of Lincoln, Neely's would not be the one to select. He does not attempt a balanced narrative, largely ignoring Lincoln as a person to analyze his management of national issues. For anyone seeking an understanding of the Lincoln presidency, however, the book offers a well-written, concise, and clear account of his leadership during the Civil War. Neely enhances the narrative by exploring Lincoln's times, making frequent comparisons to earlier and later periods. The author further provides an illuminating account of the problems and dilemmas faced by the president and explains personal values and other factors that influenced his decisions and actions. The book's major achievement lies in its exploration of the theme indicated by the title. Speaking of the Union in an address to Congress on December 1, 1862, Lincoln had said, "We shall nobly save, or meanly lose, the last best, hope of earth." The biography makes it abundantly clear that Lincoln contributed more than anyone else to nobly saving that hope.

Stanley Archer

Sources for Further Study

American Heritage. XLIV, December, 1993, p. 99.
American History Illustrated. XXVIII, January, 1994, p. 20.

Boston Globe. November 25, 1993, p. 26.
Chicago Tribune. October 6, 1993, V, p. 3.
Library Journal. CXVIII, September 1, 1993, p. 194.
Los Angeles Times Book Review. November 14, 1993, p. 11.
The New Yorker. LXIX, December 6, 1993, p. 143.
Publishers Weekly. CCXL, September 20, 1993, p. 58.
The Washington Post Book World. XXIII, December 26, 1993, p. 1.

THE LATIN DELI
Prose and Poetry

Author: Judith Ortiz Cofer (1952-   )
Publisher: University of Georgia Press (Athens). 170 pp. $19.95
Type of work: Essays, poetry, and short stories

A sensitive retelling of the author's coming of age poised between her native Hispanic culture in Puerto Rico and her newly adopted culture in the United States

El Building, a forbidding monolith that dominates the corner of Straight and Market streets in Paterson, New Jersey, once housed middle-class Jews. They have fled from Puerto Rican incursions into their territory, leaving El Building a vertical barrio occupied almost totally by people from "The Island," as the inhabitants refer to their former home. Having migrated to the United States during World War II and afterward, they have tried to establish in this cold, gray environment some semblance of the life they left behind, some replication of the sense of community they knew in their small Puerto Rican towns and villages.

Most of the people who live in El Building—especially the women—cling to the dream that one day they will be able to return to The Island and live adequately on pensions. Few of the women have jobs; few have learned English. They live within an English-speaking society, but the small center they have created for themselves on the fringes of that society is Spanish-speaking, Hispanic-thinking.

These Puerto Ricans, feeling unwelcome in their adopted environment, stay mostly to themselves, their society confined largely to the barrio they have established and the nearby *bodegas*, including the Latin Deli. Old customs die hard. The women still cook the green plaintains and dried codfish of their native land, still pay outrageous prices for the imported Bustelo coffee that is essential to their afternoon coffee and social hours, still, although they live in a larger, depersonalized society, meet almost daily in one another's apartments or in El Basement for gossip, commiseration, and emotional support.

Reflective of the solidly textured community they have created is the way the neighbors in El Building—Lydia, Isabelita, and the narrator—react when Doña Ernestina receives the devastating news that her only son, Tony, has been killed in the Vietnam War. A year earlier, when she lost her husband, Doña Ernestina had coped adequately with that death. Now that her son is dead, draped in the unrelieved black of deep mourning, she becomes frighteningly calm, almost catatonic. She gives away her most cherished possessions. When word trickles out that she is giving away everything she owns, long lines of total strangers, many of them street people, form in the hallways outside her door to grab whatever they can get.

"Nada," winner of the O. Henry Award in 1993, is the story of Doña Ernestina's emotional deterioration after her son's death. The neighbors gather, unwilling to be intrusive yet concerned about their friend's situation and her reaction to it. She has already said, "No, gracias," to the American flag and her son's medals that the army has tried to bestow upon her. Vacant inside, she sits in her room saying, "Nada, nada, nada." The narrator comments, "That word is like a drain that sucks everything down." The grieving woman now is stripping her life of all vestiges of its past, seemingly expunging from it all of her stored-up memories.

When Doña Ernestina goes so far as to begin throwing her larger possessions—her television set, kitchen chairs, stools—out the windows in the middle of the night, pedestrians on the streets below call the police. The old woman is found sitting stark naked in the corner of one of her rooms, numbed by sedatives. Her neighbors quickly run to get their best clothes for Doña Ernestina to wear so that she might dress well and be led away in dignity.

Judith Ortiz Cofer's sensitivity to language, particularly to negative terminology, recurs in "Not for Sale," the story of an itinerant salesman who comes to the narrator's house and sells her mother, on the installment plan, an expensive bedspread that depicts the Scheherazade story. The mother buys the overpriced bedspread for her adolescent daughter, whose overprotective father forbids her to date, to go on well-chaperoned school trips, or to get her driver's license. Cofer remarks on the father's *"No, no, no,* with the short Spanish 'o.' Final: no lingering vowels in my father's pronouncements."

The Salesman, El Árabe, represents another foreign culture, this one Middle Eastern. He desperately wants to bring his son to the United States, but there will be immigration problems unless the son marries an American. El Árabe, in the custom of his own country, proposes to the narrator's father that he buy the man's fifteen-year-old daughter to be his son's wife.

The narrator's father keeps screaming, "Not for sale!" but El Árabe is persistent. He has given the girl a ring, which her father pulls from her finger, breaking the skin and causing blood to flow. As the story ends, El Árabe has left the apartment and the girl is washing the blood from her hands, seemingly as an act of purification. The pictures on her Scheherazade bedspread unfold endless stories to her.

Cofer is concerned with feminist issues, yet in most of the fifteen stories and forty poems in this volume, she sees such issues in perspective and remains relatively nonjudgmental about them. In "The Witch's Husband," for example, the narrator says,

> And frankly, I am a bit appalled at what I have begun to think of as "the martyr complex" in Puerto
> Rican women, that is, the idea that self-sacrifice is a woman's lot and her privilege: a good woman
> is defined by how much suffering and mothering she can do in one lifetime.

As this story progresses, however, one learns that the old grandmother, enfeebled by severe cardiovascular problems, who is risking her life to care for her senile husband, years earlier had turned her back on that husband and on her children to go to New York for a year. Her husband, seeing how unhappy she was in her situation, had given her the money to go and had taken a second job to keep her there for a year, never knowing whether she would choose to return to him and their children. Because he had allowed her this freedom, she grew to love him completely and cannot now abandon him to the care of a nursing home.

Cofer's angriest statement comes in "The Myth of the Latin Woman: I Just Met a Girl Named Maria." In this deeply personal essay, Cofer's anger is more about ethnic stereotyping, however, than about feminism. She tells of being spotted by a man on a bus trip from Oxford, where she was doing graduate work, to London. The man burst into song, loudly singing "Maria" from *West Side Story* as he stared at her. On another occasion, as she walked with a companion from a theater in New York, a man blocked her path and burst into "Don't Cry for Me, Argentina" from *Evita*. She tells also of a Chicana friend, a Ph.D. candidate, whose physician is amazed at all the big words she uses.

One might ask whether the two men who were inspired to song upon seeing Cofer would have done something comparable had Cofer been a Latin man. It seems obvious that they would not. Would a physician have been as amazed by the vocabulary of a Chicano Ph.D. candidate as by that of a Chicana? The anger in this essay is indisputable—and it is the least temperate social commentary of any in the volume—but it is directed at the ethnic stereotyping that is obvious in each instance.

In "The Paterson Public Library," an extremely well-balanced story, Cofer again reveals her distress at ethnic stereotyping. A black girl named Lorraine has been intimidating the narrator, hating her for irrational ethnic reasons. Even though Lorraine attacks her physically, the narrator can understand Lorraine's frustration at being stereotyped by her own teachers, who, knowing nothing about Black English, view her use of the language as ungrammatical and illiterate.

A similar condemnation of ethnic stereotyping is found in "American History," where the impact is twofold. The narrator, despite her intelligence, cannot qualify for honors classes because English is not her first language. In the honors classes is Eugene, an Anglo transplant from Georgia whom the narrator finds attractive. When she finally has the courage to talk to Eugene, they find that they have much in common.

Eugene invites her to his house to study with him. On the emotionally charged day of their first study session—November 22, 1963—the young girl, despite the shock of the Kennedy assassination, goes to Eugene's house. She is rebuffed and refused entry by Eugene's mother as soon as she learns that the girl bears the stigma of living in El Building.

The parent-child relationships revealed in the prose and poetry of *The Latin Deli* present the yin and the yang of adolescent perception. Similar relationships, contradictory yet accurate, are evident in Cofer's novel *The Line of the Sun* (1989) and in her earlier collection, *Silent Dancing: A Partial Remembrance of a Puerto Rican Childhood* (1990). The narrator is not consistent in her view of her parents. What adolescent is? Cofer makes no attempt to impose an artificial consistency upon the narrator's reactions to her mother and father. She does nothing to cover up the parental warts of which the young girl becomes aware.

The father is a mysterious and enticing—if at times frightening—presence. He works two jobs, so he does not have much time at home. The daughter associates him with the smell of his cologne and thinks that it is this smell that makes her mother cry.

In "By Love Betrayed," the young girl Eva, a total innocent, finds herself in El

Building alone with her father one day when her mother is out and she has stayed home from school with a headache. Among her father's jobs is that of building superintendent. Eva, wanting to know her father better, follows the scent of his cologne to the fifth floor. Behind a door she hears his voice and that of a woman. When she knocks, the woman, hair disheveled, dressed in a red robe, answers the door. The girl asks for her father, who comes from the woman's bedroom combing his hair.

He asks why the girl is not in school. She explains that she had a headache and stayed home. Smiling his devil's smile, as Cofer calls it, he asks whether she was really sick or merely wanted a day off. He then decides that he should take a day off himself and treat her to lunch. Eva remains the innocent, unaware—or unwilling to be aware—of her father's dalliance.

In most of the stories and poems, the father is overprotective. The mother is unhappy and often argues with her husband. Still, she keeps her family together and tries to compensate for her husband's overprotection of their daughter, such as buying the girl the Scheherazade bedspread.

The stories and poems in *The Latin Deli* depict the author's coming of age with the sensitivity and verisimilitude of a James Agee, a Carson McCullers, or a Harper Lee. Despite their parochial setting, the tales woven in this collection point to universal truths that are the marks of serious and significant literature.

R. Baird Shuman

Sources for Further Study

Booklist. XC, November 15, 1993, p. 609.
Library Journal. CXVIII, November 1, 1993, p. 93.
Publishers Weekly. CCXL, November 8, 1993, p. 60.

LENIN'S TOMB
The Last Days of the Soviet Empire

Author: David Remnick
Publisher: Random House (New York). Illustrated. 576 pp. $25.00
Type of work: Current history
Time: 1988-1992
Locale: The former Soviet Union

A young American reporter shows how the sudden unveiling of the truth about the Soviet past doomed Soviet Communism to destruction

> *Principal personages:*
> VLADIMIR ILYICH ULYANOV (LENIN), founder and leader of the Soviet Union, 1917-1924
> JOSEPH STALIN, leader of the Soviet Union, 1929-1953
> NIKITA KHRUSHCHEV, leader of the Soviet Union, 1957-1964
> LEONID BREZHNEV, leader of the Soviet Union, 1964-1982
> ANDREI SAKHAROV, a leading Soviet dissident who died in 1989
> MIKHAIL GORBACHEV, leader of the Soviet Union, 1985-1991
> ALEKSANDR YAKOVLEV, a Russian reformer and adviser to Gorbachev
> BORIS YELTSIN, a politician who led the Russian Federation after 1991
> VLADIMIR KRYUCHKOV,
> BORIS PUGO, and
> DMITRI YAZOV, Soviet officials who plotted a coup on August 1991

In 1983, the French journalist Jean François Revel (*Comment les democraties finissent; How Democracies Perish*, 1984) predicted that democratic societies, with their tolerance of internal dissent, would prove no match for the ruthless single-mindedness of the totalitarian Soviet Union. As an analyst of the short term, Revel made sense; as a prophet, he could not have been more wrong. In the late 1980's and early 1990's, it was not democracy that perished but Soviet and Eastern European Communism. Barely a decade after Revel's work was published, David Remnick, a young reporter for *The Washington Post*, presents a valuable eyewitness account—based on indefatigable travel throughout the old Soviet Union and on hundreds of interviews—of the death agony of the twentieth century's most formidable totalitarian system.

Remnick's work can be compared with an eyewitness study of an earlier turning point in Russian history, also by a young American reporter: John Reed's *Ten Days That Shook the World* (1919). Reed was a partisan of the Bolsheviks and of the socialist utopia that they promised; Remnick sympathizes with those who wish to purge their country of the Bolshevik heritage and to bring democracy to a Russia so long deprived of it. Whereas Reed covered dramatic events compressed within the space of the summer and autumn months of a single year (1917), Remnick traces a process that took three years to reach its climax, in the abortive coup of 1991 and the subsequent dissolution of the Soviet Union.

The attention paid to long-term process as well as dramatic events also distinguishes

Remnick's account from another book on the 1991 events, *Russia Transformed: Breakthrough to Hope* (1992), by the Librarian of Congress, James H. Billington. Whereas Billington focuses narrowly on the abortive *putsch* of August 19-21, 1991 (that was the week he happened to be in Moscow for a librarians' conference), Remnick allots a little less than sixty pages to those three crucial days. Remnick's account of the coup is more densely packed with facts than Billington's; Billington, a historian rather than a journalist, did not take extensive notes and took absolutely no photographs. Remnick argues that it was the profound change in people's attitudes during the previous four years, and not any particular errors of judgment, that doomed the efforts of the coup plotters (KGB chief Vladimir Kryuchkov, Interior Minister Boris Pugo, and Defense Minister Dmitri Yazov) to failure. During the years 1987 to 1991, says Remnick, a fearless search for the truth about Soviet history replaced, for many Russians, the old passive acceptance of Communist mythology. Those who dug up data on the crimes of the once-revered dictator Joseph Stalin, the author suggests, did as much to end Communism as those who defied the *putsch* in August, 1991.

To give the reader a feel for the change in Russians' hearts and minds between 1987 and 1991, Remnick interviewed ordinary people as well as politicians, the obscure as well as the well-known. He talked to everyone from priests to peasants, from miners to journalists, from such dedicated reformers as Aleksandr Yakovlev (a key adviser to Soviet leader Mikhail Gorbachev) to such hard-line Communists as Nina Andreyeva and Yegor Ligachev, and from Baltic nationalists to Eskimos. By no means do all of Remnick's anecdotes deal with great political events; his report on the introduction of American baseball into Moscow, for example, is entertaining as well as insightful. In its emphasis on the effect of political change on ordinary people, Remnick's book can be compared to *The New Russians* (1990) by reporter Hedrick Smith, written just before the Soviet Union disintegrated.

The key to the overthrow of Communism in both the Soviet Union and its Eastern European satellites was a crisis of belief within the hearts and minds of members of the Soviet elite. Remnick helps American readers to understand how individuals who enjoyed privileges under the old Soviet system came to see the need to reform that system. His biographical portrait of Gorbachev, although difficult for the reader to follow (bits of information on the pre-1985 Gorbachev are found in different parts of the book, in no particular chronological order), is probably the most accurate one written up to 1993. The author views Gorbachev as a half-hearted reformer who clung too long to the notion that one could liberalize the Communist system without destroying it. Remnick also offers the reader fascinating insights into the career of Boris Yeltsin, although these, too, are scattered throughout the book (information on Yeltsin's rebellious youth in the Urals, for example, is shoehorned in to the chapter on the August, 1991, coup). The reader should compare Remnick's discussion of Yeltsin with that found in *Boris Yeltsin: A Political Biography* (1992), by the Russian émigrés Vladimir Solovyov and Elena Klepikova.

By paying attention to both ordinary people and members of the elite, Remnick helps answer a question that provokes the curiosity of many American readers: How could such a powerful wave of popular anti-Communist sentiment arise in a country where no effort had been spared to indoctrinate the young in Communist ideology? Through his interviews, Remnick points to many things that gradually eroded the Russian people's faith in Communism: the corruption among many local Communist Party bosses under the regime of Leonid Brezhnev; the emergence, during Brezhnev's rule, of the former political prisoner Aleksandr Solzhenitsyn and the nuclear physicist Andrei Sakharov as models of courageous, nonviolent resistance to Communist totalitarianism; the memories that many Russians had of family members who were persecuted unjustly by dictator Joseph Stalin in the 1930's; the impact on young future members of the Communist elite of Soviet leader Nikita Khrushchev's denunciation of Stalin in 1956; and, for some especially privileged members of that elite (such as Gorbachev adviser Aleksandr Yakovlev and KGB agent Oleg Kalugin), the broadening effects of travel to the United States. Remnick has interviewed not only the relatively well-known members of the pre-1991 elite but also some of the lesser-known figures, not only Yakovlev but also the journalist Len Karpinsky. The author ably traces the evolution of such men from careerist opportunism to determined support for liberal reform.

Perhaps understandably, Remnick's book lack's comparative perspective. The reader learns something about why Communism had, by the beginning of 1992, collapsed in the Soviet Union. One learns little, however, about why Communism had not collapsed by that time in Cuba, Vietnam, North Korea, and mainland China. Political scientist Ken Jowitt's collection of essays *New World Disorder: The Leninist Extinction* (1992) provides a starting point for those who wish to understand Communism as an international, and not merely a Russian phenomenon.

In general, Remnick's book is quite well written. He is skilled in the use of irony and is a master of the apt metaphor. His comparison of the Soviet state under Brezhnev to a senile old man is an especially powerful image. In a sense, the book's title itself is a metaphor. The constant efforts through the years to preserve the publicly displayed corpse of Vladimir Ilyich Ulyanov (Lenin), the founder of Communism (efforts that Remnick derides), did not, after all, prevent the Russian people themselves from ultimately burying Leninism.

Remnick's frequent comparison of Russian phenomena to things that Americans are familiar with is especially helpful to those readers (probably a majority) who are neither of recent Russian immigrant stock nor acquainted with Russia through travel. By calling the prominent Stalinist Nina Andreyeva an advocate of "traditional values," Remnick makes an implicit analogy between her views and those of America's religious right; such a comparison, while perhaps controversial, does drive home a point.

Remnick's physical descriptions of individuals paint vivid word pictures; his emphasis on sartorial details, however, seems a bit excessive at times. Occasionally the author slips: The effect of Yeltsin's personality and oratory on the average Russian of the late 1980's is described as "narcotic" when "intoxicating" would have been a better word choice.

Remnick is not completely unbiased; he freely confesses his sympathies for the Russian reformers against their hard-line Communist opponents. Since this bias is shared by most Americans, and indeed by most persons of goodwill outside Russia, it will arouse little controversy. Remnick is not impressed by the argument, put forward by Russian foes of reform, that moving away from the Communist economic system will increase income inequality and impoverish the Russian masses. Citing evidence from his travels across the former Soviet Union, he shows how the old Communist economic system produced equality in poverty rather than a broadly shared middle-class standard of living. Such things as the destruction of the environment (especially in Central Asia), the sorry state of collectivized agriculture, and the primitive living and working conditions of Russian miners are all described vividly, and with some indignation, for the American reader.

Remnick is honest enough, however, to concede the existence of a downside to the new freedom of the late 1980's and early 1990's. There has been a rise in crime in Moscow, including the growth of protection rackets that prey on the new entrepreneurs; there have been ugly manifestations of anti-Semitism that previously had been submerged; and quarreling has broken out between the various nationalities in the once-subordinate republics of the former Soviet Union. The author also points out that Boris Yeltsin, who built up a reputation by attacking the opulent lifestyles of Party bureaucrats, himself came to live rather luxuriously once he became President of the Russian Federation.

Remnick's book is valuable for the light it sheds on the history not only of the period from 1985 to 1991 but also of the Stalinist era (1929-1953). The book opens with the story of the official Soviet reinvestigation, in 1990 and 1991, of the Katyn Forest murders of Polish Army officers, an event that had occurred some fifty years earlier. By interviewing a man who had been one of the executioners and by digging up the remains, the head of the investigation, Colonel Aleksandr Tretetsky, discovered that these officers had been murdered not by the soldiers of Nazi Germany but by Stalin's secret police. Interviewing the very few survivors of the Stalinist terror and the surviving relatives of the victims, Remnick himself shows just how arbitrary Stalin's despotism was and how many Russians were personally affected by it. It becomes clear, for example, that some of those who were exiled or killed had committed no crimes whatsoever but were chosen by Stalin's ambitious subordinates merely in order to meet a quota. In presenting such evidence, Remnick confirms the conclusions reached earlier by such Western experts on the Stalinist period as Robert Conquest.

By jumping around chronologically, Remnick sometimes makes his account a bit hard to follow. The Chernobyl nuclear disaster of 1986, for example, is treated in the same chapter (that on Soviet nationalities) in which the nationalist revival of 1989-1990 in the Baltic states is discussed; the apparent justification for doing so is the Chernobyl disaster's role in strengthening the Ukrainian resolve for independence. If Remnick had included a timeline, he would have made it easier for readers (especially those who do not follow Russian affairs closely) to keep their chronological bearings.

Lenin's Tomb: The Last Days of the Soviet Empire includes a detailed (more than twenty-page) index. The note on sources delivers more than it promises; it not only lists the names of the better-known individuals whom the author interviewed in the Soviet Union but also provides some critical evaluations of other works written by Americans about political change in the Soviet Union between 1985 and 1991. The well-chosen photographs do much to help the reader understand the text. There is also a bibliography, which is not annotated.

Although both a diligent historian and an excellent journalist, Remnick does not have the gift of prophecy. He does note the existence of strong anti-Yeltsin sentiment among right-wing and left-wing extremists in early 1992, but he does not predict the violent rebellion against Yeltsin's reforms that erupted in October, 1993. About the two key anti-Yeltsin leaders in the 1993 crisis, Aleksandr Rutskoi and Ruslan Khasbulatov, Remnick's book says little, aside from mentioning their participation in the resistance to the August, 1991, coup. Rutskoi's reputation in 1991 as a conservative is alluded to only briefly. Nor does Remnick seem to have interviewed these two men, who came to play such a significant role in politics later on. Like most books on Russia that have appeared in the late 1980's and early 1990's, *Lenin's Tomb*—which received the 1994 Pulitzer Prize for general nonfiction—will inevitably be overtaken by events. It is nevertheless one of its time's most helpful books on Russia.

Paul D. Mageli

Sources for Further Study

The Christian Science Monitor. July 29, 1993, p. 14.
The Economist. CCCXXVIII, July 24, 1993, p. 87.
Foreign Affairs. LXXII, September, 1993, p. 167.
Los Angeles Times Book Review. June 20, 1993, p. 1.
National Review. XLV, August 9, 1993, p. 64.
The New York Review of Books. XL, August 12, 1993, p. 3.
The New York Times Book Review. XCVIII, May 30, 1993, p. 1.
Newsweek. CXXII, July 26, 1993, p. 44.
Publishers Weekly. CCXL, April 19, 1993, p. 41.
Time. CXLI, June 14, 1993, p. 74.
The Wall Street Journal. June 29, 1993, p. A12.
The Washington Post Book World. XXIII, June 13, 1993, p. 1.
World Policy Journal. X, Fall, 1993, p. 97.